WORD BIBLICAL COMMENTARY

VOLUME 19

Psalms 1-50

PETER C. CRAIGIE

WORD BOOKS, PUBLISHER • WACO, TEXAS

Word Biblical Commentary:
Psalms 1–50
Copyright © 1983 by Word, Incorporated

Library of Congress Cataloging in Publication Data
Main entry under title:

Word bibilical commentary.
  Includes bibliographies.
  1. Bible—Commentaries—Collected works.
BS491.2.W67   220.7'7   81–71768
ISBN 0–8499–0218–5 (v. 19) AACR2

Printed in Colombia

17 18 - 03 02

WORD
BIBLICAL
COMMENTARY

To Professor John Gray,
with gratitude and respect

Contents

Author's Preface

The invitation to contribute a volume to the Word Biblical Commentary on Psalms 1–50 was both an honor and a challenge. It was an honor to share in the monumental task being undertaken by Word. It was a challenge, because for years I had been mystified by many of the psalms. I belong to a tradition in the church in which the psalms continue to be used regularly in worship. And yet, as a teenager singing the psalms, their words for the most part contained little meaning for me; they were the songs of a remote and distant land, with no evident relevance to my own world. It was the custom in Scotland for boys to wear the kilt to church on Sunday; to this day I can recall singing the words of Psalm 147:10, in the Prayer Book version: "neither delighteth he in any man's legs." I pondered at that time the problem of whether Scripture condemned the kilt. It was a false problem, yet typified, I suspect, the sense of mystery encountered by many who have sung the psalms.

Later in life, I turned to the study of the Psalms and then encountered an entirely different problem. The investigation of Hebrew poetry, albeit fascinating, became so complex that it was easy to lose sight of the vitality of the Psalms, not only as a part of the Bible, but also as a vehicle of worship. An immense body of scholarship devoted to the Psalms has accumulated over the centuries, and to that must be added the wealth of new knowledge flowing from archaeological discovery. But a surfeit of knowledge in the *minutiae* may lead to confusion as surely as shortage. I have sought to find a middle path in this book, drawing on the wealth of information now at our disposal, but in the end trying to clarify the meaning of each psalm in the modern world.

No book is written without considerable assistance. I am particularly grateful to Dr. John Watts, the Old Testament Editor, for his guidance and advice throughout the period of writing. And there is an old friend I should like to have thanked, whose name appears throughout this book: Mitchell Dahood. His writings were a constant source of stimulus, and though we rarely agreed on matters Ugaritic, I have learned enormously from his insights. Over the years, through meetings and correspondence, a friendship developed; his death, on March 8, 1982, marked the loss of a colleague, friend, and a great companion of the Psalms.

Finally, I must thank Ms. Beverley Forbes for her preparation of the manuscript of this book. My writing is at times more difficult to decipher than any ancient manuscript, and I am most grateful for her painstaking preparation of the typescript.

P. C. Craigie

Calgary, September, 1982

Editorial Preface

The launching of the *Word Biblical Commentary* brings to fulfillment an enterprise of several years' planning. The publishers and the members of the editorial board met in 1977 to explore the possibility of a new commentary on the books of the Bible that would incorporate several distinctive features. Prospective readers of these volumes are entitled to know what such features were intended to be; whether the aims of the commentary have been fully achieved time alone will tell.

First, we have tried to cast a wide net to include as contributors a number of scholars from around the world who not only share our aims, but are in the main engaged in the ministry of teaching in university, college and seminary. They represent a rich diversity of denominational allegiance. The broad stance of our contributors can rightly be called evangelical, and this term is to be understood in its positive, historic sense of a commitment to scripture as divine revelation, and to the truth and power of the Christian gospel.

Then, the commentaries in our series are all commissioned and written for the purpose of inclusion in the *Word Biblical Commentary.* Unlike several of our distinguished counterparts in the field of commentary writing, there are no translated works, originally written in a non-English language. Also, our commentators were asked to prepare their own rendering of the original biblical text and to use those languages as the basis of their own comments and exegesis. What may be claimed as distinctive with this series is that it is based on the biblical languages, yet it seeks to make the technical and scholarly approach to a theological understanding of scripture understandable by—and useful to—the fledgling student, the working minister as well as to colleagues in the guild of professional scholars and teachers.

Finally, a word must be said about the format of the series. The layout in clearly defined sections has been consciously devised to assist readers at different levels. Those wishing to learn about the textual witnesses on which the translation is offered are invited to consult the section headed "Notes." If the readers' concern is with the state of modern scholarship on any given portion of scripture, then they should turn to the sections on "Bibliography" and "Form/Structure/Setting." For a clear exposition of the passage's meaning and its relevance to the ongoing biblical revelation, the "Comment" and concluding "Explanation" are designed expressly to meet that need. There is therefore something for everyone who may pick up and use these volumes.

If these aims come anywhere near realization, the intention of the editors will have been met, and the labor of our team of contributors rewarded.

General Editors: *David A. Hubbard*
Glenn W. Barker†
Old Testament: *John D. W. Watts*
New Testament: *Ralph P. Martin*

Abbreviations

1. Periodicals, Reference Works and Serials

AB	Anchor Bible
ANET	J. B. Pritchard, ed. *Ancient Near Eastern Texts*
AOAT	Alter Orient und Altes Testament
ASTI	*Annual of the Swedish Theological Institute*
ATANT	Abhandlungen zur Theologie des Alten und Neuen Testaments
AusBR	Australian Biblical Review
BAR	*Biblical Archaeologist Reader*
BASOR	*Bulletin of the American Schools of Oriental Research*
BDB	F. Brown, S. R. Driver, and C. A. Briggs, *Hebrew and English Lexicon of the Old Testament*
BeO	*Bibbia e oriente*
BHK³	R. Kittel, *Biblia Hebraica*
BHS	Biblia Hebraica Stuttgartensia
Bib	Biblica
BibLeb	*Bibel und Leben*
BJRL	*Bulletin of the John Rylands University Library of Manchester*
BSOAS	*Bulletin of the School of Oriental and African Studies*
BZ	Biblische Zeitschrift
BZAW	Beihefte zur *ZAW*
CBC	Cambridge Biblical Commentary
CBQ	*Catholical Biblical Quarterly*
CJT	*Canadian Journal of Theology*
CML	*Canaanite Myths and Legends* (G. R. Driver; 2nd ed. J. C. L. Gibson)
CTA	A. Herdner, *Corpus des tablettes en cunéiformes alphabétiques*
CTM	*Concordia Theological Monthly*
Est Bib	*Estudios biblicos*
ETL	*Ephemerides Theologicae Lovanienses*
ExpTim	*Expository Times*
FreibZ	*Freiburger Zeitschrift für Philosophie und Theologie*
FRLANT	Forschungen zur Religion und Literatur des Alten und Neuen Testaments

GKC	*Gesenius' Hebrew Grammar*, ed. E. Kautzsch, tr. A. E. Cowley
HeyJ	*Heythrop Journal*
HKAT	Handkommentar zum Alten Testament
HSM	Harvard Semitic Monographs
HTR	*Harvard Theological Review*
HUCA	*Hebrew Union College Annual*
ICC	International Critical Commentary
Int	*Interpretation*
JANES	*Journal of the Ancient Near Eastern Society of Columbia University*
JAOS	*Journal of the American Oriental Society*
JBL	*Journal of Biblical Literature*
JBL MS	Journal of Biblical Literature Manuscript Series
JCS	*Journal of Cuneiform Studies*
JETS	*Journal of the Evangelical Theological Society*
JNES	*Journal of Near Eastern Studies*
JNWSL	*Journal of Northwest Semitic Languages*
JQR	*Jewish Quarterly Review*
JSOT	*Journal for the Study of the Old Testament*
JSOT SS	Journal for the Study of the Old Testament. Supplementary Series
JSS	*Journal of Semitic Studies*
JTS	*Journal of Theological Studies*
KB	L. Koehler and W. Baumgartner, *Lexicon in Veteris Testamenti Libros*
KTU	*Die Keilalphabetischen Texte aus Ugarit*, ed. M. Dietrich, O. Loretz, and J. Sanmartin.
NewslUgSt	*Newsletter for Ugaritic Studies*
OTL	Old Testament Library
OTS	*Oudtestamentische Studiën*
PEQ	*Palestine Exploration Quarterly*
PRU	*Le Palais royal d'Ugarit*
RB	*Revue Biblique*
RevistB	*Revista biblica*
RevQ	*Revue de Qumran*
RIH	*Ras Ibn Hani*

RivB	*Rivista biblica*
RSP	*Ras Shamra Parallels,* ed. L. Fisher
SB	Sources bibliques
SBS	Stuttgarter Bibelstudien
SBT	Studies in Biblical Theology
Sem	*Semitica*
SJT	*Scottish Journal of Theology*
SR	*Studies in Religion/Sciences religieuses*
TDOT	*Theological Dictionary of the Old Testament*
ThLZ	*Theologische Literaturzeitung*
ThQ	*Theologische Quartalschrift*
TOTC	Tyndale Old Testament Commentary
TRev	*Theologische Revue*
TRu	*Theologischer Rundschau*
TyndB	*Tyndale Bulletin*
TZ	*Theologische Zeitschrift*
TTZ	*Trierer Theologischer Zeitschrift*
UF	*Ugarit-Forschungen*
UT	C. H. Gordon, *Ugaritic Textbook*
VCaro	*Verbum Caro*
VF	*Verkündigung und Forschung*
VT	*Vetus Testamentum*
VTSup	Vetus Testamentum, Supplements
WO	*Die Welt des Orients*
WTJ	*Westminster Theological Journal*
WUS	J. Aistleitner, *Wörterbuch der ugaritischen Sprache*
ZAW	*Zeitschrift für die alttestamentliche Wissenschaft*
ZNW	*Zeitschrift für die neutestamentliche Wissenschaft*
ZTK	*Zeitschrift für Theologie und Kirche*

2. Biblical and Ancient References

A. *General*

G	Greek Old Testament
L	Latin Old Testament
LXX	Septuagint

MT	Masoretic Text
NT	New Testament
OT	Old Testament
S	Syriac Old Testament
Vg	Vulgate

B. Biblical and Apocryphal Books

OLD TESTAMENT

Gen	Genesis
Exod	Exodus
Lev	Leviticus
Num	Numbers
Deut	Deuteronomy
Josh	Joshua
Judg	Judges
Ruth	Ruth
1 Sam	1 Samuel
2 Sam	2 Samuel
1 Kgs	1 Kings
2 Kgs	2 Kings
1 Chr	1 Chronicles
2 Chr	2 Chronicles
Ezra	Ezra
Neh	Nehemiah
Esth	Esther
Job	Job
Ps	Psalms
Prov	Proverbs
Eccl	Ecclesiastes
Cant	Song of Solomon
Isa	Isaiah
Jer	Jeremiah
Lam	Lamentations
Ezek	Ezekiel
Dan	Daniel
Hos	Hosea
Joel	Joel
Amos	Amos

Obad	Obadiah
Jonah	Jonah
Mic	Micah
Nah	Nahum
Hab	Habakkuk
Zeph	Zephaniah
Hag	Haggai
Zech	Zechariah
Mal	Malachi

NEW TESTAMENT

Matt	Matthew
Mark	Mark
Luke	Luke
John	John
Acts	Acts
Rom	Romans
1 Cor	1 Corinthians
2 Cor	2 Corinthians
Gal	Galatians
Eph	Ephesians
Phil	Philippians
Col	Colossians
1 Thess	1 Thessalonians
2 Thess	2 Thessalonians
1 Tim	1 Timothy
2 Tim	2 Timothy
Titus	Titus
Phlm	Philemon
Heb	Hebrews
Jas	James
1 Pet	1 Peter
2 Pet	2 Peter
1 John	1 John
2 John	2 John
3 John	3 John
Jude	Jude
Rev	Revelation

APOCRYPHA

1 Kgdms	1 Kingdoms
2 Kgdms	2 Kingdoms
3 Kgdms	3 Kingdoms
4 Kgdms	4 Kingdoms
Add Esth	Additions to Esther
Bar	Baruch
Bel	Bel and the Dragon
1 Esdr	1 Esdras
2 Esdr	2 Esdras
4 Ezra	4 Ezra
Jdt	Judith
Ep Jer	Epistle of Jeremy
1 Macc	1 Maccabees
2 Macc	2 Maccabees
3 Macc	3 Maccabees
4 Macc	4 Maccabees
Pr Azar	Prayer of Azariah
Pr Man	Prayer of Manasseh
Sir	Sirach
Sus	Susanna
Tob	Tobit
Wis	Wisdom of Solomon

C. *Rabbinic and Other Ancient References*

Ber.	Berakot
Bik.	Bikkurim
C	Cairo Geniza
Ros. Has.	Rosh Hashanah
RS	Ras Shamra
Sop.	Sopherim
Tg	Targum

D. *Dead Sea Scrolls and Related Texts*

CD	Cairo (Genizah text of the) Damascus (Document)
Hev	Nahal Hever texts
Mas	Masada texts
Mird	Khirbet Mird texts

Mur	Wadi Murabba at texts
p	Pesher (commentary)
Q	Qumran
1Q, 2Q, 3Q, etc.	Numbered caves of Qumran, yielding written material; followed by abbreviation of biblical or apocryphal book
QL	Qumran literature
1QapGen	*Genesis Apocryphon* of Qumran Cave 1
1QH	*Hôdāyôt* (*Thanksgiving Hymns*) from Qumran Cave 1
1QIsa*a,b*	First or second copy of Isaiah from Qumran Cave 1
1QpHab	*Pesher on Habakkuk* from Qumran Cave 1
1QM	*Milḥāmāh* (*War Scroll*)
1QS	*Serek hayyaḥad* (*Rule of the Community, Manual of Discipline*)
1QSa	Appendix A (*Rule of the Congregation*) to 1QS
1QSb	Appendix B (*Blessings*) to 1QS
3Q*15*	Copper Scroll from Qumran Cave 3
4QFlor	*Florilegium* (or *Eschatological Midrashim*) from Qumran Cave 4
4QMess ar	Aramaic "Messianic" text from Qumran Cave 4
4QPrNab	Prayer of Nabonidus from Qumran Cave 4
4QTestim	*Testimonia* text from Qumran Cave 4
4QTLevi	*Testament of Levi* from Qumran Cave 4
4QPhyl	Phylacteries from Qumran Cave 4
11QMelch	*Melchizedek* text from Qumran Cave 11
11QtgJob	*Targum of Job* from Qumran Cave 11

3. Translations

AV	Authorized Version
JB	Jerusalem Bible
KJV	King James Version
NAB	New American Bible
NEB	New English Bible
NIV	New International Version
RSV	Revised Standard Version
TEV	Today's English Version

An Explanation

This is the first of three volumes on the Psalms in the Word Biblical Commentary series. The Introduction that follows in this volume is a general introduction to the whole Book, but the succeeding volumes will also provide brief introductory remarks to the individual sections of the Psalms which they cover. Volume 20, Psalms 51–100, is being prepared by Dr. Marvin E. Tate, and Volume 21, Psalms 101–150, is being prepared by Dr. Leslie C. Allen.

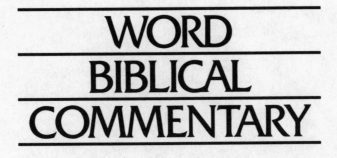

Introduction

THE ORIGINS OF PSALMODY IN ISRAEL

Bibliography

Albright, W. F. *Yahweh and the Gods of Canaan.* Garden City, NY: Doubleday Anchor Books, 1969. **Craigie, P. C.** "The Conquest and Early Hebrew Poetry." *TyndB* 20 (1969) 76–94. _____. "The Song of Deborah and the Epic of Tukulti-Ninurta." *JBL* 88 (1969) 253–65. **Cross, F. M.** *Canaanite Myth and Hebrew Epic.* Cambridge: Harvard University Press, 1973. **Freedman, D. N.** *Pottery, Poetry and Prophecy.* Winona Lake, IN: Eisenbrauns, 1980. **Robertson, D. A.** *Linguistic Evidence in the Dating of Early Hebrew Poetry.* Missoula, MT: Scholars Press, 1972.

In the OT, songs and prayers are by no means limited to the Book of Psalms. Long before the Book of Psalms came into existence, and before the major part of its content was written, there was a tradition of psalmody in ancient Israel. The evidence for this ancient tradition is to be found in the poetic texts embedded in the prose narrative concerning Israel's early period. The corpus of this ancient poetry is relatively small, consisting of the following primary texts, to which some shorter poetic fragments could be added:

> The Song of the Sea (Exod 15:1–18)
> The Song of the Ark (Num 10:35–36)
> The Oracles of Balaam (Num 23–24)
> The Song of Moses (Deut 32)
> The Blessing of Moses (Deut 33)
> The Song of Deborah (Judg 5)
> The Song of Hannah (1 Sam 2:1–10)

The general antiquity of this corpus of ancient Hebrew poetry has been established beyond reasonable doubt by the pioneering research of W. F. Albright, developed further in recent years by F. M. Cross and D. N. Freedman. Though the precise dates of all the above texts cannot be fixed, all are ancient, and the detailed work of D. A. Robertson indicates strongly that the Song of the Sea is probably the most ancient text of the group.

The origins of Israel as a nation are to be found in the Exodus from Egypt. It is that same event which marks the origin of Israel's psalmody. The Exodus was celebrated in a great hymn of praise, the Song of the Sea; that ancient hymn not only stands at the head of all Israel's hymns of praise, but it profoundly influenced many subsequent hymns and continues to be used in the synagogue to this day. The Song of the Sea was never incorporated within the Psalter, but was utilized effectively by the writer(s) of the Book of Exodus to make a theological point. God participated in Israel's history to liberate his chosen people from human bondage; that participation was perceived to be not merely an historical fact, but also a source of praise. The God who acted for his people should be praised by his people. The Song of the Sea thus reflects a human response to God's self-revelation in history; it mirrors the intimate relationship which existed between Israel and God.

The relationship between God and his people is illustrated further by other examples of poetry and song which have survived from Israel's earliest history. The Song of Deborah resembles the Song of the Sea in that it too celebrates a great victory achieved by God on behalf of his people. Though the content is military, Deborah's song reflects the same central theological conviction: God acts on behalf of his people (his "friends": Judg 5:31), and the acts of God elicit the praise of God's people.

But hymns of praise (or, more precisely, victory hymns) are not the only types of psalmody to have survived from early Israel; there are also other kinds of poetry coming from Israel's earliest period. The Song of Moses is quite different in both form and style from the Song of the Sea and the Song of Deborah. Its purpose is more that of instruction than praise, and its themes are those of the biblical wisdom literature. The Blessing of Moses, though presented in the form of a paternal blessing, has a prophetic and oracular character. The Song of the Ark indicates the more liturgical usage of poetry, namely the words and ritual which accompanied particular events in Israel, such as the departure of the Ark for war and its safe return. The Song of Hannah introduces a personal note into the poetry of praise; whereas the Song of the Sea reflected the praise of a community or nation, Hannah's Song represents the response of an individual who has experienced sorrow or hardship; David's Lament for Saul and Jonathan (2 Sam 1:19–27), from a slightly later period, provides a clear insight into the anguish of human sorrow. The ancient Oracles of Balaam, though pronounced by a non-Hebrew, indicate a further dimension of poetry, namely prophetic poetry (in this context, the prophetic blessing); the Oracles contain some parallels to the Blessing of Moses.

From these assembled examples of poetry and psalmody composed during Israel's early history, a number of points become clear. First, poetry, as a form of language, was native to early Israel, as it was to most ancient cultures; it was not necessarily a *literary* form initially, for it is probable that Israel's earliest poetry was composed orally, rather than being a literary creation. Second, poetry was the natural medium through which to give expression to the most profound of human feelings and insights; prayer, praise, liturgy, wisdom and lament were conveyed in the words of poetry. These various types of poetry are all reflected at a later date in the Book of Psalms. Third, music accompanied poetry on certain occasions. The Song of the Sea and the Song of Deborah are explicitly introduced as having been sung; the praise of thanksgiving required not only the transcendence of poetic words, but evoked also the sense of joy and beauty which may be conveyed in music. Fourth, though Israel's earliest poetry may have been composed orally, some of it was remembered and handed down to future generations. Whether it was remembered by virtue of being written down, as is explicitly stated with respect to the Song of Moses (Deut 31:22), or whether it was passed down orally from generation to generation, cannot always be known with certainty. What is fairly certain is that much of the poetry survived through constant use in worship and liturgy. Thus the Song of the Sea celebrated a single event, the Exodus, yet the significance of its theme ensured its survival; thanksgiving for Israel's liberation from Egypt became a hallmark of the religion of the Hebrews.

There is some evidence to suggest that from an early date songs were written down and collected together in "books" (presumably either scrolls or tablets) in early Israel. Two such ancient collections are referred to in the biblical text. First, there is the *Book of the Wars of the Lord* (Num 21:14), from which a poetic fragment, "Waheb in Suphah" (Num 21:14–15), is quoted. It may be that two other short poetic passages in the same chapter are also drawn from this book: the Song of the Well (Num 21:17–18) and the Song of Heshbon (Num 21:27–30). The Song of Heshbon is linked to the "ballad singers," who may have been the persons responsible for the preservation of songs in ancient times and for their compilation in the *Book of the Wars of the Lord;* Judges 5:11 may contain a further reference to such groups of singers and musicians who created and preserved Israel's poetry of war. The second ancient collection of poetry is the *Book of Yashar* (2 Sam 1:18), from which David's lament is quoted by the compiler of the Books of Samuel. This work must have been compiled during or after the time of David, and it is possible that the *Book of the Wars of the Lord* may also be dated to about the time of the beginning of the monarchy in Israel.

Though the contents of these two ancient collections are not known beyond the brief passages explicitly identified as drawn from them, they may have been the "psalters" of early Israel. The *Book of the Wars of the Lord* may have contained such passages as the Song of the Sea, the Song of Deborah and the Song of the Ark; the *Book of Yashar* may have contained other early poetry, such as Hannah's Song, in addition to David's Lament. This is clearly speculation; what is known with certainty is that there was a tradition in early Israel of collecting songs together into a book. It was this tradition and custom which, at a later period, was to culminate in the formation of the Book of Psalms. A brief insight into the period of transition is provided by David's great hymn of praise after deliverance from his enemies; the hymn is recorded first in the historical narrative (2 Sam 22), but later appears as a part of the Book of Psalms (Ps 18; see further the commentary).

THE COMPILATION OF THE PSALTER

In most contemporary forms of religion, use is made of a hymnal or service book for the purposes of worship. The hymnal is usually a collection of hymns and songs, written by many different people over the course of several centuries. It is basically an anthology, rather than the work of a single author. The individual compositions of many authors of entirely different backgrounds are brought together into a single volume by an editor or editorial team. A similar process apparently took place in the formation of the Book of Psalms. It contains the compositions of many poets and singers whose works have been brought together into a single volume, namely the Book of Psalms as it now stands. It is not possible to trace each step in the process from the composition of individual psalms to the compilation of the Psalter as a whole; nevertheless, a number of clues have survived concerning the various stages between composition and compilation. In summary form, one can trace four stages in the process: (a) a psalm is composed; (b) it is linked together with other psalms to form a small collection, analogous to the *Book of the Wars of the Lord* or the *Book of Yashar;* (c) several small collections are brought together to form a larger unit; (d) the current Book of Psalms emerged, being a "collection of collections," with various individual psalms added by the editor(s) of the final book.

There are several clues to this process of compilation contained within the Book of Psalms. First, there is the information contained in the titles which are placed at the beginning of many psalms. Although these titles are of dubious value with respect to the initial composition of the psalm they introduce, they are of considerable relevance with respect to the work of those who compiled the Book of Psalms. (The titles are examined in more detail in the next section; at this point, they are discussed only with respect to the compilation of the Psalter.) The titles identify certain psalms in relation to particular persons or according to particular types and thus may be indicative of early collections of psalms, prior to the formation of the Psalter as a whole. Second, Ps 72:20 should probably be understood as the concluding portion of an early collection of Davidic psalms: "David ben Jesse's prayers are ended." The words obviously do not apply to the Psalter as a whole, for many subsequent psalms in the Psalter are identified as Davidic. Third, there are a number of duplications within the Psalter (Ps 14 = Ps 53; Ps 40:13–17 = Ps 70; and Ps 108 = Ps 57:7–11 + 60:5–12), probably indicating that initially these psalms belonged to independent collections; when the collections were brought together, some duplication was inevitable.

Though all the early collections of psalms cannot be identified with precision, it is possible to list, by way of example, some of the basic collections which were to form part of the Psalter.

(i) *Collections of Davidic Psalms.* Several such collections can be identified: Pss 3–41 (with the possible exception of Ps 33); Pss 51–70 (with the possible exceptions of Pss 66 and 67); and Pss 138–45. These three collections do not constitute all the Davidic psalms, of which there are 73; others may have formed smaller collections (e.g., Pss 108–110) while yet others, which now stand alone, may have belonged to collections initially, but were moved to another position in the Psalter by the editor(s) for some theological or liturgical reason.

(ii) *The Psalms of Asaph.* Eleven psalms (Pss 73–83) made up the collection, to which Ps 50 may have belonged initially. Asaph was a Levite musician who played a leading role in the music of worship during the time of David (1 Chr 15:17–19; 16:4–5) and whose descendants carried on the family tradition of music (Ezra 3:10).

(iii) *Psalms of the Sons of Korah.* There may have been two such collections: Pss 42–49 (with the exception of Ps 43) and Pss 84–88 (with the exception of Ps 86). The Korahites were Levites, descended through Kohath (1 Chr 6:22), who were involved in the music of the temple.

Other psalms are identified as belonging to collections, not on the basis of association with a particular person or group, but on the basis of common type or subject matter, for example:

(iv) *Songs of Ascents* (Pss 120–134). These psalms have not only a certain similarity in content, but probably also shared a common function, namely use during or preceding Israel's great festivals, specifically the Feast of Tabernacles.

The list of collections is not complete; to it could be added the *Egyptian Hallel* [praise] *Collection* (Pss 113–118), which is traditionally associated with the Festival of Passover, and a second group of *Hallel Psalms* (Pss 146–150) for more general use in worship. But to go much further becomes a subjective process, for it is difficult to determine whether some groups of psalms, such as the two just mentioned, may have formed an original collection, or whether they may simply have been placed together in the final editorial process.

The next stage in the process of compilation is even more difficult to determine with clarity; some of the smaller collections were brought together to form larger collections. There is only one fairly firm piece of evidence to provide guidance with respect to this stage in the process of compilation; it pertains to the use of divine names in the Psalter. In Pss 1–41, the divine name *Yahweh* is used very frequently, and the name Elohim occurs only occasionally; *Yahweh* outnumbers *Elohim* by about 18 to 1 (S. R. Driver [*Introduction to the Literature of the Old Testament*, 371] specified 272 occurrences of *Yahweh*, and 15 of *Elohim*). On the other hand, in Pss 42–83 *Yahweh* is used only 43 times, in contrast to some 200 uses of the word *Elohim*. In the remainder of the Psalter (Pss 84–150), the name *Yahweh* predominates, with only about a dozen uses of *Elohim*.

This data provides the basis for postulating the existence of an "Elohistic Psalter" (Pss 42–83), in which the divine name *Elohim* was most commonly used, and the "Elohistic Psalter" in turn represents a second stage in compilation, namely the bringing together of a variety of smaller collections to form this larger collection. Although the argument is hypothetical, the hypothesis is firmly grounded. It cannot simply be argued that the author(s) or compilers of Pss 42–83 preferred to use the name *Elohim* for some unspecified reason, on at least two grounds. First, there are psalms within the "Elohistic Psalter" and outside it which are identified, for example, as Davidic; if one assumes that there were originally several Davidic collections, or a single Davidic collection that is now dispersed throughout the Psalter, the fact remains that the Davidic psalms within the "Elohistic Psalter" differ from these outside it with respect to the use of divine names. Second, two of the three psalms which are duplicated within the Psalter as a whole (as noted above) occur both within and outside the "Elohistic Psalter." In Ps 14, the name *Yahweh* occurs four times; in the duplicate Ps 53, three of the lines of Ps 14 employing *Yahweh* are precisely reproduced, except that in each case *Yahweh* has been replaced by *Elohim*. The evidence, however, is not without ambiguity, for in Ps 40:13–17, duplicated in the "Elohistic Psalter" in Ps 70, *Yahweh* (Ps 40:13) is replaced in one instance by *Elohim*, but in another place *Elohim* (Ps 40:17) is replaced by *Yahweh* (Ps 70:5)! And it must be remembered that *Yahweh* is by no means absent from the "Elohistic Psalter" (*Elohim* outnumbers *Yahweh* by 4.6 to 1).

Nevertheless, the accumulation of evidence strongly suggests that an editor compiled the "Elohistic Psalter" from earlier collections and that their editorial revisions included the deliberate and frequent revision of *Yahweh* to *Elohim*. This process may indicate that the purpose of the compilation was the production of a collection of hymns specifically designed for the temple's worship, at a time when the divine name *Yahweh* was used only with considerable hesitation. (Later in the history of Judaism, it was not used at all during normal worship and could only be pronounced by the high priest at a key moment in the observance of the Day of Atonement.) The "Elohistic Psalter" thus included various earlier collections: (i) a Korahite collection (Pss 42–49); (ii) a collection of the Psalms of Asaph (Pss 50, 73–83); (iii) a Davidic collection (Pss 51–65 and 68–72); and (iv) miscellaneous psalms (Pss 66 and 67).

Although the existence of an Elohistic Psalter can be postulated with a reasonable degree of certainty, it cannot be determined with any conviction whether or not there were other "collections of collections." In the absence of firm evidence, it is necessary to move on to the final stage, namely the compilation of the Book of Psalms as it now stands. The editor(s) of the Book of Psalms brought together the various collections and added a number of psalms which were probably not included initially in a collection, to form the hymnal of Israel. Psalm 1 (and perhaps also Ps 2; see the commentary) was placed at the beginning as an introduction to the Psalter; Ps 150, which may already have belonged to a collection of *Hallel* psalms, formed a suitable conclusion.

If the ordering of material within the book followed some grand design, it is no longer possible to discern that design with clarity; indeed, it is possible that there is no overall structure to the Book of Psalms. Sometimes a purpose can be seen in the placing of psalms alongside each other. Thus Psalm 3 was traditionally interpreted as a *morning prayer* and Psalm 4 as an *evening prayer* (see the commentary), so there was a certain logic in placing them together; but whether this was done by the editor(s) of the Book of Psalms, or by the compiler of a particular collection of Davidic psalms, cannot be determined.

The editor(s) of the Book of Psalms as a whole divided the entire Psalter into five "books" as follows:

Book I	Pss 1–41
Book II	Pss 42–72
Book III	Pss 73–89
Book IV	Pss 90–106
Book V	Pss 107–150

The end of each of these books contains a doxology: I . . . 41:13; II . . . 72:18–19; III . . . 89:52; IV . . . 106:48; V . . . 150:6 (although Ps 150 as a whole should perhaps be viewed as the doxology to the entire Psalter). Whether the doxologies were inserted by the editor(s), or whether the presence of the doxologies in particular psalms prompted the editor(s) to choose those points in the text for the division of the Psalter into five books, is uncertain. Probably the latter is the case, for there is no firm internal ground for viewing each of the five books of the Psalter as a complete or self-contained unit. If the divisions were made first on the basis of the existence of the doxologies (which initially functioned internally within the psalms of which they are a part), then the analogy of the Five Books of Moses to the five so-called Books of Psalms may have suggested itself to the editor(s). But if such were the case, the correspondence does not go beyond the number five, and no firm internal correspondences or analogies can be established between the five Books of Psalms and the Five Books of Moses.

The book thus compiled is referred to as the *Book of Psalms;* the English word *psalm* is derived from the Greek Ψαλμός which in turn is a translation of Hebrew מזמור, designating either instrumental music or song. For practical purposes, the English title of the book means "Book of Songs." The traditional Hebrew title of the book is ספר תהלים, or "Book of Praises." But neither the English title (after the Greek version) nor the Hebrew title is precise as a designation of the book as a whole. The Psalter is more than a collection of *songs,* for it contains also prayer and wisdom poetry; and for the same reason, it is more than a collection of *praises* (the Hebrew word is used only once, in the singular, viz. תהלה, in the psalm title prefixed to Ps 145). But the titles of the book, whether English or Hebrew, are useful enough, for no single word could encompass the richness and diversity of poetry and religious thought and expression contained in this extraordinary book.

It is not known precisely when the task of compiling the Psalter was completed. The psalms within it come from a variety of periods—from before the monarchy (in a few cases) to after the exile. It is probable that the Book of Psalms had reached substantially its present form by the fourth century B.C.

PSALM TITLES

Bibliography

Childs, B. S. "Psalm Titles and Midrashic Exegesis." *JSS* 16 (1971) 137–50. **Delekat, L.** "Probleme der Psalmenüberschriften." *ZAW* 76 (1964) 280–97. **Guilding, A.** "Some Obscured Rubrics and Lectionary Allusions in the Psalter." *JTS* (NS) 3 (1952) 41–55.

Of the 150 psalms in the Psalter, 116 are provided with titles. The titles are incorporated within the text of modern editions of the Hebrew Bible; they are translated in most (but not all) modern English versions of the Bible. The titles form a part of the canonical text of the Hebrew Bible. It is, therefore, unfortunate that some modern versions, such as the NEB, omit them in their translation. In many cases, however, the titles do not appear to form an integral part of the psalm to which they are attached; they may represent the work of the editors of the early collections, or of the Book of Psalms as a whole. Thus, they are frequently of more importance for understanding the role of particular psalms in the context of the Psalter and in the historical context of Israel's worship than they are for understanding the original meaning and context of the individual psalms.

The titles have often been given little importance in the contemporary study of the Psalms. Mowinckel describes them as *midrashic*, specifying the term as designating the "learned forming of legends" (*The Psalms in Israel's Worship*, II, 100), though his comment pertains primarily to the historical information contained in the titles, and he makes considerable use of their data with respect to reconstructing the compilation of the Psalter. While titles may be in some sense *midrashic* (viz. investigative), they do represent a devout and serious study of the text of the Psalms (cf. B. S. Childs, *JSS* 16 [1971] 137–50) and deserve careful examination. Though the date of the titles cannot be determined with precision, some may come from the postexilic period and the final stages in the process of compiling the Psalter. However, certain psalms outside the Psalter also contain titles, which may indicate the possibility of the transmission of individual psalms together with titles from the time of their composition or soon thereafter. David's psalm of thanksgiving (2 Sam 22:1) and Hezekiah's psalm of thanksgiving (Isa 38:9) both contain titles of an historical character; Habakkuk's psalm has a title containing the type of musical and other data found in titles in the Book of Psalms (Hab 3:1, 19b). Thus it is possible that in some cases, psalm titles may have been linked to particular psalms before their incorporation within the Psalter or in the earlier collections; this possibility is evaluated with respect to the individual titles in the commentary. The statement in Ps 72:20 concerning the ending of David's prayers (see the comment on p 28 above) may also indicate the presence of titles in psalms at an early stage in the process of compilation.

To this internal evidence, certain external evidence may be added. A Hurrian cult song, together with musical notation, which was recovered from the excavations at Ras Shamra/Ugarit, contains a colophon (see RS 15.30 +15:49 +17.387; E. Laroche, "Documents en langue Hourrite provenant de Ras Shamra," *Ugaritica* V, 463–87). The colophon specifies that the text is a song, that it is to be sung according to a certain type of tuning or scale, that it is a type of *hymn* (though the meaning of the text is uncertain), and it concludes with the name of the scribe or copyist, namely a certain Ammurapi. The presence of such a colophon on the same tablet containing the words and music for the song suggests that some psalm titles may have accompanied their respective psalms prior to their incorporation within collections internal to the Psalter. Furthermore, the reference to tuning or scale in this colophon may give a clue—in principle, at least—to the meaning of certain obscure terms in the psalm titles, such as *sheminith* (Ps 6:1), which has been translated tentatively as "octave."

In general terms, the titles contain five different types of information, though the obscurity of certain words in the titles is such that it cannot be known with certainty whether this fivefold classification is complete. (a) Some titles identify psalms with a person or group of persons (e.g., Pss 3, 72, 90; see further the discussion of authorship on p 33). (b) Some psalm titles contain what purports to be historical information concerning the psalm, particularly with respect to David (e.g., Pss 18, 34). (c) Some titles contain musical information (e.g. Pss 4, 5; see p 38). (d) Some titles contain liturgical information (e.g. Pss 38, 100). (e) Some titles designate the *type* of psalm (e.g. hymn or song) in question (e.g. Pss 32, 120, 145).

The titles were included in the earliest versions (e.g. the LXX, but there are a number of minor variations between the text of the LXX titles and that of the Hebrew Bible), though some of the words employed in the titles were apparently not understood by the translators. Some scholars believe that this lack of understanding—evident when the Hebrew Bible was translated into Greek during the third/second centuries B.C.—is indicative of the titles' antiquity (D. Kidner, *Psalms 1–72*, 32–33). This is possible, though it may simply indicate a lack of musical or liturgical knowledge on the part of the translators, or the lack of equivalent or appropriate terminology in the Greek language. The psalm titles were also apparently known and utilized as a part of the text of the psalms by the writers of the NT (e.g. Mark 12:35–37; Acts 2:29–35). For further information on particular psalm titles, see the commentary.

THE PSALMS AND THE PROBLEM OF AUTHORSHIP

A major problem pertaining to the study of individual psalms relates to the possibility of identifying authors for the particular compositions. A comprehensive listing of authors is clearly impossible, for 34 psalms have no titles and are technically anonymous; while in theory it might be possible to determine authorship on the basis of the content of these anonymous psalms, in practice the substance of the psalms is such as to make the task virtually impossible. However, the existence of titles for 116 psalms raises the possibility of identifying particular authors for particular compositions.

As has been noted, the psalm titles contain a variety of different types of information, but the majority of titles include some kind of reference to a person or persons. The persons clearly named in the psalm titles are the following: (i) David, most frequently; (ii) Solomon (Pss 72, 127); (iii) Moses (Ps 90); (iv) Asaph (twelve times); (v) Heman the Ezrahite (Ps 88); (vi) Ethan, the Ezrahite (Ps 89); (vii) the Sons of Korah (eleven times); and (viii) the musical director (or choir-master: מנצח, more than 50 times). The first part of the problem concerns whether or not this designation of persons in the titles was intended to convey authorship, or whether there was some other purpose in the designation. Depending upon the resolution of the first part of the problem, a second problem may emerge: if the designations were intended to convey authorship, are they a reliable guide or does their editorial nature result in doubtful evidence with respect to identifying authors?

In attempting to resolve these problems, it is necessary to examine first the potential meaning of the Hebrew preposition ל which is prefixed to the persons named in the titles. The preposition has a variety of possible meanings in English translation; in the normal process of translation, it is the context which helps to resolve the ambiguity in meaning, but in the psalm titles the ambiguity cannot be resolved by the context alone. The titles are for the most part in the form of notes, a kind of editorial shorthand, so that grammatical and contextual ambiguity remains. The following are possible meanings of the preposition ל in the titles: (a) "for" (e.g. for David); (b) "by" (e.g. by David; viz. belonging to David as author): (c) "to" (perhaps in the sense "dedicated to"); (d) "with reference to, concerning, about"; (e) "for the use of." Some of the earlier grammarians assumed that the second of the possible meanings listed above, the so-called *lamedh auctoris*, was intended in the psalm titles; they pointed to the common usage of the same idiom in other Semitic languages such as Arabic (e.g. *GKC* §129 c). But in the Ugaritic texts, where a similar variety in meaning for the preposition *1* is known, the expression *1b'1* would fall into category (d) above, meaning "about/concerning Baal" (or perhaps "[tablet belonging] to [the] Baal [cycle]," as proposed by D. Pardee, "The Preposition in Ugaritic." *UF* 8 [1976] 215–322 [*p. 301]).

Apart from the general ambiguity associated with ל, the contents of the psalm titles indicate that the preposition is used in a variety of different ways.

(a) The most common use is with the name of an individual, either standing alone (e.g. Ps 11:1 לדוד "for David") or following a term such as "hymn" or "song" (e.g. Ps. 3:1 מזמור לדוד "a song for David").

(b) A similar usage is seen in conjunction with the title, rather than the name, of a person (e.g. Ps 4:1 למנצח "for the musical director").

(c) It may be used with a group of persons (e.g. Ps 42:1 לבני קרח "for the sons of Korah").

(d) It may be used with the sense "for (use on)" (e.g. Ps 92:1 ליום השבת "for use on the sabbath day.")

(e) It may be used with the sense "for (the use of)" (e.g. Ps 102:1 לעני: "for the use of the afflicted.")

(f) It may carry the sense "belonging to," without connotations of authorship (e.g. Ps 30:1 הבית לדוד, "for the house of David," though if לדוד is taken as standing separately from the preceding word, this example should then be moved to [a] above.)

It is clear from the data listed above that the preposition is employed in a variety of different ways; the critical question concerns whether its use in category (a) above should be taken to imply authorship. In category (b), it almost certainly does not imply authorship, if only because the numerous examples of למנצח usually occur in titles in conjunction with another use of the same preposition (e.g. with לדוד, Ps 11:1); both uses of ל cannot imply authorship (unless one assumes joint-authorship for the more than fifty psalms concerned). The most appropriate translation of למנצח would be "for the use of/for use by the music director." The implication is that these psalms belonged to a collection, though the wide distribution of psalms including the term למנצח indicates that the collection overlaps into many of the more clearly discernible collections noted on p 28 above, and it may have been a collection based on the already compiled Psalter or approximately contemporary with the final compilation of the Psalter. Category (c), referring to a group (the "Sons of Korah"), could be taken to be analogous to category (a), though the role of the Korahites in the temple music implies rather the sense "for the use of the Sons of Korah" (indicating a collection); if the latter were correct, category (f) would be similar to category (c), and both would be similar to category (b).

From this survey of the use of the preposition, it is by no means clear what ל means in category (a). The possibility remains that it implies authorship, though there is no persuasive evidence to indicate that such is the case. It could certainly mean "for the use of David" (implying "for the use of the

Davidic Kings"), as is argued by Mowinckel (*The Psalms in Israel's Worship* I 77) and other scholars. It could imply "belonging to David," in the sense of belonging to a collection of Davidic hymns. And it could mean "(dedicated) to David," who was the patron of psalmody in Israel. Thus, it is concluded that the conjunction of the preposition ל with certain personal names (David, Solomon, Moses, et al.) need not, and probably does not, imply authorship. If the addition of names in psalm titles was intended by the editors to imply authorship, then it must be concluded that the editorial addition was not in every case accurate.

Nevertheless, the strong possibility remains that in some cases the Psalter contains psalms composed by David (though now the argument does not rest simply on the meaning of the preposition ל in the titles). In historical and prophetical narratives, David is frequently associated with music and psalmody. He is called the "sweet psalmist of Israel" (2 Sam 23:1). He is credited with inventing musical instruments (Amos 6:5). He is said to have appointed singers and musicians and assigned them to their roles in the worship of God (1 Chr 15:16–24; 16:7, 31). At a later date, music and worship were specified as being undertaken according to the directions of David (Ezra 3:10; Neh 12:24). And several poetic passages in the historical narratives are directly associated with him (David's Lament, 2 Sam 1:19–27; two hymns of thanksgiving, 2 Sam 22 and 1 Chr 16:8–36; and David's Last Testament, 2 Sam 23:3–7). The probability remains, therefore, that a number of the psalms in the Psalter which are associated with David may be Davidic compositions.

In general, however, it may be safest to recognize that the majority of psalms are anonymous and that no certain statement can be made concerning their authorship. The origin of many of the psalms may be found within the context of Israel's worship, in those servants of the temple whose names have not survived for the benefit of posterity. But the absence of precise information concerning authorship is not a serious setback with respect to understanding the Psalms, for their theme is the relationship between a person and God, and their variations on that central theme have a universality and timelessness which transcend the particularities of authorship.

HEBREW POETRY AND MUSIC

Bibliography

Alden, R. L. "Chiastic Psalms: A Study in the Mechanics of Semitic Poetry in Psalms 1–50." *JETS* 17 (1974) 11–28. **Bee, R. E.** "The Mode of Composition and Statistical Scansion." *JSOT* 6 (1978) 58–68. **Casetti, P.** "Funktionen der Musik in der Bibel." *FreibZ* 24 (1977) 366–89. **Gray, G. B.** *The Forms of Hebrew Poetry.* First published in 1915. Reprinted, with a Prolegomenon by D. N. Freedman, New York: KTAV, 1972. **Kilmer, A. D., Crocker, R. L. and Brown, R. R.** *Sounds from Silence. Recent Discoveries in Ancient Near Eastern Music.* Berkeley: Bit Enki Publications, 1976. (Booklet and stereo record.) **Robinson, T. H.** *The Poetry of the Old Testament.* London: Duckworth, 1947. **Stuart, D. K.** *Studies in Early Hebrew Meter.* HSM 13. Missoula: Scholars Press, 1976.

The psalms are poetic compositions; some were no doubt composed orally and spontaneously, whereas others were literary compositions in a more formal sense. A recognition of the poetic form of the psalms is important for their interpretation, for poetry is a special kind of language; the importance of poetic language in the biblical context is indicated by the fact that somewhere between a third and a half of the OT is poetic in form. Whereas the language of prose is utilized primarily toward direct communication, poetic language is characterized by a more transcendent quality. There are aspects of human experience, and aspects of the knowledge of God, for which the mundane language of prose cannot provide adequate expression. Poetry is, among other things, an attempt to transcend the limitations of normal (prosaic) human language and to give expression to something not easily expressed in words—indeed, it may ultimately be inexpressible in human terms. When poetry is accompanied by music, the element of transcendence may be heightened.

Thus the psalms, which in many different ways reflect the relationship between Israel and God, utilize the medium of poetry to convey insight, experience, the perception of God and the nature of the relationship with God. They are, on the one hand, profoundly theological writings; on the other hand, they defy any attempt to reduce them to theological dogma or creed. Poetry, like music, may be analyzed and dissected, yet ultimately it must be appreciated and experienced, and to divorce the element of subjectivity from the understanding of poetry is to divest it of its power. But though poetry is a form of art, and the interpretation of poetry may become a form of science, the two cannot be entirely separated, particularly for those in the modern world, who are so far removed from the cultural milieu which gave birth to the Psalms. A knowledge of the fundamental forms and canons of Hebrew poetry provides the framework within which that poetry can be appreciated and its meaning grasped. Thus the formal analysis of poetry is a useful and necessary task, though it cannot be an end in itself; it must be a means toward the end of appreciating, understanding and ultimately utilizing the Psalms.

A problem arises, however, in determining the precise nature and forms of Hebrew poetry; although there is some agreement concerning the principal characteristics, there continue to be numerous areas of debate and speculation. Unfortunately, there remain no works from ancient Israel (if they ever existed) on the nature of poetics and rhetoric, such as survived from the Classical World (Aristotle's *De Poetica*) or from the world of classical Tamil poetry (the ancient *Tolkāpiyyam*). G. B. Gray, in an important study published in 1915, stated that "the main forms of Hebrew poetry are two—parallelism and rhythm, to which as a third and occasional form, we may add strophe" (*The Forms of Hebrew Poetry*, 236). The two main forms of Hebrew poetry, parallelism and rhythm (or meter), are undisputed, though there is a good deal of dispute concerning the precise nature of each form. The third form, strophe, is at best occasional and in a technical sense, it may not exist at all, though often in English translation a kind of strophic structure may be determined on the basis of units of meaning or the recurrence of a refrain. To these basic forms can be added the variety of tools employed by poets everywhere, such as simile, metaphor, chiasmus and the like.

Of the two principal forms of Hebrew poetry, it is debatable whether *parallelism* or *rhythm* (meter) is the primary characteristic. Nevertheless, of the two,

it is parallelism which is most clearly understood and parallelism which survives translation into languages other than Hebrew. Since Robert Lowth's
magnificent study, *De Sacra Poesie Hebraeorum Praelectiones Academicae,* was published in 1753, the basic characteristics of parallelism (and many other aspects
of Hebrew poetry) have been recovered for modern scholarship. While a
knowledge of parallelism had been retained within traditional Judaism and
is reflected in a number of writings before the work of Lowth (references
occur in the writings of Ibn Ezra, Kimhi, Azariah de Rossi, and others), for
practical purposes it was Lowth's work which rediscovered parallelism for
modern scholarship.

Lowth's system has been modified and corrected in a number of details,
but his basic insights remain unchanged. A large amount of Hebrew poetry,
though not all, is characterized by thought parallelism, which may take a
variety of forms: e.g., synonymous parallelism (the repetition of the thought
of one line in the following line, with the use of different words), or antithetical
parallelism (the expression in the second line of the opposite thought to
that contained in the first line). The psalmists make frequent use of parallelism,
and the implications of parallelism in its various forms are noted in the commentary on particular psalms.

The question of rhythm or meter, however, has been debated hotly for
several centuries. In the seventeenth century, a certain Marcus Meibomius
boasted that to him had been revealed the true science of Hebrew meter;
he promised to release this secret as soon as 6,000 subscribers had promised
him five pounds sterling for a copy of his work. Unable to raise the funds,
he took his secrets of Hebrew meter with him to the grave, though as John
Jebb remarked wryly in 1820: "posterity may contentedly endure the depriva-
tion" (*Sacred Literature* 11). The incident is not untypical of many eccentric
approaches to the study of Hebrew meter prior to the advent of modern
biblical scholarship. In the scholarship of the last century, a number of different theories of meter have emerged; some theories are mutually incompatible,
whereas others may overlap or complement each other to a certain extent.
A useful survey of the principal systems of metrical analysis is provided in
D. Stuart, *Studies in Early Hebrew Meter* 1–10. Stuart's own system, which is
rooted in the earlier work of F. M. Cross, D. N. Freedman and others, is
essentially a system of scansion based upon syllable counting, in contrast
to earlier systems based upon such factors as stress (the stress of syllables
in a poetic "foot"), or word-units, insofar as they comprised the poetic line.

However, all attempts to determine a precise system of meter in biblical
Hebrew poetry are severely limited by the absence of critical data. Those
systems of meter which depend upon the vocalization of the Massoretic text
are weakened by the fact that the vocalization of the Massoretes, in all its
details, may not represent the vocalization, and hence pronounciation, of
the poetry in its original form (the original form being represented by the
consonantal text). On the other hand, systems such as that of Stuart, which
as a preliminary exercise involve the reconstruction of the supposed vocalization of the consonantal text in ancient times, are inevitably characterized
by a high degree of hypothetical reconstruction. The problem is compounded
by the fact that a large percentage of the psalms cannot be dated with any

confidence, which in turn means that the hypothetical nature of any reconstructed vocalization is even further accentuated. While it may be granted
that a system based on the reconstructed vocalization of certain datable Hebrew texts may be preferable to a system based upon the Massoretic vocalization, neither system is free from fundamental problems. And granted that
the limited materials employed by Stuart in his studies of Hebrew meter
may be dated with some certainty, the lack of similar certainty with respect
to the great majority of the psalms renders the syllabic metrical scansion,
based upon a hypothetically revocalized text, too delicate and subjective a
task to be employed in this commentary.

As a consequence, the approach to meter in Hebrew poetry which has
been adopted in this volume may seem to some to be rather old-fashioned.
In general terms, I have adopted the general system espoused by G. B. Gray
and T. H. Robinson (*The Poetry of the Old Testament* 30–46); the meter of
lines is indicated, for example, as 2+2 or 3+3, the numbers referring not
to syllables (for which larger numbers would occur) or accents (though there
may be coincidence with accent), but to "units," which may sometimes be
single words, or sometimes compound expressions. The system is by no means
entirely accurate, for no system can be in view of the limitations of the evidence. Nevertheless, it is a relatively adequate system, for any approach to
Hebrew meter is essentially *descriptive* of the phenomenon of line length or
relative line lengths, there being no evidence that a theory or system of meter
was ever articulated in ancient Israel. The very concept of the word *meter,*
drawn as it is from classical and European languages, may be inappropriate
to Hebrew poetry if it is taken to imply any rigid regularity or system, but
as a word designating approximate line length and the approximate balance
of lines, it may serve as a useful tool.

If there are problems with respect to the knowledge of meter, there are
even greater problems with respect to knowledge of music in ancient Israel.
Quite a lot is known *about* music, viz. about the organization of temple singers
and musicians, about the types of musical instruments, and about the varieties
of musical usage in ancient Israel (cf. P. Casetti, "Funktionen der Musik in
der Bibel." *FreibZ* 24 [1977] 366–89). But with respect to the form of music,
what it sounded like, whether it was a kind of chant or more rhythmic melody
(or both), little can be known with certainty. The Psalm titles (see p 31 above)
contain some musical information, though few of them can be interpreted
with precision; the information contained in the titles is examined in the
body of the commentary.

Some general light has recently been shed on music in the ancient Near
East as a consequence of archaeological research. Clay tablets (three fragments
of a single text) were recovered from Ras Shamra (ancient Ugarit), containing
the words of a Hurrian cult-song together with musical notations. The musical
notations have been deciphered provisionally and the song has been recorded
(in stereo) with the aid of a lyre reconstructed according to ancient patterns:
see *Sounds from Silence. Recent Discoveries in Ancient Near Eastern Music.* The
whole process of interpreting the musical notations, building and tuning the
musical instrument and other related matters is fraught with technical problems (see the author's review of the recording in *NewsUgSt* 15 [January, 1978]

6–7). Nevertheless, this modern recording of music from the Late Bronze Age in Ugarit, some centuries before the period of the Book of Psalms, is a remarkable achievement. Though the relationship (if any) between Hurrian cult music and Hebrew music is not known, the recording of the ancient song provides a small glimpse into the world of music which was part of the environment of the ancient Hebrews.

THEOLOGICAL PERSPECTIVES ON THE BOOK OF PSALMS

Bibliography

Amirtham, S. "To be near and to be far away from Yahweh: the Witness of the Individual Psalms of Lament to the Concept of the Presence of God." *Bangalore Theological Forum* 2 (1968) 31–55. **Burns, J. S.** "The Mythology of Death in the Old Testament." *SJT* 26 (1973) 327–40. (Reference to the Psalms, Wisdom Literature and the Prophets.) **Fischer, B.** "Zum Problem einer christlichen Interpretation der Psalmen." *TRev* 61 (1971) 5–12. **Harmon, A. M.** "Aspects of Paul's Use of the Psalms." *WTJ* 32 (1969) 1–23. **Kraus, H.-J.** *Theologie der Psalmen.* BKAT 15/3. Neukirchen-Vluyn: Neukirchener Verlag, 1979. **Lewis, C. S.** *Reflections on the Psalms.* London: Geoffrey Bles, 1958. **Parson, I. R. M.** "Suffering in the Psalms." *AusBR* 20 (1972) 49–53. **Seybold, K.** *Das Gebet des Kranken im Alten Testament. Untersuchung zur Bestimmung und Zuordnung der Krankheits- und Heilungspsalme.* Stuttgart: Kohlhammer, 1973. **Smick, E.** "The Bearing of New Philological Data on the Subjects of Resurrection and Immortality in the Old Testament." *WTJ* 31 (1968) 12–21. **Thordarson, T. K.** "The Mythic Dimension. Hermeneutical Remarks on the Language of the Psalter." *VT* 24 (1974) 212–40. **Vosbergh, L.** *Studium zum Reden vom Schöpfer in den Psalmen.* München: Chr. Kaiser Verlag, 1975.

In the few paragraphs that follow, no attempt is made to provide a comprehensive theology of the Book of Psalms: the items listed in the bibliography will provide a preliminary guide to further reading. More detailed theological comment can be found in the body of the commentary; the following comments merely set certain general perspectives within which to engage in theological reflection.

Within the OT as a whole, the biblical literature may be divided loosely into two categories. First, there is that which purports to be God's direct revelation to mankind (specifically to Israel) through the medium of the prophet; for example, much of the Law of Moses and the oracles of the prophets fall into this category. Second, there is that literature which purports to be primarily a human creation, though it is created in the religious context and pertains to the relationship between Israel and God, or in some cases to the relationship between Hebrew and Hebrew. The Psalms fall into this second category. With the exception of a few psalms which have a prophetic character, the Book of Psalms as a whole contains Israel's songs and prayers which constitute the response of the chosen people to their revelation from God. (The Book of Psalms is thus recognized as "revelation," or inspired, by virtue of its inclusion in the canon of Holy Scripture, rather than by any internal characteristics specifying God's direct self-revelation in word.)

It is this primary characteristic which provides a starting point for all theological reflection on the Book of Psalms. For the most part, the psalms do

not contain abstract theological statements or anything approaching philosophical theology. The theological richness of the psalms emerges out of
a profound knowledge of God rooted in relationship; at bottom, the framework
for all dimensions of that relationship is provided by the covenant. Thus
the psalmists are covenant writers, whether their perspective is individual,
national, or that of Israel's cult. And their knowledge of God is rooted in
the covenant; they respond to God in prayer, in praise, or in particular life
situations because of an already existing covenant relationship which makes
such response possible. In this broad sense, all the psalms may be related
to the central concept of covenant, though they are not necessarily to be
linked to a specific covenant festival, as is proposed by Weiser in his commentary, *The Psalms* (see section on *The Psalms in Recent Research* below). Because the
covenant dominated all aspects of human life for the Hebrews, to a greater
or lesser extent, there is no aspect of life which may not appear in the psalms.
The psalms may thus relate to national events such as a coronation (Ps 2),
may reflect intensely personal prayer (Ps 3), may offer praise to God in a
thunderstorm (Ps 29) or in the wonders of his creation (Ps 104), may be
identified with particular religious festivals (Pss 113–118), or may relate to
any other private or public aspect of life. This broad spectrum of the experience of God which is reflected in the psalms means that they contain *popular
theology*, in the best sense of that expression; it is not the abstract and philosophical theology limited to the intelligentsia, but that theology or knowledge of God which emerges out of a life lived in relationship with God.

But to say that theology is popular is not to undermine its significance
or importance; popular theology is theology at its best, for if the knowledge
of God is revealed to all mankind (or, in the context of the psalms, to all
Israel) then that knowledge should be grasped and articulated by all. The
Book of Psalms not only contains this popular theology, and hence teaches
it, but it also offers this theology for all to utilize. Insofar as the psalms
have been employed in both Jewish and Christian worship from their earliest
periods down to the present century, this theology has survived, though its
ultimate survival will depend upon the extent to which the psalms continue
to be understood in their modern use.

In the interpretation of the psalms, an attempt must be made to distinguish
between different layers of theological meaning and significance. The long
history of particular psalms and of the Psalter as a whole is such that their
theological significance and relevance may change. Psalm 2 provides an illustration. If it is correct, (see further the commentary) that Ps 2 was initially
a royal psalm related to the coronation of a Davidic King, then it is clear
that the significance of the psalm had changed by the time of its incorporation
into the Psalter as it now stands, for at that time the Davidic monarchy no
longer functioned in Jerusalem. The initial, quite specific role of the psalm
had been broadened to a more general role in the context of Israel's worship.
And by NT times, Ps 2 was clearly recognized as messianic, indicating yet
another dimension of its meaning and use. The words of the psalm do not
change, but its function and significance have changed over the passage of
time. Consequently there is change, or at least development, in the theological
significance of the psalm; whereas in its original form, its theology pertained

to the role of God in relation to the Davidic kings, that theology eventually blossomed into a fully messianic theology in one period of the history of the psalm's interpretation. The latter stage is not a new theology, but a growth and development from the initial nucleus.

There are two important consequences which emerge from the recognition of distinct layers of theological meaning in the psalms. (1) If a psalm is to be understood fully, it is best to begin the attempt at comprehension by determining the initial meaning, and hence the initial theological significance, of the psalm (though this may not always be possible). From there, it is possible to build toward a greater understanding. Thus, Ps 2 was not initially a messianic psalm, in my judgment; it was a royal psalm which was transformed at a later date into a messianic psalm, the transformation being evident clearly in the NT. If this is correct, then care must be taken to interpret the psalm first in its initial setting; only then may the richness of the later theological meaning of the psalm emerge. (2) The reinterpretation of individual psalms within the biblical tradition itself also provides the starting point for a contemporary reinterpretation of the psalm for our own use. The fact, for example, that a modern reader of Ps 2 may live in a republic in the modern world does not mean that this monarchic hymn of coronation has no relevance; it has relevance both from the perspective of the NT interpretation of the psalm and from a personal interpretation and appropriation of its theological insight.

Nevertheless, the modern reader may find a number of problems, which are broadly identified as theological problems, in reading the Book of Psalms and in the attempt to make the theological content of the psalms relevant and meaningful. There are many places in the Psalter, particularly in the so-called *individual laments,* where the sentiments of the psalmists seem to be harsh, unloving and vindictive, and they are thus hard to relate to the gospel and to Jesus' injunction that we love even our enemies. Of many such problematic passages in the psalms, there are few more difficult than Ps 137:8–9, in which the psalmist, crying for vengeance, declares the happy estate of those who kill Babylonian babies by dashing them upon the rocks. There are no simple solutions to problems such as these. But these psalms are not the oracles of God; they are Israel's response to God's revelation emerging from the painful realities of human life, and thus they open a window into the soul of the psalmist. The psalmists in ancient times were bound to the same commitment of love for enemies as is the modern Christian or Jew (cf. Lev 19:17–18; Exod 23:4–5), and their expressions of vindictiveness and hatred are not "purified" or "holy" simply by virtue of being present in Scripture. They are the real and natural reactions to the experience of evil and pain, and though the sentiments are in themselves evil, they are a part of the life of the soul which is bared before God in worship and prayer. The psalmist may hate his oppressor; God hates the oppression. Thus the words of the psalmist are often natural and spontaneous, not always pure and good, and yet they reflect the intimacy of the relationship between psalmist and God. The expression of hatred is in a way a confession of sin, though it is not phrased as such; it is a part of the inner life of a person which may be cleansed and transformed through the relationship with God. (For further perspectives on these and related problems, C. S. Lewis' book, *Reflections on the Psalms,* is highly recommended.)

In the commentary on the respective psalms, the various levels and dimensions of theological meaning are interpreted as far as the evidence permits. The primary theological relevance is examined in the basic interpretation of each psalm; the broader theological significance, from a NT and contemporary perspective, is treated in the concluding portion of the commentary on each of the psalms.

THE PLACE OF THE BOOK OF PSALMS IN THE OLD TESTAMENT

From an early period (at least the second century B.C.), the OT was divided into three sections, the Law *(Torah),* the Prophets *(Nebi'im),* and the Writings *(Kethubim).* The Book of Psalms belongs to the third division, the Writings, though its appropriate place within that division is uncertain. The expression, "The Law of Moses, the Prophets, the Psalms" (Luke 24:44; cf. 2 Macc 2:13), implies either that the Psalms came first in the Writings, or at least that the book was considered to be the most significant part of the third division in the first century A.D. But according to the ancient manuscripts, the Psalms sometimes come first in the Writings (in the northern or "German" tradition) and sometimes second, after Chronicles (in the southern or "Spanish" tradition) or after Ruth (in the Talmud; *Bathra* 14b). The ordering of books in the English Bible does not follow the Hebrew manuscripts at this point, but follows rather the early Christian tradition concerning the ordering of the books.

CHAPTER AND VERSE NUMBERS IN THE PSALMS

The Psalms are numbered in this commentary after the system of the Hebrew Bible, which has been adopted by most modern English translations. However, the numbering of the psalms differs between the Hebrew text and the LXX at certain points, and some older English translations (and certain currently used Roman Catholic translations) follow the LXX. In this commentary, the numbers of the Hebrew text (and most modern English Bibles) have been followed. However, as a guide to the reader, the following comparative table of numbering systems is provided.

Hebrew Text	Septuagint
1–8	1–8
9–10	9
11–113	10–112
114–115	113
116	114–115
117–146	116–145
147	146–147
148–150	148–150

The LXX also includes an additional psalm, Ps 151, though it is explicitly identified as being "outside the number." The differences in numbering, as they pertain to particular psalms, are examined in the body of the commentary; in this volume *(Psalms 1–50)*, see the commentary on Pss 9–10.

There are some differences in the numbering of verses between the Hebrew Bible and most English versions. In the Hebrew text, titles which consist of more than a word or two are normally set off as the first verse of the psalm (e.g. Ps 3:1) and on one occasion as the first two verses (Ps 51:1–2). In most English versions (e.g. KJV or RSV), the titles are separated from the psalms and the verse following the title is numbered as the first verse. Thus Ps 3:2 (Hebrew) = Ps 3:1 (English). In this commentary, which is based upon the Hebrew text, the numbers of the Hebrew text are followed. Readers are warned that there may thus be a difference of one verse between the translation of certain psalms with title in this commentary and the more familiar English translations.

THE PSALMS IN RECENT RESEARCH

Bibliography

(a) *Surveys of Current Research*
Becker, J. *Wege der Psalmenexegese.* SBS 78. Stuttgart: KBW Verlag, 1975. **Clines, D. J. A.** "Psalm Research since 1955: I. The Psalms and the Cult." *TyndB* 18 (1967) 103–26. ———. "Psalm Research since 1955: II. The Literary Genres." *TyndB* 20 (1969) 105–26. **Eaton, J. H.** "The Psalms in Israelite Worship." *Tradition and Interpretation,* ed. G. W. Anderson. Oxford: Clarendon Press (1979) 238–73. **Gerstenberger, E.** "Literatur zu den Psalmen." *VF* 17 (1972) 82–99. **Hunt, I.** "Recent Psalm Study." *Worship* 51 (1977) 127–44. ———. "Recent Psalm Study: Individual Psalms and Verses." *Worship* 52 (1978) 245–58. **Johnson, A. R.** "The Psalms." *The Old Testament and Modern Study,* ed. H. H. Rowley. Oxford: Clarendon Press (1951) 162–209. **Kapelrud, A. S.** "Scandinavian Research in the Psalms after Mowinckel." *ASTI* 4 (1965) 74–90. **Mowinckel, S.** "Psalm Criticism between 1900 and 1935." *VT* 5 (1955) 13–33. **Neumann, P. H. A.** ed. *Zur neueren Psalmenforschung.* Wege der Forschung 192. Darmstadt: Wissenschaftliche Buchgessellschaft, 1976. (This book is an anthology of significant studies on the Psalms during the previous 75 years, with essays by Gunkel, Mowinckel and others.) **Schildenberger, J.** "Die Psalmen. Eine Übersicht über einige Psalmenwerke der Gegenwart." *BibLeb* 8 (1967) 220–31. **Stamm, J. J.** "Ein Viertel jahrhundert Psalmenforschung." *TRu* 23 (1955) 1–68. **Van der Ploeg, J.** "L'étude du Psautier, 1960 à 1967." *De Mari à Qumran. Donum Natalicium Iosepho Coppens.* Vol I: *L'Ancien Testament.* Gembloux: Duculot (1969) 174–91.

(b) *Commentaries and Textual Studies*
Anderson, A. A. *Psalms.* 2 vols. The New Century Bible. London: Oliphants, 1972. **Beaucamp, E.** *Le Psautier. Ps. 1–72.* SB 7. Paris: Gabalda, 1976. **Briggs, C. A. and E. G.** *A Critical and Exegetical Commentary on the Book of Psalms.* 2 vols. International Critical Commentary. Edinburgh: T & T Clark, 1906. **Dahood, M.** *Psalms I. 1–50. Introduction, Translation and Notes.* AB 16. New York: Doubleday, 1966. **Delitzsch, F.** *Biblical Commentary on the Psalms.* 3 vols. Tr. D. Eaton. London: Hodder & Stoughton, 1887. **Durham, J. I.** *Commentary on Psalms. The Broadman Bible Commentary,* ed. C. J. Allen. Vol. 4. Nashville: Broadman Press, 1972. **Gunkel, H.** *Die Psalmen übersetzt und erklärt.* HKAT II/2. 4th ed. Gottingen: Vandenhoeck und Ruprecht, 1926. **Jacquet, L.** *Les Psaumes et le couer de l'homme. Étude textuelle, littéraire et doctrinale.* Vol 1 (Book 1

of the Psalter). Gembloux: Duculot, 1975. **Kidner, D.** *Psalms 1–72. An Introduction and Commentary on Books 1 and 2 of the Psalms.* TOTC. Leicester: InterVarsity Press, 1973. **Kraus, H.-J.** *Psalmen.* 2 vols. BKAT 15. 5th ed. Neukirchen-Vluyn: Neukirchener Verlag, 1978. **Lamparter, H.** *Das Buch der Psalmen I. Psalm 1–72.* Die Botschaft des Alten Testaments 14. 3rd ed. Stuttgart: Calwer Verlag, 1977. **Maillot, A.** and **Lelièvre, A.** *Les Psaumes. Traduction, notes et commentaire.* 2nd ed. Geneva: Éditions Labor et Fides, 1972. **Rogerson, J. W.** and **McKay, J. W.** *Psalms 1–50.* CBC. Cambridge: University Press, 1977. **Van Uchelen, N. A.** *Psalmen, Deel I (1–40)* and *Deel II (41–80).* Nijkerk Callenbach, 1971 and 1977. **Van der Ploeg, J.** *Psalmen uit de grondtekst vertaald en uitgelegd.* Roermond: J. J. Romen en Zonen. Fascicle 1, 1971; fascicle 2, 1972 (Pss. 1–68). **Weiser, A.** *The Psalms.* Tr. Herbert Hartwell. OTL. Philadelphia: Westminster Press, 1962.

(c) *Academic Studies, Form Criticism and Related Topics*
Beyerlin, W. *Die Rettung der Bedrängten in den Feindpsalmen der Einzelnen auf institutionelle Zusammenhänge untersucht.* FRLANT 99. Göttingen: Vandenhoeck und Ruprecht, 1970. **Coppens, J.** "La royauté de Yahwé dans le Psautier." *ETL* 53 (1977) 297–362. **Crüsemann, F.** *Studien zur Formgeschichte von Hymnus und Danklied in Israel.* Neukirchen-Vluyn: Neukirchener Verlag, 1969. **Culley, R. C.** *Oral Formulaic Language in the Biblical Psalms.* Near and Middle Eastern Series 4. Toronto: University Press, 1967. **Eaton, J. H.** *Kingship and the Psalms.* SBT, Second Series 32. London: SCM Press, 1976. **Eichhorn, D.** *Gott als Fels, Burg und Zuflucht. Eine Untersuchung zum Gebet des Mittlers in den Psalmen.* Bern: Herbert Lang, 1972. **Gerstenberger, E.** "Zur Interpretation der Psalmen." *VF* 19 (1974) 22–45. **Goeke, H.** *Das Menschenbild der individuellen Klagelieder. Ein Beitrag zur alttestamentlichen Anthropologie.* University of Bonn: 1971. **Gunkel, H.** and **Begrich, J.** *Einleitung in die Psalmen. Die Gattungen der religiösen Lyrik Israels.* Göttingen: Vandenhoeck und Ruprecht, 1933. _____. *The Psalms. A Form-Critical Introduction.* Tr. T. H. Horner Philadelphia: Fortress Press, 1967. **Kühlewein, J.** *Geschichte in den Psalmen.* Calwer Theologische Monographien, Series A, No. 2. Stuttgart: Calwer Verlag, 1973. **Kittel, G.** *Die Sprache der Psalmen. Zur Erschliessung der Psalmen im Unterricht.* Göttingen: Vandenhoeck und Ruprecht, 1973. **Mowinckel, S.** *The Psalms in Israel's Worship.* Tr. D. R. Ap-Thomas. Nashville, Abingdon Press, 1967. **Ridderbos, N. H.** *Die Psalmen. Stilistische Verfahren und Aufbau mit besonderer Berucksichtigung von Ps 1–41.* BZAW 117. Berlin: Walter de Gruyter, 1972. **Ringgren, H.** *Psalmen.* Stuttgart: Kohlhammer, 1971. **Tsevat, M.** *A Study of the Language of the Biblical Psalms.* JBL Monograph Series 9. Philadelphia, 1955. **Westermann, C.** *Der Psalter.* Stuttgart: Calwer Verlag, 1967. 3rd ed. 1974. _____. *Lob und Klage in den Psalmen.* Göttingen: Vandenhoeck und Ruprecht, 1977. (The fifth, revised edition of *Das Loben Gottes in den Psalmen,* 1954; for an English translation of the fourth edition, see below.) _____. *The Praise of God in the Psalms.* Tr. Keith R. Crim. Richmond, VA: John Knox Press, 1965.

(d) *General Studies, Popular Guides*
Ackroyd, P. R. *Doors of Perception. A Guide to Reading the Psalms.* Leighton Buzzard: Faith Press, 1978. **Anderson, B. W.** *Out of the Depths. The Psalms Speak for us Today.* 2nd ed. Philadelphia: Westminster Press, 1974. **Barth, C. F.** *Introduction to the Psalms.* Oxford: Blackwell, 1966. **Goldingay, J.** *Songs from a Strange Land.* Leicester: InterVarsity Press, 1977. (Studies in Psalms 42–51). **Gouders, K.** *Herr, öffne meine Lippen. Aus dem Buch der Psalmen.* Stuttgarter Kleiner Kommentar, AT 22/1. Stuttgart, 1974. **Guardini, R.** *Weisheit der Psalmen.* Würzburg: Werkbund Verlag, 1973. **Haag, H.** *Gott und Mensch in den Psalmen.* Einsiedeln: Benziger Verlag, 1972. **Hayes, J. H.** *Understanding the Psalms.* Valley Forge: Judson Press, 1976. **McEleny, N. J.** *The Melody of Israel. Introduction to the Psalms.* Pamphlet Bible Series 42. New York: Paulist Press, 1968.

Merton, T. *On the Psalms.* London: Sheldon Press, 1977. **Ringgren, H.** *The Faith of the Psalmists.* London: SCM Press, 1963. **Routley, E.** *Exploring the Psalms.* Philadelphia: Westminster Press, 1975. **Schungel, P.** *Schule des Betens. Die Klage- und Dankpsalmen.* Stuttgarter Kleiner Kommentar, AT 22/2. Stuttgart, 1974. (See the companion volume by K. Gouders listed above.) **Shepherd, M. H.** *The Psalms in Christian Worship. A Practical Guide.* Minneapolis: Augsburg, 1976. **Stradling, L. E.** *Praying the Psalms.* London: SPCK, 1977. **Troeger, T. H.** *Rage! Reflect! Rejoice! Praying with the Psalmists.* Philadelphia: Westminster Press, 1977. **Vogel, D. W.** *The Psalms for Worship.* St. Louis: Concordia, 1974.

The Book of Psalms, as is well known, is one of the most frequently quoted OT books in both the NT and in the sectarian Jewish writings from Qumran. Its ancient popularity has continued into the modern world, and there are few biblical books which have generated so voluminous a secondary literature as the Book of Psalms. The select bibliography provides only a limited glimpse into the vast quantity of writing elicited by the Psalms. In this section of the Introduction, an even more restricted perspective is provided. From the multitude of commentaries and studies I have selected only the ones I judge to be among the most significant, and I have commented on them briefly. The purpose of the concise observations which follow is to set a perspective for the present commentary and to indicate approximately where it stands in the larger context of modern Psalms studies. I have not included in the discussion some of the older commentaries, such as A. F. Kirkpatrick's *The Book of Psalms* (1906), for although they (and many like them) are still of immense value for the study of the text of the Psalms, they have not really shaped the context within which modern Psalms studies must be undertaken.

The pioneer in the modern study of the Psalms is surely Hermann Gunkel, whose commentary (*Die Psalmen übersetzt und erklärt,* fourth edition, 1926) and a companion Introduction (*Einleitung in die Psalmen,* published in 1933 shortly after Gunkel's death and completed by his former student, J. Begrich) began a new era in the study of the Psalms. Gunkel pioneered the method of study commonly referred to in English as *form-criticism.* He identified and described the basic literary types or genres (*Gattungen*) in the Psalms, attempted to identify the individual or communal life situations (*Sitze im Leben*) in which those types functioned, recognized the oral origins of much of psalmodic poetry, and stressed the importance of studying the Psalms not only in the context of the OT as a whole, but also in the literary and cultural context of ancient Near Eastern civilizations. With respect to psalm types, Gunkel identified five principal types ([i] Hymn; [ii] Communal Lament; [iii] Royal Psalms; [iv] Individual Lament; [v] Individual Song of Thanksgiving) and a number of minor categories (e.g., [i] Pilgrimage Songs; [ii] Wisdom Poetry; [iii] Communal Thanksgiving; [iv] Liturgy). Some psalms were identified as "mixed" types, which were said to be of a later date than the "pure" types. Though many of the details of Gunkel's position have been challenged and modified, almost all modern commentators reflect to a greater or lesser extent the influence of Gunkel.

The foundations laid by Gunkel were developed further by the second great pioneer of psalm-criticism in this century, Sigmund Mowinckel; though his best-known work available in English, *The Psalms in Israel's Worship,* is not a commentary, it is of sufficient significance to be included in this survey. Mowinckel built upon the foundations of form-criticism laid by Gunkel, but he pursued more rigorously and extensively than had Gunkel the relationship between the Psalms and Israel's cult; his method has sometimes been called *cult-historical*. More specifically, he argued that a high percentage of Israel's psalms (hymns, royal psalms and some laments) must be related to an Israelite New Year Festival, celebrated in the autumn, in which the Lord's kingship was annually reaffirmed over the forces of chaos. Most other psalms (with the exception of those of a wisdom type) were also to be related to the Israelite cult; those of an individual nature were to be connected with private temple services. Mowinckel effectively narrowed down the variety of life situations proposed by Gunkel and set the majority of the psalms in the context of a particular interpretation of Israel's cultic life. He drew widely upon Near Eastern sources in his reconstruction of the proposed New Year Festival in Israel, particularly upon data pertaining to the Babylonian *Akitu* festival, and major portions of his interpretation of the psalms are contingent upon the validity of the existence of a form of this festival, as reconstructed, in the life of Israel's cult.

Whereas Mowinckel found a focus for psalm interpretation in the cult, particularly in the proposed New Year Festival, Arthur Weiser (in his commentary, *The Psalms*) found a focal point for interpretation in the *covenant*, specifically in his understanding of the "covenant festival." Thus, although Weiser works within a general framework provided by Gunkel, his real concern is to interpret the psalms in the context of the "covenant festival," celebrated in the autumn. The covenant festival, reconstructed on the basis of detailed studies of portions of the Law and the Prophets, is perceived to have been the central and most comprehensive celebration in Israelite life, centered not so much on Creation and the related themes of nature and chaos, as in Mowinckel's system, but rather on Israel's annual reestablishment of its formal alliance with the Lord. This festival, Weiser proposes, so dominated the purpose and substance of the psalms, that although a variety of literary types may be identified within the Psalter, the majority of them find their life-setting in the "covenant festival."

Many commentaries on the Psalms have stayed within the broad guidelines set by Gunkel, though they have modified his system and taken account of later research. H.-J. Kraus (in his two-volume commentary, *Psalmen*) stands within the general tradition of Gunkel, though he has refined the form-critical method and taken account of the data provided by archaeological research since Gunkel's time. Gunkel's understanding of the relationship of the psalms to Israel's cultic life is modified in the light of works such as that of Mowinckel; furthermore, Gunkel's view that "pure" literary types were early, whereas "mixed" types were a later development, is called seriously into question by Kraus. His work also exhibits a somewhat more explicit theological perspective than was evinced in the writings of Gunkel.

Some recent approaches to the Psalms are presented within the context of form-critical studies, but contain newer emphases. Thus, principally within the context of French biblical scholarship, there has developed a form of analysis by which a *relecture* ("re-reading") of a psalm may be discerned. Modification of an original psalm, or the addition of verses, are proposed as indications of the process of "re-reading," by which a psalm that originally had a very specific purpose, for example in some royal setting, might be modified for different use in a later life situation. With respect to recent commentaries, the identification of messianic *relectures*, to give only one example, may be found in E. Beaucamp's *Le Psautier. Ps.1–72*.

On quite a different note, Mitchell Dahood's three-volume commentary on the Psalms, in the Anchor Bible series, has set Ugaritic Studies firmly in the center of the modern study of the Psalms. It is probably fair to say that Dahood's work on the Psalms is the most radical and far-reaching in its implications since the time of Gunkel. Drawing upon the resources of Ugaritic language and literature, Dahood has presented a new translation of the Psalms, and consequently many new interpretations of them, so that many of the psalms, in Dahood's rendition, are barely recognizable as the psalms handed down to the modern world through the Massoretes. Indeed, a fundamental characteristic of Dahood's commentary is his dependence upon the resources of Northwest Semitic languages, specifically Ugaritic, in the translation and interpretation of the Book of Psalms, often to the exclusion of the vocalization of the Massoretes through whom we have received the consonantal text of the Psalter. Dahood's work on the Psalms, and the relevance of Ugaritic for the study of the Psalms, have potentially such far-reaching implications, that the matter has been subjected to a detailed examination in the following section (THE PSALMS AND UGARITIC STUDIES).

This first volume on the Psalms in the *Word Biblical Commentary* series is written within the broad perspectives provided by this brief summary of recent commentaries and books on the Psalms. While it is influenced to some extent by all the perspectives presented above, it does not stand consciously in any of the particular schools or traditions which have been summarized. I have followed the broad principles of form-criticism set down by Gunkel, at least insofar as I have recognized the importance of attempting to classify psalms according to their type and to set them in particular life situations. But my system of classification, though rooted in Gunkel, is more flexible, and it has been necessary at times to modify the terminology describing the various types.

The principal value of the form-critical method, originating in the work of Gunkel, lies in the recognition of the necessity of a *functional* study of the psalms. Though not all psalms can be studied from a functional perspective, the majority can be, and it is the recognition of the usage of a particular psalm in some distinctive social or cultic situation which contributes so enormously to the understanding and interpretation of the various psalms. Thus the importance of determining the setting, or *Sitz im Leben*, where appropriate, cannot be overstressed; but the classical form-critical elaboration of the elements of form and type *(Gattung)* are far less convincing. To establish a *type*, in the sense of *genre*, one must build upon the commonalities of formal structure that may be determined in the data, namely the psalms as such. But though it is clear that form-critical types/genres in the Psalms have some commonality of structure, in the broadest possible terms, it is the differences which are far more notable in the examination of the examples belonging to any given type/genre. The essential commonality between the members of any given type lies in function, not in form and structure. And thus a method is required which is sensitive to the functional study of the psalms, but takes seriously the particularities and peculiarities of poetic and literary structure in the analysis of particular psalms. From this perspective, I have been very positively influenced in the study of many psalms in this volume by the work of N. H. Ridderbos, *Die Psalmen* (1972), in which a balance is achieved between form-criticism, on the one hand, and a close examination of the distinctive literary structure of each psalm (in terms of the "new stylistics"), on the other hand.

The detailed literary analysis, of the type proposed by Ridderbos (or, for those who prefer it, in terms of "rhetorical criticism"), must be undertaken first, before the more general form-critical evaluation can be undertaken. Frequently, the findings of the detailed literary analysis are so distinctive, that in *literary terms* it is difficult to identify a particular text with any of the classical genres; in *functional terms,* however, the category of genre to which the text belongs usually becomes clear, so that the form-critical setting, or *Sitz im Leben,* can be determined.

Mowinckel's work has been invaluable in many respects, though the autumnal New Year Festival, as proposed by Mowinckel, is considered to be a somewhat elusive reality with respect to Israel's early history. And Weiser's stress on the covenant has been recognized as being of considerable importance, though his emphasis on a "covenant festival" is thought to be too exaggerated; the autumnal "covenant festival" is in some ways as elusive as the proposed New Year Festival of Mowinckel. Ugaritic is recognized as being of great importance for the study of the Psalms, but while I have made considerable use both of Ugaritic and of the contributions of Mitchell Dahood, I have sought also to introduce a moderating influence. While Dahood has in many cases made notable advances in the understanding of particular psalms, in at least as many cases I consider that he has gone too far in the application of Ugaritic data toward the interpretation of the Psalms (see p 51). Though I have not trod carefully in the footsteps of the earlier masters of Psalms studies, I have benefited enormously from their contributions to the study of the Psalter.

THE PSALMS AND UGARITIC STUDIES

Bibliography

(a) *The Writings of Mitchell J. Dahood*
Dahood, M. J. *Psalms 1: 1–50* (1966); *Psalms II: 51–100* (1968); *Psalms III: 101–150* (1970). AB vols 16, 17, 17A. New York: Doubleday. For bibliographical guidance to the numerous publications of Dahood in addition to his three-volume commentary, consult the following (and the items in section (b), below): **Martinez, E. R.** *Hebrew-Ugaritic Index to the Writings of Mitchell J. Dahood* Rome: Pontifical Biblical Institute, 1967.

(b) *Bibliographical Guides to Hebrew-Ugaritic Studies*
Dietrich, M., Loretz, O., et. al. *Ugaritische Bibliographie 1928–1966.* 4 vols. Neukirchen-Vluyn: Neukirchener Verlag, 1973. **Craigie, P. C.** *Ugaritic Studies: 1972–1976.* Calgary:

Newsletter for Ugaritic Studies, 1976. _____. *Ugaritic Studies II: 1976–1979*. Calgary: Newsletter for Ugaritic Studies, 1980.

(c) *Ugaritic Studies*

Aistleitner, J. *Wörterbuch der ugaritischen Sprache*. Berlin: Akademie Verlag, 1974. **Caquot, A., Sznycer, M.** and **Herdner, A.** *Textes ougaritiques I: Mythes et Légendes*. Paris: Editions du Cerf, 1974. **Craigie, P. C.** "The Problem of Parallel Word Pairs in Ugaritic and Hebrew Poetry." *Semitics* 5 (1977) 48–58. **Dahood, M.** *Ugaritic-Hebrew Philology*. Rome: Pontifical Biblical Institute Press, 1967. **De Langhe, R.** *Les Textes de Ras Shamra-Ugarit*. 2 Vols. Gembloux: Duculot, 1945. **Fisher, L. R.,** ed. *Ras Shamra Parallels*. Rome: Pontifical Biblical Institute Press, 1972 (Vol. 1) and 1975 (Vol. 2). **Fisher, L. R.,** ed. *The Claremont Ras Shamra Tablets*. Rome: Pontifical Biblical Institute Press, 1971. **Gibson, J. C. L.** *Canaanite Myths and Legends*. Edinburgh: T & T Clark, 1978. **Gordon, C. H.** *Ugaritic Textbook*. Rome: Pontifical Biblical Institute Press, 1968. _____. *Ugaritic Literature*. Rome: Pontifical Biblical Institute Press, 1949. **Gray, J.** *The KRT Text in the Literature of Ras Shamra*. 2nd ed. Leiden: Brill, 1964. **Gray, J.** *The Legacy of Canaan*. 2nd ed. Leiden: Brill, 1965. **Herdner, A.** *Corpus des Tablettes en Cunéiformes Alphabétiques*. 2 vols. Paris: Paul Geuthner, 1963. **Van Zijl, P. J.** *A Study of Texts in Connexion with Baal in the Ugaritic Epics*. AOAT 10. Neukirchen-Vluyn: Neukirchener Verlag, 1972.

(d) *Ugaritic Studies and the Psalms*

Craigie, P. C. "The Poetry of Ugarit and Israel." *Tynd B* 22 (1971) 3–31. _____. "The Comparison of Hebrew Poetry." *Semitics* 4 (1974) 10–21. _____. "Parallel Word Pairs in Ugaritic Poetry." *UF* 11 (1979) 135–40. _____. "Ugarit and the Bible." *Ugarit in Retrospect*. Ed. G. Young. Winona Lake, IN: Eisenbrauns, 1981. **Donner, H.** "Ugaritismen in der Psalmenforschung." *ZAW* 79 (1967) 322–50. **Loretz, O.** "Die Ugaritistik in der Psalmeninterpretation." *UF* 4 (1972) 167–69. _____. *Die Psalmen, Teil II. Beitrag der Ugarit-Texte zum Verständnis von Kolometrie und Textologie der Psalmen. Psalm 90–150*. AOAT 207/2. Neukirchen-Vluyn: Neukirchener Verlag, 1979. **Moroder, R. J.** "Ugaritic and Modern Translation of the Psalter." *UF* 6 (1974) 249–64. **Mowinckel, S.** "Psalm Criticism between 1900 and 1935 (Ugarit and Psalm Exegesis)." *VT* 5 (1955) 13–33. **O'Callaghan, R. T.** "Echoes of Canaanite Literature in the Psalms." *VT* 4 (1954) 164–76. **Patton, J. H.** *Canaanite Parallels in the Book of Psalms*. Baltimore: John Hopkins Press, 1944. **Sauer, G.** "Die Ugaritistik und die Psalmenforschung." *UF* 6 (1974) 401–6.

In the study of any literature, be it prose or poetry, it is valuable to undertake a comparative evaluation in order that a more balanced assessment may be made of the relative merits and meaning of the literature under examination. The modern era in the study of biblical Hebrew poetry has been characterized by resort to comparison throughout its history, though the comparative resources and the purposes of comparison have changed with the passage of time. The pioneer of the modern study of Hebrew poetry, Robert Lowth, made numerous comparative remarks in his fundamental work on Hebrew poetry, *De Sacra Poesie Hebraeorum Praelectiones Academicae* (1753); Lowth, who was Professor of Poetry in the University of Oxford, drew principally upon the resources of classical poetry for comparative purposes. And J. G. von Herder also made use of comparative data, including Arabic poetry, in his book, *Vom Geist der Ebräischen Poesie* (1782/83). But the function of comparison in the works of these earlier scholars was principally aesthetic and illustrative; they were not attempting to argue a case with respect to the origins of Hebrew poetry vis-à-vis other poetry, or with respect to the possibility of an interrelationship between Hebrew and other poetry (see further P. C. Craigie, *Semitics* 4 [1974] 10–21). It was the discovery of the literature of the Babylonians and Egyptians which most profoundly changed the role of comparative studies; the development of "biblical archaeology" in the nineteenth century, which has continued into the present century, revealed to modern scholars the poetry of Israel's neighbors and contemporaries, and thus made possible a more specific type of comparative study. Comparativists began to formulate hypotheses concerning the origin of the forms and types of Hebrew poetry; indeed in many cases they argued that the biblical poetry of the Psalms had been borrowed by the Hebrews from their neighbors. For a while, at the beginning of the twentieth century, "pan-Babylonianism" and "pan-Egyptianism" flourished in the comparative study of Hebrew literature (see the critical appraisals of A. M. Blackman and G. R. Driver in D. C. Simpson (ed.), *The Psalmists*. London: Oxford University Press, 1926).

The whole direction of comparative studies was to be changed by a chance discovery on the coast of Syria early in the spring of 1928. A Syrian peasant, living a few miles to the north of Latakia on the coast of Syria, discovered a tomb dating from the second millennium B.C. The following year, a French team began a series of archaeological excavations at the site which have continued, with some interruptions, for more than half a century. The archaeologists have recovered for us the remains and archives of the ancient city of Ugarit, which reached its Golden Age during the fourteenth and thirteenth centuries B.C. It was the archives of ancient Ugarit which were to exert a profound influence on the study of the Psalms, for they contained among their rich resources a collection of the poetry of the ancient citizens of Ugarit. This poetry, primarily myth and legend in substance, was written in the Ugaritic language, which has close linguistic affinities to biblical Hebrew. Within a few years of the discovery of Ugaritic poetry, scholars were utilizing this new resource to make comments, explanations or clarifications on the substance and form of the Psalms and other portions of the Hebrew Bible.

The poetry of Ugarit had several advantages over Babylonian and Egyptian poetry for the purposes of comparativists. Linguistically, Ugaritic language was closer to Hebrew than were Babylonian and Egyptian, and geographically and culturally, the ancient Kingdom of Ugarit was closer to the biblical world than were the great civilizations of Mesopotamia and the Nile Valley. Thus, whereas some of the earlier hypotheses of comparativists concerning the interrelationship of Hebrew and Babylonian or Egyptian poetry taxed the credulity of more cautious scholars, comparative studies of Ugaritic and Hebrew poetry appeared to be based on a firmer footing. Indeed, H. L. Ginsberg went so far as to claim that "the Hebrew Bible and the Ugaritic texts are to be regarded as one literature, and consequently a reading in either one may be emended with the help of a parallel passage in the other" ("The Ugaritic Texts and Textual Criticism." *JBL* 62 [1943] 109). By the mid-twentieth century, "pan-Babylonianism" and "pan-Egyptianism" had virtually become historical phenomena, but a new phenomenon could be discerned in the continuing growth of comparative studies: "pan-Ugaritism."

Of the numerous scholars who have been engaged in the comparative study of Ugaritic poetry and the Psalms, few have been so prolific, creative, and influential as Mitchell Dahood. Apart from his major three-volume commentary on the Psalms, Dahood has contributed many more than one hundred articles and notes to the topic. With respect to the Psalms alone, Dahood's contribution has been the greatest and most influential since the work of Gunkel earlier in the century. Indeed some scholars would rate his influence even more highly. W. F. Albright, the most distinguished figure in American biblical scholarship and archaeology in the twentieth century, stated that Dahood had contributed more to our understanding of the vocabulary of biblical Hebrew poetry than all other scholars combined: "Even if only a third of his new interpretations of the Psalter are correct in principle—and I should put the total proportion higher—he has contributed more than all other scholars together, over the past two thousand years, to the elucidation of the Psalter" (W. F. Albright, *BASOR* 186 [1967] 54). And Sauer has suggested that there has been no more comprehensive treatment of the meaning of the Psalms since the time of the Reformation (G. Sauer, *UF* 6 [1974] 401).

With certain provisions, these assessments of Dahood's contributions are probably correct. He has made an enormous contribution to the study of the Psalms, and no criticism of his work should detract from the significance of that contribution. Nevertheless, some criticism is necessary, precisely because the pioneers often go too far in the initial excitement and creativity of their ideas (as Gunkel did, in his time), and because the more lasting worth of their contribution may not be perceived until after the process of criticism. In this commentary, which owes a great deal to the insight of Mitchell Dahood, an attempt has been made to evaluate critically Dahood's contributions to the study of Psalms 1–50. The critical evaluation is very limited, principally because the extent of Dahood's work is so massive that a complete book would be required for critical evaluation alone. In this section of the Introduction, there are stated some of the principles which have dictated the grounds for caution or disagreement; in the commentary itself, some of the more critical issues are examined in detail.

The principal issue of theory with respect to the comparative study of the Psalms and Ugaritic poetry has to do with the relative merits of two sets of data which are at the disposal of the comparativist. The relatively fixed point, upon which the evidence of the two sets of data may be brought to bear, is the *consonantal* Hebrew text of the Psalms. The first set of data is the vocalization of the consonantal Hebrew text, which has come down to us through the work of the Massoretes. The second set of data is the collection of linguistic resources made available through the rediscovery of Ugaritic and other Northwest Semitic languages during the nineteenth and twentieth centuries. Both sets of data purport to offer the resources for translating and understanding the consonantal text of the Psalms, but the issue of relative merit is a complex one. It would be unwise simply to accept the vocalization of the Massoretes and ignore the resources of Northwest Semitic and Ugaritic, but the converse would be equally unwise; and yet the help offered by these two sets of data is often in conflict, so that the scholar is forced to make a choice, either as a general principle, or else with respect to each problem which occurs in the text.

Dahood wrote in *Psalms I* (p. xxii): "The reverence of the Massoretes for the consonantal text outstripped their knowledge of archaic Hebrew poetry: the result is that their vocalization, and even their word division, must sometimes be disregarded if one is to find the way back to the original sense." The view is repeated in subsequent volumes, with an emphasis on the gap of more than one thousand years separating the Massoretes from the composition of the latest psalms (*Psalms II*, p. xviii), and it is a view which profoundly affects the translation and interpretation of the Psalms in the writings of Dahood. Implicit in this line of argument is the view that the lateness of the Massoretic vocalization of the consonantal text of the Psalms militates against its authority and reliability, and that in effect the Massoretic vocalization should be looked upon as a product of medieval Judaism. If this argument, with all its implications, were correct, then certainly it would be wise to turn first to the resources of Ugaritic and Northwest Semitic languages in the attempt to elucidate the meaning of the text of the Psalms. But the argument, particularly in its application, seems to imply that the Massoretes invented the vocalization of the texts, rather than that they simply invented the symbols with which to record an already existing tradition of vocalization. It is far more probable that the Massoretes should be accorded the role of *recorders*, rather than *inventors*, of the actual vocalization of the Hebrew text. They recorded the tradition of vocalization which had been handed down orally for centuries through the process of reading the Torah, Prophets and Writings in the synagogues and other institutions of Judaism (see further James Barr, *Comparative Philology and the Text of the Old Testament* 188–222). Thus, although the recording of the vocalization of the Hebrew text (viz. the Massoretic vocalization, as distinct from the use of *matres lectionis*) was essentially a medieval activity, the vocalization as such may in all probability be assumed to go back to biblical times, or at least shortly thereafter.

The conviction, however, that the Massoretes recorded an ancient tradition of vocalization does not mean that it is in every case correct and free from error, any more than that their recording of the consonantal text is in every case free from error. There may be mistakes in both the consonantal text and in the vocalization. Thus, with respect to the resources available for the translation of the consonantal text of the Psalms, the interpreter is not faced with a simple choice of resources, but must attempt to make judicious use of both the available sets of data. In practice, Dahood does utilize both sets of data, but the emphasis in his work, and the basis of the massive innovation in his interpretation of the Psalms, is to be found in the fact that he gives greater prominence to the use of Ugaritic and Northwest Semitic data than he does to the Massoretic vocalization. In contrast, the work of some other scholars and translators has been undertaken to the neglect of Ugaritic and similar resources (see R. J. Moroder, *UF* 6 [1974] 249–64). In this commentary, I have attempted to maintain a balance; but, in general, I have placed more weight on the value of the Massoretic tradition than is done in the writings of Dahood.

The comparative studies of Dahood are far-reaching in their scope and implications; they affect our understanding of Hebrew lexicography, Hebrew grammar, Hebrew poetry, and other technical matters. And the results of the comparison may influence significant aspects of OT theology, such as the understanding of death and the afterlife (see particularly *Psalms III*, pp. XLI–LII). Thus the interpreter who desires a critical appraisal of the merits and weaknesses of Dahood's work, faces a variety of difficulties in addition to the judgment concerning the relative merits of Ugaritic vis-à-vis the vocalization of the Massoretes. One difficulty is essentially that of *judgment* with respect to possibilities and probabilities. Thus, in the question of lexicography, the following example will illustrate the nature of the judgments required. The Hebrew word מָגֵן (e.g., in Ps 3:3) is traditionally rendered "shield"; but Dahood (*Psalms I*, p. 16), noting uses of a cognate term in Ugaritic, Phoenician and Punic, suggests the word should be translated "Suzerain" (probably to be vocalized מָגֵן, as distinct from the Massoretic vocalization מָגֵן). It must be admitted immediately that the suggestion is *possible*, but whether it is probable or correct remains a matter of judgment. Either is possible, but to accept the new suggestion appears to involve rejecting the meaning implied by Massoretic vocalization. Since the context, taken loosely, might be interpreted as permitting either possibility, the judgment is particularly difficult. The important aspect of this example is the observation that the introduction of new evidence broadens the range of options, but does not automatically lead to correct answers. Thus, if the hypothetical Hebrew word *abc* has always been known to have one clear and distinct meaning, the discovery of Ugaritic *abc*, with a quite different meaning, merely increases the options: (a) Hebrew *abc* means what it did before, the Ugaritic evidence being irrelevant; or (b) Hebrew *abc* is a homonym, the word having two possible meanings in Hebrew (and this view may or may not involve the revocalization of the Hebrew word); or (c) the original meaning attributed to Hebrew *abc* was wrong, and must be corrected in the light of the Ugaritic evidence. Given the diverse nature of the Hebrew texts, similar options and difficulties may apply not only in the area of lexicography, but also in poetic and grammatical matters. Thus, even when a principle has been established (e.g. with respect to giving priority to the resources of Ugaritic), there remains a series of difficult and subjective decisions and judgments to be made.

But still further difficulties pertain to the actual conduct of comparative studies. In any comparative study which attempts to determine interrelationships between two bodies of literature, or merely to assess influence or interdependence, certain firm controls should be employed which provide the context necessary for interpreting the comparative data. (Dahood claims that his comparative studies are concerned not so much with influence or dependence as much as they are with elucidation: *Psalms II*, p xv; nevertheless, the nature of his comparative "elucidation" is such that the use of controls would be important in attempting to establish the validity of the elucidation.) The controlling factors, which are certainly known to Dahood, are not given sufficient significance in his work, in my judgment; they pertain to matters of chronology, geography, literary forms, and the nature of the textual evidence employed in comparisons.

The chronological problem may be stated concisely as follows: any comparative study must keep in mind the gap of two to seven centuries which separate the Ugaritic texts from the Hebrew psalms. The Ugaritic texts were composed, for the most part, between the fifteenth and thirteenth centuries B.C.; in contrast, the majority of the psalms were probably composed between the tenth and sixth centuries B.C. The various types of Hebrew-Ugaritic comparison must be controlled by an awareness of the diachronic nature of the comparative study. Thus, if a direct relationship is posited between a Hebrew psalm and its Ugaritic or Northwest Semitic antecedents, as is commonly proposed for Ps 29 (see the commentary), then the diachronic nature of the comparison, and the gap of two or more centuries between the texts under comparison, requires a careful explanation or hypothesis to account for the time differential. Or again, if a Hebrew word is unknown, but a cognate Ugaritic term is discovered, the meaning of which can be determined, the transference of the meaning of the Ugaritic term to the unknown Hebrew word can only be done with caution; even if the respective terms are linguistically related, the chronological gap requires the recognition that semantic change may have taken place, and that as a consequence the Hebrew term may have acquired a different meaning or nuance from the cognate Ugaritic term. The same caution is required in the *elucidation* of some aspect of Hebrew (poetic) grammar by reference to Ugaritic grammar; even if one admits that Hebrew is dialectically related to Ugaritic, and that "proto-Hebrew" may have had virtually the same grammatical structure as that reflected in the Ugaritic (poetic) texts, the chronological differential between the actual texts under comparison requires the recognition that the "Classical Hebrew" (tenth century B.C. and after) of the majority of the psalms has undergone a variety of grammatical changes from the earlier period of the language.

The geographical control, or perhaps geo-cultural control, requires a recognition of the places in which the respective texts originated and the cultural climate which they reflect. The Ugaritic poetic texts were all found in the libraries of the ancient city of Ugarit, the capital of a small but cosmopolitan state situated on the Mediterranean coast of northern Syria. (Some additional poetic texts were recently discovered at nearby Ras Ibn Hani.) The Hebrew texts come from the far south, the geographical region of Palestine, from a culture and environment very different from that of Syria. At no point was there direct cultural or historical interchange between the Kingdom of Ugarit and the Hebrew Kingdoms, for the former had ceased to exist before the latter came into existence. This geographical and geo-cultural division clearly poses difficulties for any hypothesis which seeks to posit direct dependence of Hebrew texts on Ugaritic texts. But it also poses difficulties with respect to the elucidation of Hebrew texts on the basis of Ugaritic texts. The geographical separation, which may not seem too great in the context of the modern North American concept of distance, resulted nevertheless in considerable differences of culture, custom and language. A modern illustration will help to clarify the point. The Arabic language which is spoken nowadays in the district of Latakia (i.e., the vicinity of ancient Ugarit) has a number of dialectical differences which distinguish it from the Arabic spoken in southern Syria (the vicinity of Damascus) or from Palestinian Arabic; such differences are particularly notable with respect to matters of lexicography. But what is even more significant is that some of the peculiarities of the Arabic spoken in Latakia have direct and precise parallels in the language of ancient Ugarit!

This fact illustrates both the regional differences between forms of the same language and the peculiar linguistic conservatism of certain geographical areas. With respect to comparative studies, this observation requires that particular caution be exercised in the use of Ugaritic resources either to elucidate Hebrew texts or to argue particular hypotheses of interrelationship.

There are certain mitigating factors in the application of the geographical control. Thus, as Dahood points out (*Psalms II*, p xv), the Ugaritic script is known to have been used at several places outside Ugarit. The Ugaritic script, or forms of it, have been found on texts at a number of places outside the city of Ugarit: Ras Ibn Hani (a few miles south of Ugarit), Sarepta, Tell Nebi Mend, Tell Taanach, Tabor, Beth Shemesh, Tell Sukas and Kamid el Loz. In addition, a recently discovered Akkadian tablet from the thirteenth century B.C., recovered from the ruins of an Egyptian fortress at Tell Aphek in Israel, contains a letter from a certain Takukhlina of Ugarit to the Egyptian ruler of Canaan (see *NewsUgSt* 17 [1978] 3). Evidence of this kind may be used to argue for considerable interchange between Ugarit and the area of Palestine, from which it may be urged that the geographical control in comparative studies should not be given too much weight. But taken in a larger perspective, the evidence from outside the city of Ugarit is very slender, providing limited insight into the real nature of Ugarit's penetration of the southern region, or of the extent to which the language and poetry of Ugarit may be representative of Canaanite language and poetry in Palestine. Thus, it is wise to maintain certain controlling factors and concurrently to maintain caution.

A third factor controlling comparisons of the Psalms with Ugaritic literature has to do with literary forms. Stated simply, there are no Ugaritic psalms. There are portions of the poetic texts which have a hymnic character, there are semipoetic religious (or ritual) texts, and, from another source, there are the so-called "Canaanite psalm fragments" from the Amarna Letters (see A. Jirku, *JBL* 52 [1933] 108–20). This factor should introduce an element of caution in specifically *literary* comparisons (the comparisons of literary forms, structures, and so on), for in effect, we do not know what Ugaritic psalms were like. (The recovery of a Hurrian cult-song from Ugarit suggests that some kind of psalmody was in use in Ugarit, but no samples have yet been found in the Ugaritic language as such.)

A final controlling factor in comparisons pertains to the nature of the Ugaritic texts. The Ugaritic texts, by virtue of the manner of their survival, are frequently broken, incomplete, partially illegible, and consequently difficult to interpret. They are written in a language which still contains words of uncertain meaning and grammatical structures which are not fully understood. Enormous progress has been made in recent decades, and the Ugaritic texts are better understood today than they were following the initial discoveries half a century ago. But it is simply in the nature of the texts that their evidence is not always clear and free from ambiguity, and as a consequence the Ugaritic texts are not easy to use in comparative studies (see further P. C. Craigie, *JSOT* 2 [1977] 33–49).

None of the cautions or controlling factors noted above are intended to deny the possibility of legitimate or worthwhile comparative studies. Nor are any of these factors unknown to Dahood. They simply provide a controlled perspective within which comparative studies may be conducted: they are a constant reminder of the necessity for caution. From the perspective of the writer of this commentary, they provide an indication as to why it is that there has so often been disagreement with the suggestions or hypotheses of Mitchell Dahood. But it must also be acknowledged again that Dahood is immensely provocative and has numerous brilliant insights; without scholars of his caliber, there would be little or no progress. Any critical comments in this commentary should be perceived within this larger perspective of gratitude.

For examples of the critical treatment of the use of the Ugaritic texts in the study of the Psalms, the reader is referred to the indexes of Ugaritic texts at the end of this volume. Examples illustrating a critical appraisal of the use of Ugaritic in matters pertaining to comparative lexicography may be found by consulting the Index of Key Ugaritic Terms, also at the end of this volume.

BOOK I: PSALMS 1–41

An Introductory Psalm of Wisdom (1:1–6)

Bibliography

Auffret, P. "Essai sur la structure littéraire du Psaume 1." *BZ* 22 (1978) 27–45. **Anderson, G. W.** "A Note on Psalm 1:1." *VT* 24 (1974) 231–3. **Beaucamp, E.** "La salutation inaugurale du livre des Psaumes." *Église et Théologie* 1 (1970) 135–46. **Bergmeier, R.** "Zum Ausdruck עצת רשעים in Ps. 1:1, Hi. 10:3, 21:16 und 22:18." *ZAW* 79 (1967) 229–32. **Brownlee, W. H.** "Psalms 1–2 as a Coronation Liturgy." *Bib* 52 (1971) 321–36. **Bullough, S.** "The Question of Metre in Psalm 1." *VT* 17 (1967) 42–49. **Lack, R.** "Le psaume 1-Une analyse structurale." *Bib* 57 (1976) 154–67. **Merendino, R. P.** "Sprachkunst in Ps. 1:1." *VT* 29 (1979) 45–60. **Rinaldi, G.** "*Môšāb* nell'ultima frase del Sal. 1:1." *BeO* 17 (1975) 120. **Schedl, C.** "Psalm 1 und die altjüdische Weisheitsmystik." In *XVII Deutscher Orientalistentag vom 21. bis. 27. Juli 1965 in Würzburg,* ed. W. Voigt. Wiesbaden: Franz Steiner Verlag, 1969. **Soggin, J. A.** "Zum ersten Psalm." *TZ* 23 (1967) 81–96.

Translation

> [1] *Blessed the man who has not walked by the counsel* [a] *of the wicked,*
> *and has not stood in the way* [b] *of the sinful,*
> *and has not sat in the gathering* [c] *of scoffers.* [d]
> [2] *But in the Lord's Torah is his delight*
> *and in his Torah will he muse* [a] *by day and night.*
> [3] *So shall he be like a tree,*
> *transplanted by running waters,* [a]
> *which shall yield its fruit in its season,*
> *and its foliage shall not wither.*
> *So, in all that he shall do, he shall prosper.* [b]
> [4] *Not so the wicked!*
> *But they are like the chaff that wind tosses.* [a]
> [5] *Therefore, the wicked shall not rise up in judgment,* [a]
> *nor sinners in an assembly of the righteous.*
> [6] *For the Lord protects* [a] *the way of the righteous,*
> *but the way of the wicked shall perish.*

Notes

1.a. עצת, "counsel," in *S,* is transposed with דרך "way" in v lc; though such a change might be viewed as an improvement in the sequence of thought, it is unnecessary. The word עצה can mean either "counsel" or "council"; Dahood translates "council" in this context (*Psalms I,* 1–2). A similar alternative is the translation "fellowship" (of wicked men), on the basis of the use of the term in the Qumran literature, as proposed by Bergmeier, *ZAW* 79 (1967) 229–32. Both alternatives are possible, though it is a question of judgment rather than semantics and depends upon the translation of the rest of v 1; see notes b and c below.

1.b. דרך *"way."* Dahood (*Psalms I,* 2) translates דרך by "assembly," basing his translation upon a supposed usage of the cognate term in the Ugaritic texts. The word is used again (in v 6, twice) and thus is critical to the meaning of the psalm as a whole. According to Dahood, the Ugaritic word *drkt*, which means "dominion, power," and hence "throne" (see Aistleitner, *WUS* #792), undergoes a semantic shift from "dominion" to the place where dominion is exercised, namely the "assembly." But the argument is weak. Within Ugaritic, there is precisely such a semantic shift, but it is from "dominion" to "throne" (namely, the seat of dominion). The use of the term in Ugaritic may designate the dominion of the deities; Anat, for example, is called *bˁlt.drkt*, "mistress of dominion" (RS.24.252.7). No doubt the Ugaritic nuance of *drkt* ("dominion, power") does occur in the OT in the Hebrew usage of the root דרך (see Judg 5:21 and P. C. Craigie, *JBL* 88 [1969] 257). In the present context, however, the argument for the meaning "assembly," insofar as it is based on Ugaritic, is without firm foundation. "Throne" would be a possible translation, though it would not fit the poetic context well. Furthermore, the contrasting of two *ways* (1:6) is a common theme in both biblical literature (Deut 30:19; Jer 21:8; Prov 1:1–7; Matt 7:13–14) and in Near Eastern texts: e.g. in Gilgamesh X.vi (*ANET*, 93) and the "Hymn to Aten" (*ANET*, 371). In summary, it is better to retain the translation "way" for Heb דרך, both here and in v 6.

1.c. "Gathering" (מושב) or "seat"; on the meaning of the term, see Rinaldi in *BeO* 17 (1975) 120. The sense of this word could admittedly add to the strength of Dahood's argument (note b), in that it would provide synonymous parallelism for the first three lines as follows: "council// assembly//gathering (session)." Nevertheless, the more conventional rendering shows a progression within the parallelism. Just as the verbs demonstrate a kind of progression (or regression): "walked//stood//sat," so too do the nouns: "counsel//way//gathering."

1.d. The verb ליץ has the basic sense "to talk loosely," and the noun לץ has the sense "babbler"; but the context here suggests the nuance "scoffers." cf. H. N. Richardson, "Some Notes on ליץ and Its Derivatives." *VT* 5 (1955) 163–79.

2.a. The root הגה, which may be onomatopoeic, implies more than just "meditating"; some kind of utterance is indicated, such as "murmuring" or "whispering."

3.a. "Running waters"; viz. "irrigation channels," fed with a constant supply of water.

3.b. The syntax is ambivalent, and the line could refer to the *tree*. But the line is best taken as referring to the righteous man and as concluding the first section (vv 1–3); it is thus unnecessary to delete the line as a gloss (as suggested in *BHS*).

4.a. *G* adds ἀπὸ προσώπου τῆς γῆς (". . . from the face of the earth"). The words may have been added simply for stylistic reasons, to avoid the abruptness of MT, which is nevertheless the best text.

5.a. "In judgment" implies the *place* of judgment (cf. Deut 25:1); i.e. the wicked will have no place, or no respect, in the courts of law, where justice and righteousness are the *modus operandi*. Such a meaning is strongly implied by the second line of the synonymous parallelism (v 5b). If this interpretation is correct, then there is not any eschatological implication of a final judgment here.

6.a. "Protects": the normal sense of the verb ידע is "to know"; on the sense "protect, guard," see Dahood, *Psalms I*, 5.

Form/Structure/Setting

Psalm 1, by virtue of its language and content, must be classified with the *wisdom psalms* (cf. Pss 32, 34, and 49 in this volume). Its terminology and teaching reflect the thought of the Wisdom Literature in general and the Book of Proverbs in particular (cf. Prov 2:12–15, 20–22). The psalm was probably not composed in the first instance for use in formal worship; rather, it must be viewed as a literary and poetic composition, expressing with remarkable clarity the polarity of persons and their destinies.

There are certain basic problems pertaining to the analysis of the psalm in terms of poetry, particularly with respect to meter. While the analysis of meter is always difficult in the study of Hebrew poetry (see the critical remarks in the INTRODUCTION), there is even less regularity than usual in Ps 1. The interpretation of most scholars has proceeded on the basis of a provisional metrical analysis (e.g. Gunkel, *Die Psalmen*, 1–4), but it has been claimed by

Bullough that the psalm is not metrical at all, but is "plain rhythmic prose" (*VT* 17 [1967] 42–49). For a critical analysis of the problem of meter, see O. Loretz, *UF* 3 (1971) 101–3. The translation above has not included a metrical notation (as is done for other psalms in this commentary). Bullough is probably correct in his view that the psalm is not metrical in the normal sense; the only approximate indicator of balance is the division of lines, which are very uneven in length. But although there is not a normal metrical structure to Ps 1, it is still clearly and distinctively *poetry*. Parallelism is used in vv 1, 2, 3c–d, 5, and 6. And the psalm as a whole is a finely crafted piece of poetic literature, as various recent studies have shown. Merendino has shown that the psalm is a work of art *(Kunstwerk)*, and Lack's structural analysis has shown the closely knit structure of the whole—the text is a "tissue of interdependencies" (*Bib* 57 [1976] 167).

The structure of the psalm may be set forth as follows: (1) the solid foundation of the righteous (1:1–3); (2) the impermanence of the wicked (1:4–5); (3) a contrast of the righteous and the wicked (1:6). Within this overall structure the poet has made careful use of chiasmus in the first two sections:

vv 1–2	A
v 3	B
v 4	B'
v 5	A'

On this chiastic structure, see further N. H. Ridderbos, *Die Psalmen*, 120 and R. L. Alden, *JETS* 17 (1974) 11–28. The inner chiasmus between the first two parts of the psalm is then united in the contrast of the antithetical parallelism in v 6, which also has an internal chiastic structure.

Psalm 1, as a didactic poem, does not in the first instance have a cultic or social setting; its primary setting is literary, for it forms an introduction to the Psalter as a whole and has been placed in its present position by the editor or compiler of the Psalter for that purpose. But although the psalm is a distinct and independent literary composition, there is some evidence, in both the early Jewish and Christian traditions, to suggest that it was joined to Ps 2, and the two psalms together were considered to be the first psalm of the Psalter. In the Jewish tradition, Rabbi Johanan is credited with the following words in the Babylonian Talmud: "Every chapter that was particularly dear to David he commenced with 'Happy' and terminated with 'Happy.' He began with 'Happy,' as it is written, *'Happy is the man,'* and he terminated with 'Happy,' as it is written, *'Happy are all they that take refuge in him'."* (*Ber.* 9b). The reference here to the first verse of Ps 1 and the last verse of Ps 2 indicates that the two psalms together were considered to be a literary unit.

The evidence from the early Christian tradition is found in Acts 13:33. The writer, Luke, gives a quotation from Ps 2:7, but introduces it as coming from the first psalm; the corrections, both in the early Greek text and in modern English versions, to read "the second psalm," are appropriate given the change in the conventional system of numbering the Psalms. Nevertheless, the oldest Greek text of Acts provides evidence for the early Christian view that the first two psalms were considered to be a single unit. If the two psalms were first joined in the Psalter (despite being independent compositions prior to their incorporation in the Book of Psalms), it may be that they were intended to provide a double perspective in introduction; Ps 1 provides an introduction from the perspective of wisdom, whereas Ps 2 provides a prophetic approach to the book. It has also been suggested that the two psalms were joined together to form a coronation liturgy, perhaps for one of the last kings of Judah; the king, at his coronation, pledged himself to fulfill the Deuteronomic law of kings (W. H. Brownlee, *Bib* 52 [1971] 321–36).

Comment

The solid foundation of the righteous (1:1–3). The righteous are introduced as the "blessed" or "happy" (see further H. Cazelles, *TDOT* I, 445–48). Their happy estate is not something given automatically by God, but is a direct result of their activity. A person can be happy, from a negative perspective, by avoiding the advice, the life style and the assembly of wicked persons (v 1). The three parallel lines of v 1 are poetically synonymous and thus all describe in slightly different ways the evil company which should be avoided by the righteous. Though the three lines, taken together, provide a full picture of what is to be avoided, it would be stretching the text beyond its natural meaning to see in these lines three distinct phases in the deterioration of a person's conduct and character (see further G. W. Anderson, *VT* 24 [1974] 231–33). The righteous person avoids all the dimensions of the way of the wicked; therein lies the source of blessedness or happiness.

But a person who is to be happy must also engage in a positive task, which is identified in v 2 as being related to the Torah. Although the term *Torah* can be used of the law, or of the Pentateuch, or even (at a later date) of the whole OT, its significance here is the most fundamental one. Basically, the word *Torah* means "instruction"; specifically, it is the instruction which God gives to mankind as a guide for life. Thus it may include that which is technically law, but it also includes other more general parts of God's revelation. The Torah is to be a source of "delight" (see further the *Explanation,* below), a delight which is discovered by means of constant meditation on its meaning. Just as the king would learn to live a life of humility and righteousness through constant reflection on the meaning of Torah (Deut 17:18–20), so too could all mankind. And an understanding of Torah contributed to long life, peace and prosperity (Prov 3:1–2), for in its words God has set down the nature of a life which would reach the true fulfillment for which it was created.

The happy estate of the righteous is illuminated in v 3 by the simile of the tree. A tree may flourish or fade, depending upon its location and access to water. A tree transplanted from some dry spot (e.g. a wadi, where the water runs only sporadically in the rainy season) to a location beside an irrigation channel, where water never ceases to flow, would inevitably flourish. It would become a green and fruitful tree. The simile not only illustrates colorfully the prosperity of the righteous, but also make a theological point.

The state of blessedness or happiness is not a *reward;* rather, it is the result of a particular type of life. Just as a tree with a constant water supply *naturally* flourishes, so too the person who avoids evil and delights in Torah *naturally* prospers, for such a person is living within the guidelines set down by the Creator. Thus the prosperity of the righteous reflects the wisdom of a life lived according to the plan of the Giver of all life.

The wicked (1:4–5). "Not so the wicked" (v 4); that is, they shall not prosper as the righteous (v 3). The life of the wicked is summarized succinctly in the brief simile of v 4b. They are like chaff. The language reflects the practice of winnowing grain at harvest time. The grain would be tossed into the air with a pitchfork at the village threshing floor; the wind would separate the light chaff and husks and blow them away, while the more substantial grain fell back to the floor. Chaff is something light and useless, part of the crop, but a part to be disposed of by the farmer. The wicked are thus depicted in the simile as lightweights, persons without real substance or worth.

The "lightness" of the wicked is then elaborated in v 5. The two lines of v 5, in synonymous parallelism, reflect essentially the same thought, namely that the wicked hold no weight or influence in the important areas of human society. Where the righteous meet for the pursuit of justice and government, the wicked have no place and are not recognized. They live for themselves and cannot participate in the affairs of those who live for others and for righteousness.

The contrast (1:6). And so, in the last resort, human beings are of two kinds. They may be righteous; if so, God protects their way. But they may be wicked, and for the wicked, the final destiny is doom. The doom of the wicked, as it is expressed in this psalm, is not primarily a punishment, any more than the happiness of the righteous is a reward. Each is presented as the natural outcome of a way of life which has been chosen.

Explanation

"The fear of the Lord is the beginning of wisdom" (Prov 1:7); these words are often taken to be an expression of the fundamental principle of the Wisdom Literature, of which this psalm is a part. Psalm 1 elaborates upon this principle with respect to human behavior. The righteous person is the one whose "fear" (or reverence) of God affects his daily living; he avoids evil and learns how to live from God's Torah, and therein lies his wisdom. The wisdom, as expressed in this psalm, is essentially related to the present life; the psalm does not clearly evince any doctrine of future life (as proposed, for example, by Dahood in *Psalms I,* 3–5). The anticipated prosperity is in the present life, just as the failure of the wicked is to be a present reality.

The contrast between the two *ways* (1:6) is illuminated further in the words of Jesus in the "Sermon on the Mount" (Matt 7:13–14). Jesus speaks of two gates, a broad gate giving entrance to the "way that leads to destruction" and a narrow gate giving entrance to "the way that leads to life." (Alternatively, the text could be interpreted to mean that there are two *ways,* one leading to a broad gate, the other leading to a narrow gate). The principles of Jesus' teaching are essentially those of the psalm, yet there is an eschatological

element in the words of Jesus (see also Luke 13:24), for the kingdom of
God, represented by the way of life associated with the narrow gate, has
both a present and a future dimension of reality.

There is a further aspect of this psalm which is relevant to its application.
In the last resort, the principal wisdom of the psalm can be reduced to v 2;
the prosperity and happiness of the righteous depends upon their finding
"delight" in the Lord's Torah. But how is such delight to be found? In practical
terms, it is achieved by constant meditation upon the Torah (v 2b), which
is God's *instruction*. As instruction, it contains guidance from the Creator as
to the meaning of creation. Life is lived in futility if its fundamental purpose
is never discovered. It is the meaning of human existence which is enshrined
in the Torah, and it is the discovery of that meaning which flows from meditation upon Torah.

A Coronation Psalm   (2:1–12)

Bibliography

Auffret, Pierre. *The Literary Structure of Psalm 2.* JSOT SS 3. Sheffield, England. 1977.
Filipiak, M. "Mesjanism królewski w Psalmie 2." *Collectanea Theologica* 43 (1973)
49–65. (Polish/French summary). **Holladay, W. L.** "A New Proposal for the Crux
in Psalm 2:12." *VT* 28 (1978) 110–12. **Kunz, P. L.** "Der 2. Psalm in neuer Sicht."
BZ (NF) 20 (1976) 238–42. **Macintosh, A. A.** "A Consideration of Problems presented
by Psalm 2:11." *JTS* (NS) 27 (1976) 1–14. **Pili, F.** "Possibili casi di metatesi in Genesi
49:10 e Salmo 2:11–12a." *Augustinianum* 15 (1975) 457–71. **Robinson, A.** "Deliberate
but Misguided Haplography Explains Psalm 2:11–12." *ZAW* 89 (1977) 421–22. **Soggin,
J. A.** "Zum zweiten Psalm." In *Wort-Gebot-Glaube. Beiträge zur Theologie des Alten Testaments,
Walter Eichrodt zum 80. Geburtstag,* ed. H. J. Stoebe, J. J. Stamm and E. Jenni (ATANT
59. Zurich: Zwingli Verlag, 1970) 191–207. **Van der Kam, J.** "*Bhl* in Ps 2:5 and its
Etymology." *CBQ* 39 (1977) 245–50. **Wilhelmi, G.** "Der Hirt mit dem eisernen Szep-
ter." *VT* 27 (1977) 196–204.

Translation

1 *Why do the nations congregate in commotion*   (3+3)
        and why [a] *do the warriors* [b] *murmur murderously?* [c]
2 *Why do earthly kings take their stand*   (3+3+2)
        and why do princes join together as one,
        against the Lord and his anointed?
3 *"Let us tear off their fetters*   (3+3)
        and let us cast off their cords [a] *from us!"*
4 *The Enthroned One laughs in heaven;*   (3+3)
        the Lord mocks them.
5 *Then he addresses them* [a] *in his anger*   (3?+2)
        and in his wrath he terrifies them. [b]
6 *"I have installed* [a] *my king*   (3+2?)
        upon Zion, my holy mountain!"

[7] *"I will tell of the Lord's decree.*   (4, 4+3)
He said to me: 'You are my son.
Today, I have begotten you.

[8] *Just ask me,*   (2+3+3)
and I will grant nations as your inheritance
and as your possession, the ends of the earth.

[9] *You shall break them* [a] *with an iron rod;*   (3+3)
like a potter's vessel you shall pulverize them.' "

[10] *So now, O kings, think carefully!*   (3+3)
Be admonished, O earthly rulers!

[11] *Serve the Lord with fear*   (3+2)
and rejoice with trembling.

[12] *Kiss the son,* [a] *lest he be angry*   (2+2)
and you perish in the path,
for his anger flares up quickly;   (3+3)
happy [b] *are all who seek refuge in him!*

Notes

1.a. The word "why" (למה) is used only once at the beginning of v 1a, but it dominates the whole introductory section (2:1–3) and is implied in the following lines. Thus it is repeated four times in the translation to convey the power of the passage.

1.b. The "warriors" (לאמים): the Heb word is commonly translated "peoples," which is legitimate. But in both Hebrew and Ugaritic, the word may carry the connotation "warrior" (viz. "warlike people"); see further Craigie, *ZAW* 90 (1978) 377. It is the military context of these opening verses which suggests the nuance *warriors*.

1.c. "Murmur murderously": literally, "growl a vain thing" (הגה, "growl, murmur," probably being onomatopoeic). V 1 contains the first of several examples of chiasmus in the psalm, though the device cannot always be reflected properly in the English translation. Here, the form is: "they congregate (A) the nations (B); the warriors (B′) murmur (A′)." Other examples of chiasmus occur in vv 2ab, 5, 8bc, 10.

3.a. The words "fetters" and "cords" may simply imply captivity (viz. the foreign nations were vassal states), but *G* implies the imagery of a *yoke*, attached by cords, which the nations cast off like rebellious oxen.

5.a. Dahood's rendering of v 5a ("Then he drives away their lieutenants in his ire": *Psalms I*, 6) is ingenious and perhaps plausible. But the meaning of MT is perfectly clear as it stands and fits the context well enough; hence radical change (in meaning) is thought to be unnecessary. For criticisms of Dahood's rendering, see J. VanderKam, *CBQ* 39 (1977) 245–46.

5.b. VanderKam's suggestion (see note 5a) that the root בהל should be translated "to speak passionately" (whence the translation: ". . . in his fury he will berate them") is plausible and possible. But the assumptions that led to a search for a new meaning for בהל in the first place are not entirely convincing: (i) that בהל, "to terrify," is ill-suited to the context, and (ii) that it does not supply a semantic parallel to ידבר "he addresses." With respect to the first point, it is quite appropriate for the divine speech to *terrify* (the theme of fear reappears in v 11); with respect to the second point, parallelism need not imply synonyms (or even near-synonyms) in the parallel lines; see J. Barr, *Comparative Philology and the Text of the Old Testament*, 277–82.

6.a. The conjunction *and* (ו) which opens the line has been omitted as a possible case of dittography (v 5 ends with /w/). In *G*, v 6 is translated as the opening words of the king (see v 7), rather than God's words: "I have been made king by him on Zion, his holy mountain." This is a possible rendering, though the translation above, based on MT, is to be preferred; by maintaining MT, the parallel structure between vv 1–3 and 4–6 is kept. Dahood follows *G* in v 6a, but translates: "But I have been anointed his king. . . ." He takes MT's נָסַכְתִּי to be נְסָכֹתִי, from סוּךְ, "to anoint"; the reading is possible, though MT provides acceptable sense as it stands. With respect to the Ugaritic verb "anoint" in *CTA* 3.2.41, adduced by Dahood in support of his rendering, it must be said that the text in question is uncertain and it is not clear that it refers to anointing: see Craigie, *ZAW* 90 (1978) 380.

9.a. The pointing in MT, תְּרֹעֵם, indicates the use of the root רעע, "break." *G*'s translation, on the other hand, assumes a verbal form derived from רעה, "to pasture, graze" (hence "rule"). Although either reading is possible, depending upon the vocalization of the consonantal text, the context as a whole suggests the more powerful "break them." But this is not certain, and NT references to this verse follow *G;* see further G. Wilhelmi, *VT* 27 (1977) 196–204.

12.a. *MT*'s נשקו־בר is the *crux interpretum* of Ps 2. Although the meaning of MT as it stands is perfectly clear (viz. "kiss the son"), there are two principal grounds of difficulty. (i) The word בר ("son") is Aramaic, and is therefore thought to be unlikely in Hebrew (especially if the psalm is to be dated early in the monarchy). In v 7, the standard Heb word for *son* has already been used, namely בן. (ii) The majority of the versions, with the exception of *S*, together with the later rabbinic writings, presuppose a Heb text such as בֹּר ("purity") or בַּר ("clean, pure"). For these two principal reasons, there have been numerous attempts to solve the problem: (a) most commonly on the basis of *emendation* (e.g. Auffret, following Berthelot and others); (b) on the basis of *dittography* (Macintosh); (c) on the basis of *haplography* (Robinson); (d) on the basis of *metathesis* (F. Pili), and (e) on the basis of a redivision and revocalization of MT, together with a use of the resources of Ugaritic, to gain a new translation (so Dahood and Holladay). None of the solutions to the problem are entirely satisfactory, though the best choice from those summarized above would be that of Holladay (after Dahood), who revocalizes the text and translates: "you who forget the grave" (נשי־קבר: Holladay, *VT* 28 [1978] 110–12).

The dissatisfaction created by the multitude of solutions prompts a reexamination of the initial (supposed) problems, which gave rise to the identification of the *crux* in the first place. First, is בר "son," admittedly an Aramaic loan-word, necessarily a major problem in a psalm dated provisionally at some point in the Hebrew monarchy? It need not be; Aramaic is known to have been used widely in Syria-Palestine from at least the ninth century B.C., and the current absence of earlier epigraphic evidence does not mean that it could not have been used earlier (though it should be recalled that no precise date is known for Ps 2). Furthermore, the context of vv 11–12 should be noted. The words are addressed (in the mouth of the poet) to *foreign* nations and kings (Aramaic speaking?), whereas בן, "son," in v 7, is used by God in speaking to his king. It is possible that the poet deliberately uses a foreign word (loan-word) to dramatize his poetic intent at this point. Finally, as Delitzsch noted (*Biblical Commentary on the Psalms, I,* 128), the use of בר *bār* here avoids the dissonance בן פן *běn pěn.* These factors are presented in support of MT; they do not resolve the problem of the rendition of the words in the majority of the versions, though perhaps a variety of psychological factors might explain their ambiguity. If indeed MT should be kept and translated "kiss the son," then the reference is to an act of homage which earthly rulers would pay to the "son" (viz. the king, v 7). Thus vv 10–12 comprise a passage in which the earthly rulers are required to serve *God* and to acknowledge his *king;* this double theme nicely counteracts the rulers' rebellion, which was said to be directed against both God and his anointed (v 2).

12.b. "Happy" (or, "blessed") balances the opening word of Ps 1:1, perhaps forming an in-clusio, if the first two psalms are taken to be a single unit (see further the commentary on Ps 1).

Form/Structure/Setting

In general terms, the psalm is a *royal psalm* and must be interpreted in association with the Hebrew monarchy. More specifically, Ps 2 is a *coronation psalm;* such a classification depends primarily upon the content of the psalm, rather than any characteristic form which distinguishes it from other royal psalms. A coronation involved the setting of a crown upon the new king's head, the formal presentation of a document to the new king, and his procla-mation and anointing (cf. 2 Kgs 11:12); in the interpretation (below), the ceremonial details are drawn out more fully. The identification of the psalm with the coronation of a Davidic king is clarified by the parallels between this psalm and the promises given to David in the oracle of Nathan (2 Sam 7:8–16; see further Rogerson and McKay, *Psalms 1–50,* 19).

The psalm consists of four sections of approximately equivalent length.

(1) Foreign nations and their rulers express rebellion against God and his king (2:1–3). (2) God mocks the might of kings by announcing the installation of a king of his own choosing in Zion (2:4–6). (3) The Davidic king speaks and declares the words of God contained in his kingly deed (2:7–9). (4) The nations and their kings are warned of God's wrath and of the consequences of his anger and pleasure (2:10–12). Although it is possible that the whole psalm should be viewed as containing the words spoken by the Davidic king (so Eaton, *Kingship and the Psalms*, 111), it is perhaps better to note the change of speakers throughout the psalm. From a literary perspective, the psalmist or poet presents a variety of persons, each of whom speaks. First, he presents foreign nations and kings (2:1–2) who speak their words of arrogance (2:3). Second, he presents the Lord (2:4–5) who speaks concerning the chosen king (2:6). Third, he presents the words of the king, who in turn proclaims the divine words of royal proclamation (2:7–9). Fourth, he addresses his own words of advice to the foreign nations and their rulers. Thus, the whole psalm has a dramatic character. From a liturgical perspective, it is possible that the different sections of the psalm were spoken by different persons during the course of the coronation ceremony. The congregation, or its priestly and prophetic leaders, may have spoken the opening verses (2:1–6). Then the king may have responded (2:7–9), followed by a congregational or priestly conclusion (2:10–12). The scant nature of the evidence, however, makes any such analysis uncertain; it is equally uncertain whether the psalm may reflect the coronation liturgy of the temple or a later ceremony in the palace.

The psalm is effective and dramatic in its literary style. The poet has used fairly short lines, which highlight the drama of the moment which the psalm reflects. Parallelism and chiasmus are both commonly used poetic devices throughout the psalm (see the textual and philological notes), which contribute to its literary quality. The structure of the psalm as a whole is also distinctive, reflecting movement and completeness; beginning with the tumultuous nations, the poet then turns to God and his king, before concluding (chiastically) with the nations again, now subdued rather than tumultuous. And the sound of the psalm is also effective. In vv 3–5, the poet plays on the sound /o/, producing an effect which is like rhyme (unusual in Hebrew poetry). The sound appears first in the arrogant words of the earthly rulers (v 3); but then the same sound of arrogance is converted into a sound anticipating *woe* in the words introducing God's response (vv 4b, 5). Thus through a variety of artistic devices, the poet has crafted a psalm of power and elegance, worthy of the drama of its theme.

Comment

Foreign nations and rulers (2:1–3). The coronation of a king marks the accession of a person to a position of power and authority; for the Davidic kings, that power and authority were received from God and exercised under his dominion. It is against this background of divine and regal authority that the opening words of the psalm must be read. The nations of the world, their warriors and rulers, are gathering together in an act of rebellion against God and the king. Although it is possible to seek an historical background to the rebellious nations (e.g. in the reign of King Solomon), the psalmist is not necessarily referring to any particular event in history. The language reflects primarily all—or any—nations that do not acknowledge the primacy of Israel's God, and therefore of Israel's king. Thus, the verses contain a reflection of the opposite to a theological ideal. The ideal was that of a world in which all nations and kings recognized the kingship of God and his appointed sovereign; the reality was seen anew in each coronation, that such was not the case. Foreign nations would act violently against Israel's king and in so doing would be rebelling against divine rule. Hence the opening verses of the psalm introduce a note of immediacy and drama which permeates the entire psalm. A new king was coming to the throne, but he would rule in a world characterized by the violence and danger of foreign powers. In such a world, human strength would be insufficient; divine aid would be needed.

The human king is here identified as God's *anointed*. The royal title is derived from the fact that the king on his coronation is anointed (1 Kgs 1:45), an act symbolizing that he was set aside from other persons to perform a particular service. Although the word rendered "anointed" is the form from which comes the English title *Messiah* (derived from the Hebrew), the presence of the word in 2:2 does not necessarily mean that the psalm was initially *messianic*. Here, the reference of the term in the context of the psalm's initial use is simply to the *human* king, for whom the coronation was conducted (cf. Filipiak, *Collectanea Theologica* 43 [1973] 49–65). It was only from a more distant perspective in history that the messianic implications of the psalm could be discerned (see *Explanation*, below).

God announces his king (2:4–6). The scene now shifts from the earthly rulers and their arrogant words to the heavenly Ruler and his words evoking terror. The contrast is striking; God is the *Enthroned One*, literally "the one sitting" (on his throne) in heaven. The mockery and anger of God's words are prompted by the rebellion and arrogance of the earthly kings, and the very utterance of his words instills terror in those to whom they are addressed. Throughout these opening six verses, the entire scene is strictly imaginary; that is, imaginary nations (though they are rooted in the reality of constant historical experience) rebel and God responds. Yet this dramatic imagery serves to give international and cosmic significance to the first climax of the psalm, namely v 6. God terrifies the earthly rulers, not with any direct threat, but simply with an announcement that he has established his king in Zion.

When the liturgical dimension of the psalm is recalled, namely its use in a coronation ceremony, the words of v 6 take on further significance. Verse 2 implies that the anointing has already taken place, and v 6 indicates that the candidate was now officially king. His office as king was one of divine appointment; God had *installed* him. The king was installed "upon Zion"; Zion, in David's time, was the hill in the southeastern section of the city of Jerusalem (not to be confused with later popular tradition which located Mount Zion in the southwest), where the former Jebusite city had been located. But for practical purposes, the term Zion is virtually synonymous with *Jerusalem*, and whether the installation took place in the palace or temple cannot be ascertained (though parts of the coronation ceremony probably took place in both localities).

The king declares his mandate (2:7–9). The words of the king in this section, and the divine words which he quotes, may well be words which were formally declared by the new king after his anointing and installation, during the course of the coronation. The principal portion of the king's declaration is a quotation from the words of God which are written in the "Lord's decree" (2:7). The "decree" is a document, given to the king during the coronation ceremony (cf. 2 Kgs 11:12); it is his personal covenant document, renewing God's covenant commitment to the dynasty of David. The content of the decree establishes the nature and authority of the newly crowned king.

The divine words which the king declares are words pertaining to the royal covenant. At the heart of the covenant is the concept of *sonship;* the human partner in the covenant is *son* of the covenant God, who is *father.* This covenant principle of sonship is a part of the Sinai Covenant between God and Israel. The covenant God cares for Israel as a father cares for his son (Deut 1:31) and God disciplines Israel as a father disciplines a son (Deut 8:5). The focus of the Sinai covenant is the relationship between God and nation; in the covenant with the house of David, the focus is narrowed to a relationship between God and the king, but the concept of sonship is still integral to this covenant. Thus God, through words spoken by Nathan, declared of David: "I will be his father and he shall be my son" (2 Sam 7:14); David, in return, could say to God: "You are my father" (Ps 89:26).

The Davidic covenant was eternal, but all covenants were renewed from time to time; the principal form of renewal in the royal covenant took place in the coronation, when a new descendant of the Davidic dynasty ascended to the throne. Thus, the divine words "you are my son" mark a renewal of the relationship between God and David's house in the person of the newly crowned king. "Today" points to the fact that the words were announced on the coronation day, the day on which the divine decree became effective. (The emphasis on *today* also occurs in other types of covenant renewal ceremony; see Deut 26:17 and 30:19). "I have begotten you" is metaphorical language; it means more than simply adoption, which has legal overtones, and implies that a "new birth" of a divine nature took place during the coronation. It is important to stress, nevertheless, that the Davidic king, as son of God, was a *human being,* not a divine being, as was held in certain Near Eastern concepts of kingship. For background material and illustrations pertaining to the concept of sonship and coronation in other Near Eastern civilizations, see O. Keel, *The Symbolism of the Biblical World. Ancient Near Eastern Iconography and the Book of Psalms.* New York: Seabury (1978) 247–68.

The king's sonship carried privileges, but the privileges were to be asked of God (v 8a), who would then willingly grant them. The privileges are expressed in ideal terms as the control of all nations to the ends of the earth (v 8) and power to "break them" and "pulverize them" (v 9), words which refer back to the rebellious nature of the earthly nations (2:1–3). The poetry in v 9 presents this regal authority in a dramatic manner: an "iron rod" is something intrinsically strong, just as a potter's vessel is constitutionally fragile. This stark contrast between the power of the Davidic king and the fragility of earthly monarchs rested not in the human strength of the Hebrew king, but in the strength of God, the speaker of these words.

A warning to earthly rulers (2:10–12). The earthly kings and rulers, who at the opening of the psalm were acting rashly and arrogantly (2:1–3), are now admonished and told to think very carefully (v 10) of the implications of the coronation which has just transpired. They are advised to "serve" the Lord; the word "serve" (עָבַד) has political overtones and implies that the foreign nations should submit as vassals to Israel's God. In order to submit to God, they would have to submit to his son, the king; thus, they are called upon to "kiss the son," for kissing was a sign of homage and submission (cf. 1 Sam 10:1; 1 Kgs 19:18). Failure to submit to God through his king would result in disaster, for God's hasty wrath would culminate in their destruction (v 12). But submission, though not easy for the arrogant, would lead not only to a vassal relationship, but also would bring with it the happiness of "all who seek refuge in him" (v 12).

Explanation

Psalm 2 is one of the psalms most frequently quoted and alluded to in the NT; from the perspective of early Christianity, it was a messianic psalm par excellence. Yet in the interpretation of the psalm which has been given so far, the psalm has been presented as a royal psalm, to be associated with a king's coronation; it has not been identified as explicitly messianic. To perceive the transition of the psalm from its royal to its messianic character, it is necessary first to perceive certain transitions in biblical history and religious thought.

A central theme of the entire biblical tradition is the *kingdom of God.* In the monarchic period, the kingdom of God is identified with the state of Israel (and later Judah). That state had a human king, but ultimately its king was God; Israel was a theocracy. Psalm 2 clearly reflects this joint-kingship of the state. The Lord, the Enthroned One (v 4), was the universal king, but his earthly representative was his "son," the Davidic king. Because God is a universal God, the earthly king's jurisdiction is also presented in world-wide terms (2:8–9), though with respect to the Davidic kings, the world-wide authority always remained an ideal rather than a reality. With the decline and eventual demise of the state of Judah (587/6 B.C.), the line of Davidic kings came formally to an end; the ideal of world-wide kingship, never realized during the historical monarchy, now seemed to be an impossible dream.

The demise of the state and the end of the monarchy required radical rethinking within ancient Judaism. The new thought, which emerged during and after Exile, took a variety of forms. There would be a new covenant (Jer 31:31–34), which implied a new kingship. The covenant with David's house had been eternal, so that in some form the Davidic kings would have a role to play in the future. The concept of an "anointed one" or messiah, which had originally attached only to an earthly king (2:2), came to have eschatological and messianic overtones (in the modern sense of the term *messianic*). In one of the few other references to the word *messiah* in the OT, the office is seen to be a princely one associated with a future work of God (Dan 9:25).

When Jesus began his ministry of preaching, his central theme was the *kingdom of God* (Mark 1:14–15), and from the perspective of the Gospel writers, it is clear that Jesus was in some sense king in this newly announced kingdom. It is precisely the proclamation of the kingdom of God in the teaching of Jesus which permits the terminology of royalty in Ps 2 to be incorporated into the NT language about Jesus. The "anointed one" *(Messiah)* in Ps 2:2 was the king; hence Jesus, understood within early Christianity as the king in the kingdom of God, could be entitled *Messiah* or *Christ* (the Anointed One). Again, just as the king in Ps 2:7 was addressed by God as his *son,* so too the new King Jesus could be designated the *Son of God.*

The interpretation of Ps 2 as messianic in conjunction with Jesus involves a great insight into the nature of the entire ministry of Jesus. The psalm is a coronation psalm and its interpretation with respect to Jesus is indicative of the coronation of Jesus within the kingdom of God. Whereas the coronation of the Davidic king took place on one day, there is a sense in which the coronation of Jesus took place throughout his ministry. In the NT, the words "You are my son" are quoted and paraphrased at a number of points in Jesus' life: (a) at his baptism (Matt 3:17); (b) at the Transfiguration (Matt 17:5), and (c) with reference to the Resurrection (Acts 13:33). It is above all Jesus' resurrection from the dead which publicly declares that he is King, or Son of God (Rom 1:4).

Yet the establishment of the kingdom of God by Jesus marks a radically new concept of royal power from that depicted in the coronation of the Davidic king. In OT times, the nations of the world were portrayed as rebellious at the time of the coronation (Ps 2:1–3), yet they would (or could) be subdued by the Davidic king; the psalm breathes an atmosphere of violence (2:9). This rebellion of the nations is interpreted by the earliest Christians as referring to the opposition to Jesus of Herod, Pontius Pilate, the Gentiles and Israel (Acts 4:24–28); their violence was not confronted by further violence, but accepted by Jesus in his death. The new kingdom was established in the receipt of violence and death, but the climax of Jesus' coronation lay in his conquest of death through resurrection. It is this which distinguishes Jesus from a mere earthly king, which makes him more than human in his sonship, and which translates him higher even than the angels (Heb 1:5; 5:5).

There is a further dimension to the NT use of Ps 2 which is important for a full understanding of the messianic nature of the psalm. It was noted in the interpretation that the language of Ps 2 concerning the Davidic king was characterized by an ideal rather than reality; the Davidic kings never exercised world-wide dominion. But the same objection might be lodged against the kingship of Jesus. *Theologically,* one might affirm his universal dominion, but in reality the world is still characterized by tumultuous nations and rebellious rulers. From this perspective, the kingship of Jesus is established, but the climax of his dominion remains yet a future reality. And so it is not surprising that one of the NT books which contains many references to Ps 2 is the Revelation of St. John. The Revelation, in the symbolic and mysterious language of its writer, contains an anticipation of the ultimate rule and triumph of the man born to be King in the language and imagery of Ps 2 (Rev 1:5; 2:27; 4:2; 6:17; 12:5; 19:5 and others).

A Morning Prayer (3:1–9)

Bibliography

Eaton, J. H. *Kingship and the Psalms*, 27–29. **Loretz, O.** "Psalmenstudien III." *UF* 6 (1974) 175–201 (177–78).

Translation

¹ A psalm of David. When he fled from Absalom, his son.

2(1)* *O Lord, how many are my foes!* *How* ᵃ *many rise up against me!*	(3 + 3)
3(2) *How many are saying* ᵃ *of me:* ᵇ *"There is no victory for him* ᶜ *from God!"* SELAH	(3 + 3)
4(3) *But you, O Lord, are a shield* ᵃ *round me,* *my glory, and the One who holds up my head.*	(4 + 3)
5(4) *I will cry out loud to the Lord,* *and he will answer* ᵃ *me from his holy mountain.* SELAH	(3 + 3)
6(5) *I lay down. Then I fell asleep.* *I awakened, because the Lord sustains me.*	(3 + 3)
7(6) *I will not fear the multitudes* ᵃ *of the people,* ᵇ *who, on every side, have deployed against me.*	(3 + 4?)
8(7) *Rise up, O Lord!* *Give me victory,* ᵃ *O my God!*	(2 + 2)
Oh, that you would smite ᵇ *all my enemies on the cheek.* *Oh, that you would smash the teeth of wicked men.*	(3 + 3)
9(8) *Victory belongs to the Lord.* *Your blessing is upon your people.* SELAH	(2 + 2)

Notes

2.a. The particle מה "how?" is used only once in the opening line of v 2: מה רבו צרי "how many are my foes." But the thrust of the word carries on to the two further uses of the root רבב, namely רבים "many" in vv 2b and 3a, as is reflected in the translation.

3.a. "Saying": אמרים. Dahood's translation, "who *eye* . . . ," as from the root אמר, "see" (in Akk. and Ugaritic), is possible; but since the following line of poetry involves speech, in the form of a quotation, it is preferable to retain the conventional rendering.

3.b. "Of me": לנפשי (or "to my soul"). This expression may have been used, rather than the simpler לי for reasons of poetic balance; nevertheless, the word may imply that the critical words which follow immediately reflect upon his most *essential being*, namely his relationship with God.

3.c. S renders ". . . for *you* in *your* God," implying that the enemies address their words directly to the psalmist, rather than simply talking about him. G retains "for him," but adds a suffix to the following noun: "(in) *his* God." The sense of the words is clear, though by retaining the meaning of MT, the power is heightened; the enemies are talking of him behind his back!

* Verse numbers in parentheses are those of the standard English versions. Those without parentheses are those of the Hebrew Text.

4.a. "Shield": מגן. Dahood translates the term "Suzerain," and provides a lengthy argument drawing upon the resources of Ugaritic, Phoenician and Punic. The argument is plausible, and the fact that both terms, "shield" and "Suzerain," relate to God and imply such things as his *protective* nature, makes a decision on the most appropriate translation difficult. I have preferred to retain the conventional translation of MT for two reasons: (i) it is clear in some poetic passages that מגן must mean "shield" (e.g. in Deut 33:29, "shield" is parallel to "sword," and in Ps 91:4, "shield" occurs in conjunction with "buckler"); (ii) the translation "Suzerain" involves further the revocalizing of בעדי "round about me"; in other words, such a translation was clearly not the one implied by the Massoretic tradition. On the translation "shield," see further O. Loretz, *UF* 6 (1974) 177–78.

5.a. "He will answer": the *waw* prefixed to the verb is read as a simple, rather than a consecutive, *waw.*

7.a. "Multitudes": רבבות. Dahood translates the "*shafts* of the people," from רבב "to shoot arrows"; though such usage is attested in the OT (but in the masc. rather than fem. form), it is highly unlikely in this context. The psalmist has already employed the root רבב three times (vv 2–3) with respect to his enemies; now he employs a word from the same root to give expression to his confidence.

7.b. "People": concerning the military connotations of this word, see the remarks on military terminology in the commentary on Ps 2:1.

8.a. "Victory": see also vv 3, 9. The word, both as noun and verb, relates to "victory" and "deliverance," from whence comes the later (more theological) rendering "salvation."

8.b. On the translation of the verbs in this verse, see Dahood, *Psalms I,* 19–20.

Form/Structure/Setting

The psalm is usually classified as an *individual psalm of lament;* more precisely, it is not a lament in the fullest sense (viz., implying a disaster that has already taken place), but a *protective psalm,* reflecting a current or impending danger (Mowinckel, *The Psalms in Israel's Worship I,* 219–20). The psalmist begins with a complaint against the enemies arrayed against him, but moves on to a prayer of confidence and assurance of ultimate victory.

The language and terminology employed throughout the psalm have military overtones, which suggest that in its initial function, the psalm was more than a general psalm for individual use, but may have been a *royal protective psalm.* The military terminology may be summarized as follows:

(i) The reference to "foes" (3:2) and "enemies" (3:8).

(ii) The references to "victory" (3:3, 8).

(iii) God is described as a "shield" (3:4).

(iv) "People" (3:7) may be employed with the nuance "army"; see further Num 20:20; Judg 5:2; Ps 18:43 and the comments in Craigie, *TB* 20 (1969) 89–90.

(v) The people are "deployed" (3:7) against the psalmist.

(vi) The expression "Rise up, O Lord" (3:8) is parallel to the words spoken on the departure of the Ark for war (Num 10:35).

(vii) "Victory belongs to the Lord" (3:9) sounds like a battle cry.

This military terminology, implying that the crisis facing the psalmist was military in nature, tends to identify the psalm with the king, who was commander-in-chief of the armed forces. (It should be added that the military language is also entirely in harmony with the superscription linking the psalm with David's flight from Absalom; see the *Comment*). Interpreted as a royal protective psalm, it may be that the setting of the psalm initially was in some religious ceremony either before or during a military campaign. The king, facing a military crisis, called for God's help and victory.

There is a further dimension of the psalm which must be accounted for, namely its relationship to Ps 4, with which it has many close parallels (see Kirkpatrick, *The Book of Psalms* [Cambridge: University Press, 1906], 13). Ps 3:6 has suggested to many interpreters that the psalm was used regularly in the morning worship of the individual or of Israel; this suggestion has been incorporated within the title given the psalm in this commentary (above). Ps 4:8 has suggested that the fourth psalm was employed during evening worship. Thus the location of these two psalms next to each other in the Psalter would not be accidental; the compiler of the Book of the Psalms (or of a collection within it) has set alongside each other two standard psalms for use in morning and evening worship respectively.

From the various data which have been accumulated in these introductory paragraphs, it is possible to form a provisional history of the origin and subsequent use of the psalm. The psalm may have originated as a particular prayer during David's lifetime (see further the *Comment* on v 1), associated with his flight from Absalom. Subsequently it became a royal psalm for general use, employed by the Davidic kings in times of military crisis. But this particular use was transformed to a general use. The particular military crisis and the need for victory was analogous to the crisis and needs which may face any human being at any time; so the psalm entered the general resources of Israel's worship as a protective psalm, specifically as a psalm traditionally used during the morning worship.

The psalm falls naturally into four sections, which (with the exception of the third section) are ended by the word SELAH. (1) The psalmist complains of his many enemies (3:2-3); (2) he expresses confidence in God's ability to answer prayer (3:4-5); (3) the psalmist trusts fully in God (3:6-7); (4) he prays for God to grant victory (3:8-9).

Comment

Title (3:1). Although the historical value of the superscriptions of the Psalms is of uncertain significance (see the INTRODUCTION, p 32), it is wise to begin the consideration of a psalm in the light of its superscription, where present. The word *psalm* or *song* (מזמור) indicates that the psalm was sung, although in substance it may be viewed as a prayer. The threefold use of *Selah* (vv 3, 5, 9) is also a probable indication of the use of the psalm in a musical setting; see the discussion of *Selah* in the *Excursus* following the commentary on this psalm. The words "of David" are ambivalent; see p 33 of the INTRODUCTION. For practical purposes, the psalm is anonymous and the date of its composition is not known with certainty.

The second half of the superscription is historical in nature and purports to relate the psalm to a particular incident in David's life. The parallels between the historical incident (David's flight from Absalom) and the *substance* of the psalm are such as to give some credibility to the value of the superscription. The parallels may be summarized as follows:

Ps 3:3	David to be forsaken by God	2 Sam 16:7–8
Ps 3:4	David's head, covered on the Mt. of Olives, will be raised by God	2 Sam 15:30
Ps 3:6	Danger and confidence at night	2 Sam 17:1, 16
Ps 3:7	David heavily outnumbered	2 Sam 15:13 and 17:11
Ps 3:9	Victory eventually comes	2 Sam 19:1–2

In summary, the parallels indicate a close link between the psalm and David's flight from Absalom, but the significance to be attached to the parallels could be interpreted in a variety of ways: (1) the psalm may have been *composed* by David, during or after his flight from Absalom. (2) The psalm might have been composed at a later date, to fit the account of David's flight; thus "to David" (לדוד) would imply *"concerning* David" with respect to this psalm. (3) The parallels may be entirely coincidental, but were sufficiently striking to prompt a later editor to add the superscription, identifying the psalm with David's flight. The first of these three possibilities cannot be proved, but the parallels are sufficiently strong to suggest that Ps 3 may have originated in the context of this particular event in the lifetime of David.

The psalmist complains of his many enemies (3:2–3). The first three lines of the psalm are in poetic parallelism; the parallelism is synonymous, so that the lines express essentially the same thought, though there is an element of climax reached in the third line. The foes "rise up" against the psalmist, but their enmity is expressed in their words. The foes, however, are not merely verbal enemies, as is made clear both by their words and by 3:7. The foes are real enemies arrayed against the psalmist and their words express their own hope: "There is no victory for him from God." God alone gives victory, but the psalmist (in the eyes of his enemies, at least) has been deserted by God; thus the enemies think that it is safe to attack him.

If the psalmist, or the key figure in the psalm, were David, then it might be suggested that the period reflected is that which followed the king's adultery with Bathsheba. That event started a series of problems during David's reign, so that in the eyes of many, it seemed that God had deserted the king. But if the psalm is understood simply as a general royal psalm, pertaining to the activities of the Davidic king in war, then the words of the enemy are equally significant. In the practice of war in the Near East, the role of the gods was held to be highly significant, and it was common for one state to taunt an enemy with words to the effect that his god(s) had deserted him; an example may be seen in the Epic of Tukulti-Ninurta (see P. C. Craigie, *JBL* 88 [1969] 263–73).

The psalmist expresses confidence in God's ability to answer prayer (3:4–5). As the psalmist moves his eyes from the multitude of enemies to God, the tone of the psalm changes abruptly. The principle that is involved in this change of tone is one which is well established in the biblical literature. If one gazes too long upon the enemy and his might, the enemy grows in the mind's eye to gigantic proportions and his citadels reach up to the skies (Deut 1:28). The hypnotic power of the enemy is broken when one turns one's gaze toward God, who is able to fight and grant victory (Deut 1:29–30). The psalmist, faced by foes, now recalls that God is a "shield round about," that is, protecting him on all sides. His glory, as king, lies not in past accomplishments or present potential; God, the sovereign king, is his *glory!* The psalmist's description of God as "the One who holds up my head" (3:4b) can be interpreted in a number of ways. If the psalm applies initially to David, the words imply contrast; David, whose head was covered in shame on the Mount of Olives (2 Sam 15:30), will be helped by God to hold his head high again through this time of crisis. But if the psalm is of general royal significance, then the expression, "to hold/lift up the head" relates to a divine action, or sovereign action, which may include restoration to a former position (see Gen 40:20–21). In general terms, the lifting of the head signifies the movement from despair to hope (see Luke 21:28).

God not only protects, but answers the prayers of those who call upon him (3:5). God will answer "from his holy mountain"; this is significant in the context of a royal psalm, for the "holy mountain" was also the place of the coronation (see Ps 2:6 and commentary). The God who had installed the king on the holy mountain would also come to his aid from that place which symbolized his earthly presence.

The psalmist trusts fully in God (3:6–7). It is the psalmist's conviction that God heard and answered prayer, which makes possible the transition to this quiet statement of trust. Surrounded by enemies who want to kill him, the psalmist finds himself in a situation naturally inviting insomnia. But it is his conviction that "the Lord sustains" (3:6b) that makes sleep possible in an impossible situation. The words of trust reflect the morning after. The psalmist had already slept; God had sustained him through the night, so that now, with the confidence rooted in rest, he could look forward to another day in the presence of a God who "sustains." The rest, and its implications, had banished fear, so that those very multitudes which gave rise to the complaint at the beginning of the psalm (3:2–3), now cause no fear. The multitudes at first had merely talked in enmity (3b), but now they were ready for war, "deployed against" the psalmist (v 7). But as the military situation moved toward a climax, the spiritual situation was transformed into peace by that trust which the psalmist had discovered.

The psalmist prays for God's victory (3:8–9). The last section of the psalm contains the actual words of prayer addressed to God. In the Hebrew understanding of warfare, victory could only be achieved if God fought in and through his people; human strength alone was not sufficient. But the symbol of God's presence amongst his people was the ark of the covenant. Thus when the armies had set forth with the ark, they pronounced these words: "Rise up, O Lord, and let your enemies be scattered, and let them that hate you flee before you"; when the ark returned home again, some further words were pronounced: "Return, O Lord, to the many thousands of Israel" (Num 10:35–36). In the psalmist's prayer, he uses the opening words of this ancient prayer: "Rise up, O Lord." During the time of the Davidic kings, the ark probably remained in Jerusalem, but the theology remained the same; as the army set out for war, its departure would be futile unless God arose and accompanied them. With God's presence, victory would come and enemies would be annihilated.

The psalmist prays that God would smite his enemies "on the cheek" (3:8c). The words are symbolic; to smite someone on the cheek was to administer a gross insult (cf. 1 Kgs 22:24; Job 16:10; Lam 3:30). As the psalmist had been insulted by the words of his enemies (3:3b), so now he prays for an insult to be administered to them. The parallel line (3:8d) takes the thought further. He prays that God would "smash the teeth of wicked men"; although the words have been interpreted as the imagery of savage beasts rendered harmless through fractured teeth, it is possible that their primary significance is with respect to speechlessness. The enemies had spoken wicked words (3:3d), but mouths cluttered with shattered teeth could no longer voice their enmity.

The psalm ends with a note of supreme confidence. "Victory belongs to God" (3:9b), so that the king was asking for that which was correct and proper. God could give of his own, and victory meant not merely the conquest of an enemy, but the divine "blessing" upon God's own people (3:9b).

Explanation

In the NT, the terminology of battle and war is consistently transformed into the language of spiritual warfare and the struggle against evil. Such a transformation is not new in the NT; it is anticipated in this and many other psalms, whose initial martial purpose had already undergone transformation by the time of their incorporation into the Psalter. The particular experience of the kings of Israel and Judah was adapted for use in the spiritual experience of all God's people. The editor(s) of the Psalter, either in editorial wisdom or following an established practice, placed this psalm next to Ps 4, the former for use in the morning, the latter for the evening.

As a morning prayer, the psalm conveys a particular wisdom. For a person afflicted with troubles or "enemies," the opening moments of consciousness which mark a new day may be filled with an awareness of problems on every side. The psalm required of the worshiper a conscious movement of attention from those troubles to God, who is a source of protection and who answers prayer. After any sleep, there is cause for gratitude and trust; the moments of unconsciousness have ended and life resumes, only because God is the perpetual Sustainer. That same Sustainer of all life can grant victory for the coming day. Thus the psalm reflects a spiritual progress which is necessary for every day of human existence. The worshiper must consciously move from the natural state of anxiety, through trust and thanksgiving, to a prayer for God's victory (or salvation) and blessing in the coming day. Such a psalm is not only present in the Psalter for instruction, but it is there to be used in the daily spiritual life.

The words of v 8cd seem at first vindictive and harsh, with respect to the enemy. Yet in their transformation, it is not that one prays for God's action against the enemy as such, but against the evil which they speak and do.

Excursus I: The Meaning of SELAH (סלה) in the Psalms

The word *Selah* is used three times in Ps 3 (vv 3, 5, and 9); in the Book of Psalms as a whole, it is used a total of seventy-one times and a further three times in the psalm of Habakkuk (Hab 3:3, 9, 13). Both the etymology of the term and its precise significance remain uncertain. It is used sometimes at the end of sections which may be equivalent to strophes or stanzas (e.g. Ps 3:3, 5), sometimes at the end of a psalm (e.g. Ps 3:9), sometimes after what appears to be a quotation (e.g. Ps 44:9), but sometimes no evident significance may be determined from its location; thus it is used in Ps 68:8 in the middle of what is probably a quotation from an ancient passage of Hebrew poetry. The wide distribution of the term throughout the Psalter, and throughout the collections within the Psalter, probably indicates that the use of the word goes back to ancient times, though whether the usage goes back to the time of the composition of the psalms within which it appears cannot be certain.

One factor which seems to be fairly certain is that the term has some kind of musical significance, either with respect to the singing of the psalm or with respect to its musical accompaniment. With very few exceptions, the term is used in psalms which have titles; the majority of the titles identify the psalms containing סלה with David or the Levitical singers, and about 75 percent of the titles also make reference to the "musical director" or "choirmaster."

A variety of theories, some ancient and some modern, have offered possible solutions to the meaning of the term:

(i) *G* rendered the Hebrew term by διάψαλμα, which might be taken to imply "pause," or "instrumental interlude," or even "louder."

(ii) The Palestinian Jewish tradition, as represented in the Targum and followed by some early Christian interpreters such as Jerome, took the term to mean "for ever," though no precise etymological basis can be found for this meaning for the term. The implication would be that a benediction or chorus was to be sung at this point in the psalm.

(iii) A third possible interpretation is to understand the term as referring to points in the use of the song in the context of worship at which the congregation prostrated themselves on the ground in obeisance before God (see S. Mowinckel, *The Psalms in Israel's Worship* II 211).

Unfortunately, the absence of a clear etymology for the term means that the uncertainty as to its meaning cannot be removed. The commonest derivation is from the root סלל, "to raise, lift up," whence the possible implications: (a) "to raise the voice" (or sing louder) or (b) "to raise the volume" (of the musical accompaniment). But it is possible to suggest alternative derivations and no single etymological proposal has yet been received with the common assent of all scholars.

With respect to the interpretation of the psalms in which the word is used, it must be admitted that in the light of current knowledge no precise significance can be attributed to סלה. However, it may serve as a useful reminder to the modern reader of the Psalms that many psalms were initially sung with musical accompaniment. And in terms of probabilities, the tradition preserved by *G* should probably be considered as providing the most likely significance of the term.

An Evening Prayer (4:1-9)

Bibliography

Eaton, J. H. "Hard Sayings X: Ps 4:6-7." *Theology* 67 (1964) 355-57.

Translation

1   For the musical director. With stringed instruments. A psalm of David.[a]

2(1) *When I call, answer me, O God of my righteousness.*   (4+3+3)
    When in distress, give me room.
    Be gracious to me and hear my prayer.[a]

3(2) *O sons of man,*
    How long is my reputation to be a reproach?[a]   (3+2+2)
    How long[b] *will you love vanity?*
    How long[b] *will you seek falsehood?* SELAH

4(3) *But know that the Lord has set aside*[a] *the godly for himself!*   (4+4)
    The Lord will hear[b] *when I call to him.*

5(4) *Tremble, but don't sin!*   (2+2+2)
    Speak within yourselves,
    but be still on your bed![a] SELAH

6(5) *Sacrifice sacrifices of righteousness*   (3+2)
    and trust in the Lord.

7(6) *Many people say: "Who will show us good?"*[a]   (4+4)
    Lift up the light of your countenance upon us, O Lord![b]

8(7) *Put*[a] *more joy*[b] *in my heart*   (3+4)
    than when their corn and new wine[c] *abound.*

9(8) *In peace, I will both*[a] *lie down and sleep,*   (4+3+2)
    for you alone are the Lord;
    you make me dwell in safety.

Notes

1.a. On the possible implications of the expression "Psalm of David" see the INTRODUCTION, THE PSALMS AND THE PROBLEM OF AUTHORSHIP.

2.a. The principal difficulty in this verse relates to the forms and tenses of the verbs. Three verbs in MT are imperatives (שמע, חנני, ענני "answer," "be gracious," "hear.") but the fourth (הרחבת "give room") appears to be perfect. The older commentators debated the possibility of the existence of a precative perfect (in effect, a form of the imperative) in Hebrew, some accepting it, and others denying the existence of such a form; see Briggs, *The Book of Psalms,*

32–33. The situation is complicated by G's rendition of עֲנֵנִי (εἰσήκουσέν μου), indicating that they understood a perfect form rather than an imperative. However, the parallelism of the opening two lines of the verse strongly indicates that הרחבת should be understood as a precative perfect, parallel to עֲנֵנִי (imv.) in the previous line; see further Dahood, *Psalms I*, 23. S's rendition of v 2a implies the existence of a conjunction in the text: "my God *and* my righteousness"; though it is possible there was a conjunction in the original text, lost in the course of transmission. MT makes good sense as it stands.

3.a. The misunderstanding of Heb כבודי לכלמה "my reputation to be a reproach" in G, and the translation ("how long will you be heavy of heart?"), is best explained as the consequence of an error in the Heb. text from which the translators were working; see Briggs, *The Book of Psalms*, 33.

3.b. The interrogative ("how long?") is used only once at the beginning of the first clause, but it is to be understood as introducing all three clauses. Alternatively, the second two clauses could be rendered simply as exclamations: "You love vanity! You seek falsehood!" (and their love of falsehood and vanity is the source of the reproach upon the character of the righteous).

4.a. Numerous Heb. mss, including C, and the principal versions, suggest that הפלה "set aside" should be read as הפלא "be wonderful"; if this reading were accepted, together with changing חסיד לו "the godly to him" to חסדו לי "his love to me" (following Ps 31:22), the clause could be translated: "the Lord has shown to me his wondrous love." But MT makes good sense as it stands, and it is unnecessary to follow these possible textual changes.

4.b. G implies a pronominal suffix on ישמע "will hear *me*"; Dahood argues for an example of the double-duty suffix here (*Psalms I*, 24), but since this possibility depends upon an emendation of an earlier portion of the line, I have not added the equivalent of a suffix (which is certainly implied) in the translation.

5.a. The verse is difficult both to translate and to interpret; the key to the translation is probably to be found in recognizing the balance and parallelism between the opening two words and the following two lines, which may be set out as follows—

Tremble . . . but don't sin
speak within yourselves . . . but be still on your beds

See further the *Comment* (below). This rendition involves only one change in MT, namely the transposition of the conjunction from דמו to be placed before על, which has the support of G and S, and partial support from Heb. mss (including C). The word דמו has been translated conventionally ("to be still, silent"); Dahood's suggestion that it be translated "weep" (on the basis of Ugaritic *dmm*) is linguistically possible, though the meaning of the verse is best suited by the conventional translation (see *Comment*).

7.a. The word טוב "good" is translated by Dahood as "rain," which is described as the good par excellence in Palestine (*Psalms I*, 25). But the argument is not persuasive in this context. While in some of the examples cited by Dahood ("Hebrew-Ugaritic Lexicography, II," *Bib* 45 [1964] 393–412), the context makes it clear that "good" is in effect *rain*, the case rests primarily on context rather than on any linguistic (or etymological) argument as such. And in the Ugaritic evidence presented by Dahood, namely 1 Aqht (*CTA* 19).1.45–6, the significance of *tb* is uncertain. The relevant text is as follows: *bl tbn ql b'l*, which Dahood translates: "no rain with Baal's thunder." The context has to do with rain, certainly, but the text could be appropriately translated: "no more the good sound of Baal's voice" (implying no more *thunder;* cf. Gibson, *CML* [2], 115). A. Caquot et al., *Textes ougaritiques I*, 445, translate: "point d'agréable voix de Ba'al," noting that *tbm* is an abstract noun with the sense "charm" (*agrément*). Thus, in summary, the Ugaritic evidence is of uncertain value. The context of טוב in Ps 4 is ambiguous, and though v 8 could be taken to imply rain, it need not do so. Hence, I have preferred to adhere to the conventional translation, "good."

7.b. The difficulty in translating this verse as a whole lies in attempting to determine whether the third line should be taken within the quotation marks of the second line (viz. whether it is a part of what many people say), or whether it is the psalmist's response to the question which many people ask. The translation above assumes the latter to be the case; hence נסה is read as נשא "lift" (for which there is support in the Heb mss), which may even be an alternative form of נסה. But it is possible to translate נסה as from the root נוס "flee", and to understand על in the sense "from" (Dahood, *Psalms I*, 26), which would lead to the translation: "The light of your countenance has fled from us, O Lord" (cf. NEB and Dahood), in which case the words would continue the quotation from the previous line.

8.a. נתתה "give" is translated as a precative perfect; see the note on v 2 (a).

8.b. It is possible to render *"your* joy" (after *S*), which would provide a parallel to *"your* countenance" in v 7.

8.c. The Qumran text, with *G* and *S*, adds "oil" to the sequence "corn and new wine," which produces a sequence parallel to Hos 2:24 (ET22), but the addition is unnecessary.

9.a. Although the construction employed with the adverbial יחדו "both together" is unusual, it is unnecessary to follow Dahood here (*Psalms I*, 27) in rendering יחדו as a noun, "face." Though Ugaritic *ḥdy* is cognate to Heb חדה ("see"), the various known Heb substantives related to חדה normally have the *zayin* rather than a *daleth*.

Form/Structure/Setting

Psalm 4 is traditionally classified as an *individual lament,* but more precisely it is a *psalm of confidence* in which the innocent worshiper rises above the grounds of lamentation with sure trust in God. Whether the psalm originally, or in its subsequent use, had a setting in formal worship cannot be known with certainty. V 6 is sometimes said to contain the words of a priest to the worshiper (e.g. J. H. Hayes, *Understanding the Psalms,* 63), but the context of v 6 makes such an interpretation unlikely. The substance of the psalm is of such a general nature that various proposals for a specific life setting have failed to carry conviction. Thus Eaton's proposal for a royal interpretation (*Kingship and the Psalms,* 29–30) is based on very slender evidence; similarly, Dahood's interpretation of the psalm as a prayer for rain (*Psalms I*, 23) depends primarily on a doubtful translation of v 7 (see note a, v 7). Thus the original thrust and context of the psalm remain uncertain and its anonymity contributes further to this uncertainty.

It is clear that by the time of the psalm's insertion into an early collection of psalms (it belonged to an early Davidic collection, and was also incorporated in the Music Director's collection), it had become a regular and formal part of worship, and though written in the first person, it would have been used by members of a congregation. The reference to stringed instruments to be used in accompaniment (in the title), and the double use of SELAH, both imply the employment of the psalm in congregational worship. The location of the psalm in the Psalter, immediately following the morning prayer (Ps 3), indicates that Ps 4 was used within the regular service of evening worship. The psalm may not have been written initially as an evening prayer, but the closing words (4:9) would naturally have contributed to the custom of using the psalm during the evening.

The poetic structure of the psalm is particularly distinctive, and though the psalm lacks any clear metrical balance, the poet has achieved striking effect in the repeated use of the same words, or words derived from the same root. The following table illustrates the use of double terms or related terms in the psalm.

(a) call	בקראי (v 2)		(e) bed	משכב (v 5)
	בקראי (v 4)		lie down	אשכב (v 9)
(b) righteousness	צדקי (v 2)		(f) trust	בטחו (v 6)
	צדק (v 6)		safety	בטח (v 9)
(c) hear	שמע (v 2)		(g) many	רבים (v 7)
	ישמע (v 4)		abound	רבו (v 8)
(d) heart	לבב (v 5)			
	לב (v 8)			

The pairs of terms serve a variety of poetic purposes, such as inclusio (a, g, and possibly c), contrast between the good and the wicked (d and e), and emphasis (f).

The psalm is so closely integrated by the use of double terms that the structure cannot easily be determined, and numerous different outlines of the content of the psalm have been suggested. (The general nature of its sentiments and the ambiguity as to meaning in certain verses contribute further to the difficulty in discerning an overall structure.) The use of the term SELAH might indicate a structure as follows: (1) vv 2–3; (2) vv 4–5; (3) vv 6–9. This structure would be similar to that of Ps 3, but it probably reflects the manner of its musical performance, rather than any inner structure based upon the progression in meaning. The outline which follows in the *Comment* is based primarily on the use of double terms to form an inclusio (see above), though it is proposed only tentatively: (1) The Lord who answers prayer (4:2–4); (2) Trust in the Lord (4:5–6); (3) A prayer of confidence (4:7–8); (4) Rest in peace (4:9).

Comment

The Lord who answers prayer (4:2–4). The psalmist turns to prayer with trouble brooding in his mind; he has been accused, quite unjustly, of some crime or sin and though he knows that he is innocent, the reproach hangs heavily upon him. All he can do is turn to God; he has no particular request, other than that God hear him and grant him some peace of mind.

The source of his anxiety is described as the "sons of man" (v 3), who are persons of significance or influence, as distinct from the common people (see the distinction between the בְּנֵי אִישׁ "sons of a man" and the humbler בְּנֵי אָדָם "sons of a human" in Ps 62:9). These "sons of man," in their persistent pursuit of vanity and lies, have made the psalmist's reputation as nothing, a word of reproach, and their words come to his mind as he engages in prayer. So he prays for God to answer, for the accusers will not answer his protestations of innocence, but merely persist in their falsehood. Feeling hemmed in and constrained by his human enemies, he asks the God of his "righteousness" (the One who knows he is innocent) to give him room, or to release him from the straits and pressures to which he has been subjected. He requests God's grace, which would bring release from the human accusations.

But as he addresses the question "How long?" to his adversaries in the words of his mind (v 3), he also provides them with an answer which demonstrates the futility of their accusations. They may say what they like, but they should know that "the Lord has set aside the godly for himself" (v 4). The godly (חָסִיד) is both the one who has experienced God's faithful love (חֶסֶד) and the one who has learned to show that love to others. The adversaries should know that the one whom they accuse is one who is loved of God and therefore godly.

In a subtle manner, which recurs throughout the poem, the psalmist discovers that he is beginning to answer his own questions. He asks his enemies: Why do you continue in your lies? Don't you know that God looks after his own? And then he realizes that the words apply to him. God does look after his own, and so what began as a prayer ("when I call . . . hear my prayer," v 2) ends up as a statement of confidence ("the Lord will hear when I call to him," v 4).

Throughout these opening verses, there is no clear indication as to the nature of the accusations which are leveled at the innocent worshiper, beyond the fact that they undermine his reputation and his honor.

Trust in the Lord (4:5–6). These two verses are characterized by a series of imperatives or commands; the words are addressed still to the "sons of man" (v 3) and contain advice for them, but as before they also contain further consolation and strength for the psalmist himself.

V 5 is difficult, both with respect to translation and interpretation. It might be paraphrased as follows: "You can tremble with anger and rage, but don't sin by doing anything! You can speak your evil words within your hearts, but don't speak them out loud! Lie still and silent upon your beds, where you can do no harm." The psalmist advises his adversaries to keep their rage within themselves, to maintain control of their actions and their evil words. It was when they spoke out loud and acted (v 3) that their inner evil was released to afflict the innocent. And though silence and lack of action would not remove the rot within, it would at least curtail its evil effects.

But the psalmist has not merely negative advice to give; he has also positive counsel. His adversaries should engage in the proper forms of worship and place their trust in God; that alone would root out the deeper evil within them. "Sacrifices of righteousness" were those which were offered properly, not only in a ritual sense, but also in a spiritual sense; the one whose sacrifices were accompanied by genuine repentance and true trust was returning to a proper relationship with God, for God was the One who could become a person's righteousness (v 2).

A prayer of confidence (4:7–8). Early in the prayer, the psalmist recalled mentally the words of the arrogant adversaries (v 3), but now, as his thoughts progress, it is the words of the pusillanimous doubters which come to mind, the people who say: "Who will show us good?" And the dubious help of doubters can sometimes be as dangerous as the arrogant words of enemies! An attack by enemies can be thwarted if the innocent person has trust in God, but when nagging doubts arise, confidence can easily be undermined. Enemies are real and all too visible, but is there anybody who can really help against them? Can God really do any good? And so the psalmist, as his confidence grows, must not only transcend the attacks of opponents, but must also overcome the voice of doubt within himself. And he overcomes it by recalling an ancient blessing, the Blessing of Aaron, which he had doubtless heard hundreds of times during his participation in worship: "The Lord will make his face to shine upon you and be gracious to you; the Lord will lift up his face to you and give you his peace" (Num 6:25–26). In a shortened form, he makes that blessing his own to quash the uncertainties within him. He prays for an inner joy which would be greater than those outward manifestations of joy which characterized his society, the joy and rejoicing which stemmed from a successful harvest of corn and grapes for new wine. The greatest joy for which he prayed was not that of a harvest home, but of an awareness of the light of God's countenance.

Rest in peace (4:9). Having opened his prayer with a sense of burden and oppression, the psalmist now can close it with a sense of confidence and peace. There is only one God, his Lord, in contrast to whom the "sons of man" are of no significance. But where the accusations of the sons of man had created that inner tension and anxiety which makes sleep impossible, the Lord granted that security within which sleep could be a time of rest and tranquillity. At the end, the psalmist has seen that he is better off than his adversaries. He had advised them to lie still on their beds, in an attempt to curtail their evil (v 5), but he could lie on his bed and sleep the sleep of peace which came from God.

Explanation

While the unknown composer of this beautiful psalm was doubtless oppressed by real adversaries and specific accusations, the lack of precise identification of either adversaries or accusations is a part of the genius of the psalm, and that which makes it so appropriate for use by any man or woman. The particular crisis which the psalmist encountered may have been peculiarly his own, but the principle and the general experience are common to all mankind. Thus the identification of this psalm in the Psalter as an evening prayer, standing beside the morning prayer (Ps 3), is particularly appropriate. There are days in the lives of all human beings which require a psalm like this at their end.

It is not a psalm of penitence, arising out of the recognition of sins committed; there are other psalms for that purpose. It is rather a psalm which reflects the anguish of the innocent and oppressed, or of the righteous sufferer. And thus it is a particularly important kind of psalm, for it addresses a fundamental human experience, the experience of injustice, suffering and oppression. It was Koheleth, with his cold-eyed realism, who observed how common and fundamental oppression was to the human experience of living, and he saw that the oppressors had the power, while the oppressed seemed to have none to comfort them (Eccl 4:1–3). Conversely, the experience of oppression and injustice might turn a person away from seeking comfort in God, for the awareness of injustice creates doubt in a God whose world is supposed to be just. Psalm 4 offers no theoretical solutions to the problems of false accusations, oppression and injustice. It offers, rather, a kind of therapy: prayer. For however strong the accuser or oppressor may be, ultimately it is only God who matters. And however deep the anguish and uncertainty may be, God can provide that inner peace which makes sleep possible.

There is no suggestion in this psalm that the accusers go away or cease in their accusations. What changes as a consequence of prayer is not the external circumstance, but the inner spirit of the worshiper. The accusations are like barbs in the mind, needling and prodding, causing anxiety; prayer leads to that calmness of mind in which the accusations can be accepted and carried, for a greater peace of mind has come from God. Psalm 4 is thus a prayer which can be used by every believer, for there are none who do not experience, to some degree or another, the turmoil of mind expressed in this poignant psalm.

There is yet another side to all this; the psalm reflects the experience of the oppressed, but it arose because of the actions of an oppressor. It is in the nature of being human that we are most sensitive to being oppressed, but often insensitive to our own acts of oppression. The suffering reflected here is not rooted in some mysterious cosmic evil; it is the direct result of the words and actions of a fellow human being. One should not too quickly seek release from oppression, without also examining one's own life for the acts and sentiments of oppression toward others.

A Morning Prayer for Protection (5:1–13)

Bibliography

Koch, K. *The Growth of the Biblical Tradition. The Form-Critical Method.* London: A. and C. Black, 1969 (171–82). **Krinetzski, L.** "Psalm 5. Eine Untersuchung seiner dichterischen Struktur und seines theologischen Gehaltes." *ThQ* 142 (1962) 23–46.

Translation

1   For the musical director. To flute music.[a] A psalm of David.

2(1) *Give ear to my words, O Lord.* (3+2)
    Consider my murmuring. [a]

3(2) *Give attention to the sound of my plea,* (3+2+2)
    my King and my God,
    for it is to you that I pray.

4(3) *O Lord, in the morning hear* [a] *my voice;* (4+3)
    in the morning, I make preparations for you and watch.

5(4) *For you are not* [a] *a God who takes pleasure in wickedness.* (4+3)
    Evil may not sojourn with you.

6(5) *Boasters* [a] *may not set themselves before your eyes.* (4+3)
    You hate all workers of iniquity.

7(6) *You shall destroy those who speak falsehood.* (3+4)
    You loathe [a] *bloodthirsty and deceitful men, O Lord.*

8(7) *But I will enter your house in the abundance of your lovingkindness.* (5+4)
    I will worship toward your holy temple in reverence [a] *of you.*

9(8) *O Lord, guide me in your righteousness* [a] *because of those lying in watch for me.* (5/4+3)
    Make straight [b] *your way before me.*

10(9) *Because there is no truth in their* [a] *mouth;* (3+2,3+2)
    their inner-man is corruption;
    their throat is an open grave;
    with their tongue, they speak flattery. [b]

11(10) *Destroy* [a] *them, O God.* (2+2,3+2)
    Let them fall because of their plans.

> *Thrust them out because of the multitude* [b] *of their transgressions,*
> *for they have been rebellious against you.* [c]
>
> 12(11) *But let all who take refuge in you rejoice!* (3+2,2+2+2)
> *Let them be jubilant forever!*
> *And over them set a screen,*
> *that they may exult in you,*
> *those who love your name!*
>
> 13(12) *For you will bless the righteous, O Lord.* (4+3)
> *Like a large shield,* [a] *you will surround them* [b] *with favor.*

Notes

1.a. The precise sense of נחילות is uncertain; the translation "flute music" assumes a relationship with חליל, "flute, pipe." It is known that flutes were used in the music of Israel's worship (Isa 30:29, "pipe"), and Mowinckel has noted the association between flutes and laments in Babylonian psalmody (*The Psalms in Israel's Worship*, II, 210). But *G* offers little support, apparently deriving the word from the root נחל, "to inherit" (which, in turn, could imply the name of a tune, rather than the type of musical accompaniment).

2.a. הגיג is an onomatopoeic term, hence "murmuring" or "muttering." Etymologically, Dahood (after Zorell) subsumes the word under the root הגה "moan, growl," rather than a separate root הגג (so BDB). But the Ugaritic evidence which he cites in support of this contention is not convincing. Dahood cites *UT* 1001 (=*PRU* 2.1), rev. 13: *lthggn*, which is the only occurrence of the reduplicated /g/ form in Ugaritic. But the Ugaritic word is defectively written and could also be read *lt'iggn*. Virolleaud, who accepts the reading *lthggn* (*PRU* 2. 6–7), nevertheless lists the root as *hgg* in his glossary. Thus Heb הגיג here should still be derived from a root הגג. The Ugaritic evidence is ambiguous, though the possibility remains that Ugaritic also has two forms, namely *hgh* and *hgg*.

4.a. תשמע (formally imperfect) has been translated as an imperative, following the sequence of imperatives in vv 2–3; compare Deut 32:1 and see Craigie, *The Book of Deuteronomy*, (NICOT. Grand Rapids: Eerdmans, 1976) 376 (n.9) and Dahood, *Psalms I*, 30.

5.a. לא is interpreted as a simple negative, not part of a compound name, לא־אל, "no-god," as proposed by Dahood, *Psalms I*, 30. The use of the compound form in Deut 32:31 is clearly indicated by context, but the context here does not require it, nor is it to be inferred from either MT or the versions.

6.a. Dahood is probably correct in his observation that הוללים ("boasters") may possess pagan overtones. The term in Hebrew may carry either negative (as here) or positive overtones (*worshipers*). It is possible that the negative and pagan associations arose from the practice of praising (or boasting in) a foreign deity. Dahood illustrates this general theme by referring to Ugaritic *bnt hll*, "daughters of shouting." But it is also possible that the *bnt hll* may be the "daughters of Helel" (probably the Canaanite deity Athtar), whose name in turn is derived from a second root *hll*, "shine" (see also Heb. הלל, I). See further Gordon *UT* #769. On Helel and the Canaanite background, see Isa 14:12 and Craigie, *ZAW* 85 (1973) 223–25. In summary, the הוללים are "boasters," but the poet may imply "worshipers of the Shining One (Helel)," who cannot "set themselves before your eyes."

7.a. "You loathe" presumes תתעב (2 pers. sing., following Jerome's Latin version), rather than MT's יתעב (3 pers. sing.); this sequence is parallel to תאבד "you shall destroy" earlier in the verse. If MT is preferred, the line would be translated: "The Lord loathes. . . ."

8.a. יראתך is treated as an abstract noun: "Fear, reverence." Dahood's argument, that the term has assumed concrete significance, by virtue of its general parallelism, is possible: "among those who fear you"(*Psalms I*, 32).

9.a. Dahood translates בצדקתך by "into your meadow," and relates "meadow" to the Elysian Fields; thus he finds here a prayer for eternal happiness (*Psalms I*, 33–34). But the argument, and the additional biblical texts adduced in support of this radical reinterpretation, are not convincing, and the traditional sense of צדקה "righteous" provides an acceptable meaning in context (see *Comment*).

9.b. הושר (K) is read (Q) as הַיְשַׁר (Hiph. imv. of ישר).

10.a. "*Their* mouth": reading פיהם (for פיהו "his mouth"), for which there is manuscript evidence (De-Rossi, IV, 2), and which provides a better parallel with the pronominal suffixes of the remainder of the verse.

10.b. Dahood translates יחליקון by "they bring death," deriving it from חלק "to perish," cognate to Ugaritic *ḫlq*. But though the presence of such a verb is likely in Hebrew (KB cite two examples, both in the Pi'el, under חלק III), its use here is unlikely; it is true that the translation provides a parallel of sorts to "open grave," but the more common sense, namely of tongues employed in *flattery* or *deceit* (see also *G*), provides the most appropriate translation.

11.a. On אשם (Hiph.) with the sense "destroy," see Dahood, *Psalms I*, 35–36.

11.b. Q indicates the reading וכרב (see also *G* and Jerome): "(and) according to the multitude of their transgressions. . . ," which is possibly a correct reading, though the overall meaning would be affected little.

11.c. *G*'s addition of Κύριε (יהוה) at the end of v 11 is an unnecessary addition, given the uneven meter in the psalm as a whole.

13.a. צנה is the large body-shield, as distinct from מגן, the smaller shield; cf. O. Keel, *The Symbolism of the Biblical World*, 222–24.

13.b. The suffix translation of the singular by the plural *them* on תעטרנו refers back to the ·*righteous*, considered collectively; alternatively, the suffix of the original text may have been 1 pers. plur. (as implied by *G*) or first pers. sing. (as implied by *S*).

Form/Structure/Setting

This psalm belongs to the first Davidic psalter, and along with Ps 4 it was also a part of the musical director's collection (למנצח). The content of the psalm is of such a general nature that it is not possible to specify with certainty either the date or the author. The substance of vv 4 and 8 may imply that the psalm was composed and used during the time when the temple was functioning, but that is so extensive a period that the information is of little help.

Traditionally, this psalm has been classified as an *individual lament*, though taken alone, such a classification may be misleading (cf. Krinetski, *ThQ* 142 [1962] 23–46). In terms of Gunkel's subclassification of the lament psalms, Ps 5 would most appropriately be designated in the subcategory *psalms of innocence* (see also Dahood, *Psalms I*, 29), though even this classification may miss the main substance of the psalm. It is, with respect to substance, primarily a *protective psalm* (or psalm of confidence), as Mowinckel has correctly observed (*The Psalms in Israel's Worship*, I, 220), but whether it was a cultic psalm in its initial context or setting is a more complex issue. V 4 is often interpreted as referring to the preparations for sacrifice, though it need not carry that sense, and v 8 may be interpreted as implying the context of temple worship; but both verses are susceptible to a different interpretation (see the *Comment*, below) and it is possible that in its initial use, the psalm was noncultic. By the time of its incorporation within the Psalter, however, the psalm was certainly utilized in a liturgical setting, as the expression "to flute music" (v 1) implies. And the reference to "morning" (v 4) would have made the psalm particularly appropriate for morning worship in the temple, which may explain its present location in the Psalter, following another morning prayer (Ps 3) and an evening prayer (Ps 4).

The psalm falls into five natural sections, which alternate between prayer and the state of the righteous (sections 1, 3 and 5) on the one hand, and the nature and fate of wicked persons, on the other hand (sections 2 and 4): (1) a prayer that God would listen (vv 2–4); (2) evil persons may not

enter God's presence (vv 5–7); (3) the desire to worship (vv 8–9); (4) the
rejection of the wicked (vv 10–11); (5) a prayer for protection (vv 12–13).

Comment

A prayer that God would listen (5:2–4). The psalm begins with a series of
imperatives in which the Lord is requested to listen to the worshiper's prayer.
The psalmist asks for God to hear both his spoken "words" and also his
"murmuring," namely the inarticulate attempts to vocalize his situation, or
the silent words spoken within his heart. In prayer, he approaches with a
certain confidence, for he addresses the Lord as *my* King and *my* God; God,
who is creator and ultimate Lord of all being, is also one who can be approached in personal terms and addressed as one known and loved. The
expression "my king" is sometimes taken to indicate that the worshiper was
the king, who shared in God's rule (cf. Eaton, *Kingship and the Psalms*, 65),
and while this is possible, it is not a necessary inference. God had been
recognized as king in Israel since the time of the glorious redemption of
the Exodus (Ex 15:18), and ultimately, for every Israelite or Hebrew, God
was king. It was to God that the psalmist turned in prayer, not to a human
king, for God was the absolute Lord and the only one who could answer
prayer.

The time of prayer is specified in v 4 as the "morning" (cf. Ps 3). Whether
this was a private prayer offered by an individual at the beginning of the
day, or whether it was offered in some formal context of morning worship,
cannot be ascertained. Many interpreters assume a formal context of worship,
for the verb translated "I make preparations" (עָרַךְ) may be used with respect
to the making of formal preparations for a sacrifice (e.g. setting the wood
upon the altar). But the word may also be used of preparing one's words
(e.g. in a legal case or debate) and there can be no certainty that it is used
in any technical sacrificial sense here. Thus, although it is possible that the
context of the prayer is provided by the morning sacrifice, it is equally possible
that the worshiper is simply preparing the words of his prayer. And, having
prayed, he will "watch" (v 4) for a response from God.

Evil persons may not enter God's presence (5:5–7). The psalmist, whose opening
words indicate his own preparations for entering the presence of God, now
indicates the nature of those persons who cannot enter God's presence. God's
hatred of all forms of evil and wickedness is such that persons who live by
those norms cannot expect to enter his presence. Because God takes no
pleasure in wickedness, evil (or evil persons) may not be his guest or stand
in his presence, as the psalmist is doing (vv 2–4, 8–9). God is not merely a
God of power with whom powerful (but evil) persons might hope to stand
as guests and companions; God's nature as good and righteous specifies the
character required of human beings who desire to "sojourn" (or be as guests)
with him.

The evil persons specified here are of various kinds. They include "boasters" (either persons arrogant and confident in their own strength, or worshipers of another god; see v 6, note a), "workers of iniquity" (the most common
expression in the Psalms for wicked persons) and those who speak "falsehood"

(v 7). "Bloodthirsty. . . . men" may either be murderers, or more likely unscrupulous persons whose falsehood and deceitfulness create trouble for the weak and innocent, and could in certain cases result in the death of the innocent (e.g. through false testimony in court). But all evil persons are not only cut off from God's presence (v 5), but are also *hated* (v 6) and *loathed* (v 7); their ultimate destiny is destruction (v 7), for life lived in direct contradiction to God is doomed from the beginning.

Whether the evil persons specified in these verses are the actual enemies of the psalmist is uncertain. They are presented simply as the archetype of those persons banned from God's presence. The psalmist's reflection on such evildoers may indeed be a part of his own self-examination as he comes before God's presence; knowing the nature of God and its implications for evil, he examines himself as he brings his prayer to God. But they may also have been his enemies, and though no precise acts of persecution or evil against the psalmist are specified, it is in part the enmity of evil persons which drives the psalmist to prayer and the search for divine protection.

The desire to worship (5:8–9). Though evil persons are excluded from God's presence because of their sin, it does not follow that the psalmist is admitted by virtue of his own goodness. The psalmist's entrance into God's house would be based only upon "the abundance of your lovingkindness" (v 8); that is to say, it was only God's grace and covenant love (חסד) toward his people which made entrance into his presence possible. But those who knew and understood this love of God sought not only to turn from evil, but also sought forgiveness for the evil they had done.

The future implications of these verses may either imply that the worshiper is at home (or some other place) and desires to enter God's house, or else that he is already in the outer court of God's house engaged in worship. If the latter were the case, the words of the prayer might imply the expression of intention to worship God in true reverence. The focus of worship was the "holy temple" of God (presumably the Holy of Holies in the innermost part of the house of God), not as an object of worship, but as a symbol of God's most intimate presence. But these verses are in many ways ambiguous. Those who offer a cultic interpretation of the psalm take this section to refer to the context of the act of worship as such. Alternatively, it is possible to interpret the psalm as preparation for an act of formal worship; the worshiper declares the intention of entering God's house to worship (v 8) and seeks God's guidance and protection on the journey to the temple (v 9). Whatever the initial sense of these verses, there is a deeper thrust contained within them. The earthly temple of God was merely a symbol of God's heavenly dwelling and presence; the worshiper sought ultimately to enter not simply a building, but a living presence. And the psalm gives expression for that desire of the worshiper to enter the living presence of God, not for a temporary act of worship, but as a perpetual estate; the one perpetually in God's presence would experience God's guidance and the straight path throughout all the experience of living.

The rejection of the wicked (5:10–11). Again, the attention of the psalmist returns to the nature of wicked persons. He had prayed for guidance (v 9), because human counsel from the wicked was utterly unreliable and mortally dangerous (v 10). The evil are characterized here entirely in terms of their speech in a manner which illustrates forcefully the potential evil of the tongue (cf. Jas 3:6–12). Their words, in the absence of "truth," were without foundation or certainty, and hence altogether unreliable. The inner emotions and desires of the wicked are of such a destructive nature that their throat is like an "open grave," symbolizing death, but more forcefully (in a hot climate) an abominable stench; in the pure air of morality, their words created an unbearable smell. Their tongues articulate no truth, but only the smooth words of flattery, which are lies designed cunningly to enable the evil to achieve their ends. With respect to such evildoers, the psalmist can only pray for their destruction (v 11); their thought and words are not only a danger to the righteous, but an insult to God.

Again, it is not certain whether the psalmist has particular enemies in mind, or simply envisions all those articulators of evil whose words can be heard in every day of life. But the prayer here for their destruction does not reflect the psalmist's vindictiveness; he prays for it because they have been rebellious against God (v 11). He does not ask for thunderbolts from heaven; he asks only that their evil might reverberate upon themselves, that they might be tripped up in their own devious schemes, and thus become their own victims.

A prayer for protection (5:12–13). The psalm concludes both with a prayer for protection and with a confident exhortation to rejoice in God's protectiveness. The psalmist, who began on a very personal note (*my* words, *my* murmurings, v 2), has now gained sufficient confidence to address all the righteous: "let all . . . rejoice" (v 12). The ground for rejoicing is not the impending destruction of the wicked persons (v 11), but rather the spontaneous result which is experienced by all those "who take refuge" in God, and are delivered from anxiety about "those lying in watch" (v 9). Their rejoicing is to be "for ever," an expression denoting the furthest duration of time imaginable, though (in the context of the Psalter) probably limited to the duration of life itself. One who finds refuge in God has a life-long source of jubilation.

The psalmist prays that God will "set a screen" over (v 12; or, "overshadow, cover," תָּסֵךְ) his people, evoking perhaps the imagery of God's protection being like that of a bird covering its chicks protectively with its wings (cf. Ps 91:4). In v 13, the metaphor is expanded into the simile of the large body-shield which protects the entire body from the assaults of enemies. Both the metaphor of v 12 and the simile of v 13 develop the initial statement concerning those who "take refuge" (v 12a) in God, and that refuge makes possible both exultation in God (v 12d) and the receipt of God's blessing (v 13a).

The righteous are described as "those who love your name," and the name of God is pregnant with theological implications in the OT literature. The revelation of the divine personal name, *Yahweh* (see Exod 3:13–15; 6:2–3), was both an intimation of God's gracious movement toward Israel, and also of his impending redemption from Egyptian slavery and of the establishment of the Sinai covenant. Those who love the name are those to whom it has been revealed, the chosen people, and those to whom the blessing of the name had been granted in redemption and covenant. But more than that, the name symbolized God's presence in Israel; the sanctuary was the place in which God chose to set his name (Deut 12:5), indicating both his presence and the possibility of approaching God and calling upon his name. At the beginning of the psalm, the worshiper had used both God's name (*Lord:* יהוה, v 2) and titles ("my King, my God," v 3) in his entreaty to be heard; at the end of the psalm, he repeats God's name (יהוה, v 13), in the sure confidence of God's blessing and favor.

Explanation

Psalm 5 illustrates with clarity the polarity and tension which characterize certain dimensions of the life of prayer. On the one side, there is God: on the other, evil human beings. And the thought of the psalmist alternates between these two poles. He begins by asking God to hear him, but recalls that evil persons have no place in God's presence. He turns back to God again, expressing his desire to worship and his need of guidance, but then is reminded of the human evils of the tongue. Eventually, he concludes in confidence, praying for protection and blessing. But the prayer is not only for protection *from* wicked persons, but also a prayer for protection from becoming *like them.* Those who use their tongues to exult in God, cannot also use them to boast and flatter.

Thus, although the original psalmist was perhaps seeking protection from particular enemies, there is a sense in which this psalm may be seen as a prayer for protection from one's own tongue, from the evil that is within a person, both real and potential. St. Paul quotes from this psalm in his catalog description of sinful mankind: "No one is righteous. . . . *Their throat is an open grave, they use their tongues to flatter*" (Rom 3:10–13; cf. Ps 5:10). Thus the enemies of the psalmist may symbolize all persons without God, without the gospel; and like all sinful mankind, they require the gospel.

Psalm 5 offers not only a prayer that may be used in the worship of God, but also a mirror of mankind without God. And it is important to note that the principal characteristic of evildoers in this psalm is to be found in their speech: they are "boasters," they speak "falsehood," "there is no truth in their mouth," "their throat is an open grave," and "they speak flattery." Ancient Israel was not a primitive society where the only ills were acts, but—like our own society—it was an age in which the more sophisticated sins of speech abounded. And the sins of speech were not only an affront to God, but also caused pain in the lives of fellow human beings. Thus, from a NT perspective, it is difficult to limit this psalm as a prayer for protection; it must also be perceived as a prayer of self-examination and a request for forgiveness and deliverance.

A Prayer in Sickness (6:1–11)

Bibliography

Airoldi, N. "Note critiche al Salmo 6." *RivB* 16 (1968) 285–89. **Coppens, J.** "Les Psaumes 6 et 41 dépendent-ils du Livre Jérémie?" *HUCA* 32 (1961) 217–26. **Knuth,**

H. C. *Zur Auslesungsgeschichte von Psalm 6.* Tübingen: J. C. B. Mohr, 1971. (This extensive history of the psalm's interpretation covers in detail the early church, the medieval interpretations, the reformers, and the recent centuries of scholarship.) **Koch, K.** *The Growth of the Biblical Tradition. The Form-Critical Method,* 171–82.

Translation

1   For the musical director. With stringed instruments. Upon the octave.ᵃ A psalm of David.

2(1)   *O Lord, do not rebuke me in your anger*   (3+2)
       and do not chastise me in your wrath.

3(2)   *Be gracious to me, O Lord,*ᵃ *for I have grown feeble.*   (4+4)
       Heal me, O Lord, for my bones have become disturbed,

4(3)   *and my soul has become exceedingly disturbed.*   (3+3)
       But you, O Lord—How long?

5(6)   *Return, O Lord. Save my soul!*   (4+3)
       Deliver me because of your lovingkindness.

6(5)   *For in Death, there is no memory*ᵃ *of you.*   (3+3)
       In Sheol, who can praise you?

7(6)   *I have grown weary with my groaning.*   (2, 3+3)
       Every night, I soak my bed,
       I dissolve my couch with my tears.

8(7)   *My eye wastes*ᵃ *away because of grief:*   (3+3)
       it grows weak on account of all my enemies. ᵇ

9(8)   *Depart from me, all workers of wickedness,*   (4+4)
       for the Lord has heard the sound of my weeping.

10(9) *The Lord has heard my supplication.*   (3+3)
       The Lord will accept my prayer.

11(10) *All my enemies shall be disappointed*ᵃ *and exceedingly disturbed.*   (4+3)
       They shall turn back. They shall be disappointed in a moment.

Notes

1.a. השמינית ("the octave") is difficult to interpret; the literal sense of the word is *eighth.* The term is omitted in certain mss; see De-Rossi, IV, 2. See further 1 Chr 15:21, which might support the interpretation "octave." The implication may be that the musical accompaniment should be on a lower or base octave (*all' ottava bassa,* Delitsch, *Psalms I,* 168), which would be appropriate to the solemn theme of the psalm. A further possibility is that the expression refers to the tuning of a musical instrument, or to scale; see further the comments on the colophon to the Hurrian cult-song from Ras Shamra in the INTRODUCTION (PSALM TITLES).
3.a. It is possible that the two occurrences of "Lord" (יהוה) in this verse should be omitted as glosses, the first being absent in certain Heb. mss, and the second being absent both in certain Heb. mss and G (Vaticanus). But it is preferable to keep the words, for they fit well with the tone of entreaty in the opening portion of the prayer.
6.a. זכרך is parsed as a noun, "memory, remembrance" (after MT), rather than a participle, as implied by G.
8.a. Following MT, the subject of עתקה "grow weak" is "eye"; but it is possible that a first person sing. form of the verb should be read (after G, Aquila and Symmachus), which would be translated: "I have grown weak. . . ."
8.b. The word צוררי has caused numerous difficulties; the translation above ("enemies") assumes it is derived from צרר (II), "to show hostility to" (BDB). Dahood translates the line: "my heart has grown old from pining" (*Psalms I,* 38), deriving from Akk. ṣurru and Ugar. ṣrrt, which (he claims) mean "heart, innards." The Ugaritic evidence, however, does not clearly support

Dahood's hypothesis. Driver (*CML*, 150, cited by Dahood) gives the meaning of *ṣrrt* as "recess" or "heights," simply citing an Akk. cognate (*ṣurru*) to illustrate the etymology of "recess." Gibson (*CML²*, 156) also suggests "recess." Gordon (*UT*, #2199) offers "heights," noting also the possibility of "recesses, hiding places," as suggested by Finkel. Aistleitner proposes "heights," though with an element of doubt (*WUS*, #2363). Dietrich and Loretz propose "shining (peaks)" ("Zur ugaritischen Lexikographie (v)," *UF* 4 [1972] 29). Of the seven uses of the Ugaritic word *ṣrrt*, six occur in conjunction with *ṣpn*, and the most appropriate translation would be "heights of Ṣapon," or possibly "recesses of Ṣapon." The seventh use of the term *ṣrrt* is quite different and probably should be translated "lintel, door-pivot" (*CTA* 16.1.43; cf. Gibson, *CML²*, 95). In summary, while admitting the possible sense of Ugaritic *ṣrrt* as "recesses," and the possible etymology in terms of Akkadian, none of the Ugaritic texts uses the term in conjunction with human beings or gives strength to the possibility of a Hebrew word meaning "heart." On the general etymological difficulties with the term, in both Akkadian and Ugaritic, see B. Margalit, "Studia Ugaritica II," *UF* 8 (1976) 150 (n.33). Thus, Dahood's hypothesis with respect to the meaning of the term צורריר is to be rejected.

11.a. The editorial suggestion in *BHS* to delete יבשׁו ו "be disappointed and" at the beginning of this verse is unnecessary, and fails to appreciate the phonetic effect of the repeated use of the consonants *yodh, beth,* and *shin* in this line. As Delitzsch observed of this verse: "How much music the Psalter contains! Would that composers understood it!" (*Psalms I*, 174).

Form/Structure/Setting

Psalm 6 may be classified generally as an *individual lament*, though more precisely it is a *psalm of sickness*, reflecting the prayer for healing of a person afflicted in both body and spirit. The contents of the psalm do not give any explicit clues as to its initial association with the cult or formal worship in Israel, though such an association is possible. The marked transition in tone which takes place between vv 8 and 9 may imply that the suppliant has received an oracle or word of confidence from the priest, and gone away from God's house in faith and certainty (see further the *Comment*).

By the time of the psalm's inclusion in the Psalter (it belonged initially to the first Davidic collection, then to the music director's collection), it had become a part of Israel's resources for worship, and was sung with musical accompaniment, as is implied in the title verse. The early church used this psalm and six others (Pss 32, 38, 51, 102, 130 and 143) as the "Penitential Psalms," which were traditionally sung on Ash Wednesday. Although it is not a *penitential* psalm in the most explicit sense, the tone of the psalm is appropriate to penitence and v 2 might be taken to imply penitence.

The change in tone (between vv 8 and 9) does not undermine the unity of the psalm, as supposed by some of the older commentators, for change is vital to the spiritual progress within the psalm, whereas continuity is indicated by the use of similar and related words in both parts. Thus, forms derived from חנן "gracious" occur in vv 3 and 10, the verb נבהל "be disturbed" is used in both vv 3–4 and in v 11, and the verb שוב "return" is used in vv 5 and 11; these stylistic devices impress upon the reader both the unity and the power of the poem. But, from another perspective, the substance of Ps 6 contains a high percentage of formulaic language (viz. it shares *formulae*, clauses or phrases, both with other psalms and with OT books beyond the Psalter; see R. C. Culley, *Oral Formulaic Language in the Biblical Psalms*, 105). The nature of this common language, indicating perhaps an oral form of composition, should create caution with respect to the formula-

tion of an hypothesis concerning the interrelationship between this psalm
and other psalms or literature such as Jeremiah (see further Coppens, *HUCA*
32 [1961] 217-26, for additional arguments against dependence on Jeremiah).
The common language gives the psalm a familiar flavor, but at the same
time it is distinctive by virtue of the power and pathos of its lamentation.

Neither the form nor the content contain any clear and firm evidence with
respect to the date and authorship of Ps 6. There are differences of opinion
with respect to the structure of the psalm, but it falls most naturally into
three parts: (1) the psalmist's cry of anguish (vv 2-4); (2) a prayer for deliverance from misery (vv 5-8); (3) confidence in answered prayer (vv 9-11).

Comment

The psalmist's cry of anguish (6:2-4). The anguished cry with which the psalm
begins reflects the psalmist's experience of physical illness and spiritual travail.
The psalmist has become feeble and weak as a result of the course of his
illness, though the poetic language of the psalm does not permit the identification of the disease. Both the inner and the outer person have been affected;
the double use of the same verb (בהל "be disturbed") indicates that both
the *bones* (representing the physical being) and the *soul* (representing the
inner or spiritual being) have been profoundly disturbed.

Before specifying his sorry estate, the psalmist has prayed that God not
"rebuke" and "chastise" him in his divine wrath (v 2), and this opening
plea poses certain difficulties of interpretation. One way of understanding
it is to suppose that the psalmist perceived an intimate relationship between
sin and sickness; thus his experience of sickness presupposed acts of sin,
which in turn suggested that sickness itself was an act of divine chastisement
and rebuke. But nowhere does this psalmist explicitly confess to sin; in this,
Ps 6 differs from Ps 38, which opens with an identical plea, but which continues
to a confession of sin. Here, there is no confession of sin and there is no
explicit statement of penitence. If this interpretation of v 2 is correct, then
one must either suppose that the psalmist has committed sins in ignorance,
and therefore cannot explicitly repent, or else that, like Job, he is a righteous
sufferer whose sickness cannot be explained simply as a consequence of evil
action.

A different and more satisfactory sense can be attributed to the opening
plea, though it too is related to the concept of the righteous sufferer. It
may be that the psalmist prays not to be rebuked or chastised for bringing
this problem to God in prayer; whatever the reason for his sickness, it must
either have been sent or permitted by God, and it might seem presumptuous
of a mere mortal, albeit a suffering mortal, to complain of the experience
which God has permitted to fall upon him. If this interpretation is correct,
the psalmist first prays that God not be angry with him for raising a problem,
namely his sickness, for which God may have had a good reason. Then, immediately, he goes on to ask that God be gracious to him; that is, that God
treat him in a manner characterized by grace, the undeserved and freely
given love and mercy of God, because physically and spiritually he can no
longer bear the suffering. He does not claim that he deserves God's grace,

for by definition it cannot be deserved or earned, but he pleads for it neverthe-less on the basis of his sorry estate. He needs God's grace, knows that he needs it, and in desperation asks for God's grace.

But, eventually, the anguish exceeds words and overcomes the psalmist's power to articulate his agony; he can only ask "How long?" How much longer must he continue to suffer? How much longer will it be until he experiences the gracious action of God?

A prayer for deliverance from misery (6:5–8). Gaining strength again, the psalmist returns to his plea and explicitly asks God to deliver him from his sickness. He begins the next stage in his prayer by saying "Return" (v 5), presumably implying that the state of sickness had been an experience in which it seemed that God had deserted him; now he asks for God to return. (Alternatively, the verb שׁובה could carry the sense "again" in conjunction with the following verb, leading to the translation: "Save my soul again, O Lord." The implication of this translation would be that the psalmist asked for God to do for him now what he had already done in the past, on another occasion.) "Save my soul:" the implication is "save my *life*" (on the use of נֶפֶשׁ, "soul, life," in the Psalms, see further A. A. Anderson, *Psalms I*, 266–67). Deliverance was requested on the basis of God's "lovingkindness" or covenant love (חסד), and the request is entirely appropriate. Just as Israel as a nation received God's love in covenant in, and after, the great deliverance from Egypt, so too each member of the covenant community could request the continuing experience of God's lovingkindness in the act of divine deliverance.

Close to death as a result of his sickness, the psalmist prays for deliverance from that ultimate enemy, death itself. The conception of death and the after-life implicit here is that of the OT in general (with the exception of some of the later writings, which reflect the beginning of eschatological thought). The state of the dead is not differentiated with respect to good and evil persons; there is no clear distinction here between heaven and hell. *Sheol* was conceived as a kind of underworld; the word is translated in *G* as *hades* (ᾅδη). In Sheol, persons were believed to exist in a form of semi-life, at rest, yet not in joy, for they had not the fullness of life which made possible the richness of relationship with the living God. Death was thus to be dreaded. The psalmist feared death, for in the state of Sheol there would be neither memory of God, nor the praise and worship of God. The word "memory" does not refer to the abstract possibility of remembering God in Sheol, but rather to the role of memory in the worship and praise of God. It was memory which evoked the praise of God, for the memory of what God had done for the living was a basis for the living to both praise God and to go on living within the perspective of a good memory (see further Deut 8 and Craigie, *The Book of Deuteronomy*, 184–89).

The psalmist's sickness had created both exhaustion and insomnia. "I soak my bed" (v 7); the literal sense is that he *caused his bed to swim*, or *float*, so profuse were his tears. The insomnia was the result partly of the pain accompa-nying sickness, and partly of the spiritual anguish and sense of separation from God which resulted from that pain. As for most sufferers, it was in the long watches of the night, when silence and loneliness increase and the warmth of human companionship is absent, that the pain and the grief reached their darkest point. It is possible that this psalm reflects the time of morning prayer, when the memory of the long night was still vivid and the thought of another night was appalling; if such were the case, there would be a certain affinity between this psalm and Pss 3–5, which were also related to the morning and evening times of prayer.

The *wasting* and *weakness* of the *eye* (v 8) are indicative of the state of physical decline into which the psalmist had descended, just as conversely the clear eye symbolized strength and good health. It was said of Moses, before his death, that "his eyesight had not failed" (Deut 34:7), indicating his generally robust state of health at the age of 120 years! But the psalmist's eye had faded before its time, partly as a result of the *grief* stemming from his sickness, and partly because of "enemies" (v 8). The reference to enemies may be the result of a common experience of the sick in ancient Israel; many persons believed that the sick were sinners, being judged by God, so that even a sick man's friends might become enemies. Such was apparently the experience of Job (30:1–15). The tragedy of enmity in a time of sickness is that it compounds the pain, for the person who is ill needs friendship, not enmity, and his diseased condition undermines that robustness of character which may simply shoulder the experience of enmity and bear it as an inevitable part of the experience of living. The psalmist has no such spiritual and emotional reserves; he has reached rock bottom.

Confidence in answered prayer (6:9–11). The tone and atmosphere of the psalm change radically in these last three verses. It may have been the case that as the psalmist progressed in prayer, he eventually reached a point where faith and confidence outstripped anguish and despair. But if the initial context of the psalm's use were cultic, if it presupposes the worshiper going to the temple with his problem, it is quite possible that the change in tone is the consequence of some act or statement external to the psalmist.

Perhaps we should understand the presence of a priest or temple servant, who—having heard the opening words of the worshiper—declares a message or oracle from God which gives faith to the psalmist. Just as Hannah had poured out her lament to God, weeping profusely as she prayed, and then had received a word of confidence from Eli the priest (1 Sam 1:17), so too the psalmist's sorrowful prayer may have been met with a word from God, spoken by his representative, which restored confidence and faith. (For a fuller discussion, see Ridderbos, *Die Psalmen,* 71, 129.)

As confidence returns, the first topic to be taken up is the same as the last topic to be mentioned in the lament: "depart from me, all workers of wickedness." The "workers of wickedness" (v 9) are presumably none other than the enemies of v 8. When sorrow was in ascendancy and faith lagged, enemies caused grief and compounded injury; now that faith and hope were restored, the enemies could be confidently dismissed. The grief had been caused by enemies partly as a consequence of the sufferer's sneaking and insidious suspicion that perhaps they were right, perhaps God had indeed deserted the sufferer; but now that the psalmist has confidence that "the Lord has heard" (v 9b), the enemies no longer offer a threat. Where there is confidence in God, no human being can activate anxiety.

The tenses of the two verbs in v 10 differ. The first implies an action completed in the past: (the Lord) "has heard." The second implies an action still in the future: (the Lord) "will accept." Although some scholars have sought to change this sequence and translate both verbs as if they were in the same tense, the alternation is probably deliberate. The psalmist has opened his prayer fearfully, lacking any confidence that God would hear this, or his former, prayers, but he closes with confidence. The Lord has indeed heard him. But the answer to the prayer lay still in the future—he "will accept," implying that the act of divine healing and restoration, when it came, would be the ultimate consequence of God having heard his prayer. The psalmist's faith, in other words, outstripped the reality of any change in his physical condition.

In the concluding verse, the process of liberation can be seen. Whereas at the beginning, both his body and his soul had been "exceedingly disturbed" (vv 3–4), now the psalmist perceives that his enemies would be "exceedingly disturbed" (the same terminology is employed in v 11). And whereas early in his prayer, he had asked God to "return" to him (using the root שוב), now he perceives that his enemies would "turn back" or "return" (v 11b; the same verb is used). In his newfound confidence, he perceives not only that God will answer his own prayer, but also that his malicious enemies would find their sin boomeranging upon themselves.

Explanation

Mortality is of the essence of the human condition. In a life filled with uncertainty and an unknown future, there remains always one certainty, that one day we shall die. But whereas the healthy person knows this, yet learns to live with an awareness of mortality, the sick person may find that equanimity dissolves and the awareness of death becomes more vivid. Health is normal and it may result in praise, but sickness is a reminder and an anticipation of death. Life itself is no longer so good, for it is marred with pain, and the experience of imperfection in living evokes awareness of that ultimate enemy, death. In sickness, the body does not function properly; in death it ceases to function altogether. Thus it is that the psalms conceived on the sickbed are marked by a profound pathos, for though they contain the words of the living, they are haunted by the shadow of dying.

For the modern Christian or Jewish reader of the Bible, it is most difficult to enter fully into the spirit of the OT *psalms of sickness*. The contemporary Christian and the contemporary Jew can face the experience of sickness and the anticipation of death with a perspective denied to the psalmists, namely belief in a life in God's presence beyond the grave. Yet there was no such clearly articulated doctrine in early Israel. It emerged only in the latest writings of the OT and found fuller expression in the Jewish centuries preceding the Christian era; but even in NT times, there was a debate between the Sadducees and the Pharisees concerning the legitimacy of a belief in resurrection and life beyond the grave. To grasp the initial profundity of the psalms of sickness, we must first attempt to read them within the perspective of the beliefs of their authors. This life is the life given by God. It terminates in death, beyond which was Sheol, an existence not really known, shadowy and incomplete in its substance. Sickness, in a sense, is an anticipation of Sheol; it was hard in sickness to rejoice in God and praise him, but in Sheol it would be impossible.

It is proper that the modern reader of the Psalms understand them with an awareness of the doctrine of resurrection and everlasting life. But to add this perspective to the psalms of sickness too quickly may be questionable, especially for the healthy reader. For the awareness of joy and resurrection beyond sickness and the grave may contribute to a casual understanding of death, and a casual understanding of mortality is likely to crumble with the onset of sickness and the advent of death. It was a fact, as the psalmist knew, that this life was the gift of God; in this life God could be praised, but in death it would no longer be possible to join in the praise of the congregation of the faithful (v 6). If too easily we think that when sickness and death approach, we will trust in God and look to the life beyond, then when the reality comes, the casual faith may not sustain. Like the psalmist, we need a full appreciation of this life before we can look beyond it. And like the psalmist, we may have to undergo the anguish of pain and the sense of separation from God before we can emerge to the faith that rests confidently upon God. The sense of anguish and trouble which permeates this psalmist's words was experienced by Jesus, and indeed influenced his words (v 4; cf. John 12:27); we perceive the pathos of the psalm most clearly when it is read in the context of the Passion.

The Prayer of a Person Falsely Accused (7:1–18)

Bibliography

McKay, J. W. "My Glory—A Mantle of Praise." *SJT* 31 (1978) 167–72. Tigay, J. H. "Psalm 7:5 and Ancient Near Eastern Treaties." *JBL* 89 (1970) 178–86. Vigano, L. "Il titolo divino מרום, 'L' Eccelso'." *Studii Biblici Franciscani Liber Annuus* 24 (1974) 188–201.

Translation

¹ A Shiggaion ª of David, which he sang to the Lord concerning the words of Cush, a Benjaminite.

²⁽¹⁾ *O Lord my God, I have sought refuge in you.* (4+4/3)
Save me from all my pursuers and deliver me,

³⁽²⁾ *lest they* ª *should rip me* ᵇ *like a lion,* (3+3)
tearing ᶜ *me up, with no deliverer.*

⁴⁽³⁾ *O Lord my God, if I have done this thing,* (4+3)
if there is injustice in my hands,

⁵⁽⁴⁾ *if I have repaid my ally with treachery,* (3+3)
*and rescued his adversary*ª *empty-handed,*

⁶⁽⁵⁾ *let an enemy pursue ᵃ me ᵇ and overtake me,* (4+3+3)
   and let him trample my life onto the earth,
      and let him lay my glory ᶜ onto the dust. SELAH ᵈ
⁷⁽⁶⁾ *Arise, O Lord, in your wrath.* (3+3, 2+2)
   Lift yourself up against the furious outbursts of my enemies.
   Awake,ᵃ O Lord my God.ᵇ
   Declare ᶜ a judgment!
⁸⁽⁷⁾ *And let the assembly of peoples ᵃ gather around you,* (3+3)
   and above it ᵇ take your seat on high.
⁹⁽⁸⁾ *The Lord adjudicates the nations ᵃ!* (3,3+2)
   Judge me, O Lord, according to my righteousness,
      and according to my integrity, O Most High. ᵇ
¹⁰⁽⁹⁾ *Let the evil of wicked persons come to an end, ᵃ* (3+2, 3+2)
   but establish the righteous,
   and scrutinize the thoughts and emotions, ᵇ
   O righteous God.
¹¹⁽¹⁰⁾ *My shield ᵃ is upon ᵇ God,* (3/2?+2)
   the One who delivers the upright of heart.
¹²⁽¹¹⁾ *God is a righteous judge,* (3+3)
   but God ᵃ is indignant every day
¹³⁽¹²⁾ *if a person does not repent. ᵃ* (2,2+3?)
   He sharpens his sword;
   he has bent ᵇ his bow and prepared it,
¹⁴⁽¹³⁾ *and for it ᵃ he has made ready instruments of death.* (3+3)
   He will make his arrows fiery shafts. ᵇ
¹⁵⁽¹⁴⁾ *Lo, he ᵃ is in labor with iniquity,* (3+2+2)
   and he is pregnant with mischief,
   and gives birth to falsehood.
¹⁶⁽¹⁵⁾ *He dug a pit and excavated it;* (3+3)
   then he fell ᵃ into the hole he was making.
¹⁷⁽¹⁶⁾ *His mischief returns upon his own head,* (3+3)
   and his violence descends on his forehead.
¹⁸⁽¹⁷⁾ *I will laud the Lord because of his righteousness,* (3+3)
   and I will sing the praise of the name of the Lord Most High.

Notes

1.a. The meaning of *Shiggaion* (שִׁגָּיוֹן) is uncertain. G simply translates *psalm* (ψαλμὸς). If it is related to the root שָׁגָה, "to go astray, reel," it might indicate a psalm of a particular type (e.g. characterized by "wandering" style, uneven meter, or a type of lament characterized by distracted thoughts and words), but there can be no certainty. Mowinckel offers the reasonable hypothesis that the word is related to Akk. *šegu*, "psalm of lamentation" (*The Psalms in Israel's Worship*, II, 209). The word occurs only here in the Psalter, though a different form of the word occurs in Hab 3:1.

3.a. "They"; literally, "he," though the reference is to the "pursuers" (v 2).

3.b. "Me" is literally נַפְשִׁי, "my soul," which may often refer to the individual in the manner of the English pronoun. Dahood translates "my neck," noting the use of Ugaritic *npš*. This is possible, though if the Ugaritic nuance is to be followed, *throat* would be a more appropriate translation than *neck*; the word *npš* designates the internal organ of respiration and ingestion (cf. Caquot et al., *Textes ougaritiques I*, 125 note p). However, *me* is a better translation than *throat*, and balances the subsequent use of נפשי in v 6.

3.c. "Tearing" (פרק): the word may also carry the sense "deliver," which is implied by *G*; but this interpretation would require moving אין "there is no" to an earlier position in the line before פרק. For pictorial representation of being torn by a lion, see Keel, *The Symbolism of the Biblical World*, 86. Lions (of the Asiatic variety) were common in Palestine and the Near East in biblical times, and still survived in Syria and Iraq into the early twentieth century. They no longer exist in the Middle East.

5.a. The verse presents a number of difficulties with respect to meaning; the solution adopted here follows Tigay, *JBL* 89 (1970) 178–86. שולם is an *ally*; צוררי "my enemy" is read as צוררו "his enemy," either emending final *yodh* to *waw*, or interpreting *yodh* as a possible form of the 3rd masc. sing. suffix (after Dahood). On the meaning *enemy* as against *heart* (so Dahood), see Ps 6:8, note. On the threefold use of אם "if" (vv 4–5), in Hebrew and Ugaritic, see R. Althann, *Bib* 58 (1977) 525–26.

6.a. ירדף "pursue" is, in the words of Briggs, "a Massoretic conceit" (*The Book of Psalms*, 56), attempting to combine the Qal and Piel in a single form, and thus offering the reader a choice. There is some mss evidence to suggest that the Qal is the best reading (De-Rossi, IV, 2).

6.b. The word translated "me" is Heb. נפשי again; see v 3, note b (above). The second "me" (after "overtake") is simply implied, though *S* supports reading the pronimal suffix "it," referring back to נפש.

6.c. "My glory" כבודי: on this conventional translation, rather than Dahood's "my liver" (*Psalms I*, 43), see McKay, *SJT* 31 (1978) 167–72.

6.d. On SELAH, see the *Excursus* following Ps 3.

7.a. "Awake": MT has *and awake*, but it is best to omit the conjunction, following *G* and *S*, thus providing more force to the sequence of four imperatives. For the use of the verb עור "awake" in a military context, see Judg 5:12.

7.b. אלי could be translated "to me"; the divine name seems preferable, however, balancing *Yahweh* at the beginning of the verse. If the pointing is correct, it may indicate the plural of majesty (see Dahood, *Psalms I*, 43); alternatively, the suffix could be pointed as for a sing. noun.

7.c. "Declare": the perf. tense of the verb is translated as a further example of the precative perf. (see the note on Ps 4:2).

8.a. לאמים ("peoples") may perhaps have the nuance "warriors," partly on the basis of context, and partly by analogy with Ugaritic *l'imm:* see Craigie, *ZAW* 90 (1978) 377.

8.b. "Above it": the antecedent is the (fem.) "assembly." It has been suggested by Dahood and Vigano that מרום "on high" is a divine name, "Exalted One," but this is uncertain. The traditional meaning provides good sense.

9.a. עמים ("nations") may carry the sense "armies," providing a parallel to לאמים (v 8), particularly if that word implies "warriors" (v 8, note a).

9.b. עלי "upon me" is pointed in MT as a preposition, but should probably be read as a divine name "Most High" (עֵלִי); see also Deut 33:12 (Craigie, *The Book of Deuteronomy*, 396) and M. Dahood, "The Divine Name 'Eli' in the Psalms," *TS* 14 (1953) 452–57.

10.a. Though it is possible that the verb גמר "finish, end" may carry the sense "avenge" in certain contexts, that sense is unlikely in this context. The simplest way of interpreting the alternation from 3rd pers. (יגמר) to 2nd pers. (תכונן) "establish") is to understand רע "evil" as the subject of the first verb, and יהוה "Lord" (v 9—implied here) as the subject of the second.

10.b. "Thoughts and emotions": literally, "hearts and kidneys," the physical organs associated with thinking and feeling respectively.

11.a. מגני is "my shield" rather than "my Suzerain" (as Dahood renders it); see the note on Ps 3:4 and Loretz, *UF* 6 (1974) 178. The further references to instruments of war in vv 13–14 support the translation "shield" in this context.

11.b. על has caused some difficulties: the translation "upon God" implies that God, protecting his servant, holds the shield. Alternatively, following *S*, the word could be omitted and the line translated: "My shield *is* God." Other solutions include (a) adding a 1st pers. pronoun suff. to על (Kraus, *Psalmen*, 53), or (b) assuming a form of the divine name עלי (see v 9, note b and Dahood *Psalms I*, 45–46), though it should be noted that in compound names in the

Ugaritic texts, *'ly* normally occurs in the second position, not in the first (as here, in terms of the proposal). The best solution is either the translation above, or the omission of the preposition after *S*.

12.a. אל ("God, El") is interpreted in *G* as a negative particle, but a noun is more likely in view of the parallelism within the verse.

13.a. The syntax of the opening words of the verse is difficult. I have taken the first clause in conjunction with v 12, as explaining the reason for divine indignation, following the implication of *S*. The words could be taken with the remainder of v 13, however, either (a) "If a man (literally, "he") does not repent, he (God) will sharpen . . ." or (b) "He (God) will sharpen his sword *again*" (see GKC 120d).

13.b. "He has bent" (דרך): the verb indicates the holding of the bow on the ground with the foot, and the pulling back of the cord with the hand.

14.a. "for it": reading ולה for ולו (with some support from Heb mss, De-Rossi, IV, 2), assuming the antecedent to be "bow." Alternatively, translate "for him," referring to the one who does not repent (v 13).

14.b. "Fiery shafts": the reference may be to arrows dipped in a kind of oil or pitch and set alight before shooting.

15.a. The "he" in this verse refers back to the enemy, or the one who does not repent (v 13).

16.a. Note the word play on יפל "fell" and יפעל "was making."

Form/Structure/Setting

Traditionally identified as an *individual lament,* the psalm is more precisely an innocent man's prayer for protection in the face of the false accusations of enemies. The psalmist has been unjustly accused of an act of treachery, including the breach of covenant or treaty obligations, and asks God to vindicate him and let the false accusations and their consequences rebound onto the head of the accuser. There can be no certainty concerning whether the psalm, in its initial use, reflects a cultic context, e.g. some particular ceremony at the sanctuary (see Hayes, *Understanding the Psalms,* 70), or whether it was simply the private anguish of an individual in time of trouble. The solution of the problem will depend partly on the interpretation and evaluation of the psalm's title.

The title (v 1) associates the psalm with a particular event in the life of David, concerning the (false) accusations of a certain Benjaminite named Cush. The incident is not referred to elsewhere explicitly in the Bible, though the fact that David experienced opposition from the Benjaminites, both during Saul's lifetime and afterward, is well documented (see 1 Sam 24–26; 2 Sam 16:5 and 20:1). If the title has historical value and there was an incident with Cush, the account may have been contained in the ancient and no longer extant historical sources named in 1 Chr 29:29. In general, the obscurity of the incident tends to support both its antiquity and its authenticity. Thus, while there can be no historical certainty, it may be reasonable to suppose that the psalm reflects David's reaction to false charges laid against him (in the presence of Saul?), purporting that he had acted treacherously and in defiance of treaty obligations.

If indeed the psalm was set initially in the context of a particular event in the life of David, one may suppose that at a later date it passed into more general usage in the context of worship. The use of SELAH (v 6) may imply such usage in worship. At a still later date in the development of Judaism, the psalm was traditionally associated with the feast of Purim in the month of Adar; the plotting and other themes in Esther, which are central to the celebration of Purim, provided an appropriate context for the psalm's use.

The poetic language is colorful and effective, employing the simile of a fierce lion (v 3), the imagery of divine weapons (vv 13–14), and the metaphor of conception and pregnancy to describe the manner in which a person conceives evil and creates deception.

The psalm falls into two principal sections: (1) the psalmist sets forth his case (7:2–11); (2) God's righteousness and the fate of the wicked (7:12–18).

Comment

The psalmist sets forth his case (7:2–11). The psalm opens with two statements, each introduced by the words, "O Lord my God." The first statement is a prayer for deliverance (vv 2–3); the second is a declaration of innocence, expressed in the form of an oath (vv 4–6). The two statements are closely interrelated; the deliverance for which the psalmist prays will only be forthcoming if indeed he is innocent, for specifically he seeks deliverance from the circumstances created by false accusations laid against him.

The first statement, a prayer, requests deliverance from "pursuers." In the light of the following verses, it is clear that the "pursuers" must be interpreted metaphorically, rather than literally. Certain false charges have been laid against the psalmist which, if substantiated, could undo his good name and his position in society. In this sense, he is pursued or hounded by enemies; they are out to get him, not with swords in the first instance, but with the more powerful weapon of words. The simile of the lion is dramatic; the psalmist is like a helpless person, devoid of weapons, torn apart by the sharp teeth of a ravaging lion; he cries for help, but there is no one there to help or assist. The simile represents the psalmist's situation before prayer—being torn apart without a deliverer; the purpose of prayer is to change that situation and to ask for the advent of a deliverer. The prayer for deliverance is based upon a history of relationship with God; it is possible to say "save me" and "deliver me" now (v 2b), only because in the past "I have sought refuge in you" (v 2a). The experience of deliverance which the psalmist sought would be a part of the continuing relationship with God, not a sudden new experience of religion evoked only by the enormity of the crisis.

In the second statement, the psalmist solemnly swears his innocence before God of the charges laid against him. The oath takes the form of a series of statements introduced by "if," followed by consequences. If indeed he had done certain things, then his enemies had every right to pursue him. The consequence of pursuit by enemies (v 6) indicates the close relationship between the two opening statements. He prays first for deliverance from pursuers (v 2), and then invites pursuit (v 6), if indeed he has committed those crimes of which he is accused. It is possible to form a general understanding of the substance of the false accusations from the four declarations contained in vv 4–5. (i) "This thing" (v 4a) refers in general terms to the accusations laid against him; (ii) "injustice" (v 4b) implies the character of the action he is said to have done (the word "hands" implies evil actions; cf. 1 Sam

24:11 and 26:18). (iii) The reference to an "ally" (v 5a) indicates the person against whom the evil actions were said to have been done, namely a person to whom the psalmist was bound in a relationship of treaty or covenant, which should be characterized by faithfulness, not treachery. (iv) The reference to rescuing "his (viz. the ally's) adversary" is an example of the kind of treacherous act of which the psalmist is accused, for persons or parties committed to one another in treaty were supposed also to share both friends and enemies, as illustrated by the following quotation from an ancient Hittite treaty: "with my friend, you shall be friend, and with my enemy, you shall be enemy" (*ANET,* 204a). Thus, if the psalmist had rescued his ally's adversary, he would indeed have been acting treacherously; if that person were "empty-handed" (v 5b), the treason would be worse, for it could not even be claimed that the act had been done for personal benefit, but only out of spite or hatred.

If he had done such things, the psalmist swears, then let certain terrible things happen to him (v 6); the words are addressed to God and in effect cancel the earlier prayer for deliverance, *only if* the psalmist is indeed guilty of the charges against him. The first penalty which the psalmist invites, in the case of his guilt, is the very thing that he feared and that prompted his prayer in the first instance, namely that he be both pursued and overtaken. The consequence of being overtaken is spelled out in v 6b–c; in effect, it is death. For his "life" to be trampled onto the earth and his "glory" to be set down in the dust, implies not only the destruction of his body, but indicates poetically the departure for *Sheol,* or the nether-world (on Sheol, see Ps 6:5–8, *Comment*). The psalmist's glory was not merely his personal honor, but his capacity to praise and worship God; if he were guilty, that capacity would go, along with life itself.

The solemn oath sworn by the psalmist, and the accusations laid against him, invite arbitration and a judgment concerning innocence and guilt, so that now the psalmist's prayer turns to a petition for the establishment of a court of judgment (vv 7–11). The language is figurative, but the outcome desired was real and would have historical reality, namely the vindication and deliverance of the psalmist. The prayer for divine arbitration must be set in the context of the psalmist's experience of life; he is not merely asking for future vindication, nor is this passage to be interpreted eschatologically.

The prayer for arbitration and judgment begins with four imperatives: "Arise . . . lift yourself . . . awake . . . declare" (v 7). The language implores God to act in the most urgent tones; it was not that God was actually sitting, and should arise, or sleeping and should awake, but so long as the false accusations against the psalmist remained unanswered, it would appear that God was otiose and his enemies rampant. The language of this portion of the prayer is partly military and partly judicial. The military overtones with respect to God emerge from the words "Arise" (similar to the prayer for God's presence in battle, Num 10:35) and "awake" (reminiscent of the battle cry in Deborah's war, Judg 5:12). The military atmosphere with respect to mankind, emerges from the words "peoples" and "nations" (see the *Notes* on vv 8–9). The military terminology may reflect partly the military nature of the false accusations laid against the psalmist (the breach of a treaty), but may also evoke the image of God as Warrior, who would be fearful in judgment. But the terminology as a whole conjures the image of a court of law; peoples gather around and God takes his lofty seat of judgment (v 8). In this context, in the presence of the one who "adjudicates the nations" (v 9a), the psalmist asks to be judged according to his "righteousness" and "integrity"; he does not for one moment claim absolute righteousness or sinlessness, but only complete innocence with respect to the false charges which have been laid against him. Only in this divine court will the wicked "come to an end" (v 10) and the righteous be established; God, the Judge, is righteous, and by virtue of his divine ability to scrutinize the innermost thoughts and emotions of the persons standing in court—figuratively, the psalmist and his accusers—he will establish the righteous and terminate the wicked.

The prayer for arbitration and judgment concludes with a statement of the psalmist's confidence (v 11). The word "shield" carries further the military imagery (above); the psalmist's enemies have been casting weapons (the arrows and spears of their words) against him, but God is not only Judge, but also Defender of the defendant in court. Only because the psalmist is "upright in heart" (v 11b) can he expect the deliverance for which he initially prayed (see v 2).

God's righteousness and the fate of the wicked (7:12–18). The last portion of the psalm marks a transition from particular prayer to general praise, though the two portions of the psalm are intimately related. The transition is prompted by the high point of confidence which the psalmist had reached, as expressed in v 11. But the substance of the praise maintains the earlier themes of the psalm. There are two themes, closely intertwined; the righteous God and wicked persons. It was wicked persons, with their false accusations, who created the psalmist's plight; it was the existence of a righteous God which made possible the prayer. Now, in this closing section, the two parties are brought into conjunction; that is, the lot of the wicked is described in terms of their relationship to the righteous God.

The first portrait in words describes God (vv 12–14). He is a "righteous Judge," but the necessary implication of this positive statement is that the same God will stand in indignant judgment over the unrepentant sinner (v 13a). The description of God's potential violence against the unrepentant sinner is pursued in the military terminology which characterized the earlier part of the psalm; God does not act, as such, but makes preparations for action. "He sharpens his sword" (gets it ready for action) and "has bent his bow" (analogous to cocking a pistol), and the flaming arrows are all ready for shooting. But God is not said to act: he is set, primed, and ready, yet action does not take place until finally triggered by the evil and unrepentant sinner. So now the psalmist turns to the second portrait in words, that of the wicked.

The origin of the wicked person's sin is described in the metaphor of conception and pregnancy. The metaphor, described by Oesterley as "extremely distasteful" (cited by Anderson, *Psalms I,* 99), is forceful, particularly when used in the masculine form! As a woman labors painfully, yet lovingly, with the child soon to be delivered, so too does the unrepentant sinner with his iniquity. The seed of mischief has been planted in his mind and, after labor, it will come forth as "falsehood," namely the false accusations laid against the psalmist. And then the poet turns to another metaphor, in which he makes clear the course that evil runs; the wicked person falls into the pit he was digging for others. The principle, of both evil and its consequences, is stated clearly in v 17: evil eventually functions like a boomerang, bringing back upon its perpetrators the wickedness planned for others. And there is a sense in which the boomerang of human evil may be identified with the "sword" (v 13) and "fiery shafts" (v 14) of divine judgment; God was primed to act against the unrepentant sinner, but the nature of his action was simply to direct the consequences of evil away from the innocent and turn them back upon the perpetrators.

The psalmist began his prayer within the confines of distress which had limited his vision; he could think only of the false accusations made against him and of his need for deliverance. In the beginning of his prayer, the enemies overshadowed God in the enormity of their plotting against him. But as the prayer ends with a note of praise (v 18), a proper balance has returned. God's righteousness was greater than the wickedness of enemies, and thus praise was called for more than prayer. In praising the "name" of God (v 18c), the psalmist is rejoicing in the access to God's presence in prayer which had been made possible by the revelation of the divine name.

Explanation

It is a curious feature of the experience of human living, that the public accusation of the sins or crimes which we have committed is easier to bear, emotionally and spiritually, than the false accusations concerning crimes of which we are innocent. When an evil act or sin is committed, there is at least justice in the accusation; there is a path of restoration and repentance possible. But the false accusation is harder to bear, partly because it brings with it the experience of injustice, and partly because there may seem to be no escape from its consequences. We cannot repent of something we have not done, nor can we make restoration, and it is in the nature of false accusers that they do not easily depart and leave us in peace. The genuine anxiety evoked by false accusations, whether of a subtle and personal nature or an open and legal nature, is partly legitimate and partly illegitimate. It is legitimate in the sense that false accusations can do real damage, whether to reputation, family, or means of livelihood. But it may be an illegitimate anxiety if it is tied too intimately to pride, for such anxiety assumes that the opinion of other persons is of more significance than the opinion of God. Yet it is in the nature of false accusation, that whereas it may deceive and convince our fellow human beings, it cannot deceive God. False accusation never undermines a person's standing in the sight of God, though it may provide a testing ground for the accused's strength of character.

The psalmist begins his prayer in just such a state of anxiety, precipitated by the false charges laid against him; the anxiety is real, and for the most part legitimate, for the accusations create genuine danger. As the psalmist begins his prayer, things have understandably grown out of proportion; the false accusers appear to have gained the upper hand and turning to God is a last and desperate resort. It is only at the end of the prayer that balance is restored, and the balance involves a proper appreciation of God's righteousness and the nature of evil. It is the judgment of God that matters more than the machinations of wicked persons; and it is better to stand in integrity before God who is a righteous Judge, than to share the slippery foothold with sinners on the edge of the pit they have dug for themselves.

We do not know from the psalm whether the falsely accused was finally vindicated or his name was cleared; we know only that he came into such a knowledge of God that he could accept his lot. It is clear that the psalmist *desired,* and legitimately desired, an immediate acquittal from the charges laid against him and their consequences. And he desired it in the here and now, in the midst of his crisis, not in some far-off eschatological future. But all else remains uncertain, and we are not told that he lived happily ever after. The psalm thus provides an appropriate perspective for dealing with the common experience of false accusation. It is legitimate to take the problem to God in prayer, and since God is a righteous God, we may hope for justice and acquittal. But whether or not we perceive that justice is done, we require the proper perspective. It is better to maintain integrity and continue to suffer injustice, than to sell out to evil and form ranks with the unrighteous.

What Is Man? (8:1-10)

Bibliography

Beyerlin, W. "Psalm 8. Chancen der Überlieferungskritik." *ZTK* 73 (1976) 1–22. **Childs, B. S.** "Psalm 8 in the Context of the Christian Canon." *Int* 23 (1969) 20–31. **Donner, H.** "Ugaritismen in der Psalmenforschung." *ZAW* 79 (1969) 322–50 (*324–27). **Görg, M.** "Der Mensch als königliches Kind nach Ps 8.3." *Biblische Notizen* 3 (1977) 7–13. **Gouders, K.** "Gottes Schöpfung und der Auftrag des Menschen (Ps 8)." *BibLeb* 14 (1973) 164–80. **Hamp, V.** "Ps 8:2b, 3." *BZ* 16 (1972) 115–20. **Huppenbauer, H. W.** "God and Nature in the Psalms." *Ghana Bulletin of Theology* 3 (1969) 19–32. **Loretz, O.** "Die Psalmen 8 und 67. Psalmenstudien V." *UF* 8 (1976) 117–22. _____. "Psalmenstudien III. Poetischer Aufbau von Psalm 8." *UF* 3 (1971) 104–12. **Moloney, F. J.** "The Targum on Psalm 8 and the New Testament." *Salesianum* 37 (1975) 326–36. **Schmidt, W. H.** "Gott und Mensch in Ps 8. Form- und überlieferungsgeschichtliche Erwägungen." *TZ* 25 (1969) 1–15. **Soggin, J. A.** "Textkritische Untersuchung von Ps VIII, vv 2–3 und 6." *VT* 21 (1971) 565–71. **Tournay, R. B.** "Le Psaume 8 et la doctrine biblique du nom." *RB* 78 (1971) 18–30.

(N.B. The above is a select listing from a more comprehensive bibliography of studies of Ps 8; for additional bibliographical information, see the study of Soggin listed above).

Translation

¹ For the musical director. According to the Gittith.ᵃ A psalm of David.
²⁽¹⁾ *O Lord, our governor,*   (2, 3+3)
      how majestic your name is in all the earth.
      I will worship ᵃ *your majesty above the heavens.*

3(2) *From the mouths of babes and sucklings,* [a]   (3+3+3)
     You have established strength [b] *on account of your enemies,*
     to put at rest both foe and avenger.

4(3) *When I see* [a] *your heavens, the work* [b] *of your fingers,*   (4+4)
     the moon and stars which you have established,

5(4) *what is man that you are mindful of him?*   (3+3)
     And the son of man, that you attend to him?

6(5) *But you have made him little less than God,*   (3+3)
     and you will crown him with glory and honor.

7(6) *You will make* [a] *him master over the work of your hands;*   (3+3)
     you have set [a] *everything beneath his feet,*

8(7) *all sheep* [a] *and cattle,*   (3+3)
     and even the beasts of the field;

9(8) *birds of the air and fishes of the sea,*   (4+3)
     whatever passes through the pathways of the seas.

10(9) *O Lord, our governor,*   (2,3)
      how majestic your name is in all the earth.

Notes

1.a. The meaning of גתית (*Gittith*) is not known with any certainty. The word might designate (a) a kind of musical instrument, the "Gittite lyre" (analogous to the Spanish guitar; viz. a specific type of instrument named after a place); or (b) a musical tune or setting; or (c) a festival or ceremony of some kind (see Mowinckel, *The Psalms in Israel's Worship*, II, 215).

2.a. The *crux* in this verse pertains to the meaning of the words אשר תנה. As it stands, MT is anomolous, both with respect to the syntax of אשר and the vocalization of תנה. The various solutions which have been proposed are surveyed and analyzed critically by Soggin, *VT* 21 (1971) 566–68, and the possibility of interpreting by means of Ugaritic *tny* has been effectively undermined by Donner, *ZAW* 79 (1967) 324–27. The best solution is probably that of Dahood (*Psalms I*, 49), which involves joining the two forms into a single word (אשרתנה) and pointing it as a Piel imperf., with energic ending, from שרת ("to minister, serve"). It is this solution which has formed the basis of the translation above.

3.a. The difficulties encountered in the previous verse continue in v 3, partly because of the uncertainty as to how to translate v 3, and partly because of the difficult syntax and uncertain prosodic analysis of v 3. For a critical survey of the problems, see Loretz, *UF* 3 (1971) 104–12. For suggested emendations of MT, see Leveen, *VT* 21 (1971) 48–58. The immediate problem concerns whether the opening line of v 3, mentioning "babes and sucklings," should be taken as qualifying the praise of v 2b, or should be taken in conjunction with the remainder of v 3. For the former solution, see Dahood, *Psalms I*, 48–50. I have preferred to take the opening words with v 3b-c (see further the *Comment*).

3.b. "Strength" (עז) could perhaps be translated "stronghold, fortress" (BDB, 799), though the more general sense seems preferable; over and against the strength of his enemies, the Lord establishes his strength through the symbols of weakness, namely babes and sucklings. However, the above translation of vv 2–3 should be considered as tentative.

4.a. "I see" (אראה); *S* implies the 3 pers. plur. form of the verb, but MT's 1 pers. sing. is to be preferred; note that the presence of the 1 pers. sing. here supports the suggestion concerning the presence of a verb in the first person in v 2: אשרתנה "I will serve."

4.b. "Work": the translation assumes a sing. form of the noun, for which there is support from several mss (De-Rossi, IV, 2), including *C*, and which has the support of *S*.

7.a. The tenses in this verse (and v 6) are the source of some difficulty. Here, the imperf. is followed by the perf., which (according to Moroder, after Dahood) might perhaps both be translated as referring to past time (see Moroder in *UF* 6 [1974] 263); this is possible. Yet the four verbs in vv 6–7 appear to be in a chiastic structure, and it may be that the poet is contrasting both what God has accomplished for mankind (perf.) and also what will be mankind's future

(imperf.). It is this contrast which I have attempted to convey in the translation. See further
the *Excursus* on Heb. tenses following the commentary on this psalm.

8.a. "Sheep"; reading צאנה, for which there is extensive mss evidence (De-Rossi, IV, 2);
the word may imply "small cattle" in contrast to אלפים, "large cattle."

Form/Structure/Setting

Psalm 8 is a *hymn of praise*, in general terms, though more precisely it
may be classified as a *psalm of creation* (see Westermann, *Der Psalter*, 78). Yet
it has an originality and distinctiveness which defy any attempt to categorize
the psalm with respect to precise forms and substance. Indeed, a number
of scholars have noted the apparent mixture of forms within the psalm, claiming the presence of hymnic material, wisdom material and portions similar
to the lament (see Schmidt, *TZ* 25 [1969] 1–15; Beyerlin, *ZTK* 73 [1976]
1–22). Yet it is clearly a hymn, and the impossibility of fitting it into a precise
mold is indicative in part of the poet's genius and creativity.

The universal nature of the psalm's substance is such that there can be
no certainty whether or not the psalm was designed in the first instance for
use in the cult, in some specific act of worship. It is certainly most appropriate
for use in the cult's mode of worship, though a number of scholars consider
it to have been initially noncultic (e.g. Fohrer, *Introduction to the OT*, [Nashville:
Abingdon, 1968] 286). If the psalm were initially cultic, it would have been
appropriate for use on an occasion such as the Feast of Tabernacles (see
Anderson, *Psalms I*, 100), but its theme is so central to the Israelite tradition,
that there may have been many other occasions for which this psalm would
have been equally appropriate. The alternation between plural and singular
("our governor," v 2; "I see," v 4) would fit quite naturally within the context
of communal worship. Although there is uncertainty as to the original relationship between the psalm and the cult, the title (v 1) indicates that the psalm
came to be used regularly in the course of Israel's worship in the temple.
In Christianity, at a later date, the psalm was traditionally associated with
the worship of Ascension Day, in the light of the NT interpretation of the
psalm.

It is not possible to specify the date and authorship of the psalm with
any certainty. The contents are of such a kind as to offer little help with
dating. There are certain affinities between the psalm and Gen 1 (with respect
both to creation in general and the place of mankind within creation), but
these similarities do not permit either precise dating or even a firm judgment
as to historical sequence. Also, there is a point of similarity between the
psalm and Job (Job 7:17; cf. Ps 8:5), but again the parallel does not contribute
to dating or sequence. The theme of creation has given rise to a popular
view that the psalm must be postexilic, on the assumption that creation-
thought developed most fully in Israel during and after the Exile. But such
an assumption is surely unwarranted, given the commonality of creation
thought throughout the ancient Near East and the centrality of creation in
Israelite thought from a very early period.

The psalm forms a perfect unity, but may be examined in terms of its
four component parts. (1) God's majesty and might (8:2–3); (2) mankind's

sense of insignificance (8:4–5); (3) God's role for mankind (8:6–9); (4) concluding praise (8:10).

Comment

God's majesty and might (8:2–3). God is addressed by his proper name (יהוה, *Yahweh,* or conventionally in English, "Lord,") followed by a title (אדנינו "our lord/governor"). In later Judaism, the divine name was held to be so sacred that the title was always used in place of the name; but here, the name is enunciated, and then immediately the psalmist goes on to praise the majesty of the "name" (v 2b). The word "name" here represents not only God, but also God's revelation of himself, and it is critical to an understanding of the theme of revelation in the psalm as a whole (see below, and also Tournay, *RB* 78 [1971] 18–30). Thus God's "name" and God's "majesty" (v 2c) are poetically synonymous, for the majesty of both God's person and creation are revealed to mankind in the divine name and all that it implies. The majestic name of God both permeates the earth and transcends the heavens, thus evoking the words of mortal praise. And as this psalm begins with an exclamation of the majesty of God's name, so too it ends in the same words (v 10), indicating in part that it is the majesty of the divine name which provides the central theme of the psalm and which provides the clue to its fundamental meaning.

The interpretation of v 3 is rendered difficult by virtue of the uncertainty as to its proper translation (see v 3, note a, above). There is a contrast between "babes and sucklings," on the one hand, and the "foe and avenger" on the other; between the contrasted parties is God (v 3c). God uses the mouth of "babes and sucklings," in some manner, to establish (his) "strength," on account of the presence, or existence, of enemies. It is probable that the verse should be interpreted with specific reference to the divine "name" (v 2). Enemies symbolize human strength; they are arrogant in their self-assertion. The essence of the enemies of God is that they do not recognize the name of God or the revelation that came through that name, for if they had come to such full recognition, they would have desisted from their enmity. Babes, on the other hand, symbolize human weakness and humility, but they have a strength greater than that of God's enemies when they take the *name* of God on their lips; that is, in speaking the name, they acknowledge and in some sense understand the majesty and revelation of God which are implicit in that name. Thus God may utilize the weak of this world, even the child, both to establish his strength, reflected in his nature and in his creation, and at the same time "to put at rest" (or quiet) the opposition of enemies. Understood in this manner, v 3 sets the stage for what is to follow. Though the universe is vast and imparts to mankind a sense of smallness and insignificance (vv 4–5), nevertheless God has given to mankind a position of extraordinary strength within the universe (vv 6–9). But that position of strength is not a natural human right (persons who think that it is are enemies), but something God-given and God-revealed through the divine name. The psalmist, who will soon speak of the extraordinary honor and power bestowed upon mankind by God, first establishes in v 3 that it is not human arrogance that asserts such power, but the childlike recognition and enunciation of God's name.

Mankind's sense of insignificance (8:4–5). The spontaneous reaction of a human being, upon seeing the nighttime universe reflected in the stars and moon, is to become aware of his own insignificance. From a poetic perspective, the vastness of the universe is subtly magnified, for the heavens are the work of God's "fingers"! Though God does not have physical dimensions, the poet makes a striking point. In contrast to God, the heavens are tiny, pushed and prodded into shape by the divine digits; but in contrast to the heavens, which seem so vast in the human perception, it is mankind that is tiny. The response to this heavenly panorama is a response which so many humans have felt, whether or not they have encountered Ps 8. In such a vast space, with dimensions beyond human comprehension, "what is man?" (The expression "son of man," v 5b, is simply a poetic synonym of "man" in v 5a). The question of v 5b is phrased in such a manner that it evokes from the person without revelation (the enemies of v 3?) the answer: Nothing! In such vastness, it is inconceivable that human beings have significance or meaning; it is inconceivable that God, if there is a God, could remember each human being or give attention to each person. The poet deliberately creates this sense of despair, first, in order to make the positive answer to the question, when it comes (vv 6–9), all the more powerful. From an objective perspective, human beings are but the tiniest fragments in a giant universe; it is not conceivable that they could have significance or a central position in that universe. But the name of God, through which revelation comes, indicates that the very opposite is true.

God's role for mankind (8:6–9). God's role for mankind is that of master within the created universe; specifically, the mastery extends over living creatures within the universe. Thus mankind is only a "little less than God" (v 6a); as God, the Creator, is ultimate master, so has he delegated mastery to mankind, the creature. The early versions differ in their interpretations at this point. Many of the earliest versions took the word אלהים (literally, "God, gods") to mean "angels" (so *G, S, Tg* and *Vg*), and in some texts that would be an appropriate translation. But other versions (Aquila, Symmachus, and others) translated *God.* The translation *angels* may have been prompted by modesty, for it may have seemed rather extravagant to claim that mankind was only a little less than God. Nevertheless, the translation *God* is almost certainly correct, and the words probably contain an allusion to the image of God in mankind and the God-given role of dominion to be exercised by mankind within the created order. This position is mankind's estate (the verb in v 6a implies a past accomplishment), yet the role is not static, but requires continuous human response and action: hence, "you will crown him with glory and honor" (v 6b).

Mankind's mastery is to extend over all created things, but it is specifically living creatures that are singled out in vv 8–9. Both domestic and untamed creatures will fall beneath mankind's mastery, and both fish and birds will be set beneath his dominion. The reference to "whatever passes through the pathways of the sea" (v 9b) may simply be an all-embracing way of describing marine life, but it may indicate that even the monsters of the ocean (whales, or even mythological monsters), which were so much larger than tiny humans, were to fall under human control. The words are reminiscent of the ships and the monstrous Leviathan (Ps 104:25–26) that ply the waterways of the world.

Concluding praise (8:10). The psalm concludes on the same note as that on which it began—the praise of God's "name," for it was the name and the revelation which came through the name that transformed mankind's sense of universal insignificance into an awareness of the divine and significant plan.

Explanation

There are a few psalms in the Psalter which raise in various ways the question of nature's role in Hebrew thought and theology (cf. Pss 19, 104). Psalm 8 addresses that question in a distinctive way, though nature is not the central theme of the psalm.

Nature, or more precisely the created world which is God's handiwork, does not contain in this context any inherent qualities of revelation. The person who reflects upon nature, who perceives the vast universe with its celestial bodies, will certainly be impressed, but the impression will not imprint any truth in the mind with respect to mankind's role in the universe. In fact, the opposite is the case; the honest person's gaze into the vastness of space evokes only a sense of smallness, an awareness of human insignificance. Indeed, in some people, it may evoke a sense of awe, a sense of wonder at the extraordinary nature of the universe, but it contains no explicit revelation within it concerning mankind's place. Thus, the psalmist is not concerned here with presenting nature as a vehicle of revelation; nature rather evokes the necessary sense of nothingness which must precede a specific kind of revelation, namely the revelation of the name of God to mankind and within that, God's revelation of mankind's role within the created world. The role of human beings in the universe, in other words, is not something which can be discerned from reflecting upon nature, or from a kind of natural philosophy; it is something which may only be known on the basis of special and specific revelation.

Psalm 8 is referred to a number of times in the NT. It is used by Jesus in a fashion which brings out more profoundly its initial meaning, but its use in the early church reflects a new kind of interpretation in the context of the earliest church's christology. Jesus, after cleansing the temple, was criticized by the chief priests and scribes for his apparent acceptance of the behavior of children, who were shouting "Hosanna to the Son of David." The authorities were indignant and expected Jesus to calm this juvenile chorus. But he responded by quoting Ps 8:3: "Out of the mouth of babes and sucklings, you have brought forth perfect praise" (Matt 21:16). In his rebuke to the authorities, he brought out the inherent contrast in the original psalm; the children take the *name* upon their lips (interpreting *Son of David,* from the perspective of the early church, as a messianic title), but the authorities are indignant and complain—in effect, they are the foes and the avengers of the psalm. But, as in the psalm, it is the children who have the truer perception, not the arrogant enemies.

In the early church, the words of the psalm describing mankind's role of dominion in the world (8:6–7) are given christological significance with respect to the dominion of Jesus Christ in his resurrection and exaltation (1 Cor 15:27; Eph 1:22; Heb 2:6–8). In one sense, this is quite a new meaning, not evidently implicit in the psalm in its original meaning and context. And yet in another sense, it is a natural development of the thought of the psalm, for the dominion of which the psalmist spoke may have had theological reality, yet it did not always appear to have historical reality in the developing history of the human race. The historical reality, according to Paul and the author of the Epistle to the Hebrews, is—and will be—fulfilled in the risen Christ.

Excursus II: The Translation of Tenses in Hebrew Poetry

The translator of the Psalms constantly faces a difficulty concerning the most appropriate translation of Hebrew verbs with respect to tenses in English. The general difficulties are illustrated clearly by the four verbs in Ps 8:6–7, which might seem to be translated best into English by a single tense (a past tense?), yet the Hebrew verbs express a variety of forms: waw-consecutive-imperfect, two imperfects, and finally a perfect. The general difficulties of translation are compounded by the following factors.

(1) Hebrew is generally said to have two tenses, the *imperfect* (commonly said to refer to the *future* and sometimes the *present*), and the *perfect* (normally referring to action in the past). Yet, from a technical perspective, it may be incorrect to use the word *tense* at all with respect to the Hebrew (or Semitic) verbal system, for the word *tense* (which may be used appropriately of verbs in English or Classical languages) implies that the forms of the verb are modified in order to express primarily distinctions in *time* with respect to actions or states. Yet this is not evidently the case with respect to the Hebrew verbal system; the system defines primarily *aspect*, not time. Thus the so-called perfect tense normally indicates completed action, which, in turn, normally indicates past time, but in certain contexts may appropriately be translated into a present or future (perfect) tense. The so-called imperfect tense normally indicates incomplete action, which normally indicates a present or future tense, but a past continuous tense is possible. Thus, the very word *tense* is strictly inappropriate with respect to Hebrew, though it will continue to be used for reasons of simplicity. The expressions *prefixed-verb* (imperfect) and *suffixed-verb* (perfect) describe the two principal forms in a less prejudicial fashion.

(2) The general difficulty with respect to the two principal forms of the verb may be compounded by the Massoretic pointing, which reflects a later

and developed stage in the Hebrew language compared to that reflected in
the consonantal text (see further section [3] below).

(3) It is quite possible that in early Hebrew, there were three forms of
the verb: (a) the suffixed form (the so-called perfect tense); (b) the normal
prefixed form (the so-called imperfect tense), and (c) a second prefixed
form, probably equivalent to the so-called preterite tense of Akkadian, normally implying action completed in the past. It is possible that the Ugaritic
verbal system reflects a transitional stage between the forms of Akkadian
and the standard forms of Hebrew. (See further, on the general problems,
S. Moscati (ed.), *An Introduction to the Comparative Grammar of the Semitic Languages*, 1964, 131–34; F. C. Fensham, "The Use of the Suffix Conjugation
and the Prefix Conjugation in a few Old Hebrew Poems," *JNWSL* 6 [1978]
9–18; R. Hetzron, "The Evidence of Perfect *y'aqtul* and Jussive *yaqt'ul* in
Proto-Semitic," *JSS* 14 [1969] 1–21.) If indeed there were such forms in
early Hebrew, the Massoretic pointing did not clearly reflect any differentiation
between forms (b) and (c), (It is possible, however, that the so-called *waw*-
consecutive form may reflect survival of an older form; viz. the prefixed form
in the *waw*-consecutive imperfect may be equivalent to (c) above.)

(4) It has been argued that *early Hebrew poetry* differs from *standard Hebrew
poetry* (viz. poetry composed in or after the eighth century B.C.) in a number
of linguistic features, one of which is the distribution of tenses or forms to
designate actions clearly completed in the past. Standard poetic Hebrew normally employs the suffixed and *waw*-prefixed forms in the narration of past
events, while early Hebrew poetry uses both suffixed and prefixed forms (viz.
both perfect and imperfect) to narrate past events; see D. A. Robertson,
Linguistic Evidence in the Dating of Early Hebrew Poetry, 1966, chap. 2.

(5) Dahood (in his "Grammar of the Psalter," *Psalms III*, 361–456) notes
considerable variety in the use of forms of the verb with respect to time:

(a) *yqtl* expressing past time
(b) the sequence *qtl-yqtl* referring to past time
(c) the sequence *qtl-yqtl* referring to the present
(d) the sequence *qtl-yqtl* referring to the future
(e) the sequence *yqtl-qtl* referring to the past
(f) the sequence *yqtl-qtl* referring to the present
(g) the sequence *yqtl-qtl* referring to the future

In each of the categories listed above, Dahood cites numerous examples;
though many of the examples may be eliminated as unsubstantiated or ambiguous, nevertheless the overall facts of the case remain the same.

From the kind of evidence summarized above, it is evident that there can
be no simple rule of thumb with respect to the appropriate English tense
which may be indicated by the forms of the Hebrew verb. In practice, the
context is the principal guide to determining the most appropriate translation,
but difficulties arise precisely because context, in nonhistorical poetic texts
(which is the case with respect to the majority of the psalms), may leave
room for considerable ambiguity and uncertainty. Thus Robertson's criteria
(section [4] above) are often of little help, partly because the majority of

the psalms cannot be dated accurately, and partly because the use of the
prefixed form to describe past actions is in fact only known through unambiguous contexts (the historical portions of the Song of the Sea, Exod 15:1–18,
by way of example). In contexts where there is ambiguity, one is left with
the possibility that a prefixed form of the verb might imply past action, or
might imply present or future action. Indeed, the data adduced by Dahood
might even imply that the surviving forms as such are virtually irrelevant in
themselves with respect to the definition of time, and that the poet had relative
freedom to use the most appropriate form.

It is my view that not enough is yet known about the nature and development of the Hebrew verbal system to permit a sure translation of Hebrew
verbs *in poetic texts* with respect to tense on the basis of the form alone. A
comparison of the Ugaritic evidence, the early forms of Hebrew poetry (e.g.
the Song of the Sea, the Song of Deborah, and so on) and the later forms
of Hebrew poetry does indeed provide a fragile framework within which to
perceive development and change with respect to the forms and function
of the verb in the early history of Hebrew grammar. But the evidence is
incomplete, the consonantal text by its very nature does not retain the ancient
distinctions of vocalization and stress, and the Massoretic text has not retained
the distinctive features of the various verbal forms which must once have
existed. The uncertainty of our knowledge with respect to the historical grammar of poetic Hebrew between the twelfth and fifth centuries B.C., together
with the virtual inability to date accurately the majority of the psalms, means
that we are working partially in the dark with respect to the translation of
Hebrew verbs in poetry. In general, in my translation, I have attempted to
work in terms of the conventional understanding of *aspect* (completeness or
incompleteness with respect to verbs designating action) and *context* as providing the principal guides to the translator.

The two verses which prompted this Excursus (Ps 8:6–7) are a clear indication of the nature of the problem. My initial "translator's instinct" would
be to translate all four verbs as English past tenses:

⁶ *But you have made him little less than God,*
   and you have crowned him with glory and honor.
⁷ *You have made him master over the work of your hands;*
   you have set everything beneath his feet.

For such translations, see AV, RSV (partial), Dahood, and others. Yet if a translation in the past tense is best, one is left with the question concerning why
the poet used different forms of the verb to express the same aspect (completion) or indication of time? A possible solution might go as follows:

ותחסר (*waw*-consec. imperf.)   = *waw* + preterite
תעטר (imperfect)   = preterite
תמשיל (imperfect)   = preterite
שתה   = "perfect"

The preterite, like the so-called perfect, would normally designate *completed*
actions, and thus would normally be translated into English by a past tense.

It would be presumed that the prefixed forms, here called preterite, would originally have been distinguished from the normal so-called imperfect by both vocalization and stress (neither of which were retained in the transmission of the consonantal text, and which were therefore not represented in the vocalization of the Massoretes), and the poet's choice of verbal forms may have been determined by such features as phonetic considerations and meter (neither of which can be detected with certainty in the light of the extant evidence).

A number of factors, however, militate against this approach. First, such an approach would be more convincing if it could be demonstrated on other grounds that Ps 8 was an example of early Hebrew poetry, in which case such alternation in forms might be expected; but the date of Ps 8 cannot be fixed with any certainty. Second, the context is ambiguous and does not require a sequence of past tenses in English; a translation rendering the sequence of verbs into English as *past/future/future/past* is quite possible (cf. NEB's past/present/present/past) and the poet may be making a particular theological point (see *Comment*). Hence, I have opted for this latter solution, though it remains tentative.

At subsequent points in the commentary, where the appropriate English tense for the Hebrew verbal form is thoroughly dubious, a comment to that effect is entered in the *Notes*.

Praise and Lament (9–10)

Bibliography

Gray, G. B. *The Forms of Hebrew Poetry* (1915. Reprinted KTAV: New York, 1972). See particularly chap. 8, "The Alphabetic Structure of Psalms IX and X" (267–94). **Leveen, J.** "Textual Problems in the Psalms." *VT* 21 (1971) 48–58. **O'Callaghan, R. T.** "Echoes of Canaanite Literature in the Psalms." *VT* 4 (1954) 164–76 (*164–66). **Rosenbaum, S. N.** "New Evidence for Reading *ge'im* in place of *goyim* in Pss. 9–10." *HUCA* 45 (1974) 65–70.

(N.B. Pss 9 and 10 are taken together as a single literary unit; for an explanation, see *Form/Structure/Setting*, following the *Notes* on Ps 9).

Translation (Ps 9)

1		For the musical director. According to *Muth Labben.*[a] A psalm of David.	
2(1) (א)		*I will praise the Lord with all my heart:*	(3+2)
		I will recount all your wonderful works.	
3(2)		*I will rejoice and I will exult in you;*	(3+3)
		I will sing the praise of your name, O Most High.	
4(3) (ב)		*When* [a] *my enemies turn back,*	(3+3)
		they shall be thrown down and shall perish before you;	

5(4)	*for you have undertaken my judgment and my cause;*	(3/4?+4)
	you have sat upon the throne, judging righteously. ª	
6(5) (ג)	*You have rebuked the nations;* ª *you have made the wicked perish;* ᵇ	
		(4+4)
	you have wiped out their name forever and ever.	
7(6)	*The enemy* ª *are finished, perpetual ruins,* ᵇ	(4+4)
	and you have uprooted ᶜ *cities;* ᵈ *their memory has perished.*	
8(7) ((ד)ה)	*Behold,* ª *the Lord shall reign* ᵇ *forever;*	(4+3)
	he has established his throne of judgment.	
9(8)	*And he shall judge the world with righteousness;*	(3+3)
	he shall adjudicate ª *the peoples with equity.*	
10(9) (ו)	*And the Lord shall be a refuge for the oppressed,*	(4+3)
	a refuge for times of trouble.	
11(10)	*And the ones who know your name shall trust in you,*	(4+4)
	for you have not forsaken those who seek you, O Lord.	
12(11) (ז)	*Sing praises to the Lord, the Enthroned of Zion;* ª	(4+3)
	declare his deeds among the peoples!	
13(12)	*For the Avenger of Blood* ª *has remembered them;*	(4+3)
	he has not forgotten the cry of the afflicted. ᵇ	
14(13) (ח)	*Be gracious* ª *to me, O Lord! Look upon my affliction from*	
	those who hate me,	(5+3?)
	my guardian ᵇ *from the gates of death,*	
15(14)	*that I may recount all your praise in the gates of the daughter of Zion.*	
		(5+2)
	I will rejoice in your deliverance!	
16(15) (ט)	*Nations have sunk into the pit they have made.*	(4+4)
	Their foot was caught in the net which they hid!	
17(16)	*The Lord has revealed himself; he has executed judgment,*	(4+4)
	by the action of his hands striking ª *down the wicked.*	
	HIGGAION.ᵇ SELAH.	
18(17) (י)	*The wicked shall return* ª *to Sheol,*	(3+3)
	all nations that forget God,	
19(18) (כ)	*for the poor will not always be forgotten,*	(4+4)
	nor ª *will the hope of the afflicted* ᵇ *perish forever.*	
20(19)	*Arise, O Lord! Don't let humans prevail!*	(4+3)
	Let the nations be judged before you.	
21(20)	*Put fear* ª *in them, O Lord;*	(4+4)
	let the nations know they are only human! ᵇ SELAH	

Notes

1.a. The meaning of the expression *Muth Labben* is not known with certainty, though it probably designates the tune according to which this psalm (and probably also Ps 10) was to be
sung. Taken literally, it would mean "death to the son" (cf. Symmachus and Jerome). If, however,
על and מות are taken as a single word (עלמות), as in *BHS* (see De-Rossi, IV, 2, for the mss
evidence with respect to this alternate reading), there would be some similarity to Ps 46:1:
על עלמות, which may mean something like "by female (treble or soprano?) voices"; see the
Notes on Ps 46:1.

4.a. The בְּ, with which the verse begins (followed by inf. constr.), introduces a temporal clause, not a causal clause ("because of"), as suggested by Briggs, *Psalms*, 82.

5.a. "Judging righteously," taking צֶדֶק "righteous" in an adverbial sense; alternatively, following *S*, it is possible to assume the loss of a *yodh* in the original text, and to read צַדִּיק: "Righteous (Judge)."

6.a. גּוֹיִם "nations"; the reading גֵּאִים "proud ones" has been proposed by Duhm and other earlier scholars, and more recently by Rosenbaum, *HUCA* 45 (1974) 65–70. Though Rosenbaum makes a strong case for the possibility of the confusion or conflation of the terms, it remains in the realm of possibility rather than probability, and is determined in the last resort more by general exegetical considerations than by the possibility of an alternative reading of the text.

6.b. For MT אִבַּדְתָּ "you caused to perish," *G* presupposes a text וְאָבַד, of which רָשָׁע is the subject; "the wicked has perished".

7.a. הָאוֹיֵב "the enemy" is taken as a collective term, and thus is followed by a plural verb.

7.b. חֳרָבוֹת is understood as "ruins," though if the initial letter were pointed with *hateph pathah*, the word could be rendered "swords" (for which there is some evidence in the Heb. mss; De-Rossi, IV, 3; cf. *G*): "the swords of the enemy have been finished." But this possibility is unlikely in view of the syntax of the Hebrew line.

7.c. "You have uprooted" (reading נָתַשְׁתָּ); alternatively, "you have abandoned," reading נָטַשְׁתָּ, for which there is some evidence in the Heb mss (De-Rossi, IV, 3).

7.d. "Cities" (עָרִים); Dahood (*Psalms I*, 55) proposes to translate "gods" ("root out their gods"), deriving עָרִים from an Ugaritic root *ġyr*, "to protect" (viz. "protector," hence "gods"). But this proposal is almost certainly wrong. Ugaritic *ġyr* means "to be jealous" (though there may be at least two roots *ġyr*). Ugaritic forms such as *ġr*, *tġr*, which carry the sense "protect," are almost certainly derived from the root *nġr*, "to protect," which in turn is related to Hebrew נצר. See further Caquot et al., *Textes ougaritiques I*, 315, 595; Gibson, *CML²*, 153; Gordon, *UT*, #1670.

8.a. הֵמָּה "they," according to the current verse division, belongs with v 7: "the *very* memory of them" (cf. RSV). But the syntax is curious, and הֵמָּה looks like the first word in the strophe beginning with ה in the acrostic pattern (though a strophe is missing). Leveen, *VT* 21 (1971) 48–58, undertakes massive emendation, resulting in good sense and the restoration of both a ד-strophe and a ה-strophe; but the emendation is scarcely warranted by the text or versions. Dahood's solution (*Psalms I*, 56) is at first attractive: הֵמָּה is rendered "Behold" on the basis of Ugaritic *hm*, said to mean "behold." But it is almost certain that Ugaritic *hm* means "if" in all contexts (equivalent to Heb. אִם); see J. C. De Moor, "Ugaritic *hm*—Never 'Behold'," *UF* 1 (1969) 201–2. Thus the translation above assumes minor emendation to: הִנֵּה "behold" (see Gray, *The Forms of Hebrew Poetry*, 273). Alternatively, הֵמָּה could be retained in v 7, and v 8 translated: "But the Lord shall reign. . . ."

8.b. Literally, "shall sit" (as king).

9.a. Both *S* and a few Heb. mss (De-Rossi, IV, 3) indicate the omission of יָדִין "he shall adjudicate" and the reading וּלְאֻמִּים "and to the peoples"; but MT makes satisfactory sense as it stands.

12.a. "Enthroned of Zion"; alternatively, "the Inhabitant of Zion."

13.a. "Avenger of Blood"; see also Gen 9:5.

13.b. The words עָנִי "afflicted" (in both singular and plural) and עָנָו (in the plural) are used frequently in Pss 9–10; see 9:13, 14, 19; 10:2, 9, 17. There appears to be some confusion in MT as to the appropriate forms: (a) 9:13 עֲנִיִּים (but *Qere* עֲנָוִים); (b) 9:19 עֲנָוִים (but *Qere* עֲנִיִּים); (c) 10:17 עֲנָוִים (but some mss, *G* and *S*, imply עֲנִיִּים). The problem is compounded by semantics; while it is possible in certain contexts that עָנִי and עָנָו have different meanings, in other cases it seems clear that the two terms are virtually synonymous: "poor, afflicted, humble" (BDB, 776). The translation above assumes that the terms are virtually synonymous, but the translation may be nuanced according to context. Although the terms may have a technical sense in the Psalms, it is more likely that they simply refer to the poor and afflicted in general, and that a specific connotation may only be implied by the context in certain psalms; for a balanced discussion of the problem see Anderson, *Psalms I*, 269–70.

14.a. חָנֲנֵנִי; the preferred reading is חָנֵּנִי "be gracious to me", following the evidence of numerous Heb. mss (De-Rossi, IV, 3), including *C*.

14.b. "My guardian": literally, "the one raising me up."

17.a. נוֹקֵשׁ "striking down," following MT, is translated as a participle referring to divine action. Alternatively, after *G* and *S*, the consonants could be vocalized as Niph. perf. of יָקֹשׁ, and רָשָׁע taken as the subject: "the wicked are trapped . . ." (cf. RSV).

17.b. "Higgaion": The word appears to relate either to the manner of singing or to the musical accompaniment. Mowinckel has suggested "musical flourish"; *The Psalms in Israel's Worship,* II, 211. But if the word is derived from the root הגה ("to moan, sigh, muse"), it might imply *soft* singing or accompaniment and could thus indicate that the concluding verses of the psalm (those following *Higgaion*) should be rendered quietly, as befits the solemn theme. The word is also used in Ps 92:4 of lyre music, though that context does not remove the ambiguity.

18.a. "Shall return" (יָשׁוּבוּ): the concept of *returning* to Sheol is analogous to "returning to the dust" (viz. death), which is of the essence of mankind (see Gen 3:19).

19.a. The second line of the verse contains no explicit negative particle. Either the negative of the first line (לֹא) may be assumed to function as a "double-duty negative" (Dahood, *Psalms I*, 58), or an original לֹא must be restored in the text, with some support from Heb. mss (De-Rossi, IV, 4) and the unanimous witness of the versions.

19.b. On "the afflicted," see v 13, note b (above).

21.a. "Fear": the translation assumes the reading מוֹרָא for MT's מוֹרֶה "teaching", for which there is both mss evidence (De-Rossi, IV, 4) and support from some versions (Theodotian, Aquila, et al).

21.b. "They are only human": literally, "they are man."

Form/Structure/Setting (Pss 9–10)

The principal problem pertaining to Pss 9 and 10 concerns whether they should be treated as a unity, namely a single acrostic psalm, or whether they should be treated as separate and independent psalms. As they stand in most Heb. mss, they are two psalms, and the impression of two distinct psalms is initially reinforced by the contents: Ps 9 appears to be an *individual hymn,* whereas Ps 10 appears to be an *individual* (or perhaps communal) *lament.* On the other hand, there are a number of reasons for supposing that the psalms originally comprised a single literary unit.

(a) There is an acrostic pattern (partially obscured), which begins in Ps 9 and concludes in Ps 10.

(b) Certain versions treat the two psalms as a single literary unit (e.g. *G* and *Vg*), as do some Heb. mss (De-Rossi, IV, 4).

(c) Ps 10 lacks a title, which is unusual in Book I of the Psalter and may indicate that Ps 10 originally belonged with Ps 9.

(d) The psalms share a variety of distinctive words and expressions of which the following are only a sample: (i) "times of trouble" (9:10 and 10:1); (ii) the "afflicted" (9:13, 19; 10:2, 9, 17); (iii) "man" (אֱנוֹשׁ; 9:20 and 10:18); (iv) the "oppressed" (9:20 and 10:18); (v) the common use of the rare relative pronoun זוּ (9:16 and 10:2).

In 1906, A. F. Kirkpatrick wrote: "The two psalms present an unsolved literary problem" (*The Book of Psalms,* 42); Kirkpatrick himself preferred to understand the psalms in terms of two separate literary units. The problem remains unsolved from a technical perspective, but nevertheless, an hypothesis may be presented in an attempt to account for the variety of data.

It may be supposed that initially, there existed a single alphabetic acrostic psalm, in which each "strophe," beginning with the consecutive letters of the alphabet, comprised four poetic lines. The original psalm would have contained elements of both praise and lament, which is not in itself unusual or any indication of lack of unity (see further Mowinckel, *The Psalms in Israel's Worship,* I, 95). At the time of the incorporation of the single psalm into the Psalter (or into one of the earlier collections; see the title, v 1), one may envisage either of two possibilities. (a) The editor divided the psalm into two and modified each psalm slightly (thus partially obscuring the acrostic pattern), for reasons which are no longer clear; the use of SELAH and HIGGAION (9:17, 21) may be indicative of a liturgical reason for the modification. (b) Or, if the original psalm were ancient, the text before the editor may have been incomplete, or partially destroyed; the psalm would then be restored in two units (an examination of the *Notes* will indicate the problem areas pertaining to translation and stichometry which give rise to this suggestion). On the other hand, the translators of *G* (and other versions, and certain Heb. mss) restored the unity, basing their restoration on the clear remnants of the acrostic pattern, and perhaps also on the basis of the commonality of language and the absence of a title in Ps 10. Such an hypothesis is inevitably speculative, but if it is even partially correct, it implies that an initial interpretation should take two levels into account, that of an initial text, a unity, in which the themes of thanksgiving and lament are intimately interwoven, and that of the subsequent use of two psalms in Israel's worship, in which the emphasis on lament (Ps 10) has been separated from that of praise (Ps 9). Even if the two psalms are treated separately, the themes cannot be entirely disentangled. In Ps 9, God is at the center of the stage, though wicked persons and enemies are present; in Ps 10, the wicked stand in the limelight, though ultimately it is God who is victorious (10:12–18). Thus, although one may distinguish between praise and lament in terms of literary categories, the psalms are nevertheless intimately interrelated in the context of religious experience.

The date and authorship of the two psalms cannot be determined with certainty; the view of the older commentators that the psalms were Davidic is not without merit (e.g. Delitzsch, *Psalms,* I, 204), though it cannot be established. The substance of the psalms lends itself to a royal interpretation, at least in the initial stage of their history (cf. Eaton, *Kingship and the Psalms,* 32–33). The exclusive use of זו as a relative pronoun might be taken as a further indication of antiquity; see also its use in Exod 15:16, an ancient Hebrew victory song. (The single occurrence of אשׁר in 10:16, should be pointed as a noun, "happiness"; see the *Notes*). The use of the acrostic pattern need not imply a late date, as has sometimes been argued, though neither does it indicate an early date; see the *Excursus* on acrostic psalms following Ps 10. Probably all that can be claimed with reasonable confidence is that the two psalms come from the time of the monarchy (perhaps as early as the united monarchy) and that they continued to be used in Israel's worship in the postexilic period and beyond.

In the paragraphs that follow, the *Comment* has been given separately for each psalm; the *Explanation* is based on both psalms, though with an emphasis on Ps 10. Such an approach, together with this section on both psalms, effects a compromise with respect to the unity and distinctiveness of Pss 9–10.

Comment (Ps 9)

The acrostic pattern of Pss 9–10 imposes a literary structure on the psalms which determines to some extent the progression of the poet's thought.

Hence, in the *Comment*, the pattern is followed, rather than attempting to find larger units of thought in the grouping of several verses, as has been done in the *Comment* on nonacrostic psalms in this commentary. Psalm 9 covers the first eleven letters of the alphabet (כ–א), of which only *daleth* is missing; there is some irregularity in the length of the units or "strophes," though the normal length is four lines (usually two verses).

א (9:2–3). The psalmist begins by expressing his intention of praising God. Though the entire unit is characterized by close parallelism, the successive lines elaborate upon the nature of the praise: it involves the public *recounting* of God's work, the experience of *rejoicing* and *exultation*, and the *singing* of praise concerning God's *name*. Such praise embraces the whole being, and as an expression of love for God it comes from the whole *heart* (v 2a; cf. Deut 6:5). The two specific objects of praise are the "wonderful works" of God and the "name" of God; the two are intimately related. Through his divine name, God revealed himself to his people in redemption (viz. in historical experience) and in creation (cf. Ps 8:2 and *Comment*). It was this special understanding of both historical experience and divine creation, through God's revelation of his name, that made Israel identify these experiences, and the world within which they were set, as God's "wonderful works." But the psalmist has a more personal note, for his intention to praise God issues not only from the knowledge and remembrance of such works in the past, but from anticipation of God's deliverance from a specific situation and from a current experience. Yet it is the knowledge of God's past works which provides understanding and hope in the current experience, and thus releases the desire to praise, as expressed here.

ב (9:4–5). The grounds for confidence lie in anticipation, rather than the present experience of deliverance. The psalmist is confident that his enemies will turn back in retreat, giving up their attack on him; in panic-stricken retreat, they would be thrown to the ground and perish. The coming defeat of the enemies lay not in the psalmist's own strength; that defeat lay in the power of God, who is depicted here as a Judge. God judges righteously, but the psalmist has been attacked without cause and treated unrighteously; thus, he is confident that God has taken up his cause, and in declaring righteous judgment, he will eventually bring about the ruin of unrighteous enemies.

ג (9:6–7). Now the psalmist's words contain both remembrance of God's past acts and anticipation of his future acts. Wicked persons, enemies, even nations, have been dealt with by God in the past; they surely would be in the future. The divine rebuke had created total disaster for enemy nations: their name was wiped out, their cities destroyed, and the memory of them lost. The two ideas of the wiping out of the *name* and the loss of *memory* of nations are closely interrelated, recalling both the terrible words concerning Amalek (Exod 17:14), but also the disaster which once had threatened even Israel (Deut. 9:14). The concern for the continuation of the "name" (in effect, posterity), and hence the continuation of remembrance, is significant both in Israelite literature (e.g. in the institution of Levirate marriage, Deut 25:5–10; see Craigie, *The Book of Deuteronomy*, 313–15), and in Near Eastern literature, such as that from ancient Ugarit (the concern is expressed both in the Aqht text and the Krt text from Ugarit; cf. R. T. O'Callaghan, *VT* 4 [1954]

164–66). Thus, the psalmist recalls the total nature of God's acts of judgment in the past and anticipates his own deliverance in the future.

ז (missing).

ח (9:8–9). *The Lord shall reign:* literally, "shall sit," which is clarified in the following line—his throne is established for the execution of judgment. These verses amplify the earlier references to God as one who judges righteously (v 5). Though the judgment of God may result in disaster (vv 6–7), it is undertaken in righteousness and equity, so that only the wicked need fear the divine throne. But the word picture painted here is not one of final and eschatological judgment; the psalmist experiences present enemies and anticipates the present reality of deliverance. His anticipation is based on the conviction that God is seated, that—despite his experience of affliction—God is still on the throne!

י (9:10–11). The metaphor now changes from that of God as Judge to that of God as "refuge," a word meaning literally "stronghold, place with high fortifications" (cf. Isa 25:12). Yet the two metaphors are intimately related, for the same God who appears as awesome Judge to the wicked, offers refuge to the oppressed in their times of trouble. Whereas the Judge will wipe out the *names* of the wicked (v 6), those who know God's *name* have a foundation for trust; on God's *name*, see further vv 2–3 (above). "You have not forsaken": again, the words express the psalmist's confidence, for the nature of his crisis is precisely that it appears that God has forsaken his own and left them at the mercy of their enemies.

ז (9:12–13). The psalmist began by declaring his own intention of praising God, but now the theme of praise is broadened and the two imperatives with which this section opens are a call for all "the afflicted" (v 13) to join in the praise of God. This invitation to praise emerges spontaneously from the conviction of v 11, that God has not forsaken his own; therefore, they should praise him. God is referred to by two epithets: (a) "the Enthroned of Zion"; (b) "the Avenger of Blood." The first refers to the symbolic presence of God in the world, particularly as it was symbolized by the Ark of the Covenant in the temple in Jerusalem (Zion). The words claim God's presence, for God's throne was in heaven, yet also in a sense on the earth (cf. Ps 11:5); but the might of enemies made God seem distant, or heavenly only, yet in praising God as the "Enthroned of Zion," it was his immanent presence which was praised in hopeful expectation. The expression "Avenger of Blood" indicates that God, who was the giver of all life, also acted as judge of those who took, or attempted to take, human life (cf. Gen 4:10 and 9:5). Thus, God would act as avenger against those who sought the psalmist's life. The word translated "avenger" is literally "seeker"; God does not forsake those who *seek* him (v 11), but *seeks* out those who bring about affliction.

ח (9:14–15). The praise of the previous verses now turns into an intensely personal prayer, though the subject matter of the prayer in turn is intimately related to the substance of the invitation to praise (vv 12–13). "Be gracious to me": these words imply the context of the prayer—see also Ps 4:2. The psalmist explicitly prays for deliverance from the affliction caused by enemies, which has brought him close to the "gates of death." Thus the "Avenger of Blood" (v 13) and the "guardian" (v 14) represent two faces of the same

God: the "Avenger," who seeks out those that try to kill, will also be a "guardian" to those in danger of being killed, who stand at the gates of death in
imminent danger of gaining admission. When prayer was answered, then
the psalmist would be able to praise God "in the gates" (viz. in the public
concourses) of the "daughter of Zion," namely Jerusalem; these words tie in
the prayer with the earlier praise of God as the "Enthroned of Zion" (v 12).

ט (9:16–17). The theme now returns to the disaster awaiting the wicked
as a consequence of the judgment of God. But the nature of the judgment
is expressed once again in terms of the boomerang effect of evil (see also
Ps 5:11). The "pit" and "net" prepared for the innocent become the trap
of the guilty perpetrators of the plot. The poet expresses again the sense
of tension between past and future, though real confidence for the future
emerges explicitly only in vv 18–19. "The Lord has revealed himself": the
words refer partly to God's self-revelation in judgment, but partly they anticipate the "re-appearance of God," for to the psalmist in distress, it appeared
that God was no longer there. The revelation struck terror in the hearts of
the wicked, but hope in those oppressed by wickedness.

י (9:18). This apparently short strophe must be read in conjunction with
כ below. On "Sheol," see the *Comment* on Ps 6:6. The nations that "forget
God" shall go to Sheol where *there is no memory* of God (cf. 6:6)! On memory
and forgetfulness with respect to God and the actions of God, see further
Deut 8.

כ (9:19–21). "The poor will not always be forgotten": that God does not
forget his own is expressed by way of contrast to the nations that "forget"
God (v 18). The word "poor" is synonymous with "afflicted," in this context,
and refers not to the absence of wealth, but to those righteous servants of
God who suffer unjustly at the hands of evil persons, yet whose "hope" (or
"expectation" of God's intervention) does not "perish"—though the enemies
who are the cause of such suffering shall indeed "perish" (v 4).

"Arise, O Lord:" see further the *Comment* on Ps 7:7. The word employed
for "humans" (אנוש; v 20 and cf. v 21) explicitly refers to *mortal* humans,
with all the implications of human fragility and weakness in contrast to God:
see also 10:18; 2 Chr 14:11; and Job 4:17. Yet, for all the supposed weakness
of *humans,* the psalmist's mortal enemies seemed to be prevailing, so he prays
that they will not prevail and that they will be judged. "Fear" (v 21): the
word implies a *fearsome act,* such as the Exodus from Egypt (see the use of
the same word in Deut 4:34), which would cast terror into all those who
observed it (see Exod 15:14–16) and remind them of their mere mortality.

(For Bibliography and Form/Structure/Setting, see Ps 9, above)

Translation (Ps 10)

¹ (ל)	O Lord, why ᵃ do you stand at a distance,ᵇ		(4+3)
	why ᵃ do you conceal yourself in times of trouble?		
²	In arrogance, the wicked hotly pursue the afflicted.		(4+4)
	Let them be caught up in the devices they have planned.		
3–4 ᵃ	For the wicked has boasted of his innermost desires,ᵇ		(4+2)
	and the robber has cursed ᶜ		

(נ)	The wicked, with his haughty face,[d] has spurned the Lord.	(5+4+3)
	"He does not call to account!"[e] "There is no God!"	
	Such are all his devices!	
5	His ways[a] are always firm.[b]	
(ם?)	Your judgments are removed[c] from him;	(3+3)
	as for all his adversaries, he snorts at them!	
6[a]	He said to himself: "I won't slip throughout all generations.	(4+3)
	Happiness without misfortune!"[b]—so has he sworn.[c]	
7 (פ)	His mouth is full of deceit and oppression;	(4+4)
	under his tongue are trouble and iniquity.	
8	He lies in ambush in the villages;[a]	(3+3)
	in the secret places he slays[b] the innocent.	
(ע)	His eyes are lurking for the luckless;[c]	(3+4)
9	he sets an ambush in the secret place like a lion in its covert.	
	He sets an ambush to catch the afflicted;	(3+4)
	he catches the afflicted when he drops him into his net.	
10 (צ?)	(The righteous)[a] is crushed[b] and sinks down,	(3+3)
	and the hapless host[c] falls into his claws.[d]	
11	He said to himself: "God has forgotten.	(4+4)
	He has hidden his face.[a] He never saw!"	
12 (ק)	Arise,[a] Lord God! Lift up your hand![b]	(5+2)
	Don't forget the afflicted!	
13	Why has the wicked spurned God?	(4+4)
	He said to himself: "You do not[a] call to account."	
14 (ר)	You have seen the trouble and vexation, yes you have![a]	(4+3)
	You will continue to observe, to requite[b] by your hand.	
	Upon you, the hapless abandons[c] himself;	(3+4)
	as for the orphan, you have been a helper.	
15 (ש)	Break the arm of the wicked and evil!	(4+3)
	Call his wickedness into account—surely[a] you can find it!	
16	The Lord is king forever and ever;	(4+3)
	let the nations perish[a] from his earth!	
17 (ת)	You have heard the desire of the afflicted, O Lord;	(4+4)
	you will strengthen their heart; you will incline your ear.	
18[a]	Once again[b], he will continue to execute judgment	
	for orphan and oppressed,	(5+3)
	to terrify mere earthlings![c]	

Notes

1.a. The interrogative למה "why" is used once, but extends its meaning to both lines of the verse; see also Ps 2:1–2.

1.b. ברחוק: the more common form would be מרחוק "from afar," for which there is evidence in one Heb ms (De-Rossi, IV, 4). But, as Dahood points out, the preposition ב may have the force of "from" (as in Ugaritic); *Psalms I*, 61.

3.–4.a. The difficulties in translating vv 3–4 pertain primarily to the stichometric analysis; the analysis adopted here assumes the break between the verses after ברך, here "curse," and the נ-strophe beginning with נאץ "spurn" (the מ-strophe being incomplete or missing).

3.–4.b. "Innermost desires": literally, "desire of his soul/self."

3.–4.c. "Has cursed": for this sense of ברך, see Job 1:5.

3.–4.d. "With his haughty face": reading בגבה, for which there is extensive evidence in the Heb. mss. (De-Rossi, IV, 4).

3.–4.e. "He does not call to account": see further v 13 (below), which recapitulates the essence of v 4.

5.a. "Ways": reading a plur. noun with suffix (דרכיו), as indicated by Qere and Q.

5.b. "Are . . . firm," from חיל/חול (II); alternatively, following the implications of G, the consonantal text could be interpreted as a Niph. from חלל: "his ways (viz. God's) are profaned" (cf. De-Rossi, IV, 4–5).

5.c. "Are removed": this translation (prompted by G) assumes the emendation of מרום to סרו (ס mistaken for מ, and the final ם inserted by dittography). If this is correct, the ס-strophe in the acrostic pattern is restored. Alternatively, retaining MT, translate: "Your judgments are on high . . ." (see RSV).

6.a. The stichometric analysis again poses problems; I have taken אלה (in v 7 in MT) as the last word of v 6, thus preserving the beginning of the פ-strophe in פיהו (v 7) and revealing the chiastic structure of the original v 6: "He said to himself" (A); "I won't slip. . . ." (B): "Happiness. . . ." (B'); "so has he sworn" (A').

6.b. "Happiness without misfortune": by any standards, the line is difficult. My translation assumes pointing אשר, not as a relative pronoun (as MT), but as a noun, "happiness" (cf. Gen 30:13). The words thus indicate the wicked man's motto.

6.c. אלה—"he has sworn"; see 1 Kgs 8:31 for the use of this verb in the sense of taking an oath. Dahood translates the term cursing, citing Ugaritic ʾalt by way of evidence (plus the cognate term in a Phoenician incantation). The Ugaritic evidence is misleading. The Ugaritic word ʾalt is commonly translated "throne," or some other word generally synonymous to ksʾu, with which it stands in parallelism; Dahood has recognized this meaning of the term in Ugaritic-Hebrew Philology, 51 (cf. Gordon, UT #211). The particular text cited in support of the meaning cursing is UT 1001.2.2. (=PRU II, 1.2), which Dahood claims is in the nature of an incantation; but the opening two lines of the text are difficult to read, with breaks in the text at the beginning and the middle, which render the text difficult to translate and of uncertain syntax. Virolleaud (PRU II, 3) noted the fact that ʾalt is usually equivalent to ksʾu, but wisely left the term untranslated. For a full discussion of the possible etymology, see P. J. van Zijl, A Study of Texts in Connexion with Baal in the Ugaritic Epics, 235–36. In summary, a translation of אלה as cursing, on the basis of Ugaritic evidence, is not convincing. A more convincing argument might be made on the basis of Judg 17:2, though it remains ambiguous in that context whether general cursing is implied, or the more formal taking of an oath.

8.a. "In the villages": reading בחצרים, the initial preposition apparently having been omitted in the text by haplography. Note the chiastic structure of v 8a–b.

8.b. יהרג; G implies the inf. constr. in a causal sense (להרג): "in order to slay. . . ."

8.c. חלכה: luckless; the precise meaning of the term is uncertain (see also חלכא'ם in v 10). A few Heb. mss insert a yodh: חילכה (De-Rossi, IV, 5). For further discussion of the problems pertaining to the term, see Barr, Comparative Philology and the Text of the Old Testament, (Oxford: Clarendon Press, 1968) 228–29.

10.a. The first line of the verse is unusually short in the context of the psalm as a whole, and its position is such that one might expect it to begin the צ-strophe. Hence צדיק "righteous" has been inserted, though it must be admitted that this is a speculative restoration (cf. NEB, and Gray, The Forms of Hebrew Poetry, 283–84).

10.b. ודכה (Kethib): Qere indicates ידכה; Qere has been followed with respect to the consonants and pointed as Niph. imperf.

10.c. חלכאים could be a variant of חלכה "luckless" (v 8), but Qere indicates חיל כא'ם; Qere has been followed above and translated "hapless host." Although a variant form of חלכה is possible, it is more likely that the poet employed phonetically similar terminology for poetic effect.

10.d. בעצומיו has been the source of several problems. BDB (783) suggests "his mighty ones" (i.e. claws of a lion). Dahood, on the other hand, translates "into his pit," postulating a root עצם "to dig," on the basis of Ugaritic ʿẓm, which (he claims) means "dig, burrow" (Psalms I, 63–64); UT 75 [CTA 12] 1.23–25 is cited in support. The Ugaritic text, however, does not unambiguously support Dahood's proposal, nor does it give clear evidence of the root ʿẓm ("burrow, dig") in Ugaritic:

kry ʾamt ʿpr   "Dig (with) the forearm the dust,
ʿẓm yd ʾugrm   (with) the bone of the hand the soil."

On this translation and the meaning of *ʿẓm*, see further Caquot et al., *Textes ougaritiques I*, 339. However, the association of Ugaritic *ʿẓm* with *yd* "hand" might give further support to the meaning *claws* for עצמיו; viz., the "bones" (of the hands) are poetically described as "claws," thus heightening the simile of the lion employed in v 9.

11.a. הסתיר "he has hidden"; Hiph. of סתר. It is surely unnecessary to suppose with Dahood (*Psalms I*, 64) that this verb is an infixed-t form of סור ("to turn away"). The root סתר is far more likely, particularly since a noun from the same root has already been used (vv 8–9). Just as the wicked lies hidden, so too he vainly hopes that God has hidden his face!

12.a. "Arise": see also 7:7 and 9:20.

12.b. "Your hand": some Heb. mss indicate the plural, "your hands" (ידיך), both here and in v 14.

13.a. "You do not": alternatively, "he does not. . . ." (after *G* and *S*); see also v 4 (above).

14.a. "Yes you have": translating כי אתה "for you" as emphasizing the subject of ראתה "you have seen."

14.b. On the sense "to requite" for לתת (נתן), see Briggs, *The Book of Psalms*, 87.

14.c. יעזב "abandons": the translation assumes as reflexive sense of the verb עזב, "to leave, forsake, abandon." Dahood's proposal for a verb עזב (II), meaning "to put, place," on the basis of Ugaritic *ʿdb* is possible. It is not, however, entirely convincing for Ugaritic *ʿdb* (I) has the basic sense of "make, prepare" (cf. Gibson, *CML²*, 154), from which "set, put" emerges as a secondary sense.

15.a. בל: commonly a negative "not," the word may also function to emphasize the affirmative; see KB, 126.

16.a. אבדו "perish": the verb is interpreted as an optative perfect (see Dahood, *Psalms I*, 66, after I. Eitan).

18.a. The syntax of v 18 is difficult. I have taken לשפט "to judge" to be parallel to לערץ "to terrify," both governed by יוסיף "will continue"; God, the subject, will continue to do two contrasted things, to execute judgment on behalf of the weak, but strike terror in the hearts of mortal humans who think there is no God (v 4). בל is taken in an affirmative sense; see v 15, note a (above).

18.b. Dahood (*Psalms I*, 67) renders עוד (translated above by "once again") as "the arrogant," from a root עדד, related to Ugaritic *ǵdd* ("to swell up"). The Ugaritic root is used only once in this sense in the Ugaritic corpus, in *CTA* 3.2.25 (from which it may be restored in *CTA* 7.1.7.). In this text, it is used unambiguously of mirth: *tǵdd kbdh bṣḥq*—"her liver swells up with laughter." The Ugaritic evidence adds little to Dahood's proposed translation "the arrogant," and the Arabic evidence, such as it is, would imply no more than "the irritated."

18.c. "Mere earthlings"—literally, "man from the earth." אנוש "man," here, appears to refer to the *wicked*, in contrast to the "orphan and oppressed"; see further 9:20, *Comment*.

Comment

As with Ps 9, so here the comment follows the acrostic pattern of the psalm, though it has not been preserved as clearly as in the former psalm. Psalm 10 carries the pattern forward from ל (v 1) to ת (v 17). The letter מ, however, is missing; נ and ס have been restored tentatively (see the *Notes* on vv 3–4, and v 5) and the letters פ and ע occur in the reverse of the common sequence. (See further the *Excursus* on Acrostic Psalms following the commentary on Ps 10.)

ל (10:1–3b). *Times of trouble* (see also 9:10) are created not merely by the presence and plots of enemies, but by the apparent absence of God at the time when the need of God is sensed most urgently. It seems that God is at a distance and concealed, when his presence and visibility are immediately required, and so the psalmist expresses his question: *Why?* He requires not merely deliverance, but asks for the judgment of those wicked persons who press in on him. They are *arrogant* (v 2), for they think they can pursue the afflicted in absolute immunity from any reaction by God; the psalmist asks that their immunity be punctured by the return of their own evil plots upon themselves (see also 9:16). If God's power were self-evident, the wicked would keep their innermost desires to themselves and robbers would not dare to curse, but the problem facing the psalmist is the apparent absence of God; the wicked, also perceiving that apparent absence, do not even bother to hide their innermost desires and lusts, and the robbers openly curse, thinking themselves safe from any retribution for their evil.

מ (missing).

נ (10:3c–5a). In this section and the following (through to v 11), the psalmist dwells morbidly on the nature of wicked persons and their affliction of the innocent; for the moment, his faith and confidence have sagged, as depressing thoughts weigh upon his mind. The whole section is governed by v 1; that is, the wicked are magnified in his mind, precisely because God appears to be distant and concealed.

The imagined words of the wicked indicate cléarly their frame of mind and the structure of belief which permits their action. God "does not call to account"; literally, "does not seek"; thus the wicked deny any reality to that epithet of God, that he is the "Avenger (or Seeker) of Blood"; see further the *Comment* on 9:13. The wicked are practical atheists, affirming that with respect to their actions, God is otiose (see further *Explanation*, below), and thus they plan devices (v 4; see also v 2) against the afflicted with an unburdened conscience. To the external observer, the wicked person has all the characteristics which he should not have; his ways appear to be always *firm*, though those of the afflicted are very shaky indeed. Once again, it is the problem of injustice and the apparent inversion of values which looms so large in the psalmist's mind.

ס (10:5b–6). The theme continues: the wicked person lives in apparent freedom from either divine judgment or human oppression. Divine judgment never seems to touch him, and when human adversaries arise, he is sufficiently powerful to *snort* at them in rage and ignore their threat. He lives by two mottos, which are entirely unjust and unfair from the perspective of the righteous sufferer. "I won't slip": yet (by way of contrast) the afflicted slipped into trouble so easily, though they did not deserve it. The problem with the wicked was that they deserved to slip, but did not, and thus their ungodly motto appeared to be true. And they had another motto: "happiness without misfortune"; again, the issues of Job and all righteous sufferers are raised. Why is it that evil persons appear to live in a state of happiness with impunity, while the righteous so frequently suffer misfortune (cf. Job 21:7–16)? It was not merely affliction which disturbed the righteous, but the apparent absence of values. A practical and empirical theology, based upon experience and observation of the way people lived, appeared to indicate that the wicked were right: God did not appear to call the wicked to account, and the afflicted continued in their affliction.

פ (10:7–8b). In both speech and action, the wicked person was a source of trials to others. His speech was deceitful; his words created oppression and endless trouble. The simple villager, or the innocent passer-by, was never safe, but in constant danger of being ambushed or slain. The Hebrew poetry conveys the implication that the trouble and iniquity which are "under his tongue" are a source of pleasurable taste and genuine delight to the wicked person; see further Kirkpatrick, *The Book of Psalms I*, 53. The wicked person not only speaks evil, but positively delights in it!

ע (10:8c–9). With two metaphors and a simile, the poet describes still further the nature of the wicked person. (a) He is a brigand or robber, waiting in ambush for the innocent (v 8c; cf. v 8a–b); (b) he is like a lion in hiding, waiting and ready to pounce; (c) he is a hunter who has set his net to catch the prey. But while this poetic language illustrates vividly the nature of the wicked, it also illuminates the mental anguish of the righteous. For all the things which the wicked person did, and appeared to get away with, were precisely the things which the righteous person had been taught to avoid, from the days of his childhood education. In the proverbial instruction of the wise men, the young were explicitly instructed to avoid the company of violent persons, who sought to gain personal profit through ambushing the poor and innocent (Prov 1:11–18). Again, it was the apparent injustice of the situation which weighed so heavily on the psalmist's mind.

צ (10:10–11). The wicked plot and lie in wait, but now, as the psalmist points out, comes the real calamity—they are successful in catching their luckless and righteous prey! It was bad enough that they were wicked; that they should be successful compounded the problem. And again, the imaginary words of the wicked person illustrate his philosophy of life. God forgets such evil acts, if he sees them at all; more probably, he doesn't see a thing! The inactivity of God, which gives such great confidence to the wicked, is the same apparent inactivity which creates such grave concern for the psalmist.

ק (10:12–13). At last the psalmist breaks free from the oppressive weight of his meditation on the wicked, and he does it by proclaiming words reminiscent of an ancient battle cry: "Arise, Lord God!" (cf. Num 10:35). It is as if he has had enough of sitting trembling in the trenches; he is going to arise and face the enemy and asks God himself to arise with him. But the strength to conquer lies with God alone: "Lift up your hand." The lifting of the divine hand symbolizes not only the strength of God, but also a declaration of God's hostility against his enemies (see the use of the expression in 2 Sam 20:21). And the psalmist, in his prayer that God *arise,* provides two grounds which require the divine action: he asks that God not *forget* the afflicted, whose hope is in God, but who is in danger of perishing (see 9:19), and that God *remember* the wicked, who spurn him and live as if God did not call human beings into account for their evil actions (v 13; see also v 3).

ר (10:14). The psalmist's confidence increases as he reflects upon the "facts of faith," rather than the empirical evidence which surrounds him. The fact is that, whatever might seem to be the case, God has seen what is going on and will continue to observe it. In reality, he is not at a distance, not concealed (v 1), but merely biding his time; eventually God would act and the hand raised in hostility and power (v 12) would exact requital. Thus the present action of the "hapless," and the former experience of the "orphan" (both of whom symbolize the afflicted), would not be in vain.

ש (10:15–16). "Break the arm": the meaning is that the psalmist asks God to break the power of the wicked persons to execute their evil acts. The

powerful "hand" of God would break the seemingly powerful "arm" of the
wicked. "Call his wickedness into account" (see also vv 4, 13); he prays that
the wicked, who have boasted so long that God does not call to account,
be proved wrong. "Surely you can find it": though the wicked may have
thought that God did not see them in their evil, or could not find evidence
of their sin, the psalmist now has confidence that nothing could be concealed
from his omniscient and omnipresent God. "The Lord is king": the kingship
of God, demonstrated so convincingly against the massive mortal might of
Egypt in the Exodus (Exod 15:18), would once again cause the destruction
of wicked persons and nations from the earth, which was the realm of God's
kingship.

ת (10:17–18). The psalm ends on a note of supreme confidence. God
has heard; God will act. God has heard the desperate prayer of the afflicted
for deliverance; he would act in strengthening their courage and continually
listening to their pleas. Divine and favorable judgment could be expected
for those who requested it and needed it, namely the "orphan" (symbolizing
the one with no protection) and the "oppressed," whereas the oppressors
would be terrified with a reminder that they were "mere earthlings," or merely
mortal; see further 9:21. The psalmist began his prayerful lament with a
desperate "Why?" He has concluded with a confidence transcending the evidence of his calamity, that God is still on his throne, still "king forever and
ever" (v 16).

Explanation

Of all the striking themes raised in Pss 9–10, there is none so provocative
and haunting as that of *atheism*. The issue is raised most clearly in Ps 10 in
the imagined words of the enemy. "There is no God" (v 4). "He has hidden
his face. He never saw!" (v 11). "He does not call to account" (vv 4, 13).
It is not the theoretical issue of atheism which is raised here, but *practical*
or *functional* atheism, which is a much more dangerous and sinister matter
for the theist. The functional atheist is not concerned so much with the theoretical question as to the existence of God; rather, he lives and behaves *as if*
God did not exist. Indeed, the functional atheist may well admit the theoretical
possibility that God does exist, but affirms by his speech and behavior that
such existence is irrelevant.

Now the theoretical atheist was rare in the ancient (pre-Greek) world of
the Eastern Mediterranean. Theoretical atheism is as difficult a position to
hold as is theism; of both theist and atheist, faith of a sort is required, though
the theist's faith (in the context of Judaism and Christianity) is based upon
revelation, while the atheist can entertain no such possibility. While the theist
may find it impossible to prove the existence of God on the basis of reason
alone, the atheist may find it equally difficult to disprove the existence of
God—hence the requirement of a sort of faith. Many moderns, who employ
for themselves the title of atheist, are really agnostics, for agnosticism is an
easier view to adopt with honesty. But there is a point to be made: true,
theoretical atheists are rare, but they are not necessarily dangerous. Indeed,
many atheists are very moral people and some great religions (such as early

Buddhism) involve a technical atheism, but at the same time are accompanied by a most profound and noble system of morality.

In contrast to the theoretical atheists, the practical or functional atheists, of whom the psalmist speaks, are a most dangerous species of human being. Ultimately, their character is determined not simply by dispensing with belief in God, but more specifically by dispensing with the concepts and precepts of morality and justice, which throughout the ancient world presupposed the existence of gods or God. And it is the absence of morality which makes the functional atheist dangerous. The functional atheist, as portrayed by the psalmist, is self-confident ("I won't slip," v 6) and desires only such things as power and happiness of a sort ("Happiness without misfortune," v 6). To gain such goals as security, wealth, power and happiness, anything goes; life and behavior are not modified by morality, are not lived beneath the horizon of justice, and are not qualified by the possibility of either human or divine judgment. The weak are there to be exploited or oppressed; the stronger may be recognized, though only for safety's sake. Their goals are entirely self-centered, and in seeking to attain them, they do not hesitate to oppress and exploit their fellow human beings.

But the haunting character of atheism in Ps 10 emerges not simply from the description of wicked persons and oppressors; it lies in the nature of the temptation faced by the righteous sufferer. As the psalmist develops his theme (10:2–11), reflecting upon the nature of these functional atheists, inevitably his faith and confidence in God, in the system of morality, and in the existence of justice, must falter. It is easy to say that God exists, to affirm that morality matters, to believe in divine and human justice, but the words carry a hollow echo when the empirical reality of human living indicates precisely the opposite. The reality appears to be that the atheists have the upper hand, that morality really does not matter and that justice is dormant. At the moment that this reality is perceived, in all its starkness, the temptation is at its strongest to jettison faith, morality and belief in justice. What good is a belief and a moral life which appear to be so out of place in the harsh realities of an evil world? Indeed, would there not be a certain wisdom in the oppressed joining ranks with the oppressors?

The psalmist did not have the option, as Christians and Jews of a later period would have, of resolving the intellectual aspects of his dilemma by resorting to an eschatological solution—by believing that beyond death, morality would be recognized and justice would be done. There is a wisdom and strength in the psalmist's position, for while many believers may find consolation in the greater concepts of eschatology, many cannot. And eschatology is rarely of immediate help to the oppressed who do not believe; they may want to believe, but the apparent absence of God from a world characterized by amorality and the evident nonexistence of justice, makes such belief impossible. The psalmist, in other words, noted a great gap between what he experienced and what he perceived, and he could not simply bridge that gap by positing a solution beyond death, or a final judgment. A present solution was required, a present deliverance, and he needed a reaffirmation of the fact that God was not distant (v 1), but close at hand, and that the righteous were not abandoned in an immoral and unjust world.

As so often in the Psalms, we do not know that deliverance came. We know only that the psalmist gained confidence that it would come and, thus armed, was able to continue living. And thereby, the psalmist offers an ever-timely warning. Belief and morality are not guarantees of happiness and stability; they do not insure benefits and security. Belief in God and the morality which must accompany that belief are, in one sense, their own rewards and promise nothing more with respect to security and a trouble-free life. But, in another sense, they do offer something more than the security and superficial happiness which characterized the life of the wicked. They offer that continuing relationship with God which imparts ultimate meaning to human existence, a relationship within which the psalmist concludes his thoughts.

Excursus III: Acrostic Psalms

A number of psalms in the Psalter have been constructed on the basis of an acrostic pattern; in every case, the acrostic is alphabetical. Although the precise character of the acrostics may differ, there are two general rules governing acrostic poetry in Hebrew. (i) The initial letters of the successive sections or units must follow the sequence of the letters of the alphabet. (ii) The lines, or units, which are opened by the letters of the alphabet, are of approximately the same length. The eight acrostic psalms in the Psalter may be summarized as follows:

Psalm	Complete/incomplete	Unit Average	Comments
9–10	Incomplete. Missing: נ. ד Restored: צ. ס. ג Reversed: פ/ע	4 lines	"For David" Hymn/lament
25	Complete. ו and ק dubious. פ at the end.	2 lines	"For David" Lament
34	Almost complete; ו missing; פ at the end.	2 lines	"For David" Mixed
37	Complete	4 lines	"For David" Wisdom
111	Complete	1 line	Hallel Hymn
112	Complete	1 line	Hallel Wisdom
119	Complete	8 verses; 16 lines	No title Wisdom
145	Almost complete. ג-section missing in most Heb mss	2 lines	"For David" Hymn

It will be noted that all the psalms fall within the limits imposed by the two general rules (above), but beyond that they display considerable diversity as to the unit average (from 1 to 16 lines) and the type. Five of the eight are "Davidic." With respect to literary type, in general categories only, some are hymns, some are laments, and some are examples of wisdom or didactic poetry. The diversity as to type may be expanded by noting the presence of further acrostic poetry outside the Psalter, of various literary types: Lam 1–4; Prov 31:10–31; Nah 1:2–8(?), Sir 51:13–30. Of the examples within the Psalter, the most complete and polished example is Ps 119; in addition to having the basic characteristics of acrostic psalms, the units themselves have an additional refinement. Each unit contains eight verses, of two lines each, and each verse in the respective units begins with the same letter.

In almost every case, the alphabetic sequence is followed carefully (Pss 37, 111, 112, 119), and the apparent omission of a letter (and its unit) can sometimes be restored on the basis of manuscript evidence or the versions (e.g. Ps 145). Pss 25 and 34 pose a problem in the absence of the *waw* and the addition of a פ-unit at the end. It is probable that the two psalms reflect a particular stage (or deviation) in the history of the alphabet, in which consonantal *waw* had been repressed and replaced by a secondary *pe* at the end of the alphabet, for which there are analogies in the derivation of Greek letters from the cursive Phoenician script, as proposed by W. Johnstone, "The Punic Ship, Acrostic Psalms and the Greek Alphabet" (paper read to the Society for Old Testament Study, July 1978).

In this larger context, the problems associated with Pss 9–10 can be seen in clearer light. The joint-psalm follows the general characteristics of acrostic psalms, but omits certain letters and is much less even and regular with respect to the average unit length than are other acrostic psalms. It would be most natural to assume either editorial modification, or textual corruption (at a very early date) to account for such divergences from the norm. It has been argued by some scholars that partial acrostics were sometimes composed and that therefore Pss 9 and 10 could be viewed as two partially acrostic psalms. Evidence for partial acrostics is usually drawn from literature of a much later date, such as Syriac poetry (Delitzsch, *Biblical Commentary on the Psalms*, I, 222) or the Qumran literature, such as 11QPs 155 (for fuller discussion, see N. H. Ridderbos, *Die Psalmen*, 141), but all the parallel evidence from within the Psalter indicates that complete alphabetic acrostics were the norm for biblical psalmody.

The precise role of the acrostic pattern cannot be determined with certainty, though a number of general roles may be proposed. (1) It was an artistic device, which provided the poet with a distinctive framework within which to express his thought. (2) It may also have been a mnemonic and educational device, to assist the young in learning poetry, which would fit well with the *wisdom* background and content of much acrostic poetry. (3) The pattern may imply completeness, that a subject is covered "from A to Z," from "Alpha to Omega." But the first of the three points above is the most fundamental, and it is not necessary to suppose that the second and third points were operative in every instance.

The origin of the alphabetic acrostic is not known, though it may be assumed to have developed independently and at an early date in the literatures of those languages which employed an alphabetic script. It used to be argued by a number of biblical scholars that the Hebrew poets borrowed (at a late date) the idea of acrostic alphabetical poetry from the Hellenistic environment, for it is known that alphabetic acrostic poetry was quite common in Greek and Hellenistic literature, and still later in Latin literature. But the possibility of such influence is highly unlikely; the Greek script was derived and adapted from the Phoenician, which in turn is related to the Hebrew. It is not necessary to suppose that the Greeks borrowed the acrostic concept from the Phoenicians, for—in the absence of extensive evidence of Phoenician poetry—such a case could not be established. Independent origin is most likely.

The proposal that the Hebrew poets were influenced by classical poets in their acrostic compositions necessarily carried with it certain implications with respect to the date of Hebrew acrostic psalms; many scholars considered them to be late. But recent research in the context of Near Eastern studies has made such a view unnecessary. The acrostic device was used in Babylonian literature, though clearly it was not an *alphabetic* acrostic (for the simple reason that an alphabet was not employed in Babylonian writing). The so-called *Babylonian Theodicy* is a dialogue written in the form of an acrostic poem; the 27 initial syllables of the acrostic made up a phrase describing in pious terms the author of the acrostic poem (see further A. Leo Oppenheim, *Ancient Mesopotamia*, 273; W. Beyerlin [ed.], *Near Eastern Religious Texts Relating to the Old Testament*, 134). The existence of a form of acrostic poetry in Babylonian literature, while it does not prove anything, undermines nevertheless the supposition that acrostics *could not* have been utilized in Hebrew poetry from an early date.

The evidence from Ugaritic literature is particularly illuminating. While no acrostic poetry has survived as such (the corpus of Ugaritic poetry is relatively small and limited as to type), there are numerous texts containing alphabets. In all, twelve Ugaritic texts are known which contain an alphabet, in whole or in part; these are conveniently brought together in *KTU* 7.5. Some are simple alphabetical texts, giving the letters of the alphabet in sequence. Others are practice tablets from students learning the writing system; they contain such things as copied epistles (for practice) followed by the letters of the alphabet (e.g. *KTU* 7.5.9), and sometimes constant repetition of the alphabet, as the student has repeated his first attempt over and again to improve his knowledge and style. What the Ugaritic alphabetic texts demonstrate is that the alphabet was thought of abstractly, that it was taught within the scribal schools of ancient Ugarit and that the ordinary scribe and pupil would have had familiarity with the alphabet and the normal sequence of letters. It is not in the least unlikely to suppose that a similar state of affairs existed in ancient Hebrew society; such information provides a broader context within which to appreciate the role and function of the Hebrew acrostic psalms.

To the evidence of the Ugaritic texts may be added that of the recently discovered "proto-Canaanite" text from near Tel Aphek in Israel, which contains the earliest known example of an abecedary outside the corpus of the Ugaritic texts. If this abecedary is Israelite, as seems possible, it provides further indication of the abstract knowledge of the sequential alphabet in Israel from a very early date, namely the time of the Judges: see further A. Demski, "A Proto-Canaanite Abecedary dating from the Period of the Judges and its Implications for the History of the Alphabet," *Tel Aviv* 4 (1977) 14–27.

Confidence in Crisis (11:1–7)

Bibliography

Morgenstern, J. "Psalm 11." *JBL* 69 (1950) 221–31. **Rinaldi, G.** "Salmo 11." *BeO* 15/3 (1973) 123–27. **Sonne, I.** "Psalm Eleven." *JBL* 68 (1949) 241–45.

Translation

[1] For the musical director. For David.[a]
  In the Lord I have sought refuge.   (2, 3+3)
  How can you say to me: [b]
    "Flutter [c] like a bird to the mountain,[d]
[2] for look, the wicked are bending [a] the bow;   (5?+3+3?)
  they have fitted their arrow [b] onto the bowstring,
  to shoot in the dark at the upright in heart"?
[3] The foundations are indeed [a] being torn down!   (3+2)
  What has the righteous done?
[4] The Lord is in his holy temple;   (3+3)
  the Lord's throne is in the heavens.

  His eyes see,[a]   (2+3?)
  his eyelids [b] scrutinize the sons of man.
[5] The Lord tests the righteous,   (3+3+2)
  but the wicked and the one loving violence—
    his soul hates! [a]
[6] He rains down on the wicked coals,[a] fire and brimstone,   (5+4)
  and a burning hot wind is the portion of their cup.
[7] But the Lord is righteous, he loves righteous deeds.   (4+3)
  The upright shall see his face.

Notes

1.a. "For David": There is some support in the Heb. mss and *G* for adding "a psalm" (מזמור).

1.b. "To me": literally, "to my soul" (לנפשי).

1.c. "Flutter": the fem. sing. form of the impv. (נודי) is read *(Qere)*, with the support of numerous Heb. mss (De-Rossi, IV, 6).

1.d. "Like a bird (to the) mountain": reading הר כמו צפור (cf. *G* and *Vg*).

2.a. "Bending": on the meaning of the verb, see the note on 7:13.

2.b. "Their arrow": alternatively, read "arrows" (חצים; cf. *G*). For a pictorial representation of birds being shot by arrows, see Keel, *Symbolism*, 95.

3.a. The introductory כִּי is interpreted as emphatic; see GKC §159ee.

4.a. "His eyes see": it is possible that this line is short. A Greek papyrus of *G* (BM 37) provides an object (οἰκουμένην) which might be rendered in Hebrew as חלד *(BHS)* or תבל (cf. J. Leveen, *VT* 21 [1971] 48–58), both meaning approximately "world." But the evidence for such a restoration is quite slender.

4.b. "His eyelids" (עפעפיו); Dahood quotes H. L. Ginsberg with approval: "It is time the practice of rendering Hebrew 'ap'appayim by 'eyelids' was discontinued. . . ." The comment was made in the context of Ugaritic 'p'pm (cf. C. H. Gordon, UT 1895). It is certainly true that the *sense* of the Heb. word in this context is "eyes," but there are good reasons for retaining the translation *eyelids*. (i) The Ugaritic evidence is ambiguous. The word 'p'pm occurs only twice in the corpus of the Ugaritic literature (CTA 14. 147 and 295), and though the translation is difficult, "eyelids" offers good sense; see Gibson, CML², 86, 154, and cf. Aistleitner, WUS, #2072. If the Ugaritic word does, or could, mean "eyes," it is probable nevertheless that the initial sense of the term was "eyelids" (on the basis of etymology) and that the secondary sense "eyes" came about through the process of metonymy; cf. Caquot et al., *Textes ougaritiques I*, 525 (note e). (ii) The word is used in this context in synonymous parallelism with עיניו "his eyes," but with respect to the word "synonymous" in the context of parallelism, it indicates complementary or balancing terms; it does not necessarily indicate synonyms in any strict sense. Thus, although it is clear that in prosaic terms the word עפעפיו in this context means "his eyes," the poetic brilliance may lie precisely in the fact that the poet used the term "eyelids."

5.a. It is difficult to be certain of the stichometry of this verse. It would be possible to translate: "The Lord tests the righteous and the wicked/and his soul hates the one loving violence" (4+4). The analysis in the translation above is preferred, for it sets out more clearly the contrast between the *righteous* and the *wicked*, which is pursued further in v 6 (the wicked) and v 7 (the righteous).

6.a. *Coals:* alternatively, a plur. constr. could be read—פחמי (cf. Symmachus), "coals of fire."

Form/Structure/Setting

The psalm is an individual *song of confidence;* see Ps 4 for further discussion. The psalmist, in imminent danger from violent enemies, has sought refuge in God and rises in confidence above the inimical threat and the temptation to flee. It is possible, though not certain, that the psalm's initial setting was in the context of the temple (see v 4), though it need not be found in the context of formal worship. God is not addressed directly, as in prayer: the psalmist reflects upon his distressing situation and then rises above it with confidence in God. The title (v 1a) may be taken to indicate that in its subsequent history, the psalm was used regularly in the context of Israel's worship.

The psalm contains two basic sections: (1) the sense of despair (11:1–3); and (2) the restoration of confidence (11:4–7). In the later use of this psalm in a liturgical context, it is possible that the transition from the first section to the second was marked by a priestly statement declaring God's coming deliverance.

Comment

The sense of despair (11:1–3). The psalmist begins by stating that he has *sought refuge in the Lord,* implying either that he has come to the temple in his time of crisis (cf. v 4), or else simply that it has always been his custom in times of crisis to seek divine protection. On this occasion, the crisis has brought with it a temptation; the temptation is to not stand and face the crisis, but to *flee like a bird to the mountain* where (from a human perspective) security might be found. The temptation may have come in the words of advice offered by a well-intentioned friend: "How can you say to me . . . ?" But it is equally likely that the words in quotation marks (vv 1–2) are the psalmist's own words, the internal voice of fear, speaking silently and temptingly in his thoughts. The temptation is powerful: the wicked enemies are already arming their weapons, and to stand firm and courageous would also be to offer a target to the wicked; flight might at least put the psalmist beyond the range of the missiles aimed against him. If the psalmist, who was innocent of any wrongdoing ("upright of heart," v 2c), stood firm, he would have little chance of protecting himself against arrows *shot in the dark* (v 2); that is, he would be vulnerable to attacks from dangerous and concealed opponents. Some scholars have suggested translating v 2c: "to shoot *like a fowl* the upright in heart" (cf. *BHS*); the emendation is in some ways attractive (though it has little support), but may miss the poet's point. To "shoot in the dark" implies either that the enemies hoped to achieve their criminal goal without being seen; yet, as the psalmist eventually perceives, the eyes of God *see* all things (v 4). The reference to hunting (the *bow*, the *arrow*, and so on) has been interpreted by Morgenstern (*JBL* 69 [1950] 229) as a description of the procedures of magicians, who under the cover of darkness undertook certain symbolic acts, such as shooting arrows, in their plots against the righteous. But such an interpretation is uncertain, and it is preferable simply to interpret the hunting language of v 2 as a development of the simile of the bird in v 1. The language expresses poetically the crisis in which the psalmist finds himself.

The worshiper's critical plight made him feel that the very foundations of life and society were being *torn down* (cf. Ezek 30:4); if the foundations were standing firm, an upright person should not be in fear of his life. "What has the righteous done?"—the cry may express the sense of despair experienced by the psalmist, namely, "what has the righteous done to deserve a plight such as this?" Or it may be that the words express a sense of helplessness: "What can the righteous do" (so RSV) in the face of such a crisis? But the sense of despair or helplessness is transformed in the remainder of the psalm to a spirit of confidence.

The restoration of confidence (11:4–7). The restoration of confidence begins with the recognition that God is still on his throne; it is effected by turning the eyes away from the threatening foes and upward toward the sovereign Lord. It is possible that the reference to God's "holy temple" indicates that the psalmist, too, is in the temple, but the poet is saying more than that. "The Lord is in his holy temple," symbolizing his presence amongst his people, but his "throne is in the heavens," signifying transcendence and might greater than that of any human enemy. It is this double recognition that gives the psalmist confidence; God is both immanent, and therefore present with him in his crisis, but also transcendent, and therefore in control of the apparent chaos of that crisis.

The poet describes the reigning Lord in the metaphor of one who tests or assays metals, though the metaphor is developed in different directions for the wicked and the upright respectively. The verb ןחב, translated "scrutinize," implies "testing, proving, assaying." And the testing of metals was done by fire, as is vividly illustrated in ancient Near Eastern iconography (see Keel, *The Symbolism of the Biblical World*, 185 for illustrations). In the translation of the metaphor, it was the all-seeing eye of God that scrutinized and examined for purity the works of all mankind (viz. the "sons of man," v 4); even the deeds of darkness (v 2) were seen by God. The testing of the righteous (v 5a), though it might involve great hardship, would culminate in purity and the removal of dross, but the testing of the wicked (the reference to the "one loving violence" presumably indicates that the psalmist's particular enemies were violent persons) evoked the divine hatred. So the metaphor changes subtly: whereas fire can be a purifying element, eliminating imperfections, it can also be a symbol of judgment. The testing of the wicked culminates not in the purifying fire, but in the "fire and brimstone" which are associated with the extermination of evil. A similar double-edged metaphor of molten metal, involving both purification and judgment, may be seen in the early hymns of the Iranian prophet, Zarathustra (e.g. *Yasna* 33), which are approximately contemporary with this psalm. The reference to the "burning hot wind" draws in another metaphor, that of the scirocco, or more precisely the *hamsin* (Arabic) or *sharab* (modern Hebrew), which blows hotly over the promised land in season, bringing with it oppressive heat from the deserts to the east and south. Such would be the lot (viz. "the portion of their cup") of the wicked.

Because God is righteous, *he loves righteous deeds* (v 7), implying either that he loves to *do* righteous deeds, or loves those that do righteous deeds; in context, the latter is more likely, so that there is here a confident expression of the love of a righteous God for a righteous person. "The upright shall see his face": the words need not imply either a specific theophany in life, or even the beatific vision beyond the grave (as proposed by Dahood, *Psalms I*, 171), but may simply indicate the coming vindication and deliverance in which the psalmist has confidence. The crisis of oppression creates the sense that God's face is hidden and that relationship has been disrupted, but deliverance restores a vision of the true state of affairs, so that it seems as if God has once again revealed himself (cf. Ps 9:17).

Explanation

In the life of faith, confidence is both a necessity and a virtue. It is a necessity, for the absence of confidence may contribute to the disintegration of life in fear and anxiety; it is a virtue, for it may lead toward the fullness of life which God intended when he granted the gift of life. But such confidence is never primarily based upon an assessment of the self; it is rooted and fixed in God. Though self-confidence may be a valuable asset in a human personality, it is confidence in God which is expressed in this short psalm.

Confidence is a characteristic which must be tempered by wisdom. Thus, there are times when confidence may be false, or unwarranted, and would lead to unnecessary danger. There are other times when confidence is entirely appropriate. Jesus was exercising appropriate confidence in his conviction that God would provide for him in his time of trial, but to have submitted to the temptation to cast himself down from the pinnacle of the temple, trusting angels to protect him (Matt 4:1-7), would have been a false form of confidence. In particular situations of crisis, a person must measure circumstances to determine the appropriate form of confidence. Therein lies a certain but unavoidable danger: the assessment of the nature of a crisis is not easy to undertake in cool objectivity, and may in itself undermine the confidence.

This is the situation in which the psalmist is placed. He is in a time of crisis; he has sought refuge in the Lord. But he had been warned, either by friends or by the inner voice of conscience, that escape would be the most appropriate course of action. Also, the advice carried within it a reminder of the might of wicked persons and of the threat contained within the crisis. There are times when such advice must be heeded, not out of fear, but out of prudence. But there are also times when it is necessary to take a stand, to refuse to admit to the natural and legitimate fear precipitated by the crisis, and to be confident in God who is still on the throne, still controlling the affairs of mankind. It was just such a situation that the psalmist encountered.

It is interesting to note that the psalmist's growth in confidence was not expressed as a consequence of prayer, as is sometimes the case. Confidence may also emerge from viewing not only the crisis (vv 1–3), but also the God who is ultimately sovereign in all crises. In this balanced assessment, the psalmist perceives something more than the immediacy of the crisis. Crisis may create a time of testing, and the end result of the test would be disaster for the wicked, but the upright could emerge beyond the trial as a better person, perceiving the face of God more clearly.

So it is that the psalmist speaks not only of a crisis provoked by enemies, but also of a crisis of confidence. The culmination of the crisis was not prayer, but praise, for when the time comes to stand and be tested, it is not the grimace of endurance which is looked for, but the acceptance of praise.

Human Flattery and Divine Speech
(12:1–9)

Bibliography

Brockington, H. L. *The Hebrew Text of the Old Testament. The Readings Adopted by the Translators of the New English Bible.* U.K.: Oxford and Cambridge University Presses, 1973. **March, W. E.** "A Note on the Text of Psalm 12:9." *VT* 21 (1971) 610–12. **Weiss, M.** "Einiges über die Bauformen des Erzählens in der Bibel." *VT* 13 (1963) 456–75.

Translation

1   For the musical director. Upon the octave.[a] A psalm of David.
2(1) *Help,*[a] *Lord, for the faithful one has come to an end,*   (4+4)
      for the honest persons [b] *have disappeared* [c] *from among the sons of man.*
3(2) *They speak vanity, each man with* [a] *his neighbor;*   (4+4?)
      with flattering [b] *lip and double heart they speak.*
4(3) *Let the Lord cut off all flattering lips,*   (4+3)
      the tongue [a] *that speaks great words,* [b]

5(4) *those who have said: "By our tongues, we will establish strength.* [a]   (4+4)
Our lips are our own! [b] *Who will be our master?"*

6(5) *"Because of the devastation* [a] *of the afflicted, because of the groaning of the poor,*
(4+4+3)

I will now arise," says the Lord.
"I will set him in safety. I will shine forth [b] *for him."*

7(6) *The utterances of the Lord are pure utterances,*   (4+3+3)
silver refined in a furnace,
gold [a] *purified seven times.*

8(7) *You, O Lord, will watch us,* [a]   (3+3?)
you will guard us [a] *from this generation for ever.* [b]

9(8) *All around the wicked strut about,*   (3+3)
as the vileness of the sons of man is exalted. [a]

Notes

1.a. "Octave": see the discussion of this term at 6:1.

2.a. *G* opens with "Help *me*," implying the existence of a suffix on the opening imperative, but MT is satisfactory and conveys the appropriate sense of urgency.

2.b. "honest persons": more precisely, "(persons of) faithfulness."

2.c. פסו "disappear": several Heb mss (De-Rossi, IV, 6) read פצו, "are dispersed," which would provide equally good sense to the line.

3.a. "with" (את): several Heb mss read אל: *"to* his neighbor" (De-Rossi, IV, 6).

3.b. The word חלקות ("flattering") is derived by Dahood (*Psalms I*, p. 73) from Ugaritic *ḫlq* ("to perish") and translated *pernicious;* see the critical remarks on this possibility in the *Note* on Ps 5:10.

4.a. *G* and *S* indicate a reading ולשון, *"and* the tongue," which is possible, but not necessary.

4.b. גדולות: literally, "great ones," the sense "great *words"* being implied by the preceding participle referring to speech.

5.a. נגביר ("we will establish strength"): the precise nuance of the Hiph. of גבר is uncertain.

5.b. "Our lips are our own" (cf. *G* on this translation); literally, "our lips are with us," though the Heb. expression is difficult (see further Anderson, *Psalms I*, 125–26).

6.a. "Devastation" (שד): Dahood translates the term שד by "sobs," including among his reasons the proposed meaning of the Ugaritic term *šdm* (*Psalms I*, 74). The text in question is *CTA* 16.i (*UT* 125). 34: *ʾal.tšt. bšdm(.)mmh.* Dahood's translation ("Let her not dry up [root *nšt*] her waters by sobbing") is similar to the earlier translation of Ginsberg (*The Legend of King Keret*, 26). But Ginsberg later admitted of this text that the "sense of lines 31–37 (is) obscure" (*ANET*, 147), and his early translation is effectively criticized in J. Gray, *The KRT Text in the Literature of Ras Shamra* [2], 1964, 67–68. Gray, who had originally held a position similar to that of Ginsberg and Dahood (in the first edition, 1955, of the work cited above), later rejected that position as untenable. The line in question should probably be translated: "Let her set in the fields her clamor . . . ," reading *šdm* in the more conventional sense (parallel to the following *bsmkt,* "heights," or perhaps "heavens": cf. Aistleitner, *WUS,* #1923), and translating *mmh* not as "her waters," but as "cry, clamor" (Aistleitner, *WUS* #1587). See further Caquot et al., *Textes ougaritiques I,* 553; Gibson, *CML* [2], 95. In summary, there is no clear evidence for an Ugaritic word *šd* meaning "sobs, sobbing." Despite the other arguments adduced by Dahood, the conventional translation of שד (above) seems most appropriate in context.

6.b. "I will shine forth": MT reads יפיח ("he will puff for it"), of which the sense is uncertain. The above translation assumes the emendation אופע (Hiph. of יפע), following the suggestion of *G* and *S,* and providing a parallel to the preceding אשית, but the emendation is by no means certain.

7.a. The latter part of the verse (v 7b-c) poses a variety of problems, and the disparity between the principal versions at this point indicates the possibility of early corruption in the text (the majority of the early translators do not appear to have worked from a consonantal text identical to that which is now MT). The solution adopted above involves only two small changes with respect to לָאָרֶץ "to the land": (i) the introductory *lamedh* is removed (on the basis of dittography; see the preceding word); (ii) the initial *aleph* is emended to ח, giving חָרֶץ "gold" (cf. L. H. Brockington, *The Hebrew Text of the Old Testament*, p. 123). This minor emendation provides good sense and good parallelism: כסף//חרץ, "silver//gold" (on this parallel word pair in Hebrew and Ugaritic poetry, see Dahood in *RSP I*, p. 234–35); צרוף//מזקק, "refined//purified."

8.a. The two verbs of this verse in MT have 3 pers. plur. and 3 pers. sing. suffixes respectively. The translation above assumes 1 pers. plur. suffixes on both verbs, for which there is good support in the Heb. mss (De-Rossi, IV, 6) and the versions (cf. *G* and *Vg*).

8.b. זו לעולם could be interpreted as a divine name, "O Eternal One" (Dahood, *Psalms I*, 75).

9.a. The latter part of v 9 has been the source of difficulty for a long time, as is evident from the differences between the various Greek versions. Modern attempts at a solution have involved a redivision of the consonants and a resolution through reading ("stars, constellation"), hence finding a reference here to astral worship; cf. J. Leveen, *VT* 21 (1971) 48–58; W. E. March, *VT* 21 (1971) 610–12. In the translation above, I have retained MT (judging the proposals of Leveen and March to be too radical): כְּ is interpreted in a temporal sense (see GKC §118u) and לְ in a genitive sense (GKC §129). Thus v 9 describes "this generation" (v 8) and develops further the theme of the flattering lips and evil speech (vv 3–5). The use of the expression "sons of man" in v 9 links up the end of the psalm with the use of the same expression in v 2, to form an inclusio.

Form/Structure/Setting

Psalm 12 is in the form of a lament; it is probable that it functioned as a *communal lament*, though the internal evidence is ambiguous and the psalm could be interpreted in *individual* terms (cf. *G*'s "help *me*" in v 2). Presumably, the psalm would have been utilized in some specific context in Israel's temple worship, though a precise context cannot be determined. It is possible that v 6, expressed as the words of the Lord (in language of a prophetic character), was addressed to the worshipers by a priest or prophet (cf. Mowinckel, *The Psalms in Israel's Worship*, I, 218). But even this cannot be certain, for the use of direct speech is a useful poetic device and need not imply an additional participant in a cultic context; the imagined words of the enemy have already been utilized in v 5, and it is entirely natural, simply from a literary perspective, to balance them with the divine words of v 6.

The date and author of the psalm cannot be determined; the nature of the wicked as described here, and of the innocent sufferers, are too general and common to be fitted into a particular period or event in Israel's history. There are no good reasons for supposing that the psalm should be dated any later than the time of the Hebrew monarchy.

The psalm is finely constructed and makes effective use of repetition and contrast (cf. Ridderbos, *Die Psalmen*, 150–51; Weiss, *VT* 13 [1963] 474). The principal contrast concerns speech, the evil and flattering speech of the "sons of man" being contrasted with the pure and true utterances of God. There are two basic sections: (1) the vain speech of wicked persons (12:2–5); (2) the sure speech of God (12:6–9).

Comment

The vain speech of wicked persons (12:2–5). The psalm begins abruptly with a cry for help, and then goes on to explain the reason for the request. On the one hand, good persons appear to have disappeared from the land; on

the other hand, the wicked are rampant. In his distress, the psalmist encounters
the experience of Elijah who, in a time of testing, also felt that he was the
last upright person left in the land (1 Kgs 19:10). The psalmist could no
longer discern the existence of a "faithful one," viz. a covenant member
whose life was characterized by that faithfulness and loving kindness which
were of the very essence of the covenant relationship and life. But if honest
persons could not be seen, wicked persons could be both seen and heard.
Their speech is described as "vanity" (v 3, "emptiness, nothingness"), "flattering" (vv 3–4; "smooth") and issuing forth from a "double heart" (v 3).

The essence of evil is presented here in terms of speech, not action, though
that speech had precipitated the crisis which evoked the psalmist's cry for
help. Wicked persons spoke fine-sounding words which contained no substance. They spoke the "easy speeches that comfort cruel men" (G. K. Chesterton, cited by Kidner, Psalms 1–72, 74), but threatened the lives of the innocent.
They spoke from a "double heart": the heart, in the Hebrew conception,
was the seat of the mind. The "double heart" does not indicate the sense
of the English metaphor "in two minds" (viz. uncertainty), but rather indicates
a double standard, and hence implies lies and deceitfulness. They knew one
thing, but said another; they would not speak truth, though they knew it,
when a lie would accomplish their goal. The imagined words of the wicked
(v 5) indicate the power within their grasp through the mastery of speech
(cf. Jas 3:6–12), but their ultimate crime was that of hubris: Who will be our
master?—and they believed the answer to be "No one"! The pride within
them came forth in arrogant speech; refusing to acknowledge the mastery
of God, they oppressed with their tongues the servants of God. So the psalmist
prays that such speech be terminated (v 4).

The sure speech of God (12:6–9). The words of the wicked (v 5) are suddenly
and strikingly contrasted with the spoken words of God (v 6: on the possibility
that this verse was spoken by a prophet or priest, see *Form/Structure/Setting*
above). God declares his intention to *arise;* on the use of this verb with respect
to divine action, see further 7:7 (and *Comment*) and 9:20. God would arise
because of the sad estate of the afflicted and the *poor,* who were suffering
as a consequence of wicked persons and their words. And God states that
he will set his servant in safety (בישע); the term is a different form of the
word used by the psalmist in opening his prayer, "help" (הושיע), and indicates
that the action of God in deliverance would be a direct consequence of answered prayer. "I will shine forth" (v 6c): just as the Lord had *shone forth*
to his covenant people at Mt. Sinai in the awesome theophany (cf. the use
of the same verb in Deut 33:2), so too he would reveal himself again.

The quotation of the divine words (v 6) is followed immediately by a meditation on the nature of the divine words, in which they are contrasted sharply
with the words of wicked persons (vv 3–5). The *utterances* (or "promises,"
RSV) of the Lord are *pure;* the purity is demonstrated in the metaphor of
refining metal (see further 11:5–6 for a different use of this metaphor). The
word of the Lord is by its very nature valuable (as are silver and gold), but
through refinement and purification, in the language of the metaphor, there
is no dross in it. By implication, the speech of wicked persons is all dross,
devoid of silver and gold! That of God is pure silver, pure gold! It is devoid
of the dross of flattery, vanity, and lies, and can therefore be relied upon

absolutely. So, from a position of newly found confidence, the psalmist expresses his conviction: "You . . . will watch us, you will guard us . . ."; God had said he would arise (v 6), and that true word could be believed. Protection was coming. Yet the reality of evil circumstances continued; the wicked still strutted about, their vile speech (v 9; cf. v 5) exalted as if it were a divine word. It was not a change of circumstances which prompted the confidence of v 8, but a conviction that God's word was pure and true.

Explanation

Human life, in its normative forms, would be virtually impossible without speech, for speech provides the fundamental means of communication between human beings. Religion as we know it would also be virtually impossible without speech; though religious language borders upon the mysterious, it is through forms of speech that God has made himself known and speech is also a central part of human response to God's revelation. In the context of Hebrew theology, speech is fundamental to the creative activity of God (e.g. Gen 1), and the speech of the creature, if it is to be proper, must be marked by the characteristics of the Creator's speech. God's speech is pure (12:7), free from any falsity or impairment; human speech should also be pure.

It is generally true that the finest things or qualities within the order of creation are those most vulnerable to debasement or perversion. The more pure or good a thing may be, the more impure or rotten it may be made to become. Love, the greatest quality within creation, may be sadly abused, as the prophets (e.g. Hos 1–3) made clear. And speech, which is so central to relationships between human beings, and between persons and God, may also be radically abused. The psalmist has painted a picture of speech that has been raped—worth has been exchanged for vanity, truth for flattery, and humility for arrogance in word and thought. The gift implicit in the tongue has been twisted and tortured to evil purposes by proud mortals.

The psalmist is not merely concerned to enunciate the existence of evil speech; he suffers from its lash and falsehood, and so is compelled to seek divine help. The deliverance from the power of impure speech is to be found in hearing the pure speech of God; having heard God's speech, and having reflected upon its reliability, the psalmist achieves the trust and confidence (v 8) for which he had prayed (v 2). The danger experienced in mortal speech was to be repelled by the power inherent in divine speech. For those who experience the assault of evil speech, the solution is not to be found in the return of evil speech to enemies, but in confidence in the Word of God, which is firm and cannot be moved.

"How Long, O Lord?"   *(13:1-6)*

Bibliography

Airoldi, N. "Note ai Salmi." *Augustinianum* 13 (1973) 345–50. **Westermann, C.** *Der Psalter,* 48–51.

Translation

1 For the musical director. A psalm of David.
2(1) *How long, O Lord, will you continually forget me?*   (4+4)
      How long will you hide your face from me?
3(2) *How long must I set pain* ª *in my soul,*   (4+3(4)+4)
      grief in my heart by day ᵇ *(and night)?*
      How long will my enemy be exalted over me?
4(3) *Look! Answer me, O Lord my God!*   (4+4)
      Enlighten my eyes, lest I should fall into the sleep of death, ª
5(4) *lest my enemy should say, "I have prevailed over him,"*   (4?+4)
      (lest) my adversaries should rejoice because I am shaken.
6(5) *But I have trusted in your lovingkindness,*   (3+3)
      my heart shall rejoice in your deliverance.
      I shall sing praises to the Lord,   (2+3)
      as soon as ª *he has dealt bountifully with me.*

Notes

3.a. עצות, literally "counsels," provides a curious sense: "I will set counsels in my soul," and though such a translation is in accord with G and some other versions, it leaves the unusual combination of *counsels* (intellectual activity) with *soul* (here implying the seat of the emotions). Several scholars, following the suggestion of S, emend to עצבות, "hurts, griefs," which would provide good sense and assumes only the loss of *beth* from the consonantal text (cf. the textual apparatus in *BHS* and see also *Textual Notes on the New American Bible*, [Patterson, N.J.: St. Anthony's Guild] 380). Dahood has suggested an alternative solution, namely that the term should be translated "doubts," on the basis of Arabic *naǵaḍa*, "to shake, totter," which—he claims—is also found in the Ugaritic word *nǵṣ*, "to wobble, shake." The origin and etymology of the Ugaritic word is itself a source of considerable discussion and has provoked a variety of possible Arabic etymologies: (a) *naǵaḍa* (Dahood, Aistleitner, Caquot, Gibson, and Gordon); (b) *naǵaṣa* ("to be interrupted," Gray, *Legacy* ², 27); (c) *naǵaṭa* ("to oscillate," Driver, *CML*, 156—though this equation poses severe linguistic problems); (d) *tanaǵǵaṣa* ("to be disquieted," Speiser, *JCS* 5 [1951] 64–66). In summary, an Arabic etymology for Ugaritic *nǵṣ* is not without problems, and those problems are compounded with respect to Hebrew עצות by the absence of an initial *nun*, which (while it can be explained) leaves open a variety of other possibilities with respect to the resources of comparative Semitic lexicography (e.g. Syriac ʿeṣyānā, root ʿṣy, "contentiousness, compulsion"). The simplest and most satisfactory solution is to retain עצות and translate "pain" (literally, "pains"), a possible sense of the term for which Driver has made a plausible argument (*WO* 1 [1947–52] 410, cited by Anderson, *Psalms 1*, 129; cf. *NEB*).
3.b. יומם: "by day." G (Alexandrinus) adds "and night," which has been added provisionally above; the addition is uncertain, but see Ps 1:2. Dahood, however, reads יֹמֵם, a Qal partc. from *ymm, a by-form of Ugaritic *ybm*, which he suggests may have the meaning "to create, beget" (*Psalms I*, 77); hence, he translates: *"creating* grief in my heart." For a number of reasons, Dahood's proposal fails to be convincing. (a) MT makes acceptable sense as it stands. (b) There is considerable debate over the precise meaning of Ugaritic *ybm*, rendering unsafe any comparative philological equations which may be based upon it. For further discussion of the possible etymology and meaning of *ybm*, see Caquot et al., *Textes ougaritiques I*, 90–92; J. C. De Moor, *The Seasonal Pattern in the Ugaritic Myth of Baʿalu*, (AOAT 16. Neukirchen-Vluyn: Neukrichener Verlag, 1971) 97; Craigie, *ZAW* 90 (1978) 376–77. (c) The by-form *ymm is rare in Ugaritic, contributing still further to the precarious nature of the linguistic equation, as noted in (b) above. In summary, the suggestion of Dahood is not followed in the translation above, given the uncertain character of the comparative data.
4.a. "I . . . fall into the sleep of death": literally, "I sleep the death." Dahood has suggested

reading אִישׁ פְּנֵי, "avert the sleep. . . ." (*Psalms I*, 78), taking פְּנֵי to be a Piel impv. of פּנה (rather than the negative particle פֶּן "lest"). Though such a rendering is possible, the reoccurrence of פֶּן in v 5 suggests that it should be taken in the conventional sense in v 4, introducing a series (vv 4–5) of potential consequences which would result if God failed to *look* and *answer* (v 4a).

6.a. On the use of כִּי plus perf. to designate "as soon as," see Airoldi, *Augustinianum* 13 (1973) 345–50.

Form/Structure/Setting

The psalm is an *individual lament,* in which the worshiper comes to God with a desperate inquiry—"How long?"—and concludes on a note of hope and confidence. It is possible that the psalm, in its initial context, was utilized in the context of some ceremony in the temple, though there is little internal evidence to specify a cultic-context. It has been suggested that the change in tone between vv 5 and 6 resulted from some kind of intervention in the context of worship (cf. Ridderbos, *Die Psalmen,* 152), perhaps a word from the priest which inspired trust, but this cannot be certain. The view that Ps 13 was a national or congregational psalm (Mowinckel, *The Psalms in Israel's Worship,* I, 219) is unlikely with respect to its initial composition and purpose, though it is quite appropriate with respect to its subsequent use in the history of Israel's worship. Such general usage in worship may be implied by the reference to the "musical director" in the title.

The distress which the worshiper laments is probably the fear and proximity of death, brought on perhaps by grave illness (see further the *Comment*). The psalm begins with a series of lamenting and nagging questions, but eventually the psalmist calms down and is able to look forward to a time of deliverance and joy. As Delitzsch puts it: "The hymn as it were advances in waves that are constantly decreasing in length, until at last it is only agitated with joy, and becomes calm as the sea when smooth as a mirror" (*Biblical Commentary on the Psalms,* I, 252).

There is little in the content of the psalm to enable a firm dating of it, though its language and general sentiments are such that it may be assumed to be old, in its original form at least. There are general parallels to the psalm in Babylonian laments and the type has a long history in Israel's worship (Westermann, *Der Psalter,* 48–51). It is reasonable to assume that the psalm originated early in the period of the Hebrew monarchy.

The psalm has three basic sections. (1) The psalmist's lament (13:2–3); (2) a prayer for deliverance (13:4–5); (3) the expression of confidence (13:6).

Comment

The psalmist's lament (13:2–3). The psalmist finds himself torn between two poles. On the one side is the "Lord," to whom he addresses his lament; on the other side is the "enemy" (v 3c) who, at that moment in time, was exalted and appeared to have the upper hand. The tormented "How long?", which is repeated four times, is rooted in this tension. It is because the enemy is in ascendancy that it seems as though God has forgotten his servant and turned his face from him: he asks, how much longer must this go on? And the exaltation of the enemy and the turned face of God aggravate still further the pain and grief of the psalmist: how much longer must it continue? There is no confession or statement of sin to suggest that the trial was a judgment deserved; the urgency of the psalmist's plea springs from a sense of profound anxiety, not penitence. As a member of the covenant people, his expectation was to be remembered by God and to see the light of his countenance (Num 6:25–26), but the long absence of such privileges evoked the anguished cry of lament.

It cannot be certain, but it is probable that the enemy of whom the psalmist speaks is death (v 4). The approach of death made more acute the sense of God's distance. Death would come to all mankind, but the desire to live springs eternal, and the psalmist is not willing to capitulate to the enemy who is already in a state of exaltation. But he is near to capitulation and his hope has almost gone, for the question "How long?" expresses despair precisely because the psalmist, in his opening words, cannot provide an answer to the question. He does not know how long, but it looked like forever—and "forever" in the mind of a dying man means the grave. So he must move from lament to prayer.

A prayer for deliverance (13:4–5). In the lament, the psalmist had expressed the conviction that God's face was turned from him; but now he implores God to *look,* and to do that, God would have to turn his face back toward him. "Answer me"—that is, answer the fourfold question "How long?" in the opening lament. Thus the prayer for deliverance takes up the themes of the lament; lament is pointless unless it culminates in prayer. Specifically, the psalmist prays that the Lord would "enlighten" his eyes; the eye that was dim was clouded with both ill health and its consequent grief (cf. Job 17:7), so that the prayer is a request for restoration to health and deliverance from grief. When the eye was enlightened, it would signify a state of health (cf. Deut 34:7). But there is more than a prayer for physical health in the psalmist's plea; at a deeper level, he desires to return to close fellowship with the Lord. Thus, when God's face was hidden, the light of his countenance could not shine upon the psalmist (see vv 2–3), but when God turned to him again, not only would the psalmist see the light of the divine countenance, but his own eyes would be enlightened. When his eyes were enlightened, both spiritually and physically, he would not fall into the sleep of death which seemed so imminent.

In v 5, there is reference to both a singular "enemy" (v 5a) and to the plural "adversaries" (v 5b). Some interpreters have taken the singular term in a collective sense and interpreted both terms as referring to the psalmist's enemies in a general way, but it is probable that the distinction in number has been made deliberately. The singular enemy is no doubt the personification of death; the plural enemies are the psalmist's foes in general. If the psalmist should "fall into the sleep of death," then that great enemy of mortal mankind would be able to say: "I have prevailed over him!" If he should die, all his enemies could rejoice because he was "shaken," which is probably a euphemistic expression for death (see Anderson, *Psalms I,* 129–30). The psalmist prays for deliverance both from death and from the exaltation of evil persons which would accompany such death.

The expression of confidence (13:6). The confidence is expressed within the tension which exists between past experience and future hope. The past experience of the psalmist has been one of *trust* in God's "lovingkindness," namely the faithful covenant love of God which characterized all his dealings with his chosen people. The present reality was of such a nature as to undermine that past experience of trust, but it is in the nature of confidence to transform the present on the basis of past experience and thus to create hope for the future; and so the psalmist can affirm that he will "rejoice" in God's deliverance, even though it has not yet come. The actual song of praise would burst forth once deliverance had been accomplished, but the knowledge that deliverance was coming created an anticipatory calm and sense of confidence.

Explanation

The divine gift of life brings with it many mysteries, not least of which is the intimate connection between what we commonly call "body and soul." From the perspective of Hebrew anthropology, the essence of a person could not be conveniently split into parts—for example body, spirit and soul—as was done at a later date in the context of Greek thought. Human life was a whole, a single entity. Yet, from a more practical perspective, there were clearly different dimensions to the life of a person: there was the physical body, the mind (in Hebrew "heart"), and the emotions ("soul," v 3). But, as is demonstrated so clearly in this poignant lament, the parts did not function independently. The health of the physical body affected the mind and the emotions; conversely, the mind and the emotions could affect the physical body, or at least the interrelationship between the parts.

It is the dominance of the body with which the psalm begins; the physical body was engulfed in sickness and near to death. But because, in the Hebrew conception, there could be no life apart from the body, the inner person was profoundly affected by the state of the physical body. The nearness of death created a chasm in the sense of relationship with God; when death came, that relationship could not continue. Yet the inner being of the psalmist was not willing simply to submit in resignation to the affliction of the body; if such were the case, the psalm would end after v 3. Recognizing the danger, the psalmist calls for help and deliverance; the cry comes from within, though it relates to the external life of the body as much as to the torment of mind and emotion.

The confidence which finally comes (v 6) is based primarily upon a change of attitude, not a change in physical well-being. The essence of life was a relationship with God—for that, the inner and outer beings existed. And so the personal threat afflicting the body was countered by memory of past trust (v 6a) and anticipation of future deliverance (v 6b). Such a counterattack did not in itself change the state of the body; it simply provided the framework of confidence within which the present could be accepted and the future anticipated with joy.

A Meditation on the Fool   (14:1-7)

Bibliography

Bennett, R. A. "Wisdom Motifs in Ps. 14–53—*nābāl* and *'ēṣāh.*" *BASOR* 220 (1975) 15–21. Donald, T. "The Semantic Field of 'Folly' in Proverbs, Job, Psalms, and Ecclesiastes." *VT* 13 (1963) 285–92.

Translation

[1] For the musical director. For David.[a]
   The fool has said in his heart: "There is no God."   (5+5)
   They are perverse, they do horrible deeds; there is not one doing good.
[2] *The Lord has looked down from heaven upon the sons of man,*   (4?+5)
   to see if there is one acting prudently, one seeking God.
[3] *"The whole lot have turned aside; together they are corrupt.[a]*   (4+4)
   There is not one doing good, not even one.
[4] *Don't they understand,[a] all the workers of iniquity who are consuming my people?"*
                                     (5?+5)
   They have eaten bread: on the Lord they have not called.[b]
[5] *They were in great fear,[a] but God is in the assembly[b] of the righteous.*   (6?+5)
[6] *You would confound the counsel of the poor, but the Lord is his refuge.[a]*
[7] *Would that Israel's deliverance would come out of Zion!*   (4+4+4)
   When the Lord restores the fortunes of his people,
   Jacob shall exult, Israel shall rejoice.

Notes

1.a. Some Heb. mss add מזמור: "a *psalm* of David" (De–Rossi, IV, 7).

3.a. Some Heb. mss have the reading נאלח (sing.) "it is corrupt"; a change in number may not be necessary, for the initial verb (סר) "turn aside" may simply be singular in conjunction with the collective כל "all," so that a return to the plur. in the following verb is not surprising. (G and 2 Heb. mss have a section inserted between vv 2 and 3 which is not in MT; see further *Form/Setting/Structure,* below.)

4.a. The verb ידעו is vocalized as imperf., with the support of some Heb. mss (De-Rossi, IV, 8). The stichometric analysis of this verse is difficult. The analysis above assumes two long lines (in harmony with the previous verses); the second line has a chiastic structure (A:B::B':A'), which emphasizes the contrast being made (see further the *Comment*).

4.b. Dahood provides a very different translation of v 4b, translating לחם "bread, food" as "grain," and the verb קרא "call" as "to collect, harvest." The translation is somewhat forced and may miss the point of the passage (see below, *Comment*). Dahood suggests in support of his argument that the Ugaritic cognate term *lḥm* may mean "grain" (*Psalms I,* 81). The evidence for Ugaritic *lḥm,* "grain," is very slender. The basic evidence is to be found in *CTA* 16 (*UT* 126). iii.13–16; in that text, there occurs the triple parallelism *lḥm//yn//šmn,* which Dahood renders "grain//wine//oil" (see *RSP I,* #333). Elsewhere, Dahood defines the parallel terms in the same text as *dgn//lḥm,* "grain//wheat" (*RSP I,* #151); it is the latter reference which suggests the translation "grain" (or "wheat"). For several reasons, the Ugaritic equation *lḥm* = "grain" must be opposed. (i) In *CTA* 16.iii.13–16, the parallelism is clearly *lḥm//yn//šmn,* and *dgn* belongs to the previous unit. The text is as follows:

kly lḥm (b)dnhm	"Bread (or food) had failed in their bins,
kly yn bḥmthm	Wine had failed in their skins,
k(l)y šmn bq(. . .	Oil had failed in . . ."

The parallelism of *lḥm* with "wine" and "oil" simply indicates the meaning "bread/food," and does not require "grain." And in some Hebrew contexts where the same triple parallelism occurs, Dahood translates לחם by "food" or "bread," presumably on the basis of the context (*RSP I*, 250). (ii) The general sense of לחם, namely "food," is such that it may carry a variety of meanings by virtue of the implications of context: e.g. honey, goat's milk, meat, and so on (cf. BDB, 537). The same is true of Ugaritic *lḥm*, which may indicate (e.g.) "meat" (which is the primary sense of Arabic *laḥm*), but only on the basis of context (cf. J. C. De Moor, *UF* 1 [1969] 170). But in both Hebrew and Ugaritic, the term still has the strict sense "food," which by its very nature may incorporate the specific foodstuff designated or implied by the context. The context in Ps 14 does not clearly specify the sense "grain" (and if קרא may indeed mean "to harvest," its rarity is such that it does not clearly establish the present context), and so the translation of Dahood is not accepted. Furthermore, the Hebrew text makes good sense in terms of the conventional vocalization and interpretation of MT.

5.a. פחד "dread, fear": the use of both verb and noun, from the same root, emphasizes the state or action; on this example of the *cognate accusative*, see further GKC § 117p. While it must be admitted that there are problems in the translation of v 5a, Dahood's translation is not convincing: "See how they have formed a cabal" (*Psalms I*, 80). His translation of פחד ("family, clan, tribe," hence "cabal") is based on Ugaritic and Palmyrene cognate terms. The supposed Ugaritic evidence should be removed from the discussion. Ugaritic *pḥd*, which occurs only twice in the Ugaritic texts (*CTA* 17 [2 Aqht]. 5.17 and 23, in parallel passages), may possibly mean "flock." But more probably, it has the basic sense "lamb" (cf. Akk. *puḥādu*, which does not mean "herd"); see further M. Dijkstra and J. C. De Moor, "Problematical Passages in the Legend of Aqhatu," *UF* 7 (1975) 181–82. The translation of Caquot et al. (*Textes ougaritiques I*, 428), namely "farine," on the basis of the rare Akk. word *paḥidu*, is not entirely convincing. In summary, Dahood's argument must rest primarily on Palmyrene *pḥdʾ*, "clan," to which could be added the Arabic cognate *faḥid*, "clan," but the existence of such a meaning for Heb. פחד is far from certain.

5.b. On the sense "assembly" for Heb דור, see the following: Dahood, *Psalms I*, 82; F. J. Neuberg, *JNES* 9 (1950) 216; Caquot et al., *Textes ougaritiques I*, 363; Gordon, *UT* #697.

6.a. The problems of syntax and meaning, which are latent in v 5, emerge clearly in v 6. The stichometric analysis assumes that vv 5–6 are to be taken together as two long, balancing lines (in keeping with the style of the rest of the psalm). But the translation above (which follows MT closely) nevertheless poses certain problems. A possible solution, though fairly radical, would be as follows:

| v 5a | שם הפחידו פחד . . . |
| v 6a | עצתיעני הבישו . . . |

Translation: "There they caused great fear, but God is in the assembly of the righteous. The counsel of the poor they confounded, but the Lord is his refuge."

There are two changes in this rendering: (i) פחדו (Qal) is emended to Hiph. (cf. Job 4:14); (ii) תבישו is emended to הבישו, for which there is support in one Heb ms. The solution is attractive in providing good sense and balanced parallelism, but it remains conjectural.

Form/Structure/Setting

Psalm 14 is commonly designated as an *individual lament* with respect to form (e.g. Fohrer, *Introduction*, 286), but such a designation is uncertain. As Bennett and others have noted (*BASOR* 220 [975] 15), the psalm is of mixed type, containing resemblances to wisdom, prophetic and hymnic material. Dahood has noted that though the psalm is commonly classified as a lament, it "could, with equal justice, be put into the category of wisdom psalms" (*Psalms I*, 80). Assuming that the psalm is an integrated whole (see Bennett, art. cit.), it would appear to be the case that the wisdom theme is dominant and that the qualities of lament and praise are subsumed within this larger framework. The origin of Ps 14 should thus be sought within the wisdom traditions of ancient Israel (cf. Ps 1), though no precise setting can be determined with respect to the psalm in its initial form. It is an adaptation of wisdom; the more reflective tone of other wisdom psalms (e.g. Ps 1) is exchanged for a lament and the hope of deliverance, which emerge from the initial meditative wisdom (v 1).

Psalm 14 has a duplicate in Book II of the Psalter, namely Ps 53. The principal difference between the two texts lies in the use of the divine name, Ps 14 using the divine name יהוה "Lord" four times, while Ps 53 consistently uses the divine title אלהים "God." There are minor textual variations in the opening verses, and more substantial differences between 14:5–7 = 53:6–7. The latter differences may indicate editorial reworking or revision at an early date, or more probably they may be indicative of early textual corruption, and the two versions may thus reflect two different attempts to resolve the difficulties in the text. Of the two versions, Ps 14 is probably the earlier, being contained in the musical director's collection and the first Davidic collection, whereas Ps 53, in the so-called "Elohistic Psalter" (see INTRODUCTION, THE COMPILATION OF THE PSALTER), reflects a later stage in the development of the Psalter. The double occurrence of the psalm in the Psalter, together with the implications of the titles to Pss 14 and 53, indicate that over the course of time both psalms became used frequently in Israel's worship and they were not confined in use to the wisdom schools, despite their origin there.

Some editions of *G*, several versions, and a few Heb. mss (De-Rossi, IV, 7) have an additional piece of text inserted between vv 2 and 3 of MT, which may be translated as follows:

> Their throat is an open grave;
> (with) their tongue they have used deceit.
> Viper's poison is under their tongue,
> whose mouth is replete with oath and deceitfulness.
> Their feet are swift to shed blood.
> Destruction and misery are in their ways,
> and the way of peace they have not known.
> There is no fear of God before their eyes.

The entire passage is contained in Rom 3:10–18. It is probable that these lines were not a part of the original text of the psalm; several lines bear striking similarities to portions of other psalms (e.g. see the similar language in Ps 10). Probably Paul, in Rom 3:10–18, joined together several familiar lines from the Psalms to make his point about the corruption of all mankind. Briggs has suggested, with persuasive argument, that the lines then entered *G* at an early date by way of being a marginal reference to Rom 3:10–18, and eventually were incorporated within the text; then (to account for the

Heb. ms) they were translated back into Hebrew and so survived in the Heb. mss tradition: *The Book of Psalms,* 104.

The author of Ps 14 is not known. With respect to date, it is commonly argued that the psalm must be a postexilic composition, first on the basis of the mixed form, and second on the basis of v 7b, which could be translated: "when the Lord brings back the captivity of his people" (cf. AV), which in turn could be interpreted as a reference either to the Diaspora or the Exile. But the mixed form need not imply a late date and may even be indicative of pre-exilic composition (cf. Bennett, art. cit.), the Heb expression in v 7b requires a more general translation (see Dahood, *Psalms I,* 82, with references to further literature), and the long history of the psalm implied by the textual variations (discussed above) might indicate considerable antiquity. Thus, although uncertainty remains, a pre-exilic date for the composition of the psalm is likely.

The psalm is examined in two sections: (1) wisdom's lament (14:1–6); (2) the anticipation of deliverance (14:7).

Comment

Wisdom's lament (14:1–6). That which gives rise to the entire psalm is the "fool" (v 1) and the nature of his folly. The fool is opposed to God, threatens the life of the righteous, and thus evokes both lament and prayer for deliverance from those whose lives he affects. But the fool is not simply one lacking in mental powers; indeed, the fool may be a highly intelligent person. The fool is one whose life is lived without the direction or acknowledgment of God. Thus, the precise opposite of *fool* and *folly* is not *wise man* and *wisdom;* the opposite of *folly* in the wisdom literature is *lovingkindness* (חסד; see Donald, *VT* 13 [1963] 285–92). That is to say, the fool is defined by the absence of lovingkindness, which in turn is the principal characteristic of the relationship of the covenant; he lives as if there were no covenant, and thus as if there were no God—"There is no God" (v 1). Hence, the description of fools (v lc) is of a moral nature; they are "perverse, they do horrible deeds" (the Heb. implies deeds which are an abomination in the eyes of God) and do no *good;* see further the *Explanation* at Pss 9–10.

Vv 2–4 provide a theological perspective on the fool and his folly. The designation "fool" is not a human label, for those so named in the psalms were anything but fools in a human perspective; the ultimate reason for the status of "fool" was provided by God, who "looked down from heaven" and saw the acts of human beings. It was by the measure of divine love and wisdom that human folly emerged in all its tragedy, while to human eyes alone the same person might appear to be wealthy, powerful and successful. God perceived that the mass of mankind (the "sons of man," v 2) did not act prudently and did not seek God.

After God has looked down and surveyed the acts of human beings, he speaks; translators differ concerning the limits of the Lord's words; I have enclosed vv 3–4a in quotation marks as the divine speech, though it is possible that only v 4a should be so designated. The words reflect God's response to what he saw when he looked down from heaven on the "sons of man";

all humans appeared to be corrupt. The problem was not mental deficiency
or lack of intelligence; it was lack of understanding ("Don't they understand?"
v 4) of the fundamental principle of human life, namely that it should reflect
loving kindness, not folly, just as God loved and was the antithesis of foolishness. The absence of understanding culminated in evil acts against the people
of God ("my people," v 4a), which in turn transforms the wisdom reflection
into lament. The psalmist does not simply reflect on the sad fact that there
are fools in the world, but laments the grief and oppression which such fools
bring down upon the righteous. The fool's lack of understanding is such
that his priorities in life are entirely wrong. These fools have "eaten bread,"
thinking that to be the staple of life, but have not called upon God; the
wisdom of Moses, "that man does not live by bread alone" (Deut 8:3), was
entirely foreign to them, and they could not live by "every utterance of the
mouth of the Lord," for in not calling upon God, they could not hear him
respond.

The meaning of vv 5–6 is difficult to determine; see further the *Notes*. It
is probable that the psalmist contrasts the passive and active estates of the
wicked with those of the righteous. To paraphrase: "the wicked lived in a
state of fear as a result of their folly, but the righteous had peace of mind
(greater than their oppression) as a consequence of God's presence in their
midst. The fool attempted to do ill to the righteous, but found that the righteous benefited from the presence of God as a refuge." It is this contrast
and reflection that leads naturally to the prayer with which the psalm concludes.

The anticipation of deliverance (14:7). The psalm, which began as a meditation
and turned to lament, now concludes as prayer with anticipation of hymnic
celebration of deliverance. The psalmist prays for deliverance from the work
of fools and their oppressive folly; Mt. Zion, the place where God's presence
with his people was symbolized most forcefully, would be the place from
which deliverance would come. In other words, for the righteous, God's presence among his people could not be merely a passive symbol, but must become
an active force in securing real deliverance from actual trouble. That deliverance, when it came, would result in the joy and exultation of the people of
God.

Explanation

Paul's use of Ps 14 (Rom 3:10–18) provides an appropriate context for
the contemporary reading of the ancient psalm. It is too easy for the modern
reader to identify quickly with the oppressed and to think always of the "fool"
in terms of other people. But Paul uses the passage to establish beyond
any theological doubt the universal evil and folly of mankind. The fool is
not a rare subspecies within the human race; all human beings are fools
apart from the wisdom of God. And the works of the fool can never secure
justification in the sight of God, devoid as they are of that lovingkindness
which is of the essence of God. The fool has neither love nor righteousness;
for such, he must seek the wisdom of God. And though wisdom speaks of
love, insight and morality, in the NT context, wisdom has a more profound

component; the ultimate wisdom of God is to be found in the gospel of Jesus Christ (1 Cor 1:23–25), which from a certain human perspective may appear to be foolishness, but in reality it is the power of God in deliverance or salvation. Thus, whereas in the original psalm, there is a gap between the fool and the righteous, from a NT perspective the entire psalm may be read as a spiritual pilgrimage. The reader begins, standing where the fool stands, but as he continues to read he perceives and laments the nature of folly and its consequent evil. And, with the psalmist, he must pray for deliverance from that folly.

On the theme of atheism in this psalm, see further the explanation at Pss 9–10.

Preparation for Worship (15:1–5)

Bibliography

Dahood, M. J. "A Note on Psalm 15,4 (14,4)." *CBQ* 16 (1954) 302. **Koole, J. L.** "Ps. 15—eine königliche Einzugsliturgie?" *OTS* 13 (1963) 98–111.

Translation

1 A psalm of David.
  O Lord, who may reside in your tent? [a]   (3+3)
  Who may dwell on your holy mountain?
2 *He who walks blamelessly,*   (2+2)
    and does what is right,
    and speaks truth in [a] *his heart.*   (3+2?)
3   *He has not tripped* [a] *over his tongue.*
  He has not done evil to his friend.   (3+3)
    He has not taken up reproach against his neighbor.
4 *In his eyes, the reprobate is despised,*   (3+3+3?)
    but he honors those who fear the Lord.
    He has sworn to do no wrong [a] *and does not falter.*
5 *He has not lent his money* [a] *on interest,*   (3+3, 4)
    nor taken a bribe against the innocent.
  The one doing these things shall not be shaken forever

Notes

1.a. A number of Heb. mss read the plur. "tents," and add the conjunction *and* between the two questions (". . . and who may dwell?").

2.a. It would be possible to translate: "speaks truth *from* his heart" (cf. RSV), taking the preposition ‎ב‎ in the sense "from." But the primary truth is the inner truth of the heart (viz. the mind), which in turn results in the outward speaking of truth, which contrasts with evil persons who speak with *double heart* (see Ps 12:3); thus the psalmist is probably concerned primarily with inner truth, hence the translation "*in* his heart."

3.a. On ‎רגל‎, with the sense "to trip," see Dahood, *Psalms I*, 84.

4.a. "To do no wrong": the translation follows Dahood (*CBQ* 16 [1954] 302) and *Psalms I*, 84, taking *lamedh* in the separative sense; but the form remains curious and the sense of the passage is uncertain.

5.a. "Lent his money": literally, "given his silver."

Form/Structure/Setting

Gunkel, and many interpreters since his time, defined Ps 15 as an *entrance liturgy* (*The Psalms. A Form-critical Introduction*, 22). As such, it is characterized by a typical form: (i) the worshipers inquire of the priest as to the qualifications for admission to the holy place (15:1); (ii) the priest responds by specifying the requirements (15:2–5b), and (iii) concludes with a blessing (15:5c). The analysis is suggestive and may well be correct, in which case the psalm would be interpreted in the context of Israel's formal worship; possibly, such a liturgy might have been utilized upon the arrival of pilgrims at the gates of the sanctuary for participation in one of Israel's great festivals.

The classification of the psalm as an *entrance liturgy* (whether of a general or a royal character: cf. Koole, *OTS* 13 [1963] 98–111) cannot be entirely certain. Psalm 15 also has the flavor of the wisdom literature, particularly in the moral (as distinct from cultic or ritual) requirements for admission to the sanctuary (vv 2–5b). There are Near Eastern parallels to such entrance liturgies, but in them the requirements for admission include ritual as well as moral qualities. Thus it is possible that Ps 15 is a wisdom poem, based perhaps upon the form of the entrance liturgy; its didactic role would have been in the instruction of young people concerning the moral implications of participating in worship. On this interpretation, the concluding line (v 5c) is not a blessing, but a promise concerning the outcome of a life based upon morality and worship.

As Mowinckel and other scholars noted (*The Psalms in Israel's Worship*, I, 179), the conditions for admission appear to be *ten* in number; there is some uncertainty about this "decalogical" structure, for it depends in part on the stichometric analysis and interpretation of vv 2–5b. Nevertheless, the number ten is fairly certain, and may be confirmed by the inner grouping of positive and negative conditions. Three positive conditions are followed by three negative conditions, then two positive followed by two negative—total ten. The structure may be set forth in four groups as follows:

A. *Positive Conditions* (v 2)   B. *Negative Conditions* (v 3)
(i) walking blamelessly   (iv) no falsity
(ii) doing right   (v) no evil
(iii) speaking truth   (vi) no reproach

C. *Positive Conditions* (v 4)   D. *Negative Conditions* (v 5)
(vii) despise reprobates   (ix) no usury
(viii) swear to do good   (x) no bribery

This tenfold structure of conditions is analogous to the Decalogue in principle and with respect to the sense of wholeness, though there are no precise inner correspondences between the conditions and the Commandments. Rather, the tenfold structure suggests once again the didactic context of the wisdom school; young persons were being instructed to tick off, as it were, on their ten fingers the moral conditions prerequisite to participation in worship. Thus the conditions for admission to worship are apparently presented here in the curriculum of moral instruction and symbolically represent morality in its entirety, rather than covering every facet of the moral life in detail.

Neither the date nor the author of Ps 15 can be specified with certainty, though the reference to the "holy mountain" (v 1) may indicate almost any period from the establishment of the sanctuary in Zion. (The reference to "tent" need not imply tabernacle, but may be synonymous to the word *temple*, indicating the dwelling place and refuge of the righteous; see BDB, 14a). If Isa 33:14–15 may be understood as an adaptation of Ps 15, then the psalm was composed before Isaiah's time, though such a conclusion must remain uncertain. The presence of the psalm in the first Davidic Psalter indicates that, if its origin were indeed in the wisdom tradition, nevertheless it was incorporated eventually within the regular worship of Israel. The use of this psalm on Ascension Day, within the history of Christian worship, is entirely appropriate to its sense; the psalm speaks of admission to the presence of God, just as Christ was admitted to that full presence on his ascension.

The psalm is treated in three parts: (1) the question (15:1); (2) the answer (15:2–5b); (3) the promise (15:5c).

Comment

The question (15:1). The psalmist begins with a question: there is basically a single question, though it is asked in two different ways as required by the structure of (synonymous) parallelism. The question pertains to the nature and character of the person who desires to enter God's presence. Though the question might have a general sense, it is here quite specific: if a person is to enter the special place in which God's presence is symbolized most intimately (the "tent," or temple, on the "holy mountain," namely Zion), what must that person be like? The question is vital, for the answer given to it will affect the questioner in preparation for worship. The question, if genuinely asked, will elicit an answer which invites examination of the self and hence appropriate preparation for admission to worship and to the divine presence.

The answer (15:2–5b). The answer is provided in a series of ten positive and negative conditions (see *Form/Structure/Setting*, above). Both the positive and negative are important, for the person who would enter God's presence must have a life characterized not only by active goodness, but also by the absence of evil. The first three conditions are positive: such a person's walk in life must be blameless, free from evil. The second and third principles elaborate upon the first general principle with respect to both action and speech: action must be "right," the positive doing of good, and speech (which is rooted in the thoughts of the mind) must be *truthful*. There then follow three negative conditions which are in a sense repetitive, for they contain the antithesis of the initial positive prescriptions. The person who "has not tripped over his tongue" (v 3) is one who speaks truth; there is no internal falsity or "double heart" (see Ps 12:3) to contribute to stumbling speech or dubious intent. The precise sense of not taking up "reproach against his neighbor" is uncertain; the implication may be that such a person has not contributed to slander, spread rumors or perpetuated gossip about his neighbor.

The sixth condition is stated more fully: it involves both despising the "reprobate" (the perpetual undertaker of evil) and honoring the God-fearing. In other words, the sixth condition speaks of attitudes, both positive and negative, toward fellow human beings, but more than that, it may refer to companionship. The one who despises the reprobate avoids the company and influence of evil persons; in honoring the God-fearing, he seeks also their companionship and positive influence. The seventh condition indicates not merely a determination to do good, but the swearing of a solemn oath to avoid doing wrong, and the accompanying determination never to falter or waver in the performance of that oath.

The last two conditions are in some ways the most specific of the ten. The person who would enter God's presence must have avoided both usury and bribery. The implied condemnation of usury reflects a quite specific concern in ancient Israel. It is not the case that lending on interest was wrong in principle, but that it normally involved exploitation and abuse. Thus the Hebrew law prevented loans on interest to fellow Hebrews, but permitted them in business transactions with foreigners (see Deut 23:19–20, and Craigie, *The Book of Deuteronomy,* 302–3). The reason was that a fellow Hebrew who was in need of a loan was almost certainly in distress; to make a loan to such a person and charge exorbitant interest would culminate in the aggravation of distress rather than its removal, so that if a loan were to be made at all to a fellow Hebrew, it could only be secured by a pledge (cf. Deut 24:6), without interest. On bribery, see Exod 23:8 and Deut 16:19.

The promise (15:5c). The promise does not merely concern itself with security or freedom from trouble, oppression and the like. Indeed, the righteous very often were "shaken" (cf. Ps 13:5) in a literal sense, to the rejoicing of their enemies. The promise pertains to a more fundamental stability, indicated in the opening verse: "Who may reside in your tent?" (v 1). Answer: the righteous person (vv 2–5b), and come what may, he would not be shaken from that residence in the divine presence. Thus the "answer" of Ps 15 sets a useful perspective for the many laments contained within the Psalter. From a human perspective, the psalmists were constantly shaken by their experience of human oppression and the vicissitudes of life, and so they issued their laments; but the only possibility of transforming lament into confidence or praise lay in the fact that there was an unshaken position transcending the vicissitudes of a shaken and uncertain life. That position was in the presence of God, whether in public worship or private devotion.

Explanation

In the history of Christian and Jewish worship, there have emerged two extremes toward which the worshiper may be tempted to move. On the one hand, there have been times when the holiness of God has been stressed so powerfully, that the ordinary mortal has felt it impossible to approach

God in worship or prayer. On the other hand, the open access to God in prayer has sometimes been so stressed that admission to God's presence becomes a thoughtless and casual matter. Between these two poles, there is a proper median: there is indeed access to the Holy God in worship and prayer, but it must be employed carefully, not casually, with appropriate preparation and reverence. Psalm 15 provides a guide to such access; it reflects the wisdom, prior to entering the divine presence in worship, of reflecting upon the requirements presupposed of the worshiper.

The moral substance expressed in this psalm (vv 2–5) is of such a kind that if one were to reflect too long upon its substance, without insight, worship would never be possible. There may be many who have earnestly sought the moral integrity reflected in these ten conditions of admission, but none who could claim complete accomplishment. Psalm 15 could effectively become a barrier, closing off all from worship; since none qualify fully, none may worship.

What transforms the psalm from a barrier to a gateway is the realization that the preparation for worship illuminates also the necessity for worship. On the one hand, we must live in such a way that we may prepare for worship with integrity, without hypocrisy; on the other hand, the introspection involved, prior to worship, clarifies beyond any doubt the need for forgiveness. Failing to have fulfilled the ten conditions, we require forgiveness before we can enter the divine presence. Only then do we realize that the privilege may never be casually exploited and also that the Holy God is not inaccessible.

Confidence in the Face of Death   (16:1–11)

Bibliography

Boers, H. W. "Psalm 16 and the Historical Origin of the Christian Faith." *ZNW* 60 (1969) 105–10. **Lindblom, J.** "Erwägungen zu Psalm XVI." *VT* 24 (1974) 187–95. **Mannati, M.** "Remarques sur Ps. XVI. 1–3." *VT* 22 (1972) 359–61. **Schmitt, A.** "Ps. 16:8–11 als Zeugnis der Auferstehung in der Apg." *BZ* NF 17 (1973) 222–48.

Translation

[1] A *Miktam* [a] of David.
   Guard me, O God,   (2+2)
      for I have sought refuge in you.
[2a] You have said [b] to the Lord: (2+2+2)
   "You are my master!
   My welfare indeed [c] rests on you."
[3] (You have said) to the holy ones [a] who are in the land: (2+2+2)
   "They are my mighty ones! [b]
   All my pleasure is in them."

⁴ They will multiply their pains: (2+2)
  they have acquired ᵃ another (god).
  I will not pour out their libations of blood,   (3+3)
  and I will not take their names upon my lips.
⁵ The Lord is my chosen portion ᵃ and my cup.   (3+3)
  You are the one who holds my lot.
⁶ The lines have fallen to me in pleasant places.   (3+3)
  Indeed, I have a beautiful heritage.
⁷ I will bless the Lord who has given me counsel.   (4+3)
  Indeed, my heart ᵃ adominishes me in the dark night. ᵇ
⁸ I have always put the Lord in front of me.   (4+3)
  Because he ᵃ is my right hand, I shall not be shaken.
⁹ Therefore, my heart ᵃ shall rejoice,   (3+2+3)
  and my glory shall exult.
  Indeed, my body ᵇ shall dwell in safety, ᶜ
¹⁰ for you do not abandon ᵃ me to Sheol,   (4+4)
  you do not permit your godly one to see the Pit.
¹¹ You make me to know the path of life,   (3+3+3)
  the full rejoicing ᵃ of your presence,
  the perpetual pleasantness ᵃ by your right hand.

Notes

1.a. *"Miktam"*: the meaning of this term is not known with certainty, though many interpretations have been offered over the centuries: (a) "an inscription, inscriptional poem" (implied by G, Theodotian, *Tg*); (b) "a *golden* psalm" (from כתם, *gold,* as in some early rabbinical interpretations); (c) an epithet of David, "humble, blameless" (Symmachus, Jerome—but the grammar makes this suggestion unlikely); (d) "a silent prayer" (Eerdmans, cited by Kidner, *Psalms 1–72,* 38); (e) "an *atonement* psalm" (from Akk. *katāmu,* "to cover (atone)": Mowinckel, *The Psalms in Israel's Worship,* II, 209); (f) the name of an early collection of psalms (Briggs, *The Book of Psalms,* lx). These are only a few of numerous interpretations. The most probable of the above interpretations is the first, namely that the term means *inscribed* (G στηλογραφία). It is possible to postulate a Hebrew root כתם, "to inscribe," closely related to כתב, "to write" (cf. Isa 38:9, מכתב). From this root, there developed the word employed in the psalm title, and it may be that the only other occurrence of a form related to this root is in Jer 2:22—נכתם: usually translated "stained" (cf. the later Syriac verb *ktham,* "to stain"), the word should perhaps be translated "inscribed" (viz. "your iniquity is inscribed before me"—and hence cannot be removed or washed out). Tentative support for this interpretation may come from the six psalms entitled *Miktam* in the Psalter; four, in their titles, are associated with times of crisis, which might have been events of sufficient moment to warrant recording in an inscription. The possibility of such significance in the present psalm is examined below. (If this interpretation were correct, then it might be assumed that the title *Miktam* was a part of the psalm from early in its history.)

2.a. There are numerous difficulties in vv 2–4, and the translation above is by no means certain; for alternative translations, interpretations, and emendations, see: Leveen, *VT* 21 (1971) 52–53; Mannati, *VT* (1972) 359–61; Lindblom, *VT* 24 (1974) 190–92, together with the standard commentaries. The following notes clarify the principal problems and provide the reasons for the translation provided above.

2.b. אמרת: most translators (ancient and modern) have assumed the verb is first pers. sing. and have restored a final *yodh.* There is some evidence in the Heb. mss for the final *yodh* (De-Rossi, IV, 8) or the form without *yodh* may be interpreted as an example of Phoenician-type orthography (Dahood, *Psalms I,* 87). But it is best to keep the consonantal text (which could be vocalized as either masc. or fem. (as in MT), 2 pers. sing.). If the second person is maintained, it brings out clearly the contrast between the psalmist's view (vv 1, 4b–11) and that of the person with whom he is in dialogue (vv 2–4a); see further the *Comment*.

2.c. בל, which may function either as a negative or affirmative particle, is here interpreted as affirmative: see O'Callaghan, *VT* 4 (1954) 166–67 and the *Note* on Ps 10:15.

3.a. לקדושים "to the holy ones" is parallel to ליהוה "to the Lord," and therefore implies the preceding verb of speech.

3.b. MT ואדירי: I have omitted the conjunction, with the support of several Heb. mss (De-Rossi, IV, 9), and pointed the final *yodh* as a pronominal suffix. Though the translation deviates from the punctuation of MT, it provides good sense and helps retain the 2+2 balance which permeates vv 2–4a. The "mighty ones" are parallel to the "holy ones," both expressions designating foreign gods, as pointed out by Dahood (*Psalms I*, 87–88).

4.a. מהרו: the meaning of the term is uncertain. The translation assumes a denominative verb מהר (BDB, 555), "they have acquired by paying the purchase price (of a wife)." But it must be admitted that such a sense is uncertain, given the masc. object and antecedents. Dahood's proposal of a verb הרר, "to lust," on the basis of Ugaritic, is attractive, but lacks strong support. Ugaritic *hrr* occurs only once in the Ugaritic texts (*CTA* 12.i.39; it may be restored in one other text), and though "lust" is a possible interpretation, "burned, scorched" (thus relating the root to *hrr*) is a more likely rendition; see Caquot et al., *Textes ougaritiques I*, 343.

5.a. חלקי: "(chosen) portion." Dahood translates "my smooth (wine) and my cup," hence "my cup of smooth wine" (*Psalms I*, 89). He derives the word from a verb חלק, "to be smooth," and bases his argument on the Ugaritic phrase *yn ḥlq*, which he translates "smooth wine." There are two Ugaritic texts which Dahood employs in his argument for a verb חלק, II "to be smooth" (*Ugaritic-Hebrew Philology*, 59). (i) *UT* 1084 (*PRU* 2.84), in which the expression *yn ḥlq* is used; this is an economic text, listing various wines, their qualities, quantities, and the vineyards from which they came. Almost certainly, however, the expression means "bad wine," occurring in the sequence *yn ṭb* ("good wine"), *yn l ṭb* ("not good wine"), and *yn ḥlq* ("bad wine"). On this translation, see Virolleaud, *PRU* II, 108 (who cites Akk *ḥulqu*), and O. Eissfeldt, *Kleine Schriften* II, 389. (ii) *UT* 117 (*CTA* 50). 16–17; in this instance, there are problems with the text. Dahood reads: *l(ḥ)lqt*. The text, however, is exceptionally difficult and many have despaired of retrieving the sense: see R. de Langhe, *Les Textes de Ras Shamra–Ugarit*, I, 178 and Gordon, *Ugaritic Literature*, 117. The most recent reexamination and collation of the Ugaritic texts has suggested that the best reading is *l lq(h)t* (*KTU*.2.13.16–17; cf. M. Dietrich, O. Loretz, J. Sanmartín, *UF* 6 [1974] 46–52). In summary, there is no unambiguous evidence for an Ugaritic word *ḥlq*, "smooth," nor has it been clearly established that there is a Hebrew verb חלק (II), "to be smooth." Hence, Dahood's translation is to be rejected.

7.a. "Heart": literally, "kidneys," the seat of the emotions, in Hebrew thought, hence equivalent to English "heart."

7.b. "Dark night": the plur. form (לילות "nights") conveys the intensive sense (Briggs, *The Book of Psalms*, 126).

8.a. הוא ("he") is inserted, as is implied by the sense of the line.

9.a. "Heart"—viz. the mind, in this context.

9.b. "Body": literally, "flesh."

9.c. There is a problem pertaining to the translation of tenses in v 9. In MT, the third verb is imperf., the second *waw*-consec. imperf., and the first perf. All three are translated above in a future sense, after לכן "therefore"; for שמח "rejoices", I read ישמח "shall rejoice", with limited support from the Heb mss (De-Rossi, IV, 9), and ויגל is interpreted as imperf. with simple *waw* "and shall exult" (contra MT).

10.a. On Dahood's proposal to relate תעזב "abandon" to a verb meaning "to put," see the *Note* on Ps 10:14.

11.a. The plur. forms, שמחות "rejoicing" and נעמות "pleasantness," are intensive and are thus translated as sing.

Form/Structure/Setting

Psalm 16 may be classified in the most general terms as a *psalm of confidence* (cf. Pss 4, 5, and 11), but beyond such a descriptive statement, it is difficult to be precise. The difficulty of precise analysis and interpretation follows from the problems in translating the psalm (especially vv 2–4a). There are numerous different interpretations as to its type and initial life setting (see Anderson, *Psalms I,* 140, for a survey), and the differences stem largely from the various alternative translations and interpretations of the opening verses.

The data giving rise to the classification of the passage as a *psalm of confidence* are seen clearly in vv 5–11; what is not certain is whether the psalmist expresses confidence in *the midst of* crisis, or *as a result of deliverance from* a crisis. The opening words (v 1) might imply a prayer for protection in crisis, or a prayer for continuing protection similar to that recently experienced in the deliverance from crisis. And if the word *Miktam* in the title does indeed mean "inscription, inscriptional poem" (see v 1, note a), then it is conceivable that this psalm began its life as an inscription on a monument, celebrating some specific deliverance from crisis, for which there are general analogies in Near Eastern texts.

The introductory verses of the psalm, as translated here, contain the words of an imagined (or former) dialogue between the psalmist, a true worshiper of God, and some other person. The other person, if the translation is correct, was typical of a class of people common in ancient Israel, against whom the prophets railed fiercely, namely the syncretists, who continued to worship the God of Israel (as they thought), but also worshiped the pagan deities (the "holy ones," the "mighty ones," v 3), whose cults existed in the land. Presumably the other person, a friend or acquaintance, represented the temptation faced by the psalmist in time of crisis; when trouble comes, it would surely be better to have both God and the "mighty ones" standing alongside, for together they could offer more protection than a single deity. But the psalmist had refused such temptation and had risen (or was rising) in confidence above the temptation to seek help elsewhere; his help would be found in the deliverance of God alone. If there is any merit in this approach to the interpretation of the psalm, then it is possible that its origin should be sought in individual (non-cultic) circumstances.

There is no certainty with respect to the date or authorship of the psalm. All six *Miktam* psalms in the Psalter belong to Davidic collections; four of the six (56, 57, 59, 60) are identified in their titles with particular incidents in the life of David. But the substance of Ps 16 contains no precise information which might permit dating or the identification of the author.

The psalm is examined in three sections: (1) introduction (16:1); (2) the words of an acquaintance (16:2–4a); (3) a song of confidence (16:4b–11).

Comment

Introduction (16:1). The opening prayer for protection could refer to a special crisis, from which the psalmist seeks deliverance, or it may simply express the desire for continuing divine protection in the future, as it had already been experienced in the recent past. Taking the psalm as a whole, there were two dangers from which protection was sought: first, the danger of death (Sheol, the Pit, v 10), from which the psalmist might recently have been delivered, and second, the dangerous temptation to succumb to a syncretistic faith, such as is expressed in the words of an acquaintance (vv 2–4), which the psalmist still hears ringing in his ears.

The words of an acquaintance (16:2–4a). (The translation of this section is so problematical—see the *Notes*—that the *Comment* is deliberately kept short, lest too much should be built on too fragile a foundation.)

The psalmist recalls the words of an acquaintance (or a typical fellow citizen of his time), which in one sense represent temptation and in another sense represent something abhorrent to the psalmist. The acquaintance is a syncretist, wanting the best of two worlds: he vocalizes the appropriate words to God—"You are my master!"—but his faith has an elastic quality, so that he can also trip off his tongue the appropriate words to the foreign deities (the "holy ones")—"they are my mighty ones!" The acquaintance represents temptation, for he appears to have double protection in a time of crisis; he represents something to be abhorred, for his words are clearly in contravention of the first commandment.

The word "they" (v 4) now includes all such persons (introduced as *you* in v 2): though their double indemnity approach to life was attractive, it would culminate in pain, for another god (in addition to the Lord) had been acquired. Having now dispensed with temptation, by seeing it for what it really is (v 4a), the psalmist is able to move on to his own affirmation of integrity and confidence.

A song of confidence (16:4b–11). In vv 4b–5, the psalmist contrasts his own position with that of the acquaintance. While the acquaintance sought to serve two masters, the psalmist renounces one and affirms the other in closely parallel language. He refuses to participate in the worship of false gods or take their names upon his lips, as his acquaintance had done (v 3). God was his "portion" and "cup"; only the lips that abstained from pronouncing the names of foreign deities could drink of the cup of blessing provided by God. (See also Hos 2:17 [Heb 3:19]: "I will remove the names of the *Baals* from her mouth and no more shall they be mentioned by name.")

In vv 6–7, the psalmist reflects upon his experience of life, and that reflection issues forth in praise. His life has been a good one. He describes it in the metaphor of the allocation of "promised land," saying that he had been awarded "pleasant places" (viz. the measuring lines have marked out for him a good location in the promised land which is life) and a "beautiful heritage." But it is not of the literal possession of land that he speaks; it is the divine "counsel" (v 7a) which has led him to so bountiful an experience of life and which makes him bless God. The general reflection on the goodness of life returns to the particular crisis, either threatening or recently experienced, in vv 8–9; the crisis appears to take the form of the threat of death, as is implied by the words, "I shall not be shaken" (viz. I shall not die: see also Ps 13:5 and the *Comment*). The psalmist's confidence in the face of mortal threat is based first upon the fact that the Lord is in front of him (v 8), indicating both God's protective presence and also the psalmist's obedience to the divine law (cf. Ps 119:30), and second upon the fact that the Lord is his "right hand" (v 8b), holding him firmly through the tremors that seek to shake him into death. With such confidence, the psalmist rejoices and exults.

In the concluding portion of the psalm (vv 9c–11), the psalmist expresses assurance both that he was delivered from the immediate threat of death and that he was restored to a full life in God's presence. With respect to the initial meaning of the psalm, it is probable that this concluding section should not be interpreted either messianically or in terms of individual eschatology; on the later Christian interpretation along these lines, see the *Explanation* (below). The acute concern of the psalmist was an immediate crisis and an immediate deliverance. His body had been endangered and his life threatened with untimely termination in *Sheol:* on Sheol see the discussion at Ps 6:5 *(Comment).* The word *Pit* is poetically synonymous to Sheol. But emerging confidently from that crisis of mortality, the psalmist acknowledges that God makes him know, or experience, the "path of life," not the afterlife, but the fullness of life here and now which is enriched by the rejoicing which emerges from an awareness of the divine presence.

Explanation

I have suggested in the *Comment* that the psalm, with respect to its initial meaning, is neither messianic nor eschatological in nature. Yet it is apparent that in the earliest Christian community, the psalm was given a messianic interpretation with respect to the death and resurrection of Jesus Christ. Both Peter, in his sermon at Pentecost (Acts 2:25–28), and Paul, in the synagogue at Antioch (Acts 13:35), reflect this interpretation of the psalm in their preaching. From one perspective, this change in meaning attributed to the text may be examined in the context of the history of interpretation: see Schmitt, *BZ* 17 (1973) 222–48; Boers, *ZNW* 60 (1969) 105–10. From another perspective, it is an example of the double meanings which may be inherent in the text of Scripture, a dimension of their inspiration, as expressed with such clarity by C. S. Lewis (*Reflections on the Psalms,* 92–100). From either perspective, the new meaning imparted to the text suggests not only progress, but contrast. The psalmist was faced with imminent death; he rose in confidence above that danger to know the fullness of life in God's presence. But in the new interpretation, Jesus not only faces imminent death—he goes on to die; whereas from the psalmist's theological perspective, death would end it all, in the experience of Jesus, death became a door. The psalmist rose up in confidence against the danger of death: Jesus rose up in confidence from the actual stronghold of death. While God did not abandon the psalmist to Sheol, he delivered Jesus from Sheol.

And the progression of meaning in the history of the psalm's interpretation also suggests for us a progression in our experience of living. While with the psalmist we may seek deliverance from an untimely death and may rise confidently above that danger, eventually a timely death will come, as it does to all mankind. Yet there is a new ground for confidence for all mankind, for the untimely death of Jesus was consummated in resurrection; that resurrection offers hope to all who read the sermons of Peter and Paul, whether their deaths be timely or untimely. The psalmist wrote from a particular experience, and yet his words touched upon the experience of all mortal beings, namely the fear of death. It is a fear which must be controlled confidently if life is to be lived fully, yet it is a fear which can never be controlled absolutely. Yet its sting is removed in the new meaning of Ps 16: the terminal threat of Sheol was conquered in the resurrection of Jesus.

A Prayer for Deliverance (17:1–15)

Bibliography

Gaulandi, D. "Salmo 17 (16):13–14." *Bib* 37 (1956) 199–208. **Leveen, J.** "Textual Problems in Psalm XVII." *VT* 11 (1961) 48–54.

Translation

¹ A Prayer of David.
Hear my plea for vindication, [a] *O Lord.* (3+2)
   Give attention to my cry.
Give ear to my prayer, (2+3)
   (spoken) without [b] *deceitful lips.*
² *Let my judgment come from you!* (3+3)
   May your eyes [a] *see the right things!*
³ *You have tested my heart,* (2+2)
   you have visited by night,
   you have refined me, but you will find nothing: (2+2)
   I have determined [a] *my mouth shall not transgress.*
⁴ *As for the deeds of mankind—* (2+2, 2+2 or 4+4)
   by the word of your lips,
   I have kept myself
   from robbers' roads.
⁵ *My steps held firmly* [a] *in your tracks,* (3+2)
   my footsteps have not been shaken!
⁶ *I have called on you,* (2+2)
   for you will answer me, O God!
   Incline your ear to me (2+2)
   and [a] *answer my utterance!*
⁷ *Reveal* [a] *the wonder of your lovingkindness,* (2+2+2)
   you who deliver by your right hand
   those seeking refuge from assailants. [b]
⁸ *Guard me as the apple of your eye;* [a] (3+3)
   hide me in the shadow of your wings
⁹ *from wicked ones who have assaulted me.* (4+4)
   My mortal enemies encompass me!
¹⁰ *They have become rebellious.* [a] (2+3)
   Their mouths have spoken with arrogance.
^{11a} *They have tracked me down. Now they have surrounded me!* (3+4)
   They set their eyes to pitch me to the ground.

12 *His appearance* ª *is like a lion, longing to lacerate,*   (4+3)
   and like a young lion lurking ᵇ *in secret places.*
13 *Arise, O Lord! Confront him to his face. Make him bow!*   (5+4)
   Deliver my soul from wickedness by your sword. ª
14 *Kill them* ª *by your hand, O Lord!*   (3+2+2)
   Kill them ª *from the world,*
   their portion from among the living.
   But your treasured ones ᵇ*!—you will fill their belly,* ᶜ   (3+2+3)
   sons will be sated,
   and they will bequeath their surplus to their children.
15 *I, in vindication* ª, *shall see your face;*
   on awakening, I shall be satisfied by your form ᵇ.   (4+3)

Notes

1.a. צדק causes problems, though the parallelism implies that it must mean something like
"(plea for) vindication, righteousness." The pronominal suffix must either be provided by minor
emendation, צדקי, following G (cf. Brockington, *The Hebrew Text of the Old Testament*, 124), or
by the principle of the "double duty suffix" (Dahood, *Psalms I*, 93).

1.b. The last phrase in v 1 creates further difficulties; I have interpreted בלא in the sense
of "without," implying a previous verb of speech. Dahood offers the following attractive possibility: "*Destroy* deceitful lips," assuming a Piel impv. from * בלא, "to wear out, destroy," a by-
form of בלה. But the philological grounds are uncertain: Heb. בלה means "wear out, grow
old," but does not clearly carry the sense "destroy," in either Qal or Piel. Dahood claims the
Ugaritic root *blᵖ* is preserved in *nblᵖat*, "flame," but the etymology of this word is uncertain; it
may not be related to Ugaritic *bly* ("become worn, withered"); Driver cites Akk. *nablu* and Ethiopic
nabal "flame," in *CML*, 158.

2.a. עיניך "your eyes": G implies עיני "my eyes," which (if correct) would indicate the
consequence to the psalmist of the judgment coming from God. But MT gives good sense,
providing a double petition, and is to be retained.

3.a. זמתי "I have determined": the word is taken by G to be a noun, object of the preceding
verb, but this is probably incorrect. The translation above follows MT, in which the form is
pointed as a verb and introduces a new clause, as indicated by the *athnaḥ* under the preceding
word.

5.a. תמך, pointed in MT as an infinitive absolute, is interpreted as an imperative in G, *Vg*,
and *Tg* ("support/direct my steps . . ."). But context indicates that a plur. form of the verb
should be read (as indicated in *BHS*); the translation above assumes a reading תָּמְכוּ. Alternatively
(achieving the same translation), the inf. absol. of MT may be interpreted as functioning as a
finite verb; cf. GKC 113, v and gg.

6.a. A conjunction is read before שמע "hear, answer," with the support of some Heb. mss,
G and S.

7.a. הפלה "separate": the translation assumes the reading הפלא "reveal," which has massive
support in the Heb. mss (De-Rossi, IV, 10), including C; see also G.

7.b. The last four words of v 7 pose problems with respect to word order. The translation
takes בימינך "by your right hand" with מושיע "the deliverer" in sense, though actual transposition may not be necessary to achieve the required sense; viz. "the one delivering those-who-
seek-refuge-from-adversaries by your right hand." Dahood proposes an attractive alternative,
reading חסם (impv. from חסם, "to muzzle"; *Psalms I*, 96). Following this suggestion, there
would be a 3+3 line as follows: "Reveal the wonder of your lovingkindness, O Deliverer.
Muzzle the assailants with your right hand." (This is my translation, not Dahood's, who makes
various other changes in the text in addition to the one noted.)

8.a. "Apple of your eye": literally, "little one of (the) daughter of (the) eye." A similar
idiom is employed in Deut 32:10. The suffix ("*your* eye") is implied, and may be provided
from the second part of the verse on the principle of the double duty suffix.

10.a. "They have become rebellious": literally, "they have closed their fat." The precise meaning of this idiomatic expression is uncertain, but a possible solution is provided by Deut 32:10–15, which employs a series of similar idiomatic expressions: (a) "apple of the eye" (17:8 and Deut 32:10); (b) the metaphor of protective wings (17:8 and Deut 32:11); (c) "Jeshurun grew fat and kicked" (Deut 32:15), clearly indicating rebelliousness, which is the basis for the interpretation of the idiom in the translation above.

11.a. The verse has several problems. The initial word is read as אַשְּׁרֵנוּ (cf. *G's* ʾΕκβαλόντες με, "they have cast out"). The third word is read as סָבְבוּנִי (*Kethib*) "surround me." Finally, לנטות "to spread out" is read with a 1st pers. sing. pron. suff., לִנְטוֹתִי "to pitch me," with the support of *S* (or else the suffix may simply be supplied in sense, on the principle of the double duty suffix).

12.a. דְּמִינוֹ: "his appearance." *G* (ὑπέλαβόν με) implies a verb, e.g. דִּמּוּנִי (cf. *BHS*), but it is best to retain MT; as Delitzsch noted, the poet now singles out the most threatening member of the enemy host (the chief) and focuses upon him (*Biblical Commentary on the Psalms*, I, 300).

12.b. "Lurking": literally, "dwelling, sitting."

13.a. On the syntax of חרבך "your sword" (viz., a double subject, which must be translated by an adverbial phrase), see GKC 144, 1-m; the unusual construction apparently caused confusion among the translators of *G*, who linked the word to the following verse.

14.a. V 14 is exceptionally difficult to translate and the wide disparity between the various versions indicates the possibility of textual corruption at an early date; cf. the notes in *BHS* and Gaulandi, *Bib* 37 (1956) 199–208. The translation adopted here involves pointing the duplicated form ממתים in each case as מְמִיתָם "kill them," Hiph. ptc. of מות "die," plus suff.; cf. *G* (on v 14d) and Dahood, *Psalms I*, 98–99.

14.b. "Your treasured ones": the translation follows *Qere*: צְפוּנֶךָ (Qal pass. ptc.); the sing. expression is interpreted as collective and translated as plur..

14.c. "You will fill their belly"—so MT, but if *G* is followed, תמלא could be pointed as Niph. imperf.: "your belly *will be filled.*" Either rendering makes good sense.

15.a. בצדק: the translation "in vindication" is implied by the nuance of צדק in v 1, where it was translated "plea for vindication." Thus the closing verse neatly rounds out the psalm which began with a plea.

15.b. תמונה means "likeness, form." Several versions avoid the translation "form" (cf. *G* δόξαν "glory"; *Vg gloria*), presumably for theological reasons (see Deut 4:12). But there is no good reason to doubt the text of MT, and the parallelism with פָּנֶיךָ "your face" indicates that both terms should be interpreted as symbolizing the divine presence.

Form/Structure/Setting

The title appropriately designates this psalm as a *prayer.* The expression "prayer of David" has sometimes been taken to indicate that the prayer was written by David, yet the words may simply designate a collection of prayers; see the INTRODUCTION, THE PSALMS AND THE PROBLEM OF AUTHORSHIP, and compare the use of the plural form of the same expression in Ps 72:20.

In general terms, the prayer is in the form of an individual lament, yet more precisely it is an innocent person's *prayer for protection* (cf. the analogous Ps 5, which is a *protective psalm*). It may not be possible to gain further precision with respect to type and the implied social or religious setting of the psalm in its original context. Eaton interprets the psalm as royal prayer or supplication (*Kingship and the Psalms*, 33–34), which is an attractive possibility; although the language is susceptible to such an interpretation (particularly the words describing the enemies, vv 7, 9–14), it might also be interpreted as general poetic language in which a military metaphor has been employed to depict the violent threat of opponents in general (see the *Comment*).

Thus all that can be certain is that the psalm reflects the situation of an innocent person under extreme pressure. It may be the case that it should be interpreted as a *morning prayer* (cf. Ps 5), on the basis of the references to *night testing* (v 3) and *awakening* (v 15), presumably in the morning; see further the *Comment.* The general substance and language of the psalm do not provide the criteria necessary for establishing either author or date.

The psalm is carefully constructed in three parts in which the double themes of the innocent person and the opponent are skillfully interwoven (see particularly Ridderbos, *Die Psalmen,* 160–61, for a fuller analysis): (1) A prayer based on the psalmist's innocence (17:1–5); (a) prayer vv 1–2, and (b) a description of the psalmist's testing and innocence vv 3–5. (2) A prayer based on the enemy's attack (17:6–12); (a) prayer vv 6–8, and (b) description of the enemy attack vv 9–12. (3) A prayer for the enemy's destruction and the psalmist's deliverance (17:13–15).

Comment

Prayer based on testing and innocence (17:1–5). (a) The psalmist begins his prayer with a series of requests addressed directly to the Lord (vv 1–2). It is the first part of the prayer which sets out most clearly the nature of the psalmist's predicament; he is praying for "vindication" (literally, "righteousness"), or the divine affirmation of his innocence with respect to the charges and attacks launched against him. The words of the psalmist are not those of a self-righteous person asserting absolute innocence; they emerge in a particular context, and the affirmation of innocence and the prayer for vindication must be interpreted specifically in the context of the unjust charges and attacks set against the psalmist. Nevertheless, his prayer is genuine; he does not pray simply out of desperation under attack, but prays truthfully, "without deceitful lips" (v 1). The first part of the prayer requests God in the most urgent tones to attend (v 1); the second part (v 2) specifies the required action. The psalmist asks for his "judgment" (viz. the declaration concerning his innocence) to come from God, for the nature of his crisis is that unjust judgment and consequent persecution are descending upon him from his fellow human beings. While his enemies make false and lying claims concerning him, the psalmist prays that God's "eyes see the right things," namely discern the true from the false and thus separate true innocence from guilt.

(b) The psalmist then elaborates upon his initial request by a declaration of integrity (vv 3–5). God has already tested him (v 3: alternatively, if the tenses of the verbs are interpreted as precative perfects, v 3 contains an invitation for God to test him), but there is no crime to be found (viz. he is not guilty of that which the enemies claim in their attack upon him). The testing is described in two overlapping metaphors, that of refining metal (the verbs בחן "test" and צרף "refine") and that of interrogation or investigation (the verb פקד "visit": cf. Job 7:18). The words "visited (or *investigated*) by night" may refer to hours spent at night in prayer and self-inspection, perhaps indicating that the prayer was uttered at night with the expectation of an answer in the morning (cf. v 15). Whereas in v 3, the affirmation pertains primarily to innocence with respect to speech ("my mouth shall not transgress"), there is a progression in v 4 to affirmation of innocence with respect to action. The psalmist has avoided the evil deeds typical of mankind as a whole, which are represented here by one of the most common of violent crimes—robbery. The psalmist affirms that he has kept himself from such evil, but what made it possible was the "word of your lips," namely the divine revelation and guidance. In poetic language, the psalmist avoided "robbers' roads," and similar language continues in v 5 with a contrast: his feet have held firmly to God's "tracks," which suggests a walk of life entirely different from that of wicked persons. Thus, the poet is utilizing with striking effect a modification of the metaphor of the *two ways* which was employed in Ps 1; because his feet held firmly to the tracks of God, avoiding the way of the wicked, he could assume the privilege of the righteous and pray for vindication.

Prayer based on the enemy's attack (17:6–12). The second part of the psalm is characterized by the same structure as the first part. An opening prayer is followed now by a second reason, given in descriptive terms, as to why the prayer should be answered.

(a) The psalmist asks for three things: that God hear him, that God reveal himself in deliverance, and that God protect him (vv 6–8). The psalmist's confidence is revealed most clearly in v 6. He has called on God in prayer because he knows that it is in God's nature to hear and answer prayer, and as the prayer continues (vv 7–8), it becomes clear that what is requested is in keeping with God's covenant character. He prays for a revelation of God's "lovingkindness," namely that covenant characteristic of God which had been demonstrated most clearly in acts of deliverance. More precisely, the language of v 7 mirrors that of the Song of the Sea (Exod 15:1–18), in which Israel celebrated its deliverance from the Pharaoh in the Exodus, as the following parallels indicate:

Ps 17:7	*Exod 15:11–13*
הפלא "reveal the wonder"	פלא "wonder"
חסדיך "your lovingkindness"	בחסדך "in your lovingkindness"
בימינך "by your right hand"	ימינך "your right hand"

From this memory of the Exodus arose both the psalmist's confidence that God would answer his prayer and also his request that God deliver him from his assailants in a personal "exodus." The covenant theme continues still further in v 8, where the language parallels that of Moses' Song of the Covenant (specifically Deut 32:10–11); the psalmist prays for God's protection as his people had known it in the past, both in the wilderness, but more exactly in the trials in Egypt (cf. Craigie, *The Book of Deuteronomy*, 380–81).

(b) There now follows a description of the wicked persons from whom the psalmist sought deliverance (vv 9–12). The enemies are first described in general terms (vv 9–11), and then, heightening the poetic tension, the psalmist focuses on just one, perhaps the most powerful enemy whose presence created the most immediate threat (v 12). The enemies in general are characterized as *rebellious* (see further the *Notes*); that is, they have grown fat and prosperous on the basis of divine provision, but have forgotten the divine Provider, and in their amnesiac state have attacked the Lord's faithful servant. The arrogance with which they speak against the psalmist is a further indication of the loss of humility inherent in their rebelliousness. But their assault is not merely the attack of words; they have also *tracked down* (v 11) the innocent psalmist, who in turn was walking firmly in God's *tracks* (cf. v 5). The language of v 11 is military in nature, though it is probable that it should be interpreted metaphorically; and the metaphor of v 11 is heightened by the simile of the lion (v 12), ready to leap on the psalmist and tear him to pieces. It is the urgency of the crisis, as described here, which contributes to the sense of urgency permeating the poem as a whole.

Prayer for deliverance and the destruction of enemies (17:13–15). The concluding portion of the psalm rounds out the prayer in a chiastic fashion. The psalmist began by describing his innocence (vv 3–5) and followed that with a description of his enemies (vv 9–12); now he prays for the destruction of his enemies (vv 13–14a) and expresses confidence in the coming deliverance of the innocent (vv 14b–15). The chiastic structure is reinforced in other ways. He begins with a *plea for vindication* (צדק, v 1) and uses the same word in the concluding verse (v 15). He begins by praying that God *see* the right things (v 2, using the verb חזה) and concludes with confidence that he would *see* God's face (v 15, using the same verb again).

The prayer for the destruction of enemies appears to be particularly violent in tone, but it is probable that the words should be interpreted metaphorically rather than literally. The military metaphor, already noted in the descriptive language of v 11, is here worked into the prayer for deliverance. On the military associations of the word "arise" (v 13), see the *Comment* on Ps 7:7. Likewise, the words "sword" (v 13) and "kill" (v 14, twice) should be seen as part of the military metaphor, rather than as a literal expression of the psalmist's desire. Furthermore, the antecedent upon which the psalmist was basing his hope of deliverance was the Exodus (see the *Comment* on v 7, above), in which the Pharaoh and his forces were killed; the prayer in vv 13–14a continues in the same tone.

In his concluding statement of confidence, the psalmist first describes the blessed estate of God's righteous ones in general (namely the "treasured ones," v 14), and then becomes more precise in expressing his personal confidence and hope (v 15). In terms of poetic structure, vv 14b–15 are analogous to vv 11–12; in the latter passage, the poet moved from enemies in general to a specific enemy, as now he moves from God's "treasured ones" to himself. God's own people would be filled with such abundance that enough would be left for their children and grandchildren after them; though the words indicate the material provision of food (that which would "fill their belly"), the more general poetic sense implies that all of God's provision would be thus abundant. Receiving God's adequate provision for his people and for future generations, the psalmist is able to conclude with confidence. He would receive that vindication for which he had prayed and it would come in the full awareness of God's presence, here described as seeing God's face and being satisfied with his form. Though the precise sense of v 15 is uncertain, the general sense indicates the conscious awareness of the divine presence. It would no longer be enemies that dominated the psalmist's vision, but God's face; on awakening from the restless sleep of night (see also v 3), God's *form* or actual presence would be a reality, not an elusive phantom of the troubled dreams of night.

Explanation

One of the most significant aspects of this finely proportioned psalm is the way in which it gives expression to covenant theology. The psalmist is in dire straits, pressed hard on every side, but in confidence he is able to rise above the threatening circumstances. Yet the ascent to confidence is not merely a testimony to the psalmist's stalwart faith and his ability to transcend his perilous circumstances; it is primarily a testimony to the faith of the covenant community.

That which makes hope, and therefore confidence, possible is an awareness of the nature of the covenant God. The psalmist was not the first to be in trouble, nor would he be the last, but he believed in a God of covenant, whose most fundamental characteristic was *lovingkindness* (חסד, v 7). And the first and greatest demonstration of lovingkindness which Israel had experienced was in the Exodus from Egypt. Thus the psalmist belonged to a delivered community; in his own crisis, he could call upon God who was known above all as a God of deliverance in crisis. Fundamental to belonging to the covenant community was sharing in the covenant memory, which in turn had its focal point in the fact that the covenant only existed because God had delivered. And it is this conscious awareness of the psalmist, expressed most distinctly in v 7 (see the *Comment*), which is the focal point of the psalm. Though the psalm is written in the language of individuality, it does not contain the words of a lonely and bold pioneer of crisis; it contains rather the words of one sharing in the past and present experience of a community that had known God as deliverer. The psalmist thus draws upon the strengths of both history and community in reaching his confidence. And when he closes his prayer, he thinks not only of himself, but of all God's "treasured ones" (vv 14b–15). The psalmist stands firmly in a particular history, the history of deliverance or salvation, and renews that ancient reality in his own temporal experience.

It is from this sense of the continuity of the history of salvation that v 15 may assume, for the modern reader, a new theological dimension; it may refer to the awareness of the divine presence which lies beyond the awakening from that sleep which is death. Although there are several interpreters who would give such an eschatological sense to the psalm in its initial meaning (e.g. Dahood, *Psalms I*, 99–100), such an interpretation is unlikely on an initial basis; the psalmist seeks immediate deliverance from a present crisis. But from the perspective of Christian theology (or later Jewish theology), the history of salvation has assumed deeper and wider proportions. The psalm, in its current usage, may provide both hope for the immediate crisis, as for the psalmist of old, but beyond that a deeper hope for ultimate deliverance from a more dangerous and insidious enemy, a hope that reaches beyond the sleep of death itself.

A Royal Thanksgiving Psalm   (18:1–51)

Bibliography

Cross, F. M. and Freedman, D. N. *Studies in Ancient Yahwistic Poetry*, 125–60. _____.
"A Royal Song of Thanksgiving: II Samuel 22 = Psalm 18." *JBL* 72 (1953) 15–34.
Freedman, D. N. "Divine Names and Titles in Early Hebrew Poetry." In F. M. Cross,
et al., *Magnalia Dei: The Mighty Acts of God* (Doubleday, 1976). 55–102 (*75–77). **Schmut-
termayr, G.** "RḤM—Eine lexikalische Studie." *Bib* 51 (1970) 499–532. **Stuart,
D. K.** *Studies in Early Hebrew Meter*, 171–86.

Translation

1 For the musical director. Belonging to the servant of the Lord, to David, who addressed
to the Lord the words of this song on the day that the Lord delivered him from
the hand of all [a] his enemies and from the hand [b] of Saul.[c]

2(1) *And he said:*
I love [a] you, O Lord, my strength.[b]

3(2) *The Lord is my cliff and my stronghold and my deliverer;* [a]   (4+3+3)
my God is my rock in whom I seek refuge,
my shield and my horn of salvation, my safe retreat.

4(3) *I called [a] upon the Lord, who is worthy of praise,*   (3+2)
and I was delivered [a] from my enemies.

5(4) *The [a] cords [b] of death have entwined me,*   (3+3)
and the torrents of Belial have overwhelmed me; [c]

6(5) *the cords of Sheol have surrounded me,*   (3+3)
the snares of Death have confronted me.

7(6) *In my distress, I called [a] upon the Lord,*   (3+2)
and I cried out [a] for help to my God.
He heard [a] my voice from his temple,   (3+4?)
and my shout entered [a] into him,[b] into his very ears.

8(7) *Then the earth shook and quaked,*   (3+3+3)
and the foundations of the mountains [a] quivered,
and they shook back and forth because he was angry.

9(8) *Smoke has gone up from his nostrils,*   (3+3+3)
and consuming fire from his mouth;
coals and fire flame forth from him.

10(9) *Then he spread apart the heavens and came down,*   (3+3)
with dense cloud under his feet;

11(10) *and he rode [a] upon a cherub and flew,*   (3+3/2)
and soared [b] upon the wings of the wind.

12(11) [a] *He made darkness his den;*   (3+2+3?)
his lair round about
was dense clouds, dark with water.

13(12) *From the brightness before him, clouds [a] burst into flames,[b]*   (4+3/2)
hail and fiery coals.

14(13)   *Then the Lord thundered from heaven,*[a]   (3+3+3/2)
and Elyon gave forth his voice—
hail and fiery coals! [b]

15(14)   *And he dispatched* [a] *his arrows and scattered them,*   (3+3)
and multiplied [b] *bolts of lightning and routed them.*

16(15)   *And the beds of the ocean* [a] *were revealed,*   (3+3)
and the foundations of the earth were laid bare
at your rebuke [b]*, O Lord,*   (2+3)
at the breath of wind from your nostrils. [c]

17(16)   *He reached down from on high, he took hold of me,*   (3+3)
he drew me out from the deep waters.

18(17)   *He delivered me from my powerful foe,*[a]   (3+3)
and from those hating me, for they were too strong for me.

19(18)   *They confronted me on the day of my distress.*   (2/3+3)
but the Lord was my support.

20(19)   *And he led me out to the broad place;*   (2+3?)
he delivered me, because he delighted in me.

21(20)   *The Lord has dealt fairly with me according to my righteousness;*   (3+3)
according to the cleanness [a] *of my hands, he has rewarded me.*

22(21)   *For I have kept the ways of the Lord*   (3+2)
and have not departed in wickedness [a] *from my God.*

23(22)   *For all his judgments have been before me,*   (3+3)
and his statutes I have not put aside from me; [a]

24(23)   *and I have been blameless with him,*   (3+2)
and I have guarded myself from my iniquitousness. [a]

25(24)   *So the Lord has rewarded me according to my righteousness,*   (3/4+4)
according to the cleanness [a] *of my hands in his sight.*

26(25)   *With the faithful, you show yourself faithful;*   (2+3)
with the blameless, you show yourself blameless.

27(26)   *With the pure, you show yourself pure,*   (2+2)
and with the twisted, you deal tortuously.

28(27)   *For you deliver an afflicted people,*   (3+3) [a]
and you bring down haughty eyes.

29(28)   *For you light* [a] *my lamp, O Lord.*   (4+3)
O my God, you enlighten my darkness.

30(29)   *For by you, I run up to a troop,*[a]   (3+2)
and by my God, I scale a wall.

31(30)   *The God—his way is perfect!*   (3+3?+4?)
The Lord's utterance is free of blemish.
He is a shield [a] *for all who seek refuge in him.*

32(31)   *For who is a god,* [a] *apart from the Lord?*   (5+4)
And who is a rock, except our God?—

33(32) [a] *the God who girded me with might,*   (3+3)
and made perfect my way.

34(33)   *He is the one making firm my feet like the hinds' feet,*   (3+3)
and he makes me stand upon high places. [a]

35(34)   *He is the one training my hands for battle,*   (3+3)
so that my arms can depress [a] *the bow of bronze.*

36(35)   *And you gave me your shield of deliverance,*   (3+2+2)
          and your right hand supported me, [a]
          and your help [b] *made me great.*

37(36)   *You lengthened my stride* [a] *beneath me,*   (3+3)
          so that my ankles have not slipped.

38(37)   *I pursued my enemies and I overtook them,* [a]   (3+2)
          and I did not return until they were finished.

39(38)   *I wounded them, so they were not able to rise;* [a]   (3+3)
          they fell beneath my feet.

40(39)   *And you girded me with might for the battle;*   (3+3)
          you made my opponents [a] *bow down beneath me.*

41(40)   *And my enemies—you have given me (their) neck;* [a]   (3?+2)
          and those who hate me—I have exterminated them.

42(41)   *They cried for help, but there was no deliverer;*   (3?+3)
          even upon the Lord!—but he did not answer them.

43(42)   *And I pulverized them as dust, wafted by wind;* [a]   (3+3)
          as mud of the streets, I poured them out. [b]

44(43)   *You have delivered me from contentions of people;*   (3+3)
          you have made me [a] *head of the nations.*
          A people I knew not served me;   (3+3?)

45(44)   *On the ear hearing, they became obedient to me.*
          Foreigners shrink at my presence. [a]   (2+2+2)

46(45)   *Foreigners sink down exhausted,*
          and come forth quaking [a] *from their strongholds.*

47(46)   *The Lord is alive, and blessed be my rock!*   (3+3)
          And may the God of my deliverance be exalted,

48(47)   *the God who is giving me vengeance,*   (4/3+3+2)
          and who has subdued [a] *peoples beneath me,*

49(48)   *the one delivering me from my enemies.*
          Indeed, you have raised me higher than my opponents;   (3+3)
          you have delivered me from the violent [a] *man.*

50(49)   *Therefore I will praise you among the nations, O Lord,*   (4+2)
          and I will sing the praise of your name.

51(50)   *He is the one giving great victories to his king,*   (3+3+3)
          and enacting lovingkindness toward his anointed,
          toward David and his seed forever.

Notes

1.a. One Heb. ms omits כל "all" before איביו "his enemies" (De-Rossi, IV, 11).

1.b. מיד "from the hand": many Heb. mss and the parallel passage in 2 Sam 22 contain the reading מכף "from the palm," but the sense is clear in either case, and מיד is the kind of free variant one might expect in an alternate transmission of the text.

1.c. Dahood (*Psalms I*, 104) suggests the translation *Sheol* for MT's שאול ("Saul"), which is possible in the light of v 6; but the context provided by 2 Sam 21 for the parallel version makes *Saul* equally appropriate.

2.a. The denominative verb רחם is used only here in the Qal, with the sense "love." See Schmuttermayr, *Bib* 51 (1970) 499–532 for a full discussion of the verb in this text.

2.b. This introductory poetic line is absent in the parallel passage.

3.a. Several Heb. mss (De-Rossi, IV, 11) and 2 Sam 22:2 add לי "to me" after ומפלטי "and my deliverer." MT is to be preferred, though the sense is affected little by either reading.

4.a. On the translation of tenses here, see v 5, note c, below.

5.a. Some Heb. mss (De-Rossi, IV, 11) and 2 Sam 22:5 prefix כי "for" to the line, thus implying a closer connection to v 4; the addition is possible.

5.b. חבלי "cords": many scholars prefer the variant reading משברי "breakers" here; but חבלי may be preferable for phonetic reasons, the sound being echoed in the consonants of the parallel term נחלי "torrents" which follows. The repetition of the term in v 6 is not surprising in the context of early Hebrew poetry.

5.c. יבעתוני "overwhelmed me": here, and frequently in Ps 18, the so-called imperfect tense is used to describe action completed in the past; the form here is parallel to the perfect tense with which the line begins: אפפוני "entwined me." For further discussion, see *Excursus II.*

7.a. On the use of tenses in this verse, see v 5, note c (above). See also *G.*

7.b. לפניו "before him": it is possible that the word should be deleted, being absent in 2 Sam 22:7; *BHS* suggests the omission on metrical grounds. Alternatively, MT may preserve a conflation of two alternate readings; see Stuart, *Hebrew Meter,* 174.

8.a. הרים "mountains": 2 Sam 22:8 has a variant, השמים, "the heavens," but the text of MT is to be preferred; for similar language, see Deut 32:22.

11.a. וירכב. The precise sense of the verb רכב has been debated and possible meanings include: (a) "to ride"; (b) "to mount"; (c) "to gather." I have preferred the usual connotation, "to ride," in the translation above, though "to mount" also provides good sense; see Dahood, *Psalms I,* 107. For discussion of the possible etymology of the word, see the following: M. Weinfeld, " 'Rider of the Clouds' and 'Gatherer of the Clouds'," *JANES* 5 (1973) 421–26; E. Ullendorff, "Ugaritic Studies in their East Mediterranean Setting," *BJRL* 46 (1963) 243–44; S. P. Brock, *VT* 18 (1968) 395–97; Mowinckel, "Drive and/or Ride in the OT," *VT* 12 (1962) 278–99.

11.b. וידא "soared": some Heb. mss (De-Rossi, IV, 11), and 2 Sam 22:11, read וירא "saw," but this reading is almost certainly an error and the text of MT should be retained; see further Barr, *Comparative Philology and the Text of the OT,* 192–93, 218, and Dahood in *RSP I,* 162.

12.a. This verse poses numerous textual problems and contains several differences from the parallel text, 2 Sam 22:12. The translation above is an attempt to make sense out of MT, but there is probably textual corruption. For hypothetical attempts at reconstruction of the text, see Cross and Freedman, *JBL* 72 (1953) 25; Stuart, *Hebrew Meter,* 175.

13.a. עביו: literally, "his clouds": *G* is followed here, indicating a plur. form without pron. suff. (עבים).

13.b. עברו: literally, "they passed over." But 2 Sam 22:13 has בערו "burned," indicating metathesis has taken place in the present text; בערו is the preferred reading in the light of the context (cf. v 9).

14.a. בשמים: the prep. is interpreted in the sense "from"; alternatively, with the support of several Heb. mss (De-Rossi, IV, 11), and 2 Sam 22:14, the prefixed prep. מן could be read.

14.b. The final phrase, duplicated in v 13 ("hail and fiery coals") could perhaps be omitted on the basis of dittography. But the variations between Ps 18 and 2 Sam 22 are considerable at this point, and Ps 18 has effective poetry through the duplication of the line. As repetition is a distinctive feature of some early Hebrew poetry (e.g. Judg 5), it is better to retain the phrase in both verses.

15.a. שלח "dispatches": Dahood (*Psalms I,* 109), translates "he *forged* his arrows" arguing for a distinction between Heb. שלח (I) "to send" and (II) "to forge," on the basis of Ugaritic *šlh,* which he claims has the meaning "to forge, hammer." However, the meaning of the Ugaritic term is not well established. In the critical text in which it *might* have the sense "forge," *UT* 51/*CTA* 4.1.26–27, it could equally mean "plate" (Gibson, *CML* [2], 56) or perhaps "filed" (Arabic *saḥala*), or "polished" (Akk. *šuʾulu*), as proposed by Driver, *CML,* 148. The translation "forged" appears to go back to Ginsberg (cf. Caquot, *Textes ougaritiques I,* 194), but the cognate Syriac term, on which the etymology is based, is *ḥṣal,* "to forge, found." In summary, the sense of Ugaritic *šlḥ* (II) is not sufficiently secure to form the basis for the interpretation of Heb. שלח (II), "to forge." In addition, the normal (I) sense of שלח, "to send, dispatch," provides a perfectly good translation in context.

15.b. רב is treated as a verb ("he multiplied," from רבב, though the form is unusual), on the basis of *G*'s ἐπλήθυνεν "he multiplied."

16.a. מים "water": the reading ים "sea, ocean" is adopted on the basis of several Heb mss (De-Rossi, IV, 11) and 2 Sam 22:16; the reading also provides an appropriate parallelism with the following תבל "world."

16.b. מגערתך: the conventional translation, "rebuke," is preferable to Dahood's proposed "roar" (Psalms I, 110), which is based in turn on the view that Ugaritic gʿr may have two meanings: (a) "rebuke"; (b) "roar." The former meaning is undisputed; the latter sense, however, is tenuous and based on a single text, UT 56/CTA 161, rev. 23. The text is a hippiatric text, and the line in which ygʿr occurs is in a portion of the text which is broken (the first five lines of the reverse of the text are all incomplete, the tablet being broken). If one grants that the term refers to some kind of noise emitted by a horse, then "neigh" might be an appropriate translation (cf. Aistleitner, WUS, #681). But the Ugaritic evidence is too fragile a foundation on which to propose the meaning "roar" for Heb. גערה.

16.c. אפך "your nostril": a plur. form is read (אפיך), with the support of a few Heb. mss, including C.

18.a. "My powerful foe": G and S imply a plur. form, but the sing. is to be preferred; cf. 2 Sam 22:18.

21.a. כבר: "according to the cleanness" . . . ; some Heb mss suggest the reading כבוד ("honor"), but MT is to be preferred, since the prep. כ provides a parallel to the earlier part of the verse (כצדקי "according to my righteousness"). Cf. v 25, where the problem re-appears.

22.a. רשעתי: the literal sense of the verb is "to do wickedness," but the unusual construction of this verb with following מ ן, plus the parallelism, imply the sense "depart, wander in wickedness" (from the ways of the Lord).

23.a. The latter part of the verse is rendered in 2 Sam 22:23 as: "and his statutes—I have not turned aside (אסיר) from it (ממנה)." But the lack of agreement in the pron. suff. (מהן or מהנה would be expected) lead one to suspect that MT of Ps 18:23 is the preferred reading.

24.a. מעוני (literally, "from my iniquity") poses several problems. Dahood proposes the translation—"not to offend him," taking the pron. suff. (yodh) to be an example of the 3 masc. sing. suff. -y in Hebrew (analogous, Dahood claims, to Ugaritic and Phoenician). But the argument for a Heb. 3 masc. suff. -y is based on fragile evidence and is by no means certain; for a critical assessment, see Z. Zevit, "The Linguistic and Contextual Arguments in support of a Hebrew 3 m.s. suffix -y," UF 9 (1977) 315–28. The solution above, however, is not without difficulties; עוני is treated in an abstract sense, "iniquitousness" (viz. tendency toward iniquity).

25.a. On textual problems concerning the reading כבר, see note a, v 21 (above).

28.a. Dahood (Psalms I, 112) renders v 28 as 2+2+3, and translates עם (normally "people") as "Strong One," a divine epithet. Against this translation and analysis of the line, see Loretz, "Psalmenstudien III," UF 6 (1974) 183–84.

29.a. In 2 Sam 22:29, the verb תאיר "light" is omitted, providing equally good sense; but the verb should be retained here (cf. G).

30.a. The translation of ארץ גדוד is difficult. The translation above assumes the presence of a root רוץ "to run," but the sense "run up to" is unusual. Alternatively, the root might be רצץ "to crush"; this sense might indicate the emendation of גדוד "troop" to גדר "wall," as implied by Lucian's translation of 2 Sam 22:30. But the precise sense of the verse is uncertain (cf. Stuart, Hebrew Meter, 185, n. 33) and the safest course is to stay with the sense implied by MT.

31.a. מגן ("shield"); against Dahood's translation "Suzerain" (Psalms I, 114), see Loretz, UF 6 (1974) 178, and the Note on Ps 3:4.

32.a. אלוה (god); this is a relatively rare noun, and there is some evidence in the Heb mss suggesting the reading אל "god"; cf. 2 Sam 22:32. On the use of the term אלוה, see Freedman in Magnalia Dei, 90. Though the translation is affected little, it is best to retain MT, providing variety in the usage of divine names in vv 32–33; אל is used in v 33.

33.a. There are several differences between this verse and 2 Sam 22:33, but they are of such a kind as to reflect a variant tradition, rather than textual corruption.

34.a. במתי "my high places": following the implications of G, the form is read without pron. suff. (במת), the yodh presumably having arisen through dittography.

35.a. נחתה "depress" (Piel) is sing., the subject זרועתי "my arms") being interpreted in a collective sense.

36.a. The second of the three lines is omitted in 2 Sam 22:36, but it is preferable to retain MT.

36.b. The meaning of the line is unclear, especially the meaning of וענותך; probably the best solution is that of Stuart (*Hebrew Meter*, 185, n. 40), reading עזרתך "your help," on the basis of *Q*.

37.a. צעדי ("my stride"): MT has a sing. pron. suff.; *G* implies a plur. suff., which is equally possible.

38.a. ואשיגם "overtook them": 2 Sam 22:38 has a variant reading, ואשמידם "destroyed them."

39.a. 2 Sam 22:39 has a longer first line than Ps 18, but it probably reflects a conflation of two variant readings; hence MT of Ps 18:39 is to be preferred.

40.a. קמי "my opponents": *G* adds πάντας, implying כל־קמי, "all my opponents."

41.a. ערף is "neck," rather than "back" (cf. rsv). The expression means that the victor places his foot on the neck of the fallen foe (cf. vv 40–41) as a sign of victory. See further Dahood, *Psalms I*, 116.

43.a. "Wafted by wind": literally, "upon wind's face"; 2 Sam 22:43 has a variant reading כעפר־ארץ "as dust of the earth."

43.b. אריקם "I empty": many Heb. mss, 2 Sam 22:43 (plus *G, S*, and *Tg*) indicate the reading אדקם "I crushed, pulverized him," which may be correct in view of the parallelism.

44.a. ותשימני "you have made me": 2 Sam 22:44 has the variant reading תשמרני "you have kept me."

45.a. יכחשו: on the translation "shrink at my presence," see Eaton, "Some Questions of Philology and Exegesis in the Psalms," *JTS* 19 (1968) 603–9.

46.a. ויחרגו "were quaking": many Heb mss (De-Rossi, IV, 13) and 2 Sam 22:46 have the reading ויחגרו "and they girded," but this is presumably an error and MT should be retained.

48.a. וידבר: many scholars prefer the reading of 2 Sam 22:47, ומוריד "and the one who causes to go down"; cf. Cross and Freedman, *JBL* 72 (1953) 34. But MT's use of דבר with the sense "subdue" can be sustained without resorting to Aramaic (see Briggs, *The Book of Psalms*, 162); on this sense of דבר, see Dahood, *Psalms I*, 118; cf. Arabic ʾadbara, "to cause retreat, defeat."

49.a. חמס "violent": several Heb mss (De-Rossi, IV, 13), and 2 Sam 22:49 read a plur. form (חמסים), but the sing. form of MT is appropriate after the singular איש "man."

Form/Structure/Setting

In general terms, Ps 18 may be classified as an individual psalm of thanksgiving, but the royal references (specifically in the title and v 51) indicate that it should be grouped with royal psalms. It is thus a king's psalm of thanksgiving. It has certain general similarities to *victory songs* or *victory hymns* (cf. Judg 5 and Exod 15:1–18), but the content is less specific than would be expected in a victory song, so that the designation royal psalm of thanksgiving is probably as precise a description as is possible.

The title verse indicates that the song was sung *on the day* of deliverance, but no precise event is known with which the psalm may be associated. As a royal psalm, it could have functioned as a general thanksgiving psalm for use on any and every day of victorious celebration. Alternatively, it may have been used in one of Israel's great annual festivals, e.g. the Feast of Tabernacles, in which the king's annual deliverance and victory may have been celebrated. Again, there can be no certainty.

A parallel text to Ps 18 occurs in 2 Sam 22. In general terms, the texts are the same, though there are numerous minor divergencies between them (see the *Notes*). There can be no certainty as to which may be the oldest and most authentic of the two texts; it is clear that they represent two variant traditions (perhaps northern and southern?) in the history of the psalm's transmission. In terms of certain forms and characteristics (e.g. orthographic forms), 2 Sam 22 appears to be the most archaic text, but that is partly to be expected. The text in the Psalter was clearly utilized in the context of Israel's worship long after the time of its initial composition, and the modernizing of such matters as orthography would be expected, whereas the text in 2 Sam 22 would have a more static history from the time of its incorporation into one of the sources of the Books of Samuel. But it does not follow that the text of Samuel is always the best text, or the nearest to the original. It may not even be proper to talk of an "original" if the initial transmission/ composition was oral and the psalm was itself composed orally, in which case a number of variants may represent oral alternatives going back to the earliest period of the text's history. The various manuscript traditions represent a constant tendency in later times toward the harmonization of the two texts; an examination of the variant readings in De-Rossi (IV, 11–13) indicates that for all the variants between Ps 18 and 2 Sam 22, some mss of Ps 18 have preferred the reading of 2 Sam 22. In the translation (above), the text of MT has been followed, except in those cases where there are very good reasons for preferring the reading of 2 Sam 22.

There is some degree of unanimity among scholars that Ps 18 is ancient, to be dated in the eleventh or tenth century B.C.; see Freedman, in *Magnalia Dei*, 96, for a tabulation of proposed dates. The evident antiquity of the psalm, taken in conjunction with the content of the title, make it most reasonable to suppose that the original form of Ps 18 comes from the time of David or shortly thereafter. (The psalm apparently preserves the old Hebrew tense system, in which the so-called imperfect tense is commonly utilized to express past time; see further *Excursus II.*)

Although a number of scholars have argued that there is no unity in the psalm, but that originally there were two separate psalms (e.g. Fohrer, *Introduction*, 286, who notes [a] vv 1–31, a post-exilic individual thanksgiving; [b] vv 32–51, a pre-exilic thanksgiving for victory), there are no convincing reasons for doubting the unity and integrity of the psalm as a whole. The structure may be set out as follows:

> Title (v 1)
> 1. Introductory praise (vv 2–4)
> 2. The psalmist's plea and the theophany (vv 5–20)
> 3. The goodness of God (vv 21–31)
> 4. The incomparable God and his servant (vv 32–46)
> 5. Concluding praise to the Living Lord (vv 47–51)

Comment

Title (18:1). Though the title as a whole indicates that the psalm was utilized originally in a specific setting related to the Davidic king (presumably King David), the expression "for the musical director" may indicate that later in the psalm's history it was incorporated within a collection of hymns which found a more general usage within Israel's worship.

The title indicates that the song was used *on the day* that David was delivered from enemies in general and from Saul in particular. Yet the context of the title in the parallel passage (2 Sam 22) does not permit the identification of the psalm with a particular event or military victory; it follows an account of Saul's death and then a summary account of a series of military campaigns against the Philistines (2 Sam 21:15–22). It may have been employed in a celebration of victory after a series of campaigns, or it may be interpreted as having been used in one of Israel's great annual festivals.

Introductory praise (18:2–4). The psalmist begins his magnificent hymn of praise with a profoundly personal statement: "I love you." The verb is unusual, but indicates an intimacy in the relationship with God which is reflected throughout the psalm, and it becomes clear as the psalm progresses that the intimacy arose from an awareness of God's companionship in a series of dangerous and mortal crises. The psalmist continues by piling up a series of words and epithets, in a kind of staccato style, which express pungently the nature of God as he has been experienced. The names reflect two themes, though each is closely related to the other; one theme is *military* (God is deliverer, shield, and safe retreat) and the other evokes the *rocky wilderness* which was for so long a part of David's experience (God is cliff, stronghold, and rock); it was in the wilderness that David in his military campaigns experienced God's intimate presence. Having begun with praise, the psalmist then provided the specific reason for praise (v 4); having called upon the Lord for help, he had experienced the divine deliverance from enemies. It is this past deliverance which becomes the focal point of the psalm in the section which follows.

The psalmist's plea and the theophany (18:5–20). This main section of the psalm has a simple theme which has been most powerfully and dramatically expressed in colorful poetry. The simple theme may be expressed as follows: the psalmist, in mortal danger, cries for help, and God appears to deliver him from his danger. But in the amplification, the whole theme has been given cosmic dimension; this cosmic dimension has been achieved by the utilization of language which is rooted in Near Eastern mythology, but which has been transformed to express the Lord's deliverance of his human servant. The transformed mythological background to this section of Ps 18 has many parallels to the mythological background of the Song of the Sea (Exod 15:1–18; cf. Craigie, *TyndB* 22 [1971] 19–26). While the poetic language has some similarities to that of the Babylonian myth of Marduk and Tiamat, the more precise antecedents are to be found in the Canaanite (Ugaritic) myths of Baal, Mot, and Yam. The general parallels may be expressed as follows.

Psalm 18	*Canaanite myth*
(1) The psalmist is caught in the *cords of death (mot)* and torments of Belial (viz. Yam), vv 5–6.	(1) Mot and Yam, gods of death and chaos, are ascendant (e.g. *CTA* 2.iii and 5.i).
(2) The Lord comes to deliver him in the theophany characterized by storm and earthquake: vv 7–15.	(2) Baal demonstrates his character as the god of storm (*CTA* 4.vii).
(3) The Lord rebukes *ocean (Yam)* and *earth* (viz. the underworld, realm of Mot) and thus delivers his servant: vv 16–20.	(3) Baal conquers Yam and Mot and establishes order (*CTA* 2.iv and 6.vi).

It is clear from the nature of the parallels that we are dealing with adaptation, not simple borrowing. The dominant motifs of the Baal traditions in Canaanite mythology have been adapted to give cosmic dimension to the psalmist's difficulties and divine deliverance.

If the historical background to the psalm is to be found in a series of events, rather than a particular occasion, then the opening description (vv 5–6) typifies the psalmist's perpetual estate. Faced with constant mortal danger, it was as though death and the underworld had already bound him and were drawing him inexorably toward demise. So the psalmist called upon God, and God heard from "his temple" (v 7); the reference is probably not to the Jerusalem temple, given the nature of the poetic language, but to the heavenly abode of the Lord which symbolized his cosmic dominion. Having heard, God reacted angrily; the violence depicting God's reaction to having heard his servant's plea is appropriate, for the God who is king of life and order has been challenged by the assaults of death and disorder on his servant. But from another perspective, the divine reaction (vv 8–9) is depicted in language reminiscent of the Sinai theophany, which language in turn had become a fundamental manner of expressing God's preparation for warfare in the early Hebrew poetic tradition (Deut 33:2–3; Judg 5:4–5; Ps 68:7–8). Thus God, in response to his servant's plea, was preparing for battle against those who were afflicting his servant.

The initial description of divine reaction (vv 8–9) is followed by a description of divine movement (vv 12–13), indicating God's passage (poetically speaking) from his cosmic abode or temple to the place of his servant's affliction. The description is of one riding upon clouds ("cherub" is poetically synonymous with cloud) and wind, in the kind of language associated with a powerful god of storm. On his arrival on the scene, he thunders (representing the divine voice, v 14: see further Ps 29) and sends forth his "arrows" (and "bolts of lightning"—v 15). This demonstration of divine power *rebukes*, in effect conquers, the "beds of the ocean" and the "foundations of the earth" (v 16), which symbolize the tyrannical enemies threatening the Lord's servants with death (vv 5–6). The rebuke of the enemies was followed by the deliverance of the Lord's servant, described in language reminiscent of the Exodus and the Reed Sea deliverance (vv 17–20): "he drew me out from the deep waters" (v 17), as Israel had formerly been delivered through the sea, and "he led me out to the broad place" (v 20), the Promised Land that lay beyond the act of deliverance.

The goodness of God (18:21–31). In this moving description of the goodness of God, the poet alternates between reflection on God's goodness to him (vv 21–25), God's goodness to mankind in general (vv 26–28), and then returns to a more personal reflection (vv 29–30), before concluding with an exclamation of praise.

The first section comprises a carefully constructed poetic unit (vv 21–25), beginning and ending with a reference to God's actions "according to my (viz. the psalmist's) righteousness" and "according to the cleanness of my hands." From a theological perspective, the passage must be understood in context; the righteousness of the psalmist placed him in that intimate relationship with God from which he could call upon God in distress and expect God's deliverance. He had lived a life of moral integrity, he had walked in

God's ways and avoided wickedness, he had lived within God's judgments and statutes and had been blameless, yet nevertheless he had been attacked by enemies. But the assault of enemies had not been a consequence of his behavior; it did not reflect divine judgment. So he had been able to call for divine deliverance, and deliverance had come. That deliverance was a reflection of God's fair dealings with him.

As the meditation continues, the psalmist remembers that his good experience of God was no fluke. It was cause for thanksgiving, but not for surprise, for God acted toward mankind in a comprehensible fashion (vv 26–28). There was a reciprocal dimension to the relationship with God, by which the faithful, the blameless, and the pure could expect God's faithful response, while the twisted could expect tortuous returns. Again, the theological perspective of this meditation is only a part of the whole picture and does not attempt to encompass an experience like that of Job; it is valid, nevertheless, for it represents faithfully one dimension of the goodness of God toward his servants, and the retributive action of God toward the tortuous and arrogant.

Again, the psalmist returns to a personal reflection (vv 29–30), in which he recalls the crisis from which he had sought deliverance, and the deliverance which came. He has almost been trapped by Death and Sheol (vv 5–6), which are symbolized by darkness, but in that darkness, God had given him light (v 29) and had warded off the ultimate darkness of death in defeat. He had been threatened by enemies (v 4), but had been enabled by God to attack a greater enemy force ("a troop") and "scale a wall" (namely the walls of enemy forts or cities, v 30).

Such meditations on God's goodness can only conclude with praise of the God whose "way is perfect" (v 31). The "utterance" of God, which holds forth the promise of deliverance (Ps 12:6–7), is entirely reliable, and God is a shield for all those who seek his refuge (cf. Ps 3:3).

The incomparable Lord and his servant (18:32–46). This portion of the psalm forms a poetic parallel to section (2) above (vv 5–20). In the former section, the focus was upon God's advent to deliver his servant, but now the focus changes; it is now the military activity of the Lord's servant which is given prominence in the poetic language, though it is made clear right at the beginning that his help came entirely from God (vv 32–33). The two passages thus tell the same story from different perspectives, but the culmination is the same in both instances—deliverance and victory for God's servant. Again, the poetic language is pregnant with meaning, and the beginning of the section recalls another victory on another occasion. When the Israelites sang of their great victory at the Reed Sea, they praised the God who was incomparable with any other supposed deity (Exod 15:11); the theme reappears here, for the two questions raised in v 32 invite a resounding answer, None!—none other can be compared with the Lord!

The psalmist then describes himself as the divinely equipped warrior, mighty in battle—yet only because of his God-given equipment. The description may be condensed as follows:

Feet: the warrior's feet are firm and fast like those of a hind (v 34).
Stance: the stance is on good strategic territory, high ground (v 34).
Hands and arms: trained for battle in the use of the mighty bow (v 35).

The expression "bow of bronze" may either indicate a wooden bow with bronze decoration, or the bronze tipped arrows shot from large bows, or it may merely be a poetic way of describing the great strength of the warrior's bow. For pictorial representation of a deity instructing his servant in the use of the bow, see Keel, *The Symbolism of the Biblical World*, 265; the deity stands behind the warrior, holds firmly the arms which grasp the bow and draw back the bowstring. On the bow as a symbol of royal dominion in Israel and Egypt, see Keel, "Die Bogen als Herrschaftssymbol. Einige unveröffentliche Skarabäen aus Ägypten und Israel zum Thema 'Jagd und Krieg'." *ZDPV* 93 (1977) 141–77.

Support and protection: provided by God's right hand and shield (v 36).

Stride: the stride is long, enabling the warrior to overtake enemies, and his firm ankles keep him from slipping (vv 37–8).

Victory: comes to the warrior in the defeat of enemies (v 39).

The psalmist's deliverance from enemies and concurrent victory over enemies are described graphically in the following verses (vv 40–46), and again, although the warrior's activity is described, it is clear that the heroic action was only possible because of God-given strength (v 40). "You have given me their neck" (v 41): the words evoke the picture of the enemy lying prostrate on the ground, the victorious warrior's foot placed on the neck in a symbol of triumph. "They cried for help . . . even upon the Lord" (v 42); the implication may either be that the enemies were Israelites (see the reference to Saul in the title) and so called upon the Lord for help, or else that they were foreign enemies who called upon the Lord for help when no aid was forthcoming from their own gods. (In the practice of warfare in the ancient Near East, it was frequently considered advantageous to seek the assistance of foreign gods, as well as of one's own gods, in order to increase the advantage over the enemy. A general reflection of this practice may be seen in Balak's attempt, through Balaam, to curse Israel in the name of *Yahweh* [cf. Num 22–24]). But the enemies' plans were to no avail; unlike the psalmist, they were not in such a relationship to God that they could expect the Lord's help when they cried, as could the psalmist (vv 21–31). Thus they were thoroughly conquered by the warrior psalmist and became cringingly subservient to the one whom they had sought to oppress and conquer.

Concluding praise to the Living Lord (18:47–51). The concluding verses bring together the various dimensions of the psalm's theme—distress, deliverance, and victory—and focus them in the praise and thanksgiving of God.

The praise begins with a declaration of joy and faith: "the Lord is alive," an expression for which the whole preceding psalm has given evidence. It was only because God was the Living Lord that deliverance and victory had been possible: an idol, or a figment of the pious imagination, could not have provided real deliverance from the threat of real disaster. But more than that, the words "the Lord is alive" may draw once again on the mythological background which was employed by the poet in vv 5–20. Just as Baal was referred to as the "alive one" (*CTA*.6.iii.2, though there are problems pertaining to the understanding of this text), so too the Lord, who had delivered his servant from death (vv 5–6), was to be extolled as the living Lord. The

Lord, as conqueror of death, was cosmic King, but the psalm ends with a reference to the human king, the authorized representative of the cosmic King. The human king has victory (v 51), but only because the divine King grants victory as a sign of his covenant faithfulness "toward his anointed" (namely, David and the Davidic kings who would succeed him). It is this closing reference to David and his seed which, taken in conjunction with the title (v 1), lends strong probability to the view that the psalm's historical situation is to be located in the life of King David.

Explanation

Like Ps 2, Ps 18 is a royal psalm and refers to the king as the *anointed one* (18:51; cf. Ps 2:3) or *messiah*. But neither the former nor the latter are messianic psalms in any prophetic or predictive sense; their primary concern is with the Davidic king and with the first manifestation of the Kingdom of God in ancient Israel. Whereas Ps 2 is one of the psalms most frequently quoted in the NT, however, Ps 18 did not gain the same significance. Paul does draw briefly upon the psalm (Rom 15:9, quoting Ps 18:50) in some comments concerning the Gentiles, but does not draw out the full significance of the psalm in any messianic sense. Yet from the NT perspective, Ps 18 has latent messianic meaning, and the deliverance of God's *anointed* from the "cords of death" (vv 5–6) finds deeper significance in the deliverance of Jesus from death itself. (For more general comments on the historical and theological perspectives of a psalm such as this, see the *Explanation* at Ps 2).

Nature and Law   (19:1-15)

Bibliography

Clines, D. J. A. "The Tree of Knowledge and the Law of Yahweh (Psalm XIX)." *VT* 24 (1974) 8–14. **Donner, J.** "Ugaritismen in der Psalmenforschung." *ZAW* 79 (1967) 322–50 (*327–31). **Loretz, O.** "Psalmenstudien III." *UF* 6 (1974) 175–210 (*186–87).

Translation

1   For the musical director. A psalm of David.
2(1) *The heavens are recounting God's glory,*   (4+4)
    and the firmament is declaring the work [a] *of his hands.*
3(2) *Day to day pours forth speech,*   (4+4?)
    and night to night makes known knowledge.
4(3) *There is no speech and there are no words;*   (4+3)
    their voice is inaudible. [a]
5(4) *Their voice* [a] *has gone forth into all the earth,*   (3+3)
    and their words to [b] *the extremity of the world.*
    For the sun, he pitched a tent in them, [c]   (4+4+4)

⁶⁽⁵⁾ *so it is like a bridegroom going forth from his chamber;*
    it rejoices like a warrior to run his course. ᵃ

⁷⁽⁶⁾ *From the extremity of the heavens is its going forth,*   (3+3+3)
    and its circuit is to ᵃ *their extremities,*
    and there is none hidden from its heat. ᵇ

⁸⁽⁷⁾ *The law of the Lord is perfect,*   (3+2)
    reviving the life.

    The testimony of the Lord is sure,   (3+2)
    making wise the simple.

⁹⁽⁸⁾ *The precepts of the Lord are upright,*   (3+2)
    making the heart rejoice.

    The commandment of the Lord is pure,   (3+2)
    enlightening the eyes.

¹⁰⁽⁹⁾ *The fear* ᵃ *of the Lord is radiant,* ᵇ   (3+2)
    enduring forever.

    The judgments of the Lord are true;   (3+2)
    they are entirely righteous,

¹¹⁽¹⁰⁾ *more desirable than gold,*   (2+2)
    and than much pure gold,

    and sweeter than honey,   (2+2)
    even honey from honeycombs.

¹²⁽¹¹⁾ *Moreover, your servant is illumined* ᵃ *by them;*   (3+3)
    in observing them is great reward.

¹³⁽¹²⁾ *Who can discern errors?*   (2+2)
    Acquit me of hidden sins!

¹⁴⁽¹³⁾ *Withhold your servant even from presumptuous persons,*   (3+2?)
    and let them not rule over me!

    Then I shall be whole ᵃ   (2?+3)
    and I shall be acquitted from great transgression.

¹⁵⁽¹⁴⁾ *May the words of my mouth find favor,*   (3+3+3)
    and may the meditations of my heart be according to your will, ᵃ
    O Lord, my rock and my redeemer.

Notes

2.a. מעשה: some Heb. mss and versions (*Vg* and *Tg*) indicate a plur. constr. form: "works. . . ."

4.a. "Inaudible": literally, "was not heard."

5.a. קום: literally, "their line, cord." A variety of proposals have been offered to resolve the difficulty pertaining to the meaning of this term: see Anderson, *Psalms I*, 169; Dahood, *Psalms I*, 121–2. But *G*, indicating that the appropriate translation is "their voice," suggests that MT was originally קולם and that the *lamedh* was accidentally omitted.

5.b. ובקצה: literally, "and *in* their extremity," but the prep. ב may carry the sense "to." Alternatively, emend to ולקצה (cf. Aquila).

5.c. בהם "in them": the suff. apparently has "heavens" (v 2) as antecedent; but the line is difficult and בהם is omitted in *G:* "in the sun he has set his tabernacle."

6.a. ארח "course": there is no pron. suff., though it is implied by parallelism, or may be provided from the preceding מחפתו "from his chamber" on the principle of the double-duty suff.

7.a. על has here the sense "to, toward" (synonymous with אל: see BDB, 757), or may be emended to עד ("up to, as far as") with the support of a few Heb mss.

7.b. חמתו: "its heat." Dahood suggests revocalizing and translating "from its pavilion," translating the entire line: "never turning aside from its pavilion" (*Psalms I*, 120). The translation "pavilion" is based on the Ugaritic-Arabic cognate *ḫmt*, "tent, pavilion." There is distant support from Arabic (*ḫaymat*), but the Ugaritic evidence is very slender. There is only one clear attestation of *ḫmt* in the Ugaritic texts (*CTA* 14/KRT.3.159), from which it may plausibly be restored in one other (broken) text, *CTA* 14/KRT.2.65. Although it is possible that the Ugaritic word may mean "tent, pavilion" (cf. Gordon, *UT* #956; Aistleitner, *WUS* #1039, and others), the context of the word's usage in Ugaritic makes the meaning "pen, enclosure" more likely; cf. Gray, *The Legacy of Canaan*[2], 136 (n.2) and *The KRT Text*[2], 36; Caquot et al., *Textes ougaritiques I*, 513. Consequently, the Ugaritic evidence is not sufficiently certain to be used in support of the translation of the Heb. term by "pavilion."

10.a. יראת: "fear." The parallelism has suggested to some scholars that a word such as "saying, command" is implied. Thus *BHS* suggests emending to אמרת "you said". And Dahood reads מראת (removing the initial *yodh* and prefixing *mem* from v 9), translating "edict" on the basis of Ugaritic-Aramaic *mrʾ*, "to command." The Ugaritic evidence is dubious. There is no Ugaritic noun derived from *mrʾ* with the sense "edict" and though there may be a noun formation with the sense "commander," the etymology and the sense of the term remain dubious; for discussion and literature, see B. Cutler and J. MacDonald, "Identification of the *naʿar* in the Ugaritic Texts," *UF* 8 (1976) 32 (n.33). In summary, it is best to retain יראת, which (while not precisely synonymous with the preceding and following terms) is a good *wisdom* term in keeping with the character of the second half of the psalm.

10.b. טהורות: on the translation "radiant," see Eaton, "Some Questions of Philology and Exegesis in the Psalms," *JTS* 19 (1968) 603–9.

12.a. נזהר "illumined." Though often interpreted as from זהר (II), Niph. "to be instructed," the more appropriate translation, given the context of sun and light, is from זהר (I), Niph. "to be illumined"; cf. Eaton, *JTS* 19 (1968) 603–9.

14.a. איתם is interpreted as Qal imperf. 1 pers. from תמם, "to be whole, complete." Some scholars consider the line short and in need of an additional word (e.g. Loretz, *UF* 6 [1974] 187], but such a view presupposes fairly rigid regularity in metrical structure.

15.a. לפניך: the translation "according to your will" follows Dahood and others (see *Psalms I*, 125).

Form/Structure/Setting

In the attempt to classify Ps 19 according to its type and social setting, there is an initial problem which must be resolved, namely the issue of the unity of the psalm. The psalm clearly falls into two parts: (1) vv 2–7 are a hymn to creation, with particular emphasis upon the sun; (2) vv 8–15 have the general character of wisdom poetry and contain a meditation upon the law, or *Torah*, of the Lord. Apart from the difference of substance, there are also further distinguishing points between the two parts of the psalm: (a) אל "God" is used as the divine name in the first part, whereas יהוה "Lord" is employed consistently in the second half; (b) the style differs, the first part being characterized by generally long lines, the latter half by shorter lines, especially 3+2. As a consequence of this type of evidence, many scholars have interpreted the psalm as consisting basically of two separate units classified as *hymn* and *wisdom poetry* respectively (e.g. Fohrer, *Introduction*, 286). On the other hand, there are numerous points of contact between the two portions of the psalm; see further the *Comment* (below), Clines, *VT* 24 (1974) 12 (n.4), and Ridderbos, *Die Psalmen*, 176–78. It is reasonably certain that the psalm in its present form is a unity, either composed as a single piece, or else the author took a fragment of an old hymn (vv 2–7) and extended it by means of a theological commentary and comparison; see Mowinckel, *The Psalms in Israel's Worship*, II, 267 (note XL); Loretz, *UF* 6 (1974) 187. If

the first part of the psalm belonged originally to a sun (creation) hymn, it
is probably no longer possible to determine its origin, given the commonality
of sun/creation hymns in the ancient Near East: see the discussion of the
analogous problem in Ps 104 in Craigie, "The Comparison of Hebrew Poetry:
Psalm 104 in the light of Egyptian and Ugaritic Poetry," *Semitics* 4 (1974)
10–21. Attempts to fix the background of Ps 19:2–7 in Ugaritic poetry have
proved generally unsuccessful. Jirku attempted to show that *CTA* 3.C.17–28
was a kind of *Vorlage* to Ps 19:2–5 ("Die Sprache der Gottheit in der Natur,"
ThLZ 76 [1951] 631), but the hypothesis has been undermined effectively
by Donner (*ZAW* 79 [1967] 327–31). The literary background to the entire
psalm should most probably be traced to Gen 1–3, as proposed by Clines
(art.cit.).

Granted that the psalm is a unity (in its present form, at least), it should
probably be classified as a *wisdom hymn* (though it also has some features of
a prayer, vv 13–14). With respect to its initial composition, it should probably
be read primarily as a creative and literary work, though later it came to be
used within the regular worship of Israel, as is indicated by the title verse
(19:1). While several scholars have taken the wisdom character of the psalm
to be indicative of an exilic or postexilic date, there is no unambiguous evidence that might determine either the author or the date of this beautiful
psalm.

The commentary treats the psalm in its two principal portions: (1) the
praise of God in nature (19:2–7); (2) the praise of the Lord in the *Torah*
(19:8–15).

Comment

The praise of God in nature (19:2–7). The opening hymn of praise falls into
three distinct parts, though the common theme, linking all three parts together, is stated in v 2: it is the *glory of God*.

(a) The first part of the hymn (vv 2–3) contains an affirmation that the
world of nature testifies, by its very existence, to God's glory. But it is a
specific part of the world of nature which the poet has in mind; it is the
"heavens," or sky, and the associated aspects of light and darkness. "Heavens"
and "firmament" (in effect, a poetic synonym for "heavens") are mentioned
first (v 2), and then "day" and "night" are introduced (v 3) as the two fundamental perspectives from which the heavens may be perceived. By day, the
sky is characterized by sun and light, and by night its darkness is punctuated
by the light of moon and stars; both these dimensions combine to recount
God's glory. Their declaration of glory rests upon the fact that, though they
are inanimate entities, they are the "work of his hands" (v 2), and so reflect
positively upon the Maker. But the speech of the heavens and firmament,
of day and night, has a twofold thrust: it is addressed to God as praise, yet
it is also addressed to mankind as a revealer of "knowledge" (v 3). That is,
as mankind reflects upon the vast expanse of heaven, with its light by day
and its intimation of a greater universe by night, that reflection may open
up an awareness and knowledge of God, the Creator, who by his hands created
a glory beyond the comprehension of the human mind.

(b) In the second part of the hymn (vv 4–5), the poet draws out the paradox of "inaudible noise." On the one hand, there is no speech, no noise, from a literal or acoustic perspective (v 4); on the other hand, there is a voice that penetrates to the furthest corners of the earth. The poet conveys something of the subtlety of nature's praise of God: it is there, yet its perception is contingent upon the observer. To the sensitive, the heavenly praise of God's glory may be an overwhelming experience, whereas to the insensitive, sky is simply sky and stars are only stars; they point to nothing beyond. In this hymn of praise, it is not the primary purpose of the psalmist to draw upon nature as a vehicle of revelation, or as a source of the knowledge of God apart from the revelation in law (or *Torah*, v 8); indeed, there is more than a suggestion that the reflection of God's praise in the universe is perceptible only to those already sensitive to God's revelation and purpose.

(c) Having begun with an affirmation of the heavenly proclamation of divine glory, the psalmist himself now joins the chorus of praise and describes the sun as the crowning achievement of God's creation of the heavens (vv 5c–7). God "pitched a tent" in the heavens for the sun: in poetic language, the reference is probably to the place of the sun's night-time rest, from whence it comes forth each day at dawn. The two similes of v 6 vividly illustrate the sun's glorious emergence on the eastern horizon each morning of the year. Sunrise is like a "bridegroom going forth from his chamber," implying either the groom's emergence from the chamber in which the marriage was conducted, or from the nuptial chamber on the morning following the wedding. Sunrise is also like a warrior, or hero, who in his vigor rejoices to run and exercise his strength. During the course of a day, the sun passes from one end of the heavens to the other, shedding its heat on all that lies beneath it.

While the hymnic features of the opening part of the psalm have general antecedents in the hymnody of the ancient Near East, it is the biblical text itself which provides the most precise antecedents. The Babylonian hymns to Shamash, the Egyptian hymns to various sun-gods, even the glorious hymn to Aten, differ in one remarkable respect from Ps 19. In those psalms, nature itself is deified; the gods are praised in nature. Yet in Ps 19, nature is personified, not deified, and personified nature raises the chorus of praise to the only Creator and only deity, the one true God. The antecedents to this poetic conception are to be found in Gen 1:3–19, in which it is clear that the heavens and firmament, day and night, light and darkness, are a part of creation: they are not gods.

The Praise of the Lord in Torah (19:8–15). The second part of the psalm begins with a reflection on the law or *Torah* (v 8a) of the Lord, written in a wisdom style reminiscent of Ps 119. The passage is carefully constructed, specifying six aspects of the *Torah* (law, testimony, precepts, commandment, fear, and judgments); from a poetic perspective, these terms may be seen as synonymous, though from a theological perspective, they may be seen as all-embracing. In every sense and dimension, the Lord's *Torah* is good: it is "perfect," "sure," "upright," "pure," "radiant," and "true." And each of these six characteristics of *Torah* is illustrated by reference to its role with respect to human beings:

(i) "reviving the life": it is the fundamental force, restoring to full vigor and vitality the flagging spirit of mankind, and providing him with the enduring inner food without which life cannot be fully lived.

(ii) "making wise the simple": it provides that wisdom without which life would culminate in the disasters of folly (cf. Ps 14).

(iii) "making the heart rejoice": it creates that rejoicing which is rooted in a life of uprightness before God.

(iv) "enlightening the eyes": it reveals the dimensions of truth and reality in human existence, for it is given by God, the giver of life.

(v) "enduring forever": here, the nuance shifts, for it is the "fear of the Lord" which endures—namely, the reverence for God, which is rooted in response to the *Torah* of God, is a permanent foundation for human life.

(vi) "they are entirely righteous": this concluding statement draws together the sum total of law, which is righteous as a consequence of its origin in God, and righteous with respect to its destination, mankind. And the poet adds force to this final description of *Torah* by likening its worth and desirability to fine gold and sweet honey: the treasures for which humans strive so ardently, and the food which imparts such sweetness to the tongue, are both less desirable than the Lord's *Torah*.

This description of the bountiful nature of the Lord's *Torah* is presented in carefully balanced poetry, but the deeper force of the language may emerge from the imagery and allusions underlying the language. Clines has argued persuasively that each of the characteristics of the *Torah* listed above contains an allusion to the tree of knowledge (Gen 2–3), and that by means of these allusions the psalmist is expressing the superiority of the *Torah* to the tree of knowledge (*VT* 24 [1974] 8–14). But more than that, the allusion to Gen 2–3 in the description of the *Torah* takes further the parallels between the initial portion of the psalm (vv 2–7) and Gen 1. The psalm as a whole is a subtle elaboration on Gen 1–3, beginning with creation and its praise of God, but moving to something greater, the *Torah* of God and its place in the life of mankind. And when this internal progression within the psalm is perceived, then a further progression may be noted—a progression in revelation. The glories of nature indicate *God* (אל v 2) in general terms, whereas the glories of the *Torah* reveal the *Lord* (יהוה, vv 8–10), that is, the God who has revealed himself to his people by name in redemption and covenant. And while the sun sheds forth light and heat (v 7), the divine law "enlightens the eyes" (v 9) and "illumines" (v 12) the servant of God.

In the concluding portion of the psalm (vv 13–14), the tone changes once again; the initial praise of God in nature and law evokes in the psalmist a sudden awareness of unworthiness. Although the transition is sharp, it is entirely natural. The psalmist began by looking at the heavens and reflecting on the divine law, and such reflection naturally evoked praise; but, as his eyes turn back from this double and glorious vision to gaze upon himself, the shock is almost too much. He becomes aware of his own insignificance and unworthiness in so glorious a context and can only pray. He prays for acquittal, or forgiveness; he asks to be protected from presumptuous persons and the control which they could so easily exert over him. Only with forgiveness and deliverance would he be a complete person, delivered from the "great transgression" (v 14). The expression "great transgression" is difficult to interpret; Near Eastern analogies indicate that adultery was commonly identified as the *great sin*; see J. J. Rabinowitz, "The 'Great Sin' in Ancient Egyptian Marriage Contracts," *JNES* 18 (1959) 73; L. R. Fisher, *The Claremont Ras Shamra Tablets*, 14–19. But in this context, the expression may refer to gross sin in general, or (by way of poetical allusion) to the fall of mankind, thus carrying even further the analogies between Ps 19 and Gen 1–3 (see Clines, art. cit., 13).

The last verse ties together the themes of praise and prayer. The psalmist began by describing the speech of the heavens, extolling God's glory; he concludes by praying that his own mouth, in its speech, may be acceptable to God. The heavens praise God by their very existence: he too wishes to join that chorus of praise and prays for such worthiness to God, who is his "rock" and "redeemer." The final words, describing the psalmist's relationship to God, transform God's universal and cosmic glory, with which the psalm began, into the glory of an intimate relationship between a human being and God, who offers solidarity and redemption.

Explanation

C. S. Lewis wrote of Ps 19: "I take this to be the greatest poem in the Psalter and one of the greatest lyrics in the world" (*Reflections on the Psalms*, p. 56). Indeed, it is hard to disagree with such a judgment, for the psalm combines the most beautiful poetry with some of the most profound of biblical theology. And for those who think too easily of the Psalms merely as literature, it is wise to recall that they were also sung (as Ps 19 may have been sung, following the implications of the title verse) and that the music added still further to the beauty and profundity of the poetry. Though we do not know the forms and sounds of ancient Hebrew music, we may nevertheless grasp something of the power that music may add to words though listening to Ps 19 in the setting of Haydn's *Creation;* the music is relatively modern, but the understanding expressed in that music is surely original and genuine.

The psalmist moves in a climactic fashion from macrocosm to microcosm, from the universe and its glory to the individual in humility before God. But the climax lies in the microcosm, not in the heavenly roar of praise. For the heavens declare the glory of God, but the law declares the will of God for mankind, the creature. And though the vast firmament so high above us declares God's praise, it is the *Torah* of God alone that reveals to mankind that he has a place in the universal scheme of things. It is not a place which gives ground for human boasting or declaration of human might over the cosmos: when the psalmist's praise of God's revelation in the *Torah* dawns upon him personally, it issues immediately in a prayer for forgiveness and acceptance.

The key clause, as Lewis has pointed out, is in v 7: "there is none hidden from its (the sun's) heat." The clause marks the transition between the two parts of the psalm and at the same time links them intimately together. Just as the sun dominates the daytime sky, so too does *Torah* dominate human life. And as the sun can be both welcome, in giving warmth, and terrifying in its unrelenting heat, so too the *Torah* can be both life-imparting, but also scorching, testing, and purifying. But neither are dispensable. There could be no life on this planet without the sun; there can be no true human life without the revealed word of God in the *Torah*.

A King's Departure for Battle   (20:1-10)

Translation

¹   For the musical director. A psalm of David.

2(1) *May the Lord answer you on the day of distress.*   (4+4)
       May the name of Jacob's God make you secure.

3(2) *May he send you help* ᵃ *from his sanctuary,* ᵇ   (3+2)
       and from Zion, may he sustain you.

4(3) *May he remember all your offerings* ᵃ   (2+2)
       and regard with favor your burnt offerings. ᵃ SELAH.ᵇ

5(4) *May he give you your heart's desire* ᵃ   (2+2)
       and fulfill all your purpose.

6(5) *May we shout for joy in your victory*   (2+2, 3)
       and raise a banner ᵃ *in the name of our God.*
       May the Lord fulfill all your requests.

7(6) *Now I know that the Lord will deliver* ᵃ *his anointed:*   (5+3+3)
       he will answer him from his holy heavens,
       with a mighty act ᵇ *of deliverance, by his right hand.*

8(7) *Some (boast) in chariotry and some in horses,*   (4+4)
       but we boast ᵃ *in the name of the Lord our God.*

9(8) *They will bow down* ᵃ *and fall,*   (3+3)
       but we shall rise ᵃ *and stand upright.*

10(9) *O Lord, save the king* ᵃ   (3+3)
       and answer us ᵇ *on the day that we call.*

Notes

3.a. "May he send you help": literally, "may he send *your* help." On the unusual grammatical construction, see GKC §135m.

3.b. מקדש "from sanctuary": the translation assumes a text מקדשו "from his sanctuary", the suffix having been omitted through haplography (cf. the following *waw*); cf. S and Tg.

4.a. "Offerings . . . burnt offerings": the plural of *both* terms is read, with some support from Heb. mss, S, Tg and Vg. In each case, G has a singular form.

4.b. On *Selah*, see *Excursus I*.

5.a. "your heart's desire:" literally, "according to your heart."

6.a. נדגל "may we . . . raise a banner:" G's μεγαλυνθησόμεθα "we shall be magnified," presupposing לגדל, is probably an error, or was based on a Heb. text in which (erroneous) metathesis had taken place.

7.a. הושיע "will deliver": the perf. tense indicates the aspect of completion, though the context implies action lying in the future. Thus, the perf. form, indicating certainty or completion of action in the future, is emphatic (the so-called "prophetic perfect").

7.b. "mighty act," reading the sing. בגבורת (with many Heb. mss, Aquila, Symmachus, and other versions), for MT's plur. form (in which it may be assumed that the *waw* has been misplaced).

8.a. "boast:" on the use of זכר (II, Hiph.) plus בְּ, meaning "to boast," see Driver *VT*Sup 16 (1967) 53–54.

9.a. Again (see v 7), the verbs in this verse are perfect (two with simple *waw*), though the reference is to future action concerning which certainty is expressed by means of the perf. forms of the verb.

10.a. The caesura is interpreted as occurring after הַמֶּלֶךְ, following the suggestion of *BHS* that the *athnaḥ* be moved to הַמֶּלֶךְ from its present position under the second word in the line.

10.b. יַעֲנֵנוּ "he will answer us": the reading וַעֲנֵנוּ "and answer us" (*waw* + impv.) is preferred, following *G* and *Tg*, to MT's *yodh*-prefix.

Form/Structure/Setting

The psalm is a *royal liturgy*, presumably designed for use in the service of the sanctuary. It begins with intercessory prayer (vv 2–6), in which the congregation prays for God's help on behalf of the king (viz. *you* in vv 2–6). The prayer is followed by a declaration (v 7), from a priest, Levite, or prophet, which may have been preceded by some ritual act. It concludes with the praise of the congregation in its entirety (vv 8–10).

The psalm as a whole is closely integrated by the repetition of key terms. The first and last line (vv 2a and 10b) use the verb עָנָה "answer" and the noun יוֹם "day," which together constitute an inclusio. There is an emphasis on the *name* of God (שֵׁם; vv 2, 6, 8) and several other words are used twice: forms of the following roots reappear: (a) מלא "fulfill" (vv 5–6); (b) זכר "remember" (vv 4, 8); (c) קֹדֶשׁ "sanctuary" (vv 3, 7); (d) יֵשַׁע "deliver, save" (vv 6, 7, 10). The psalm as a whole is characterized by parallelism, both synonymous (e.g. vv 2–6) and antithetical (e.g. v 9). Many verses are also characterized by a chiastic structure: e.g. vv 3, 4, 5, 6a–b.

The precise occasion on which this liturgical psalm would have been used remains uncertain. While some scholars propose a setting in an annual festival or anniversary of the kingship, or even a New Year festival (cf. Eaton, *Kingship and the Psalms*, 117), it is more probable that the liturgy was used in a special service prior to the departure of the king and his army for a battle or military campaign (cf. Mowinckel, *The Psalms in Israel's Worship*, I, 225). A description of a similar ritual occasion is provided in 2 Chr 20: (a) the king's prayer (20:5–12); (b) an oracular pronouncement from a Levite (20:13–17); (c) concluding praise (20:18–19). On this interpretation, Ps 20 would have been the liturgy employed for one part of the larger ritual. Similar rituals were common in ancient Near Eastern religions as a whole. The title verse (v 1), and the indication that this psalm was incorporated in the musical director's collection, may imply that at a later date, the psalm passed into general liturgical usage and lost its particular associations with the royal ritual preceding a military campaign.

Comment

The intercessory prayer (20:2–6). The opening verses contain the intercessory prayer of the congregation on behalf of the king, yet they are not intercessory in the normal sense. That is, the words are addressed specifically to the

king, not to God, though they contain an expression of the people's prayer
on behalf of the king. It is probable that the liturgical setting explains the
form. Early in the religious ceremony, the king would offer certain sacrifices
to God; it is implied in v 4 that this activity was going on while the congregation
expressed the words of vv 2–6. (On the practice of making offerings prior
to departure for war, see 1 Sam 7:9–10 and 13:9–12.) The background of
vv 2–6 thus emerges in the liturgical and ritual context: the king, who would
be commander in warfare, offered sacrifices and the peole joined him in
words. The words which they spoke, addressed formally to the king, vocalized
the prayer and desire of the king who was engaged in the activity of worship.

The synonymous parallelism of the opening verses amplifies the fundamental theme of the sacrificial act: the people are expressing their desire that
the king's prayer for help and victory, externalized in the act of sacrifice,
be heard and answered. Yet the words, for all their synonymous character,
bring out the various dimensions of the people's desire. (a) They pray for
safety, sustaining power, and victory. (b) The expression "the name of Jacob's
God" (v 2), though poetically parallel to "Lord," evokes specifically the protective dimension of the Lord's activity; see the very similar language, in the
context of the Jacob story, in Gen 35:3. (c) God's help is requested "from
his sanctuary // from Zion" (v 3); that is, when the king and his people left
the temple (where the liturgy took place), they would not leave alone, but
with the presence of God. (d) The people prayed not only for the king, but
also for themselves, for he was their representative; thus victory would not
only be an answer to the king's sacrifice and prayer, but also a ground for
the people's rejoicing and celebration (v 6).

The declaration (20:7). At the completion of the sacrificial acts undertaken
by the king and the concurrent words spoken by the people, there came a
formal declaration spoken by an individual. The identity of the individual is
not known, though a priest, Levite, or prophet is likely. The declaration begins
with the word *now* (עתה), which is an emphatic term, indicating a turning
point in the ritual. What prompted the turning point is uncertain: it may
have been the completion of the sacrificial acts and accompanying ritual, or
it may have been the receipt of a positive oracle in the person of the declarer.
The declaration affirms that God has responded positively to the royal request
and would answer the prayer in the granting of "deliverance" or victory.
The answer is "from his holy heavens," namely from the divine presence,
which is merely symbolized in the sanctuary in Zion (v 3). The use of the
so-called perfect tense in v 7a could be translated "the Lord has delivered";
it implies completed action. From the perspective of the one delivering the
oracle, the action was already complete, though from the mundane perspective
of the king ("his anointed"), the actual battle remained to be fought: hence
the translation by means of an English future tense. The king would only
depart for battle, following the completion of the ritual, on the basis of this
firm declaration that victory had already been won and need only be claimed,
or appropriated.

Concluding praise (20:8–10). In the concluding words, the congregation expresses its new-found confidence by means of striking poetic contrasts. (a)
Whereas "some" (the enemy is implied) boast in the power of their military

resources, *they* boast only in "the name of the Lord." The words "chariotry" and "horses" should probably be taken as poetically synonymous. Chariots, and the horses which pulled them, represented the most powerful military resources available in the ancient Near Eastern practice of warfare; see further D. R. Ap-Thomas, "All the King's Horses," in J. I. Durham and J. R. Porter (eds.), *Proclamation and Presence*, 135–51, and G. Morgan, "The Heavenly Horses," *History Today* (Feb. 1973) 77–83. The sentiment expressed in v 8 is not merely poetic, for the Hebrew kings were specifically prohibited from accumulating large numbers of horses and, by implication, from depending upon the military might which they represented (Deut 17:16). Ultimately, the strength of the king was the strength of God, not that of a horse. (b) The enemy, now standing in their arrogance and might, would bow down and fall (v 9), whereas the king and his people, now bowed down in the worship of God, would ultimately stand upright in victory.

The concluding verse is part prayer, part praise; it reiterates dramatically and concisely the earlier portion of the liturgy (vv 2–6) and gives expression to the sure-founded confidence with which worship ceased and the march to battle commenced. (V 10a is the foundation of the exclamation still used in monarchic states, "God save the Queen/King.")

Explanation

A fundamental characteristic of the experience of ancient Israel was the frequency of warfare. It characterized the historical experience of Israel, as it did that of all nations in the ancient (and modern) world. The practice of warfare in ancient Israel was intimately related to religion; the Lord, a "Warrior" or "Man in Battle," participated with his people in the experience of warfare (Exod 15:3). For an examination of the theological problems raised by the predominance of warfare in ancient Israel, see Craigie, *The Problem of War in the Old Testament* (1978).

Psalm 20 provides an insight into one dimension of the interrelationship between war and religion. The psalm presupposes that a battle or military campaign is about to begin, though no details are provided. From a military perspective, such a battle required careful planning, well-trained troops, superior military resources (e.g. chariotry) to those of the enemy, and the courage to fight. But in Israel, something more was required before departure for battle. It was fundamental to the faith of the Hebrews that success in battle depended primarily upon God, not only upon military planning and strategy. And so, before a campaign could commence, there must first be a retreat to the temple. The king, who both led the army and was the representative of God among the people, had a key role to play in the service of the sanctuary. He did not demand divine aid as a royal right; rather, he offered sacrifices to God, indicating on the one hand his unworthiness before God, and on the other hand his need of God's assistance. The sacrifice was a royal act, but the worship of which it was a part involved the people as a whole. All joined in his acknowledgment of unworthiness and prayer for assistance; all shared in the joyful anticipation of victory.

The psalm reflects the tension that runs through all Hebrew history and theology. On the one hand, the necessities of historical existence imposed certain requirements upon the chosen people: the presence of enemies made warfare a necessity. On the other hand, human action which involved no divine participation was doomed from the beginning; at the heart of Hebrew theology lay the conviction that God was involved in their historical experience. So the preparation for war was twofold. First, there must be practical and military preparation, for it would be impossible simply to sit back and wait for a miracle to happen. Second, there must be religious preparation, which is here reflected in Ps 20, for it would be equally irresponsible to hope that anything lasting could be achieved merely in human strength. The formal act of worship, prior to battle, which is reflected so clearly in Ps 20, would affect and influence the actual action on the battlefield which was to follow.

A Royal Liturgy *(21:1-14)*

Bibliography

Fensham, F. C. "Ps 21—A Covenant Song?" *ZAW* 77 (1965) 195–202. **Morrow, F. J.** "Psalm 21:10; An Example of Haplography." *VT* 18(1968) 558–59.

Translation

¹   For the musical director. A psalm of David.

²⁽¹⁾ *O Lord, in your might* ᵃ *the king rejoices,*   (4/3+3)
     and in your victory, how ᵇ *greatly* ᶜ *he exults!* ᵈ

³⁽²⁾ *You have given to him his heart's desire*   (4+3)
     and you have not withheld the request ᵃ *of his lips.* SELAH.ᵇ

⁴⁽³⁾ *For you meet him with blessings of goodness;*   (3+3)
     you set on his head a crown of fine gold.

⁵⁽⁴⁾ *He asked life from you: you gave it to him,*   (5+4)
     length of days for ever and ever.

⁶⁽⁵⁾ *His honor is great through your victory;*   (3+4)
     you bestow upon him splendor and majesty.

⁷⁽⁶⁾ *For you give* ᵃ *him blessings forever;*   (3+3)
     you make him see ᵇ *your face in joy.*

⁸⁽⁷⁾ *For the king is trusting in the Lord,*   (3+3)
     and in the lovingkindness of the Most High, he will not be shaken.

⁹⁽⁸⁾ *Your hand will find out all your enemies;*   (3+3)
     your right hand will find out all ᵃ *who hate you.*

¹⁰⁽⁹⁾ *You will set them against* ᵃ *your face like a fiery oven:* ᵇ   (5+5)
     the Lord will consume them in his anger, and fire will devour them.

¹¹⁽¹⁰⁾ *You will destroy their fruit from the earth*   (3+3)
     and their seed from among the sons of man.

¹²⁽¹¹⁾ *Though they have extended evil against you,*   (3+3)
     have planned evil devices, ᵃ *they will not succeed.*

13(12) *For you will make them turn back* (3+3)
    with your bowstrings, you will aim against their faces.
14(13) *Arise, O Lord, in your might!* (3+3)
    Let us sing and praise your strength!

Notes

2.a. בְעֻזֶּךָ ("in your might"): on the various nuances of the noun עֹז, see Craigie, *VT* 22 (1972) 146.

2.b. מה ("how") is omitted in *G* and *S*, though the word is best retained with MT.

2.c. מֹאד ("greatly"): Dahood translates this as "the Grand One," a divine name or title, vocalizing מָאֵד; see *Psalms III* pp. xxvi–xxviii (contra *Psalms I*, 130). But this translation is most unlikely: see O. Loretz " '*d m'd*, 'Everlasting Grand One' in den Psalmen," *BZ* 16 (1972) 245–48; ibid., "Die Umpunktierung von *m'd* zu *mā'ēd* in den Psalmen," *UF* 6 (1974) 481–84; D. Marcus, "Ugaritic Evidence for 'The Almighty/The Grand One'?," *Bib* 5 (1974) 404–7.

2.d. יגיל ("he exults"): K יָגִיל, but Q (יָגֶל) is to be preferred if the preceding particle is retained.

3.a. ארשת ("request"), though a *hapax legomenon* in Heb, is well attested in other languages: Ass. *erēšu*, Ugar., *'iršt*, and probably also Arabic *'arš* ("blood price").

3.b. The word is omitted in *S*. On the meaning of *Selah*, see Excursus I (following Ps 3).

7.a. On the verb שית, with the sense "to give," see Briggs, *Psalms*, 187.

7.b. The tranlation "see" assumes that the verb חדה may be a dialectal variation of חזה; see Dahood, *Psalms I*, 133. Alternatively, a more conventional translation would be: "You make him joyful in joy with your face."

9.a. Reading לכל־שׂנאיך, with two Heb. mss, *G* and *Tg*; the reading balances the opening part of the line and the grammatical structure in a manner superior to MT.

10.a. לעת: assuming the omission of a letter, לְעֻמַּת ("opposite, against") is read; see Morrow, *VT* 18 (1968) 558–59.

10.b. There are problems in the stichometric analysis of this verse; יהוה is taken as opening the second stichos, rather than as a vocative form closing the first, and thus provides clearer meaning and approximate metrical balance.

12.a. MT is singular; the plural translation is based on a few Heb. mss, with the support of *G* (A and L), *Tg* and *Vg*.

Form/Structure/Setting

There are various types of material integrated into the psalm as a whole. The first major section (vv 2–7) is expressed in language reminiscent of the thanksgiving psalms; the second major section (vv 9–13) contains the language of confidence. The varieties of formal language are to be understood as constituting the parts of a royal liturgy in which various persons participated. The liturgy begins with the priest or congregation expressing thanks to the Lord for what he has done on behalf of his king (vv 2–7). There is then a sentence of transition (v 8), in which both the king and the Lord are addressed in the third person, though the person pronouncing this sentence cannot be identified. In the next section (vv 9–13), a prophet or priest addresses the king (in the second person) and declares the future successes which will come the king's way as a consequence of God's blessing. The liturgy ends with a congregational response (v 14), which is part prayer and part praise.

The entire psalm is constructed in a finely balanced manner:

> (i)   vv 2–7   : 6 distichs
> (ii) vv 8   : 1 distich
> (iii) vv 9–14 : 6 distichs

The unity of the entire psalm is emphasized by the *inclusio* device, namely the phrase יהוה בעזך in vv 2, 14. Several other words (derived from a common root) are used repeatedly in the psalm to heighten further the poetic effect: (a) שמח (vv 2,7); (b) ישועה (vv 2,6); (c) נתן (vv 3, 5); (d) שית (vv 4, 7, 10, 13); (e) ברכות (vv 4, 7); (f) מצא (v 9).

Though the classification of the psalm as a *royal liturgy* is fairly certain, the precise social setting within which the liturgy should be interpreted remains uncertain. The military associations of the language have suggested that the psalm should be interpreted in the setting of thanksgiving for a military victory (on the basis of vv 2–7) or in preparation for departure in battle (on the basis of vv 9–13), but the presence of language indicating both past victories and the prospect of future triumphs makes unlikely either suggestion with respect to a specific setting. The inference regarding the setting must take into account not only the language pertaining to past and future victories, but also the covenant character of the psalm (both in the terminology of v 8, in the blessings of vv 2–7, and in the divine protection implied in vv 9–13: see further Fensham, *ZAW* 77 [1965] 193–202). It is probable that the liturgy was associated with some ceremony pertaining to the anniversary or renewal of a king's coronation in the Davidic tradition. The anniversary involved recollection of past victories and anticipation of future triumphs because of the king's steadfast trust in the Lord of the covenant (v 8); at the same time, the references to the king's crown (v 4) and splendor (v 6) indicate a distinctly regal occasion. In summary, although precise information on the setting cannot be ascertained, the psalm should be interpreted with respect to its initial sense as a liturgy utilized in a royal ceremony associated in some fashion with the commemoration of a coronation.

Comment

The Lord's goodness to the king (21:2–7). The words of this section are addressed to the Lord and, with respect to substance, they concern the divine goodness toward the king; the element of thanksgiving is implicit throughout the section. All the language refers to God's general goodness toward the king, but the major subtheme throughout these verses is the awareness of God's goodness in granting the king "victory" (or "deliverance") from enemies; "victory" is referred to in both v 2 and v 5. The military victory which the king appeared to win in battle was in reality the victory which God, in his might, had granted. It is most probable that the king's "desire/request" (v 3) alludes to his prayer for divine aid and victory prior to departing for battle. And, having set out for war in faith, the king was then met by God with "blessings" (v 4a). The crown set upon the king's head (v 4b) symbolized the divine approval, for ultimately only God was king, and the human representative of the divine kingship could only receive that royal status from God. For pictorial representation of a king being crowned by a deity, see Keel, *The Symbolism of the Biblical World* (1978), 259–60.

It has been argued by some scholars, notably M. Dahood, that the substance of v 5 is indicative of the view that "the king was thought to receive the gift of immortality on the day of his coronation" (*Psalms I*, 132). It is certainly the case, as Dahood points out, that very similar language is used in the Ugaritic texts with respect to immortality (see *CTA* 17. vi. 27–28). Ultimately, though, the meaning of such words and expressions as "life," "length of days," and "for ever and ever," must be determined in the light of context— both the immediate literary context and the broader context of ancient Hebrew theology. Here, it is said of the king that he asked for life and received it: but when did he ask? And when did he receive it? The immediate context (see the *Comment* on vv 2–3 above) implies that the verses express thanksgiving following a military victory and refer back, by implication, to the prayer of the king prior to his departure for battle. In such a context, it is best to assume that the king, prior to departing for battle, asked that his life be preserved in the time of conflict; on returning home alive, his prayer had been answered in the gift of "life" and "length of days." The expression "for ever and ever," in context, implies that such life would extend into the future as far as was conceivable, but there need be no implication of a future life or afterlife. And since a royal psalm such as this reflects the theology of the period of the monarchy, the broader context need not imply any view of eternal life; such a view did not clearly emerge in Israel until the period after the Exile. It must be concluded, then, that v 5 need not be interpreted to imply any doctrine of immortality. At most, it might imply the continuity which would exist through the continuation of the Davidic kings, even beyond the life of the reigning monarch (2 Sam 7:29); such a view would be in harmony with the covenant character of the psalm, as noted by Fensham (art. cit.).

The king had received not only life, but also "honor," "splendor" and "majesty" as a consequence of the God-given victory (v 6); such attributes, which are essentially the attributes of God, constitute the *reflected glory* of the king. They derived not from his person or achievement, but from the one whom he represented by virtue of office.

The king's steadfastness (21:8). It is presumed that this verse represents a further stage in the liturgy, for now not only the king, but also the Lord, are referred to in the third person. Although a change in person is not always a sure guide to a change in speaker (see Anderson, *Psalms I*, 182), the liturgical character of the psalm as a whole makes a change in speaker likely in this context. Whereas the first part of the psalm (vv 2–7), presumably spoken by the congregation, referred primarily to God's past actions on behalf of the king, which were a source of thanksgiving, this single verse—the midpoint of the entire psalm—serves to bring the focus to the present, the actual moment of proclamation in the liturgy. Just as the king had trusted in the past, so now in the present moment the solemn declaration is made (presumably by a priest): "the king is trusting in the Lord." Consequently, in all future moments, "he will not be shaken" as he continues to trust moment

by moment in God (see further the *Explanation,* below). The language of
the declaration is the language of covenant, especially notable in the words
בטח and חסד, and these two words sum up, in a sense, the entire theology
of the psalm. There are two partners to the covenant, God and Israel (represented by the king); God's fundamental character in the covenant relationship
is *lovingkindness* (חסד), and the king's response was to be one of *trust* (בטח).
The former is unchangeable, but the latter must be constantly maintained
if the covenant relationship is to prosper. Thus, in this solemn moment in
the progress of the liturgy, the fundamentals of the covenant faith are declared
and affirmed.

The king's future victories (21:9–13). The principal difficulty in the interpretation of this portion of the psalm lies in identifying the person addressed
("you"). The majority of scholars interpret the verses as being addressed
to the king (see, Ridderbos, *Die Psalmen,* 182), but Dahood interprets this
section as words addressed to the Lord (*Psalms I,* 131). Ultimately, there is
a fusion between the two views: viz. if it is the king who is here promised
future victories, they could only be achieved through divine aid, as is made
clear in the first section of the psalm. Nevertheless, it must be admitted that
there is some ambiguity. There are two critical issues. (i) There is the problem
of the translation of the tenses of the so-called imperfect verbs in this section.
Dahood consistently translates them as past tenses and interprets the passage
as a description of God's triumphs in the past. Yet, though it must be admitted
that such a possibility exists with respect to the translation of Hebrew tenses
(see *Excursus II,* following Ps 8), the argument for such a translation in this
context is not compelling. The regularity in the use of the so-called imperfects
in this section, together with the argument from substance, namely a progress
from *past* (clearly identified in vv 2–7 by the so-called perfect tenses) to *present*
(in v 8), leads one to interpret the so-called imperfects as *future* tenses in
vv 9–13 (in deliberate contrast to the tense structure of vv 2–7). (ii) The
analysis of v 10 is also critical: if the word יהוה is taken at the end of the
first line, as a vocative exclamation, it would clearly indicate that "you" should
be interpreted as the *Lord.* But such an analysis is unlikely (see note b on v
10, above). It is concluded, therefore, that vv 9–13 are addressed to the
king and should be interpreted in a future sense. The substance of the verses
indicates that they should be read in a declaratory sense and were, perhaps,
addressed to the king by a prophet or priest participating in the liturgy.

Whereas vv 2–7 recounted the *blessings* of God received by the king, vv
9–13 express the *curses* which would be executed by the king, namely the
defeat of the king's enemies and those who oppressed the covenant people
of God. (Defeat could be a curse *upon* Israel, if it failed in its covenant commitment, but so long as the people, through their representative the king, remained *trusting,* defeat of others would be the other face of the coin which
was God's covenant blessing upon them.) The simile of v 10 expresses powerfully the manner in which the king, with divine aid, would conquer the enemies
referred to in v 9. The king would set his enemies before him "like (fuel
in) a fiery oven;" God, through the agency of fire, would consume them.
So complete would be the victory, that the defeated enemies would leave
behind no progeny in this world.

Concluding prayer and praise (21:14). Again, the military language is apparent in the prayer that the Lord "arise"; note the words proclaimed prior to the departure for battle in early Israel (Num 10:35). The prayer forms the congregational response to the declaration of vv 9–13: they pray that the future victories described in those verses might be converted into historical reality. The anticipatory praise of v 14b follows as a consequence of v 14a: as God granted future victories, so would the people respond by singing God's praise, just as they had done earlier in the liturgy (vv 2–7) because of past victories.

Explanation

The Davidic covenant affected every aspect of the reign of a king: his coronation, his conduct of war, his administration of the state and other matters. While nothing lay beyond the scope of the covenant, nevertheless there were moments in the year when the covenant was not merely the background to all that was done, but was consciously brought into the foreground. A royal liturgy was an occasion of ceremony and worship in which, self-consciously, the centrality of the covenant in the entire life of the nation was recalled and reaffirmed. Although the precise setting of this cultic liturgy cannot be determined with certainty, the general context is clear enough. Out of necessity, given the historical conditions of the nation's existence, much of the king's time and attention had to be devoted to war: there were enemies on every side striving for control of the kingdom. But the kingdom existed only because of the covenant; hence, the conduct of war had to be undertaken within the context of covenant. And in liturgy, there was a return to basics: the king and his co-worshipers recalled that victory and deliverance had not been achieved, and would not be achieved, on the basis of military strength alone, but only in the strength of God. In the constant struggle to survive the assaults of enemies, there had to be times set aside to remember why survival was necessary.

The particular liturgy reflected in Ps 21 clarifies one of the most fundamental aspects of the life of the covenant community, namely the close interrelationship between past, present and future (see further Craigie, *The Book of Deuteronomy*, 40). The remembrance of the past evoked not only past victories, but also the fact that those victories had been a result of divine activity (vv 2–7). Because God had acted in the past, he could certainly also grant victory again to his people in the future (vv 9–13); remembrance of the past established a precedent for the future. But always, past and future remained contingent upon the present moment, and it was the present moment which formed the central point of the liturgy (v 8). The memory of the past created present trust, which in turn would form the basis of future success and victory. The expression of this complex of ideas and time inevitably must utilize the language of both praise and prayer: praise for what had been done, anticipatory praise for what would be done, and prayer that the potential blessings of the future would materialize. In the liturgy, there are crystallized all the hopes and aspirations which constituted the covenant people's reason for living.

A Liturgy for One Threatened with Death (22:1-32)

Bibliography

Fisher, L. R. "Betrayed by Friends: An Expository Study of Psalm 22." *Int* 18 (1964) 20–38. **Frost, S. B.** "Psalm 22: an Exposition." *CJT* 8 (1962) 102–15. **Holladay, W. L.** "Background of Jeremiah's Self-understanding: Moses, Samuel, and Psalm 22." *JBL* 83 (1964) 153–64. **Jirku, A.** "Ajjelet haš-Šaḥar (Ps 22.1)." *ZAW* 65 (1953) 85–86. **Keel-Leu, O.** "Nochmals Psalm 22:28–32." *Bib* 51 (1970) 405–13. **Killian, R.** "Ps 22 und das priesterliche Heilsorakel." *BZ* 12 (1968) 172–85. **Krahlmalkov, C.** "Psalm 22:28–32." *Bib* 50 (1969) 389–92. **Lipinski, E.** "L'hymne à Yahwé Roi au Psaume 22:28–32." *Bib* 50 (1969) 153–68. **Martin-Achard, R.** "Remarques sur le Psaume 22." *V Caro* 65 (1963) 78–87. **Roberts, J. J. M.** "A New Root for an Old Crux." *VT* 23 (1973) 247–52. **Schmid, H. H.** " 'Mein Gott, mein Gott, warum hast du mich verlassen?' Ps 22 als Beispiel alttestamentlicher Rede von Krankheit und Tod." *Wort und Dienst* NF 11 (1971) 119–40. **Tournay, R.** "Note sur le Psaume 22.17." *VT* 23 (1973) 111–12.

Translation

1 For the musical director. According to "Doe [a] of the Dawn." A psalm of David.

2(1) My God, my God, why have you forsaken me? (4+4)
My moaning [a] is of the distance of my salvation!

3(2) O my God, I cry out by day, but you don't answer, (4+3)
and by night, but there is no rest for me.

4(3) But you are holy, [a] (2+3)
enthroned upon the praises of Israel.

5(4) Our fathers trusted in you; (3+2)
they trusted and you delivered them.

6(5) They cried out to you and were delivered; (3+3)
they trusted in you and were not disappointed.

7(6) But I am a worm, and not a man; (4+4)
scorned by mankind and despised by people.

8(7) All that see me deride me; (4+4)
they curl their lips, [a] they shake their heads.

9(8) "He trusted [a] in the Lord! Let him deliver him. (4+4)
Let him rescue him, since he takes delight in him! "

10(9) You are the one who drew me forth [a] from the belly, (3+3)
the one who made me safe upon my mother's breasts. [b]

11(10) I was cast upon you from the womb; (3+3)
from my mother's belly, you have been my God.

12(11) Don't be distant from me, (2+2+2)
for trouble is near;
there is certainly [a] no helper! [b]

13(12) Many bulls have surrounded me; (3+3)
mighty bulls of Bashan have encircled me.

14(13) *They have opened their mouths against me,*   (3+3)
     like [a] *a lion about to rend and roar.*

15(14) *I have been poured out like water,*   (2+2)
     and all my bones have become disjointed;
     My heart was like wax;   (3+3)
     it melted within my inwards.

16(15) *My strength* [a] *dried up like a potsherd,*   (3+3+3)
     and my tongue was fused [b] *to my jaws,*
     and you deposited [c] *me in death's dust.*

17(16) *For dogs have surrounded me;*   (3+3+3)
     a pack [a] *of thugs have encompassed me;*
     my hands and my feet were exhausted. [b]

18(17) *I count all my bones;*   (2+3)
     They stare and look at me!

19(18) *They divide my garments among themselves*   (3+3)
     and cast lots for my clothing.

20(19) *But you, O Lord—do not be distant!*   (3+3)
     O my Help [a]*, hasten to my aid!* [b]

21(20) *Deliver my soul from the sword,*   (3+3)
     my life [a] *from the paw of the dog.* [b]

22(21) *Save me from the mouth of the lion,*   (3+2,1)
     from the horns of wild oxen,
     You have answered me! [a]

23(22) *Let me tell of your name to my brethren;*   (3+3)
     I will praise you in the midst of the congregation.

24(23) *You who fear the Lord, praise him!*   (3+3+4)
     All you descendants of Jacob, honor him!
     And all you descendants of Israel, stand in awe of him!

25(24) *For he has not despised and has not detested*   (3+2)
     the affliction of the afflicted;
     and he has not hidden his face from him, [a]   (3+3)
     but when he [a] *cried for help, he heard him.* [a]

26(25) *From you comes my praise in the great congregation.* (4+4)
     I will fulfill my vows before those who fear him.

27(26) *The afflicted shall eat and shall be satisfied;*   (3+3+3)
     those who seek him shall praise the Lord—
     may your [a] *hearts live forever!*

28(27) *All the ends of the earth shall remember and turn to the Lord,* (4+4)
     and all the clans of the nations shall worship before you. [a]

29(28) *For the dominion belongs to the Lord,*   (3+2/3)
     and he [a] *is the one ruling over the nations.*

30(29) *Indeed,* [a] *all those about to sleep* [b] *in the earth*
     shall bow down [c] *to him*   (4?+4)
     all those about to descend to the dust shall bend down to him.
     And he who did not keep [d] *his life—*   (3+2)

31(30) *his descendants* [a] *shall serve him.*
     It shall be told concerning the Lord to a generation
     that will come; [b]   (4+4+2)

32(31) *and they shall declare his righteousness to a people about to be born* ª—
what he ᵇ *has done!*

Notes

1.a. "Hind" or "doe" (אַיֶּלֶת) is rendered by G as "help" (אֱיָלָת); if this is the correct reading, the expression in the psalm title might be taken as an indication of the content of the psalm which follows. Alternatively the expression may designate the name of the tune to which the psalm was to be sung. The association of *deer* with the sun-god (in archaeological data from Anatolia) has suggested to Jirku (*ZAW* 65 [1953] 85–86) that originally the title was associated with sun-god Šaḥar, also known from the Ugaritic texts.

2.a. Literally, "the words of my roaring." The translation of this verse as a whole presents problems. G renders v 2b by: "the account of my transgressions is distant from my salvation," apparently reading שִׁאָתִי ("transgressions") for MT's שַׁאֲגָתִי; but G was probably working from a different text, for it also contains an additional clause after "My God," namely: "attend to me" (πρόσχες μοι). It is preferable to retain MT, though G's syntax is followed, taking v 2b as a separate line, not governed by למה "why" in v 2a (as is implied in RSV and other translations).

4.a. The translation of this line is difficult and depends in part upon the location of the *athnaḥ*; the translation above follows MT, but it would be possible to place the *athnaḥ* under יושב. G (cf. *Vg*) assumes such a division of the line, but also renders קדוש as "sanctuary" (ἐν ἁγίῳ): "but you dwell in a sanctuary, the praise of Israel."

8.a. Literally, "they separate with a lip"; the idiom refers to sneering.

9.a. Reading גַּל (perf.: cf. G and S) for MT's imperative form. The literal sense of the verb is "to roll"—viz. "he rolled (his burden) to the Lord."

10.a. The etymology of גֹחִי is uncertain, though it appears to be a participle from גיח. A possible emendation is suggested by Leveen (*VT* 21 [1971] 53), who reads נחי "my rest, security," though it is best to retain MT.

10.b. There is some ambiguity in v 10b; G (with some support from Heb mss) translates: "my hope (apparently reading מִבְטָחִי) from my mother's breasts (reading מִשָּׁדָי)."

12.a. The second כִּי is interpreted as serving an emphatic function: GKC 159 ee.

12.b. Alternatively, the nuance of עוזר may be "(to) deliver"; for a discussion of the etymology and meaning, see B. Q. Baisos, "Ugaritic ʿḏr and Hebrew ʿzr I," *UF* 5 (1973) 41–52.

14.a. Reading כאריה (after G). כארי (in v 17) may originally have been a marginal gloss to indicate the absence of the preposition כְּ; see further v 17, note b.

16.a. כֹּחִי: "my strength." Alternatively, to provide better parallelism with "tongue," it is possible to read חִכִּי, "my palate" (on the assumption that accidental metathesis has occurred).

16.b. מדבק (Hoph. ptc. of דבק): literally, "was made to cling."

16.c. תשפתני: a denominative verb (from שפה), though it is probably not related to Ugaritic *ṭpd*, as suggested by Dahood (*Psalms* I, 140) and other scholars. On the etymology of Ugaritic *ṭpd*, see Craigie, *JSOT* 2 (1977) 41–42.

17.a. On the nuance "pack" for עדח, see Dahood, *Psalms* I, 140.

17.b. MT's כָּאֲרִי ("like a lion") presents numerous problems and can scarcely be correct. One must suppose that incorrect vocalization of the consonantal text occurred, perhaps through association with a marginal gloss at v 14; see note a at v 14 and L. C. Allen, "Cuckoos in the Textual Nest," *JTS* 22 (1971) 148–50. It is probably best to read a consonantal text כארו or כרו; see the massive discussion of the manuscript evidence in De-Rossi, IV, 14–20. G's translation, "*they pierced* my hands and feet" (ὤρυξαν), may perhaps presuppose a verb כרה, "to dig," or כור (II), "to pierce, bore" (though the latter verb is dubious). Some scholars have supposed a verb אָרָה ("to pluck, pick clean"), prefixed by כְּ ; for different approaches to this solution of the problem, see Dahood, "The Verb ʾĀRĀH, 'pick clean,'" *VT* 24 (1974) 370–71, and Tournay, *VT* 23 (1973) 111–12. Still another solution is the proposal of a verb כרה (V), "to be shrunken, shriveled" (on the basis of Akk. and Syriac), as proposed by Roberts, *VT* 23 (1973) 247–52. The starting point for the translation which is adopted above is provided by E. J. Kissane (*The Book of Psalms*, 97–101). He proposes an original text כלו , changed to כרו (noting the occasional interchange of ל and ר), and translates "consumed." This is basically the position adopted above; on the consonantal interchange, see A. Fitzgerald, "The Interchange of L, N and R in Biblical Hebrew," *JBL* 97 (1978) 481–88. Thus the verb is a form of כלה (3 plur. perf.); on the nuance "to be exhausted," for this verb, see BDB, 477.

20.a. אֱיָלוּתִי "my help" is a *hapax legomenon;* on the meaning, see BDB, 33. On the basis of Ugaritic *ʾul,* Dahood (after Ginsberg) translates: "O my army" (*Psalms* I, 141). But Ug. *ʾul* means more generally "might, strength" (Aistleitner, *WUS* #186, Gibson, *CML,* 143, and others); in the text adduced by Dahood (*UT* Krt. 88), it may either have this sense (see Caquot, et al., *Textes ougaritiques I,* 517) or it may have the sense "freeman" (cf. Akk. *awilu;* Gray, *The Krt Text in the Literature of Ras Shamra,* 1964, 13, 39–40). The specific sense "army" is not clearly attested in Ugaritic, so that (given the nature of the Hebrew evidence) the precise sense of the word in this verse must remain uncertain.

20.b. Or, "to my rescue"; see Baisos, *UF* 5 (1973) 41–52, and v 11, note b (above).

21.a. Literally, "my only one."

21.b. Dahood, finding the parallelism "sword // dog's paw" to be curious, understands כלב to be a by-form of כלפות "axe," and translates: "from the blade of an axe" (*Psalms* I, 141). But in v 17, there is the parallelism "dogs // hooligans" and the present parallelism refers back to that verse. The metaphor of the dog is continued with further animal imagery in v 22. Thus, it is better to stick with the conventional translation, which demonstrates more clearly the poet's striking use of poetic language.

22.a. MT עניתני: "you have answered me"; but the overall sense of MT is unclear. *G* renders τὴν ταπείνωσίν μου, "my lowliness," apparently reading a noun (עניתי ?). The parallel in grammatical structure between vv 21 and 22 lends some support to *G*'s rendition. But the structure of the psalm as a whole implies that the text and meaning of MT should be retained: see the structure (below) in *Form/Structure/Setting.*

25.a. In each case, *G* presupposes the first person singular suffix ("me"), but the opening lines of the verse make the third person suffix more appropriate.

27.a. Two Heb mss (cf. *G* and *S*) indicate a 3 m. pl. suffix: לבבם, which is possible in the light of v 27 a–b, though not necessary.

28.a. Or, "before him" (cf. *S* and *Vg*).

29.a. Reading והוא משל (cf. *G*), thus providing a balanced line 3+3.

30.a. MT reads אכלו, "they have eaten." The translation above assumes two words (accidentally joined in the text represented by MT), namely לו אך.

30.b. Reading ישני ("these that sleep") for MT's דשני ("fat ones"), thus providing a more appropriate parallel to יורדי ("those who descend") in the following parallel clause. The participle, from ישן ("sleep"), serves to express the immediate future ("about to . . ."), as does the participle in the following clause: cf. GKC, 116 p.

30.c. The verb is treated as a simple imperfect form (ישתחוו), the initial *waw* being a dittography, presumably arising as a consequence of the confusion noted in note a (above).

30.d. חיה (Pi'el perf.), "to keep, preserve life."

31.a. Literally, "(a) seed."

31.b. יבאו is taken with v 31 (cf. *G*) and read either as יבוא(the *aleph* and *waw* having been accidentally interchanged) or יבא, the final *waw* being a dittography.

32.a. נולד: Niph. ptc. from ילד, designating the immediate future: see v 30, note b (above).

32.b. *G* adds ὁ κύριος, viz. "what *the Lord* has done," but the short line of MT may provide a more fitting climax.

Form/Structure/Setting

The initial problem in determining the form of Ps 22 lies in the fact that the psalm contains at least three different kinds of material: (a) *lament* (vv 2–22), within which there are elements of (b) *prayer* (vv 12, 20–22), and finally (c) *praise* and *thanksgiving* (vv 23–32). The sharp distinction between the two main sections (vv 2–22 and 23–32) has prompted some scholars to suggest that originally there were two separate psalms which were fused into one; while this view is a possibility with respect to the pre-history of the psalm, it fails to take into account the evident unity of the psalm as it now exists. The mixture of forms and types of language suggests strongly that the text of Ps 22 is the basis of a liturgy, in which the worshiper moves from lament to prayer, and finally to praise and thanksgiving. The psalm should probably

be interpreted primarily as an *individual* psalm, though the liturgy sets the
problem of the individual in the context of the community as a whole; thus,
the liturgy was clearly a communal affair.

The liturgical dimension of the psalm emerges most clearly from an analysis
of its structure, which may be set out as follows:

> I. *Lament* (vv 2–22b): the sick declares his sorrow.
>   1. Forsaken by God and mankind (vv 2–11).
>   2. Prayer for help (v 12).
>   3. Surrounded by trouble (vv 13–19).
>   4. Prayer for deliverance (vv 20–22b).
> II. *Response* (v 22c): presupposing an oracle.
> III. *Thanksgiving* (vv 23–27): declared by the sufferer.
> IV. *Thanksgiving* (vv 28–32): declared by the congregation.

There are several clues to the liturgical structure of the psalm as a whole.
The most distinctive one is the declaration of trust and confidence by the
worshiper at the end of v 22: "You have answered me!" The words come
in such striking contrast to the preceding lament and prayer, that one must
presuppose the declaration of an oracle (cf. Killian, *BZ* 12 [1968] 172–85)
announcing healing and health, after the prayer (vv 20–22b), which gives
rise to this sudden declaration of confidence. In the praise which follows,
the individual worshiper twice makes reference to the congregation (vv 23,
26) that forms the larger context of the liturgical proceedings. The change
of person and of tone in the final section (vv 28–32) indicates the congregational response and conclusion to the liturgy.

The words of the lament imply the worshiper's deep state of distress prior
to the liturgy; although in their original composition, the words presumably
indicated the particular experience of a particular person, in the normal use
of the liturgy they are simply words spoken by individuals whose personal
circumstances may have differed. Consequently, it is difficult to determine
the precise purpose and setting of the liturgy. In all probability, the liturgy
was used for those persons who were severely sick and threatened by death;
they participated in the liturgy, in the context of the community as a whole,
who gathered as a congregation in the temple; see further Schmid, *Wort und
Dienst* 11 (1971) 119–40. In participating in such a liturgy, the worshiper
hoped for a priestly oracle favorable to his plea, which would enable the
great declaration of confidence (v 22c). In the concluding portion of the
ritual, the worshiper would fulfil his vows (v 26), both through offering praise
to God and through participating in the sacrificial feast (v 27). It is probable
that a liturgy such as this was used for any person who was sick and threatened
with death, though it is possible to interpret the liturgy as a *royal ritual* (cf.
Eaton, *Kingship and the Psalms*, 34–36); the evidence for such a view, however,
is at best indirect, and the royal hypothesis must remain uncertain.

Comment

Forsaken by God (22:2–6). The worshiper begins by expressing the darkest
mystery of his suffering, namely the sense of being forsaken by God. It is a

mystery because it appears to be rooted in a contradiction, namely the apparent contradiction between theology and experience. Theology, based upon the tradition and experience of the past, affirmed unambiguously that *trust* (the verb is used three times, for emphasis, in vv 5–6) resulted in deliverance. Indeed it was of the essence of the covenant faith that those who trusted in the holy God would not be disappointed—hence the praise of Israel upon which God was enthroned (v 4). But experience was altogether at odds with theology; whereas the fathers trusted and were delivered, the essence of the psalmist's complaint ("my moaning," v 2) was "the distance of my salvation." The God of covenant, who was believed not to have deserted his faithful people, appeared to have forsaken this worshiper who, in sickness, faced the doors of death. And it was the sense of being forsaken by God that was the fundamental problem—more grave than the actual condition of sickness and the threat of death.

Despised by fellow human beings (22:7–11). Whereas the problem of God is expressed most powerfully in the divine silence (v 3a), the problem of fellow human beings arose from the derisory words which they addressed to the ailing person. Scorned and despised by fellow human beings, the worshiper is treated as a *worm,* implying both a state of decay and unpleasantness (cf. Exod 16:20), and by implication the nearness of death itself (cf. Isa 14:11). Again it is clear that the primary problem was not sickness or death as such; the primary problem was the silence of God (v 3) and the secondary problem was the terrible reaction of fellow human beings, who—rather than offering comfort and consolation—spurned the sick person as if an object less than human, tainted already with corruption and death. But the secondary problem of the scornful fellow humans reintroduces the primary problem of God; their taunting words (v 9) remind the sufferer that God appears to have deserted him. Though the words are spoken in derision, they strike home in the heart of the worshiper precisely because they appear to have the essence of truth in them. Now the sufferer perceives a further contradiction; this time, the contradiction lies in his own experience from birth onward to the present moment. From the moment of his birth and his mother's initial care, the sufferer had been dependent ultimately upon God (vv 10–11); but now in the time of crisis, that past experience seemed like a hollow mockery of reality. The only reality was the distance of God, aggravated by the taunting nearness of fellow human beings.

A prayer for help (22:12). In such desperate straits, the psalmist is compelled to move from lament to prayer; the substance of the prayer illustrates the true nature of his condition. There is no explicit prayer for healing or deliverance from death (though such may be implied); the prayer begins with the request for the removal of the divine distance. Feeling forsaken by God, the worshiper asks that God be no longer distant. While it is true that the sense of distance would disappear in an act of healing, there is something more immediate in the desire of this prayer; more than anything else, the worshiper requires to know once again the intimate presence of God. If such presence brought with it healing, so much the better, but even if it did not, sickness and death could be faced squarely in the presence of God, who would be a *helper.*

Surrounded by trouble (22:13–19). As the lament continues, it is the awareness of enemies which dominates the psalmist's thought. He is trapped; his experience is presented dramatically as one who is "surrounded, encircled" (v 13), "surrounded, exhausted" (v 17). The words evoke the abject terror of one who is powerless, but surrounded, with no avenue of escape; those who look upon him in his miserable estate assume the proportion of beasts (in the language of the poetry). They are like bulls (Bashan, v 13, produced the fattest and largest cattle in the territory), like a lion hungry for its supper (v 14), like dogs sniffing about for something to eat. It is these enemies, devoid of comfort, who confound the physical malady with spiritual terror, for though the sick person is not yet dead, they are already dividing up his clothes (v 19), as if he were deceased. In each case, the description of the threatening dominance of enemies (vv 13–14, 17) is followed by a description of the fear instilled in the sufferer (vv 15–16, 18). The words of vv 15–16 should not necessarily be taken as indicative of the disease as such; rather, they describe the fear evoked by enemies who are waiting and watching for death to come. The sufferer feels as if "poured out like water" ("completely washed out," in modern idiom) and as if all his bones were disjointed—he was merely a bag of useless bones! Though not yet dead, he felt already that he had been deposited in *death's dust; "you* deposited me" (v 16c) implies that the psalmist understood God to have set him in this mortal predicament, so although it is the derisory enemies that surround him, it is God who is at the root of his dilemma.

Prayer for deliverance (22:20–22b). Again, the desperate situation pushes the psalmist to prayer and again he begins the prayer in a similar fashion, pleading for the removal of the divine distance (v 20; cf. v 12). But then he prays specifically for deliverance, not explicitly from sickness and death, but rather from the enemies (again, animal metaphors are introduced) that stand around him, awaiting his death with such morbid anticipation.

The sufferer's response to an oracle (22:22c). "You have answered me"; the perfect tense expresses the worshiper's confidence (cf. Killian, art. cit.). His confidence is based upon the faith that God would answer his prayers, but specifically it was elicited by the oracular statement declared by a priest (or perhaps by a prophet) that God would answer. The oracular proclamation presupposed by this statement of confidence is implied, not stated; presumably it could not be stated in the text of the liturgy, for the officiating priest (or prophet) would be waiting for the divine word and would proclaim only the word that was given to him. Since the substance of the divine word, in cases such as sickness and the nearness of death, could not always be anticipated, it was not written as a formal part of the liturgy. But faith was such that the response was included. (One may suppose that the general use of such a liturgy presupposed in the first instance a particular situation and a particular outcome; viz., it was derived from a situation in which a sufferer did receive a favorable Word from God and did proclaim this statement of confidence.)

Thanksgiving of the one about to be delivered (22:23–27). The opening words of praise and thanksgiving are addressed to God (v 23); the remaining and major portion of the declaration is addressed to the congregation as a whole (vv 24–27). Because the worshiper has received the assurance of God's response in the context of a congregational liturgy, his immediate response is to say to God that he will offer him praise in that same congregation. Thus, the praise of God that follows is not addressed to God in a vacuum; it is addressed to God through the congregation, with the invitation that they too honor and praise God. The psalmist's invitation to the congregation (viz., the "descendants of Jacob . . . of Israel") is taken up in vv 28–32, where the whole congregation joins in the praise.

It is clear in v 25 that the worshiper has experienced a total reversal of his predicament as expressed in vv 2–3. He began feeling forsaken (v 2), but now knows that God did not in fact despise his affliction. He began by crying out for help, with no apparent answer (v 3), but now perceives that God had in fact heard him and that an answer was coming. Specifically, the answer to his prayer came in the proclamation presupposed by the statement of confidence contained in v 22c. It is this priestly (or prophetic) proclamation which is again presupposed in the words: "from you comes my praise . . ." (v 26); it was the Word which came from God, promising deliverance, that prompted the praise offered in the midst of the congregation. God's faithfulness, in promising deliverance, required also faithfulness from the sufferer; he was to fulfil those vows and commitments made to God in the earlier time of distress. "The afflicted shall eat" (v 27): though the psalmist speaks of all the afflicted who are promised relief from their affliction, he speaks also of himself as one just relieved. The reference to *eating* and consequent satisfaction implies the worshiper's participation in a communal meal which formed a part of the ritual; though his previous experience was one of being "scorned by mankind" (v 7), he now sits with his fellow human beings and participates in a feast which symbolizes fellowship with God. And perhaps the last words he speaks, "May your hearts live for ever!" (v 27), should be interpreted as a toast to his fellow diners—a significant toast from one who stood so recently on the threshold of death!

Thanksgiving of the congregation (22:28–32). In the concluding words of thanksgiving, there is a move away from the individual perspective of the earlier portion of the liturgy to a more cosmic perspective. Although at first the change seems abrupt, it is entirely appropriate; it sets the particular event of deliverance into a broader and more balanced perspective, and yet it is still related intimately to the earlier liturgy. Hence, it is unnecessary to suppose that the last section is not an integral part of the original psalm, as proposed, for example, by Martin-Achard (*VCaro* 65 [1963] 78–87). Ultimately God is king and controls the affairs of all mankind and all nations (v 29); all persons need to remember that and to worship—the psalmist who forgot it in his sense of desolation (v 2), the enemies who implied that God was not in control (vv 8–9). The particular incidents of desolation and deliverance need to be set in the larger perspective—"dominion belongs to the Lord" (v 29). But the concluding praise also ties in with another theme of the liturgy, namely the nearness of death. Though the psalmist had been delivered from death, its nearness was no excuse to cease from worshiping God; those about to die should also bow down in worship before the God of the universe (v 30). Survival is not so much important for its own sake as it is important for providing a further opportunity for participation in the worship of God,

so that if one died, there was at least the possibility of descendants worshiping
God (v 31). "He who did not keep his life" (v 30)—these words, in context,
may refer to those who did not receive a positive oracle from God, who
did not escape death; see further the discussion of v 22c above. The deliverance of a sufferer was ground for praise, but the death of a sufferer was
not the end, for God's mighty acts would still be told in the future, beyond
the funeral, to generations yet unborn (vv 31–32). It is this sentiment which
sets the perspective for the whole liturgy, regardless of the specific will of
God for the individual sufferer. Death, after all, comes to all mankind sooner
or later, but the mighty acts of God will continue to be told from generation
to generation.

Explanation

To Pascal has been attributed the saying that at the end of life, "one
dies alone" ("on mourra seul"). The psalmist begins his lament with an expression of the loneliness of dying; it is loneliness in the absence of God,
compounded by the presence of evil human beings who offer neither companionship nor consolation. Thus, at its beginning, the psalm supplements those
other writings in the OT which express profound desolation—the dreadful
curse of Job (3:1–26) and the lament of Jeremiah (20:14–18). And like both
Job and Jeremiah, the psalmist thinks back to the time of his birth and wonders
why life has come to this (22:10–11). Yet the psalm differs finally from the
record of the experiences of Job and Jeremiah by virtue of its liturgical character; the liturgy immediately sets the loneliness of dying into the context of
a caring community. And the worshiper, who begins his words in utter desolation, ends by inviting his fellow worshipers to join in the praise of God (22:23).
The agent of deliverance from desolation is God himself, but the context
in which that deliverance is declared is none other than the community of
God's people.

Though the psalm is not messianic in its original sense or setting (though
some scholars would interpret vv 28–32 as a messianic relecture: see Martin-
Achard, art. cit.), it may be interpreted from a NT perspective as a messianic
psalm par excellence. It is clear, from the recorded words of Jesus on the
cross, that he identified his own loneliness and suffering with that of the
psalmist (Matt 27:46; Mark 15:34). And it is clear that the evangelists interpreted the crucifixion in the light of the psalm, utilizing its words in their
description of the scene (Matt 27:39; Mark 15:29; cf. Luke 23:35; Ps 22:8).
Indeed, the psalm takes on the appearance of anticipatory prophecy; the
high priests, scribes and elders employ the modes of words of the psalmist's
enemies against Jesus (Ps 22:19; cf. John 19:24; Matt 27:35; Mark 15:24;
Luke 23:34). It is not without reason that the psalm has been called the
"Fifth Gospel" account of the crucifixion (Frost, CJT 8 [1962] 102–15).

What is most significant about the NT perspective is the self-identification
of Jesus with the suffering psalmist, for it provides an insight into one part
of the meaning of the crucifixion. The sufferer of Ps 22 is a human being,
experiencing the terror of mortality in the absence of God and the presence
of enemies. In the suffering of Jesus, we perceive God, in Jesus, entering

into and participating in the terror of mortality; he identifies with the suffering and the dying. Because God, in Jesus, has engaged in that desolation, he can offer comfort to those of us who walk now where the psalmist walked. But there is also a remarkable difference between the experience of the suffering psalmist and that of Jesus. The psalm concludes with praise because the sufferer escaped death; Jesus died. Yet the latter half of the psalm (vv 22–32) may also be read from a messianic perspective. The transition at v 22 is now understood not in deliverance *from* death, as was the case for the psalmist, but in deliverance *through* death, achieved in the resurrection. And it is that deliverance which is the ground of praise, both for the sufferer (vv 23–27) and for the "great congregation" (vv 28–32).

The Shepherd Psalm (23:1–6)

Bibliography

Ammassari, A. "Il Salmo 23." *BeO* 16 (1974) 257–62. **Freedman, D. N.** "The Twenty-third Psalm." *Michigan Oriental Studies in Honor of George C. Cameron,* ed. L. I. Orlin. Ann Arbor: University of Michigan, 1976, 139–66. **Johnson, A. R.** "Psalm 23 and the Household of Faith." *Proclamation and Presence,* ed. J. R. Durham and J. R. Porter (1970), 261–71. **Koehler, L.** "Psalm 23." *ZAW* 68 (1956) 227–34. **Loretz, O.** "Psalmenstudien III." *UF* 6 (1974) 187–91. **Meek, T. J.** "Old Testament Notes, I: the Metrical Structure of Psalm 23." *JBL* 67 (1948) 233–35. **Merrill, A. L.** "Ps 23 and the Jerusalem Tradition." *VT* 15 (1965) 354–60. **Milne, P.** "Psalm 23: Echoes of the Exodus." *SR* 4 (1974/75) 237–47. **Morgernstern, J.** "Psalm 23." *JBL* 65 (1946) 13–24. **Power, E.** "The Shepherd's Two Rods in Modern Palestine and Some Passages of the Old Testament," *Bib* 9 (1928) 434–42. **Vogt, E.** "The 'Place in Life' of Ps. 23." *Bib* 34 (1953) 195–211. **Von Rohr Sauer, A.** "Fact and Image in the Shepherd Psalm." *CTM* 42 (1971) 488–92.

Translation

[1] A Psalm of David.
    The Lord is my shepherd;   (2+2)
    I shall not want.

[2] *In grassy meadows he will make me lie down;*   (3+3)
    beside placid waters he will lead me.

[3] *He will refresh my soul;*   (2+2?+2)
    he will lead me in paths of righteousness
    for his name's sake.

[4] *Even though I shall walk*   (2+2+2)
    in the valley of death's shadow,
    I shall fear no evil.
    For you are with me: (2+2+2)
    your rod and your staff—
    they[a] shall comfort me.

⁵ *You will spread a table* ^a *for me*   (3+2)
   before my enemies.
  You have anointed my head with oil: (3+2)
   my cup is full. ^b
⁶ *Surely goodness and lovingkindness shall pursue me*   (3?+2)
   all the days of my life,
  and I shall dwell again ^a *in the house of the Lord*   (3+2)
   for days without end. ^b

Notes

4.a. המה: "they." Dahood translates "behold," on the basis of Ugaritic *hm* (*Psalms I,* 147; also Freedman, "The Twenty-third Psalm," 157–58, and others). Against this translation, see the note on Ps 9:8 (above).

5.a. Power has suggested emending שֻׁלְחָן, "table," to שֶׁלַח ("weapon, spear, javelin"), on the basis of dittography (*Bib* 9 [1928] 434–42); he translates: "thou preparest arms for my defence against my enemies" (cf. Koehler, *ZAW* 68 [1956] 234, and Morgernstern, *JBL* 65 [1946] 13–24). The translation is possible, but the substance of v 5 c-d, and the absence of support from the versions, makes such a change from the standard reading of the text unnecessary.

5.b. G renders vv 5c-6a differently from MT: "And your cup cheers me like the best (wine?). Also, your mercy shall follow me. . . ." G joins the first two words of v 6 with the last word of v 5 (cf. S and *Vg*), but such a construction would be anomalous in Hebrew and it is best rejected.

6.a. וְשַׁבְתִּי: literally, "*and I shall return* in the house of the Lord." The construction is pregnant, implying "and I shall return and I shall dwell (וְיָשַׁבְתִּי) in the house of the Lord" (Cf. Delitzsch, *Biblical Commentary on the Psalms,* I, 40).

6.b. Literally, "length of days."

Form/Structure/Setting

Although Ps 23 is short and relatively free from textual and translation problems, it is nevertheless particularly difficult to interpret with respect to such matters as its form and original social or cultic setting. There has been general agreement since Gunkel's time that the psalm is a *psalm of trust* or *confidence.* Those who do not accept such a view differ more in nuance than in substance; thus Vogt (*Bib* 34 [1953] 195–211) considers the psalm to be a *thanksgiving psalm,* basing his view in part on a particular interpretation of the setting (below). But, as Loretz (*UF* 6 [1974] 187–91) has indicated, at certain points in its history the psalm could be related to either genre. The identification of the psalm as a *royal psalm* poses more serious problems (so Merrill, *VT* 15 [1965] 354–60 and Eaton, *Kingship and the Psalms,* 36–38): the view is not implausible, but the substance of the psalm is so general and so laden with metaphor, that a specific interpretation in terms of royal psalmody is, of necessity, highly hypothetical.

The structure of the psalm is also difficult to define with clarity or certainty. There is some consensus that the psalm falls into two main sections: (1) the Lord as shepherd (23:1–4); (2) the Lord as host (23:5–6). Yet even this basic analysis is subject to criticism. There is little disagreement that the first four verses utilize the metaphor of the divine shepherd; there is considerable debate, however, as to the interpretation of vv 5–6. Traditionally, the verses have been interpreted as reflecting a change in imagery from the Lord as shepherd to the Lord as host. But several scholars have argued that the shepherd metaphor is retained throughout the psalm (so Koehler, *ZAW* 68 [1956] 227–34). Yet another possibility is that vv 5–6 do not contain metaphorical language at all, but should be interpreted more literally with respect to a sacrificial banquet, which provides the setting for the psalm (see Vogt, art. cit.).

The problems pertaining to form and structure naturally culminate in a variety of views with respect to the setting of the psalm. At one end of the spectrum is the view of Morgernstern (*JBL*, 65 [1946] 13–24) that the psalm was not composed for use in temple worship, but was a pious Jew's expression of faith and confidence in the Lord. Vogt, on the other hand, proposes a fairly elaborate hypothesis, inferring from the substance of the psalm a liturgical ritual of thanksgiving, of which a sacrificial banquet was a part. Still another proposal is that of Milne, who interprets the psalm in an exilic context (*SR* 4 [1974/75] 237–47); the shepherd metaphor, which contains within it reminiscences of the Exodus (cf. Freedman, art. cit.), provides hope for an exiled community cut off from home and temple.

The sheer diversity of views is a clear indication of the most fundamental problem with respect to the interpretation of the psalm: it is that the language of the psalm is not sufficiently explicit to establish beyond dispute its original sense and setting. Thus, several of the various interpretations noted above are plausible, but several also go beyond the clear evidence of the psalm (e.g. royal interpretations, liturgical interpretations, or exilic interpretations); they are not thereby wrong, merely hypothetical. In the interpretation presented in the comment that follows, it has been impossible to avoid hypothesis; nevertheless, a relatively simple interpretation is given to reduce the element of hypothesis as far as possible.

It is proposed that the psalm must be interpreted as a *psalm of confidence* in the context of some ritual or the context of thanksgiving, without being so specific as Vogt. Such a setting is implied in vv 5–6 (especially v 6c: see *Comment*), though the possibility of a noncultic interpretation such as that of Morgernstern remains open. It is presumed that initially the psalm was an *individual psalm*, utilized in such a setting, though later in its history, it may well have come to function as a *communal psalm*. The following basic structure is proposed: (1) the divine shepherd (23:1–4); (2) anticipation of future thanksgiving in God's house (23:5–6). The metrical and stichometric analysis is fraught with difficulties (cf. the analyses of Meek, Loretz, Freedman, and others): the translation above reflects an attempt to show the simplest analysis of the lines, though a more complex structure may in fact be present.

Comment

The divine shepherd (23:1–4). The first four verses contain an extended metaphor: God is the shepherd, and the psalmist is a sheep belonging to his flock. The fundamental points expressed in the metaphor are the interrelated dimensions of *protection* and *provision*. Yet the metaphor is pregnant with meaning; it is not merely a picture drawn randomly from nature to illustrate the character of the relationship between God and the psalmist. It is a metaphor drawing on the ancient resources of the Hebrew tradition; thus the psalmist, in utilizing the metaphor, is linking his thought to a broader concept, namely that of God who had been experienced as shepherd by many persons over many generations. And the metaphor is loaded in another sense, too; the terminology of the metaphor associates it with the Exodus from Egypt and the Hebrews' travels in the wilderness, when God's provision and protection had been known like that of a shepherd. Thus, in a subtle fashion, the psalmist is expressing confidence and trust in such a manner that his sentiments are linked to the great acts of divine salvation of the past, which in turn formed the basis of the covenant faith. Yet, in spite of this rich background to the use of the shepherd metaphor, it is possible that the particular words employed in the psalm may give some insight into the background of the psalm, namely the circumstances giving rise to such a profound expression of trust and confidence.

The Lord (v 1). The opening word (יהוה) sets the theme for the psalm as a whole and occurs again in the last verse to form an *inclusio*. The Lord is called "shepherd"; the metaphor, at this point, draws upon one of the oldest epithets of God in the Hebrew tradition (cf. Gen 49:24), an epithet which has parallels in Near Eastern religions (e.g. it is used of Shamash: *ANET*, 387). The poet takes the ancient epithet of God as a starting point, but then develops its metaphorical content by drawing out its inherent implications with respect to God's care for his people. In moving from the epithet to the metaphor, the psalmist is doing nothing distinctive, for the metaphor is employed in various psalms (e.g. 80:2; 77:21; 95:7). The distinctiveness in the opening words of this psalm lies in the use of the pronoun, *my* shepherd; the shepherd theme, traditionally interpreted communally of the "flock" (or nation), is here given its most personal interpretation in the entire biblical tradition. (Even if the use of "I/my" was intended, or later interpreted, in a communal sense, the implications of a personal association with the shepherd remain.)

As a consequence of the fact that the Lord is his shepherd, the psalmist can say: "I shall not want." Koehler's translation (art. cit., 228–29) expresses clearly the consequence implicit in the construction: *Solange weil Jahwä mein Hirte ist, leide ich keinen Mangel*—viz., "so long as the Lord is my shepherd, I suffer no lack." In general terms, the words reflect simply the shepherd's provision. But more than that, they recall God's provision for his people during the travels after the Exodus; see Deut 2:7, "you have not lacked a thing" (the same verb, חסר, is used as in Ps 23). This is one example of the undertones of the Exodus which extend throughout the shepherd metaphor, as demonstrated clearly in the studies of Milne and Freedman.

Verses 2–3 extend the metaphor further, illustrating the nature of the shepherd's guidance and provision. It is these verses which form a central part of the evidence for Dahood's hypothesis, namely that the psalmist speaks of the Lord's guidance through the vicissitudes of life to the eternal bliss of Paradise (*Psalms I*, 145–46); specifically, the verses are said to contain a description of the "Elysian Fields." But such an hypothesis reads more into the text than it can clearly sustain; it is more suited to the later allegorical interpretations of the psalm in the early church than it is to the original intent of the psalmist (see further Loretz, *UF* 6 [1974] 191). The verses develop primarily the role of the shepherd with respect to his sheep,· but at a secondary level they elaborate still further the echoes of the Exodus. Thus the "meadows" (נאות) appear to recall the "holy *pasture*" (נוה: Exod 15:13) which was the immediate goal of the Hebrews in their Exodus from Egypt. (Note also that the verb נהל, "to guide," is used both in Exod 15:13 and Ps 23:2). The "placid waters" (literally, "waters of *placidity*": מנחות, an intensive plural) may recall the "resting place" or "placidity" (מנוחה) associated with the ark in the wilderness wanderings (Num 10:33). The climactic point in vv 2–3, "for his name's sake," also associates the metaphor with the Exodus, as is indicated by the use of the same expression in Ps 106:8 in the context of the deliverance from Egypt. On the one hand, the psalmist speaks in confidence of the guidance and refreshment which he believes the Lord will continue to give to him; the implication is that he has recently experienced such blessing and expects the experience to continue in the future. On the other hand, the anticipation of this future refreshment and guidance is based upon something more solid than his own past experience; the undertones of the Exodus indicate that his expectation is established on the bedrock of Israel's faith, namely the precedent of God's refreshment and guidance in the Exodus and wilderness journeys.

The meaning of the expression "the valley of death's shadow" (v 4) poses some difficulty. The Hebrew צלמות may properly be understood as a compound noun, with the literal sense "very deep shadow" (see D. W. Thomas, "*ṣlmwt* in the Old Testament," *JSS* 7 [1962] 191–200), or even "total darkness" (Dahood, *Psalms I*, 147). As such, it is not only a part of the metaphor of the shepherd, but again has associations with the Exodus and the wandering through the "deep shadow" of the wilderness (Jer 2:6). But the expression may have been used deliberately to convey the threat of death, as is done in the poetry of Job (10:21–22). Thus the psalmist's confidence rests in the fact that even in the shadow of death itself, he need fear no evil. The reason for such confidence is found in God's protection, described in the metaphor as the shepherd's "rod" and "staff." Power (art. cit., 435) has illuminated the poetry from a modern context; the Palestinian shepherd normally carried two implements, a *club* (or rod) to fend off wild beasts and a *crook* (or staff) to guide and control the sheep.

Anticipation of future thanksgiving in God's house (23:5–6). Although the focus of the psalmist now shifts, v 5 forms a transition from the imagery of the shepherd to that of present and future banquets of thanksgiving. That is, although the shepherd imagery no longer dominates in the last two verses, it is still present in the transition, though some efforts to locate it may possibly be misguided. Thus the view of von Rohr Sauer that the word "table" continues the metaphor and is to be understood as "grass" is not entirely convincing; equally unconvincing is his suggestion that the contents of the *cup* were for the sustenance of weak sheep (*CTM* 42 [1971] 488–92). But Freedman's reference to Ps 78:19 (art. cit., 159) is convincing; in that psalm, containing allusions to the rebellion in the wilderness, there is reference to God "spreading a table," in which similar terminology to Ps 23 is employed. The psalmist, already participating in a banquet and anticipating further such occasions in the future, recalls (by implication) God's provision of a "table" in the past. The reference to "enemies" is also difficult to interpret. To identify the term with specific enemies, such as the original inhabitants of Jerusalem (as proposed by Ammassari, *BeO* 16 [1974] 257–62), is a precarious task; at most, there may be allusions in the language of the poetry to enemies who were encountered in the wilderness. It is safer to assume that the psalmist had endured affliction in the past at the hands of enemies and had risen above that affliction in confidence. Now, as he anticipates the future, he has no illusions; there would still be enemies, perhaps even enemies present in the temple when he offered thanks, but God's provision would come, even in the presence of those enemies.

While v 5a-b appears to anticipate future banquets, v 5c-d makes reference to the banquet of thanksgiving in which the psalmist is actively engaged. "You have anointed . . ."; viz. prior to the banquet the traditional anointing ceremony of preparation had taken place. "My cup is full (or "overflowing")": the immediate reference is to the banquet cup from which the psalmist drank, but the symbolism is deeper. The banquet was a celebration of God's provision and protection; the psalmist's experience of life (*viz.* his *cup*) had been so bountiful, that it was life itself which was full of blessing, overflowing with thanksgiving. The experience of the past and the rejoicing of the present gave rise to the magnificent expression of confidence in the future in v 6. He would be pursued by "goodness" and "lovingkindness" (חסד), the latter term specifically associating future blessing with the covenant of God. In a sense, the language of Exodus and wilderness which permeates the entire psalm comes to a head in the expression *lovingkindness;* the God of covenant, who in the past had expressed his lovingkindness to his people so bountifully in their redemption, would continue to do so in the future.

With this confidence, the psalmist rejoices not only in the present moment of festivity and thanksgiving, but also anticipates future occasions when he would return and dwell again in the *house of the Lord* (the temple), in order once again to give thanks. The thanksgiving of the given moment was merely part of a larger series of thanksgiving ceremonies which would punctuate the entire life of the psalmist (see further the articles of Vogt and Johnson in the *Bibliography*).

Explanation

There are few psalms in the Psalter which are so well-loved and well-known as Ps 23. Its appeal lies partly in the simplicity and beauty of its poetry, strengthened by the serene confidence which it exudes. But more than that, the genius of the psalmist is to be found in his extraordinary expression of a trusting relationship with God. To express such a relationship in simple language is no easy task; on the one hand, the psalm could sink to a monotonous repetition of affirmations, while on the other hand it could defy the abilities of language for articulate expression as a consequence of its profundity. The psalmist has avoided the extremes and found a middle path which is at once simple, yet also profound. The simplicity arises from the use of the shepherd metaphor, involving language which would be understood readily by all living in a world where the landscape was dotted with sheep and shepherds. The profundity emerges in the beauty of the poetry, which transforms simple metaphor into profoundly spiritual expression. And the appeal of the psalm has continued through subsequent generations, partly because the beauty of the poetry has survived the process of translation, and partly because (until very recently) the pastoral metaphor has retained its significance and accessibility to the majority of human beings. The psalm is written consistently from the perspective of the sheep; that is, its expression of trust and confidence presupposes an awareness of helplessness and need on the part of the one who trusts. In a distinctive fashion, the psalmist has set forth the fundamentals of the covenant relationship, not in terms of Lord and servant, but in the more intimate language of shepherd and sheep.

Though its words are not explicitly quoted in the NT, Ps 23 is important nevertheless for understanding the substance of the Gospels. When Jesus said: "I am the good Shepherd" (John 10:11), he was not merely utilizing a metaphor familiar to his audience from their knowledge of the Hebrew Scriptures. He was also implying something about his person, for in Ps 23 and other psalms in which the metaphor is employed, it is God who is the shepherd. It is the words of Jesus himself, amplified by the early church (cf. 1 Pet 2:25 and 5:4), which make possible a "re-reading" of Ps 23 in the light of the gospel of redemption. The echoes of the Exodus and the redemption from Egypt in the psalm are transformed into echoes of the redemption won by the shepherd who lays down his life for his sheep (John 10:11).

A Hymn to the King of Glory   (24:1–10)

Bibliography

Cross, F. M. *Canaanite Myth and Hebrew Epic* (1973) 91–99. **Dijkstra, M.** "A Ugaritic Pendant of the Biblical Expression 'Pure in Heart' (Ps 24:7, 73:1)," *UF* 8 (1976) 440. **Treves, M.** "Date of Psalm 24," *VT* 10 (1960) 428–34.

Translation

[1] A Psalm of David.[a]
>The earth and its contents belong to the Lord,   (3+3)
>   the world and those who dwell [b] therein;
>[2] for [a] he has fixed it upon the seas   (3+2)
>   and established it [b] upon the rivers.[c]
>[3] Who shall ascend into the mountain of the Lord   (3+3)
>   and who shall stand up in his holy place?
>[4] He who has innocent hands and a pure heart,[a]   (4+4+3)
>   who has not raised his mind [b] to what is false
>   and has not sworn [c] deceitfully.[d]
>[5] He will receive blessing from the Lord,   (4+3)
>   and righteousness from the God of his salvation.

6 *This is the generation of those* ᵃ *who consult him,*   (3+2+2)
   of those who seek your face,
   O God ᵇ*of Jacob.* SELAH
7 *Lift up your heads, O gates!*   (3+3+3)
   And be uplifted, O eternal doors! ᵃ
   Then the King of Glory shall come in!
8 *Who, then, is the King of Glory?*   (3?+3+3)
   The Lord, strong and mighty!
   The Lord, mighty in battle!
9 *Lift up your heads, O gates!*   (3+3+3)
   and be uplifted, ᵃ *O eternal doors!*
   Then the King of Glory shall come in!
10 *Who is he, then,*   (3+2)
   the King of Glory?
   The Lord of Hosts,   (2+3)
   he is the King of Glory! SELAH.

Notes

1.a. *G* adds to the title: Τῆς μιᾶς σαββάτου ("for the first day of the week"), reflecting no doubt early Jewish tradition concerning the psalm's usage in worship.
1.b. *G* implies a text: וכל־ישבי, by the use of πάντες, but the addition is not well supported and is unnecessary; the same phrase is used in Ps 98:7 without כל, and it is also absent in *G* at that text (*G*, 97:7).
2.a. The introductory particle (כי) is absent in the text presupposed by *G*, but the causal link implied in MT is preferable to the text of *G*.
2.b. Reading כוננה (viz. perf. for imperf.; cf. *BHS*); a perfect tense is implied, given the tense in the preceding parallel line.
2.c. "Rivers" is the normal rendering of נהרות. Dahood translates "ocean currents," with reference to Ugaritic (*Psalms I*, 151). But Ugaritic does not clearly support such a translation, and elsewhere Dahood has recognized the more appropriate translation of Ugaritic *nhr*, namely "river," or perhaps "river current" (*RSP I*, 203).
4.a. The expression "pure heart" is illustrated in the Ugaritic texts: *brt. lb(k)*, "pure in your heart," with reference to moral integrity (*CTA* 54. Obv. 5); cf. Dijkstra, *UF* 8 (1976) 440.
4.b. *BHS* reads נפשי ("my mind, soul"). But most Hebrew mss read נפשו (*Kethib*), with נפשי as *Qere;* see the detailed discussion in Delitzsch, *Biblical Commentary on the Psalms, I,* 411–12. The ms. of the Cairo Geniza and the majority of the versions support נפשו, which is translated above.
4.c. Or, "taken an oath."
4.d. *G* adds τῷ πλησίον αὐτοῦ ("to his neighbor": viz. לרעהו); the addition is possible, on the grounds of parallelism and meter, but uncertain.
6.a. The translation assumes a plural participle, plus plural suffix: so *Qere*, with the support of several Hebrew mss (cf. *G*).
6.b. MT reads "your face, O Jacob." The translation above assumes the addition of אלהי, "*God* of Jacob," to provide appropriate sense (with limited support from Heb mss, *G* and *S*); see further Ps 75:10 for the same phrase. An alternative, but more radical solution is that of T. H. Gaster ("Old Testament Notes," *VT* 4 [1954] 73–79), who reads ועקב (for יעקב) and moves it to the beginning of the line: "and the reward of those that seek him is his face."
7.a. *G* renders: "lift up your gates, you princes," which is grammatically possible, with respect to the Hebrew text, but stylistically it is improbable; the parallelism implies both "gates" and "doors" should be interpreted as vocatives.
9.a. Reading והנשאו (as in v 7): MT reads ושאו ("and lift up"). But the line is in other respects identical to v 7, and the duplicate form is more likely (cf. *G*).

Form/Structure/Setting

It is difficult to determine the form, and hence the setting, of the psalm as a whole, principally because the component parts of the psalm appear to be diverse in form and background. Thus, prior to appraising the problem of the whole psalm, it is wise to examine the constituent parts, of which there appear to be three.

The first part (vv 1–2) is hymnic in substance, praising the Lord for his establishment of the world and his dominion over it.

The second part (vv 3–6) appears to be liturgical in form and content; it may be compared with Ps 15 (on the similarities, see Ridderbos, *Die Psalmen,* 198–99) and Isa 33:14–16. In terms of type, it would belong to the category designated by Gunkel as an *Entrance Liturgy.* As such, it may be divided into three parts: (1) *Question:* "Who shall ascend . . . ?" (v 3); the question was perhaps asked by pilgrims, or their representative, at the foot of Mount Zion. (2) *Response:* "He who has innocent hands . . ." (vv 4–5); the words were probably declared by a priest. (3) *Affirmation:* "This is the generation . . ." (v 6: viz. these people are qualified to ascend); the affirmation was probably made by the representative of the pilgrims.

The third part of the psalm (vv 7–10) is of the kind associated with a procession of the Ark; again, it is liturgical in form, having a question-response format. (1) The Ark bearers' declaration (v 7). (2) The question posed by the gatekeepers of the temple (v 8a). (3) The response of the bearers of the Ark (vv 8b–9). (4) The further question of the gatekeepers (v 10 a-b). (5) The response of the arkbearers (v 10 c-d). The original kind of setting presupposed by such a procession is provided in 2 Sam 6:12–19, a passage describing the transportation of the Ark from the house of Obed-edom during King David's reign.

The problem of the psalm as a whole pertains to the nature of the interrelationship between the three parts. Is the whole psalm, in its present form, a liturgical piece? Or have the parts been joined together to form a *literary* whole, the end result being in effect a *hymn?* At a later date in its history, it is clear that the whole psalm was used as a unity within the regular worship of Judaism. The psalm's title, in *G,* designates it as a psalm for use on the day after the sabbath, and in the Talmud the reason for such association is related to the history of creation, implied in the first two verses (*Roš. Haš.* 31a; cf. *Tamid* vii. 4). But if one assumes that the psalm achieved its present unity prior to incorporation within the Psalter, the possibility remains that the entire psalm was a liturgical piece with a setting in some specific cultic activity. It is difficult to be more precise because of the difficulty in discerning a single theme unifying the three parts.

The most notable such theme is the worship of God as King. The opening verses (vv 1–2), referring to creation, establish the foundation of God's kingship in creation and the subjugation of the waters of chaos. The second part of the psalm specifies the conditions to be met by those who would worship the God of creation. The third part celebrates the kingship of God in military language, having associations with the Ark of the Covenant, which in turn symbolized God's victorious presence in battle in early Israel. Thus the setting of the psalm should be interpreted in a festival such as the autumnal festival, the celebration of the kingship of God and of the foundation of worship in the sanctuary in Jerusalem (see Cross, op. cit., 93). But a strictly liturgical interpretation has problems associated with it. It is not known with any certainty whether, in the history of Israel's worship during and after the reign of Solomon, the Ark was actually carried in liturgical processions, as is implied by the interpretation of vv 7–10 in their present context. Once the Ark was established in Jerusalem, it tended to lose its practical function; the development of the Ark traditions became more and more *literary* in character (cf. O. Eissfeldt, "Die Lade Jahwes in Geschichtserzählung, Sage und Lied," *Das Altertum* 14 [1968] 131–45). Thus it remains possible that Ps 24, in its present form, is essentially a *hymn*, for use in the celebration of the Lord's kingship, within which ancient liturgical materials have been utilized and united into a fine literary structure. The early use of the hymn in the annual celebration of the Lord's kingship was later transformed to weekly usage in the worship services of temple and synagogue.

Comment

The God of Creation (24:1–2). The hymn begins with an affirmation of the Lord's dominion over the created world and its inhabitants; that dominion is based upon the fact that God himself "fixed" and "established" the world. At first sight, it appears as if the language of v 2 reflects primitive cosmology: the world, like a floating saucer, is anchored "upon the seas." Yet the language is more profound and contains within it a transformation of Canaanite (Ugaritic) cosmogony. *Yam* (literally, "Sea"), who is also called *Nahar* (literally, "River"), represented a threat to order in Canaanite mythology; the conquest of Yam by Baal represented the subjugation of chaotic forces and the establishment of Baal's kingship. The Hebrew poet, using the terms *yam* and *nahar* in a demythologized and depersonified sense (נהרות, ימים, v 2), depicts forcefully the Lord's creation of an ordered world, "upon" seas and rivers, symbolizing the subdued forces of chaos. (On other passages employing similar transformation of Ugaritic-Canaanite mythological language, see Craigie, *Tynd B* 22 [1971] 3–31 and *Semitics* 4 [1974] 10–21.) The symbolism of the language is significant: just as in the underlying Ugaritic myth, the conquest of *Yam* culminated in kingship, so too the Lord's creative work, as described here, is linked with kingship in vv 7–10.

The Worship of the Lord (24:3–6). In the original liturgical significance of this passage, a ritual was enacted which was the necessary precursor to participation in worship. The worshipers, or pilgrims, were approaching "the mountain of the Lord"; that mountain, with its temple, was the earthly symbol of the kingship established by God in his creative acts. They ask a question, prior to climbing Mount Zion: "Who shall ascend . . . ?" The question is significant in terms of the creation theme of the opening verses. In those verses, the poetic motifs are those of *order* and *chaos;* the Lord established *order* (the created world) by virtue of the subjugation of *chaos* ("seas," "rivers"). But now, in the context of worship, the motifs of order and chaos are transformed into moral concepts, *good* and *evil*. The place symbolizing God's creation and order is a "holy place" (v 3b); order is good. Hence the question—who may ascend to such a place? The answer given to the pilgrims, pronounced by a priest, specified that only the *good* could ascend to the *holy place*. The qualifications for worship are elaborated in moral terms, rather than ritual terms. The worshiper must have "innocent hands and a pure heart"; that is, he must have maintained moral integrity with respect to both actions and thoughts. The idiom "raised the mind" (v 4b) implies an attitude of adoration and worship; the potential worshiper must not have been so bound to falsity, or vanity, as to have been a worshiper of such emptiness. And he must not have "sworn deceitfully"—viz. undertaken a solemn oath with no intention of fulfilling it. The qualifications given here are only a partial list; a much fuller list of moral prerequisites is provided in Ps 15. Persons of such moral integrity would receive "blessing" and "righteousness" from God (v 5); in context, the terms refer to both the practice and consequence of participating in the worship of God in his place.

After the priest had declared the qualification for ascending to the temple for worship, the pilgrims—or their representative—declare their worthiness so to worship (v 6). The declaration is not one of absolute moral integrity, for no person could make such a claim; it is a declaration rather that the potential worshipers are aware of the implications of their desire to worship—they must be innocent. They are described, in the declaration, as those that "consult" God and "seek" his "face"; they are prepared in the sense that the desire to worship God has become an integral part of their lives, providing direction and focus. Though they lacked absolute righteousness, they desired it; in part, they would receive it as a consequence of worship.

The King of Glory (24:7–10). The kingship of God is the central theme in the last section of the psalm. The basic concept involved was in no sense unique to Hebrew theology, for many ancient Near Eastern nations attributed the role of kingship to their deities. The kingship of Baal, following his conquest of Yam, was central to Ugaritic mythology (see the comment on vv 1–2 above). Other Ugaritic-Canaanite gods are also accorded the title and role of king. In a recently discovered text from Ras Ibn Hani, just south of Ras Shamra-Ugarit, Shapash is entitled "righteous king, king of kings" (*mlk.ṣdq.mlk.mlkm: RIH*, 1978, #3). The kingship of God in the psalm has analogies to such ancient Near Eastern concepts, but also differences. The Lord's kingship was rooted in the act of creation (vv 1–2), but it was also established in a historical sense. The Exodus from Egypt, which was viewed as a second act of divine creation (viz. the creation of Israel; see Deut 5:13–15 and Craigie, *The Book of Deuteronomy*, 157), resulted in the acclamation of the kingship of God (Exod 15:18). And the Lord's participation in Israel's wars symbolized the constant reaffirmation of the kingship of God. It is this latter aspect of kingship which dominates the concluding verses of the psalm.

The basic image underlying vv 7–10, and reflected in the original liturgical usage of the passage, is that of the return of the Ark from war. In battle, the Ark symbolized God's presence; in victory, the return of the Ark symbolized the victorious return of the warrior God to his people (Num 10:36).

More precisely, the original setting of the liturgical piece may have been the arrival of the Ark in Jerusalem in David's time (2 Sam 6:12–19), which marked on the one hand the establishment of the sanctuary in Jerusalem, and on the other hand the crowning achievement of Israel's wars. The transportation of the Ark into Jerusalem, whether on the original occasion or in annual reenactment, marked the arrival of the victorious warrior king in his holy place. Once again, though the language can be interpreted against an original liturgical background, it may also be read in terms of its transformed mythological undertones. Thus Baal, in words very similar to Ps 24:7 and 9, says to the gods who cower in fear at the threat of chaos: "Lift up your heads, O gods" (*š'u* [.] *'ilm . r'aštkm: CTA* 2.i.27; cf. Gibson, *CML²*, 41). But the mythology is transformed in the psalm; it is the *gates/doors* of the temple that are invited to lift up their heads in hope at the approach of the creating and conquering King. (The language is transformed further in liturgical usage, so that the "gates/doors" represent the gatekeepers of the temple; as the procession approaches them, twice they ask: "Who is the King of Glory?" [vv 8, 10], and twice they are answered by those in the Ark's procession.)

The language describing God in these verses is thoroughly military in tone; the Lord is "mighty in battle" (cf. Exod 15:3) and the "Lord of Hosts" (viz. armies). Although, to some extent, this language is rooted in Israel's experience of warfare interpreted religiously, in the context of the psalm it is cosmogonic language, as is indicated by vv 1–2. In the poetry of transformed mythology, the Lord is the warrior king who has defeated the forces of chaos and established the order of creation. The primeval victory had implications for Israel's understanding of warfare, but fundamentally it is creation—not military victory—which is here extolled in the affirmation of the Lord's kingship. On the theological difficulties pertaining to the concept of God as warrior, see Craigie, *The Problem of War in the Old Testament*, (Grand Rapids: Eerdmans, 1978) 33–43.

Explanation

There are few themes more central to the Old Testament literature than the kingship of God. It is a concept rooted in creation and elaborated in historical experience, and the presence of the theme in Israel's earliest poetry (Exod 15:18) is indicative of its centrality throughout the history of Israel's religion. Psalm 24 is one of the central texts for understanding the breadth and the significance of the concept; the kingship of the Lord is not merely a religious affirmation—it is a basis of worship and praise. Those who worship are those who recognize the kingship, who accept the rule of the sovereign God. But the genius of the psalm lies in the linking together of cosmological belief and historical experience; the link is achieved, from a literary perspective, by the composition of the psalm from fragments of hymn and liturgies. From the perspective of cosmology, the world is created and thus represents order (vv 1–2); that order was established by God the King. But historical experience, characterized as it is by war and conflict, suggests a different reality, namely that the world is marked in actuality by chaos. The psalm offers a resolution of the dilemma. It is God, the Creator of order, who is also the Warrior of Israel, subduing the military threats (the chaos) that undermine Israel's orderly existence. Order in creation, and victory and peace in historical existence, are part and parcel of the same concept: God is King. And both evoke from Israel the worship that belongs to God. But just as the order of creation is a moral order, symbolized by God's "holy place" (v 3), so too the peace and victory achieved by the Warrior King belonged to Israel only so long as they possessed "innocent hands and a pure heart" (v 4). The recognition of the kingship of God must result in the worship of God by those who recognize his royal authority; to worship presupposes moral integrity—and that, in a sense, is the central point in the psalm. There could be no separation between the Creation, deliverance in historical experience, and moral integrity; if there were, chaos would triumph again. Thus there is a certain logic attached to the traditional use of this psalm within Christianity on the celebration of Ascension Day. As the psalm affirms the origin of God's kingship in creation (vv 1–2) and the advent of the Warrior King in the worship of the temple (vv 7–10), so in its later usage it affirmed the victory achieved by Jesus Christ in death and resurrection and anticipated the ultimate and triumphant Advent of the King.

A Prayer of Trust (Ps 25:1–22)

Bibliography

Möller, H. "Strophenbau der Psalmen." *ZAW* 50 (1932) 240–56. **Ruppert, L.** "Psalm 25 und die Grenze Kultorientierter Psalmenexegese." *ZAW* 84 (1972) 576–82.

Translation

1-2   Of David. [a]
    (א) *For you I have waited,* [b] *O Lord.*   (3+3)
            I will lift up my soul to [c] *my God.*
    (ב) *In you I have trusted—let me not be put to shame;*   (3+3)
            Let not my enemies exult over me.
3   (ג) *Indeed, all who are waiting for you will not be put to shame:*   (3+3)
            the ones who act treacherously without reason will be
            put to shame. [a]
4   (ד) *Cause me to know your ways, O Lord;*   (3+2)
            teach me your paths.
5   (ה) *Make me walk in your truth and teach me,*   (3+3)
            for you are the God of my salvation.
    (ו) *And* [a] *I have waited for you all day long,*   (3+3)
            on account of your goodness, O Lord. [b]
6   (ז) *Remember your acts of mercy* [a] *and lovingkindness,*   (3+3)
            for they are from of old.

7 (ח) *Do not remember the sins of my youth or my transgressions;* [a]   (3+3)
     please [b] *remember me according to your lovingkindness.* [c]

8 (ט) *Good and upright is the Lord;*   (3+4/3)
     therefore, [a] *he is showing sinners the way.*

9 (י) *He will make the humble walk in judgment*   (3+3)
     and he will teach the humble his way.

10 (כ) *All the Lord's paths are lovingkindness and truth*   (4+3)
     for the ones who keep his covenant stipulations. [a]

11 (ל) *For your name's sake, O Lord,*   (3+4?)
     please forgive [a] *my iniquity, for it is great!*

12 (מ) *Who, then, is the one who fears the Lord?*   (4+3)
     He will show him the way that he shall choose.

13 (נ) *His soul shall dwell in prosperity,*   (3+3)
     and his seed shall inherit the earth.

14 (ס) *The friendship* [a] *of the Lord belongs to those who fear him,*   (3+2)
     and, indeed, he makes them to know his covenant.

15 (ע) *My eyes are constantly toward the Lord,*   (3+4)
     for he is the one who brought forth my feet from the net.

16 (פ) *Turn to me and be gracious to me,*   (2+3)
     for I am alone and afflicted.

17 (צ) *Troubles alarm* [a] *my heart—*   (3+2)
     bring me forth from my straits!

18(ק?) *Meet* [a] *my affliction and my trouble,*   (3+3/2)
     and take away [b] *all my sins.*

19 (ר) *See how numerous my enemies are!*   (3+3)
     And they have hated me with violent hatred!

20 (ש) *Guard my soul and rescue me;*   (3+3)
     don't let me be put to shame, [a] *for I have sought refuge in you.*

21 (ת) *May integrity and uprightness protect me,*   (2+2?)
     for I have waited for you, O Lord. [a]

22   *O God, ransom Israel from all its troubles.*

Notes

1–2.a. *G* adds ψαλμός: *"psalm* of David."

1–2.b. The translation assumes the conjectural reading of קִוִּתִי after אֵלֶיךָ, as suggested in *BHS*. The acrostic structure requires that אֱלֹהַי be taken with v 1, but without the addition of a word (as above), the syntax and meaning become uncertain. The addition of the verb קוה resolves the difficulty; the same verb is used in v 3 and its restitution here forms an inclusion with the use of the same verb in v 21. An alternative resolution of the problem would be to transpose יהוה, placing it before אֱלֹהַי, and translate "To you I have lifted up my soul, O Lord my God" (see *Textual Notes on the NAB*, 381). But such a solution does not provide the metrical and stichometric balance (as in the translation above); the structure of the psalm as a whole leads one to expect two lines in v 1.

1–2.c. Reading אֶל־אֱלֹהַי (cf. *BHS*), the אֶל having been omitted by haplography.

3.a. The second יבשׁ is not dittography (cf. *BHS*), but typical of the repetitive style of the psalm, forming an inner chiastic structure within the verse and contributing to the chiastic structure of the psalm as a whole; v 3 has both קוֹיך and יבשׁו, and the same verbs are used in reverse sequence in vv 20–21.

5.a. "And": reading וְאוֹתְךָ, after *G* and *S*, with some Hebrew mss., in order to maintain the chiastic structure. MT may reflect a later tradition in which *waw* was suppressed and replaced by final *pe*: see v 22 (which falls outside the basic alphabetic acrostic pattern) and compare Ps

34 in which the suppression of *waw* is more complete. See *Excursus III* (following Pss 9–10) and W. Johnstone, "The Punic Ship, Acrostic Psalms, and the Greek Alphabet" (paper read to the S.O.T.S., July, 1978).

5.b. The line is restored from v 7 (which is too long), thus restoring the balance in the *waw*-section: cf. *BHS*.

6.a. MT's יהוה is provisionally omitted, after *C, G* (Vaticanus) and *L* (Parisinus), to maintain the stichometry (cf. *BHS*).

7.a. ופשעי "or my transgressions" is omitted in *S,* and should perhaps be omitted from the Hebrew text on metrical grounds, though the evidence is not strong.

7.b. This translation is an attempt to represent the force of the emphatic אתה "you."

7.c. The last phrase in MT has been transposed to v 5 (see note 5.b.).

8.a. It is possible that על־כן should be deleted on metrical grounds (cf. *BHS*), though there is no strong support for such a deletion.

10.a. Literally, "his covenant and his testimonies," but the structure is best interpreted as hendiadys: cf. Dahood, *Psalms I,* 157.

11.a. וסלחת: the *waw* is interpreted as emphatic, represented in translation by "please"; the tense is precative perfect (cf. Dahood, *Psalms I,* 157).

14.a. On סוד ("friendship"), cf. RSV and Gunkel, *Die Psalmen,* 108; alternatively, the word could be translated "counsel."

17.a. Literally, "make large"; alternatively, the form could be read as an imperative (הַרְחִיב) and the final *waw* taken with the following clause: ". . . as for the troubles of my heart, make room, and bring. . . ."

18.a. MT reads ראה ("see"; cf. v 19), but a ק-verse is expected in the acrostic structure. The translation assumes an original text קראה ("meet"; cf. Briggs, *Psalms,* 229); the ק was probably omitted accidentally by virtue of the similarity with the following ראה.

18.b. נשא plus ל has the nuance "to take away"; BDB, 671.

20.a. The negative clause is omitted in *S,* but it is best retained, both for the metrical balance within the verse and because of the characteristic structure of the psalm as a whole: cf. אל־אבושה "let me not be put to shame." in v 2.

21.a. *G* adds κύριε: "O Lord," which may be original and provides a more balanced metrical structure. It also balances the chiastic-inclusion structure opened in vv 1–2; see note 1–2b.

Form/Structure/Setting

Ps 25 is commonly designated an *individual lament,* though the tone of the language suggests a more appropriate description as a *prayer of confidence.* But such a classification of the psalm need not have implications as to its setting; for a variety of reasons, it may be advisable to view the psalm primarily as a literary creation (see Ruppert, *ZAW* 84 [1972] 576–82). In the later history of the psalm, it was in all probability employed in communal worship, as is indicated both by the title (viz. it belonged to a Davidic collection) and by v 22, which appears to be a postscript to the psalm (see *Comment*).

The most dominant characteristic of the psalm is its alphabetic acrostic structure; see further *Excursus III* (following the commentary on Pss 9–10). The acrostic employs a bicolon for each letter of the alphabet. But inevitably the acrostic pattern imposes certain limitations on the poet, and as a consequence there is not a clearly developed internal sequence of thought within the psalm. The verses alternate between prayers or petitions and expressions of the psalmist's confidence in God.

Some scholars have sought to define an inner structure to the psalm within the overall confines of the acrostic structure. Thus Möller (*ZAW* 50 [1932] 240–56), followed by Ruppert, has sought to discern an overall chiastic structure in the psalm. The structure may be represented as follows:

A			vv	1–3
	B		vv	4–7
		C	vv	8–10
			D	v 11
		C′	vv	12–14
	B′		vv	15–18
A′			vv	19–21

The analysis is at first attractive and to some extent it accounts for the constant duplication of words and phrases which characterize the language of the psalm. Thus, the following duplications may be noted:

A/A′ אל־אבוש "not be put to shame" (v 2; cf. v 20); קוה (v 1?; v 3; v 21); איבי "my enemies" (v 2; v 19); נפשי "my soul" (v 1; v 20).
B/B′ חטאות "sins" (v 7; v 18); יהוה "LORD" (v 4; v 15)
C/C′ טוב "good, prosperity" (v 8; v 13); יורה "show" (v 8; v 12); בדרך "way" (v 8; v 12); בריתו "his covenant" (v 10; v 14).

But for all the appeal of the chiasmus-hypothesis, it is not entirely convincing with respect to the detailed substance of the respective sections and must remain in the realm of hypothesis (cf. Ridderbos, *Die Psalmen*, 206, n. 8).

The language of the psalm is ambivalent in another sense. Some of the terminology suggests a covenant background to the psalm (e.g., חסד "loving-kindness" in vv 6, 7, 10; ברית "covenant" in vv 10, 14). But a more dominant characteristic of the psalm is the preponderance of language typical of the Wisdom Literature (e.g. דרך "way" in vv 4, 5, 8, 9; ירא "fear" in vv 12, 14; טוב "good" in vv 8, 13); see further Ruppert, art. cit., 581. It is the acrostic structure of the psalm, together with the frequency of terminology associated with the wisdom tradition, which suggests that it should be interpreted primarily as a literary work, which was only employed within Israel's worship at a later date in its history.

For the purpose of commentary, the psalm is divided into three main sections, though the division does not necessarily reflect the internal structure of the psalm: (1) vv 1–7; (2) vv 8–14; (3) vv 15–21.

Comment

Opening prayer (25:1–7). The opening words of prayer are intermixed with statements of confidence upon which the prayer is based. The petitioner comes to God in an appropriate manner: (1) he has "waited" on the Lord, implying an attitude of both patience and hope, together with the recognition that the initiative of response lies with God; (2) he is preparing to worship ("lift up [the] soul") the God for whom he waits; and (3) he has "trusted." The attitude of trust is the key to the psalmist's preparation, for trust signifies dependence and hope based upon the *covenant* character of God. He *trusts* because God is faithful as the God of the covenant promises; he trusts because those who have trusted in the past have experienced the presence and help of God. Trust, then, is neither naive and misplaced confidence, nor is it self-confidence; it is a human response to God's self-revelation in covenant and in historical experience, both personal experience and that of the community. But inevitably the confident statement of trust (v 2a) is mixed with anxiety until such time as God actually responds, and so the words of trust pass into prayer—"let me not be put to shame" (v 2b). Immediately, the broader context of the worshiper becomes evident: the scene is not that of a lonely worshiper praying to God in solitude, for there is, as it were, an audience of enemies awaiting the outcome. The psalmist waits upon God, and the enemies wait upon the outcome; if God does not respond, the psalmist will be put to shame and the enemies will exult in his plight. But the anxiety of the psalmist is not merely over the possible reproach that might fall upon him, but it includes the implications for the attitude of enemies toward God; if God did not answer, the implication might be that God did not exist or that God did not matter in human life. And then, as confidence builds, the psalmist passes again from prayer (v 2) to confidence (v 3). Those who wait for God will not be put to shame—the enemies will! The enemies are defined as those who "act treacherously without reason," and it is reasonable to suppose that they are fellow Hebrews. The verbs ("wait"/"act treacherously") are in contrast, so that the treachery is not directed primarily toward the psalmist, but toward God. Such persons, who do not *wait* for God, hope that the righteous will receive no response, for divine silence would give support to their lives which were lived as if God did not matter. Thus the psalmist's confidence (v 3) expresses not only hope for himself, but also a kind of hope for his enemies. If they were put to shame, then they might come to the realization that the Lord was no otiose deity, but one with whom they must reckon in the treachery that was their life.

The psalmist prays next for guidance and instruction (vv 4–5). He needs to know not only the ways of God (v 4), but also to be made to walk in them (v 5); that is, he requires both enlightenment and strength. And this is the first part of the petition for which he is awaiting the Lord's response. He has walked in God's ways and desires to continue to walk in them; but such continuance depends upon the divine aid, specifically *deliverance* from a present crisis (hence, God is called "the God of my *salvation*" or *deliverance*, [v 5b], reflecting both past experience and present anticipation.) But the desire to be strengthened to walk in God's ways recalls in the mind of the psalmist his failure to walk consistently in those ways in the past; hence, the petition progresses to a prayer for forgiveness (vv 6–7). Three times he uses the word "remember"; first, in asking God to recall his past acts of mercy (v 6); second, in asking that his own past sins not be remembered (v 7a); and finally, he asks that he, as an individual, be remembered (v 7b). The sequence is significant; the psalmist first establishes God's own history of forgiveness and then seeks to participate in that history through the forgiveness of his own sins. While he prays for forgiveness from all sins ("transgressions" being a broad and general term in this context), he specifically refers to the sins of his youth—not those of childhood, but those of early adulthood which were rashly committed and live on to haunt him in the middle years of life. He cannot honestly pray to be directed on God's path (vv 4–5) without first dealing with his past wanderings away from that path. But he can confidently pray for forgiveness, for God is no distant judge, but a covenant God who acts in "mercy" (the word may imply the attitude of a mother toward her child) and in "lovingkindness" (חסד: the word designates the fundamental character of the covenant God). His prayer, in effect, separates sin from the sinner; he prays "do not remember the sins" (v 7a), but "please remember me" (the sinner).

Confidence in God's goodness (25:8–14). In the verses that follow the opening prayer, the psalmist now expresses more fully his confidence in God, in words which are occasionally hymnic in form and substance; his confidence is not just stated, but directed as praise to the God in whom he trusts. But right at the center of this section, indeed at the center of the whole psalm (v 11), there comes a further prayer for forgiveness; the focus of God's goodness reintroduces to the mind of the psalmist his own unworthiness and need of pardon.

The opening verses (8–10) continue the theme of the foregoing prayer. The Lord, by virtue of his goodness, is "showing sinners the way" (v 8b). It is not of the enemies that he speaks, but of himself, for he had prayed to be shown the way (vv 4–5) and he was a sinner needing forgiveness (v 7b). His confidence that both earlier petitions would be answered was rooted in his perception and confidence in the nature of God as "good and upright." At first impression, the terms seem mutually exclusive with respect to the psalmist's plight. If God was upright, he could hardly overlook the psalmist's transgressions or the sins of youth; if he was good, he would desire to overlook them as the psalmist bowed in repentance. But God was both good and upright; because he was upright, God could not ignore sin, but because he was good, he could forgive sin. And so the psalmist was confident that he would receive both the deliverance and the guidance that he sought (v 9). Again, it is the covenant character of God which dominates this expression of confidence; as is emphasized in the terminology of v 10; the confidence in God's "lovingkindness" is linked intimately to the prayer for "lovingkindness" in vv 6–7. But all covenants have two parties, and the lovingkindness of God, the senior partner in the covenant (v 10a), was related to the psalmist's obedience to the covenant stipulations (v 10b). It is this reminder that launches the prayer for forgiveness in v 11; if God's response depended upon *sinlessness* with regard to the covenant stipulations, then there could be no response. And so the psalmist prays again for forgiveness, aware that his "iniquity . . . is great." (Dahood has suggested that the "great sin" was that of idolatry: *Psalms I,* 157. In other contexts, the "great sin" is adultery; see Craigie, *The Book of Deuteronomy,* 305, note 3. In this context, the words should be interpreted generally, as referring to the psalmist's awareness of the magnitude of his sin in the past.)

The psalmist, pursuing his confident statement once again, now raises a rhetorical question: "Who, then, is the one who fears the Lord?" (v 12). The question is analogous to Ps 24:3, but whereas that question asks who may *worship* God, this one raises the fundamental point of the Israelite wisdom tradition. Who is the truly God-fearing person? (The term "fear" here implies not terror, anxiety, but an attitude of reverence and awe toward God, which is transformed into an appropriate manner of living.) The God-fearing person is directed by God to the way of life which he must consciously choose to live (v 12). Indeed, the way of wisdom, as it is expressed here, is the way of covenant, for there can be no division between the two traditions. The prosperity and inheritance of the God-fearing person (v 13) are the blessings of the covenant. The inheritance of his seed (or "posterity") would be the *earth* (or "land"); the implication is not that he and his descendants would become great landowners, but that they would continue to share in the possession of the land promised by God to the covenant people (Deut 4:1). But the more profound blessing was to be found in the "friendship" of God (v 14), for the covenant was not merely a conditional contract, offering rewards in return for obedience; more than that, it was a privileged and intimate relationship, offered by God to his covenant people. To those who feared, or revered, God, there was held out the promise of an intimate relationship of friendship. It is this bright prospect that prompts the psalmist to return to prayer for the concluding verses of the psalm.

Concluding prayer (25:15–21). The psalmist returns to his waiting for God (see vv 1–3), which is now described as a fixed gaze toward the Lord (v 15a). And again, the patient gaze is grounded in experience, for God had delivered the psalmist from trouble (the "net," v 15b) in the past. A sense of loneliness emerges clearly in these verses. He is still surrounded by troubles and enemies, nothing in his world offers either fellowship or consolation; he desires the friendship of God, of which he spoke so confidently (v 14), and so prays that the Lord will "turn" to him (v 16) and end his loneliness and affliction. The acuteness of the loneliness and the sense of distance from God are amplified by their dual source; they are partly a consequence of the psalmist being surrounded by enemies who create trouble and partly a consequence of the awareness of sin within (v 18b) which, if not removed, would bar him from the divine friendship.

Specifically, the psalmist prays for the protection of "integrity and uprightness" (v 21); the two terms are personified, as if guardian angels. But there is some doubt as to whether the terms reflect the divine characteristics, which may be a source of protection, or whether they are the characteristics of the psalmist, which form the basis of his prayer. Dahood (*Psalms I*, 159) and others argue that they cannot be the virtues of the psalmist, in view of his earlier confession of sin. But such a view is uncertain. The same words are used to describe David in God's address to Solomon (1 Kgs 9:4); it is clear that they do not imply that David was sinless, for the following words in that text amplify the expression, indicating that they refer to David's determination to act according to the divine law. (Job is also described in similar terms; cf. 1:1.) Thus it is probable that the words "integrity" and "uprightness" do refer to the psalmist, indicating not sinlessness, but his penitent state and determination to obey God (v 11). His prayer is not based on self-confidence with respect to his worthiness, but rather in the trust that his attitude toward God, of repentance and worship, is of such a kind that he may legitimately expect God's answer and protection. And so he continues to *wait for* God (v 21), as he had been doing when first he opened his mouth in prayer (v 1). Though there is no reference in the psalm to the divine response, the psalmist has moved closer, both by praying for forgiveness as he became more aware of his own unworthiness and by converting his confidence into praise (vv 8–14).

Postscript (25:22). The last verse is interpreted as a postscript principally because it falls outside the basic alphabetic acrostic pattern which ends in v 21. It is also different in tone, introducing "Israel" into the psalm for the

first time. The occasion for the addition may have been provided by a change
in the developing alphabetic system in postexilic times, when *waw* may have
been suppressed and an additional (compensatory) *pe* added at the end of
the alphabet; see note a on 25:5 (above). The effect of the postscript is to
transform the more individual prayer of the psalm into a prayer suitable
for Israel as a nation; the "troubles" (v 17) of the psalmist are analogous
to the *troubles* of Israel. As the whole community utilized this psalm in their
worship, they rose above their own troubles and prayed that God would
"ransom Israel" from those enemies who were the source of the entire nation's
troubles.

Explanation

The prayer of Ps 25 complements the wisdom of Ps 1. The latter, in the
more didactic tradition of wisdom, established the two ways, that of the righteous and that of the wicked. But taken alone, the dispassionate wisdom of
Ps 1 could be misleading; it might be taken to imply that the essence of
life was simply choosing the right road—once the choice had been made,
all would be well. But in Ps 25, the wisdom themes reappear, though now
in a context of prayer. The prayer is that of a person who has made the
choice and is walking the road of the righteous; but the dispassionate wisdom
has been transformed to passionate petition, for the right road is not an
easy one on which to walk. It is lined with enemies who would like nothing
better than to put the walker to shame; and the traveler on the road is also
plagued with internal doubts, as he recalls in his mind previous wanderings
from the path and former sins. The essence of the road of the righteous is
this: it is a road too difficult to walk without the companionship and friendship
of God. The psalmist, troubled from without and within, has stopped for a
moment in the way; he knows he cannot turn back, but scarcely knows how
to continue. And so he prays that God would show him the road and make
him walk in it (vv 4–5). He knows that he does not deserve such guidance
and strength, but as one forgiven of sin, he is confident that God will show
him the road again (v 2b). Ps 1 is a signpost which directs the wise to the
choice of the right road; Ps 25 is a companion for use along the way.

Preparation for Admission to the Temple (26:1–12)

Bibliography

Vogt, E. "Psalm 26, ein Pilgergebet." *Bib* 43 (1962) 328–37.

Translation

[1] For David.
   Judge me, O Lord, for I have walked in my integrity   (5+4)
   and have trusted in the Lord. I shall not slip. [a]

² *Examine me, O Lord, and try me;*   (3+3)
   test ᵃ *my kidneys* ᵇ *and my heart.*

³ *For your lovingkindness is before my eyes*   (3+2)
   and I have walked constantly in your faithfulness.

⁴ *I have not sat with men of falsehood,*   (3+3?)
   nor will I consort with dissemblers.

⁵ *I have hated the assembly of evildoers*   (3+3)
   and I will not sit with the wicked.

⁶ *I will wash my hands in innocence*   (3+3)
   and I will go around your altar, O Lord,

⁷ *to hear* ᵃ *the sound of praise*   (3+3)
   and to recount all your wondrous deeds.

⁸ *O Lord,*ᵃ *I have loved the habitation* ᵇ *of your house*   (4+3)
   and the place where your glory dwells.

⁹ *Do not gather up my soul with sinners*   (3+3)
   or my life with bloodthirsty men,

¹⁰ *in whose hands* ᵃ *is wickedness*   (3+3)
   and their right hand is full of bribes.

¹¹ *But I shall walk in my integrity—*   (3+2?)
   redeem me ᵃ *and be gracious to me.*

¹² *My foot has stood on level ground;*   (3+3)
   in the assemblies of worship, I will bless ᵃ *the Lord.*

Notes

1.a. The metrical structure is uncertain; it is possible that v 1 should be interpreted as four short lines rather than two long lines. But the parallelism links the two middle clauses, contributing to the uncertainty of the analysis.

2.a. The translation follows *Qere* (cf. *C*): צָרְפָה (Qal imv.).

2.b. The "kidneys" were considered to be the seat of the emotions, the "heart" the seat of the mind; hence, in the English sense, "test my heart and my mind" (RSV).

7.a. The vocalization in MT suggests a defectively written Hiph. form: לְהַשְׁמִיעַ. But the consonantal text, together with the use of בְ in the next word, imply Qal inf. constr. (לִשְׁמֹעַ), for which there is support in *G* and in two Heb. mss; the translation is based on reading a Qal inf. form.

8.a. *BHS* (n.) suggests the omission of יהוה on the basis of meter. While the omission would result in a balanced 3+3 line, there are such uncertainties pertaining to meter in Hebrew poetry that all deletions, *metri causa*, are uncertain.

8.b. *G* translates εὐπρέπιαν ("the *beauty* [of your house]" . . .), implying an original text with נעם ("delightfulness, pleasantness"); this is possible, on the supposition that the consonants of מעון ("habitation") have been accidentally transposed. But the parallelism of the verse supports MT against *G*.

10.a. Dahood translates "left hand," interpreting the form as singular; the meaning *"left hand"* emerges from the parallelism with ימין, "right hand." See *Psalms I*, 163 and *RSP I*, 195 (#218). But for a number of reasons, this interpretation is not convincing. (i) In MT's vocalization, the parallelism is "hands" (plur.)//"right hand" (sing.). *Wickedness* is a general term going with the plural *hands; bribe* is a specific term going with the singular *right hand.* (ii) The Ugaritic evidence adduced in support is equally uncertain; thus Dahood's claim that *yd//ymn*= "left hand"//"right hand" (*RSP I*, 195) is hardly strengthened by the other parallel terms in Ugaritic, specifically *ymn//šm'al* (cf. *RSP I*, 206, #240), where the *left* hand is clearly specified. Other Semitic languages employ the parallel word pair "right hand"//"left hand" and always specify the *left* hand: (a) in Akkadian, the parallelism is *imittu//šumelu* (cf. Craigie, *Semitics* 5 [1977] 51); in Arabic poetry, the same distinctive specification is maintained in *Qur'an* 90,17–19 (cf. Craigie, *JETS* 20 [1977] 21). It is certainly possible that in some contexts Hebrew יד may

have the nuance *"left* hand," but in general it means simply "hand"; the general sense is clearly
specified here by MT's use of the plural form (Dahood's analysis of the form as singular with
an archaic genitive ending, *yodh,* is not entirely convincing).

11.a. Possibly יהוה "LORD" should be added, following *G* (A and L), thus providing a metrical
balance, 3+3. But see note a on v 8.

12.a. *G* ("I will bless you, O Lord") implies אברכך, which is possible (MT representing
haplography); but equally, *G*'s text may have suffered through dittography in the original.

Form/Structure/Setting

Gunkel classified Ps 26 as an *individual lament,* placing it in the sub-category
psalms of innocence (The Psalms, 35–36), and supposed that it should be interpreted as the prayer of a sick man *(Die Psalmen,* 1926, 109). But neither the
form nor the substance provide strong support for such a classification; while
the element of innocence is clear throughout the psalm, there is no explicit
reference to sickness or any other situation of distress, nor are false accusers
or accusations against the psalmist specified. Hence Mowinckel's designation
of the psalm as a *protective psalm* is equally uncertain *(The Psalms in Israel's
Worship,* I, 220). The basic components of the psalm fall into three categories:
(1) prayer; (2) declarations of integrity and innocence; and (3) the certainty
of divine hearing (cf. Ridderbos, *Die Psalmen,* 206–07). The classification must
take into account these component parts and the particular substance of the
psalm's language.

The most appropriate interpretation of the psalm's form and setting is
that proposed by Vogt *(Bib* 43 [1962] 328–37), who identifies the psalm
with a ritual for pilgrims at the temple gates. Thus the psalm should be
viewed in its original form and setting as part of an *entrance liturgy* utilized
in a ritual at the temple prior to participation in worship. It is thus closely
associated with Pss 15 and 24, though more limited than they in its scope,
for it reflects only the worshiper's declaration and prayer during his participation in such a ritual. The psalmist prays for the divine judgment (v 1) and
testing (v 2) prior to admission to worship. He declares his innocence (in
the sense of integrity and preparation) as qualification for admission in language reminiscent of the admission requirements established in Ps 15 (on
the close parallels between the declarations of innocence in Ps 26 and the
qualifications for admission in Ps 15:2–5, see Hayes, *Understanding the Psalms,*
73). He further indicates his intention of undertaking ritual purification (v
6a), prior to entering the temple and participating in the worship of God.
Although the psalm could be associated with admission to worship in general,
it is more probably to be linked with admission to one of the great pilgrim
festivals; the expression "assemblies of worship" (מקהלים v 12) occurs elsewhere in the OT only in Ps 68:27 (in the fem. form), in a context implying
the great religious processions associated with particular festivals. Thus the
setting of the psalm, though no longer certain, is probably to be associated
with a ritual at the entrance to the temple, where the pilgrim worshipers
were met by priests. The words of the psalm would be spoken by each worshiper (presumably as a group) in response to an initial question or statement
from the priest. And the statements providing the assurance that God has
heard their prayer (vv 1b, 12) may have followed certain priestly declarations
not contained in the text of the psalm.

The substance of the psalm cannot easily be subdivided, for the three basic themes (prayer, affirmation and certainty) are intertwined throughout the psalm. Verse 1 and vv 11–12 contain all three themes and make use of the expression הלך בתם ("walk in integrity"), thus forming an inclusio for the psalm as a whole. The intervening verses contain a mixture of prayer and affirmation of innocence (vv 2–10). Within this general structure, a number of poetic techniques are used to good effect, such as chiastic parallelism (vv 4, 5) and contrast (e.g. between קהל "assembly" v 5 and מקהלים "assemblies of worship" v 12); see further Ridderbos, *Die Psalmen*, 208. For the purpose of commentary, the psalm is divided as follows: (1) opening statement (v 1); (2) prayer and affirmation (vv 2–5); (3) the intention of worship (vv 6–7); (4) affirmation and prayer (vv 8–10); and (5) concluding statement (vv 11–12).

Comment

Opening statement (26:1). The opening verse contains the three basic elements of the psalm and sets out, in summary form, the essence of the psalm as a whole: (1) *prayer:* "Judge me, O Lord"; (2) *affirmation:* "for I have walked . . ."; (3) *certainty:* "I shall not slip." These three themes are taken up and developed in the subsequent verses of the psalm; (1) *prayer:* vv 2, 9–10, 11b; (2) *affirmation:* vv 3–8, 11a; (3) *certainty:* v 12.

The prayer to be *judged* by God is a necessary prerequisite to entering the temple and participating in worship; it presupposes the (priestly) questions concerning admission to the temple: "who shall dwell . . .?" (15:1) and "who shall ascend . . .?" (24:3). To such questions, the psalmist responds: "Judge me," implying "see if I am worthy to enter your house." Having invited judgment, he then affirms his "integrity" and "trust," that is the moral nature of his living and the spiritual nature of his trust. His affirmation is not one of sinlessness, only of the integrity of his desire and trust as a qualification for participation in worship. And on the basis of his affirmation, and perhaps also on the basis of a statement from the priest and servants at the gate (implied, rather than stated), the worshiper expresses certainty that his prayer has been heard and that "he shall not slip," viz. he would stand in God's house among the worshipers (cf. v 12).

Prayer and affirmation (26:2–5). The prayer of v 2 elaborates upon the initial prayer of v 1 ("judge me"), making use of language associated primarily with the smelting and refining of metal (cf. Ps 11:4). God, who symbolically occupies the temple, is portrayed in the metaphor of a refiner of metal, who tests the 'metal' of those who would enter his house to worship. But the terminology is significant in another sense, for it implies not only testing, but also refining and purifying. In praying to be tested, the potential worshiper affirms integrity (v 1), but is also aware of the need for purification. (On the metaphor of testing and refining, see further Keel, *The Symbolism of the Biblical World*, 183–86.) The affirmation that follows the prayer is reminiscent both of the description of the righteous person at the beginning of the Psalter (Ps 1:1) and of the liturgical requirements for admission to worship (Ps 15:2–5). The integrity of the worshiper is affirmed in both positive and negative terms. In positive terms, it consists in a walk of life in which there was constant awareness of God's covenant characteristics, "lovingkindness" and "faithfulness" (v 3), which in turn had implications for the moral and spiritual life. Negatively, the psalmist's integrity had been maintained through the avoidance of evil persons (vv 4–5), whose influence could distract the righteous from the fundamental relationship with God. The negative assertion encompasses both past and future; the psalmist had avoided and hated evil company (vv 4a, 5a) and would continue to avoid such company in the future (vv 4b, 5b). The psalmist's affirmation, that he had hated the "assembly" (קהל) of evildoers, contrasts vividly with that which he desires and anticipates so avidly, the "assemblies of worship" (מקהלים, v 12).

The intent to worship (26:6–7). The pilgrim now declares his intention of washing his hands "in innocence"; indeed, the words may have been declared while the washing took place. The washing was symbolic, signifying both innocence and yet, at the same time, the need for purification; the act was a symbolic fulfilment of the prerequisite of "clean hands" for the would-be worshiper (see Ps 24:4) and was apparently a regular ritual at the entrance to the temple (cf. Ps 73:13). No doubt fonts of water were located at the temple's door, similar to those on a ceramic model of a shrine excavated at Gezer (cf. Keel, *The Symbolism of the Biblical World*, 123). Only when the hands were clean, which in turn symbolized the inner cleansing of heart and mind (cf. v 2b and Ps 24:4), was it possible for the pilgrim to pass beyond the gates into the temple, where he could walk around the altar, the symbol of God's presence and mercy. The altar was more than just the place of sacrifice; it symbolized God's table, where his fellowship and presence could be known. Verses 6b–7 are anticipatory; they express the basic desire of the psalmist toward which the entire entrance liturgy was directed, namely admission to God's house and the particular experience of his presence there, which in turn evoked from the worshiper both "praise" and a recounting of God's "wondrous deeds" (v 7). If, as has been suggested, the occasion for worship was one of Israel's great annual festivals, the "wondrous deeds" would include such divine acts as creation, exodus and covenant.

Affirmation and prayer (26:8–10). The opening affirmation (v 8) follows immediately from the preceding ritual (vv 6–7), with its anticipation of entrance into God's house or temple. As the psalmist anticipates entering again, he recalls past occasions when he had been in the temple; he "loved" that place, not for its architectural splendor, but because God's presence or "glory" (v 8b) was present there. But the affirmation turns quickly to prayer (vv 9–10). The prayer is partly in the form of a contrast; to be in the temple is vastly preferable to being in the presence of evil men and women. But more than that, the prayer returns again to the theme of the qualifications for admission to the temple. For "sinners" or "bloodthirsty men" to enter God's house would be a suicidal act, for God would destroy such evildoers (Ps 5:7). Thus the psalmist, in praying that he be delivered from *death* (which is the implication of the words "gather up my soul" in v 9), is again praying for purification, while at the same time affirming his integrity (cf. vv 4–5).

Concluding statement (26:11–12). The concluding statement takes up the three aspects of the opening statement (see the *Comment* on v 1) and thus brings the ritual to a close, after which the pilgrim worshiper would be admitted to the temple. The prayer (v 11b) reintroduces the worshiper's awareness of the need for redemption and grace, already implicit in the earlier verses of the psalm. The psalmist has declared his past integrity (v 1a) and his commitment to future integrity (v 11a) and has undergone ritual purification; nevertheless, even when all the qualifications for admission have been met, the worshiper can still proceed only tentatively into God's house, depending ultimately on redemption and grace. The prayer perfectly balances the approach to God, for the worshiper must qualify, but the fundamental and final qualification for admission is God's mercy. Access to God presupposes qualification, but it cannot be earned and maintained as a right.

"My foot has stood on level ground" (v 12a): these words may perhaps be interpreted as a further affirmation of integrity, as a consequence of which the psalmist would stand in the worshiping assembly. Alternatively, the perfect form of the verb may designate the certainty of future action, viz. "I will indeed stand. . . ." The line as a whole is the positive affirmation of the negative statement in v 1: "I shall not slip." The thought is expressed partly in conscious contrast to the plight of the wicked, who stood on very slippery ground indeed (cf. Ps 73:18–20). But more than that, it is an affirmation of the true solidarity of the worshiper. The "level ground" is on the one hand a metaphor for moral integrity and uprightness (the word may also be translated "uprightness"; cf. Ps 67:5), but on the other hand, it may refer to the floor of the temple on which the worshiper would stand. Standing there on solid ground, he would join with the other pilgrim worshipers in blessing the Lord. Again, it may be that this statement of certainty followed a declaration or oracle delivered by the guardians of the temple's door.

Explanation

Although the omnipresence of God was affirmed in Hebrew religion, the specific presence of God was associated from early times with the mobile sanctuary, and later with the permanently established temple in Jerusalem. The presence and glory of God could not be confined to the temple (1 Kgs 8:27), but it could be experienced there in a particular way. And the particular experience of God in the temple could be accentuated even more dramatically in the great festivals that punctuated Israel's religious calendar; in those festivals, in which the fundamentals of the faith were recalled and reaffirmed, the presence and the glory of God were perceived more intimately than on other occasions. But there was a certain danger associated with the localization of the divine presence in a particular place; the fundamental danger was that of familiarity, which in turn could lead to a casual approach to worship, from which hypocritical and superficial attitudes could easily emerge. Thus the presence of God in the temple differed radically from the experience of God's presence in theophany. In the latter case, the phenomena accompanying the theophany were so awe-inspiring that the worshiper was immediately aware of his unworthiness and insufficiency. Moses, Job, Isaiah and others, in their encounter with God in theophany, were struck by the awesome nature of the divine presence. But the divine presence in the temple, though no less real, was not accompanied by such awesome phenomena; hence, there arose the danger of familiarity.

The preparations for entering the temple, such as those reflected in Ps 26, are part of a conscious attempt in the Hebrew tradition to prepare the pilgrim for the presence of God. There must always be a double focus in such preparations—the glory of God and the basic unworthiness of the worshiper to enter the divine presence. The two themes inform each other. Reflecting on God's glory, the worshiper is made aware of unworthiness; but reflecting on that unworthiness, the worshiper becomes aware of the need for forgiveness and mercy, for moral integrity and spiritual faithfulness, which propel him toward the worship of God. And so the preparation to enter God's presence involves two dimensions. First, the integrity and lifestyle of the worshiper must be such that he can say to God, in honest humility, "judge me" (v 1). But it is in the very nature of such integrity and honest desire that there is evoked recognition of the fact that integrity alone is not enough, although it is essential. The worshiper must also pray, with the same humility and expectation, "redeem me and be gracious to me" (v 11); only then may he proceed into the divine presence and participate in worship.

A Royal Ritual   (27:1-14)

Bibliography

Birkeland, H. "Die Einheitlichkeit von Ps. 27." *ZAW* 51 (1933) 216-21. **Leveen, J.** "Textual Problems in the Psalms." *VT* 21 (1971) 48-58. **Niehaus, J.** "The Use of *LÛLĒ* in Psalm 27." *JBL* 98 (1979) 88-89. **Pardee, D.** *"YPH,* 'Witness' in Hebrew and Ugaritic." *VT* 28 (1978) 204-13.

Translation

[1] For David.
>   The Lord is my light and my salvation;   (3+2)
>   whom shall I fear?
>   The Lord is the refuge of my life;   (3+2)
>   of whom shall I be afraid?
> [2] When evildoers approached me   (3+2)
>   to devour my flesh,
>   they [a] were my opponents and my enemies;   (3+2)
>   they stumbled and fell.
> [3] Even though an army encamps against me,   (3+2)
>   my heart shall not fear.
>   Even though war rises up against me,   (3+2?)
>   in spite of this, I am confident.
> [4] One thing I have asked of the Lord—   (3+2?)
>   I will seek it!—
>   to dwell [a] in the house of the Lord   (3+2)
>   all the days of my life,[b]

to gaze upon the beauty of the Lord (3+2)
and to inquire [c] in his temple.
[5] For he will conceal me in a booth [a] (3+2)
on the evil day;

he will hide me in the hiding place of his tent; (3+2)
he will place me high on a rock. [b]
[6] And now my head will be raised [a] up (3+3)
above my enemies round about me. [b]

And I will sacrifice in his tent (2+2,3)
sacrifices of joy; [c]
I will sing and I will make music to the Lord.
[7] O Lord, hear my voice when I cry; (4/3+2)
be [a] gracious to me and answer me!
[8] My heart said to you: (3+2)
"I have sought your face." [a]

Your face, O Lord, I will seek; (3+3)
[9]   do not hide your face from me!
Do not turn away your servant in anger (2?+2)
you who have been my help!
Do not reject me and do not forsake me, (2?+2)
O God of my salvation!
[10] For my father and my mother have forsaken me, (3+2)
but the Lord will take care of me.
[11] Teach me your way, O Lord, (3+3+2)
and lead me on a level path,
because of my enemies.
[12] Do not deliver me to the greed of my opponents (3+3+2)
for false witnesses have arisen against me,
violent witnesses [a] too!
[13] I[a] believe [b] that I will see the goodness of the Lord (4/3+2)
in the land of the [c] living.
[14] Wait for the Lord! Be strong, (3+2+2)
and let your heart be bold.
Yes, wait for the Lord!

Notes

2.a. The *athnaḥ* in v 2b is placed after המה ("they"), and לי ("to me") is omitted, following
G and S, thus retaining the 3+2 metrical balance of the opening verses. It is unlikely that המה should be
translated as an interjection, "Lo," on the basis of Ugaritic *hm*, as suggested by
Dahood, *Psalms I*, 167. See note a on Ps 9:8.

4.a. שבתי: inf. constr. of ישב ("dwell"), without ל because it is in apposition to אחת ("one
[thing]"); the two following inf. constrs. in this verse have ל, introducing circumstantial clauses
(see Dahood, *Psalms I*, 167).

4.b. The second bicolon of v 4 is sometimes said to be a gloss from Ps 23:6 (cf. *BHS*),
and the absence of ל with שבתי is taken as evidence that the glossator did not assimilate the
line to its new context (Briggs, *Psalms*, 243). But this view is incorrect; (a) on the absence of
ל, see note a above; (b) the similarity with Ps 23:6 is probably to be accounted for by the high
percentage of formulaic language in the psalm as a whole (cf. Culley, *Oral Formulaic Language
in the Biblical Psalms*, 103).

4.c. לבקר ("to inquire"); the meaning of the term has caused considerable debate, conveniently summarized in Anderson, *Psalms I*, 222–23. Ugaritic *bqr* may have the sense "to divine," and the parallel Hebrew term used here probably implies "inquire (by seeking a divine oracle)"; cf. Gray, *The Legacy of Canaan*, 2, 194 (note).

5.a. *Kethib* סכה ("booth"); *Qere* סֻכּוֹ ("his lair"; cf. *Q*). *Kethib* is to be preferred, providing an appropriate parallel to the following אֹהֶל ("tent"; viz. the temple).

5.b. The transition from the imagery of *hiding* to that of exposure on a rock is abrupt; it may be that בְּצוּר ("on a rock") should be read בְּצַר ("in straits"), providing a parallel to the preceding "evil day" (Briggs, *Psalms*, 243).

6.a. Alternatively (after *G*), it is possible to read יָרִים ("he will raise," Hiph.), which might be implied by the subject of the verbs in v 6.

6.b. *G* indicates a break after "my enemies," followed by a verb (אסבבה ?) which goes with the next line ("I will go around and I will sacrifice . . ."). But MT probably has the better text, making good sense (and balance) as it stands.

6.c. Literally, "sacrifices of a *shout of joy*."

7.a. The conjunction is omitted, with the support of several Heb. mss, *G* and *S*.

8.a. The text of MT is difficult in the context: בַּקְּשׁוּ פָנָי, "seek (plural) my face." The second person plural form (בַּקְּשׁוּ) causes problems after the second person singular. Leveen solves the problem by radical means (*VT* 21 [1971] 54); the offending words are omitted as pleonastic, and the first three words of v 8 are emended to: כִּי מַר לִבִּי ("for my heart is bitter"). But the solution is too radical, and the versions, though apparently based on a text different from MT, offer no support for such major emendation. A possible solution is that of Dahood (*Psalms I*, 168), who translated: "Come, said my heart, seek his face." The translation involves the pointing לֵךְ (impv. of הָלַךְ) and transposing the *waw* to provide the text: בַּקֵּשׁ פָּנָיו ("seek his face"). But probably the best solution (that taken above) is to follow *G* (ἐξεζήτησα τὸ πρόσωπον σου) and emend the Hebrew text as follows: בִּקַּשְׁתִּי פָּנֶיךָ ("I have sought your face"). The variety of renditions in the versions indicates the possibility that the original text was corrupt at an early stage, probably as a result of confusion arising from the threefold use of פָנֶ״ךְ.

12.a. יָפֵחַ is traditionally translated "breathing, puffing" (BDB; cf. RSV, NIV). But Heb. יָפֵחַ is a verbal adjective, functioning as a noun, meaning "witness," cognate to Ugaritic *yph* and parallel to עֵדֵי in the preceding line. For the most comprehensive analysis of the meaning of the Hebrew and Ugaritic terms, see Pardee, *VT* 28 (1978) 204–13.

13.a. In MT, the line begins with לוּלֵא ("unless, if not"); but this term normally introduces a protasis clause, and in v 13 there is no apodosis (though it is possible that the apodosis clause could have been suppressed: GKC, § 159 dd). One solution is to provide the apodosis from v 12b (the clause introduced by כִּי "for"), as proposed by Niehaus (art. cit.). But the extraordinary pointing in MT (six points above and below the main consonants) indicates that the term was suspect to the Massoretes (cf. Briggs, *Psalms*, p. xxiv) and in five Heb. mss it is omitted, as in the translation above. (It is also omitted in *G*, though the equivalent of לֹ is added to the last clause of v 12.)

13.b. The perfect form of the verb is used.

13.c. The definite article is provided in several Heb mss, including *C*.

Form/Structure/Setting

From the time of Gunkel's pioneering work on the Psalms into recent times, Ps 27 has commonly been divided into two psalms, the first (vv 1–6) a *psalm of confidence* and the second (vv 7–14) an *individual lament* (e.g., Fohrer, *Introduction to the OT*, 287). But there are a number of arguments against the division of the psalm (the classic argument against Gunkel's division being that of Birkeland, *ZAW* 51 [1933] 216–21); although there are indeed two principal sections in the psalm, the whole should be perceived as a unity. The first part differs from the second in both form and substance; (a) in form, the Lord is referred to in the third person in vv 1–6, but addressed directly in vv 7–13; (b) in substance, the first section is characterized by confidence and trust, whereas the second contains the words of prayer. But the unity binding the two principle parts is to be perceived in the overall liturgical setting of the psalm (below) and in the use of key words common to both sections. The following terms are used in both sections of the psalms: (a) יֵשַׁע "salvation" (vv 1, 9); (b) צַר, "opponent" (vv 2, 12); (c) לֵב "heart" (vv 3, 8, 14); (d) קוּם "rise" (vv 3, 12); (e) בקש "seek" (vv 4, 8); (f) חיים "life" (vv 4, 13).

The liturgy, which provides the context within which the psalm must be interpreted, has three parts, interrupted perhaps by two ritual actions which are implied, rather than explicitly stated, in the text: (1) a statement of confidence, in which the worshiper (probably the king: see below) publicly declares his faith to the congregation and declares his intention of offering his sacrifices and praise (vv 1–6); (2) a prayer addressed directly to God (vv 7–13), and (3) an oracle, delivered by a priest or temple servant (v 14). It is likely that between stages (1) and (2), the spoken part of the liturgy ceased while sacrifices were being offered. Between stages (2) and (3), the priest or temple servant may have undertaken certain actions in order to determine or receive the divine oracle.

The evidence for the royal interpretation of the psalm is indirect, though a number of scholars support a royal interpretation: e.g., Mowinckel, *The Psalms in Israel's Worship*, I, 238; Eaton, *Kingship and the Psalms*, 39–40. The precise details giving rise to the royal interpretation are elaborated in the *Comment* (below); they include such matters as the military language (e.g. v 3) and the concept of sonship (v 10). But if the royal interpretation is correct, it is difficult to be precise in determining the setting for this liturgical psalm; it could be a ceremony undertaken prior to a king's departure for battle, but it is perhaps more probable that the setting is to be found in an annual event such as the anniversary of a coronation (cf. Ridderbos, *Die Psalmen*, 210).

In the later history of Judaism, and continuing into the present century, Ps 27 has played a central role in the "Days of Awe" (*Yamim Noraim*), being recited in the synagogue during each of the ten holy days. The psalm's substance, concerning God's compassion and love for his people, is most appropriate for the season in which judgment and deliverance are the central themes in the Jewish liturgy.

Comment

A statement of confidence (27:1–6). The first part of the statement of confidence (vv 1–3) expresses the absolute certainty that banishes fear, regardless of the dimensions of the threat. The confidence is based upon the Lord, who is described by three terms: *light, salvation* and *refuge.* (1) The first metaphor, *light,* implies a force that automatically dispels darkness (here representing the psalmist's enemies); the language is reminiscent of Ps 23:4, in which fearlessness is expressed despite death's dark shadow. But the metaphor may also be associated specifically with military dangers, as is implied by the same kind of language in Ps 18:29. Thus the psalmist is affirming that even in the darkness of the terrible threat of war, he has no fear, for God is the light that can dispel such darkness. (2) The Lord is also *salvation* (or "victory," or "deliverance"); again, the metaphorical language emphasizes God's ability to give victory, regardless of the military odds against success. (3) The third term is ambiguous. It may mean "refuge" (from the root עוז) or it may mean "stronghold" (from the root עוז). But, in either case, the term carries connotations of a place of safety in a military context. The military associations of all three terms, together with the substance of v 3, are part of the basis for associating this psalm with the king, who was commander-in-chief of Israel's armies.

Both v 2 and v 3 refer to enemies; if the tenses implied by the forms of the Hebrew verbs have been rendered correctly, v 2 refers to past victories (one of the sources of confidence) and v 3 expresses confidence in the future, regardless of the scale of the military crisis. The precise sense of the idiom "to devour the flesh" is uncertain; it might imply "speech" (viz. slanderous speech; cf. RSV and see v 12 below) or it might be a metaphorical description likening the enemies to wild beasts, who hope to devour the flesh of the fallen. But these enemies, as opponents of the king, were also opponents of God and hence *fell* (or were defeated) in battle. (N.B.: if the perfect tenses of v 2d were translated as implying the certainty of future action, then the whole verse could be taken with v 3 as expressing the psalmist's confidence in future victories.) The military language emerges most explicitly in the synonymous parallelism of v 3; no military threat can undermine the psalmist's confidence.

In the second part of the statement of confidence (vv 4–6), the focus changes, and the psalmist makes one of the most single-minded statements of purpose to be found anywhere in the OT. The expression "one thing I have asked" has no parallels among the biblical numerical sayings; see further W. M. W. Roth, "Numerical Sayings in the Old Testament. A Form-Critical Study," *VTS* 13 (1965) 70. The central point of this single request is stated in v 4c: "to dwell in the house of the Lord;" the statement should not be taken literally, as if referring to a temple servant who would actually live perpetually within the temple precincts. It refers rather to living permanently in God's presence; such a life was regularly punctuated by actual visits to the temple, such as that in which the psalmist was engaged. This central thrust in vv 4–6 is intimately related to the substance of vv 1–3. It was deliverance from military threats that would make possible the permanent dwelling in God's house; and it was faith in God, renewed in his house, that contributed to fearlessness in the face of military threats.

The psalmist specifies two consequences that would follow from his permanent residence in God's presence. (1) He would be able "to gaze upon the beauty of the Lord," not to be interpreted literally, but as implying the extraordinary experience of God's beauty and glory as symbolized in the temple, specifically in the Ark. (2) He would be able to "inquire in his temple" (see v 4, note c). The military context may provide the specific nuance of the expression; the king, prior to departing for war, would be able to enter the temple and to seek an oracle from God pertaining to his military plans. But the expression may have more precise implications with respect to the actual liturgy in which the king was participating; he was about to sacrifice (v 6) and sought guidance from God, and v 14 (see below) may contain the oracle for which he made inquiry.

The desire to dwell in the Lord's house is elaborated still further in v 5; the house *(booth // temple)* symbolized the divine protection which gave rise to the psalmist's great confidence. The temple was the king's asylum in time of trouble, not in a literal sense, but in the more figurative sense of the word "refuge" (v 1). It was both a refuge in which he could be protected "on the evil day" (presumably the day of danger, when enemies attacked) and a "rock," as stronghold, giving strength in the face of enemy attack.

Verse 6 must be interpreted with respect both to the liturgical proceedings and to the implications of those proceedings for the king's reign and military affairs; the word "now" may carry this double nuance. The immediate sense of "now" emerges in the liturgical context; the king was now about to offer sacrifices and praise to God as a part of the liturgical proceedings. But the sacrificial offerings were related to the divine activity; the king's "head will be raised up" (v 6a), referring to the anticipated divine protection and victory in battle (see Ps 3:4 and *Comment*, where the same kind of language is used). The sacrifices about to be offered "in his tent" (a poetic description of the temple, rather than an indication that the psalm was composed prior to the construction of the temple) are linked with "joy" (תְּרוּעָה), a word which may carry the nuance of "battle cry, victory cry." The sacrifices, in other words, appear to have been associated specifically with the king's role as warrior and they anticipate (with both prayer and joy) the coming victory shout that could only be a consequence of the divine aid.

A prayer for divine aid (27:7–13). The prayer is expressed in common language, reflecting no doubt the cultic background to the psalm's composition; but the formulaic language is of such a kind that there must inevitably be uncertainty as to the extent to which the psalm's language may be used for interpreting the specific background and setting of the prayer. The following formulaic expressions should be noted (based on Culley's tables in *Oral Formulaic Language in the Biblical Psalms*, 35–96): (1) v 7 (see 64:2 and 141:1); (2) v 9a (see 102:3 and 143:7); (3) v 9d–e (see 38:22); (4) v 11a (see 86:11 and 119:33); (5) v 11b–c (see 5:9); (6) v 12 (see 41:3); (7) v 14a, c (see 37:34) and (8) v 14b (see 31:25).

The movement of the prayer is from the general to the particular; the general opening petitions (vv 7–10) culminate in two particular requests in vv 11–12. The general petitions express the psalmist's determination to seek God's face, as he had done in the past (vv 8–9a); but the determination is modified by the recognition that a divine answer would be an act of graciousness (v 7b) and that the petitioner's qualifications (moral and otherwise) might result in God's turning from him in anger (v 9b–c). It is thus a prayer of determination, modified by humility and a sense of unworthiness. But the psalmist also conveys clearly that there is none other than God to whom he can turn. His parents have forsaken him (v 10a); the expression should not be interpreted literally, but should be understood in terms of the king's role as God's son (see Ps 2:7). Thus, the Lord functions as a parent to the king, and the petition is based in part on the intimacy of that relationship (v 10b).

The first of the two specific petitions (v 11) is to be instructed to walk in God's way. If, as has been suggested above, the specific setting of the liturgy was the celebration of an anniversary of the royal coronation, the words may contain the king's request to be kept firmly to his royal role and task (cf. Deut 17:14–20). To carry out his royal task, however, the king required freedom from the oppression of enemies, and so the second specific petition is closely related to the first; the king prays to be delivered from opponents. It is difficult to be certain whether precise significance should be given to the description of the opponents as "false and violent witnesses," or whether the language simply refers to the clamorous nature of the enemies (cf. Ps 2:1–3). If the language has precise significance, it may be that the background is to be found in a treaty or covenant. As a king in the context of international affairs, the king may have had imposed upon him treaties demanding his subservience to foreign powers; as a king in the covenant tradition of David, he could have allegiance only to God. The commitment to God in covenant could be perceived as a treacherous act by foreign nations, who sought to control the king as a vassal; thus, in poetic language, they are described as witnesses, giving evidence in court concerning the king's breach of treaty obligations. And their words of witness contain within them the threat of violence; from such violence, the king prayed for protection. On the treaty-covenant tension in the military setting of the Hebrew monarchy, see further Craigie, *The Problem of War in the Old Testament*, 69–70.

The prayer concludes (v 13) with a statement of confidence. Looking to the future, which held in store another year of battle and the problems of ruling a nation, the king is confident that he will survive and continue to see God's goodness. "The land of the living" means no more than the king would survive the attacks of his enemies and still be alive to see God's goodness in this life. It is going beyond the plain meaning of the text to perceive here (as does Dahood, *Psalms I*, 170) a reference to the afterlife; such a view would be anachronistic in the context of Hebrew theology during the monarchy.

A response (27:14). The last words were declared to the king by a priest or temple servant. The words are an answer to the prayer, not merely an injunction to wait for an answer. The answer, in other words, is to wait constantly for the Lord, because he would respond in the future as each crisis and need appeared. The intervening words ("be strong . . . be bold") are also a part of the answer and recall the words of Moses to Joshua at the time when the leadership in the covenant community was being transferred to Joshua (cf. Deut 31:7). Joshua was to be strong and bold because the Lord was definitely going to give him success in the conquest of the Promised Land. Likewise, the king was to be strong and bold, because he would receive the divine aid in ruling his country and conquering his enemies.

Explanation

If it is correct that background to this liturgical psalm is to be found in a royal event such as the anniversary of a coronation, then the psalm provides considerable insight into the continuity required throughout the reign of a monarch in the tradition of the Davidic Covenant. There was a sense in which that covenant was eternal (2 Sam 7:16), yet it was also renewed in the coronation of every new monarch. And within the reign of each king, the covenant tradition was susceptible to two dangers. From within, there was the danger that the king would forget his covenant obligations and wander from the divinely prescribed path. From without, there was the danger posed by foreign powers; their military threat hung not only over the life of a particular monarch, but also over the continuity of the royal covenant tradition.

Within the kingdom, there were certain structures established to preserve the self-conscious awareness, in the person of the king, of the nature of the covenant tradition. The king would not depart for war without first consulting God and offering sacrifice and prayer. And he would annually renew his coronation commitments, in which the role of his reign was clearly enunciated. It is on this context that the psalm sheds light. It begins with a declaration of confidence, entirely appropriate from the mouth of the king whose throne was established in perpetuity by divine fiat. The statement of confidence is by nature a statement of humility; the words of its proclamation undermined that most dangerous and subtle of attitudes in a person endowed with considerable influence and power, namely the arrogance of self-confidence. The single-minded request of the king, to dwell permanently in God's presence, ensured the proper exercise of his dominion, namely the awareness that he who reigned was also ruled.

But the strength and success of a good monarch in each year of his reign was not rooted only in a conviction about the permanent nature of his dynasty; it was also rooted in a living and constant relationship with the Lord of the royal covenant. Thus the declaration of the opening part of the liturgy moves to the prayer of the second part of the liturgy, and the fitting confidence is transformed into an urgent plea for divine aid in the immediate future. The prayer is answered, partly because it is legitimate within the framework of the covenant, and partly because it is offered humbly in a son's awareness of his need for his father's help.

A Liturgy of Supplication (28:1–9)

Bibliography

Dahood, M. "Ugaritic *mšr*, 'song', in Psalms 28:7 and 137:3." *Bib* 58 (1977) 216–17. Gelston, A. "A Note on the Text of Psalm XXVIII.7b." *VT* 25 (1975) 214–16.

Translation

[1] Of David.
   O Lord, I call out to you.   (3+3)
      O my Rock, do not turn a deaf ear to me,
   lest, if you are silent to me, [a]   (2+3)
      I should become like those who go down to the pit.
[2] Hear the voice of my supplications,   (3+2)
      when I cry to you for help,

when I lift up my hands   (2+2)
   toward your most holy place.
3 Do not drag me away with the wicked   (2+2)
   and with those who do wrong; [a]
those who speak peace with their neighbors,   (3+2)
   but evil in their heart.
4 Requite them according to their action   (2+2)
   and according to the evil of their practices.
Requite them for what their hands have done   (3+3)
   and render to them their recompense.
5 Because they do not understand [a] the works of the Lord   (4+2+2)
   and what his hands have done,
he will tear them down and not rebuild them.
6 Blessed be the Lord,   (2+3)
   for he has heard the voice of my supplications.
7 The Lord is my strength and my shield;   (3+3)
   my heart has trusted in him.
So I was rescued [a] and my heart exulted   (3+2)
   and I will praise him with my song. [b]
8 The Lord is strength for his people [a]   (3+4)
   and he is a refuge of deliverance for his anointed.
9 Deliver your people and bless your inheritance,   (4+3)
   and be their shepherd and lift them up for ever.

Notes

1.a. This line is omitted in a few Heb. mss (and *L*); the omission may have been made on the basis of irregular meter (2+3), but it is best to retain MT.

3.a. *G* apparently worked with a longer text for the first two lines of v 3: in the first line, a noun replaced the pronominal suffix (אל־תמשך נפשי "do not drag my soul away"), and a verb was added to the second line: אל־תאבדני ("do not kill me"). There is, however, little support for *G*'s longer text among the extant Heb. mss.

5.a. בין, plus אל, is the Hiph.: "to understand."

7.a. On the sense "rescue" for the verb עוז, see Ps 22:20 (note b).

7.b. וּמִשִּׁירִי is the source of long-standing difficulties; the pointing indicates prefixed מן־ ("from"), which would be peculiar in the context. Gelston has proposed emending to בישירי "with my song," which has support from Symmachus, Jerome, and *S*. But emendation may be unnecessary if it is supposed that Hebrew, like Ugaritic, has two nouns for *song*: שיר and משיר; see Dahood, *Bib* 58 (1977) 216–17. On the evidence for Ugaritic *mšr*, "song," see particularly Dietrich, Loretz and Sanmartín, "Lexikalische und literarische Probleme in RS.1.2 = *CTA*.32 und RS.17.100 = *CTA* Appendice I," *UF* 7 (1975) 150–51.

8.a. Reading לעמו ("for *his* people") with *G, S, Vg,* and some Heb. mss) for MT's למו; the reading is also supported by the parallelism with משיחו ("his anointed").

Form/Structure/Setting

Psalm 28 is commonly classified as an *individual lament*, in which the opening verses contain the lament as such (vv 1–5), followed by a hymnic expression of thanksgiving (vv 6–9). Viewed in this context, the psalm has close parallels to Ps 6, but though such a categorization is generally appropriate, it is not sufficiently specific to take note of the distinctive features of Ps 28. A fourfold division, reflecting a liturgical proceeding, conveys more accurately the structure, and hence the form, of the psalm (the analysis which follows is essentially that of Ridderbos, *Die Psalmen,* 214–17). (1) The suppliant offers prayer from the perspective of lament (vv 1–4); (2) a priest or temple servant declares divine judgment against the psalmist's enemies (v 5); (3) the psalmist, responding in faith to the declaration, offers thanksgiving and praise (vv 6–7); (4) the priest or temple servant concludes with a declaration and prayer on behalf of all the people (vv 8–9). If this analysis is correct, the psalm must be interpreted as a part of a *liturgy of supplication,* conducted in the temple (cf. v 2). It begins with the individual expressing his prayer and, after hearing the declaration, moving on to praise; it concludes with the emphasis shifting from the individual to the nation as a whole, thereby providing an appropriate communal context, which is the larger setting of every act of individual deliverance.

Whether such rituals could be conducted at any time of need, or whether the general setting is to be found in one or other of the great annual festivals, is not known. Nor is it known with certainty precisely what kind of trouble afflicted the psalmist or, more generally, qualified for the use of the liturgy in which the supplication was made. Though a number of scholars have identified the psalm with the affliction of sickness (e.g., Mowinckel, *The Psalms in Israel's Worship,* I, 74), such an interpretation is uncertain. The danger of death referred to in v 1 ("those who go down to the pit") is expressed in formulaic language (cf. Pss 30:4 and 143:7) and should be interpreted generally of the threat to the psalmist's life, without necessarily being identified with sickness. The declaration of v 5 indicates that enemies were the source of affliction and that the psalmist would be delivered when the enemies were judged. The nature of the enmity toward the psalmist, while uncertain, could have been in the form of unjust accusations or general deceitfulness (v 3 c–d). In the *Comment* that follows (see particularly vv 3–4), it is suggested that the psalmist's difficulty is to be interpreted in terms of a covenant with certain persons (here described as enemies) who accused him of breach of contract. It follows from the above analysis of the psalm that it need not be interpreted as a *royal psalm.* The reference to the "anointed" (or king, in v 8) is not a part of the psalmist's self-designation (as supposed by Eaton, *Kingship and the Psalms,* 40–41), but a part of the liturgical pronouncement addressed both to the psalmist and to others participating in the liturgy.

In terms of literary style, the poet has made effective use of repetition, both to link the parts of the liturgy together and to convey contrast. The words of prayer in v 2 ("Hear the voice of my supplications") reappear dramatically in the thanksgiving (v 6) to indicate answered prayer. Forms of the root פעל are employed effectively to contrast the deeds of evil persons (vv 3, 4) with divine deeds (v 5); likewise, "what their hands have done" (v 4) contrasts sharply with "what his (viz. God's) hands have done" (v 5). The psalmist *blesses* (ברוך) the Lord, while the priest or temple servant implores the Lord to *bless* (ברך) his inheritance. Thus the language of the different portions of the liturgy is closely interrelated, creating unity and continuity between the different sections.

Comment

The suppliant's prayer (28:1–4). The psalmist begins his prayer by asking God to hear him (vv 1–2); the words convey a sense of desperation, as though his situation had lasted for some time, but God had not answered. The Lord to whom he prays is addressed as "my Rock"; in general terms, the word "rock" designates permanence, strength and security. It is an old appellation for God in the Hebrew tradition, being used in the earliest poetry (cf. Gen 49:24, "stone"; Deut 32:4, "rock"); in early Israel, the rock symbol was probably linked to the rocky Mount Sinai, which symbolized the enduring and everlasting covenant (see J. G. Herder, *The Spirit of Hebrew Poetry*, I, 280). But in the context of Ps 28, the word "rock" may be linked with the "most holy place" (v 2), which in turn was built upon a rock foundation; the psalmist prayed to God, his rock, whose earthly presence was symbolized by the holy place (דביר) founded upon rock.

The psalmist's anxiety that he not become "like those who go down to the pit" (v 1d) is related to his prayer as such; the fear of death, implied by these words, is not the actual crisis which precipitated the supplication in the first place (contra Lamparter, *Das Buch der Psalmen*, I, 144). The psalmist's fear is this: if God were silent, then he would be one of the dead, for the realm of death was a realm of silence (Ps 94:17. cf. Keel, *The Symbolism of the Biblical World*, 67–68). The blessing of life was fellowship with the living God, but if in life's crises God were silent, then for practical purposes the psalmist became like the deceased, who lived in the silent darkness of the pit (namely, the underground tomb or burial chamber, which here symbolizes the realm of death as a whole).

The words of prayer were accompanied by actions, so that both mind and body were engaged in the ritual proceedings. The suppliant's hands were lifted and directed toward the holy place, in a gesture typical of supplication in the Near East in general (for an illustration of the practice in Egyptian religion, see *Biblisch-historisches Handwörterbuch*, I, 521, fig. 2). It may be that the hands were raised in a gesture symbolizing the anticipation of receiving something in the hands, namely the divine response to prayer. But the reference to the "pit" (v 1) suggests an alternate symbolism; the psalmist is like one standing on the edge of the pit of death in danger of falling in, and his hands are stretched out in desperation. If God would only answer his prayer, it would be as though he had taken his hands and rescued him from that threatening abyss. The reference to the most holy place (the Holy of Holies) is the principal basis for the assumption that the psalm is to be associated with a temple liturgy; the worshiper is in an outer court of the temple, directing himself toward the innermost sanctum, which symbolized God's earthly presence. (It must be conceded, however, that such an interpretation is not certain, for worshipers in the Diaspora directed themselves toward the temple in worship and prayer.)

The psalmist comes to the specific point of his prayer in v 3: it is that he not be consigned to judgment with the evildoers. While the general sense of the request is clear, the reasons giving rise to such a request are less clear. It appears as if the psalmist had some kind of association with wicked persons, but did not participate in their evil acts; nevertheless, the association in itself was worrying, for the evildoers were inevitably bound to be judged for their acts. It may be that the larger context in which the suppliant's anxiety is to be understood is that of a contract or covenant. A covenant context is implied both by the curse-like character of vv 3–4 and perhaps also by the use of the word "peace" (שׁלום). (a) The psalmist prays that he not be cursed with the fate of the wicked, but that the wicked themselves be cursed (v 4); (b) the evildoers are described as speaking "peace," but villainy was in their hearts. The covenant bond (viz. a covenant or contract between two parties) carried curses, penalties for breach of contract, and positively it was to be characterized by peace between the parties. (On the role of "peace," שׁלום and Akk. *salīmum*, in vassal treaties, see Craigie, *The Book of Deuteronomy*, 276.) If the psalmist were party to a covenant or contract, which was then broken, he would be in a dilemma; if the guilty party claimed he was the one responsible for breach of contract, then technically he was in danger of the covenant curses falling on him. But, as the innocent party, his innocence would not be known until the covenant curses were executed upon his enemies (those who had broken the covenant), as he prays in v 4. Interpreted in this manner, the specific prayer in vv 3–4 is a prayer for vindication in a covenant context and such a prayer must have two parts, corresponding to the two parties to the covenant: he prays for his own deliverance from the covenant curse (v 3) as vindication of his innocence, and for the evildoers to be "requited" (a legal term) as they deserved by virtue of their crime. The prayer for requital is not malicious; the evildoers, in their covenant commitment, had asked for such curses to fall upon them if they should be unfaithful to the covenant stipulations.

The pronouncement of judgment (28:5). These words are distinguished from the preceding part of the liturgy partly by their declarative substance and partly by the change in the form of address; whereas in the supplication, the psalmist addressed the Lord in the second person, now the speaker refers to the Lord in the third person. The words would presumably have been declared by a priest or temple servant. On the other hand, if the ritual were associated in some way with a legal case before the central tribunal in Israel (Deut 17:8–13), the declaration may have been made by a judge or officer of the law.

The judgment of the psalmist's enemies is based upon their actions, which spoke loudly as if in testimony; their actions and "what their hands have done" (v 4) testify clearly that they do not follow God's actions and what "his hands have done" (v 5). God, as a covenant God, was characterized by integrity; their lack of integrity, in a covenant relationship with the psalmist, indicated their fundamental lack of understanding of the nature of covenant. Hence, the precise judgment is declared: "he will tear down and not rebuild them" (employing a metaphor from construction/demolition). The language of the judgment is reminiscent of the prophetic judgments (Jer 45:4, cf. Jer 24:6 and 42:10). Though the date of the psalm cannot be determined precisely, it is probable that the psalm reflects the earlier usage of this type of language; employed first in the settlement of contract-covenant disputes, it was later adapted in prophetic usage to apply to the covenant between God and Israel.

The psalmist's response (28:6–7). Following the declaration of judgment, which is at the same time a declaration of the psalmist's integrity in his dealings, it is possible for him to proceed immediately to thanksgiving and praise. The thanksgiving (v 6) is linked directly to the earlier words of supplication (v 2a). Whereas frequently in the Psalms the transition from prayer to thanksgiving is marked by anticipatory faith, namely that the Lord had heard and would answer, in this context it is probable that the thanksgiving is based on an answer already given in the pronouncement of v 5. The pronouncement affirmed the psalmist's innocence of the false charges laid against him (and hence his deliverance from the curse which his enemies wished upon him). Hence, the psalmist can say: "I was rescued" (v 7); the deliverance had already been achieved and naturally flowed out in praise of God, who is described in military terminology as a source of strength and defense. The interrelationship between covenants emerges in the word "trust" (בטח) in v 7, for it describes the proper attitude of the covenant member toward the covenant God. Because the psalmist had trusted in the God of the covenant, that same God has delivered him from the crisis precipitated by a human covenant in which there was no trust.

The final declaration (28:8–9). The final declaration, which includes a prayer (v 9), relates the specific situation in the liturgy of supplication to the national situation of the king and the people as a whole. The covenant crisis in which the individual found himself was analogous to that in which the king and his people frequently found themselves; owing allegiance only to God, they were nevertheless threatened frequently by foreign powers that would make vassals of them. With respect to such external threats, the priest or temple servant first declares the Lord's strength and protective capacity (v 8, parallel to v 7 in the individual's praise) and then prays that in fact they might be delivered and perpetually cared for. The imagery of the prayer in v 9b is that of the caring shepherd, similar in tone to the language of Ps 23:1 and Isa 40:11.

Explanation

The life of the Hebrew was bound not only by the fundamental covenant with God, but also by particular covenants or contracts with fellow human beings. The word "covenant" (ברית), apart from its religious usage, may have a secular sense, referring to such things as alliances, treaties, agreements and contracts. The precise nature of individual contracts in ancient Israel is not known, though it may be assumed that they were generally similar to Near Eastern treaties: two persons or parties undertook certain obligations toward one another and sealed their intent both by solemn pledge and by the invocation of curses, to become effective if a partner to the covenant or contract was unfaithful to its stipulations. A similar situation may be seen with respect to the Mesopotamian *kudurru* ("boundary stone"), which functioned as an official deed pertaining to real estate holdings and called down divine curses upon those who sought to change its substance or contest its contents. Some such covenant situation is presupposed by the psalm. The psalmist had been bound to certain other persons in covenant or contract;

the relationship was sealed not only by law, but also by God who could execute the contractual curses explicit in the agreement. But, in a case of breach of covenant, the psalmist faced a dilemma if his innocence was not evident, or if the other party claimed he was guilty. Such a case could go to the courts, but the ultimate judge was God, who was witness to the covenant and executor of its curses. The starting point of the liturgy marks in a sense the psalmist's plea to the final court of appeal—the divine court. His request is simple: judge this case and carry out the curses of this covenant. In his innocence, he does not fear divine judgment, but in terms of the false accusations directed against him, he has every reason to fear human judgment, for human justice can be perverted.

If this interpretation of the psalm is correct, it provides insight into the theological dimensions of Israel's legal system. There were local courts and a central tribunal, local magistrates and itinerant judges, but the Chief Justice was God. But if appeal was to be made to God in a legal matter, the setting of that appeal was the liturgy of the temple, rather than a local court of law. And the pronouncement of the Chief Justice would be delivered through a servant (v 5) to whom the divine decision was revealed. Beyond this, the psalm provides little insight, though one must suppose the liturgy was conducted in conjunction with, or following, certain prescribed legal proceedings such as those set down in Deut 17:8–13.

The declaration of blame and innocence (v 5) gives rise to hope for the nation as a whole (vv 8–9), and this broadening of the psalm's implications for justice in its initial context provides the basis for its perpetual relevance. The plea of the innocent psalmist (v 2) may become the plea for every person falsely accused; the answer to that plea (v 6) in the receipt of justice may become the hope of all who seek deliverance and justice.

A Hymn to God's Glory   (29:1-11)

Bibliography*

(*Note: the literature on this psalm is so extensive that the list which follows is necessarily selective; the works of Cunchillos and Mittman, noted below, contain more extensive bibliographies.)

Cazelles, H. "Une relecture du Psaume XXIX?." *A la rencontre de Dieu: Mémorial Albert Gelin* (1961) 119–28. **Craigie, P.** "Psalm XXIX in the Hebrew Poetic Tradition." *VT* 22 (1972) 143–51. ———. "Parallel Word Pairs in Ugaritic Poetry: a Critical Evaluation of Their Relevance for Psalm 29." *UF* 11 (1979) 135–40. **Cross, F. M.** "Notes on a Canaanite Psalm in the Old Testament." *BASOR* 117 (1950) 19–21. **Cunchillos, J. L.** *Estudio del Salmo 29* (Valencia, 1976). **Fensham, F. C.** "Psalm 29 and Ugarit," in *Studies in the Psalms* (1963) 84–99. **Fitzgerald, A.** "A Note on Psalm 29." *BASOR* 215 (1974) 61–63. **Freedman, D. N.** and **Frank-Hyland, C.** "Psalm 29: A Structural Analysis." *HTR* 66 (1973) 237–56. **Gaster, T. H.** "Psalm 29." *JQR* 37 (1946–47) 55–65. **Ginsberg, H. L.,** "A Phoenician Hymn in the Psalter." *XIX Congresso Internazionale degli Orientalisti* (Rome, 1935) 472–76. **Loretz, O.** "Psalmenstudien III." *UF* 6

(1974) 185–86, 191–95. **Margulis, B.** "The Canaanite Origin of Psalm 29 Reconsidered." *Bib* 51 (1970) 332–48. **Mittmann, S.** "Komposition und Redaktion von Psalm XXIX." *VT* 28 (1978) 172–94. **Strauss, H.** "Zur Auslegung von Ps. 29 auf der Hintergrund seiner kanaanäischen Bezüge." *ZAW* 82 (1970) 91–102.

Translation

¹ A psalm of David.ᵃ
   Ascribe to the Lord, O sons of God,ᵇ   (4+4)
   ascribe to the Lord glory and strength.
² Ascribe to the Lord the glory of his name.   (4+4)
   Worship the Lord in holy attire.ᵃ
³ The voice of the Lord is upon the waters.   (3+2+3)
   The God of glory thunders.
   The Lord is upon the mighty waters.
⁴ The voice of the Lord is powerful;   (3+3)
   the voice of the Lord is majestic.
⁵ The voice of the Lord breaks the cedars,   (4+4)
   and the Lord breaks up the cedars of Lebanon.
⁶ He makes Lebanon skip ᵃ like a calf,   (3+3)
   and Sirion like a young wild ox.
⁷ The voice of the Lord strikes with flashes of lightning.ᵃ   (4) ᵇ
⁸ The voice of the Lord makes the desert writhe;   (4+4)
   The Lord makes the holy desert writhe.
⁹ The voice of the Lord makes hinds ᵃ writhe in travail,   (4+2)
   and he strips bare ᵇ the forests. ᶜ
   But in his temple, every one ᵈ is saying: "Glory!   (3?)
¹⁰ The Lord sat enthroned over ᵃ the flood,   (4+4)
   and the Lord will sit ᵇ enthroned as king for ever.
¹¹ The Lord will give protection ᵃ to his people;   (4+4)
   the Lord will bless his people with peace!"

Notes

1.a. *G* adds: ἐξοδίου σκηνῆς, associating the psalm with the end of the Feast of Tabernacles; but this addition to the title reflects later usage, rather than the psalm's initial setting. For a detailed discussion of later Jewish evidence associating the psalm with the Feast of Tabernacles, see Delitzsch, *Biblical Commentary on the Psalms*, I, 446.

1.b. Literally, "sons of gods" (בני אלים), but the expression may be interpreted simply as a plural form of בן אל ("son of God"; cf. GKC § 124 q), analogous to Ugaritic *bn 'ilm*, "sons of El" (cf. M. Pope, *El in the Ugaritic Texts* [VTS 2. Leiden: Brill, 1955] 9). Some Heb. mss read אילים ("rams"), and this was apparently the text presupposed by *G*, υἱοὺς κριῶν ("young rams"), but the context supports MT (see *Comment*).

2.a. הדרת ("attire, adornment") has been the source of numerous difficulties. *G* apparently read חצרת (αὐλῇ, "court"), but the Heb. mss provide little support for this reading, which also requires the addition of a suffix, *waw*, to the following קדש ("in *his* holy court"; cf. *G* and *S*). The Hebrew word has traditionally been translated "attire," but many scholars, in the light of Ugaritic *hdrt*, have translated the term "apparition, vision"; see e.g. Cross, *Canaanite Myth and Hebrew Epic*, 152–53 (n. 28) and Dahood, *Psalms I*, 176. But Ugaritic *hdrt* is a *hapax legomenon* in the Ugaritic texts (*CTA* 14.3.155) and offers only a slender basis for the interpretation of Heb הדרת. The Ugaritic interpretation is thus opposed by Caquot (*Syria* 33 [1956] 40) and by Donner (ZAW 79 [1967] 331–33). In addition, it is quite possible that Ugaritic hdrt is a scribal error for d(h)rt; see Loretz, UF 6 (1974) 185–86, and on the meaning and form of d(h)rt, see Gordon, UT, #735. This possibility makes even less secure the supposed Ugaritic etymology of Hebrew הדרת, which is therefore rejected.

6.a. The translation of the first line of v 6 involves reading the final mem of וירקדם, not as a suffix, but as enclitic mem, analogous to Ugaritic usage (cf. Gibson, CML² 150); the athnaḥ is placed under לבנון.

7.a. Literally, "flames of fire."

7.b. The verse appears to be short, lacking a second line. Various suggestions have been made with respect to filling the gap, either through transposing lines from other verses in the psalm (e.g., the middle line of v 3), or through conjecturing what has been omitted; for critical discussion, see Mittmann, VT 28 (1978) 179. Perhaps the best suggestion is that of Ginsberg (Orientalia 5 [1936] 180), who suggests the following: "The voice of Yahweh kindleth flames, (4+4) (קול יהוה חצב להבות), yea, Yahweh kindleth flames of fire" (ויחצב יהוה להבות אש). But any restoration must remain uncertain; hence only the text of MT has been provided in the translation.

9.a. Alternatively, it is possible to vocalize the consonantal text אֵילוֹת ("large trees, oaks"; cf. RSV, NIV); this translation would provide a parallel to "forests" (see note c) in the following line. But MT is to be preferred, being similar to Job 39:1; see Dahood, Psalms I, 179.

9.b. Alternatively, the verb could be read ויחסף, meaning (on the basis of Ugaritic ḥsp) "to drench, pour water," alluding thus to the rain accompanying the lightning and thunder; see Strauss, ZAW 82 (1970) 91–102; Cunchillos, 103–4; Cross, Canaanite Myth and Hebrew Epic, 154.

9.c. The translation "forests" is fairly certain, though the fem. plur. form (יערות) is unusual (a masc. plur. form being expected). The existence of the feminine form in an Ugaritic place name (yʿrt) may support the reading in MT; cf. Strauss, art. cit., 96.

9.d. The third line is difficult, with respect to both meaning and meter. כלו ("every one") could be deleted as dittography, though there is no evidence to support such deletion. On the possible meaning of the line, see the Comment.

10.a. The preposition ל has here the nuance of על ("over, upon"); see Cross, Canaanite Myth and Hebrew Epic, 155 (n. 43).

10.b. The verb is interpreted as imperf., plus simple waw. But the interpretation of tenses in this psalm as a whole is difficult, given its antiquity; see Excursus II, following Ps 8.

11.a. עז, in v 1, was translated "strength," but the parallelism here with שלום ("peace") suggests the nuance "protection." Hebrew עז is probably a homonyn, the sense "protection" deriving from the root עוז and the sense "strength" from the root עזז. On Ugaritic ʿz, "protection," see J. C. de Moor, "Studies in the New Alphabetic Texts from Ras Shamra, I," UF 1 (1969) 176. For fuller discussion, see Craigie, VT 22 (1972) 145–46.

Form/Structure/Setting

Psalm 29 is a *hymn;* it contains three basic parts. (1) The call to praise (vv 1–2), addressed to the "sons of God"; (2) the praise of the Lord's "voice" (vv 3–9); (3) a concluding section, describing the praise of the Lord in the temple (vv 10–11). Though the classification of the psalm as a hymn, for use in the worshiping community, is clear, the precise setting in Israel's life and worship is less clear. There are two principle problems to be solved in seeking to determine the setting: (a) the significance of the Canaanite aspects of the psalm; (b) the significance of the praise of God's "voice" (viz. thunder).

(a) The Canaanite/Ugaritic aspects of the psalm formed the basis of an hypothesis presented by Ginsberg in 1935 ("A Phoenician Hymn in the Psalter"; see also Orientalia 5 [1936] 108–9), in which he proposed that Ps 29 may originally have been a Phoenician hymn, which found its way into the Hebrew psalter after suitable modification. This basic hypothesis has been developed and modified by several scholars since 1935 (for a brief history of interpretation, see Craigie, *TyndB* 20 [1971] 15–17); many scholars now consider the evidence for the original Canaanite/Phoenician character of the psalm (it is proposed that it was originally a hymn to Baal) is "conclusive" (e.g. Cross, *Canaanite Myth and Hebrew Epic*, 151–52). Only a few scholars have maintained that, while there is clearly Canaanite influence, some other interpretation of the data may be appropriate (e.g. Margulis, *Bib* 51 [1970] 332–48; Craigie, *VT* 22 [1972] 143–51).

Ginsberg based his hypothesis on features such as the following: the "pagan notions" in the psalm (e.g., the emphasis on the glorification of the Lord's "voice"), the Phoenician nature of the topography and toponymy, Canaanite linguistic features, and the "formula of Baal's triumph" (v 10). Subsequent evidence in support of the hypothesis has developed the various aspects of the poetic language of the psalm in the context of current knowledge of Ugaritic poetry (below). The evidence is certainly sufficiently extensive to require some kind of interpretation of the psalm which takes into account the Canaanite/Ugaritic background; the more critical problem concerns whether the evidence requires that the psalm be treated, in its original form, as a Canaanite or Phoenician hymn.

In general terms, it must be noted that there are numerous difficulties in proposing an hypothesis such as that of Ginsberg. In summary form, the difficulties are as follows: (1) Though there is a limited knowledge of Phoenician poetry available to us from the ancient world, there are no unambiguous examples of Phoenician hymns. The principal evidence utilized in the formation of the hypothesis is (pre-Phoenician) Ugaritic poetry; though there is fairly extensive knowledge of Ugaritic poetry, again it must be emphasized that there are no extant "psalms" or "hymns" in the Ugaritic literature (though some of the literary texts have "hymnic" portions). (2) The evidence of content is piecemeal; there are no sustained and precise parallels in wording between the psalm and Phoenician or Ugaritic texts. In summary, there are chronological, geographical, and genre problems in this comparative literary hypothesis; for a more detailed critique of the hypothesis on these grounds, see Craigie, *TyndB* 20 (1971) 18–19.

More recent formulations of the hypothesis have drawn upon new types of evidence. Dahood has noted the high percentage of common Hebrew-Ugaritic parallel word pairs in Ps 29 which, he argues, support the hypothesis concerning the Canaanite antecedents of the psalm (*RSP II*, 4). But the common parallel word pairs are not distinctive, having further parallels in Akkadian, Arabic and Egyptian poetry, and they do not clearly support Dahood's formulation of the hypothesis (see further Craigie, *UF* 11 [1979] 135–40). From another perspective, Fitzgerald has argued that if the name *Baal* is "restored" in the psalm in place of *Yahweh*, then remarkable alliterative patterns (involving the consonants ל, ב, and ע) emerge, which may support the view that the psalm was originally a Baal-hymn (*BASOR* 215 [1974] 61–63). But this hypothesis, too, runs into difficulties; the consonants of the name *Baal* (בעל) are those of three common Hebrew prepositions which are used frequently in the psalm: ב five times, ל seven times, and על two times. It is not surprising, therefore, that alliterative patterns emerge (cf. *UF* 11 [1979] 139–40).

To summarize with respect to the Canaanite aspects of Ps 29: it is clear that there are sufficient parallels and similarities to require a Canaanite background to be taken into account in developing the interpretation of the psalm, but it is not clear that those parallels and similarities require one to posit a Canaanite/Phoenician original of Ps 29.

(b) The second point pertains to the significance of the central emphasis of the psalm, namely the focus on the "voice" of the Lord. The context makes it clear that vv 3–9 contain the description of a thunderstorm in which the divine voice is the dominant motif (on the Canaanite background to the voice, see the *Comment*). It must be asked: in what context would the praise of the divine voice (thunder) be appropriate? In general terms, it could be argued that since God was worshiped as the Lord of Nature, Ps 29 is a general hymn of praise addressed to the Lord of Nature, analogous in some ways to Pss 8 and 19. It might further be supposed that this hymn was associated with the Feast of Tabernacles (cf. the title in *G*), or with some other major festival such as a Covenant Festival (as proposed by Weiser), and that, either originally or in its later usage, the psalm was used in conjunction with the so-called enthronement psalms (on the continuity between Ps 29 and the enthronement psalms, see J. D. W. Watts, "Yahweh Malak Psalms," *TZ* 21 [1965] 341–48). While suggestions such as these have considerable merit with respect to the history of the psalm's use in Israel's worship, they are insufficiently precise to account for the central emphasis on the Lord's "voice" in the psalm.

There are two further key points to be taken into account in attempting to discern the original setting of the psalm: (1) the continuity between the Song of the Sea (Exod 15:1–18) and Ps 29, and (2) the role of the *storm* in old Hebrew war poetry (both these points are developed more fully in Craigie, *VT* 22 [1972] 143–51). The continuity with the Song of the Sea may be seen in the following points: the use of עז "strength" in both texts (Exod 15:2, 13 and Ps 29:1, 11); the conjunction of עז and שם "name" (Exod 15:2–3 and Ps 29:1–2; see further the *Comment*); the reference to the divine assembly (Exod 15:11 and Ps 29:1), and the stress on the kingship of God (Exod 15:18 and Ps 29:10). On the basis of these parallels it is suggested that Ps 29, like the Song of the Sea, must be interpreted initially as a *hymn of victory*. An understanding of the role of the storm in old Hebrew war poetry provides further strength to this preliminary identification of Ps 29 as a *hymn of victory*. In the Song of the Sea, the poet describes the Lord's victory by using the terminology of storm and wind (Exod 15:8, 10); likewise, in the Song of Deborah, the victory is associated with the phenomenon of storm (Judg 5:4–5 and 19–21). Storm imagery is also utilized in other Near Eastern war poetry, the Epic of Tukulti-Ninurta for example (see R. C. Thompson, "The Excavations on the Temple of Nabu at Nineveh," *Archaeologia* 29 [1926] 131–32 [lines 41–43]). The association of storm language with war poetry is not surprising, given that weather/storm gods were frequently also war gods (as was Baal, in the Canaanite pantheon).

The significance of the "voice" of the Lord may now be interpreted in the light of the above observations. In battle, the name of the war god was called out in battle cries; thus, a description of an Egyptian pharaoh in battle includes the following words: "his battle cry is like (that of) Baal in the heavens" (*ANET*, 249). The poet, in Ps 29, has developed the general storm imagery of war poetry and highlighted the "voice" of God as an echo of the battle cry; the details of this poetic imagery are developed more fully in the *Comment*.

Although the emphasis throughout vv 3–9 is on the thundering voice of the Lord, the allusion throughout is to the weaker thunder of Baal. That is to say, the general storm image of battle has been subtly transformed into a tauntlike psalm; the praise of the Lord, by virtue of being expressed in language and imagery associated with the Canaanite weather-god, Baal, taunts the weak deity of the defeated foes, namely the Canaanites. Thus, the poet has deliberately utilized Canaanite-type language and imagery in order to emphasize the Lord's strength and victory, in contrast to the weakness of the inimical Baal.

In summary, it is argued that Ps 29 reflects a particular stage in the development of the Hebrew tradition of *victory hymns*. In the earlier stage, the hymns that have survived (e.g. the Song of the Sea, the Song of Deborah) are associated with particular victories. Ps 29 reflects a slightly later period in development (though it is one of the earliest psalms in the Psalter, to be dated provisionally in the eleventh/tenth centuries B.C.); it is a *general* victory hymn, though it was probably devised for use in the specific celebration of victories over Canaanite enemies (as implied by the Canaanite allusions). The initial setting for its use would have been in a victory celebration undertaken on the return of the army from battle or military campaign. At a later stage in the history of the psalm's use, it came to be a more general part of the resources for Israel's worship, though it was probably associated primarily with the Feast of Tabernacles.

Comment

The call to praise (29:1–2). The psalm begins with a call to praise addressed to the divine council or assembly, who are here referred to as the "sons of God." The precise sense of this expression is difficult to determine; it is translated by G, in other contexts, as "angels" (cf. Deut 32:8 [G] and the comment in Craigie, *The Book of Deuteronomy*, 378, n. 18). But the same expression is used in the Ugaritic texts, *bn 'ilm* (*CTA* 4.iii.14), referring to the deities belonging to the divine council, and it is likely that this background forms part of the context of Ps 29:1. But further background is provided by Exod 15:11, where "gods" (אלם) provide the context for an expression of the incomparability of the Lord following his mighty victory. Thus, in Ps 29:1–2, the congregation who are singing the psalm call upon the members of the divine council, or heavenly court, to join with them in the praise of God.

The military connotations of this initial call to praise emerge primarily in the use of the word "strength" (v 1). The Lord's strength is to be praised in that it has been demonstrated in the victory following the battle. And the reference to "his name" (שְׁמוֹ) strengthens the military associations still further. In the Song of the Sea, the poetry begins with a reference to the Lord's prowess as a warrior: "the Lord is a man of battle—the Lord is *his name* (שְׁמוֹ)" (Exod 15:3). So too, in Ps 29:1–2, the praise is to be directed toward the Lord's name, which was a source of strength and victory to Israel. The divine assembly was to worship the Lord "in holy attire"; the reference is probably a poetic reflection of the holy (or purified) attire in which the human worshipers were dressed for their celebration of the Lord's victory.

The praise of the Lord's voice (29:3–9). Seven times, the Lord's voice is referred to explicitly in this section and it forms the central focus; again, the background is to be found in language associated with Baal and his "holy voice" (*qlh qdš;* see Caquot et al., *Textes ougaritiques I,* 216). Baal, the Canaanite weather-god, was associated with the storm, thunder and lightning. He is portrayed in Ugaritic iconography with lightning as a weapon in his hand (cf. C. F. A. Schaeffer, "Les fouilles de Minet el-Beida et de Ras Shamra," *Syria* 14 [1933] pl. 16); in the Ugaritic texts, his *voice* is explicitly identified with thunder (*CTA* 4.vii.29–31). But the psalmist, who rejects the possibility of any real power of Baal over weather or the outcome of battle, adapts the language of storm and integrates it with his description of God's glory.

The praise begins with an affirmation that the Lord's voice is "upon the waters." At a primary level of interpretation, the words might be taken to imply that the psalmist is describing a thunderstorm at sea, perhaps a storm approaching the land from the sea. But the undertones of the language go deeper and again reflect an adaptation of Canaanite/Ugaritic religious thought. In the Ugaritic texts, Yam ("sea") is the "god of the mighty waters" (*CTA* 3.D.36; cf. Gibson, *CML²,* 50); yet the chaotic god, Yam, was conquered by Baal. An allusion to this mythological incident is already contained in the Song of the Sea, where the Lord is described as using "sea" *(yam)* as a tool of conquest (Exod 15:8). In Ps 29:3, the Lord is described not merely as a deity whose thunderous voice is heard, but as one victorious over the chaotic forces symbolized by the "mighty waters." The poetry amplifies the theme of the Lord as "warrior" (Exod 15:3).

The northern topography of the psalm emerges most clearly in the references to Lebanon in vv 5–6; these references formed a part of the evidence in Ginsberg's original hypothesis concerning the Canaanite/Phoenician origin of the psalm. But it is important to note the particular fashion in which the poet has utilized these northern references to make his point. He has taken two symbols of power and strength—"cedars" (v 5) and the mountainous area of "Lebanon/Sirion"—and illustrated in his poetry the weakness of those great symbols of strength in relationship to the *Lord's* strength (cf. עֹז, "strength," v 1). The famous cedars of Lebanon are easily broken by the Lord's voice; the immobile mountains of Lebanon skip like calves frightened at the sound of a voice. The language here is not drawn from Canaanite (Phoenician or Ugaritic) texts, but takes Canaanite symbols of stability and mocks them through a demonstration of their instability in the context of the Lord's thundering voice. Dahood has suggested that the parallelism in these verses (cedars//Lebanon and Lebanon//Sirion) is similar to Ugaritic parallelism, but this is only partially correct, and the Hebrew parallelism also

occurs in Akkadian texts, thus undermining any distinctively Canaanite background with respect to toponymy (cf. Craigie, *UF* 11 [1979] 135–40). "Sirion,"
specifically Mount Hermon (see Deut 3:9), is here poetically synonymous
with "Lebanon"; Sirion may occur in the Ugaritic texts in parallelism to Lebanon, but the reading of the texts is uncertain (*CTA* 4.vi.18–19, 20–21; cf.
de Langhe, *Les Textes de Ras Shamra-Ugarit,* II [1945] 190).

The identification of the Lord's voice with lightning (v 7) not only develops
further the associations with Baal, who has associations with lightning (above),
but also highlights the warrior role of the Lord, for lightning was a traditional
weapon in the depiction of ancient Near Eastern warfare (see Keel, *The Symbolism of the Biblical World,* 216).

The last two verses of the central section of the psalm (vv 8–9) develop
still further the power of the divine voice in the context of various aspects
of the world of nature: the desert, wild animals and forests. The principal
difficulty here concerns the significance of the "desert" (מדבר); the Hebrew
word designates, strictly speaking, not the desert proper, but the semidesert
steppe country that was not permanently settled. But the Hebrew expression
translated "holy desert" (v 8b) could equally be rendered "Desert of Qadesh"
and the problem concerns whether the latter translation is appropriate and,
if so, which geographical area is intended (for a full discussion, see Cunchillos,
op. cit. 100–02). Some scholars argue that the expression should be interpreted as a place name and that the Qadesh referred to in the Sinai traditions
is intended. But others, noting the same expression in the Ugaritic texts
(*mdbr qdš; CTA* 26.65), prefer to identify the area with the Syrian desert,
perhaps the area near Qadesh on the Orontes (e.g. Dahood, *Psalms I,* 178;
Cross, *Canaanite Myth and Hebrew Epic,* 154). The reference to northern locales
in vv 5–6 may seem to support such an interpretation, but it must remain
uncertain. The context of the Ugaritic expression, *mdbr qdš,* is so difficult to
interpret that even the interpretation of that "desert" in strictly geographical
terms is open to doubt; see further H. Gese, *Die Religionen Altsyriens, Altarabiens
und der Mandäer* (Stuttgart: Kolhammer, 1970) 81–82; P. Xella, *Il Mito di
Šhr e Šlm* (Studi Semitici 44. Rome: University of Rome, 1973) 96–106. It
must be concluded that the reference to desert in Ps 29:8–9 should be interpreted generally, rather than specifically, along with the general reference
to "hinds" and "forests."

It is probable that v 9c should be taken in conjunction with the last section
of the psalm (vv 10–11 below). If the word "temple" (היכל) refers to God's
earthly house, then the line may be a liturgical rubric introducing the final
praise of vv 10–11 (cf. Cunchillos, op. cit. 109). On the other hand, if היכל
is to be linked with "divine house," namely the setting in which the "sons
of God" are worshiping in "holy attire" (vv 1–2), then v 9c may be interpreted
as the concluding line of the central section of praise (vv 3–9).

Concluding Praise (29:10–11). The poetic imagery of v 10 draws upon the
resources of both the Canaanite and the Hebrew traditions. The Canaanite
tradition may be seen in the depiction of the enthronement of Baal over
the conquered "flood" (Ugaritic *mdb;* see RS. 24.245.1–2), and there has
already been allusion to this incident in Ps 29:3 (above). It is the Lord, not
Baal, who is enthroned victoriously "over the flood," which symbolizes the

subjugation of chaotic forces. But the Hebrew background draws upon the flood traditions of the Genesis flood story, which is the only other context in the Hebrew Bible in which the word "flood" (מבול) is employed (cf. Gen 7:17, etc.). The allusion to the Genesis narrative is a part of the transformation of mythological language in Ps 29:10; the deified *flood* or *sea* of Canaanite tradition has become merely the inanimate tool of the Lord. Nevertheless, the enthronement of the Lord, expressed in the powerful imagery of v 10, conveys clearly the concept of the Lord as victorious, not only over chaotic forces in general, but over Baal, the conqueror of chaos, in particular; God's power is greater than the greatest power known to the Canaanite foes.

The implicit language of victory in v 10 becomes explicit in v 11: the Lord, as a consequence of his victory, gives *protection* (עז; see note a on v 11, above) and *peace* to his people. It is on this note of supreme confidence and praise that the psalm ends.

Explanation

In the history of Hebrew religion, it is clear that one of the hard lessons for the Hebrews to learn was that their God was not only Lord of History, but also Lord of Nature. The prophets constantly harangued their people for resorting to the religion of Baal (e.g. Hos 1–3), and such deviations from the path of religion reflected a deeper lack of faith concerning the Lord's real control of the world of nature, specifically of the forces of storm and rain which were so fundamental to harvest and survival.

Psalm 29 is one of the most distinctive affirmations in the Bible, not only that God was Lord of Nature, but also that all the forces of nature so commonly attributed to Baal by the persons living in and around the Promised Land were actually attributes of the Lord. The language and imagery of the psalm not only transfer all attributes of weather control from Baal to the Lord, but also by implication mock the supposed powers attributed to Baal. It was T. H. Gaster, some years ago, who drew the analogy between the composer of Ps 29 and General Booth, founder of the Salvation Army. Just as Booth had determined that the devil should not have all the best tunes and so adapted the popular music of his day for the expression of worship, so too the psalmist has adapted the popular conceptions of his world and utilized them to express the worship of his God.

But if the correct interpretation of Ps 29 has been presented above, namely that it is a *victory hymn*, then we perceive that the genius of the poet goes beyond his depiction of God as the Lord of Nature. The ultimate praise of God is praise for his gift of victory, a gift given by virtue of his strength as Lord of History. God was sovereign in the realms both of history and of nature, and the two realms could not be easily separated. To be sovereign in human affairs, God must also be sovereign over the human environment, the world of nature; conversely, God's sovereignty in nature, demonstrated in the fertility-giving rains and storm, was a part of his provision for the continuity of human history.

There are no explicit references to Ps 29 in the NT, though it has been suggested that the "seven thunders" of Rev 10:3 have Ps 29 as their background; such a view is far from certain.

Praise for Deliverance from the Danger of Death   (30:1-13)

Bibliography

Dahood, M. "Vocative *waw* in Psalm 30, 9." *Bib* 58 (1977) 218. **Ohler, A.** "Auferweckt zu einem Leben des Lobes. Eine meditation zu Ps 30." *BibLeb* 15 (1974) 71–73. **Schreiner, J.** "Aus schwerer Krankheit errettet. Auslegung von Psalm 30." *BibLeb* 10 (1969) 164–75.

Translation

1	A psalm.[a] Dedication song for the house.[b] Of David.	
2(1)	*I will extol you, O Lord, for you have drawn me out*	(4+3)
	and have not allowed my enemies to rejoice over me.	
3(2)	*O Lord my God, I called to you for help and you healed me;*	(5+4+3)
4(3)	*O Lord, you brought up my soul from Sheol;*	
	from those going down [a] *to the pit, you made me live.*	
5(4)	*Sing praise to the Lord, O you saints of his,*	(3+3)
	and praise his holy name. [a]	
6(5)	*For in his anger is death,* [a]	(3+2)
	but [b] *in his favor is life;*	
	Weeping may tarry in the evening	(3+2)
	but joy comes at dawn.	
7(6)	*But I!—I said in my security:*	(3+2)
	"I will never be moved!"	
8(7)	*O Lord, in your favor you made me stand more erect than* [a] *the*	
	mountains [b] *of strength.*	(5+4)
	You hid your face—I was dismayed!	
9(8)	*To you, O Lord, will I cry!*	(3+3)
	And to you, [a] *my Governor, will I plead for mercy.*	
10(9)	*What profit is there in my weeping,* [a]	(2+2)
	in my going down to the pit?	
	Will dust [b] *praise you?*	(2+2)
	Will it declare your faithfulness?	
11(10)	*Hear,* [a] *O Lord, and be merciful* [a] *to me!*	(3+3)
	O Lord, be [a] *my helper!*	
12(11)	*You have changed my wailing to dancing for me;*	(4+4)
	you have removed my sackcloth and girded me with rejoicing,	
13(12)	*so that my* [a] *soul* [b] *shall sing your praise and not weep;* [c]	(5+4)
	O Lord my God, I will praise you for ever.	

Notes

1.a. *G* adds Εἰς τὸ τέλος ("for the end"), implying למנצח ("for the musical director").
1.b. The word "house" may imply *temple,* though there can be no certainty. If the root

חֲנֻךְ does not mean "dedicate," but "initiate, begin to use," then an alternative possible translation would be: "song for use of the household (or temple)." Cf. S. C. Reif, "Dedicated to *ḥnk*," *VT* 22 (1972) 495–501; J. Parkhurst, *An Hebrew and English Lexicon* (1811), 225. On the use of the verb חֲנֻךְ with the sense "begin to use," see Deut 20:5.

4.a. *Kethib* יוֹרְדִי (Qal ptc; cf. *G, S*) is preferable to *Qere:* יָרְדִי (inf. constr. plus suffix; cf. *Tg*); the normal infinitive construct form occurs in v 10, רִדְתִּי, and an alternate form, as implied by *Qere*, is unlikely. Furthermore, the *Kethib* is more in line with the normal form of this formulaic expression, cf. Pss 28:1; 143:7.

5.a. Literally, "remembrance, memorial." But the term is used in synonymous parallelism with שֵׁם ("name") elsewhere, implying the appropriate nuance here; cf. Ps 135:13.

6.a. On the sense "death" for רֶגַע (usually "instant, moment"), see Dahood, *Psalms I*, 182 and note the (antithetical) parallelism with חַיִּים ("life").

6.b. The translation "but" involves reading a conjunction, *waw*, at the beginning of the clause (with *G* and *S*).

8.a. The *lamedh* (in לְהַרְרִי) is interpreted as comparative *lamedh;* see the discussion and literature cited in Dahood, *Psalms I*, 183.

8.b. הַרְרִי (in MT, "my mountain") is difficult; *G* presupposes הֲדָרִי ("my beauty"). The translation above assumes the pointing הֲדָרַי (plur. constr.; cf. *Tg*).

9.a. Reading וְאֵלֶיךָ (with the support of *S* and *Tg*) for MT's אֶל. Dahood (*Bib* 58 [1977] 218) proposes to translate the *waw* as vocative, and the consonantal text (אֵל־אֲדֹנָי) as "El my Lord." This is a possible rendering and avoids emendation; but the minor emendation above (with the support of *S* and *Tg*) provides better parallelism with the previous line.

10.a. MT's דָמִי ("my blood, death") is pointed as דֹּמִי (inf. constr. plus suffix from דמם, II, "weep, wail"). Cf. Gunkel, *Die Psalmen*, 129. Note also the references to weeping in vv 6, 12.

10.b. Dahood (*Psalms I*, 184) translated Hebrew עָפָר as "slime," arguing that such a translation is more appropriate to the North Semitic motifs employed in the description of the Netherworld as a place of mud and filth. But Heb. עָפָר clearly means "dust" (cf. A. F. Rainey, "Dust and Ashes," *Tel Aviv* 1 [1974] 77–83), and such a translation fits well enough in the Near Eastern context. When Ishtar descended to the Netherworld, she found it covered in *dust* and its citizens consuming mud (*ANET*, 107).

11.a. The three verbs in this verse are pointed in MT as imperatives; *G* interprets all forms as indicative. But MT is to be preferred, the imperative form being expected after the note of supplication in v 9.

13.a. Reading כָּבוֹד, but adding the pronominal suffix ("my") with the support of *G*.

13.b. On כָּבוֹד, "soul," see Ps 7:6 and the parallelism with נֶפֶשׁ.

13.c. The translation assumes that יִדֹּם is from דמם (II), "weep"; see v 10 (note a, above).

Form/Structure/Setting

Psalm 30 may be classified either as an *individual psalm of thanksgiving* (Fohrer, *Introduction*, 287; Schreiner, art. cit.), or as an *individual declarative psalm of praise* (Westermann, *Der Psalter*, 65); on the difference in nuance between these two approaches to describing the form, see Becker, *Wege der Psalmenexegese*, 52–57. It is a song of praise in that the substance of the psalm throughout is the praise of God (see vv 2, 5, 13). It is a song of thanksgiving in that it was a divine act of *healing* (v 3) which prompted the praise in the first place. As a psalm offering praise, by way of thanks for deliverance from sickness and near death, the psalm has parallels with Hezekiah's psalm (Isa 38:10–28), both in general terms and in specific types of language (with Isa 38:18–19, compare Ps 30:5–6, 10).

As an individual psalm of thanksgiving/praise, the passage contains a number of key features common to most such psalms: an introductory declaration (v 2) and introductory summary (vv 3–4); a reference to the earlier crisis (vv 7–8); a recollection of the former lament (vv 9–11) and deliverance (v 12); and a final declaration of praise (v 13). For a tabular presentation of these elements in Ps 30 and similar psalms, see Westermann, *Lob und Klage in den Psalmen* (1977) 77. But while these elements are common to individual psalms of thanksgiving/praise, the structure and the sequence in which they appear vary considerably from psalm to psalm. Thus, with respect to Ps 30, the structure in the formal elements is not in itself distinctive, and attempts to analyze the structure of the psalm in terms of its formal elements vary considerably in their overall conclusions; compare, e.g., the different analyses of Ridderbos, *Die Psalmen*, 222–23; Westermann, *Der Psalter*, 65–69; Schreiner, art. cit., 164–75. The overall structure must be determined on literary, not strictly form-critical, grounds.

The basic literary structure may be expressed as follows: (1) introductory declaration of praise (vv 2–4); (2) the detailed declaration of praise (vv 5–13). Both sections open with a statement of praise (vv 2, 5) and the psalm concludes with a further statement of praise (v 13). The key to the division of the psalm into these two major sections is to be found in vv 5 and 13; in both these verses, the verbs ידה ("praise") and זמר ("sing praises") are employed and form an *inclusio* for the second section as a whole. The summary statement of the opening section is elaborated in retrospective detail in the second section.

The key theme of the psalm is *praise,* and the key word is the verb ידה (vv 5, 10, 13). As Ridderbos puts it: *Das Schlüsselwort dieses Psalms,* ידה, *ist auch das Schlusswort* "the key word of the psalm is also the closing word" (see v 13; *Die Psalmen,* 224). But the significance of the key theme is brought out more significantly by two sub-themes: (a) the nearness of death (*Sheol* and the *pit,* v 4; *death,* v 6; the *pit* and *dust,* v 10); (b) the psalmist's *weeping* in the face of death (vv 6, 10, 12, 13). At each point in the psalm, the expression of praise is rooted in the memory of recent deliverance from death and of the removal of tears of grief.

A cultic setting of the psalm may be supposed, namely a ceremony of thanksgiving, presumably held in the temple. But the contents of the psalm provide little clue as to the nature of the setting. Thus, there is no reference to the offering of sacrifices or payment of vows (cf. Ps 66:13–14), and no indication that the ceremony included participation in a meal or banquet (cf. Ps 22:27). Nevertheless, the reference to "saints" (v 5) probably indicates the presence of fellow-worshipers in the thanksgiving ceremony. And the recollection of the former lament in the crisis of sickness (vv 9–11) may recall a former occasion in the temple, perhaps participation in a liturgy such as that contained in Ps 22. The transition from "sackcloth" to "rejoicing" (v 12) may further reflect the transition from a liturgy in time of crisis (Ps 22) to the present occasion of thanksgiving and praise.

The title of the psalm indicates that the initial function and setting of the psalm changed radically at a later period in the history of the psalm's use in the cult. It was used, according to the Talmud, in the celebration of *Hanukkah* (*b. Sop* 18b), established in the cleansing and dedication of the temple under Judas Maccabaeus after the desecration at the hands of Antiochus Epiphanes (ca. 164 B.C.): but whether the title reflects this usage, or whether it was interpreted to mean that this was how the psalm was used, remains uncertain. The use of the psalm was not restricted to *Hanukkah*, for according to the Mishnah the same psalm was also to be used at the presentation of the first fruits (*Bikkurim* 3.4; cf. Deut 26:1–11). But none of the later uses of this psalm reflect clearly its original usage, namely that of thanksgiving and praise consequent to healing and deliverance from death, and how such changes in usage occurred cannot be determined with certainty.

Comment

The introductory declaration of praise (30:2–4). Verse 2 presents in summary form the entire substance of the psalm: the psalmist will extol the Lord as a consequence of deliverance from death and enemies. "You have drawn me out": the Hebrew verb (דלה) may be used of drawing from a well, and its use here is entirely appropriate to the description of the psalmist's crisis as portrayed in the psalm. The psalmist, critically ill, had been in danger of going down to the "pit" (v 4, בור), a word which may also mean "well." As water is drawn from a well in a bucket, so too the psalmist had been drawn from the pit of death by the divine hand.

The reference to "enemies" (v 2b) could be interpreted in different ways. Dahood (*Psalms I*, 182) takes the term to be a "plural of excellence," denoting *death*; such a translation is appropriate to the context. But it may be preferable to retain the simple sense, as above, and interpret the term with reference to the "enemies" that the sick frequently encountered; see further the *Comment* on Ps 6. In other words, the psalmist's basic problem had been a sickness which took him to death's door; in that crisis, even friends became enemies, for they assumed that the sickness was a divine judgment on the sick person.

In v 3, the psalmist recalls that in his time of medical crisis he had prayed for help, and as a consequence had been delivered. It is possible to interpret the words generally, namely that the psalmist had prayed and had been answered. But probably the words should be taken to refer to an earlier occasion in the temple (perhaps a liturgy such as that reflected in Ps 22); the psalmist had prayed at that time and received assurance (from priest or temple servant) that God would answer. The occasion for the present act of worship and praise is not merely the assurance that God would answer, but the experience of actual healing because God had answered.

On the meaning of *Sheol*, see Ps 6:6 (*Comment*). The meaning of v 4a is not that the psalmist had died and been restored to life; rather, he had been so close to death that it was as if he were already dead, and from that grave situation he had been rescued by God's act of healing.

The detailed declaration of praise (30:5–13). The psalmist, who has already declared his own praise (v 2), now invites his fellow worshipers to join him in singing praise to the Lord. The fellow worshipers, perhaps friends and relatives, are described as *his* (God's) *saints* (חסידיו), that is, fellow members of the covenant community who, having experienced God's lovingkindness (חסד), have sought to incorporate that divine characteristic into their own lives. For the fellow worshipers to participate meaningfully in the act of praise, they must know more about the psalmist's deliverance; it is this which forms the main substance of the section.

The psalmist begins his descriptive statement, which is the basis of praise, with words describing the basic character of the relationship between God and mankind. *Anger* is the divine response to human sin; *favor* is the divine response to goodness, but also to repentance and contrition. The consequence of divine anger is death, for the sinner cannot live in God's presence; the consequence of favor is life. But the stark contrast is mellowed in the psalmist's words. Anger, as experienced by humans, may prompt confession and repentance; as such, it may lead into a return to the divine favor. Hence weeping, the human reaction to the experience of God's anger, need not be a permanent estate; if it contributes to repentance, joy is experienced again. The reference to *evening* and *dawn* (or "morning") in this context should be interpreted poetically, not literally. Evening and the coming of night symbolize the experience of anger; the breaking of dawn symbolizes deliverance or salvation (cf. N. Airoldi, *Augustinianum* 13 [1973] 345–50).

With this statement of principle established, the psalmist continues to a description of his own downfall (vv 7–8). In his health and prosperity, he had come to a position of self-confidence, thinking that what he had was a consequence of his own achievement. In the context of the Hebrew covenant, self-confidence could be one of the most fundamental sins, for it assumed that health and prosperity were a consequence of human achievement, rather than the gift of the God of the covenant (Deut 8:17–18). In v 8, the poet presents starkly the real state of affairs, which penetrates the folly of his former superficial self-confidence (v 7). The contrast is made all the more vivid by the antithetical parallelism and asyndeton which characterize the structure of the verse. He had indeed been prosperous and upright, like the mighty mountains, not for anything he had done, but simply because of divine favor. The moment God turned his face away, disaster struck. Thus it is clear from vv 7–8 that the psalmist's thanksgiving had a double thrust. First, he is thankful for healing from sickness, and second, he is thankful for the forgiveness which made that healing possible; he had not been a righteous sufferer, but suffered as a consequence of his sinful self-confidence. From the perspective of his new health, the judgment could be seen to fit the sin. His self-confidence had suddenly been shattered by the awareness of mortality. In self-confident health, he had said: "I will never be moved" (v 7), but with the advent of disease, he had begun to slide toward the "pit" that was death (v 4). He perceived, in other words, that sickness was not merely judgment in the sense of retribution, but a correctional judgment that restored him to his senses and gave him back a knowledge of the necessity of God-confidence, not arrogant self-confidence.

In vv 9–11, the psalmist recalls his prayer of lament in the time of his crisis. The future tenses in v 9 reflect the time perspective of the crisis; when he was in danger of death, he spoke these words. The language of the prayer has a formulaic character, and in both words and substance it is reminiscent of other similar prayers; with v 9, compare Pss 28:1, 142:1, and Joel 1:19, and with v 10, compare Isa 38:18–19, Pss 6:5, 88:10–12 and 115:17. It may be presumed that this was the prayer, or at least a portion of it, that the psalmist used in a temple ritual at the time of his crisis. Verse 10 provides the groundwork for the actual request which is stated in v 11, and it makes use of argumentative logic; the psalmist urges that his death can serve no good purpose, for he cannot worship god from the dust (viz. the grave). But the essence of the argument is implied, not stated: the argument implies that there has been repentance on the part of the psalmist, as is made clear in the contrast with v 7. His self-confidence, as expressed in that verse, was such that in his former state of health, he was praising himself, not God. To return to his former position of health, without repentance, would not achieve the goal stated in the argumentative prayer. Only after repentance would a return to health enable the psalmist to praise God and to declare his faithfulness. On these grounds, he makes the formal request of v 11. And in v 12, the answer to prayer is recalled, in terms which are similar to the contrast already noted in v 6. As evening weeping could be transformed to morning joy, so had the psalmist seen his wailing changed to dancing and his mournful sackcloth to a garment of praise. And so the psalmist concludes as he began, in the singing of praise to God in conjunction with his fellow worshipers (v 13).

Explanation

The significance of Ps 30 emerges clearly in the context of the Hebrew covenant. Central to the covenant promise of God was life; death was the antithesis of that promise (Deut 30:15–20). But the continuity of life depended upon faithfulness to God, in a life characterized by both love and obedience to the covenant stipulations. The focus of the covenant, in its ancient form, was upon *this life* as the arena in which the blessing and prosperity of God could be experienced; death, before the fulfilment of years, was not merely the demise of the body, but also the disruption of the covenant relationship with God.

The psalmist fell prey to that false sense of confidence which so easily besets those whose lives have been attended by health and prosperity. He thought he was secure, standing firmly in a changing world. But sickness shattered the illusion and brought him to the edge of his mortality. Facing death, it was not empty fear that confronted the psalmist; there came also the realization of sin and the awareness that his living relationship with God could not continue if Sheol became his home. And so he started on the road back to health, first to spiritual health and then to physical health. This psalm of thanksgiving reflects the last stage in the path back to physical health. He did not just get better and continue living as before; he recovered as a consequence of God's merciful intervention so that his first formal act (reflected in this psalm) was to return to God's house with his fellow human beings, there to thank God for intervening in his crisis. But although the psalm reflects the last stage on the journey back to physical health, it reflects only the first stage in the renewal of spiritual health. His new awareness of the source of health and of the meaning of existence would accompany him for the remainder of his life, and so he determines that his praise of God should be not a single event, but should continue *forever* (v 13b).

Prayer and Thanksgiving (31:1–25)

Bibliography

Airoldi, N. "Note ai Salmi." *Augustinianum* 13 (1973) 345–50. **Auffret, P.** " 'Pivot Pattern': Nouveaux examples." *VT* 28 (1978) 103–08. **Roberts, J. J. M.** "*Niškaḥti . . . millēb*, Ps. xxxi.13." *VT* 25 (1975) 797–801. **Winckler, C.** " 'In deiner Hand ist meine Zeit.' Besinnung zu Ps 31, 16." *BibLeb* 10 (1969) 134–37.

Translation

1   For the musical director. A psalm of David.[a]

2(1) *In you, O Lord, have I sought refuge;*   (3+2+2)
   let me never be ashamed,
   deliver me [a] *in your righteousness.*

3(2) *Incline your ear toward me,*   (3+3)
   rescue me quickly, O Lord. [a]
   Be a rock of refuge for me,   (3+3)
   a fortified place to deliver me.

4(3) *For you are my rock and my fortification;*   (3+2+2)
   so for your name's sake, [a]
   lead me and guide me.

5(4) *Deliver* [a] *me from the net*   (2+2+2)
   which they hid for me,
   for you are my refuge. [b]

6(5) *Into your hand I commit my spirit.*   (3+4?)
   Redeem me, O Lord, God of truth.

7(6) *I have hated* [a] *those who keep vain idols,*   (3+3)
   but I have trusted in the Lord.

8(7) *I will exult and I will rejoice in your lovingkindness,*   (3+3+3)
   you who have seen my affliction;
   you knew about the distress of my soul. [a]

9(8) *And you have not delivered me into the hand of an enemy;*   (3+3)
   you have set my feet in a broad place.

10(9) *Be gracious to me, O Lord,*   (2+2)
   for I have distress;
   my eye was wasted with grief,   (3+2)
   my soul and my belly, too.

11(10) *For my life was consumed with grief,*   (3+2)
   and my years with groaning;
   my strength staggered in my distress, [a]   (3+2)
   and my bones were wasted.

12(11) *Because of all my adversaries*   (2+2+2)
   I have become a reproach,
   and to my neighbors, a calamity, [a]
   a fearful thing to my acquaintances—   (2+2+2)
   those who see me in the street
   and retreated from me!

13(12) *I have passed* [a] *from memory* [b] *like one who is dead;* (3+3)
I have become like a broken vessel. [c]

14(13) *For I have heard the whispering of the multitude—* (3+2)
terror all around!—
in their scheming together against me, (3+3)
they have determined to take my life.

15(14) *But I—I have trusted in you, O Lord;* (4+3)
I have said: "You are my God."

16(15) *In your hands is my future* [a]*—deliver me* (3+3)
from the hand of my enemies and from my pursuers.

17(16) *Let your face shine upon your servant;* (3+2)
deliver me in your lovingkindness.

18(17) *O Lord, let me not be put to shame,* (2+2)
for I have called upon you.
Let the wicked be put to shame; (2+2)
let them be silent in Sheol.

19(18) *Let lying lips be sealed,* (3+3+2)
that speak arrogantly against the righteous,
in pride and contempt.

20(19) *How abundant is your goodness,* (2+2)
that you have set aside for those that fear you,
that you have done [a] *for those who seek refuge in you* (3+3)
in the sight of the sons of man.

21(20) *You will hide them in the hiding place of your face,* (3+2)
from the conspiracies of man;
you will set them aside in a shelter (2+2)
from strife of tongues.

22(21) *Blessed be the Lord,* (2+3?+2)
who [a] *has revealed his lovingkindness to me,*
in a time [b] *of distress.*

23(22) *But I said in my alarm:* (3+3)
"I have been cut off [a] *from the sight of your eyes."*
But you heard (2+2+2)
the sound of my supplication,
when I cried to you for help.

24(23) *Love the Lord, all you his saints—* (3+3)
the Lord preserves the faithful!
But he requites the other, (2+2)
the one acting arrogantly.

25(24) *Be strong and take heart,* (3+3)
all you who are waiting on the Lord.

Notes

1.a. G adds: ἐκστάσεως ("ecstasy"); the addition may have come from v 23, בחפזי ("in my trepidation"), rendered in G by: ἐν τῇ ἐκστασει μου.

2.a. G adds: ἐξελοῦ με ("and rescue me"); cf. Ps 71:2. But the addition is unnecessary (on metrical grounds); Ps 31 has a high percentage of formulaic language (see *Form/Structure/Setting*) and the addition in G represents the accidental addition of (familiar) formulaic language, or presupposes a text with הצילני, a dittography based on v 3b.

3.a. יהוה ("O Lord") is restored tentatively, with the support of two Heb. mss, in one of which it occurs as translated here, and in the other as a variant of the following היה (De-Rossi, IV, 23); the omission in MT was probably a result of partial haplography (note the preceding *yodh* and following היה).

4.a. One Heb. ms (and *S*) adds יהוה ("O Lord"); but the addition is uncertain, *S* conflating the two following verbs into a single verb (probably Hebrew נחמני) and apparently being based on a different Hebrew text.

5.a. The Hiph. of יצא has the sense "deliver," analogous to the Shaph. form of Ugaritic *yṣ'a;* cf. Caquot et al., *Textes ougaritiques I*, 422.

5.b. The meter of the verse is difficult; the analysis here (2+2+2) follows Kraus, *Psalmen 1–59*, 394. Airoldi, (*Augustinianum* 13 [1973] 345–50) takes the last line of v 5 (in this analysis) in conjunction with the opening words of v 6, translating: "For in you, my protector—in your hand. . . ." The rendering is plausible, though it lacks the support of the versions, and MT (despite metrical ambiguities) makes good sense as rendered above.

7.a. The principal versions (*G, S,* and *Vg*) and one Heb. ms (De-Rossi, IV, 23) indicate that the verb should be read as 2nd pers. sing. masc. ("you have hated . . ."; cf. RSV), which is possible; but MT gives good sense.

8.a. *G* renders the third line: "you have delivered my soul from distresses," which is either a paraphrase of MT, or presupposes a different text: הושעת מצרות, "you have delivered me from distresses."

11.a. Reading בעניי ("distress"), with Symmachus, rather than MT's "in my iniquity."

12.a. MT's מאד ("exceedingly") makes little sense; the translation assumes אד (or איד), the *mem* being attached as enclitic to the preceding word, after Dahood, *Psalms I*, 189; for alternative emendations, see Kraus, *Psalmen 1–59*, 393.

13.a. נשכחתי: literally, "I have been forgotten." Dahood translates: "I have shriveled up" (*Psalms I*, 190), proposing a cognate Ugaritic term *ṯkḥ*, "to wither." But this proposal is almost certainly wrong. For a detailed argument against the (supposed) problems in the Hebrew text giving rise to Dahood's interpretation, see Roberts, *VT* 25 (1975) 797–801. Furthermore, Ugaritic *ṯkḥ* does not clearly carry the sense "to wither." In *CTA* 11.1 and 24.4, it means "to be hot, inflamed," and in *CTA* 5.i.4, it may carry the same sense, or perhaps "bend down." For a discussion of the etymology of the Ugaritic word, see Caquot et al., *Textes ougaritiques I*, 239–40; for further critique of Dahood's use of Ugaritic in interpreting this verse, see Loretz, *Die Psalmen*, Teil II, 443–47.

13.b. מלב: literally, "from heart" (the heart representing the mind; hence the seat of memory).

13.c. The verse is analyzed as 3+3, but it would be possible to interpret it as 2+2+2 (cf. v 12), as proposed by Auffret, *VT* 28 (1978) 103–8.

16.a. Literally, "my times."

20.a. פעלת: Dahood (*Psalms I*, 191) translates: "you have *gathered*," on the basis of the parallelism with צפנת, and the Phoenician usage of *p'l*. But the parallelism does not require such a translation, and the root may mean "do, make," in Phoenician as also in Hebrew; cf. the use of *p'l* in the recent inscription in Ugaritic script from Sarepta (J. B. Pritchard, *Sarepta. A Preliminary Report on the Iron Age* [Philadelphia: University Museum, 1975] 102–4). On the possible occurrence of *p'l* in the Ugaritic language, see Caquot et al., *Textes ougaritiques I*, 199.

22.a. Reading אשר ("who"), for MT's כי ("for"), with four Heb. mss, *S* and Symmachus.

22.b. MT reads: in a beseiged *city* (עיר). On the emendation עת ("time") for עיר, see Kraus, *Psalmen 1–59*, 393. The entire line is omitted in *S*.

23.a. נגרזתי: "cut off"; MT's text is uncertain. Many Heb. mss read נגרזתי (meaning approximately the same) and two mss read נגרשתי, "I have been driven away" (De-Rossi, IV, 23).

Form/Structure/Setting

Psalm 31 is commonly designated an *individual lament,* and the classification is appropriate enough in general terms. More precisely, the principal portion of the psalm is a prayer (vv 2–19), followed by thanksgiving and praise (vv 20–25; see further below). A cultic context for the psalm may be supposed, though the internal evidence with respect to setting is at best vague. One must suppose a setting, perhaps, in an act of worship in which the worshiper comes to express prayer and lament, and in which he received assurance of having been heard by the Lord, which in turn prompts the concluding praise and thanksgiving.

The psalm falls into two major sections and several minor sections within the larger units, though there is no firm agreement amongst scholars as to the correct analysis. Kraus (*Psalmen 1–59*, 393) identifies vv 2–9 and 10–25 as two major sections, as does Ridderbos (*Die Psalmen*, 225–26). But it is best to separate vv 20–25 (thanksgiving and praise) from the preceding portion of the psalm for two reasons: (a) the transition from v 19 to v 20 appears to presuppose some cultic act, such as the proclamation of a prophetic or priestly word assuring the suppliant that God has heard and will answer his prayer (cf. Mowinckel, *The Psalms in Israel's Worship*, I, 219); (b) vv 2–19 appear to have an inner chiastic structure, indicating their coherence as a unit. The structure of Ps 31 may thus be set out as follows:

I. *Prayer* (1) prayer (2–6)   A
            (2) trust (7–9)   B
            (3) lament (10–14) C
            (4) trust (15)   B′
            (5) prayer (16–19) A′
[Declaration of oracle between v 19 and v 20]

II. *Thanksgiving and Praise* (vv 20–25)

A number of scholars have argued against the unity of the psalm, noting the various types of material contained within it. But the structure (as analyzed above) suggests unity, as does the use of common terminology, repeated words and phrases extending throughout the psalm, and providing a framework of coherence. The following repeated words (or words derived from the same root) should be noted (the list is not comprehensive):

(a) חסה "seek refuge" (vv 2, 20)   (e) יד "hand" (vv 6, 9, 16)
(b) בוש "be ashamed" (vv 2, 18)   (f) בטח "trust" (vv 7, 15)
(c) נצל "rescue, deliver" (vv 3, 16) (g) חסד "lovingkindness" (vv 8, 17, 22)
(d) ישע "deliver" (vv 3, 17)

It must be concluded, therefore, that despite the variety of types of language, the psalm is a unified whole, and that the major transition (between vv 19 and 20) is to be explained in a liturgical context (see *Comment*).

The language of Ps 31 has a high percentage of formulaic language in common with other psalms, estimated by Culley to be about 40 percent (*Oral Formulaic Language in the Biblical Psalms*, p 103). The percentage would be slightly higher if the material in common with Jeremiah and Lamentations were included. The common formulaic language may be summarized as follows (verse numbers refer to Heb. Bible):

(a) *Ps 31:2–4 parallel to Ps 71:1–3.*
(b) *General formulaic language: Psalmaic*
    31:2—119:40   31:5—9:16 and 71:5
    31:3—102:3   31:8—118:24

            31:10—6:8 and 69:18   31:21—61:5
            31:11—102:4   31:23—116:11; 28:2
            31:15—140:7   31:25—27:14
            31:17—109:26
(c) *Formulaic language: extra-Psalmaic*
    (1) 31:7—Jonah 2:9   (3) 31:11—Jer 20:18
        31:23—Jonah 2:5   31:13—Jer 48:38
    (2) 31:10—Lam 1:20   31:14—Jer 20:10
        31:22—Lam 3:54   31:18—Jer 17:18

The high percentage of common formulaic language makes it difficult to specify the background to the psalmist's distress; it is safest simply to admit that the language does not permit the identification of the specific crisis prompting the prayer. And if, as is implied by the title (v 1), the psalm entered the general resources of Israel's worship, it would have been entirely suitable for use by any person in distress, whether threatened by enemies (vv 5, 12), idolaters (v 7), or sickness and nearness of death (vv 10–11).

Comment

Prayer (31:2–19)

(a) *Opening words of prayer* (31:2–6). The worshiper has come to God from a specific situation of distress and prays to God for deliverance and protection from the source of that distress. The formulaic language is such that the nature of the source of distress cannot be determined with certainty. The entire thrust of the prayer, however, assumes that enemies of some kind are at the root of the psalmist's problems. In the metaphor of hunting (v 5; cf. Ps 9:16), the enemies have set a net to entrap the innocent person; the psalmist prays not only for deliverance from that net, but constantly reiterates his need of refuge and protection from God (vv 2, 3, 4, 5).

The words addressed to God are expressed in such a way as to elicit God's act of deliverance as covenant God. Thus, the reference to "righteousness" (צדקה: v 2) recalls God's character as one committed to his people in covenant. And the covenant commitment included a commitment to deliver from distress, as in the Exodus of old; the words "for your name's sake" (v 4b) refer back to that Exodus deliverance as a precedent for the present request for deliverance (see further Ps 23:3 and *Comment;* Ps 106:7–8).

At the conclusion of the opening words of prayer, the psalmist reaches a preliminary stage of confidence: he commits himself into God's hands (v 6a); the words do not imply resignation to certain fate (cf. *Explanation*), but confidence in God's ability to deliver and protect. The prayer to be *redeemed* (v 6b) has a temporal sense; the psalmist requires redemption from the present crisis. But again, the word "redeem" recalls the Exodus; as God had redeemed his people in the Exodus from Egyptian slavery (cf. Deut 7:8), so too the psalmist prays for redemption.

(b) *An expression of trust* (31:7–9). The point of confidence reached in the preceding prayer (v 6) now issues forth into a statement of confidence. The two sections, prayer and trust, are closely linked; the prayer had ended with a reference to the "God of truth" (v 6b), and the statement of trust begins with a contrast, namely the expression of hatred for "vain idols" (v 7a). In addition to the contrast, the words continue in the tone of the covenant theme of the opening prayer. The psalmist had prayed for protection as a covenant member; such a person shunned idolaters (v 7), who by definition could not be faithful covenant members. Thus the statement of v 7 is both a statement of trust and a declaration of integrity; the psalmist had trusted in the Lord, as was required of every member of the covenant community. God's *lovingkindness* (חֶסֶד, v 8) toward his people required, in response, their *trust* (בָּטַח, v 7).

The confident anticipation of praise in v 8 is based upon the psalmist's realization that the Lord has seen and does know about his crisis. Divine deliverance has not yet actually come, but neither has he yet been fully delivered into his enemy's hand. There is a sharp contrast, for poetic effect, in v 9. In the opening prayer, he prayed to be delivered (v 2) and committed himself into God's hand; now (v 9) he expresses confidence that he will not be delivered into the hand of an enemy. But this expression of trust in vv 7–9 is still anticipatory; the real distress remains, and to this theme the psalmist returns in the following verses.

(c) *Lament* (31:10–14). In the description of distress, which is central to the lament, it is difficult to know whether the terminology should be interpreted literally or metaphorically; the formulaic language, in common with other psalms and Jeremiah (see *Form/Structure/Setting*, above), might suggest that a general metaphorical interpretation is most appropriate. Thus the metaphor begins with language which describes primarily bodily sickness and the nearness of death (vv 10–11; on the wasting of the eyes, see the *Comment* on Ps 6:8, a psalm of sickness). Then the metaphorical language passes to a description of the psalmist's treatment at the hands of neighbors and acquaintances (v 12), to whom he has become an object of reproach. As a consequence of physical (vv 10–11) and social (v 12) distress, the psalmist has become like a dead man, quickly forgotten (v 13a) and like a "broken vessel," no longer useful and therefore discarded (v 13b: cf. Jer 22:28 and 48:38). But it is possible that the entire description of distress in physical and social terms (vv 10–13) should be subsumed under v 14: the introductory כִּי ("*for* I . . .") provides the explanation for the foregoing description of distress, all of which stems from the scheming multitudes who are the enemies of the psalmist (cf. vv 2–6, *Comment*). "Terror all around" (v 14) is probably a common saying, or cliché, used by an oppressed person who feels surrounded on every side by adversaries (cf. Jer 6:25; 20:10; 46:5; 49:29). Basically the source of distress and the subsequent lament is to be found in enemies, but the nature of their enmity and the basis of the persecution cannot be determined.

(d) *A further statement of trust* (31:15). Following the chiastic structure of the first main portion of the psalm, there is now a further statement of trust in the Lord (see also v 7b).

(e) *Concluding words of prayer* (31:16–19). The final prayer has parallels to the opening prayer; the focal point of the request is once again deliverance from enemies. Whereas the first prayer had concluded confidently with a statement of commitment into God's hand (v 6a), the closing prayer opens with a similarly confident statement; the psalmist's future is in God's "hand" (v 16a), and so he prays to be delivered from the hand of enemies (v 6b). On the request for God's face to "shine" (v 17) upon his servant, see Ps 4:7 and *Comment*. On *Sheol* (v 18), see Ps 6:6 and *Comment;* on Sheol and death as characterized by silence, see Ps 94:17 and 115:17. Verse 19 suggests that one manifestation of the enmity of the psalmist's oppressors was in the form of speech; in praying that their lying lips be sealed (v 19a), he is in effect praying for their demise and entry into the silence of Sheol (v 18).

Thanksgiving and praise (31:20–25)

The transition from prayer and lament to thanksgiving and praise is abrupt, and if it is correct that the psalm's setting is to be located in some cultic act, then one must assume that something has happened in the cultic or liturgical context which has made so sharp a transition possible. Presumably the event external to the psalmist which prompted the change was the declaration of an oracle by a prophet, priest or temple servant, to the effect that God had heard the worshiper's lament and prayer and that divine deliverance would come. On the basis of this assurance of coming deliverance, the psalmist concludes with words of absolute confidence, as if the actual deliverance had already been experienced. Thus the words of thanksgiving are not of a general nature, but are tied intimately to the substance of the foregoing prayer and lament, as the following clarifies:

Thanksgiving	Background: prayer/lament
v 20 For God's goodness to those who sought refuge . . .	v 2 . . . as the psalmist had sought refuge in God.
v 21 God protects his own from conspiracies and the *strife of tongues* . . .	v 17 . . . as the psalmist had experienced conspiracies and verbal attacks (v 19)
v 22 God reveals his *lovingkindness* . . .	v 17 . . . as the psalmist had prayed that he would.
v 23 God *heard* the prayer of the psalmist . . .	v 3 . . . as the psalmist had prayed that he would.
v 24 God loved his saints and hated his enemies . . .	v 7 . . . as the psalmist hated idolaters and trusted God.

In summary, the thanksgiving is directly rooted in answered prayer, or the anticipation of answered prayer, rather than being a general statement of praise. But the personal spiritual experience of the psalmist with respect to God's deliverance and response could not be kept to himself; it was the basis of an invitation to all God's people (vv 24–25) to love God and take courage in the face of adversity.

Explanation

The theme permeating the entire psalm is trust and the fulfilment of that trust. The psalmist, lamenting his distress, comes to God in prayer, but even as he prays, his spirit soars upward toward trust in God (vv 6, 7–9, 15).

That his trust was fulfilled and properly placed becomes evident in the concluding praise and thanksgiving.

It is from an understanding of this central theme of trust that we perceive the significance of the psalm in the NT. Jesus, dying on the cross, quoted Ps 31:6 in his dying words: "Father, into your hands I commit my spirit" (Luke 23:46). There is certainly a different perspective from that of the psalm in this quotation. The psalmist sought (v 18) and received deliverance *from* death and trusted in the coming of such deliverance; Jesus, on the other hand, gave expression to the same statement of trust as he died. He anticipated not deliverance from death, but trusted God even in dying and death (a trust that was later fulfilled in resurrection). It is in the light of the use of the psalm in the words of Jesus that its transformation for contemporary faith becomes clear. The psalmist prayed for life, for deliverance from death, and that is the psalm's fundamental and legitimate sense. But in the context of resurrection faith, the psalm may also be used as a prayer in death, expressing trust and commitment to the life lying beyond the grave. It was a perspective denied to the psalmist, but follows naturally from the use of his words in the mouth of Jesus.

The psalmist's lament, with respect to his physical grief and the enmity directed against him (vv 10–12), though not identified specifically as messianic in the NT, nevertheless assumes messianic overtones when read in conjunction with Jesus' quotation of v 6. In this sense, Ps 31 has close parallels with Ps 22 and its messianic interpretation.

The Blessing of Forgiveness *(32:1–11)*

Bibliography

Gertner, M. "Terms of Scriptual Interpretation: a Study in Hebrew Semantics." *BSOAS* 25 (1962) 22–24. **Kuntz, J. K.** "The Retribution Motif in Psalmic Wisdom." *ZAW* 89 (1977) 222–33. **Leveen, J.** "Textual Problems in the Psalms." *VT* 21 (1971) 55. **Macintosh, A. A.** "A Third Root עדה in Biblical Hebrew?" *VT* 24 (1974) 454–73.

Translation

[1] For David. A Maskil.[a]
  Blessed is he whose transgression is lifted,   (3+2)
  whose sin is covered.
[2] *Blessed is the man against whom the Lord counts no iniquity*   (5?+3)
  and in whose spirit [a] *there is no deceit.*
[3] *When I kept silence, my bones became old* [a]   (3+2)
  through my groaning [b] *all day long.*
[4] *For by day and by night, your hand was heavy upon me;*   (5+4?)
  my tongue [a] *was turned as in summer droughts.* SELAH.
[5] *I have made known* [a] *to you my sin*   (2+2)
  and I have not covered my iniquity.

> *I have said: "I will confess against myself* [b] (5+4/5)
> *my transgressions* [c] *to the Lord."*
> *And then you forgave the iniquity of my sin.* SELAH.

6 *Therefore, let every godly one pray to you at a time of stress;* [a] (5+5?)
   at the flood of mighty waters, they shall not reach him.

7 *You are a hiding place for me:* (3+2+3/4)
   you will protect me from trouble,
   you will surround me with shouts [a] *of deliverance.* SELAH.

8 *"I will instruct you and teach you in the way you must walk;* (4+3)
   I will give counsel with my eye upon you."

9 *Do not be* [a] *like a horse, like a mule without understanding,* (5+4+3)
   whose gallop [b] *must be restrained with bridle and halter,*
   or it will not stay near you.

10 *Many griefs are to the wicked,* (3+2+2)
   but the one who trusts in the Lord—
   lovingkindness shall surround him!

11 *Rejoice in the Lord and exult, you righteous ones!* (4+3)
   And shout aloud, all you upright in heart.

Notes

1.a. *Maskil:* the precise sense of the term is not known with certainty. The use of the same root in v 8, with the sense "teach, instruct," suggests that the term could mean "didactic psalm," but while such a sense would be appropriate for this psalm and Ps 78:1, it is not entirely appropriate for the other eleven psalm titles in which it is used (in this volume, see further Pss 42, 44, and 45). Other possible senses include: (a) "a meditation"; (b) "a psalm of understanding" (cf. *G*); (c) "a skillful psalm." All these senses are entirely appropriate to the form of the word, namely a participial formation from the Hiph. of שכל. The principal source of uncertainty concerns whether the term refers to the psalm as such or to the musical accompaniment. Gertner (art. cit.) claims that the word contains two notions, (a) that of insight and analytical understanding, and (b) that of harmony and synthesis. The double notion finds integration in that the interpretation and exegesis of the text emerges from the musical performance of the text. This proposal is possible, but by no means certain.

2.a. For MT's רוח ("spirit"), *G* presupposes פי ("mouth"), and *S* presupposes לב ("heart"); but the Heb. mss unambiguously support the reading רוח.

3.a. Alternatively, "were consumed," reading כלו, with good support from Heb. mss (De-Rossi, *IV*, 23).

3.b. Two Heb. mss. (De-Rossi, *IV*, 23) read בשגאתי; taking שגא as a form of שגה, the sense would be "through my errors/sins of ignorance."

4.a. MT's לשדי ("my juice"?) makes little sense; on the emendation לשני ("my tongue"), see Kraus, *Psalmen 1–59*, 400.

5.a. The imperfect verb is translated into a past tense on the basis of context.

5.b. Reading עלי, with some support from Heb. mss (De-Rossi, *IV*, 23) and *G*.

5.c. Reading the singular, פשעי, with some support from Heb. mss and *G*.

6.a. MT's רק מצא ("a time of *finding only*") is unclear; from the variety of possible solutions, the simplest is to emend to מצוק ("stress"); if the *waw* was written erroneously as *resh*, the *aleph* in MT may then have been introduced to resolve the anomalous form. This general solution is adopted by RSV, NAB and NEB.

7.a. MT's רני פלט has been a source of difficulty for a long time, partly because רן ("cry") is a hapax legomenon in the masc. form, and פלט ("deliverance") is rare as a noun. Leveen (*VT* 21 [1971] 55) emends רני to אדני: "rescue me, O *Lord,* and encompass me . . . ," but the difficulty scarcely warrants such radical emendation. The same objection applies to Budde's emendation of רני to מגני ("shields"), adopted by Kraus, *Psalmen 1–59*, 400. The literal translation of MT (above) provides acceptable sense.

9.a. The sing. form תחי is read (in place of MT's plur), with the support of two Heb. mss; the sing. form is in accord with the sing. suffixes of the foregoing verse.

9.b. The difficult form עדיו is translated "gallop," following the proposal of Macintosh (*VT* 24 [1974] 454–73), that there is a Hebrew root עדה (III), the sense of which is determined by the nuances of the Arabic verb *ġaḍā* (and the adjective *ġaḍawān*, "swift," of horses). Against Dahood's translation, "petulance," see Ps 10:18 (note b) and Ps 39:2.

Form/Structure Setting

Ps 32 is commonly classified as an *individual psalm of thanksgiving* (e.g. Fohrer, *Introduction*, 287; Mowinckel, *The Psalms in Israel's Worship*, II, 35–39); as such, its setting would have been in some temple ritual, perhaps the thanksgiving ceremony in which the worshiper offered a sin offering and gave thanks for deliverance (possibly from some form of sickness, on the basis of vv 3–4). But this classification of the psalm is not entirely satisfactory, partly because vv 1–2 would form a most unusual introduction to a thanksgiving psalm (cf. Ridderbos, *Die Psalmen*, 232), and partly because a number of features in the psalm may be taken as indicative of the literary tradition of wisdom. Hence it is not surprising that a number of scholars have classified the text as a *wisdom psalm* (e.g. R. E. Murphy, "A Consideration of the Classification 'Wisdom Psalms,' " VTSup 9 [1963] 161; J. K. Kuntz, art. cit., 224). The wisdom language of the psalm is most distinctive in vv 1–2 and 9–10. And yet, just as the wisdom characteristics of the text tend to undermine the classification as an individual thanksgiving psalm, so too the thanksgiving elements (and particularly the concluding verse) tend to undermine the classification of the text as a wisdom psalm in any conventional sense.

It is probable that the psalm should be interpreted as a literary composition, in which a basic thanksgiving psalm has been given literary adaptation according to the wisdom tradition; the literary structure, with its inherent chiasmus, is outlined below. The concluding verse (v 11) may either be original to the literary composition, or may reflect a development in the psalm's history, when it moved from the sphere of literary creation to that of cultic usage. The overall structure of the psalm may be outlined as follows, demonstrating the chiastic relationship between the two principal parts.

Part I	(1) Wisdom (vv 1–2)	A
	(2) Thanksgiving (vv 3–5)	B
Part II	(1) Thanksgiving (vv 6–8)	B'
	(2) Wisdom (vv 9–10)	A'

Conclusion (v 11)

In Part I, the wisdom introduction (vv 1–2) is developed in the psalmodic section, the two parts being integrated closely by the use of identical or similar terminology, as follows: (a) פשע "transgression" (vv 1, 5); (b) חטא "sin" (vv 1, 5); (c) עון "iniquity" (vv 1, 5); (d) כסה "cover" (vv 1, 5). In Part II, similar integration is achieved by the double use of terms between vv 6–7 and v 10: (a) חסיד "godly one" and חסד "lovingkindness" (vv 6, 10); (b) רבים "mighty, many" (vv 6, 10); (c) סבב "surround" (vv 7, 10);

see further Ridderbos, *Die Psalmen,* 235. The more detailed inner structure of the various parts of the psalm is developed in the *Comment.*

Within the early history of Christianity, Ps 32 was included among the seven penitential psalms; see further the commentary on Ps 6. The psalm is not in any strict sense a penitential psalm, though the language of v 5 makes an association with such psalms quite appropriate.

Comment

The blessing of forgiveness (32:1–2). The opening wisdom portion of the psalm expresses a general principle concerning the "blessed" or happy estate of a person whose sin is forgiven. On the word "blessed," see further Ps 1:1, which is also a wisdom psalm. The description presupposes throughout not a sinless person, but a person whose sins are forgiven; the psalmist views humans as sinning beings, whose possibility of happiness lies in the removal and forgiveness of that sin. Three principal terms are employed to designate the dimensions of human evil: (1) *transgression* (פשׁע), namely acts reflecting rebellion against God; (2) *sin* (חטאה), the most general term, designating an offense, or turning away from the true path; (3) *iniquity* (עון), indicating distortion, criminality, or the absence of respect for the divine will. The terms are used within the poetic structure of synonymous parallelism, and thus their potentially distinctive nuances should not be taken too precisely; yet the three terms as a whole specify the full dimensions of human evil, and hence the situation from which a person might be delivered through divine forgiveness, thus finding happiness. (Likewise, the three terms designating the manner of forgiveness are poetically parallel, but taken together, they indicate the completeness of the divine deliverance from evil which makes happiness possible.) The fourth line of the parallel structure (v 2b) refers to the absence of *deceit;* while this too is a sin, it is not here specified as something forgiven. The relevance of the term is to be seen in the means by which forgiveness is granted; the forgiveness implied in the first three lines presupposes repentance and confession (cf. v 5), and only when that repentance and confession are honest, devoid of deceit, will the happy estate of forgiveness be experienced.

A personal testimony of repentance (32:3–5). The general principle of wisdom expressed in the opening verses is now clarified in a personal statement. The psalmist first describes the grief which characterized his unrepentant state (vv 3–4), and then by way of contrast declares the deliverance consequent upon repentance and confession (v 5). Though the language is now personal, these verses retain the contrast typical of wisdom poetry; just as Ps 1 contrasts the wicked and the righteous, so here there is a striking contrast between the unrepentant sinner and the sinner who repents and finds forgiveness.

The unrepentant state (vv 3–4) is described as one of "silence"; the silence in context is specifically the absence of confession, in contrast to the speech of confession in v 5. The consequences of unrepentant silence are poetically evoked in physical terms; indeed, the physical language has led some commentators to suggest that there is here a reflection of psychosomatic illness, a bodily reaction to the internally contained conflicts of guilt. But it is more likely that the words should be interpreted in a more general poetic sense. The "groaning" is a consequence of living with guilt and a stifled conscience; the "aging bones" portray the growing weakness of the spiritual life which follows the unhealthy practice of bottling up one's evil within the soul, steadfastly retaining silence, rather than finding the emancipation of forgiveness through speech. The "heavy hand" of God, experienced within the mind and conscience, indicates an awareness of the need for repentance, but a stubborn refusal to yield to God. And the sinner's silence, aggravated by the heavy hand of God, contributed to the dry curling of the tongue, as in one desperate for water in a desert; so long as the tongue refused to speak the words of repentance, it curled in speechless pain.

In the words of confession (v 5), the psalmist uses the same three words that appeared in the wisdom introduction (*sin, iniquity,* and *transgression*) to indicate the comprehensiveness of his confession. And the confession of the first three lines (v 5a-c) immediately results in the divine forgiveness (v 5d). Confession is like opening the floodgate of a dam. When there is no confession, the waters pile up behind the dam, creating immense pressures on the wall, but as soon as the floodgate is opened, the waters subside and the pressures diminish.

The summoning of the godly to prayer (32:6–8). This section of the psalm has a threefold structure. (1) The psalmist, reflecting upon his own emancipation, summons all the godly to join in prayer for similar deliverance (v 6). (2) There follow the words of the prayer, as spoken by all the godly (v 7). (3) The prayer in turn is followed by the divine words, in oracular form, of the kind that might be delivered by a priest or temple servant in a liturgical context (v 8).

The godly are invited to pray at "a time of stress" (v 6); the precise nuance of these words is probably to be understood in terms of vv 3–4. Whenever the stress of unrepented sin is experienced, that person must turn to God in a prayer of repentance. The metaphor of the "flood of mighty waters" may imply a torrential flood following rain, whose waters would not reach the person who had prayed in confession to God (cf. the "deep waters" in Ps 18:17 [16], where the context implies the ocean).

The words of the prayer specify in various ways the kind of protection the suppliant sought from the Almighty. God would be a hiding place (cf. Ps 27:5); he would offer protection and be a victorious deliverer (the expression "shouts of deliverance" may evoke the battle cries of a conquering warrior). But the response to the prayer (v 8) promises instruction and counsel, rather than direct deliverance. In language reminiscent of the wisdom literature, the words of God contain primarily the promise of instruction concerning the path in which the godly should walk (cf. Ps 1), but contain also the assurance of protection (". . . with my eye upon you") for the one who walked in the divinely ordained path.

The conclusion of wisdom (32:9–10). Although v 9 is sometimes interpreted as part of the divine speech along with v 8 (Kraus, *Psalmen 1–59*, 405), it is preferable to interpret the verse as the opening of a concluding wisdom-type admonition, although it follows naturally from the wisdom language of the divine speech (v 8). The simile of v 9 develops in more detail the wisdom of Proverbs: "the whip for a horse, the bridle for an ass, the rod for the fool's back" (Prov 26:3). The godly one is advised not to be stubborn, like a mulish horse (cf. Anderson, *Psalms I*, 259), that constantly requires restraint lest it gallop away by itself. While it is possible that the psalmist is referring to stubborn sinfulness in general, the more immediate implication of the words is to be found in the stubborn resistance to confession of sin, already stated in vv 3–4. Such stubborn resistance brings only grief, whereas the one whose trust in the Lord leads to confession of sin may know God's loving kindness. In other words, the "godly one" (חסיד, v 6) will experience the divine lovingkindness (חסד, v 10).

Concluding praise (32:11). The concluding words, urging the praise of God, are typical of a hymn of thanksgiving. Nevertheless, they are integrated with the substance of the psalm, particularly in the reference to the "righteous ones" (צדיקים), who in the tradition of wisdom are those that choose to walk in the right path (Ps 1:5–6).

Explanation

When perceived primarily as a literary composition, Ps 32 conveys to its reader some fundamental wisdom. In the words of St. Augustine, that wisdom is: *intelligentia prima est ut te nôris peccatorem* ("the beginning of knowledge is to know oneself to be a sinner"; cf., Delitzsch, *Biblical Commentary on the Psalms*, I, 474). Indeed, it is recorded that Ps 32 was Augustine's favorite psalm, that he read it frequently, and that before he died, he had its words inscribed on the wall by his sickbed, to be both exercised and comforted by them (Kirkpatrick, *The Book of Psalms*, 161).

The psalm progresses smoothly from the statement of principle (vv 1–2) to the illustration of the principle (vv 3–5), and from the invitation to pray (v 6) to the admonition not to be stubborn (vv 9–10); it concludes on a mighty note of praise. It is a fundamental psalm, illustrating powerfully the prerequisite of spiritual health, namely a self-conscious awareness of one's sinful life and of the necessity of acting upon that awareness in confession before God. And further, the psalm establishes (as St. Paul was later to write) that justification and forgiveness for mankind are not achieved on the basis of law, or of circumcision, but on the basis of the divine grace, which flowed in response to the faith of the one who confessed and sought forgiveness (Rom 4:6–9). The psalm is thus central to the gospel and points out the path of true happiness to sinners aware of their need for forgiveness.

A Hymn to the Creator   (33:1–22)

Bibliography

Brekelmans, C. "Some Considerations on the Translation of the Psalms by M. Dahood." *UF* 1 (1969) 5–14. **Dietrich, M.** and **Loretz, O.** "Die ug. Gewandbezeichnungen

PĠNDR, KND, KNDPNṬ." *UF* 9 (1977) 340. **Loretz, O.** "Psalmen Studien, III." *UF* 6 (1974) 178. **Ouellette, J.** "Variantes Qumrâniennes du Livre des Psaumes." *RevQ* 7 (1969) 108. **Vincent, J. M.** "Recherches éxégetiques sur le Psaume 33." *VT* 28 (1978) 442–54. **Vosberg, L.** *Studien zum Reden vom Schöpfer in den Psalmen.* Munich: Kaiser, 1975.

Translation

1a *Exult in the Lord, you who are righteous!*	(3+3)
O [b] *you upright ones, praise is fitting!*	
2 *Praise the Lord with a lyre.*	(3+3)
Make music for him with a ten-stringed harp.	
3 *Sing to him* [a] *a new song;*	(3+3)
play beautifully with a joyful sound.	
4 *For the word of the Lord is right,*	(3+3?)
and all his works are indeed truth.	
5 *He is the one loving righteousness and justice;*	(3+4)
the earth is full of the Lord's lovingkindness.	
6 *By the Lord's word, the heavens were made,*	(4+3)
and by the breath of his mouth, all their host.	
7 *He gathers together the waters of the sea like a heap;* [a]	(3+3)
he puts the deep waters in his storehouses.	
8 *Let all the earth fear the Lord;*	(3?+4)
let all the world's inhabitants be in awe of him.	
9 *For he spoke, and it was;*	(3+2)
he commanded and it stood forth.	
10 *The Lord frustrates the plan of nations,*	(3+3)
he restrains the schemes of peoples. [a]	
11 *The Lord's plan shall stand for ever,*	(4+4)
the schemes of his heart from generation to generation.	
12 *Blessed is the nation whose God is the Lord,*	(4+4?)
the people he has chosen for his own possession.	
13 *The Lord has looked from heaven;*	(3+3)
he has seen all the sons of mankind.	
14 *He has gazed from his established throne* [a]	(3+3)
at all the inhabitants of the earth. [b]	
15 *He is the One who fashions their hearts, individually;* [a]	(3+3?)
he is the One who discerns all they do.	
16 *The king is not saved by a great army;*	(3+3)
the warrior is not delivered by great strength.	
17 *The horse is hopeless for victory,*	(3+3)
and by its strength, it cannot deliver.	
18 *Lo, the Lord's eye is upon those that fear him,*	(3?+2)
upon those that depend on his loving kindness,	
19 *to rescue their soul from death*	(3+2)
and to keep them alive in famine. [a]	
20 *We* [a] *long for the Lord;*	(3+3)
he is our strength and our shield. [b]	

²¹ For in him, our heart rejoices;   (3+3)

     for in his holy name we have trusted.

²² May your loving kindness be upon us, O Lord,   (3+3)

     as we have depended on you.

Notes

1.a. In *G*, the psalm is prefixed by a title: τῷ Δαυιδ, and a title is to be expected in this portion of the Psalter. The Qumran evidence also indicates a title: "To David, a song: a psalm" (cf. 4QPs: Ouellette, art. cit.). It is probable that the absence of a title is to be explained by a tradition linking Ps 33 with the preceding psalm; eight Heb. mss join Pss 32 and 33 (De-Rossi, IV, 24). But there cannot be certainty as to whether or not the psalm originally had a title, though the Qumran evidence might suggest an original title that was later omitted. Certainly the internal structure of the psalm (below) implies a composition independent from Ps 32.

1.b. The *lamedh* in לישרים is interpreted as a vocative, with Dahood, *Psalms I*, 201.

3.a. Several Heb. mss and *Tg* replace the suffix in לו with the divine name יהוה; but metrical balance suggests retaining לו, given the regularity (3+3) of the opening three verses.

7.a. The Heb. בַּנֵּד ("like a heap") has caused some difficulty. *G* reads ὡσεὶ ἀσκόν ("as [in] a bottle"), implying נֹאד, "wineskin, skin bottle." More radically, Dahood incorporates the initial particle ("like, as") into the basic form and reads בְּכַד ("jar") on the basis of Ugaritic *knd* (and Akk. *kandu*), translating: "He gathers into a jar. . . ." Dahood's proposal should be rejected. The Ugaritic word *knd* occurs only twice in the Ugaritic texts, and both occurrences are on the same tablet (*CTA* 140: 2–3 = *KTU* 4.4. 2–3). The text is an economic text, apparently an inventory of clothes or garments, as proposed by Herdner in *CTA*. Dahood's translation *jar*, following Aistleitner, is very unlikely, and Aistleitner himself noted the uncertainty of his proposal (*WUS*, #1337). As Dietrich and Loretz point out (*UF* 9 [1977] 340), the meaning of Ugaritic *knd* is almost certainly a *garment* of some type (for which, in addition, there is strong support from Akkadian cognate terms). In summary, it is best simply to accept the term נד *(heap)* as in MT, and to interpret the term in conjunction with the parallel passage in Exod 15:8; see further the *Comment*.

10.a. *G* adds an extra line ("and he restrains the plan of princes"), but it is probably duplication, rather than original; the two-line structure is retained in 4QPs^q, though that text has the singular form מחשבת ("scheme") in place of MT's plural (as also in v 11).

14.a. Some Heb. mss and *Tg* (De-Rossi, IV, 24) replace שבתו ("his throne") by קדשו ("his holy. . . ."); but MT is to be preferred, particularly in view of the parallel expression in Exod 15:17; see Comment.

14.b. 4QPs^q has a variant reading, תבל "world" which is not a surprising variant given the parallel use of the terms in v 8.

15.a. יחד ("together") is rendered in *G*: κατὰ μόνας ("alone"), apparently with the implication "individually," which appears to be the best sense of the Hebrew. Dahood (*Psalms I*, p. 202) renders itיֶחֱזֶ (יֶחֱזֶ) "he inspects," but the rendition is most unlikely in this context; cf. O. Loretz, *Die Psalmen, Teil II*, 499.

19.a. Dahood, *Psalms I*, 203, renders רעב by "the Hungry One," taking the preposition in the sense of "from," and translates: ". . . to preserve their lives from the Hungry One" (viz. Death). Although the rendering is possible, it is unnecessary and unlikely: see Brekelmans, *UF* 1 (1969) 9. The translation above, following the conventional interpretation of MT, has the support of the obvious meaning of ברעב in Job 5:20, a similar context.

20.a. Literally, "our soul" (נפשנו).

20.b. On the sense "shield" for מגן in this context, see Loretz, *UF* 6 (1974) 178.

Form/Structure/Setting

The psalm should be classified as a *hymn of praise*, in which the principal theme is the praise of the Lord as Creator in the world of nature and his concomitant mastery of human history. The structure of the hymn, in general terms, may be set out as follows:

1. Invocation to praise (vv 1–3)
2. Substance of praise (vv 4–19)
   a. The Lord's *Word* (vv 4–9)
   b. The Lord's *Plan* (vv 10–12)
   c. The Lord's *Eye* (vv 13–15)
   d. The Lord's *Might* (vv 16–19)
3. Conclusion (vv 20–22).

The psalm was certainly designed for use in Israel's congregational worship, though it may not be possible to determine the cultic setting more precisely; an autumnal festival or covenant festival are possible but uncertain settings, and it may be wisest simply to identify the psalm as a general hymn of praise, in which are present some of the most central themes of Israel's worship.

The psalm is characterized by a number of distinctive stylistic features. It may be described first as an "alphabetizing" psalm, not acrostic, but similar to the acrostic psalms in the number of verses and certain other formal features (cf. Ridderbos, *Die Psalmen*, 83, 236; Kraus, *Psalmen 1–59*, 409). One feature of the "alphabetizing" character is the considerable regularity of the internal structure and balance, as is demonstrated clearly in the study of Vincent (art. cit., 450). The psalm also makes use of a fairly high percentage of formulaic language (Vincent, 448); the repeated use of the same words, or word forms derived from the same root, throughout the psalm adds further to the overall sense of unity (see Ridderbos, *Die Psalmen*, 244–45).

Just as the cultic setting cannot be determined with precision, so also it is difficult to be precise about the date or general period to which the psalm might originally have belonged. A number of criteria have been suggested to indicate that the psalm is late, perhaps postexilic, such as its stylistic characteristics, its theology of creation (by the *Word*), or the general internal developments in theology (e.g. that in times of historical crisis, worshipers were encouraged to praise the Lord of Creation; see Vosberg, *Studien zum Reden vom Schöpfer in den Psalmen*). But neither the style (cf. *Excursus III* on Acrostic Psalms, following Pss 9–10) nor the theology (see the *Comment* below) require a postexilic date, and certain similarities between Ps 33 and Judg 5 (notably the episodic structure of the substance and the use of repetition; cf. Ridderbos, *Die Psalmen*, 238–39) might suggest an earlier date. While the date remains uncertain, there are no overwhelming reasons to oppose a general setting in the cult as practiced during the period of the Hebrew monarchy.

Both Ridderbos (*Die Psalmen*, 238) and Vincent (art. cit., 451) have suggested the possibility of determining, on the basis of the internal structure, the manner in which the psalm might have been sung. While such a reconstruction is of necessity hypothetical, Vincent's suggestion is instructive: (a) the officiating person addressed the entire congregation (v 1) and (b) addressed the accompanying musicians (vv 2–3); (c) the entire choir sang vv 4–5 and

vv 20–22; (d) vv 6–12 and vv 13–19 were sung antiphonally by the two parts
of the choir.

Comment

Invocation to praise (33:1–3). The first and general call to praise is addressed
to the "righteous," or the "upright ones"; the use of the same terms in
32:11 may account for the linking together of Pss 32 and 33 in some Heb.
mss (see v 1, note a, above), or it may be the basis of the sequence of the
psalms in their current editorial placement. On the "righteous," see Ps 1:1–
3, 5.

Two musical instruments are specified in v 2, the "lyre" (כנור) and the
"ten-stringed harp" (נבל עשור), though no doubt these two instruments
merely symbolize the entire array of instruments in the orchestra that would
be utilized in the accompaniment of praise (cf. Ps 150). On the recently discovered musical text of the Late Bronze Age, found at Ras Shamra, see HEBREW
POETRY AND MUSIC in the INTRODUCTION; the text contains the chords to be
played on a lyre in accompaniment to a Hurrian cult hymn. For pictorial
representations of harps and lyres in the biblical world, see Keel, *The Symbolism
of the Biblical World*, 346–49.

The precise significance of the expression "new song" (v 3) is uncertain.
The words might have eschatological overtones, as noted by Kraus (*Psalmen
1–59*, 410), and certainly in the NT the expression is used in an eschatological
context (Rev 5:9). But in the Psalter, the expression "new song" is used
frequently in a formulaic clause (cf. Culley, *Oral Formulaic Language in the
Biblical Psalms*, 58), and it is probable that the words designate basically the
ever-new freshness of the praise of God in his victorious kingship (Pss 96:1,
98:1, 149:1).

The praise of the Lord's word (33:4–9). In the analysis of the psalm, it is
possible to distinguish vv 4–5 from vv 6–9; see Vincent, art. cit., 450 and
Ridderbos, *Die Psalmen*, 237. Verses 4–5 are thus understood as the introduction to the central hymn of praise (vv 4–19) and at the same time they provide
in essence the reason (introduced by כי "for" in v 4) for the preceding call
to praise. Nevertheless, the entire unit (vv 4–9) is united by the basic theme
of the *Word* (vv 4, 6) and the divine speech (v 9). It was by means of the
spoken Word that God created all things.

The concept of creation being effected by the divinely spoken word is
very ancient in the Near East. Perhaps the oldest manifestation of the doctrine
is to be found in Egypt; in the so-called Memphite Theology, the god Ptah
first conceives a thought in his heart and then declares that thought in the
spoken word. The spoken word of command results in creation; see further
S. Morenz, *Egyptian Religion*, 1973, 163–66. There are similar, though less
distinctive, theologies of creation involving thought and speech in other Egyptian texts. It is unlikely that the biblical texts dealing with creation by the
spoken word have any direct dependence on the parallel Egyptian material.
Nevertheless, the antiquity of the general concept in ancient Near Eastern
thought offers a warning against too easy an assumption of the late date of
the Hebrew theology of creation by word. In all probability, the concept of

creation by the divine Word arose independently in a variety of cultures, linked no doubt by the common concept that things do not exist unless they are named. Thus the biblical doctrine expressed in Ps 33, the Egyptian Memphite doctrine, and the later Greek concept of *logos* are initially independent, though they may share certain fundamental conceptions about the nature of reality. In Ps 33:4–9, the background to the language and thought is primarily that of Gen 1, reflected most clearly in v 9: "he spoke and it was." But the explicit references to the divine word make it clear that the word not only brought things into being (v 6), but also that the character of the word as "right" (v 4) imparted to the created order the divine characteristics of the Creator—*truth, righteousness, justice,* and *lovingkindness* (vv 4–5).

In addition to the overtones of Gen 1, there is a second creation theme present in this section which is most evident in vv 7–8; it is a reflection of the "Song of the Sea" (Exod 15:1–18), which is both a victory hymn and a celebration of God's creation of his people Israel (cf. Craigie, *The Book of Deuteronomy,* 157–58). The theme is evident first in the reference to God gathering the "waters of the sea like a heap"; this was precisely God's action at the Reed Sea (Exod 15:8), and the latter verse also refers to the "deeps" (תהומות), as does Ps 33:7. The language of the "Song of the Sea" explicitly adapts the Canaanite mythology of creation to demonstrate God's work in history in the creation of his people (cf. Craigie, *TyndB* 22 [1971] 3–31). Thus in Ps 33, the psalmist utilizes two types of creation language: (a) that reminiscent of Egypt and creation by the word (Gen 1); (b) that reminiscent of Canaanite and Mesopotamian cosmogonies involving conflict and the primeval waters. The parallels with the "Song of the Sea" extend further in Ps 33:8: God's creative acts, in his control of *waters* and *deeps,* evoke *fear* and *awe* from human beings, as they do in Exod 15:14–15. Thus, in summary, the overtones of the language in vv 4–9 indicate not only the divine creation of the natural order, but also the creation of God's holy nation in the redemption from Egypt accomplished at the Reed Sea.

The praise of the Lord's plan (33:10–12). There is now a transition from the praise of God in creation to the praise of God in his control of human history. Whereas creation rests upon the divine *Word,* history rests upon the divine *plan* (עצה, or "counsel") and *scheme.* The poetic unit is constructed in a finely balanced manner. Human plans//schemes (v 10), for all their strength, are subject to divine restraint. The Lord's plans//schemes are powerful and perpetual, not subject to human restraint. The essence of these two verses, which are parallel in construction and word use but contrasting in significance, is then summarized in v 12. The "nation whose God is the Lord" (v 12) is blessed precisely because its national existence is based upon the divine *plan* or *scheme,* not merely upon human aspirations.

The themes of God's dominion in creation and in history are intimately related. God's control of history presupposes his mastery of creation, and the great examples of divine presence in history in the OT often contain within them the divine use of the forces of nature, which in turn belong to God as the Creator of the natural order. Thus, the Exodus from Egypt in the escape at the Reed Sea is on the one hand a testimony to God's masterful participation in the course of the history of his chosen people. On the other

hand, the event is testimony to God's control of substance and power within
the order of his creation. Hence, the progression in Israel's worship from
praise of God's word in its creative force to praise of God's plan in human
history is a natural and necessary consequence of the fundamental Hebrew
theology.

The praise of God's eye (33:13–15). The Lord's eye is not mentioned explicitly
in these verses, though it is in v 18. Here it is the process of divine vision
which is the focus of praise: God "has looked, has seen" (v 13), "has gazed"
(v 14), and "discerns" (v 15). He sees from his position of dominion, namely
"heaven" (cf. Ps 11:4), wherein is his "established throne" (v 14); this expression may be a further allusion by the psalmist to the "Song of the Sea," in
which a parallel expression is used (Exod 15:17). The precise focus of praise
in these verses is the divine, all-seeing omniscience, but the omniscience in
turn is related to the beings and actions of individual human persons. Thus,
within the psalm there is a transition from the cosmos (the creation theme
of vv 4–9) to international affairs (vv 10–12), to the microcosm in the lives
and actions of individuals, in these verses. And with respect to the appreciation
of the divine might upon which praise is based, the microcosm is at least as
vital as the macrocosm. But the creation theme reappears in these verses,
for God is identified as the "one that fashions" (v 15, הַיֹּצֵר) human hearts,
alluding no doubt to God's initial role in "fashioning" (Gen 2:7; the same
verb is used) human beings in creation. As Creator of each individual person,
God perceives the thoughts and actions of each individual person; the awareness of such all-seeing omniscience may only be a source of praise, as it is
here, for those who can stand the divine scrutiny. For others, it may be a
source of terror.

The praise of God's might (33:16–19). The preceding verses in praise of God's
greatness are heightened in this section of the hymn by a striking contrast;
the traditional human sources of strength are as nothing in contrast to God's
might. The first two verses (vv 16–17) demonstrate the futility of depending
upon the humanly recognized sources of strength; the next two verses (vv
18–19) demonstrate God's life-saving power.

Verses 16–17 appear to reflect the traditions of Israel's early poetry of
war. Armies (v 16a), a warrior's prowess and strength (v 16b), and the war
horse (v 17), do not offer dependable strength in crisis, nor do they bring
victory. In the "Song of the Sea," the Lord was recognized as the only true
warrior (Exod 15:3); armies and horses offered no military hope of success
for Israel's pursuers (Exod 15:1, 4). In the "Song of Deborah," kings fought
with their armies and their war horses (Judg 5:19–22), but they were defeated
by the might of Israel's God. These ancient traditions are here established
by the psalmist as a fundamental principle of human history; though there
are formidable forms of human strength, they can never balance the divine
power.

In reaffirming God's power, the psalmist returns to God's omniscient vision
(v 18; cf. vv 13–15). Specifically, he sees those that "fear him" (or "stand
in awe of him") and that depend on his covenant characteristic of lovingkindness (חֶסֶד: v 18b); and seeing, he naturally responds to their submission
and commitment to him in providing the might and defense that they require.

The psalmist specifically refers to divine deliverance from "death" and "famine" (the lines are poetically parallel); by implication, the deliverance is not only from the terminal disasters which face a living person, but into a fullness of life in relationship with God.

Concluding words (33:20–22). Throughout the section of praise (vv 4–19), the Lord's nature and might were at the focal point of worship; the concluding lines contain introspective reflection, in which the worshipers reflect upon the personal implications of their praise. The expression of longing (v 20a) is in recognition of the need for help and protection; the military overtones of the language ("shield," v 20b), though in a poetic sense continuing the military terminology of vv 16–19, nevertheless indicate on the part of the worshipers a general recognition of their need for help and protection in every facet of life. And so the psalm ends on a note of prayer (v 22), in which the worshipers specifically ask for the experience and blessing of God's lovingkindness (v 22a; cf. v 18), which brings with it all the privileges of the covenant relationship.

Explanation

In Ps 33, there are integrated some of the most basic themes of Hebrew theology: creation, history, covenant, and the human response of worship. And the integration of these themes indicates their fundamental inseparability in Hebrew religion; they are interdependent, not independent. Creation is not an abstract doctrine, providing answers to human intellectual curiosity concerning the origin and nature of the world; rather, creation doctrine deals with the world in its relationship to God, to human history, and to individual human beings. The created world is the stage on which the drama of human history unfolds; but the Hebrew concepts of God's providence and might in the developing drama of history must presuppose God's mastery of the created world as such. God is not simply another actor, along with humans, within the created world; he is Creator and thus controls the sphere within which history moves and develops. And the covenant, in turn, which is at the heart of Hebrew religion, presupposes God's roles both as Creator and as sovereign in human history.

Thus, the profoundly theological doctrines which permeate the verses of this psalm are separated by a great distance from the cool abstractions of philosophical theology. Their setting in the words of worship provides them with a personal base, related both to Israel as a nation and to each worshiper as an individual. And though the themes of God's creative role and might are central to the psalm's substance, it is perhaps his *lovingkindness* that dominates the whole; it permeates the created earth (v 5), it is in the Lord's deliverance of his people (v 18), and it is integral to the concluding prayer (v 22).

This ancient hymn of praise, with its balanced and integrated theology, is a timely reminder of the essence of biblical theology. In an age when the biblical doctrine of creation is all too frequently discussed in conjunction with *science*, the psalmist offers a reminder that creation must be reflected on in conjunction with *history*. For in engaging in the creation-science debate, it is possible to miss entirely the powerful thrust of the Hebrew doctrine of creation, namely that God's providence and dominion in history, whether ancient or modern, presupposes his role as Creator and orderer of human existence in this world.

An Acrostic Psalm   (34:1–23)

Bibliography

Roberts, J. J. M. "The Young Lions of Psalm 34:11." *Bib* 54 (1973) 265–67.

Translation

¹   For David. When he feigned madness ^a before Abimelech, so that he drove him out; and he left.

²⁽¹⁾ (א) *I will bless the Lord at all times;*   (3+3)
           his praise shall constantly be in my mouth.

³⁽²⁾ (ב) *My soul makes its boast in the Lord;*   (3+3)
           the humble shall hear and shall rejoice.

⁴⁽³⁾ (ג) *Magnify the Lord with me,*   (3+3)
           and together let us exalt his name.

⁵⁽⁴⁾ (ד) *I have sought the Lord, and he has answered me,*   (3+3)
           and he has delivered me from all my terrors.

⁶⁽⁵⁾ (ה) *Look ^a at him and be radiant ^b*   (3+2)
           and let not your ^c faces be ashamed.

⁷⁽⁶⁾ (ו) *This poor man called, and the Lord heard*   (4+3)
           and delivered him from all his troubles.

⁸⁽⁷⁾ (ה) *The Lord's angel is encamped*   (3+3)
           around those who fear him, to rescue them.

⁹⁽⁸⁾ (ט) *Taste and see how good the Lord is;*   (4+3)
           blessed is the man who seeks refuge in him.

¹⁰⁽⁹⁾ (י) *Fear the Lord, O you his saints,*   (3+3)
           for they who fear him have no lack.

¹¹⁽¹⁰⁾ (כ) *The young lions ^a are in need and are hungry,*   (3+4)
           but they who seek the Lord shall not lack
           any good thing.

¹²⁽¹¹⁾ (ל) *Come, children, listen to me;*   (3+3)
           I will teach you the fear of the Lord.

¹³⁽¹²⁾ (מ) *Who is the man that takes pleasure in life,*   (4+4)
           that loves days, so that he may see goodness?

¹⁴⁽¹³⁾ (נ) *Keep your tongue from evil*   (3+3)
           and your lips from speaking deceit!

¹⁵⁽¹⁴⁾ (ס) *Turn from evil and do good;*   (3+3)
           seek peace and pursue it.

¹⁶⁽¹⁵⁾ (ע) *The eyes of the Lord are upon the righteous,*   (3+2)
           and his ears open to their cry for help.

17(16) (פ) *The Lord's face is against* ᵃ *those who do evil,*   (3+3)
      to cut off the memory of them from the earth.

18(17) (צ) *They cry out,* ᵃ *and the Lord hears*   (3+3)
      and delivers them from all their troubles.

19(18) (ק) *The Lord is close to the broken hearted*   (4+3)
      and saves those who are spiritually crushed.

20(19) (ר) *The righteous one's afflictions are many,*   (3+3)
      but the Lord delivers him from them all.

21(20) (שׁ) *He watches over all his bones;*   (3+3)
      not one of them shall be broken.

22(21) (ת) *Evil shall slay the wicked,*   (3+3)
      and those who hate the righteous will be desolate.

23(22) *The Lord redeems the soul of his servants,*   (4+4)
      and all those who seek refuge in him will
      not be desolate.

Notes

1.a. Literally, "when he changed his discernment."

6.a. הביטו ("look at"): the form should be pointed as an imperative (with the support of some Heb. mss; cf. *G*). The pointing in MT (indicative) leaves unsolved the problem of the absence of a subject (viz., who are "they"?).

6.b. The verb should be pointed as imperative (cf. *G*, and note a above).

6.c. Following the two imperatives, a second person plural suffix is read (ופניכם), with *G* and *S*.

11.a. כפירים "young lions." *G* renders πλούσιοι, "the rich," perhaps Heb כבדים or כבירים (see further Kraus, *Psalmen 1–59*, 417; Dahood, *Psalms I*, 206). But Roberts prefers to keep MT (*Bib* 54 [1973] 265–67), noting parallels to the language in Job 4:7–11 and in Babylonian wisdom literature. MT is retained in the translation; see further the *Comment*.

17.a. The preposition ב, in context, has the sense "against," as also in Ugaritic; cf. *bhm* in *CTA* 12.I.30 and Caquot et al., *Textes ougaritiques I*, 342.

18.a. The syntax is ambivalent with respect to the subject of the verb. *G*, *S*, and *Tg* add the equivalent of צדיקים "righteous ones" (cf. v 16), which is certainly correct in terms of sense, but probably an unnecessary addition to MT. It is possible that vv 16 and 17 have been inverted, thus creating the syntactical ambiguity.

Form/Structure/Setting

Psalm 34 is an acrostic psalm; for further discussion of the principles of acrostic poetry in Hebrew, see *Excursus III*, following Pss 9–10. The alphabetic units are of two lines each and are for the most part in 3+3 meter. There are two peculiarities in this particular acrostic psalm, shared with Ps 25: (a) the apparent suppression of a *waw*-verse, and (b) its replacement by a final *pe*-verse (v 23; see further *Excursus III*). Within the acrostic structure, the poet has created a sense of literary unity by the repeated use of the same or related words. The following words are used three or more times (omitting any reference to words used only twice): (a) שׁמע "hear" (vv 3, 7, 12, 18); (b) הציל "deliver" (vv 5, 18, 20); (c) ירא "fear" (vv 8, 10a, 10b, 12); (d) טוב "good" (vv 9, 11, 13, 15); (e) רע "evil" (vv 14, 15, 17, 20, 22); (f) צדיק "righteous" (vv 16, 20, 22).

It is difficult to come to any firm judgment as to the form or type of the psalm. The opening verses (vv 2–9) have certain characteristics indicating associations with the *individual thanksgiving psalms*. The latter portion of the psalm (vv 10–23) has the general characteristics of wisdom or *didactic* poetry, but in the form of a literary creation within the acrostic structure, analogous to Ps 25. It is possible that the poet utilized and adapted older poetry in this literary creation. If vv 2–9 (or a portion thereof) originally constituted a more ancient psalm of thanksgiving, the poet has now worked that ancient unit into a larger literary whole. But the possible prehistory of the opening words of praise and thanksgiving may account for the association of the title verse (v 1: see *Comment*) with the psalm in its present form. If it is correct that the psalm should be viewed primarily as a literary creation, then it is not possible to state any social or cultic setting for the psalm in its present form.

Given the somewhat artificial restrictions imposed on the poet by the acrostic structure, the psalm is not subdivided into thought units longer than the verse; the commentary deals with verse units only.

Comment

(1) *Title.* The title alludes to the event described in more detail in 1 Sam 21:10–15. David feigned madness in the presence of Achish, king of Gath. But the use of the word "Abimelech" in the psalm title has been a source of some difficulty; at first sight, it appears to be an error for Achish. Regardless of the date of the title in relation to the psalm, it is most unlikely that so fundamental an error would have been committed by a scribe, or that it would have been perpetuated by subsequent scribes and editors. It is more plausible to assume that "Abimelech" (literally, "my father is king") was an official title for Philistine kings, just as *Pharaoh* was an official title for Egyptian kings. The word "Abimelech" in the psalm title, in other words, presumably refers to the Achish of 1 Sam 21:10 (see further Delitzsch, *Biblical Commentary on the Psalms*, I, 490).

The more difficult problem with the psalm's title concerns its relationship, if any, to the psalm as a whole. It is possible, but unlikely, that the title was affixed artificially, the editor being impressed by the correspondence between טעמו in the title and in v 9; but the sense of the terms differs in each context. And equally, the lack of correspondence between the psalm as a whole and the title tends to militate against the addition of the title to the psalm at a later date; there are no evident or strong grounds for adding such a title to the psalm. Hence, it is probable that the title is ancient and is to be associated with the prehistory of the present psalm. One may suppose (and it is no more than an hypothesis) that the title was joined to an ancient hymn of thanksgiving, traditionally associated with the Achish incident in David's life. This ancient hymn (or a portion of it) became the basis of the artistic and literary composition which is now in the Psalter, but in the process of adaptation the title remained.

(2) א The opening verse of the psalm proper contains an affirmation of intent; in character and form, it has the appearance of a formal *vow* (cf.

Kraus, *Psalmen 1–59*, 419). In context, however, the words express a commitment that finds partial fulfilment in the following two verses.

(3) ב The essence of praise is now clearly expressed. It is "boasting in the Lord"; to boast, in itself an unpleasant human characteristic by virtue of its self-centeredness, is here transformed by the object of the boasting, external to the self. Hence, the "boasting in the Lord" creates not aversion toward the boaster among those who are near; it directs them too toward rejoicing as they hear the praise of another. On the "humble," see Ps 9:13 (note b).

(4) ג "Magnify" (גדלו), or "make great"; in one sense, it is impossible to conceive of mankind making God great. God is already great, without any human help. Yet the essence of praise is the acknowledgment and public declaration of God's greatness; such praise does not change the divine essence, but creates awareness of God's greatness in the perception of others. And, as an expression of awareness, it is also a personal acknowledgment of divine majesty and glory.

(5) ד The psalmist's affirmation here has all the characteristics of a declaration of confidence on the part of the worshiper, after receiving a divine oracle from the Lord through a temple servant; see further the *Comment* on Ps 22:22c. If the opening verses originally formed part of a thanksgiving psalm (see *Form/Structure/Setting* above), the declaration of confidence would have followed an oracular statement. But in the present context, it is preferable to interpret the words as a part of the artistic literary structure of the acrostic psalm, expressing general confidence (based on experience) in God's ability to answer prayer.

(6–9) ה-ט The psalmist's own experience of God's gracious deliverance compels him to invite others to share his own experience. Hence the section opens (v 6) and closes (v 9) with imperatives ("look," v 6., "taste," v 9); the imperatives are presumably addressed to the "humble" (v 3), who have already been invited to join in the praise (v 4). Between the imperatives, the psalmist gives a personal testimony ("this poor man . . ."; v 7), in which he affirms God's deliverance in answer to prayer. Though the nature of the deliverance is not specified, the language of v 8 implies deliverance from a military crisis; the "Lord's angel" is reminiscent of the angel of God encountered by Joshua at Jericho (Josh 5:13–15). It is probable that a precise military situation may lie behind this portion of the psalm in its prehistory; in its present literary form, however, the military associations have become merely metaphorical. The psalmist, having experienced directly God's delivering power, invites others also to "taste and see"; the metaphor of invitation is powerful, for it suggests action on the part of those invited in order to perceive the greater delivering action which is God's. The divine deliverance, or salvation, requires movement, namely the response of faith that *tastes*, thereby releasing the goodness pent up in what is tasted.

(10–11) י-כ At v 10, the psalm assumes the more didactic character of the wisdom literature, but the link with the preceding section is provided by the "fear" of the Lord (vv 8, 10). In the manner of a wisdom teacher, the psalmist now invites all God's people ("saints," קדשיו, or "holy ones") to participate in that fear of the Lord which delivers (v 8) and provides for every need (v 10). In the injunction to fear the Lord, the psalmist is standing in the mainstream of the wisdom tradition, for all wisdom is established on this fundamental principle (cf. Craigie, "Biblical Wisdom in the Modern World, I," *Crux* 15 [1979] 7–9). The fear, or reverence, of the Lord was the basis upon which wisdom built, for the awe and reverence implied by the word "fear" created within the individual the attitude within which the spiritual and moral life was to develop. Hence the fear of the Lord was the *beginning* of wisdom (Prov 1:7); those who feared the Lord had no lack (v 10), for their lives were rooted at the true center of existence, namely the reverence of the One who granted human life in the first place. By way of contrast, "young lions" (v 11) do lack and grow hungry. The lion metaphor is powerful in its contrast and is employed elsewhere in the wisdom literature (Roberts, *Bib* 54 [1973] 265–67). Of all the beasts, the lion is most powerful and least likely to lack prey and go hungry. And among the lions, though old lions may lack prey, young lions are active and successful as hunters (cf. Job 4:10–11). The young lions thus symbolize the essence of self-sufficiency in the provision of physical needs. In contrast, those who fear the Lord are not self-sufficient; they depend on another, God, for the provision of their basic needs. And yet, as the psalmist demonstrates, it is the self-sufficient predators of this world who would lack, while the God-fearing would have all their needs met.

(12–13) לְמֹ In these verses, the psalm takes on an even more explicitly didactic tone. The psalmist will "teach" (לְמֹד) the fear of the Lord of which he speaks; one of the principal roles of the wise men in the Hebrew wisdom tradition was that of education. And the words are addressed to "children" (בָּנִים: literally, "sons"); the sense is not precisely *children*, but *pupils* or *students*, the Hebrew word being the conventional form of address employed by the wise men (viz. teachers) toward the members of their class (cf. Prov 4:1). The question of v 13 is a pedagogical question and establishes the subject matter which will be the essence of the instruction to follow. The lesson concerns the most fundamental of all issues—the meaning of human life! To "take pleasure in life," to "love days" (v 13b), and to "see goodness," are expressions which designate a person who has found the fulfillment of human existence by discerning its divine purpose and by living appropriately and properly. Who is such a person? How may such fulfillment be found? The instruction follows.

(14–15) נְ֫ם The question in v 13 is followed by a series of imperatives; the answer is contained in an exhortation to live a life which embodies the principles of the fear of the Lord (v 12). And the response makes it clear that the moral life embraces both speech and action. With respect to speech, there is to be neither "evil" nor "deceit." With respect to action, there is to be a *shunning* of evil, and an embracing of the good. It is clear that the required integrity of speech and action presupposes integrity of mind, for words and works are rooted in a person's inner intentions. And it is also clear that the life of speech and that of action are intimately related, for evil words can be as destructive as evil acts. Thus the tongue may be an enormously powerful force for evil (Jas 3:4–6), and wars are spawned within human hearts (Jas 4:1); hence, the imperative to integrity in speech and action is supplemented by an imperative enjoining the pursuit of *peace* (v 15). Wars arise within human beings and are activated by evil speech and action; conversely, peace is not a natural environment in the world of sinful human beings, but an environment which must be sought and pursued.

(16–17) עַ-פ In the tradition of the wisdom literature, there is now a contrast between the estate of the righteous and that of the wicked. The righteous are blessed and protected; there is no place where they are beyond the divine vision and there is no crisis so distant that God cannot hear their cry for help. The positive metaphor of the all-seeing eye of God is converted in v 17 to the negative imagery of a divinely angry countenance, set firmly against the perpetrators of evil. The divine opposition quells not only the evil of wicked persons, but also eliminates the memory of them from the earth, thereby nullifying the ambitions of those whose evil deeds have goals of personal greatness outlasting even the limits of their mortality. On the elimination of the "memory" of people from the world, see further Ps 9:6–7 and *Comment.*

(18) צ "They cry out": the antecedent of "they" is presumably the "righteous" (v 16); see v 18, note a (above). It is possible, however, that the antecedent is the evildoers of v 17, who are here depicted as repenting and receiving deliverance from God in time of trouble.

(19–21) קֹשׁ The psalmist now speaks of the Lord's salvation and help to the righteous; the striking feature of these verses is provided by the contexts within which the divine aid may be experienced. The righteous may be "broken-hearted" and "spiritually crushed"; they may have many afflictions (v 20). God's presence is experienced *within* these crisis situations; there is no divine guarantee that the righteous will escape the crises and trials of mortal existence. Thus, the psalmist espouses a more sophisticated form of wisdom theology than that of the friends of Job. The "fear of the Lord" (v 16) which was the substance of the psalmist's instruction could well lead one into a path of life characterized by hardship and difficulty, but it brought with it the divine presence which made possible triumph in the midst of trial. On the other hand, it was equally the case that the fear of the Lord did carry with it the promise of divine protection; God does watch over the physical welfare of his people and protect them (v 20). The wisdom theology offers no easy alternatives with respect to life's hardships; there may be protection from evil or deliverance in evil, but the only thing common to the lives of the righteous is the continuation of the divine oversight and care.

(22–23) ת The psalmist concludes with another contrast of the estate of the wicked and of the righteous (see also vv 16–17). The end of evil persons once again illustrates the boomerang effect of wickedness. The "wicked," who are defined as those who do evil, would be slain by evil. Those who hate and thereby make desolate the righteous, shall be desolate themselves. The judgment is thus a kind of divinely ordained freedom to remain within the terrible horizons of life—desolation and evil—which wicked persons have freely established for themselves. In contrast, God's servants would be redeemed (cf. Ps 25:22) and delivered from desolation.

Explanation

The acrostic psalms, by virtue of their literary structure, embrace a variety of thoughts and insights that cannot easily be subsumed under a single heading. Such is the case with Ps 34 with its internal blend of thanksgiving and wisdom. And so it is not surprising that through the course of its history, the psalm has had different associations for different persons and different periods. The most ancient association is that reflected in the title, the association with an incident of stress and inner anguish in David's life. And in NT times, it may well be the case that the psalm was related in a marginal sense to the suffering of the Messiah, for John appears to quote the psalm in his account of the crucifixion (John 19:36; cf. Ps 34:21). By the time of the early church, the psalm was identified and utilized as an eucharistic text, for its invitation ("taste and see how good the Lord is . . .", v 9) appeared to be so appropriate to the eucharistic meal. And if one were to pick a theme from this ancient psalm for the twentieth century, it would probably be from v 15: "seek peace and pursue it!" For although the understanding that peace does not merely arrive, but must be pursued ardently, has been in this world for a long time, the history of the present century gives little evidence that the ancient lesson has been learned.

In the context of OT theology, one of the psalm's most profound insights concerns the instruction on the *fear of the Lord* (v 12). This *fear* is not only the foundation of the wisdom tradition, but it is also one of the biblical doctrines most easily abused or misunderstood. The fear of the Lord is indeed the foundation of life, the key to joy in life and long and happy days. But it is not a guarantee that life will be always easy, devoid of the difficulties that may seem to mar so much of human existence. The fear of the Lord establishes joy and fulfilment in all of life's experiences. It may mend the broken heart, but it does not prevent the heart from being broken; it may restore the spiritually crushed, but it does not crush the forces that may create oppression. The psalm, if fully grasped, dispels the naiveté of that faith which does not contain within it the strength to stand against the onslaught of evil.

A Royal Psalm for International Crisis (35:1–28)

Bibliography

Asensio, F. "Sobre la marcha del salmo 35." *EstBib* 31 (1972) 5–16. **De Moor, J. C.** "Frustula Ugaritica." *JNES* 24 (1965) 359–60. **Dietrich, M., Loretz, O., Sanmartín, J.,** "Der Eilbrief PRU 2.20 (= RS 15.07)." *UF* 6 (1974) 471–72. **Gaster, T. H.** "Old Testament Notes." *VT* 4 (1954) 73. **Miller, P. D.** "Ugaritic ĠZR and Hebrew 'ZR II." *UF* 2 (1970) 159–75. **Ouellette, J.** "Variantes qumrâniennes du Livre des Psaumes." *RevQ* 7 (1969) 105–23.

Translation

¹ For David.[a]
   Strive, O Lord, with those who strive against me; [b]   (3+2)
   fight with those who fight me.
² *Take up shield and buckler*   (3+2)
   and rise up in my aid. [a]
³ *And draw out spear and pike* [a]   (3+2)
   to meet my pursuers.
   Say to my soul: (2+2)
   "I am your victory!"
⁴ *They shall be humiliated and put to shame,*   (2+2)
   the ones who seek my life;
   they shall be turned back and ashamed,   (3+2)
   the ones who devise my downfall.
⁵ *Let them be like chaff before the wind,*   (3+3)
   with the Lord's angel chasing them. [a]
⁶ *Let their path be darkness and slippery surfaces,* [a]   (3+3)
   with the Lord's angel pursuing them.
⁷ *For without cause,* [a] *they hid their net* [b] *for me;*   (3+3)
   a pit [c] *they dug to entrap me.* [d]
⁸ *Let ruin come upon him unawares,*   (3+3?+2)
   and let the net that he hid enmesh him;
   he shall indeed fall into ruin!
⁹ *Then my soul shall rejoice in the Lord;*   (3+2)
   it shall exult in his victory.
¹⁰ *All my bones shall say:*   (3+3)
   "O Lord, who is like you?
   One who delivers the weak from the one too strong for him,   (4+3)
   and the weak and poor from the one who robs him."
¹¹ *Violent witnesses shall arise;*   (3+3)
   they shall interrogate [a] *me on matters of which I am ignorant.*
¹² *They repay me evil*   (2+2+2)
   instead of good;
   they lie in wait [a] *for my life.*
¹³ *But when they were sick, I wore sackcloth,*   (4+3+3)
   I afflicted myself with fasting,
   but my prayer returned unanswered. [a]
¹⁴ *As for a friend, as for one like a brother to me,*   (3+2+2)
   as with one mourning a mother, I walked about,
   dressed in black, bowed in grief.
¹⁵ *But when I stumbled, they rejoiced and gathered together;*   (3+2)
   they gathered together against me!
   Oppressors [a]—*I didn't even know them!—*   (3+2)
   they tore me apart and would not desist. [b]
¹⁶ *With the profanities of derisive mockery,* [a]   (3+3)
   they gnash their teeth against me.

¹⁷ *O Lord, how long will you look on?*   (3+3+2)
  Rescue my life from their ruin,
  my existence from the young lions.
¹⁸ *I will thank you in the great congregation;*   (3+3)
  I will praise you in the mighty crowd.
¹⁹ *Let not my enemies rejoice over me wrongfully,*   (3+3)
  or those who hate me without cause maliciously wink the eye.
²⁰ *For they do not speak of peace,*   (3+2+3)
  but against the quiet ones of the land ᵃ
  they devise deceitful declarations.
²¹ *And they opened wide their mouths against me;*   (3+3+2)
  they said, "Aha! Aha!
  our eyes have seen it!"
²² *You have seen it, O Lord; don't be silent;*   (3+3)
  O Lord, do not be far away from me.
²³ *Awake, and rise up to my defense,*   (3+3)
  to contend for me, O my God and my Lord.
²⁴ *Judge me in* ᵃ *your righteousness, O Lord my God,*   (4+2)
  and let them not rejoice over me.
²⁵ *Let them not say in their hearts,*   (2+2+2)
  "Aha, just what we wanted!" ᵃ
  Let them not say, "We have devoured him!"
²⁶ *They shall be both ashamed and humiliated,*   (3+2)
  they who rejoiced in my misfortune.
  They shall wear shame and ignominy,   (3+2)
  they who made themselves mighty at my expense.
²⁷ *They shall shout out and rejoice,*   (2+2)
  they who delight in my vindication!
  And they shall say continuously: (2+2+3)
  "May the Lord be magnified,
  He who delights in his servant's peace."
²⁸ *Then my tongue shall proclaim your righteousness,*   (3+2)
  nothing but your praise all day long.

Notes

1.a. *G* (A, L) adds "a psalm" (מזמור).

1.b. Eight Heb. mss (De-Rossi, IV, 24) and *S* read ריבי; "my case, my strife." But the parallel line suggests the above translation (after MT) is preferable.

2.a. Dahood translates: "to my battle," taking עזרתי as from עזר (II) = Ugaritic *ġzr*, "lad, warrior." The rendition is unlikely; while the Hebrew-Ugaritic term has military associations (including "hero, mighty one"), it does not clearly signify battle and is probably incorrect in this context; see P. D. Miller, *UF* 2 (1970) 168.

3.a. On סָגַר meaning "pike, javelin," see Dahood, *Psalms I*, 210, with the literature cited there.

5.a. Reading דְּחָם (with plural suffix) after *G*.

6.a. Dahood's rendition, "destruction," is possible, relating the root חלק to Ugaritic *ḫlq*, "to perish" (*Psalms I*, 211); but the translation above, based on חלק (II), "to be slippery," makes equally good sense and is better attested in Hebrew.

7.a. Dahood (*Psalms I*, 211) translates חנם by "stealthily," claiming a root חנן, "to be stealthy," related to Ugaritic *ḫnn*. The Ugaritic evidence for *ḫnn* "to ambush" (and hence "be stealthy") is not strong. Dahood cites as a key text *UT* 1020: 8–10 (= PRU. 2.20); apart from two texts in which ḫnn is used in personal names, this is the only text in which the Ugaritic term is used. Its meaning is almost certainly not "ambush" (contra Dahood), but "incapacitate, disarm" (even "seize"). See further de Moor, *JNES* 24 (1965) 359–60 and M. Dietrich, *et al.*, *UF* 6 (1974) 471–72.

7.b. שחת, "pit," is omitted from the first line and transposed to the second line, following the implication of *S*, thus providing better sense and grammatical structure.

7.c. On "pit," see note b (above); the second חנם (occurring also in the first line) is omitted (cf. *S*), being replaced by שחת, thus creating a more balanced bi-colon.

7.d. Literally, "for my soul."

11.a. The verb שאל "ask" is used here in the technical legal sense of questioning a witness, cross-questioning, similar to Akkadian ša'alu; see Gaster, *VT* 4 (1954) 73.

12.a. Reading שכול (with Kraus, *Psalmen*, 426), the ל in MT's שכול being deleted as dittography. Dahood's reference to a Shaphel form of כלה is possible *(Psalms I*, 213), but the reference to Ugaritic škllt is misleading; the Ugaritic form is almost certainly not an "obscure personage in a class with š'tqt," but a noun meaning "enclosure," analogous to Akk. šuklultu (Gibson, *CML²*, 97, 158).

13.a. Literally, "my prayer returned upon my breast."

15.a. Reading תכים with 4QPsᵃ, in place of MT's anomalous נכים; see Ouellette, *RevQ* 7 (1969) 108.

15.b. Dahood adds to v 15 בחנפי (from v 16) and translates: "did not desist from slandering me" *(Psalms I*, 214). The Ugaritic evidence adduced gives little support to the translation of חנף by "slander"; Ugaritic ḫnp (like Hebrew חנף) has the sense of "profane, irreligious" (cf. Gibson, *CML²*, 147, "haughty" and Aistleitner, *WUS*, #1053). The term ḫnp is used to describe Anat's character, but to deduce the sense "slander" from the character of that deity (cf. Gordon, *UT* #981, and Dahood, 214) is a dubious procedure, given the multitude of negative characteristics attributed to Anat.

16.a. The translation of this line, which is uncertain, is based on the reading לעגי לעג, interpreted as a superlative, "the worst of all possible mockery."

20.a. The phrase, רגעי־ארץ ("the quiet ones of the land"), a *hapax legomenon*, is a poetic description of the pious congregation or nation as a whole; see further Mowinckel, *The Psalms in Israel's Worship*, II, 87.

24.a. Reading בצדקך, with six Heb. mss (De-Rossi, IV, 25).

25.a. Literally, "Aha, our soul!"

Form/Structure/Setting

Psalm 35 is commonly described as an *individual lament* or a *prayer;* both descriptions are appropriate in general terms, though neither do justice to the particular language of the psalm and its military overtones. Attempts to relate the psalm to the situation of an accused man facing trial are also unsatisfactory, as noted by Rogerson and McKay *(Psalms 1–50*, 160); some of the language does indeed have legal overtones (cf. Asensio, *EstBib* 31 [1972] 5–16), but it requires interpretation in a context larger than that of the law courts. Eaton is almost certainly correct in interpreting the psalm as a royal psalm to be interpreted in an international context *(Kingship and the Psalms*, 41–42).

The psalm may be divided into three sections. (1) In the first section, the psalmist (identified as the king) prays for God's assistance in battle (vv 1–3), declares the eventual downfall of the enemy (vv 4–8), and anticipates the praise that will emerge from victory (vv 9–10). (2) There follows a lament-like passage (vv 11–16), describing the king's enemies, which moves to a prayer for rescue (v 17), followed by further anticipation of praise after deliverance (v 18). (3) The last major section begins with a prayer directed against enemies (vv 19–26); the assurance that the prayer would be answered is expressed both in the anticipated worship of the people as a whole (v 27) and of the psalmist individually (v 28).

The external situation which must be envisaged is one that is both military and legal; almost certainly, the king faces the threat of war from foreign enemies, who in turn are using as an excuse for war certain purported violations of a treaty agreement. It is the background of an international treaty, between the king (representing Israel) and a foreign power, which provides the appropriate framework within which both the military and the legal language may be interpreted. The details giving rise to the international treaty context are elaborated in the *Comment* (below).

Though the evidence is not firm, it is reasonable to suppose that the psalm would have been utilized within the temple, perhaps in a liturgical setting, either as a consequence of the grave military threat, or else prior to the king's departure for battle to meet his adversary. If the latter were the case, then there are clearly general parallels between Ps 35 and Ps 20. The congregational setting of the ritual is indicated by the reference to the "great congregation" (v 18), to the "quiet ones" (v 20; see note a), and by the substance of v 27, which may be interpreted as a congregational response of praise (though it is anticipated, rather than actual, in the ritual).

Comment

The threat of war (35:1–10). The king begins by praying for God's military aid against his enemies. He prays that God *strive* and *fight* for him; at first sight, the two terms appear simply to be poetic synonyms, but the nuance of the first term may be particularly significant in the context of the psalm as a whole. The word "strive" (ריב) is commonly used as a legal term; here, the parallelism with *fight* (לחם) suggests a military nuance, but the psalm as a whole suggests that the military conflict in turn has legal ramifications, namely those associated with an international treaty. Thus, the king's opening prayer is that God would fight both his legal case with respect to treaty and also his battle (which might be the same thing, ultimately). The wording of the prayer in vv 2–3 indicates that the military nature of the threat is uppermost in the mind of the king, who prays that God the warrior (cf. Exod 15:3; Ps 24:8) would rise up on his behalf. The poetic language describes God as a hero of the infantry, with both hand-shield and buckler (the large body-shield, probably carried by an aide), and armed with spear and pike. The words "I am your victory" sound like either an oracle, pronounced by a priest prior to departure for war, or a battle cry shouted on the battlefield (perhaps by one of the priests, who traditionally accompanied the army into battle). In context, however, it is neither oracle nor battle cry, but an anticipation of the victory that would come when God rose up on behalf of the psalmist.

Confident in ultimate success, the king proceeds to a declaration concerning the coming doom that would meet the enemy (vv 4–8). The declaration is intermixed with prayer, as the king's confidence struggles with natural anxiety. His prayers, or wishes, introduced by "Let" (vv 5, 6, 8), sound like adaptations of the kind of treaty curses that would have been written into the treaty agreement between the king and the foreign power; hence, the desire that those curses come into effect represents the king's desire for vindication in the case against him. The treaty curses affected the party that was unfaithful to the treaty stipulations; the fulfillment of those curses, as is desired in vv 5–8, would simultaneously be a vindication of the king's own integrity with respect to the treaty stipulations.

Again, in vv 9–10, the psalmist returns to the anticipation of victory and vindication. The expression of the Lord's incomparability (v 10b) is typical of victory songs (cf. Exod 15:11), for in granting victory, the Lord demonstrates that he is the real master of history, superior to the so-called gods of other nations (cf. C. J. Labuschagne, *The Incomparability of Yahweh in the Old Testament* [1966], 22–24).

The background to the coming conflict (35:11–18). The legal context reappears in v 11 with the words "witnesses" and "interrogate." Figuratively (or perhaps even literally), the king is interrogated and hears witnesses give evidence against him with respect to some supposed violation of treaty obligations. And yet, as he protests, he is the one who has been faithful to the treaty stipulations while his enemies, even in the act of bringing charges against him, are being unfaithful (v 12); the good he has done is repaid by the evil they seek to do to him. In vv 13–14, the psalmist recalls his own positive actions in fulfillment of treaty obligations. Again, the actions described are typical of those stipulated in international treaties. The sickness of a fellow monarch, linked by treaty relationship, evoked acts of fasting and sorrow in the king; in terms both of duty and of fellow feelings, the king had been faithful in these obligations. The reference to "friend" and "brother" (v 14) is partly a poetic description of his (former) attitude to his treaty partner, but partly also a description utilizing the language of treaty (cf. Eaton, *Kingship and the Psalms*, 42). But again, the psalmist complains, his own faithful fulfillment of treaty obligations was never reciprocated in similar acts by his partner; the treaty partner had become an enemy, rejoicing in the king's misfortunes and illegally oppressing him (vv 15–16).

The king's reflection on the inconsistency between his own and his partner's responses to treaty obligations culminates once again in prayer (v 17). "How long will you look on?"—the words are highly significant, in that the Lord was the king's own witness in the sealing of the treaty relationship and thus was ultimately responsible for overseeing the integrity and faithfulness of the two partners toward their obligations. The prayer seeks to bring about the divine action which was explicitly agreed upon by the partners to the treaty at the time it was signed. And again, the prayer is followed by an anticipation of the thanksgiving and praise that would follow God's response to prayer. Though the reference to the "great congregation" is formally anticipatory, to be enacted in the future, there is little doubt that the same "great congregation" (the representatives of the nation of Israel) provided the context in which the present ritual was undertaken.

A prayer for victory (35:19–28). The king continues to pray both for his own vindication and for the downfall of his unfaithful treaty partner. "They do not speak of peace" (v 20 שלום); the word "peace" was a central term in the language of international treaties, specifying the relationship between the treaty partners. (On the use of the cognate term *salīmum* in the Mari texts, see A. Glock, *Warfare in Mari and Early Israel,* 62 [n. 79], 215–16. On "peace" and "friendship" in Near Eastern treaty terminology, see W. L. Moran, "A Note on the Treaty Terminology of the Sefire Stelas," *JNES* 22 [1963] 173–76 and D. R. Hillers, "A Note on Some Treaty Terminology in the Old Testament," *BASOR* 176 [1964] 46–47.) That the partner "did not speak of peace" was an indication that his actions were in contravention of the treaty stipulations. Verses 21–22 raise again (cf. v. 17) the issue of the witness to the treaty relationship. The enemy claim that they "have seen it" (v 21; viz. an act by the king in breach of treaty obligations), but God was the true and legal witness to the treaty. The psalmist, knowing that God had "seen it" and therefore knew the truth of the matter, prays that God not remain silent, but arise to his defense and aid. Hence, the king's prayer to be judged (v 24) is in effect a prayer for a legal declaration by the witness to the treaty concerning where innocence and guilt lie in the treaty dispute.

Confident that his vindication would eventually come, the psalmist anticipates the praise that his own people (the "great congregation" of v 18) would eventually offer to God (v 27). God himself would eventually grant the peace (v 27) which should have been guaranteed by the treaty itself. And the psalmist concludes with anticipation of his own praise of God's righteousness, which would become evident eventually in his answer to the king's prayer (v 28).

Explanation

Psalm 35 may be perceived as a royal, or national lament, equivalent to Ps 28, an individual psalm which has as its background difficulties arising from some kind of human covenant relationship. Here, in Ps 35, the scene is a larger one, for though it is a king who has difficulties with a foreign partner, the two individual persons represent two nation states. Thus the psalm provides some insight concerning the response of a nation's leader to a crisis of awesome proportions with respect to Israel's survival as a nation. The crisis of surviving a foreign military threat was difficult enough, but what added to the frustration was the fact that the threat rose in the form of an ally, one toward whom the psalmist had behaved properly in every legal respect. Innocent of any evil acts which might have justified the emergence of such a crisis, the king falls back on the ultimate defense of his nation, namely God, who as witness to the treaty perceived precisely where the fault lay with regard to the breaking of the treaty regulations. Hence the psalmist's declarations of innocence and his desire to be judged do not rest in any false piety or self-righteousness; they are based only on the conscious awareness that the treaty stipulations have been faithfully observed. And his prayer that defeat and disaster fall upon his one-time ally is not simply human vindictiveness, but a desire that the treaty curses come into effect, thereby delivering the king from the unwarranted crisis and at the same time vindicating God as the Lord and King of Israel.

The broader theological implications of the psalm are brought out clearly by the quotation of v 19 (cf. v 7) in the NT (John 15:25). Jesus warns his disciples that when they experience the world's hatred, they should remember the world hated him first and that its hatred was *without cause*. But the purpose of the psalm is transformed in the life and ministry of Jesus. Whereas the Hebrew king prayed for deliverance from the hatred of enemies, Jesus eventually succumbed to that hatred in his death. And whereas the Hebrew king invoked the curses of a treaty to escape hatred, Jesus underwent human hatred to eliminate the curses suspended over human lives as a consequence of their sin. In other words, the death of Jesus as a consequence of human hatred became the act by which a new treaty, or new covenant, was to be forged between God and mankind. It was not a treaty between the nation states of this world, but rather a covenant making possible for all mankind citizenship in the kingdom of God.

A Meditation on Wickedness and Lovingkindness (36:1-13)

Bibliography

Le Mat, L. A. F. *Textual Criticism and Exegesis of Psalm 36. A Contribution to the Study of the Hebrew Book of Psalms.* Utrecht: Kemink and Zoon, 1957. **Leveen, J.** "Textual Problems in the Psalms." *VT* 21 (1971) 48–58.

Translation

¹ For the musical director. For the Lord's servant. For David.
² (1) *An oracle.*[a]

Transgression belongs to the wicked person; (2+2)
it is in the midst of his [b] *heart.*
There is no fear of God (2+2)
before his eyes.
³ (2) *For he flatters himself too much in his own eyes* (3+3)
to find his iniquity and to hate it.
⁴ (3) *The words of his mouth are wickedness and deceitfulness;* (3+3)
he has given up being wise, doing good.
⁵ (4) *He devises wickedness upon his bed;* (3+3+3)
he sets himself on a path that is not good;
he does not reject what is wrong.
⁶ (5) *O Lord, your lovingkindness is in* [a] *the heavens,* (3+3?)
your faithfulness reaches to the clouds.
⁷ (6) *Your righteousness is like the marvelous* [a] *mountains,* (3+3)
your judgment like the mighty deep.
You deliver both man and beast, O Lord; (4+4+4)
⁸ (7) *how precious is your lovingkindness, O God,*[a]
that human beings find refuge in the shadow of your wings.

9 (8) *They are refreshed from the rich provision of your house,*   (3+3)
     and you make them drink from the river of your delights.

10 (9) *For with you is the fountain of life;*   (3+3)
     in your light, we shall see light!

11(10) *Prolong your lovingkindness to those who know you*   (3+3)
     and your righteousness to the upright of heart.

12(11) *May the foot of the proud not come against me,*   (3+3)
     and the hand of the wicked not drive me away.[a]

13(12) *The workers of wickedness were desolated* [a]*; they fell down.*   (4+4)
     They were thrown down and unable to rise.

Notes

2.a. In MT, נאם ("oracle") is linked to פשע ("transgression") as if in construct, meaning "an oracle of transgression." But such a usage of נאם is without parallel in the OT and has provoked numerous efforts to resolve the apparent problem in the Hebrew text; for a perceptive survey of the earlier attempts to solve the problem, see Delitzsch, *Biblical Commentary on the Psalms*, II, 2–4. Leveen (art. cit., 55–56) proposes to point פשע as a participle and translates: "the transgressor says within his heart . . . ," but the solution involves too radical a reorganization of the Hebrew text to be convincing. For further analysis of the critical problems in the text, see Le Mat, *Textual Criticism*, 4–9, and Kraus, *Psalmen 1–59*, 431–32. The solution adopted above is to take נאם as a word standing independently, describing the entire first part of the psalm (vv 2–5), rather than being bound to the following word.

2.b. Reading לבו, with several Heb. mss (De-Rossi, IV, 25), as also in *G, S,* and *Vg.*

6.a. MT's בהשמים ("in the heavens"), where one would expect בשמים is unusual, but probably correct; see Briggs, *Psalms*, 321 and compare with 57:11: עד־שמים ("unto heaven") (without the article).

7.a. Literally, "mountains of El," though here אל functions to express the superlative magnificence of mountains in the comparison.

8.a. אלהים is taken with the preceding words in v 8, parallel to יהוה in v 7; ובני (אדם) ("human beings") is thus taken as opening a new line and the *athnah* is removed from under אדם.

12.a. תנדני is parsed as a Hiph. form of נוד. Dahood translates "fling me down," assuming a root נדה (Ugaritic *ndy*); see *Psalms I*, 224. The evidence for Ugaritic *ndy* is far from certain (cf. M. Held, *JAOS* 88 [1968], 93), though the sense "drive away, expel" is reasonably well attested: Aistleitner, *WUS*, #1756. But Dahood's translation remains a strong possibility.

13.a. שם ("there") is anomalous in context, having no antecedent or clear sense. שממו ("*were* desolated") is read, as suggested by the parallelism with two verbs in the following line (after Kraus, *Psalmen 1–59*, 432, and others).

Form/Structure/Setting

A variety of types have been proposed with respect to the classification of Ps 36: *individual lament, national lament,* and *wisdom poetry.* Dahood, not unreasonably, remarks that "the coexistence of three literary types within a poem of thirteen verses points up the limitations of the form critical approach to the Psalter" (*Psalms I,* 218). The problem of classification arises from the recognition that the three principal parts of the psalm appear to belong to different form-critical categories: (1) vv 2–5, wisdom (with overtones of lament); (2) vv 6–10, hymnic; (3) vv 11–13, principally prayer. While in some instances diversities of type in a single psalm can be explained against the background of a liturgical setting, no such solution is readily available for Ps 36.

The problems of this psalm are analogous to those of Ps 14, and a similar solution to the problems is proposed. The psalm must be viewed primarily as a literary and devotional composition, in which the poet has blended different literary types in his creative purpose. Against this background the psalm should be set in the wisdom tradition, though it does not adhere to any distinctive literary form. The basic structure is like that of Ps 1, though in reverse. The psalmist begins with a meditation on the wicked person and his evil deeds (vv 2–5). Then he passes on to a reflection of the righteous person, not in terms of his positive characteristics, but describing in hymnic language the Lord's *lovingkindness* (vv 6, 8) toward mankind. The last three verses (vv 11–13) revert to the first two themes, in a chiastic structure, with a kind of double *inclusio,* as follows:

A.   The behavior of the *wicked* (vv 2–5)
     (note רשע in v 2)
B.   The Lord's *lovingkindness* (vv 6–10)
     (note חסד in v 6)
B′.   Prayer for *lovingkindness* (v 11)
     (note חסד in v 11)
A′.   Prayer for protection from the *wicked* (vv 12–13)
     (note רשע in v 12).

When the overall literary structure of the psalm is perceived, the unity of the psalm is evident. While it stands in the wisdom tradition, the psalm does not remain at a dispassionate distance from its subject matter, but identifies itself intimately with the subject in the concluding words of prayer (vv 11–13).

Comment

The behavior of the wicked (36:2–5). The initial problem is to determine the intent of the word "oracle," standing independently at the head of the psalm (cf. note a, on v 2). The term "oracle" (נאם) is almost always followed by the divine name יהוה, who is the source of oracles (e.g. Isa 30:1; 31:9). One may propose as a working hypothesis the view that the poet takes a divine oracle concerning the wicked as a starting point for his literary composition; the oracle would have contained vv 2–5, as a descriptive portion, and v 13, which may originally have had a more declarative and judgmental form. The fate of the wicked was then separated from the more descriptive portion of the oracle, and a striking literary contrast created by the insertion of the passage concerning God's *lovingkindness.* Whereas the original oracle would have been introduced by נאם יהוה, the divine name was removed in the new literary creation which has survived as Ps 36.

The description of the wicked person indicates that the source of his error was deep-seated in the mind (literally, "heart," v 2). Having no fear of God, he effectively blinded himself with self-adoration; having then only himself to go by as a measure for morality, he was totally unable either to know or to hate his own iniquity (v 3). Having dispensed with the fear of God, which was the foundation of wisdom (Prov 1:7), he had become a moral cripple. In both speech and action (v 4), he was totally dedicated to wickedness. In bed at night, rather than reflecting on God's goodness (Ps 63:7 [6]), he devised new mischief for the morning. Instead of choosing the good path, he deliberately chose the path that is not good, apparently not knowing that its end was destruction (Ps 1:6)

The Lord's lovingkindness (36:6–10). "Lovingkindness," which is God's basic characteristic in the context of covenant, is amplified by "faithfulness" (poetically synonymous); the expression "in the heavens" does not imply distance, but something which has no boundaries or limits (as is also implied by the reference to "clouds," v 6b). The extolling of God's virtues in relation to mankind is pursued further in v 7; the "marvelous mountains" and the "mighty deep" (viz. the ocean, not the chaotic waters of mythology) are vast in terms of human conception, and thus begin to indicate the immenseness of God's "righteousness" and "judgment" (in effect, his *justice* in dealings with human beings).

God's provision of protection is expressed by the words "shadow of your wings" (v 8), sometimes taken to allude to the wings of the seraphim in the temple, though Le Mat holds, somewhat improbably, that the metaphor is adapted from the familiar Egyptian symbol of the winged sun-disc (Le Mat, *Textual Criticism*, 23; cf. Keel, *The Symbolism of the Biblical World*, 28). It is more likely that the metaphor of protection is drawn directly from nature and is thus comparable to another metaphor derived from birds in Deut 32:11, and known also in Near Eastern literature (e.g. lines 38–46 of the Epic of Lugalbanda; C. Wilcke, *Das Lugalbanda-epos*, [1969] 94–95).

While the "house" referred to in v 9 might be an allusion to the temple of Jerusalem, with its sacrificial meals and libations, it is more likely that the poet is describing God's world as a whole, in which for mankind and animals alike (v 7) God provides both rich sustenance and ample refreshing drink.

In v 10 God is described as the source of all life in this world, but the reference is to mortal life, not everlasting life, as proposed by Dahood (*Psalms I*, 221–22). The entire context strongly implies that it is life in *this world* of which the poet writes. And the Ugaritic texts which Dahood draws on in his argument are misleading: UT 2 Aqht (*CTA* 17), vi. 27–31. The lines do indeed refer to eternal life, but they are addressed to Aqhat by Anat; as the hero clearly recognizes, Anat is lying in her promise of eternal life, for death is the lot of all mankind, according to the standard convictions of Canaanite theology (which, in this matter, were practically the same as Hebrew theology). Thus the expression "fountain of life" (v 10) must be understood as the divine source of life in this world, just as the teaching of the wise men may be a fountain of life in the present world (see Prov 13:14).

"In your light" (v 10) is probably an abbreviated form of the familiar expression "in the light of your countenance"; see further Ps 4:7 and the *Comment*.

A prayer for God's lovingkindness (36:11). While the lovingkindness of God extends in a certain sense to all living beings (v 8), the psalmist now converts the preceding hymnic meditation into a prayer that those who know the Lord may perpetually experience such goodness. The expression "those who know you" could also be rendered "those who love you," given the various nuances of the verb ידע. The "upright of heart" (v 11b) are contrasted with the wicked, for whom transgression is "in the midst of the heart" (v 2b).

A prayer for protection from the wicked (36:12–13). The meditation on the character of the wicked (vv 2–5) is also converted into a prayer, for the wicked not only cut themselves off from God's lovingkindness, but may also be a constant and powerful threat to the survival of the righteous. The final verse (v 13) appears to be a modified form of the original divine oracle concerning the wicked; see further *Comment* on vv 2–5 above.

Explanation

Whereas Ps 1 contrasts the way of the wicked with that of the righteous person, Ps 36 contrasts the way of the wicked with the lovingkindness of God. And the folly of the wicked person emerges not only from the error of his way, but from the fact that God's lovingkindness and deliverance are extended to human beings and beasts alike; nothing precluded them from the goodness of God, except their own folly and self-induced blindness (v 3). It is no doubt the human blindness to sin which makes the psalm ultimately appropriate in a broader setting. When St. Paul quotes v 2, "there is no fear of God before their eyes" (Rom 3:18), he is demonstrating in his catalog description of human unrighteousness, that, apart from the lovingkindness of God, all human beings would fall within the category described in Ps 32:2–5. But in describing the righteousness which may come by faith (Rom 3:21–31), he is developing the new meaning which the gospel imparts to the *lovingkindness* of God in the hymnic portion of the ancient psalm (36:6–10).

An Acrostic Psalm of Wisdom   (37:1-40)

Bibliography

Allegro, J. M. "A Newly Discovered Fragment of a Commentary on Psalm XXXVII From Qumran." *PEQ* 86 (1954) 69–75. **Ouellette, J.** "Variantes qumrâniennes du Livre des Psaumes." *RevQ* 7 (1969) 105–23.

Translation

1   For David
    (א) *Do not fret because of evil persons;*   (2+3)
        do not envy those who do wrong.
2   *For like grass they will wither quickly,*   (3+3)
        and like green sprouts they will die away.

³ (ב) *Trust in the Lord and do good;*   (4+4)
   dwell in the land and find safe pasture;
⁴   *and take delight in the Lord,*   (2+3)
   and he will give you your heart's desires.
⁵ (ג) *Commit your way to the Lord*   (4+4)
   and trust in him; then he will do it.
⁶   *And he will make your righteousness come forth as a light*   (3+2)
   and your justice like the midday sun.
⁷ (ד) *Be still before the Lord*   (2+2)
   and wait patiently for him.
   Do not fret because they make their way successful,   (3+3)
   because people carry out their schemes.
⁸ (ה) *Cease from anger and forget fury;*   (4+4?)
   do not fret—it only brings grief!
⁹   *For evil persons will be cut off,*   (2?+4?)
   but they that hope in the Lord shall inherit the land.
¹⁰ (ו) *But a little while, and the wicked will be no more!*   (4+4?)
   And I ᵃ *will watch his place carefully, but he won't be there.*
¹¹   *And the meek shall inherit the land*   (3+3)
   and shall take delight in great peace.
¹² (ז) *The wicked plot against the righteous*   (3+3)
   and gnash their teeth upon them;
¹³   *the Lord laughs at them,*   (2+3)
   *for he has seen that their time has come.*ᵃ
¹⁴ (ח) *Wicked persons drew the sword*   (3+2)
   and bent their bow
   to ᵃ *bring down the weak and the poor,*   (3+3)
   *to slaughter honest wayfarers.*ᵃ
¹⁵   *Their sword will enter their own heart,*   (3+2)
   and their bows will be broken.
¹⁶ (ט) *The little the righteous have is better*   (3+3)
   than the abundant ᵃ *wealth of wicked persons;*
¹⁷   *for the arms of the wicked shall be broken,*   (3?+3)
   but the Lord is watching over the righteous.
¹⁸ (י) *The Lord knows the days of the blameless,*   (3?+3)
   and their inheritance shall be forever.
¹⁹   *They shall not be ashamed in an evil time*   (3+3)
   and they shall be provided for in days of famine.
²⁰ (כ) *But the wicked shall perish,*ᵃ   (3+2)
   the Lord's enemies, too;
   they are consumed like the best of the pasture; ᵇ   (3+2)
   they are consumed in smoke.
²¹ (ל) *The wicked borrow and do not repay,*   (4+3)
   but the righteous are generous and give.
²²   *Surely those whom he blesses shall inherit the land,*   (3?+2)
   but those whom he curses shall be cut off.
²³ (מ) *A man's steps are established by the Lord,*ᵃ   (3?+2)
   and he takes pleasure in his way.

24 If he falls, he won't fall flat on his face,	(4+4)
for the Lord is holding his hand.	
25 (נ) I was young and now [a] I am old,	(3+3+3)
but I have not seen the righteous forsaken,	
or his posterity seeking food.[b]	
26 Every day they are generous and lending	(3+2)
and their posterity have become a blessing.	
27 (ס) Turn from evil and do good,	(3+2)
and dwell securely forever,	
28 for the Lord loves justice	(4+3?)
and will not forsake his pious ones.	
(ע) The unjust are destroyed forever,[a]	(3+3)
and the posterity of the wicked is cut off.	
29 The righteous shall inherit the land	(3+3)
and shall dwell in it forever.	
30 (פ) The righteous man's mouth utters wisdom,	(3+3)
and his tongue speaks justice.	
31 His God's instruction is in his heart,	(3+3)
and [a] his footsteps do not slip.	
32 (צ) The wicked lie in wait for the righteous	(3+2)
and seek to kill them.	
33 The Lord will not abandon them into their hand	(3+3)
and will not pronounce them guilty when they are brought to trial.	
34 (ק) Wait for the Lord	(2+2)
and observe his way,	
and he will exalt you to take possession of the land;	(3+3)
you will see when the wicked are cut off.	
35 (ר) I have seen the ruthlessly wicked,	(3+3)
flourishing [a] like a luxuriant native tree;	
36 But I [a] passed over and—lo!—he is no more;	(3+3)
and I sought him, but he could not be found.	
37 (ש) Observe the blameless and watch the upright,	(3+3)
for a peaceful man has a future.	
38 But transgressors shall be destroyed together;	(3+3)
the future of transgressors shall be cut off.	
39 (ת) The [a] victory of the righteous comes from the Lord,	(3+3)
their stronghold in time of stress.	
40 And the Lord helps them and rescues them;	(3+3+2)
he rescues them from the wicked and delivers them,	
for they sought refuge in him.	

Notes

10.a. The first person form of the verb is read, with 4QpPs 37, rather than MT's third person (Ouellette, art. cit., 107; Allegro, art. cit., 71).

13.a. Reading בא ("has come") for MT's יבא ("will come"), as suggested by the tense of the preceding verb (ראה "has seen"), with support from five Heb. mss (De-Rossi, IV, 26) and from 4QpPs 37 (Ouellette, art. cit., 108).

14.a. It is possible that these two lines are an addition to the original text. With them, the

ח-stanza has six lines, whereas the norm in this alphabetic acrostic is four lines. Verse 15 appears to be original, employing the same terminology as v 14 a-b. But the suggestion is conjectural, and the two lines make good sense in the context.

16.a. Reading רב ("abundant"), singular (after G, S), as qualifying wealth, rather than MT's רבים ("many").

20.a. Dahood suggests the translation "shrivel" for the verb אבד; Psalms I, 230. While the proposal might possibly be sustained on the basis of other usages in Hebrew, the Ugaritic evidence should be eliminated from the argument. Dahood argues that in UT 2031 (=PRU 5.31), the expression šd ubdy may mean "parched field," whence the sense "parch, shrivel" for the verb 'bd. But ubdy almost certainly has to do with "landholdings" provided in recompense for service (e.g., military service); hence šd ubdy means "grant of land" or "fields given for service." See further M. Heltzer, The Rural Community in Ancient Ugarit (1976), 67, and J. Gray, The Legacy of Canaan ², 233. In summary, it is preferable to remain with the commonly accepted meaning of אבד ("perish") in the translation of the psalm.

20.b. The translation of this line is uncertain; the rendition above assumes כַּר, "pasture," and moves the athnaḥ from כרים to the first כלו ("consumed"). But the disparity between MT, 4QpPs 37, and G, is such that any translation must remain dubious.

23.a. On the use of מן, in מיהוה, see GKC §121f.

25.a. וגם ("and now") is read (adding a conjunction to MT), with 4QpPs 37.

25.b. The third line of the verse is suspect, since it apparently increases the ל-stanza beyond the common four-line standard.

28.a. The translation of the line is based on the following text: עולים לעולם נשמדו. The initial word, required to introduce the ע-stanza, was presumably dropped accidentally by virtue of its similarity to the following לעולם ("forever"). The reading נשמדו ("are destroyed") follows the implication of G (cf. v 38).

31.a. A conjunction is added to לא after G and S.

35.a. MT's מתערה is problematic. The best solution is that of Fitzgerald who retains the text, interpreting it as a dialectal form of מתעלה "flourishing" (the Qal of עלה "ascend, grow" being used of trees and vegetation), in which the ל and the ר have been interchanged. See A. Fitzgerald, "The Interchange of L, N, and R in Biblical Hebrew," JBL 97 (1978) 486.

36.a. First person is read (for MT's third person), with 4QpPs 37 (Ouellette, art. cit., 109), G and S, as suggested by the parallelism.

39.a. The conjunction in ותשועת is omitted, as required by the acrostic pattern, with the support of a few Heb. mss (De-Rossi, IV, 26).

Form/Structure/Setting

Psalm 37 must be viewed primarily in terms of its alphabetic acrostic structure; for a general discussion of acrostic psalms, see further Excursus III, following the commentary on Pss 9–10. The basic unit in the acrostic structure of this psalm contains four lines, the only exceptions occurring in vv 14–15 (six lines) and vv 25–26 (five lines). Although there have been various attempts to define structures within the psalm other than the acrostic pattern (e.g. Ridderbos, Die Psalmen, (268–70), the acrostic is the only structure clearly established and, as is commonly the case in such psalms, it limits to some extent the inner development of thought.

The psalm stands firmly within the tradition of Wisdom and should be interpreted as an instructional poem. Its original purpose and setting is to be found in the wisdom schools, and like the Book of Proverbs it contains a sample of the curriculum employed in ancient Israel's moral and religious educational system. Like Proverbs, the psalm is a kind of anthology of wisdom sayings, the stanza for each letter of the alphabet containing a more or less complete proverb. A further parallel to the Book of Proverbs is to be found in the occasional autobiographical element introduced by the teacher (e.g.

vv 10, 25, 35, 36; cf. Prov 24:30–34). The alphabetic pattern of the psalm doubtless had a mnemonic function, the sequence of the letters prompting the students' memories as they sought to learn its contents by heart.

Though there is considerable diversity in the content of the psalm, the overall theme linking its parts together is *retribution* and *recompense*. The instruction provided guidance concerning how to live a moral and God-fearing life, and set a broader context within which to understand the apparent success and prosperity of those who lived irreligious and immoral lives. But the instruction is essentially practical, concerning how to live; it does not address in any theoretical sense the larger issues of justice and injustice (as is done in the Book of Job).

Comment

As was the practice with other acrostic psalms, the *Comment* follows the alphabetic units of the psalm.

א (37:1–2). With this section, compare Prov 24:19, 23:17, 24:1. There is a natural temptation to be upset and envious at the success of evil people, especially when the moral life creates hardship. But their success is superficial and not to be envied, for having no deep roots, they shrivel up as soon as testing comes along.

ב (37:3–4). The second proverb contains a contrast to the first, advocating not envy of the wicked, but *trust* in the Lord (cf. Ps. 4:6). Whereas the wicked live for themselves and by themselves, the righteous trust in God and receive from God their legitimate desires.

ג (37:5–6). See also Prov 16:3. The essence of living faith is concisely described. The acts of commitment and trust function like a trigger, releasing God's capacity to act. But it is not always evident that God acts in response to faith, and consequently the "righteousness" and "justice" of the faithful may often be veiled. The conviction expressed in v 6 is that setbacks are temporary, like clouds obscuring the sun, but that eventually God will move the clouds away to let the true light appear.

ד (37:7). This proverb advocates patience, not to be achieved by observing the instant-success schemes of this world, but by learning to wait patiently for God's appropriate time.

ה (37:8–9) The type of "anger" against which this warning is issued is almost certainly "anger against God;" it arises from the experience of trouble in a world where the wicked are evidently trouble-free, and as a consequence all of human experience seems to be grossly unfair. Again, patience is required, partly because such anger is futile, bringing only grief, and partly because the evil will eventually be cut-off (as the Canaanites were before them) and the faithful will eventually inherit the land (as their predecessors did).

ו (37:10–11). The theme of the preceding proverb is developed further. The personal touch "I will watch . . ." adds a note of authenticity to the instruction, indicating the teacher's faith is such that he is willing to watch for empirical evidence. "The meek shall inherit:" it is not so much that they inherit by virtue of their meekness, but that their inheritance is won by God, not by their own strivings. Likewise, it is only God who can ultimately give the "great peace" in which the faithful would take pleasure.

ז (37:12–13). The substance of this proverb was an experience common to the faithful, as is evident from the large number of *individual laments* in the Psalter. The problem with the wicked was not merely that they prospered, but also that very often their prosperity seemed to emerge directly from their oppression of the faithful and innocent. A larger perspective is provided; knowing that God sees it all and that the power of the wicked is limited in time, makes possible hope and patience on the part of the oppressed.

ח (37:14–15). The proverb enunciates the "boomerang principle" of evil; see further the commentary on Ps 7:12–16.

ט (37:16–17) See also Prov 15:16 and 16:18. The criticism is aimed not at wealth as such, nor does it imply that poverty is a lofty estate. The contrast is between the *righteous* and the *wicked*, yet it is an error easily committed by the righteous who are poor to think that wealth would improve their lives. The error required correction in the minds of the young, lest the pursuit of wealth for its own sake detract from the goal of righteous living. The "arms of the wicked shall be broken:" the language is probably metaphorical, indicating that the capacity to acquire wealth (symbolized by the *arms* which work) would be removed from the evil rich.

י (37:18–19). "The days of the blameless:" viz. each day of their lives is known to God and comes within his protective care. To translate "days" by "possessions," as does Dahood (*Psalms I*, 229) is misleading; (a) in part, because the Ugaritic data on which the translation is based is dubious (see note b on Ps 13:3, above), and (b) because it misses the overall sense of the passage and the parallelism with "time" in v 19. On God's provision in a time of famine, see 1 Kgs 17:1–16.

כ (37:20). The translation, and hence the meaning, of the second part of v 20 is uncertain. The implication may be that they will quickly perish, just as the green pasture of spring quickly dies and disappears with the heat of summer (so Rogerson and McKay, *Psalms 1–50*, 175).

ל (37:21–22). See also Prov 3:33. The contrast here is between takers and givers, the perpetual takers being cursed and the constant givers being blessed. The language of the proverb recalls the blessing and curse section of the Hebrew covenant: cf. Deut 28:12 and 28:44.

מ (37:23–24). See also Prov 24:16. The latter part of the proverb expresses succinctly the nature of divine support and protection. The righteous retain their humanity and still may fall in the walk of life; the divine hand ensures that the fall will not be so grave as to prohibit them from ever rising again and continuing to walk life's road.

נ (37:25–26). Again (see also v 10), the teacher inserts a personal observation, drawing on the length of his experience of this life to make a point; God does not abandon his people, but provides for both them and their children after them. But he could only proffer this wisdom from the perspective of age, for in the short run it might often appear that the righteous were forsaken. Hence the benefits of old age are offered to the young students, who simply have not lived long enough in this world to know the truth of this bit of instruction.

ס (37:27–28). See also ב (vv 3–4 above), which is similar in content (Cf. Prov 2:8 with Ps 37:28). On the meaning of "pious ones" or "saints" (חסידים), see the *Comment* on Ps 30:5.

ע (37:28–29). The expression "forever" (v 28c) implies *completely* or *totally*, without any reference in this context to life beyond death. With v 29, compare v 9.

פ (37:30–31). See also Prov 10:31–32. The intimate connection between thought and speech is evident in this proverb. The mind (in Hebrew idiom, the "heart") directs the tongue and mouth in speech. Hence the mind imbued with God's *instruction* (literally, *Torah*) utters wisdom and justice.

צ (37:32–33). See also Prov 1:11. On the threat that the evil pose to the righteous (v 32), see also v 12. Taking the proverb as a unified whole, it may be that the "killing" referred to (v 32) is not simple murder, but "legal" murder—viz. securing a death penalty in a capital case by giving false evidence in court (contrary to the ninth commandment). God, who is ultimately Israel's Chief Justice, declares that the innocent will not be declared guilty when they are brought to trial.

ק (37:34). Similar sentiments are expressed in vv 7, 9, 11, and elsewhere in the psalm.

ר (37:35–36). In this proverb, a metaphor from Ps 1:3 is developed in reverse. The righteous, in Ps 1, are like a tree planted by water that flourishes and grows. Here, the wicked flourish at first "like a luxuriant native tree"; the teacher, portraying himself as a country hiker, sees the tree one day, but it is gone the next, for it has no deep roots, no constant supply of water, and hence no resilience and staying power.

ש (37:37–38). See also Prov 23:18. The word "future" (in v 37b and v 38b) may refer to a person's prospects in this life. Or the word (אחרית) could be translated "posterity" and hence refer to the legacy of children that a person leaves in this world. On the lack of posterity as a sign of the covenant curse, see Deut 28:62–63.

ת (37:39–40). The psalm concludes with a summary proverb affirming the ultimate victory (or "salvation") of the righteous, and their deliverance from wicked persons.

Explanation

The difficulty in most forms of moral instruction is justifying the instruction to the student. Anyone can learn something by heart given enough time, and the alphabetic structure of Ps 37 provides assistance in such memorization. But still the problem remains: why should morality be adopted, when it is self-evident that wicked persons seem to get along fine in this world? It is not enough, if education is to be profound, simply to answer the question *why* with "God says so!" To indicate also why God might say so, why he requires morality, would be a considerable advance toward the educational goal of teaching morality and righteousness. Ps 37 provides this additional element, not in a profound theoretical fashion, but in a practical and functional manner. In the short run, the wicked seem to prosper, whereas the righteous very often seem to suffer at their hands. But it is the longer run that counts, and in the long run the only true satisfaction is to be found in the righteousness which is the hallmark of the one who lives in relationship with the living God. The motive is not entirely self-interest, though that may be a part of it. Rather, it is a question of determining the God-given purpose in human life and then living in accord with it; that is the essence of life and the essence of morality. Thus the psalm provides a clear insight into the educational role and responsibility of the wisdom teachers in ancient Israel; they were not primarily speculative thinkers or philosophers, as Qoheleth may have been, but educators who had a responsibility to fulfil toward the present and future generations.

The use and interpretation of the psalm among the Essenes of Qumran indicate that in their time it had lost its primarily educational function. In the Qumran commentary on the psalm, its words were taken to refer to the Elect Community, the Teacher of Righteousness, the Prince of Wickedness, and the eventual apocalyptic destruction of evildoers. But in the NT, both in the teaching of Jesus (Matt 5:5, cf. Ps 37:11 and Matt 6:8, cf. Ps 37:18) and in the Epistles (1 Pet 5:7, cf. Ps 37:5 and 1 Thess 5:24, cf. Ps 37:5), the more natural moral implications of the psalm are drawn forth and presented for use by a new community in a new era. For though the psalm belonged originally to Israel, its wisdom may be beneficial to all mankind.

A Sick Person's Prayer   (38:1–23)

Bibliography

Leveen, J. "Textual Problems in the Psalms" *VT* 21 (1971) 48–58. Martin-Achard, R. "La prière d'un malade: quelques remarques sur le Psaume 38." *VCaro* 45 (1958) 77–82. Ouellette, J. "Variantes qumrâniennes du Livre des Psaumes." *RevQ* 7 (1969) 105–23.

Translation

1   A Psalm of David. "To bring to remembrance."

2(1) *O Lord, do not rebuke me in your wrath*   (3+2)
   or discipline me in your anger.

3(2) *For your arrows have pierced me*   (3+3)
   and your hand has come down heavily upon me.

4(3) *My flesh has no soundness because of your indignation*   (4+4)
   and a *my bones have no health because of my sin.*

5(4) *For my wicked deeds have passed over my head;*   (4+4)
   like a heavy burden, they are too weighty for me.

6(5) *My wounds reeked and* a *festered*   (3+2)
   because of my folly.

7(6) *I bowed down, I stooped very low,*   (3+3)
   I walked in mourning all day long,

8(7) *for my loins are full of burning pain,*   (3+3)
      and my flesh has no soundness.

9(8) *I became numb and felt terribly congested;*   (3+3)
      I cried in distress because of my heart's growling.

10(9) *O Lord, all my desires are before you,*   (3+3)
      and my groaning is not hidden from you.

11(10) *My heart palpitated,* [a] *my strength forsook me,*   (4+4)
        and the light of my eyes—even that is gone from me!

12(11) *My companions and those that love me stood back from my plague,*   (5+3)
        and my neighbors stood at a distance.

13(12) *And they who sought my life set traps,*   (3+4+3)
        and they who looked for my downfall spoke of destruction,
        and they muttered deceptions all day long.

14(13) *But I am like a deaf man; I do not hear!*   (4+4)
        and like a mute who doesn't open his mouth.

15(14) *And I have become like a man who doesn't hear*   (4+3)
        and has no arguments in his mouth!

16(15) *But I have waited for you, O Lord;*   (4+4)
        you will answer, O Lord my God.

17(16) *For I said: "Lest my enemies* [a] *should rejoice."*   (4?+4)
        They exalted themselves over me when my foot slipped.

18(17) *But I am prepared for limping,*   (3+3)
        and my pain is continually before me.

19(18) *Indeed, I will declare my wickedness;*   (2+2)
        I am concerned about my sin.

20(19) *My enemies without cause* [a] *are numerous*   (3+3)
        and those who hate me for no reason are countless.

21(20) *And those who repay evil for good*   (4+4)
        are my adversaries in my pursuit of the good!

22(21) *Do not abandon me, O Lord.*   (2+3)
        O my God, do not be far from me.

23(22) *Come quickly to my aid,*   (2+2)
        O Lord, my Victory!

Notes

4.a. Reading ואיך, the conjunction being present in several Heb. mss (De-Rossi, IV, 26).

6.a. The conjunction is provided, as indicated by the sense, with the evidence of *G* and *S*.

11.a. The sense of סחרחר is not entirely certain. BDB takes it to be a *Pe'al'al* form of סחר, "to go around," hence "palpitate." Alternatively, it could be an error for חמרמר (cf. Lam 1:20), which is used of abdominal turmoil (see Briggs, *Psalms*, 342), but the notion is not characteristic of cardiac complaints. Dahood (*Psalms I*, 236) interprets the term as a "de-emphaticized form" of a root צחר which, on the basis of Ugarit, is said to have the meaning "to burn." The Ugaritic term *ṣhrrt* does indeed mean "burn, blaze" (cf. Gibson, *CML* [2], 125), but the linguistic equation between the respective Hebrew and Ugaritic terms is too precarious to provide a sure meaning of the Hebrew term in Ps 38:11.

17.a. MT is anomalous as it stands, there being no clear antecedent to ישמחו (*rejoice*). Leveen (art. cit., 56) resolves the problem by adding אשמרה דרכי and translates the line: "For I said: *I will take heed of my ways*, lest they rejoice over me. . . ." The proposal is possible, though the change is rather extensive. In the translation above, אֹיְבִי ("my enemies") has been provided, after G, and parallel to v 20.

20.a. חַיִּים "life" makes little sense in this context. In its place, חִנָּם "without cause" (cf. 35:19) is read, which is the reading of 4QpPs [a] (Ouellette, art. cit., 109).

Form/Structure/Setting

Psalm 38 is a *prayer;* it is evoked by the experience of sickness and the consequent sense of alienation from both God and fellow human beings. The specific elements of prayer are contained in the opening and concluding verses (vv 2, 22–23); the central section of the psalm (vv 3–21) is in the form of a lament, elaborating both upon the sickness as such and upon the effect of the sickness on the psalmist's acquaintances. The entire psalm is written from an individual perspective and is pervaded by a sense of isolation from God and from former friends and acquaintances.

Though a variety of proposals have been ventured as to the inner structure of the psalm, the following analysis appears to describe most naturally the substance of the psalm. (1) Opening prayer to God (v 2); (2) a description of the psalmist's physical malady (vv 3–11); (3) the reaction of friends and acquaintances to the psalmist's sickness (vv 12–21); (4) a concluding prayer for God's presence and deliverance (vv 22–23). But the internal structure must be set within a larger context; the psalm, like Ps 33, is an "alphabetizing psalm"; it is not an acrostic psalm, but it has the same number of verses (viz. two-line poetic units) as the number of letters in the alphabet (see further Ridderbos, *Die Psalmen,* 88). The verses are balanced two-line units throughout, with the exception of v 13 (a three-line unit), which is the opening verse of the second half of the psalm (viz. of the second group of 11 verses making up the whole).

It is difficult to know whether the psalm should be linked to any specific cultic activity. The substance of the psalm provides no clear clue as to a cultic or liturgical setting. And though the disease described by the psalmist appears to have symptoms that include dermatological disorders (e.g. vv 4, 6, 8), there is no suggestion in the psalm that it should be related to any of the rituals and procedures prescribed for dermatological problems in Lev 13–15. Furthermore, Ps 38 differs in a number of ways from other psalms pertaining to sickness. Thus Ps 6, also a prayer of sickness, does not contain strong evidence of cultic associations, but the radical change in tone in the progress of the psalm may indicate an oracular pronouncement of coming healing, implying a setting of worship and the presence of a priest. But, in contrast to Ps 6, Ps 38 has no change in tone and no thanksgiving in anticipation of healing; it begins and ends with prayer, with no indication of divine response, either in an oracular fashion or in terms of inner spiritual confidence. Ps 22 concerns a person in a similarly critical medical condition, but in that psalm the liturgical context is clear both from explicit words used and from progress and change within the substance of the psalm. But Ps 38 has no clear evidence to suggest that, like Ps 22, it should be interpreted in relationship to a liturgy for the sick.

It is thus safest to conclude that the psalm had initially no formal associations with cultic or liturgical practice. It is primarily a literary composition (as is suggested by the "alphabetic" structure), probably designed for use in the personal devotional life of the person who is sick and afflicted. It is a personal prayer, reminding God (see the *Comment* on v 1) of the continuing affliction of his servant.

Comment

Title. "To bring to remembrance" (לְהַזְכִּיר). The same expression is also used in the title of Ps 70. The word is sometimes associated with the "memorial offering" (אַזְכָּרָה), as described in Lev 2:2 and 24:7. But equally, the term might imply no more than it says, namely that the psalm was for regular use by a sufferer in bringing his plight to God's remembrance. In other words, the title may or may not imply cultic usage; but since it cannot be determined whether or not the title is a part of the original psalm, the resolution of the meaning of the term would not clarify the problem of the psalm's original purpose and setting. It might only be indicative of the psalm's later usage in the history of Israel's worship.

An opening prayer (38:2). The opening prayer is almost identical to that in Ps 6:2; see the commentary on that verse for the implications of the words. The poet attributes his sickness to the divine discipline and rebuke, but it should be recalled that his own perception of the state of affairs was not necessarily correct; he spoke and prayed from the depth of physical and mental despair, a situation within which it was easy for theological perspectives to go haywire. The facts were these: (a) he was terribly sick; (b) God, as omnipotent, must at the very least have permitted the sickness; (c) the psalmist had sinned as he freely confesses (v 19). From the facts, he drew the "logical" conclusion that the sickness must be a consequence of sin. But such was not the case in Ps 6, nor was it the case in the Book of Job: we do not really know whether it was the case in Ps 38, or whether it was only the psalmist's lonely despair which impelled him to such a conclusion. But whether or not the psalmist's self-understanding was correct, it was necessary and appropriate introduction to prayer; that is what he felt and that is what, in all honesty, he had to say to God.

A description of the psalmist's sickness (38:3–11). The description begins, following naturally from the prayer, with a metaphorical description of the divine origin of the malady; it was caused by God's "arrows" (an adaptation of the Canaanite theme of Resheph the Archer, god of pestilence) and his "hand." See further the *Comment* on v 2. The link between sin and punishment is expressed most forcefully in the parallelism of v 4, where divine indignation and human sin are linked as a primarily spiritual diagnosis of a physical complaint. In the following verses, it is the human sin that is developed further as one root of the problem (vv 5–6).

It is tempting, but probably misleading, to try to diagnose the nature of the complaint from the poetic description of it which is provided. At first sight, it appears that the patient has almost every disease in the book; the opening description of unhealthy "flesh" and "bones" is a blanket description, the "flesh" specifying dermatological or surface complaints, the "bones" covering all internal complaints. The specific complaints are staggering in their proportions: open wounds, burning loins (ulcers?), numbness, congestion, a "growling heart," palpitations, and trouble with the eyes. (Note: the loss of "light of the eyes" in v 11 may imply impotence, as is suggested by the close association of vision and potency in Deut 34:7.) As Rogerson and McKay have reasonably remarked, "no one in the terrible condition he describes would be fit to recite this psalm as a prayer, let alone compose it" (*Psalms 1–50*, 181). Thus it would be misleading to propose a particular diagnosis of the disease on the basis of the poetry, which draws together the symptoms of a variety of afflictions to portray the human condition in sickness. By the same token, the breadth of the description makes this psalm more appropriate for general usage as a prayer. There are few, fortunately, who will suffer all these symptoms at once, but many of the sick would be able to enter easily into the physical and emotional atmosphere of the psalm and participate in its prayer. Thus, though it is possible that the psalm contains a conflated description of a lifetime of disease in the person of the poet, its universal appeal lies in its applicability to the experience of sickness that so many undergo.

The reaction of friends and acquaintances to the psalmist's sickness (38:12–21). Whereas the first consequence of sickness is to create a sense of guilt and distance from God, as in vv 3–11, the second consequence is the development of a sense of alienation from fellow human beings, as described in these verses. The alienation may be partly paranoia and partly real, as some evil persons take advantage of the psalmist's weakened condition. Verse 12 may reflect near-paranoia—even friends and loved ones stand back, and though they may have stood back to avoid infection or because of the stench of infected and open wounds (v 6), their simple action creates deeper anxieties in the patient. But v 13 is closer to reality, for it is simply a fact of life that some people, like beasts of prey, close in to seek their own advantage when one who was strong becomes weak.

Verses 14–16 should probably be taken together, developing the last line of v 13; rather than listen to the muttered deceptions of his enemies, the psalmist acts like one who is deaf and mute, refusing to talk to them or argue with them. Like Job, he has said his piece and now his case rests with God, from whom he awaits an answer. The quoted words of v 17a may reflect an earlier prayer, in which the psalmist prayed for healing, in part lest the rejoicing of his enemies should reflect negatively upon God and cast doubts on his ability to heal. The sense of v 18 is not entirely clear; it may be that the psalmist is willing to continue in his affliction, but unwilling to continue with the sense of alienation from God and man, so that he declares again his penitence and sorrow over the sins he has committed (v 19). But though he freely confesses his sin and is courageous in his willingness to continue in physical suffering, all he can see around him are multitudes of enemies, hating him for no reason, and opposing his pursuit of the good. So he turns once again to prayer.

A concluding prayer (38:22–23). The sense of being abandoned by God (v 22a) is aggravated by the conscious proximity of a multitude of enemies (vv 20–21). In the prayer, the sense of separation from God and the agony of sickness are intimately related; first he prays for a return of the awareness of God's nearness, which in turn would bring him aid in the time of crisis. It is a distinctive feature of the closing prayer that it is full of the overtones of the liturgical psalm of sickness, namely Ps 22:

> v 22a: "do not abandon me" . . . see Ps 22:2
> v 22b: "do not be far from me" . . . see Ps 22:12
> v 23a: "come quickly to my aid" . . . see Ps 22:20.

It would appear that the personal prayer here employs the language of the liturgy toward the same goal, the desire for healing.

Explanation

The human experience of sickness and disease differs from one person to the next. For many, fortunately, sickness is a temporary state in life, from which there will be a return to health. In other psalms of sickness (Pss 6, 22), it is the termination of sickness and transition to health which are the central focus. But sometimes there is no transition to health, or more commonly (for the person who is sick for a long time) there does not seem to be a transition to health; in the absence of healing, sickness seems to the sufferer to be a permanent condition. The danger of physical sickness, especially over a long period of time, is that what starts as an affliction of the body can gradually become an affliction of the mind and spirit. Like rust and rot, diseases can eat away at the very foundations upon which life is established. The foundations of life, in Hebrew theology, rested upon two fundamental relationships, the first with God and the second with fellow human beings. Disease, in its prolongation, began to undermine these two relationships, as is so evident in this psalm. God becomes distant; his wrath is more evident than his love and there is a perpetual awareness of the fact that God appears to have forsaken the sufferer. Human beings also become distant: acts of love become distorted into hatred and real enemies grow beyond the proportions of reality. It is all a part of the process of illness, whereby the various agonies of the body become eventually the agonies of the mind.

The psalmist offers no ready solution to these problems, nor does he have anything more than hope that his estate in life will be changed. The only possibility of a solution to the problem is to be found in the very existence of the psalm; the psalmist, in other words, *continues to pray* despite his despair. There is little logic in his act, for he believes God caused the sickness and he thinks God has forsaken him. But still he prays, as do all those who have used this psalm and made it their own. And the very act of praying, in the context of perpetual sickness, reveals a deep-seated belief in God, beyond logic and beyond the evidence of the present circumstances. God may be a judge of sin; He may be distant from the sinner. God may even activate appalling disease as part of his purpose, at least from the point of view of the psalmist. But he continues to pray, because beyond all the evidence, he continues to believe that God is loving and merciful. It is this rock-bottom conviction that God cares which prompts the prayer. And the act of praying—even though no answer appears to come—functions as a lifeline in mortal life, for to pray is to keep open the relationship with God, in which ultimately is to be found the meaning of life itself. As so often is the case in the Psalter, Ps 38 survives not merely as a tribute to the poetic artistry of an era long since passed, but as a prayer for use in the modern era, in which sickness remains as an ever-present reality.

A Meditation and Prayer on the Transitory Nature of Life   (39:1-14)

Bibliography

Beuken, W. A. M. "Psalm 39: Some Aspects of the Old Testament Understanding of Prayer." *HeyJ* 19 (1978) 1–11. **Stolz, F.** "Der 39. Psalm." *Wort und Dienst* 13 (1975) 23–33.

Translation

¹ For the musical director. For Jeduthun. A psalm of David.

2(1) *I said: "I will guard my ways,*   (3+2)
   taking care not to sin with my tongue.
   I will put [a] *a muzzle in my mouth,*   (3+3)
   as long [b] *as the wicked are before me."*
3(2) *I was dumb with silence;*   (2+2)
   I kept quiet even about good matters.
   But my agony was aroused;   (2+2)
4(3)   *my heart grew hot within me.*
   A fire burned in my mutterings;   (2+2)
   I spoke with my tongue.
5(4) *"O Lord, explain to me my end*   (3+3+3)
   and the meaning of the measure of my days.
   I would like to know how transitory I am."
6(5) *Behold, you have made my days mere handbreadths,*   (4+3+4)
   and my lifetime is as nothing before you.
   The totality of mankind, standing firm, is merely [a] *vapor.* SELAH
7(6) *Man walks about, merely an image;*   (3?+3+3?)
   he heaps up wealth, [a] *merely vapor;*
   and he knows not who will gather it.
8(7) *And now, what have I hoped for, O Lord?*   (3+3)
   My hope is for you!
9(8) *Deliver me from all my transgressions;*   (3+3)
   don't make me the object of a fool's reproach.

10(9) *I have become silent. I will not open my mouth,*   (3+3)
    for you have acted.

11(10) *Turn your stroke away from me.*   (3+4)
    I have been destroyed by the hostility [a] *of your hand.*

12(11) *You have disciplined man with reproofs because of wickedness,*   (4+3+3)
    and you make his desires melt away like a moth.
    All mankind is merely vapor! SELAH

13(12) *Hear my prayer, O Lord,*   (3+2+2)
    and give heed to my cry;
    do not be deaf to my tears.
    For with you, I am an alien,   (3?+3)
    a sojourner like all my fathers.

14(13) *Look away from me, that I may be cheerful,*   (3+3)
    before I go and no longer exist.

Notes

2.a. The second אשמרה "I will guard" is probably a scribal error; the translation is based on the reading אשימה, implied by *G*.

2.b. Dahood translates עד by "full of glee," linking it to the Ugaritic root *ġdd*, which he says has the meaning "to be gleeful" (*Psalms I*, 240). The suggestion is particularly curious in the light of other suggestions made by Dahood in the same volume. At Ps 10:18, he proposed that עיד meant "arrogant," citing Ugaritic *ġdd*; see my note b on 10:18. At Ps 32:9, he proposed that עדי meant "petulance" on the basis of Ugaritic *ġdd*. Here, citing the same Ugaritic cognate and the same Ugaritic text (but with a different translation than in the previous note!), he suggests עד means "glee." The irony is that only in the present context might the suggestion be possible (though it is not probable), for Ugaritic *ġdd* does indeed seem to designate "laughter, mirth." But from a philological perspective, the entire procedure is unconvincing and betrays an elastic concept of the semantic range of roots and forms derived from them.

6.a. The first כל ("all"), preceding הבל ("vapor"), is omitted (being presumably a dittography), with the support of many Heb mss (De-Rossi, IV, 27).

7.a. MT יהמיון (from המה, with the sense "bustle about") is curious, both in its plural form (where a singular is expected), and in its failure to provide antecedent sense to the following clause. המון is read, with the sense "wealth," as in Ps 37:16.

11.a. Hebrew תגרה (rendered "hostility") is a *hapax legomenon* of uncertain meaning. For a general discussion of the problem, see Dahood, *Psalms I*, 241–42. Possibly the idea of "reach" is implied: viz. there is no place beyond the *reach* of the divine hand (cf. Caquot, et al., *Textes ougaritiques*, I, 308).

Form/Structure/Setting

Psalm 39 is an *individual lament*, containing a mixture of sad reflection and prayer. It is not only an *individual* psalm in general terms; it is much more personal and intimate than many laments, being characterized by an autobiographical nature in parts. The background to the psalmist's lament and prayer is not entirely certain; some scholars have suggested it was prompted by grave sickness, as was Ps 38. But sickness may be incidental to the principal element in the background, which appears to be the reflective consciousness of old age. Sickness may be a part of the experience of age, but it is primarily the awareness of the nearness and inevitability of death that provokes the lament and prayer.

The sentiment of the psalm is mixed; while parts would be fully at home in the cultic tradition of Israel's worship, other parts are more typical of the reflective tradition of wisdom. Hence there can be no certainty concerning whether or not this psalm was employed within the Israelite cult (cf. F. Stolz, art. cit). The weight of the evidence might suggest that the psalm was the private composition of a poet in the wisdom tradition. The mood of the opening verses is akin to that of Qoheleth (though it is a little more positive). And though the psalm ends in fairly conventional prayer (vv 13–14), it ends with a twist—it is the kind of prayer Qoheleth might have prayed, if he could have summoned sufficient faith. So although uncertainty remains, it is perhaps preferable to interpret the psalm as a private song of a literary, non-cultic nature.

The psalm is introduced by a description of the psalmist's state of mind (vv 2–4) and then moves to a reflection on the transitory nature of human existence (vv 5–7), concluding with the principal portion which is the prayer as such (vv 8–14).

Comment

Title. "For Jeduthun" (39:1). It is generally assumed that Jeduthun, in the psalm titles (cf. 62:1 and 77:1), is a personal name, specifically one of David's principal musicians along with Asaph and Heman (1 Chr 9:16; 16:38, 41; etc.). Mowinckel, however, has suggested that the term should be interpreted as a noun, not a personal name (*The Psalms in Israel's Worship*, II, 213); derived from ידה, it would have the meaning "confession" (though it might be added that "thanksgiving" would be equally possible in terms of the root derivation). Mowinckel goes on to propose that these psalms of "confession" would have been employed in some liturgical context of penitence. But the argument is not entirely convincing, principally because the names of David's other chief musicians (Asaph and Heman) also occur in psalm titles. It is most likely then, that the term is a personal name, but still its significance remains uncertain. The title could be rendered: "For the musical director, Jeduthun." Alternatively, the name of the person could have become the name of the tune, or musical setting, according to which the psalm was to be sung, which may be the implication of the use of the preposition על ("on, upon") with the name in the two other psalm titles in which it is employed.

The psalmist's state of mind (39:2–4). The psalmist's opening words are addressed to himself; within his own mind, he expresses his determination to keep quiet, come what may. Aware that he already has sufficient trouble for one person, he determines not to compound his problems by saying anything evil; so, in the metaphor, he "muzzles" himself. But this determination to keep silent presupposes the urge to speak, and the urge to speak was presumably provoked by the wicked people in his presence (v 2d). The very presence of the wicked, in other words, provoked the desire to speak, and at the same time created the self-imposed discipline of silence, presumably because any words he would use would run the risk of being sinful. At the root of his dilemma, one must suppose that the psalmist had within him questions, such as those Job raised, about the prosperity of the wicked (Job 21:7–16); the sin would lie in answering such questions in anger and haste, which could only imply that God was not just and fair in his dealings with human beings.

But the determination to keep silent, even on "good matters" (v 3b) or safe ground, was too much for him. The questions were burning within him and couldn't be contained (cf. Jer 20:9). The expression "my heart grew hot" is used in Deut 19:6 to describe the angry and uncontrollable reaction of a person who learns that a loved one or relative has been killed; it is the same kind of uncontrollable reaction that is growing within the psalmist and finally converts the fiery mutterings into full-blown speech.

The transitory nature of human existence (39:5–7). Nevertheless, when the psalmist does speak, he addresses his subject indirectly, still attempting to keep his tongue from sin (cf. v 2). He does not say directly: "evil people prosper, while I suffer," for that would be to imply directly that God was unjust. He asks, then, for an explanation of the meaning of his existence, and even in phrasing the question (v 5) begins to point to a part of the answer. The very ability to articulate a question about the transitory nature of human life betrays an insight that was lacking in wicked persons, who were the immediate source of his grief. Though the question is addressed to the Lord, the psalmist begins to answer it himself (vv 6–7), for in framing the question, he has begun to perceive its solution.

His days are mere "handbreadths" (v 6). The "handbreadth" (1 Kgs 7:26; the measurement was that of four fingers, Jer 52:21) was one of the smallest measures in the Hebrew system of measuring, so that the metaphor reduces the span of human life to something tiny from the perspective of God. In v 6c, he expands the comparison from his individual life to the corporate existence of mankind, but even that is insubstantial ("merely vapor") in the divine presence. The point of the question and its preliminary answer emerges in v 7. The psalmist's anger, provoked by evil persons, their success and accumulation of wealth at his expense, was based on something insubstantial. To become so upset and angry because of the wicked was to grant them an importance and permanence they did not really have (they could indeed acquire wealth, but did not know who would possess it when they died: v 7c). By beginning to perceive clearly the transitory nature of human existence, the psalmist was also beginning to gain a broader perspective within which to interpret its difficulties and hardships; value in life and appreciation of life must somehow be grasped within a full knowledge of its transitory nature.

The psalmist's prayer (39:8–14). Sobered by his reflection on the impermanence of human existence, the psalmist begins the more formal part of his prayer; in the opening words, he gets right back to basics. "What have I hoped for?" Was it wealth, success, victory over enemies, freedom from persecution, or things of that nature? No! When he got right down to his most fundamental aspirations in life, the palmist's hopes and desires focused upon God himself. And the realization that his ultimate focus in life was God created a new issue for the psalmist; it was no longer his enemies who were a primary source of external vexation, but an awareness of his own transgressions which became a primary source of internal vexation. If life was so transitory, and if God was its principal goal and meaning, then it was vital that transgressions (or sin) be dealt with, lest they destroy the potential and meaning of existence. His failure to perceive this truth made him vulnerable in another sense; he claimed to be a man of faith, but his obsession with enemies and the trappings of mortal life had become such that even a fool could see he had missed the point of life (v 9b). The fool might not agree with this perspective on life, but could reproach him for the double standard by which he lived. So the psalmist becomes silent again (v 10); this time, it is not self-imposed restraint to stop himself from speaking sinful words, but the silence of perception, for he has seen how God has acted.

He prays for divine mercy (vv 11–12), recognizing now that his former suffering at the divine hand has brought him to a point of insight and understanding. The word "stroke" (v 11a) may indicate disease or "plague" (cf. Ps 38:12), but in this context it probably refers metaphorically to God's chastisement of the psalmist. The general principle of divine action in v 12 is now understood by the psalmist at a personal level. Human beings so easily have "desires" (the word is a form of חמד, "to covet"), which may turn to wickedness, a contravention of the tenth commandment. The desires come to dominate life to such an extent that they become the meaning and end of existence, and life's transitory nature is forgotten. God's discipline may make those desires "melt away like a moth" (v 12b). Their disappearance may be a terrible judgment to those who had established their lives on desires and ambitions; but it may be a blessing to those who had been sidetracked by desires, forgetting that the only permanent meaning in a transitory life was to be found in the relationship with God.

In the concluding portion of the prayer (vv 13–14), it is clear that the psalmist has traveled a great spiritual distance from the point at which he began. His prayer is clearly one of repentance, characterized by tears, as has already been articulated in v 9. He has come to the realization that life's meaning cannot be related only to land and all that goes with it; he is a transient sojourner in the land, whose only home is God (cf. Beuken, art. cit). In this sense, the ethos of the prayer contrasts sharply with Ps 37 and its constant emphasis on the "inheritance of the land." But Ps 37 was directed toward the young, and Ps 39 reflects the wisdom of old age (cf. v 14b), and perhaps also the wisdom of another era, when the land was more dream than reality. The "alien," or "sojourner," lived in the land with the permission of its owners, but had no permanent stake in it. He received protection and certain privileges from its citizens, but never had full legal status (cf. Deut 24:17–22). "Look away from me" (v 14a): the sense is "turn aside the face of anger and discipline" (cf. v 11), so that I can live and die in peace. "Before I go. . . ;" though any person could make such a remark, it has the ring of a person who, in old age, has regained his perspective on the transitory nature of human life and can face death with calmness.

Explanation

The central concern of the psalm is that of an appropriate *perspective* within which to live out the single, but short human life which each person has received. Standing reflectively at a distance from human life, it is obvious that if any human being is to find meaning and fulfilment in existence, there must be some understanding and perspective. But the nature of the daily press and grind, which is the common experience of human living for many people, is such that the daily pressures and concerns, often legitimate in themselves, become subtly magnified into the meaning of life itself. Land, income, desires, enemies, friends—these are things that may become the stuff of life, as if it were somehow going to continue forever. But life is limited in its span; if its meaning is to be found, it must be found in the purpose of God, the giver of all life.

The psalmist, in his reflection and prayer, begins in the bustle of life and the pressure of everyday evils, which cloud his vision and disrupt his sense of values. He begins to doubt the purpose of it all and doubts, by implication, divine justice. But his doubt is rooted in a judgment based on a false measure: namely, that meaning is to be found in such things as freedom from enemies, wealth, security and the like. It is only when he rises to a mountain top that he regains the true perspective; life is extremely short, and what matters above all else is the relationship with God. Perceiving this, he confesses his sin. But the vision from the mountain takes him further; as he now looks down on the bustle of life from a distance, he perceives that though he is a part of that world, he is only a sojourner there. His deeper life was rooted in God; the world was the stage in which it was lived out. And it is this perspective of the psalmist which is taken up and developed in the NT. Peter, in his ethical admonitions to his readers, reminds them that they are "strangers and pilgrims" in this world (1 Pet 2:11; cf. Ps 39:13). But above all, it is the writer of the Epistle to the Hebrews who develops the theme. In developing the great catalogue of men of faith, he says of them: "they admitted that they were aliens and strangers on earth" (Heb 11:13), again employing the words of Ps 39. In the psalm, the perspective is developed as one appropriate for living *this life;* in the NT, it is broadened to incorporate the life beyond as well. But it is healthy to begin with the psalm; in this life, our permanence is not to be found in the world as such, but in God who granted us life in the world. To combine an awareness of the transitory nature of human life as a whole, with the wisdom that "sufficient for the day is the evil thereof," is a starting point in achieving the sanity of a pilgrim in an otherwise mad world.

A Royal Liturgy of Supplication   (40:1–18)

Bibliography

Airoldi, N. "Il Psalmo 40 B." *RevistB* 16 (1968) 247–58. **Braulik, G.** *Psalm 40 und der Gottesknecht.* Würzburg: Echter Verlag 1975. **Johnson, A. R.** *The Cultic Prophet and Israel's Psalmody.* Cardiff: University of Wales Press, 1979. **Leveen, J.** "Textual Problems in the Psalms." *VT* 21 (1971) 48–58.

Translation

¹ For the musical director. For David. A Psalm.
²⁽¹⁾ *I have waited patiently for the Lord,*   (3+3)
    and he turned to me and heard my cry.
³⁽²⁾ *And he raised me from the pit of desolation,*   (3+2)
    from the slimy mud,
    and he set my feet upon a rock;   (3+2)
    and he made firm my footsteps.
⁴⁽³⁾ *And he put a new song into my mouth,*   (3?+2)
    a hymn of praise to our God.
    Many will see and will fear,   (3+2)
    and they will trust in the Lord.
⁵⁽⁴⁾ *Blessed is the man who made the Lord his trust,*   (5+5?)
    and has not turned to the defiant, the fabricators of falsehood. [a]
⁶⁽⁵⁾ *Many are your wonders, O Lord my God,*   (3+3)
    that you have done,
    and your plans for us—   (2+3)
    no one can arrange them for you!
    I will declare, I will speak—   (2+2)
    "They are too many to count!"
⁷⁽⁶⁾ *You have not desired sacrifice and offering—*   (3+3+3)
    you have dug two ears for me! [a]
    you have not requested burnt offering and sin offering.
⁸⁽⁷⁾ *Then I said, "Look, I have come!*   (3+3)
    It is written about me[a] in the scroll of the book."
⁹⁽⁸⁾ *I have desired to do your will, O my God,*   (4+3)
    and your instruction is in the midst of my being.
¹⁰⁽⁹⁾ *I have declared glad tidings of righteousness*   (2+2)
    in the great congregation;
    Lo, I do not restrain my lips;   (3+3)
    you know that, O Lord.
¹¹⁽¹⁰⁾ *I have not hidden your righteousness within my heart;*   (4+3)
    I have been outspoken concerning your faithfulness and your salvation.
    I have not hidden your lovingkindness   (2+2?)
    or your truth from [a] *the great congregation.*
¹²⁽¹¹⁾ *Come* [a]*, O Lord, do not hold back*   (3+2)
    your mercies from me.
    Your lovingkindness and your truth   (2+2)
    continually protect me.
¹³⁽¹²⁾ *For troubles have surrounded me,*   (3+2)
    too numerous to count.
    My wicked deeds have overtaken me,   (2+2)
    so that I cannot see.
    They are more numerous than the hairs on my head, (3+2)
    and my heart has failed me!
¹⁴⁽¹³⁾ *Please deliver me, O Lord!*   (3+3)
    O Lord, hasten to my help!

15(14)	*They shall be both ashamed and humiliated,*	(3+3)
	they who sought to snatch away my life.	
	They shall be turned back and put to shame,	(3+2)
	they who desired my ruin.	
16(15)	*They shall be desolate because of their shame,*	(3+3)
	they who said to me, "Aha! Aha!"	
17(16)	*They shall exult and rejoice in you,*	(3+2)
	all they who seek you,	
	and a *they shall continually say,*	(2+2+2)
	"The Lord is great,"	
	they who love your victory.	
18(17)	*Yet I am poor and needy;*	(3+3)
	think on me, O Lord.	
	You are my help and my rescuer;	(3+2)
	do not delay, O my God.	

Notes

5.a. The expression שֹׂטֵי כָזָב (literally, "those that turn aside falsehood") is of uncertain meaning. Dahood suggests "fraudulent images" (*Psalms I*, 243); cf. NIV "false gods." Leveen, art. cit., 56, reads שָׂטְחֵי, "those who spread lies."

7.a. The sense of v 7b is difficult; the translation above is literal, based upon כרה, "to dig." On the meaning, if the translation is correct, see the *Comment*. But G has a quite different text: "but you prepared a body for me" (cf. Heb 10:5, which is based on G). כרה may have the sense "to pierce," implying that God's word penetrates deafness (Delitzsch, *Biblical Commentary on the Psalms*, II, 44); on this sense of the root, see further note b on Ps 22:17 (above). The safest approach is a literal translation, based on the assumption of ancient idiomatic usage of which the precise sense is no longer clear.

8.a. Dahood translates v 8b: ". . . it is written to my debit"; see *Psalms I*, 243. In support he cites Job 13:26 and Ugaritic texts to indicate the sense "debit" for על (Ugaritic '*l*. The interpretation is possible, depending essentially on judgment as to the sense of the passage as a whole.

11.a. The preposition ל here has the sense "from," as in Ugaritic; cf. Gibson, *CML²*, 149.

12.a. אתה is interpreted as the verb "to come" (cf. Airoldi, art. cit.), rather than the personal pronoun, "you."

17.a. The conjunction is added with strong support from Heb. mss (De-Rossi, IV, 28, and also C), and also the versions (*G, S, Tg*).

Form/Structure/Setting

Psalm 40 is commonly identified as a composite psalm containing two originally independent units which have been linked into the present unified whole: *A*, vv 2–11 and *B*, vv 12–18 (though there is disagreement among holders of this view concerning where the precise point of transition might be; v 12 and/or v 13 could be viewed as a redactional link). The evidence giving rise to the two-psalm hypothesis is essentially twofold. (1) In form-critical terms, *A* is an *individual thanksgiving* psalm and *B* is an *individual lament*. (2) Verses 14–18 of this psalm are duplicated (with only minor changes) in Ps 70. If the latter is an independent composition, then Ps 40 might either be a composite work in which two psalms are joined by an editor, or a new composition in which the poet takes an older psalm (Ps 70) and develops it by additions into a new work. The two-psalm hypothesis, whatever its faults, is based on a particular interpretation of the evidence and has many adherents (Airoldi, Braulik, Kraus, et al.).

Yet, for a number of reasons, the two-psalm hypothesis must be rejected. The problem and evidence are directly parallel to those encountered in the study of Ps 27; the argument for unity and the overall interpretation follow essentially along similar lines. First, it should be noted that the language in the two supposed "parts" of the psalm is intimately interrelated (see further Ridderbos, *Die Psalmen*, 290–97, who argues for the overall unity of the psalm). Forms of the following roots are found in both "parts" of the psalm (the list omits duplicate forms in one or other part). (1) חשׁב (vv 6, 18); (2) עצם (vv 6, 13); (3) מספר (vv 6, 13); (4) אמר (vv 8, 11, 16, 17); (5) ראה (vv 4, 13); (6) הפץ (vv 7, 9, 15); (7) רצה (vv 9, 14); (viii) תשׁועה (vv 11, 17). The overlap in language and repetitive style strongly suggest a single, unified composition.

But more persuasive than the argument of language, is that based on form and setting. As was the case in Ps 27, the apparent diversity of form is in reality not diversity at all; the two-psalm hypothesis, in fact, rises in part from too rigid a view of form-critical categories. The essence of Ps 40 is that it is a part of a *liturgy*, and the formal and substantial changes within the psalm are to be understood against the background of progression within the liturgy. The liturgy begins with *thanksgiving*, thereby establishing precedent and laying a foundation for what is to follow. It then moves on to *lament* and *prayer*; it is only in the prayer that the overall purpose of the liturgy emerges, and the preparatory role of the thanksgiving is clarified.

In terms of classification, the liturgy must be viewed as a *royal liturgy of supplication*, as is persuasively argued by both Eaton (*Kingship and the Psalms*, 42–44) and Johnson (op. cit. 399–412). The details of the royal interpretation are elaborated upon in the comment which follows. The overall parallels between Pss 27 and 40 are clear from the foregoing remarks.

The relationship between Pss 40 and 70 remains somewhat uncertain. The hypothesis is proposed that Ps 40 is the original, and hence oldest, composition, dating from the monarchical period. Ps 70 is an adaptation and abbreviation, possibly undertaken to permit "popular usage" of a part of the psalm, but more likely dating from a period when royal psalms and liturgies were no longer in use. Psalm 70 could then be viewed as a "salvaged psalm" for use in a nonmonarchical age, perhaps during the Hebrew Exile.

Comment

Thanksgiving (40:2–11). The psalm begins with a general thanksgiving for past acts of divine deliverance; by this introductory act of thanksgiving, the king establishes the ground of precedent, framed in the appropriate praise, by which he will move forward to a prayer for further deliverance in a new crisis that threatens his life and kingdom. Just as past prayers had been answered after patient waiting (v 2), so too would his present prayer.

The language of v 3 ("the pit of desolation," the "slimy mud") is indicative of a former occasion in which God had saved the suppliant's life. Although it is possible that the former deliverance was from severe sickness (cf. Ps 30:3–4), the royal context of this psalm makes it more likely that the deliverance was experienced in a military crisis. Near disaster and death were turned into victory and stability (v 3b), and a hymn of praise had been sung (v 4). The hymn of praise was in all probability a victory hymn, celebrating not only God's deliverance, but also the impact of the victory on observers; in perceiving God's act, they would *fear* (v 4b), just as various foreign nations had feared after the great victory at the Sea (Exod 15:14). Likewise, the divine "wonders" celebrated in this psalm (v 6) are reminiscent of the wonders celebrated in the victory hymn following the Exodus (Exod 15:11). These past victories and acts of deliverance now form not only the precedent for the king's supplication, but also the substance of his public declaration of God's greatness and past achievements.

The following verses (vv 7–9) have often been interpreted as a condemnation of the sacrificial cult in ancient Israel, but to read them in such a fashion is almost certainly to misinterpret them; the context of the royal liturgy provides the appropriate setting for interpretation. The king is now engaged in a liturgy of supplication; he can only participate in such a liturgy (which may well have included sacrifices) after having faithfully performed all his royal tasks as king, which included the offering of appropriate sacrifices. But the offering of sacrifices alone was not enough; more was required of him. The general background, then, to these verses is to be found in the "law (or *Torah*) of kings" (Deut 17:14–20); when the suppliant states: "it is written about me in the scroll of the book" (v 8), he is referring to the Deuteronomic law and its cultic requirements of kings. But the Deuteronomic law, while imposing on the king certain cultic requirements, had a deeper spiritual dimension to it; it was to instill in the king the fear of the Lord and keep him humble amongst his brethren (Deut 17:19–20). These verses in Ps 40 thus point to the characteristics required of the king *beyond* the cultic offerings and sacrifices; the king, after all, had "two ears" (v 7) and had heard the basic requirements of the law, which concerned sacrifice. But now he has progressed further and when he says: "your instruction is in the midst of my being" (v 9b), he is perceiving that God's "instruction" *(Torah)* has the deeper and spiritual requirements of the *Torah* (Deut 17:18) of kings. For further commentary on these verses, see particularly Eaton, *Kingship and the Psalms*, 42–44 and Johnson, op. cit., 402–3.

Having thanked God for past deliverance, and having affirmed his adherence not only to the external requirements of royal law, but also to its inner requirements, the king now goes on to declare the manner in which he had publicly announced God's righteousness in the "great congregation" (vv 10–11). The great congregation might either be the actual congregation in an act of worship, or it might refer symbolically to the people of the entire nation. The statement of past declarations of God's "righteousness" (v 10a, v 11a) becomes in itself a new and present declaration. The "righteousness" of God is here celebrated as a possession of Israel, received and experienced in God's acts of deliverance. Thus the individual note of the thanksgiving in vv 3–4 is here broadened in public declaration, so that God's acts of righteousness become the property of the community as a whole. And the public declaration is appropriate, for the words central to this declaration of praise ("righteousness," v 10; "faithfulness, salvation, lovingkindness," v 11) are all indicative of God's covenant character and his actions toward the chosen people as a nation.

Prayer (40:12). The brief element of prayer forms an appropriate transition between the thanksgiving for former acts of deliverance, and the lament (vv 13–17) which will culminate in an explicit prayer for a future act of deliverance (v 18). The whole thrust of the prayer is to be found in the imperative: "come." The king prays for the divine presence in the approaching crisis, for it had only been that presence which converted former crisis into victory. The divine presence would bring with it those covenant characteristics of God ("mercies, lovingkindness, truth") that would provide the necessary protection (v 12b) in crisis and would culminate in victory. But the prayer, which begins in v 12 and culminates in v 18, is now interrupted by a lamenting account of the dimensions of the crisis which launched the entire liturgy of supplication, interspersed by a further brief prayer (v 14).

Lament over a coming crisis (40:13–17). The opening verse of the lament (v 13) suggests two sources of the immediate crisis: (a) external troubles (v 13a), presumably foreign enemies in the light of vv 15–16; (b) "wicked deeds," presumably the king's own evil acts of the past. The first of these two is no doubt the principal cause of the crisis; the second source of trouble reflects the profound state of spiritual awareness which the king had achieved earlier in the liturgy. It is clear, on the one hand, that he is not burdened with unconfessed sin, for his relationship to God is healthy, as expressed in the foregoing verses. On the other hand, he is aware that former evil acts, albeit forgiven by God, may nevertheless have contributed to the present crisis in which he now finds himself. Hence, the sense of anxiety is produced by a profound awareness of the possible consequences of his extremely "numerous" (v 13c) past failures. So he pleads in the midst of the lament for deliverance (v 14).

While this section of the psalm clearly begins as a lament (v 13), the principal portion (vv 15–16) hovers somewhere between lament and a statement of confidence. On the one hand, the king is aware of enemies that desire his death and ruin; on the other hand, he affirms that they themselves will be devastated and made desolate. But the tension between lament and confidence is finally resolved in v 17, when confidence triumphs in an expression of exultation and the magnification of God that would follow victory. The "they" of vv 15–16 is thus the enemies of the king and nation, but "they" in v 17 refers to the king and his people who, in seeking God's aid, would find it in victory.

Concluding prayer (40:18). The exulting confidence of v 17 is now appropriately muted in the concluding prayer of the liturgy. The king and his people would rejoice in victory, but they could not achieve it by their own strength. Hence the prayer, which has punctuated the earlier portion of the psalm (vv 12, 14), reaches its climax precisely in the humility of these closing words.

The prayer is very personal, yet as the king prays for himself, he prays as one who carries the burden of an entire nation upon his shoulders. And though he opened his liturgical act with a reminiscence of how he had *waited patiently* (v 2), now the immediacy of the crisis propels him to the prayer: "Do not delay, O my God."

Explanation

In a remarkable manner, Psalm 40 unfolds the relationship between the one and the many in Israelite thought. The "one" in this context is the king, and the psalm as a whole is in the first person, for the king is the principal participant in the liturgy of supplication. The "many" are the citizens of the kingdom, who are referred to both in the expression "great congregation" (vv 10, 11) and in the anticipation of future exultation (v 17). The interrelationship is to be found in the king's representative role, for within the covenant context, he carried individually upon his shoulders the responsibility for his people. And his desire for the nation, as expressed in this liturgy of supplication, was deliverance or salvation (v 14). Thus, implicit in the psalm is a principle of representation within the kingdom of God, though here the kingdom is in the form of a nation state, Israel (and/or Judah). In one sense, every individual person shared in the covenant relationship with God. In another sense, given the context of kingdom, the relationship was channeled through the person of the king, for in a very real sense the future of the kingdom, as a national and political entity, depended on the king's role.

In the NT the theme to be developed most explicitly from Ps 40 is the passage on sacrifice, vv 7–9. The writer of the Epistle to the Hebrews develops the passage in his account of the permanent nature of the sacrifice of Christ. The words of the ancient psalm are now set in the mouth of Christ (Heb 10:5–10), though with some modification, for the writer of the Epistle employs the slightly different text of the Septuagint at this point (see note a on v 7). In one sense, Hebrews goes beyond Ps 40; the perpetual sacrifices of the past have become obsolete in terms of the permanent sacrifice of Christ. But in another sense, the writer of the Epistle grasps the fundamental sense of the psalm and neatly reverses it. The king in the ancient kingdom had been required to offer sacrifices, but that was not all; beyond the formalities of the cult, obedience and profound spirituality were required of him, for sacrifices in and of themselves achieved nothing. In Christ, says the writer of the Epistle, there is a reversal; first, he affirms his intention to do the divine will (Heb 10:9), and that intention in turn leads back inevitably to sacrifice, but now to the sacrifice that ends all sacrifices.

It is this theme of the sacrifice of Christ which made Ps 40 an appropriate passage for use as one of the proper psalms on Good Friday, during the development of Christian worship. The usage is appropriate to the intention of the writer of the Epistle to the Hebrews. But in a certain sense, it is also appropriate to the original sense of the psalm, recalling the supplicatory role of the king on behalf of his kingdom.

A Liturgy for the Sick   (41:1–14)

Bibliography

Coppens, J. "Les Psaumes 6 et 41 dépendent-ils du livre de Jérémie?" *HUCA* 32 (1961) 217–26. **Dietrich, M.; Loretz, O.** and **Sanmartín, J.** "Zur ugaritischen Lexikographie (VII)." *UF* 5 (1973) 85. **Eaton, J. H.** "Some Questions of Philology and Exegesis in the Psalms." *JTS* 19 (1968) 603–9. **Rainey, A. F.** "Observations on Ugaritic Grammar." *UF* 3 (1971) 160–62.

Translation

1 For the musical director. A psalm of David.

2(1) *Blessed is the one who gives consideration to the weak*   (4+4)
   and the poor [a]*;*
   in an evil time, the Lord will deliver him.

3(2) *The Lord will keep him and give him life;*   (3+2+3)
   he will bless [a] *him in the land*
   and will not [b] *give him up to the desire of his enemies.*

4(3) *The Lord will support him on his sickbed;*   (4+3)
   in his illness, you [a] *have changed his whole bed.*

5(4) *I said: "Have mercy on me, Lord.*   (4+4)
   Heal me, for I have sinned against you."

6(5) *My enemies speak evil of me:*   (4+4)
   "When will he die and his name perish?"

7(6) *And even if one came to see me,*   (3+3)
   he would speak falsehood in his heart.
   He would gather for himself wicked thoughts;   (3+3)
   he would go and speak them outside.

8(7) *All my haters whisper about me amongst themselves;*   (4+4)
   against me, they are plotting my misery.

9(8) *"A devilish disease* [a] *has been put upon him.*   (4+4)
   [b] *He has lain down; he will not rise again."*

10(9) *Even my good friend* [a] *whom I trusted,*   (5+5)
   my dining companion, [b] *has raised up his heel* [c] *against me.*

11(10) *But you, O Lord, have mercy upon me*   (3+3)
   and raise me up that I may recompense them.

12(11) *By this, I know that you are pleased with me,*   (4+4)
   for my enemy does not shout in triumph over me.

13(12) *As for me, you have supported me in my integrity*   (4+3)
   and have made me stand in your presence for ever.

14(13) *Blessed be the Lord, God of Israel,*   (4+3)
   from everlasting and to everlasting.
   Amen and Amen.

Notes

2.a. "The poor" (ואביון): the word is added to MT, following the suggestion of G (καὶ πένητα), thus providing (provisionally) metrical balance to the verse.

3.a. The verb is pointed and translated as Piel (with suffix), rather than MT's Pual; the rendering has the support of Q and *G*, and is implied by context and syntax.

3.b. וְלֹא is read for MT's וְאֹל; cf. *G*.

4.a. A third person form of the verb is expected: there is limited support for such a reading from one ms of *G*. On the sense, see the *Comment*.

9.a. Literally, "a thing of *beliyya'al*."

9.b. MT's וַאֲשֶׁר is puzzling in terms of syntax, and is here omitted either as a gloss, or as dittography (on the basis of אֲשֶׁר in v 10). Dahood (*Psalms I*, 251) interprets the term as a compound relative, "that he who. . . ." He claims also that Ugaritic *aṯr* functions in the role of a compound relative. Ugaritic *aṯr* in the use cited by Dahood occurs in *UT* 2060 (= RS.18.38 = *PRU* V. 60): 34–35. But in this text, the term almost certainly means "where, wherever" (see Dietrich, Loretz and Sanmartín, art. cit., 85), and Dahood's interpretation of the term as a relative pronoun cannot be sustained on the basis of the Ugaritic texts (Rainey, art. cit., 160–62).

10.a. Literally, "man of my peace."

10.b. Literally, "the one eating my bread (food)."

10.c. The expression is curious, the preceding verb (lit. "making great") seeming out of place with the noun "heel"; though the idiom is rare, the sense is clear enough. Dahood translates "spun slanderous tales," which is possible, though it rests on rare nuances (if they can be sustained) of both the Heb. verb and noun in question (*Psalms I*, 251). The Ugaritic evidence in support of the sense "malign, slander" for Heb. עָקֵב should be removed from the discussion. In Ugaritic, the noun *'qb* "heel," is well established, but the verb *'qb* has the sense "hinder, hold back." In the text cited by Dahood, 3 Aqht. rev. 19 (=*CTA*.18.i.19), *m'qbk* does not clearly mean "he who maligns you"; the more obvious sense is "he who hinders you." See further Gibson, *CML* [2], 154; A. Caquot, et. al., *Textes ougaritiques* I, 436; Aistleitner, *WUS*, #2086.

Form/Structure/Setting

There has been some debate as to the most appropriate classification of Ps 41. While many scholars have classified it as an *individual thanksgiving* psalm, others have interpreted it as an *individual lament*. The difficulty arises in that the psalm appears to be characterized by a variety of forms of language, including didactic poetry reminiscent of the wisdom tradition (vv 2–4), prayer (vv 5, 11), lament (vv 6–10), and confidence or praise (vv 12–14). The most appropriate description in general terms is to recognize the psalm as a psalm of illness (Mowinckel, *The Psalms in Israel's Worship*, II, 1–9).

Nevertheless, it is possible to be more precise in the descriptive analysis of the psalm. The variety in forms of language is to be explained in a liturgical context; the text must be interpreted as a liturgy (or a part of a liturgy) for use within a ritual in which a sick person comes to the temple in quest of healing. The analysis which is provided here follows essentially that of Ridderbos, *Die Psalmen*, 298–300. The ritual begins with some words addressed to the sick person by the priest (vv 2–4). Then the sick person declares his lament, framed in a prayer for healing. Between vv 11 and 12, one must suppose the priestly declaration of an oracle from the Lord. The liturgy closes with the sick person's declaration of confidence in God's intention to heal him. In summary form, the psalm's structure can be expressed as follows.

1. Introductory words of the priest (vv 2–4).
2. The sick person's words (vv 5–11)
   a. Prayer for healing (v 5)
   b. Lament over the crisis (vv 6–10)
   c. Prayer for healing (v 11).
3. (A priestly oracle from God is supposed.)
4. Concluding statement of confidence by the sick person (vv 12–13).

More precise details of this analysis are provided in the *Comment*. The psalm, as a liturgy for a sick person, thus has general similarities to Pss 6 and 38, though the cultic and liturgical associations are much clearer in the case of Ps 41 than is the case with the parallel psalms. As was the case with Ps 6, the similarities between the language of this psalm and Jeremiah need not form the basis of any theory of literary relationship or interdependence (cf. Coppens, art. cit.).

The concluding verse of the psalm (v 14) functions as a doxology for Book I of the Psalter (see further THE COMPILATION OF THE PSALTER in the INTRODUCTION).

Comment

The introductory words of the priest (41:2-4). The opening words are typical in style of the didactic tone of wisdom poetry (cf. Ps 1:1), but they may also be interpreted as characteristic of a statement of priestly blessing (or of the nature of a person who might expect to be blessed by God). The background to the words is to be found in the setting; the sick person comes to the temple to seek divine healing, but before speaking, he must hear a statement from the priest concerning the basic character of the kind of person who could legitimately seek God's blessing and healing.

The first words of the priest (v 2a) indicate that the person who would seek divine deliverance must be one who had given active consideration to the needs of the weak and the poor. One who had never helped a fellow human being had little right to look for divine help in a time of crisis. Eaton has argued that this first qualification is one of several pieces of evidence for associating the psalm with the king, and interpreting it as a *royal psalm*, for the king's responsibilities included the care of the weak (J. H. Eaton, art. cit., and *Kingship in the Psalms*, 44-46). While it is possible to interpret both the verse and the psalm as a whole in a royal context, the evidence is far from decisive and the possibility must remain as an hypothesis. It is equally likely that the concern for the weak and poor, reflected in v 2, is that which was incumbent on all Israelites as members of the covenant community (cf. Deut 10:18-19; 24:17-18).

The general principle contained in the priest's words is that the one who has shown concern for the weak may legitimately seek God's blessing in his own time of weakness. The general characteristics of God's blessing, as stated in v 3 (protection, long life and a fruitful existence), are then brought into focus in v 4 with respect to the immediate situation; the sick person may expect God's support (though the words do not contain any guarantee of healing as such). Verse 4b is difficult to interpret, partly for grammatical reasons; for "*you* have changed," one might expect "*he* will change" (see note a on v 4). If it is correct to assume that the subject of the verb *change* is God (regardless of the correct form of the verb), then the metaphor is that of God the nurse, who constantly changes the bedclothes and provides the sick person with some comfort and consolation.

The sick person's words (41:5-11). Having heard the opening declaration of the priest, the sick person immediately expresses his most urgent concern in prayer to God; the vocalizing of the prayer in the liturgy presupposes the worshiper's understanding of the implications of the priest's opening words. From the words of the prayer, it is clear that the suppliant has two things on his mind: sin and sickness. And so he prays both for the divine mercy (experienced in the forgiveness of sin) and for the divine healing. In the sick person's mind, the sin and sickness appear to be interrelated. In reality, there may have been no interrelationship; that is, the advent of sickness was not necessarily a direct consequence of sin. But the words of the prayer are nevertheless entirely appropriate, for full healing must encompass both body and soul.

Having expressed the basic prayer, the suppliant now expresses the words of lament (vv 6–10). The lament does not have its focus on the sickness as such, but on the sick person's enemies, who seem to hover round the sick bed like vultures, awaiting the end. In this focus on the sick person's enemies, Ps 41 has similarities to Pss 6 and 38, though in this context, the focus is much more sustained and virtually excludes specific reference to the nature of the illness. In a literary sense, however, the substance of the lament is striking; it is framed by prayer (vv 5, 11) to God who is the only possible source of help, given that human beings, foes (v 6) and friends (v 10) alike, appear to have turned against the sick person in the time of distress. As in the other laments, it is difficult to know the extent to which the enmity toward the psalmist is real, and the extent to which it is the result of a paranoid imagination inflamed by sickness (see further the *Comment* on Ps 38:12–21). Verse 7 may well reflect the paranoia of disease; the visitors come to the sick person's room and speak the common pleasantries, but all the patient can think of is the words which he supposes them to be formulating in their minds, which they will make public the moment they leave his room. The greatest sense of betrayal is expressed in v 10; even the good friend, the one with whom so many a pleasant meal had been passed, would "raise up his heel" against the sick person. On the inimical metaphor of the "heel," see Jer 9:3 (Hebrew) where the verb עקב is used in the sense of the modern idiom, "to be a heel"; Gen 3:15 may also illustrate the metaphor.

After the lament of enemies, the sick person then turns to the final words of prayer (v 11), asking again for mercy and healing. Then, in the context of the liturgy, he must await the outcome of his plea, while the priest seeks a divine oracle, "yes" or "no," with respect to his request addressed to God.

The concluding statement of confidence (41:12–14). The words "by this" (בזאת, v 12) are the key to the supposition of an antecedent priestly declaration of an oracle. In a strict grammatical sense, there is no antecedent to the word זאת ("this"); in the larger cultic context, the antecedent is clearly the positive oracle from God indicating the coming of healing. It is the oracle which provides the sick person with the knowledge of the divine pleasure (v 12a); the *word* from God has eliminated the possibility of a triumphant *shout* from the threatening human enemies (v 12b). The divine response is a reflection in part of the sick person's "integrity" (v 13a); that is, the qualifications contained in the priest's opening remarks (vv 2–4) have been met and rewarded. But basically, the positive response from God was an act of mercy, and it was for mercy that the sick person had prayed (vv 5, 11). The expression

of confidence is for the healing that would come, even though it was not
yet experienced at the time the words were offered. But the degree of confidence is clear in v 13b: the sick person was confident that he would "stand
in (God's) presence," referring specifically to future visits to the temple for
worship, but generally to the survival in life beyond the threat of death which
had come so close. On v 14, see *Form/Structure/Setting* (above).

Explanation

For general reflections on the *psalms of sickness,* see particularly the *Explanation* at Pss 6 and 38.

In John's Gospel (13:18), the lamenting words of the psalmist concerning
betrayal by an intimate friend are used by Jesus in anticipation of his own
betrayal. Thus, words which were originally part of a liturgy of sickness in
the face of death, are transformed into what amounts to a prophetic prediction
of betrayal in the life of Jesus. This quotation of the psalm in the NT is a
further illustration of the manner in which the evangelists have set forth
their passion narratives in the context of what is, in effect, a liturgy of dying,
as was so evident in the NT quotation of Ps 22 (see above).

BOOK II: PSALMS 42-72
The Lament of an Individual (42-43)

Bibliography

Alonso-Schökel, A. "The Poetic-Structure of Psalm 42-43." *JSOT* 1 (1976) 4–11. Responses, in the same issue, by M. Kessler, 12–15, and by N. H. Ridderbos, 16–21. ——, "Psalm 42-43. A Response to Ridderbos and Kessler." *JSOT* 3 (1977) 61–65. **Donner, H.** "Ugaritismen in der Psalmenforschung." *ZAW* 79 (1967) 333–36. **Leveen, J.** "Textual Problems in the Psalms." *VT* 21 (1971) 48–58. **Schreiner, J.** "Verlangen nach Gottes Nähe und Hilfe. Auslegung von Psalm 42/43." *BibLeb* 10 (1969) 254–64. **Tournay, R.** "Notes sur les Psaumes." *RB* 79 (1972) 39–58. **Waldman, N. M.** "Some Notes on Malachi 3:6; 3:13; and Psalm 42:11." *JBL* 93 (1974) 543–49.

Translation (Psalm 42)

(Note: Psalms 42 and 43 are interpreted as a single psalm. For convenience, the translations, notes, and comments are given separately, in the normal fashion. The section entitled *Form/Structure/Setting*, below, covers both psalms, as does the *Explanation*, following the *Comment* on Ps 43.)

¹ For the musical director. A *Maskil* [a] for the sons of Korah.[b]

²⁽¹⁾ *As a deer [a] longs for streams of water,*	(4+4)
so does my soul long for you, O God.	
³⁽²⁾ *My soul thirsts for God, the God of life;*	(5+5)
when may I enter and see [a] the face of God?	
⁴⁽³⁾ *My tears were my food by day and night*	(5+5)
when they [a] said to me all day long: "Where is your God?"	
⁵⁽⁴⁾ *Let me remember these things*	(2+2?)
and let me pour out my soul,	
how I used to cross with the multitude,	(3+3)
I used to walk [a] with them to God's house,	
with the sound of shouting and thanksgiving,	(3+2)
amid the pilgrim crowd.	
⁶⁽⁵⁾ *O my soul, why are you downcast*	(2+2)
and so disturbed within me?	
Wait patiently for God, for I will praise him again,	(4+3)
the victories of my God's presence. [a]	
⁷⁽⁶⁾ *My soul is downcast within me;*	(3+2)
therefore, I will remember you	
from the land of Jordan and the Hermon range,	(3+2)
from the mountain of Mizar. [a]	
⁸⁽⁷⁾ *Deep is calling to deep,*	(3+2)
to the clamor of your cataracts.	
All your breakers and waves	(3+2)
have swept over me.	

9(8) *By day, the Lord commands his lovingkindness,*   (4+3+3)
  and by night, his ᵃ *song is with me,*
  a prayer to the ᵇ *Living God.*

10(9) *I say to God, my Rock:*   (3+2)
  "Why have you forgotten me?
  Why must I walk in darkness   (3+2)
  because of an enemy's oppression?"

11(10) *With a breaking* ᵃ *in my bones,*   (2+2)
  my foes taunted me,
  by saying to me all day long: (3+2)
  "Where is your God?"

12(11) *O my soul, why are you downcast*   (2+2)
  and why are you so disturbed within me?
  Wait patiently for God, for I will praise him again,   (4+3)
  the victories of my God's presence.

Notes

1.a. On the meaning of *Maskil,* see Ps 32:1, note a.

1.b. On psalms associated with the sons of Korah, see THE COMPILATION OF THE PSALTER in the INTRODUCTION.

2.a. For MT's איל ("hart, stag"), the more normal form אילת ("deer") is read, the ת apparently having been omitted (haplography). There may be a parallel to this line in the Ugaritic texts with respect to general poetic imagery (*CTA* 5.i.16–17; *CML* ², 68), though see the cautionary remarks of Donner (art. cit.) with respect to the meaning of Ugaritic *'aylt.*

3.a. The verb is pointed in MT as Niphal (*"be seen* (by) the face of God"); the pointing, which is grammatically difficult, presumably reflects the imposition of later orthodoxy, unhappy with the implication that God's face could actually be seen. But this is poetry, not dogmatic theology: the Qal (as in the translation) is more natural grammatically and has the support of some Heb. mss (De-Rossi, IV, 28).

4.a. Reading באמרם (De-Rossi, IV, 28, four Heb. mss): cf. v 11.

5.a. MT's אדדם is interpreted as Hithp. of דדה "move slowly" (cf. BDB). Dahood interprets the term as derived from נדד, "to bow down, prostrate" (*Psalms I,* 257), making his claim principally on the basis of Ugaritic. He cites the form *ydd (ndd)* in UT 76 (*CTA* 10).ii.17–18 and UT 51 (*CTA* 4).iii.11–12. But the supposed Ugaritic evidence is a highly uncertain basis upon which to propose a Heb. verb meaning "bow down." First, there is the problem of the root form of Ugaritic *ydd* in the two texts cited. Gibson, *CML* ², 145, identifies the form in each case to be *dwd* ("stood up"). But even if one grants that the root form is *ndd,* as is likely, it remains likely that *ndd* means "hasten, run" (cf. Arabic *nadda*); this sense is given in the translation of Caquot, et. al., *Textes ougaritiques I,* 200, 284 (cf. Driver, *CML,* 157; Gordon, *UT,* #1615).

6.a. Reading פני אלהי (cf. v 12), taking the first word of v 7 as belonging to v 6.

7.a. On the sense of the geographical terms in this verse, see the *Comment.* Dahood (*Psalms I,* 258–59) renders MT's מהר מצער as מהרם צער (and then, on the assumption of metathesis, renders צער as עצר), translating "mountains at the rim" (viz. of the netherworld). The principal basis for the suggestion is Ugaritic *ġsr* in UT 51.viii.4–8 (=*CTA* 4), which, he claims, means "edge, rim." But, for three reasons, the Ugaritic basis of the proposal should probably be rejected: (1) Ugaritic *ġsr* is a *hapax legomenon* in the Ugaritic texts, and is naturally of uncertain meaning (as Dahood admits); (2) an equally probable sense of the term is "ruler" (in context, "ruler of the world"); see M. Tsevat, "Sun Mountains at Ugarit," *JNWSL* 3 (1974) 73; (3) apart from all the difficulties with the Ugaritic term, the assumption that metathesis has occurred in the Hebrew term weakens the case still further.

9.a. On the variant form of the suffix in שירה, see Tournay (art. cit.).

9.b. MT has "*my* living God," but many Heb. mss omit the suffix (De-Rossi, IV, 29).

11.a. On the nuance "break, crush," for the verb רצח (by analogy with Akkadian terminology), see Waldman, art. cit., 548–49. An alternative, though less likely solution, is to emend to ברדץ, *"with a dagger* in my bones. . . ," as proposed by Leveen (art. cit., 57).

Form/Structure/Setting

There is extensive agreement among the majority of interpreters that Pss 42 and 43 should be interpreted as a single psalm, for the following reasons: (a) many Heb. mss present the psalms as a single unit; (b) Ps 43 has no title, which is surprising in Book II of the Psalter; and (c) they are joined by a common refrain (42:6, 12; 43:5). The reason for the separation into the two extant units is not known; it may originate with *G*, which provides a title for Ps 43 ("a psalm of David"), which in turn may have reflected an interpretation of the distinction between *lament* (Ps 42) and *prayer* (Ps 43). If the division of the original psalm was as early as *G*, then it is also the case that the unity (after the division) was recognized from an early period, at least as early as the time of Eusebius (cf. Alonso-Schökel, *JSOT* 1 [1976] 4).

With respect to form, Pss 42–43 is an *individual lament.* Although it is possible to interpret the psalm as *national lament,* taking the "I" to represent the nation (cf. Mowinckel, *The Psalms in Israel's Worship,* I, 219), or as a *royal lament,* dealing with the plight of the king (Eaton, *Kingship and the Psalms,* 69–71), the evidence for such views is slender. It is more probable that the psalm should be interpreted in the conventional sense of *individual,* reflecting the spiritual plight of a particular, but unknown person. The precise background to the lament is also uncertain. It might be that of one in the Exile, or of one cut off from this homeland while the royal cult still flourished. But it is equally possible that the background is to be found in sickness, which limited the poet's possibility of going to Jerusalem and participating in the worship in the temple.

The structure of the psalm falls into three sections, each concluded with a refrain, which provides the overall framework for the psalm.

1. 42:2–6   (a) Lament (vv 2–5)
                   (b) *Refrain* (v 6)
2. 42:7–12   (a) Lament (vv 7–11)
                   (b) *Refrain* (v 12)
3. 43:1–5   (a) Prayer (vv 1–4)
                   (b) *Refrain* (v 5)

At first impression, the framework of refrain may appear to give a static quality to the psalm as a whole, but in reality it provides the context for movement from near despair to surging confidence. After each lament, the refrain recalls the possibility of future praise, and in the prayer of the third part of the psalm, the movement occurs which begins to make the possibility a reality.

The psalm should probably not be associated directly with Israel's cultic life. Indeed, the nostalgia for worship (42:5) and the hope of future participa-

tion in the temple's worship (43:4) strongly imply that his individual lament
should be interpreted in a noncultic fashion. If the psalm were late and a
product of the Diaspora, its use would have been entirely appropriate to a
worshiping community, but there can be no certainty as to the psalm's background, and as a consequence its original setting remains unknown.

Comment

Lament and refrain (42:2–6). The psalmist begins to describe his plight with
a simile drawn from nature, to convey powerfully his spiritual *thirst.* Imagining
the dry steppe country, the poet envisages a deer thirsty for water; though
the simile focuses on the deer, it is the *water* which is to be one of the principal
poetic motifs running throughout the psalm. Like a thirsty animal in a dry
place, the psalmist thirsts for God, but it is specifically the worship of God
in the temple for which he longs (as is implied by "the face," or presence,
of God: v 3b). The opening simile is converted into a metaphor in v 4, linked
by the motif of water; the one who longed for a refreshing drink, tasted
instead the bitter water of tears. The question posed to the psalmist, "Where
is your God?" (v 4; see also v 11), could perhaps be taken to imply the
Exile, where it must have seemed that God had deserted his people. But
the more immediate sense is provided by any context of despair; in sickness
or in trouble, it seemed both to the psalmist and to his enemies that God
had departed (cf. Ps 22:2). Feeling deserted by God, and cut off from the
joy of participating in the temple's worship, the psalmist determines to remember better times (v 5). He determines to think back to the times when, amid
the great crowds of pilgrims, he had gone to Jerusalem to participate in
the festivals of worship. But a forced nostalgia is no substitute for reality,
and the first occurrence of the refrain (v 6) merely emphasizes the depth of
his plight. At this stage in the psalm, it is the first part of the refrain which
dominates (v 6a-b), while the second part (v. 6c-d) remains a distant hope.
The psalmist is still downcast and the praise is distant.

Second lament and refrain (42:7–12). The second lament begins with the
words of the refrain and develops them further. Recognizing that he is still
"downcast" (v 7a), the psalmist determines once again to draw on the resources of memory. But now, rather than remembering the pilgrim crowds
and festivals (as in v 5), he determines to remember God. The action is
significant; at the heart of the psalmist's predicament is an awareness of the
absence of God, and through the tool of memory he is determined to attempt
to dispel that sense of absence and distance. The geographical references
that follow are difficult to interpret; they may refer to the psalmist's homeland
(the hills of Hermon, the source of the Jordan, and the unknown Mt. Mizar),
or they may be terms which imply the whole land, or places visited by the
psalmist during the course of a lifetime. But in either case, they must be
interpreted in the context of the psalmist's attempt to harness his memory
toward the resolution of his plight. He is deliberately thinking of those places
in which, in one fashion or another, he had known and experienced the
presence of God; the memories should dispel the sense of wilderness and
dryness evoked in vv 2–3. But the attempt to harness memory is unsuccessful;

as he thinks of the great mountain range, whose western flank is lapped by the ocean, with the streams of the Jordan rising in the east, it is only the springs of chaos and despair which are released in his mind. Now the motif of water (vv 2–3) is reversed. He longed for water in thirst, but thinking of the waters of the ocean and those of the river, it is their waves and waterfalls that dominate his mind, like one chaotic deep calling to another (v 8a). He had longed for the waters of refreshment, but somehow in the effort to remember God, he had unleashed the primeval waters of chaos, which seemed to depict so powerfully his terrible situation.

Verse 9 is difficult to interpret, appearing at first to be out of context, but again it must be interpreted in the light of the determination to exercise memory (v 7). What he could remember in a literal sense was the good old days reflected in the words of v 9, when his relationship with God had been healthy and characterized by the orderly experience of God's lovingkindness. That was the literal memory he called to mind, but in the mental image, it was jaundiced and twisted by the reality of his present situation. Things had been good, but what could that mean when since then he had been over-whelmed by the divine waves (v 8) and now had to walk in darkness, apparently forgotten by God but remembered well enough by his enemies (v 10)? Thus vv 10–11 demonstrate the awful situation to which the psalmist was reduced by his exercise of memory; as he remembered, he could only conclude that God had forgotten. For though he used to know God's lovingkindness (v 9), now he knew only the taunting of enemies (v 11). The psalmist has not yet escaped his lament, and the repeated question, "Where is your God?" (v 11, cf. v 4) only reinforces the present depth of his distress. And so the refrain comes again (v 12) and drolls a kind of epitaph on the possibility of deliverance through memory. For twice the psalmist had remembered, and still he was *downcast* (v 12a), the latter part of the refrain offering only a hope that was as elusive as before.

Translation (Ps 43)

[1] *Judge me, O God,*   (2+2+2)
  and plead my case
    against a loveless people.
  From deceitful people   (2+2)
    and the unrighteous, rescue me.
[2] *For you are the God of my stronghold;*   (3+2)
    why have you rejected me?
  Why must I wander about in darkness,   (3+2)
    because of an enemy's oppression?
[3] *Send your light and your truth.*   (3+2)
    They shall guide me; [a]
    they shall bring me to your holy mountain   (3+2)
      and to your dwelling place. [b]
[4] *And let me go into God's altar,*   (3+2)
    to the God of my [a] *gladness.*

> *I will rejoice* [b] *and praise you on a lyre,*   (3+2)
>   *O God, my God.* [c]
> [5] *O my soul, why are you downcast*   (2+2)
>   *and why so disturbed within me?*
> *Wait patiently for God, for I will praise him again,*   (4+3)
>   *the victories of my God's presence.* [a]

Notes

3.a. Alternatively, יְנַחֲמוּנִי could be read (with the support of a few Heb. mss and S): "they shall comfort me."

3.b. The plural form of the Hebrew noun should probably be taken as an intensive plural, indicating the sanctity of the place.

4.a. שִׂמְחָתִי is read, with the addition of the pronominal suffix; MT's pointing, linking the term with following גִּילִי upsets the metrical (qinah) balance. See Brockington, *The Hebrew Text of the Old Testament*, 129.

4.b. For גִּילִי ("my rejoicing"), אָגִילָה ("I will rejoice") is read; cf. Kraus, *Psalmen 1–59*, 472.

4.c. The expression "O God, my God" is the Elohistic version of the more familiar "O Lord, my God" (e.g. Ps 7:2). Ps 42 is the first psalm in the so-called "Elohistic Psalter" (Pss 42–83); see THE COMPILATION OF THE PSALTER in the INTRODUCTION.

5.a. On the reading presupposed by this translation, see note a at Ps 42:6.

Comment

Prayer and refrain (43:1–5). The lament of the two preceding sections of the psalm is now converted into a prayer, and the form of the transition is striking. In the lament sections, the psalmist is introverted, dwelling on memory and trying to summon it to his aid; for practical purposes, he is talking to himself. But now, in this section of the psalm, the internal dialogue of lament is turned into an external dialogue with God. And the change from introvertive reflection to external plea is the beginning of real progress for the psalmist; he has already learned that there is no help to be found in the weak ally of memory, and aid must come directly from God.

First, he turns in prayer to the enemies (vv 2–3) who were so significant in his lament (42:4, 10, 11). Rather than merely lamenting their enmity, he asks God to act as his defense counsel and to take up his case. The nature of the enemies is no more specific here than in the earlier portions of the text. While the reference to "people" (v 1) might imply "nation," and hence be indicative of a king's foe, the parallelism of v 1 (the "deceitful" and "unrighteous") indicates that the verse refers simply to enemies in general. While there is still the thread of lament running through the prayer (v 2c–d is almost identical to 42:10c–d), the lament is subsumed within the purpose of the prayer, namely the plea for rescue. The conversion process of prayer is seen most clearly in the petition that God "send light and truth" (v 3); while there was no escape from "darkness" in 42:10, now the light is asked for to dispel the darkness of inimical oppression. Light would bring the psalmist out of darkness and into the divine presence in the temple, here symbolized by the "holy mountain" and divine "dwelling place." Again, the way in which prayer converts lament can be observed, for in 42:5 God's temple had been merely the object of nostalgic remembrance; now it comes closer to the reality of experience in the prayer addressed to the living God. In v 4, the prayer and the confidence that it will be answered are finally fused. "Let me go in," he prays, but then confidence outstrips petition as he states: "I will rejoice. . . ."

It is the transformation of the prayer, and specifically the transition that takes place in v 4, that finally changes even the refrain, despite the fact that the words remain the same. For in the laments and their culmination in refrain, it was inevitable that the accent fall on the first part of the refrain, namely the "downcast soul," because those lines reflect precisely the internal dialogue between a person and his soul from which there was no liberation. While the dialogue remained within, the possibility of praise remained without. But the prayer has changed that; the situation creating sorrow still exists, but as the question is asked again, "why are you downcast?", the response can now be given with the conviction that God has heard and answered his prayer.

Explanation

It is characteristic of the human condition, that in health and happy times it is easier to be outgoing and positive in one's view of life than it is in times of distress. The situation is clearly exemplified in the religion of ancient Egypt, which was for the most part a religion characterized by a cheerful view of this life and a positive view of the life beyond. But there is a remarkable text which has survived from the second millennium B.C., giving a deeper insight into the human psyche: it is commonly entitled a "Dispute over Suicide" (*ANET*, 405–7). A man engages in a dialogue with his own soul. He suggests to his soul that the miseries of life are such that suicide seems attractive, but his soul has an equally gloomy view of death and sees no solution in suicide. The text (as it has survived) contains no solution to the problem of the dialogue, but its very existence is a testimony to an experience which was common not only in the biblical world, but also in our modern world: despair. Despair destroys the positive, outgoing view of life and turns a person in upon himself. As in ancient Egypt, so in Pss 42–43, the literary form by which expression is given to the sense of despair and lament over life is the dialogue between a person and his soul. And the literary form is rooted in a human reality, the psychological tendency toward introversion that is created by external pressures.

But while the basic structure of the psalm, and notably its refrain, is that of dialogue between a person and his soul, the latter part of the text (Ps 43) breaks the literary bind by bringing a third person into the "dialogue." When the psalmist stops speaking to himself (Ps 42) and addresses his words to God (Ps 43), the beginning of his deliverance is in sight. And again, the literary structure may reveal the solution for reality; when one turns from the memories and burdens within the mind and boldly addresses to God a plea for deliverance, the first step is taken on the path that leads ultimately to a restoration of the life of praise and to mental and spiritual health.

A National Lament after Defeat in Battle (44:1–27)

Bibliography

Beyerlin, W. "Innerbiblische Aktualisierungsversuche: Schichten im 44. Psalm." *ZTK* 73 (1976) 446–60. **Gross, H.** "Geschichtserfahrung in den Psalmen 44 und 77." *TTZ* 80 (1971) 207–21. **Parker, H. M.** "Artaxerxes III Ochus and Psalm 44." *JQR* 68/3 (1978) 152–68.

Translation

1 For the musical director. For the sons of Korah. A *Maskil.*

2(1) O God, we have heard with our ears—   (3+2)
    our fathers told us!—
    the deed you did in their days,   (3+2)
    in the days of old.

3(2) By your hand,[a] you dispossessed nations, but
    planted them;[b]   (4+3)
    you crushed peoples, but set them free.

4(3) For they did not take possession of the land by
    their sword,   (4+3)
    and their arm did not bring them victory;
    but it was your right hand and your arm,   (2+2+2)
    and the light of your countenance,
    for you took pleasure in them.

5(4) You are my king and[a] my God,[b]   (3+3)
    the one who commanded[c] Jacob's victory.

6(5) With you, we push back our enemies;   (3+3)
    in your name, we trample our foes.

7(6) For I will not trust in my bow,   (4?+3)
    and my sword will not give me victory.

8(7) But you have given us victory over our enemies   (3+2)
    and have put to shame those who hate us.

9(8) In God we boasted all day long   (3+3)
    and we shall praise your name for ever. SELAH.

10(9) But now you have spurned and humiliated us   (3+3)
    and do not go forth with our armies.

11(10) You make us retreat from an enemy,   (3+3)
    and those who hate us have plundered at will.[a]

12(11) You hand us over like sheep for food   (3+2)
    and have scattered us among the nations.

13(12) You sell your people cheaply   (3+2?)
    and have not profited from the price of their sale.

14(13) You make us a reproach to our neighbors,   (3+3)
    an object of mockery and derision to those around us.

15(14) *You make us a by-word among the nations,* (3+3)
  an object of sorrow [a] *among the peoples.*
16(15) *My ignominy is before me all day long,* (3+3)
  and shame has covered [a] *my face,*
17(16) *because of the voice of the reproacher and reviler,* (3+3)
  because of the enemy and the avenger.
18(17) *All this happened to us, but we did not forget you* (4+3)
  and we did not act deceitfully in covenant with you.
19(18) *Our heart did not turn back* (4+4)
  nor did our foot [a] *turn aside from your path.*
20(19) *But you crushed us in a place of jackals* (3+3)
  and covered us with deathly darkness.
21(20) *If we had forgotten our God's name* (3+3)
  and spread our hands in prayer to a foreign god,
22(21) *would not God discover this,* (4+4)
  for he knows the heart's secrets?
23(22) *Yet on account of you, we have been slain all day long;* (3+3)
  we have been reckoned as sheep for slaughter.
24(23) *Wake up! Why do you sleep, O Lord?* (4+3)
  Awake! don't reject us for ever.
25(24) *Why do you hide your face* (3+3)
  and forget our affliction and oppression?
26(25) *For we* [a] *have been prostrated in the dust;* (3+3)
  our belly clings to the earth.
27(26) *Arise! Help us!* (3+3)
  And redeem us because of your lovingkindness.

Notes

3.a. Reading בידך, and omitting אתה (with *G* and *S*).
3.b. The antecedent of "them" is the "fathers" referred to in v. 2.
5.a. The conjunction is read, after *G*.
5.b. Reading אלהי (with suffix); cf. *G*. On the final *mem*, see note c.
5.c. מצוה (participle) is read (cf. *G* and *S*), the *mem* being provided from the previous word (note b).
11.a. Literally, "for themselves."
15.a. Literally, "a shaking of the head."
16.a. Reading כסתה, with Kraus, *Psalmen 1–59*, 479–80.
19.a. The singular form is read, אשׁרנו, with several Heb. mss.
26.a. Literally, "our soul."

Form/Structure/Setting

Psalm 44 is a *national* (or communal) *lament*, reflecting the religious activity of the community following a military disaster of national proportions. The language alternates between the first person singular ("I, my, me") and the first person plural ("we, us"), and though the alternation may be merely a literary convention, it is more likely to reflect alternation of speakers. The king, who was commander-in-chief of the armed forces, speaks in the first person singular; the people (whether the army or a national congregation) speak the words in the plural.

The overall structure of the psalm falls into three parts, and the alternation with respect to speakers pervades the whole.

1. God's past acts as basis for current confidence (44:2–9)
   a. *People:* God's acts in the past (vv 2–4)
   b. *King:* the appropriation of the past (v 5)
   c. *People:* the normal grounds of confidence (v 6)
   d. *King:* declaration of trust (v 7)
   e. *People:* declaration of confidence (vv 8–9)
2. The Lament (44:10–23)
   a. *People:* lament of the present crisis (vv 10–15)
   b. *King:* declaration of shame (vv 16–17)
   c. *People:* declaration of innocence (vv 18–23)
3. Concluding prayer (44:24–27)
   King and *people* pray for deliverance and help.

The two principal sections of the psalm appear to have an inner chiastic structure with respect to speakers, which is resolved finally in the concluding prayer. One may suppose that the psalm was employed in an antiphonal fashion.

The setting in which the psalm was used is not known with certainty. It is unlikely that the psalm was used merely with the threat of disaster facing the nation. Thus 2 Chr 20:4–13 (cited by Kraus, *Psalmen 1–59*, 480, and Anderson, *Psalms I*, 336), in which Jehoshaphat proclaimed a fast in Judah in view of the impending military attack by Moab and Ammon, does not provide in principle an appropriate type of setting for Ps 44. The lament of this psalm presupposes the battle has already been lost (vv 10–11), prisoners have been taken and made slaves (v 13), and the army has been decimated in a long day of slaughter (v 23). The lament, then, was used following a defeat, not merely when disaster threatened. And though it is possible to suppose a national setting in the temple in Jerusalem, it is more likely that one should think of the lament being used at the end of the day of battle and defeat. Thus Ps 44 should be seen as the precise counterpart of the *victory hymn* (e.g. Judg 5); just as the latter was employed after battle to celebrate victory, so this psalm was used to lament defeat.

The information contained within the psalm is not sufficiently precise to allow it to be linked to any particular occasion or military defeat, though there have been numerous attempts to do so. The psalm has been linked to disasters in the Maccabean period, the Persian period, and to various periods within the history of the Hebrew monarchy. The recent attempt by Parker (*JQR* 68 [1978] 152–68) to link the psalm to the crushing of the Phoenician Revolt of 345–44 B.C. by Antiochus III Ochus, unconsciously demonstrates the impossibility of finding hard evidence to date the psalm. On the other hand, it is likely that in the psalm's history in Hebrew life and worship, it was used in a variety of situations from the time of the monarchy, through the Maccabean period, and beyond (see further W. Beyerlin, art. cit.). All that can be reasonably proposed is that the psalm's origins are to be found at some point in the history of the (preexilic) monarchy, when the king continued to function as the commander of Israel's armies.

Comment

Title (44:1). On the meaning of *Maskil,* see note a at Ps 32:1. On psalms associated with the Sons of Korah, see THE COMPILATION OF THE PSALTER in the INTRODUCTION.

God's past acts as a basis for current confidence (44:2–9). The relatively cheerful and positive note with which the psalm begins is deceptive, for it merely sets the stage for the terrible lament which is to follow. Everything they had learned about the past should have led them to hope for victory that day, but such had not been the case, so there is a certain irony in the opening words. The people knew the great deeds God had done in the past; they had learned of them as children from their fathers (v 2). Indeed, the very existence of their state was a direct consequence of God's actions in the past, conquering foreign enemies and establishing their ancestors in the land (v 3). Those past achievements had not been human achievements; they had been a direct consequence of God's participation in the history of his chosen people (v 4). And it was the essence of the Hebrew faith that the past could always be appropriated for the present, that the people in faith could look in the present moment for the continuation of those mighty acts of God in the past which had been so pregnant with future implications. Hence the king affirms his faith in that same God, who in the past had given *Jacob* (viz. Israel) victory (v 5).

In v 6, the people affirm what should have been the present reality, in continuity with the past, namely the defeat of enemies. And the king's declaration of v 7 indicates that his theology was right! He knew that he would not win victory merely by virtue of his prowess as a warrior, but only through the strength that God could give (cf. Ps 20:8 [7]; Ps 33:16). And so the people join in again, affirming that God alone can give victory and he alone deserves the praise and credit for victory (vv 8–9). If Ps 44 ended with v 9, it would be a marvelous *victory hymn,* but because it continues directly to lament, the puzzled and perplexed tone of the opening verses becomes clear. The opening verses set the stage for the striking contrast which now follows.

The Lament (44:10–23). The present reality is introduced by the words "but now" (v 10); now, for some reason beyond the comprehension of the people, things are not what they ought to be. God had not been with the army on the day of battle (v 10), and so there had been terrible defeat, some escaping, some being killed and some being taken captive and becoming, in effect, slaves. The defeat made Israel an object of pity and scorn in the eyes of other nations (vv 14–15). The nature of the defeat was particularly puzzling, for the words describing it are reminiscent of the curses of defeat that would come upon Israel if the nation was unfaithful to the covenant stipulations (e.g. Deut 28:15–69). And not only had the nation been humiliated in defeat, but so too had the king been covered with shame (vv 16–17); as the representative of God, he felt particularly humiliated by the defeat in which God should have been victor. As the representative of the people, the weight of the defeat rested on his shoulders and he carried the awful burden.

The real sense of perplexity finally emerges explicitly in vv 18–23. If the king and the nation had failed miserably in their covenant obligations to God, then at least their defeat in battle would be explicable. But they had not been unfaithful; they had maintained their integrity in the covenant relationship (v 18) and they had honestly walked in the path God set before them (v 19). They had not broken the first commandment (v 21) or kept any secrets from God (v 22). According to their understanding of the covenant theology, God should have been with them and given them victory; instead he had crushed them (v 20) and permitted them to be slaughtered (v 23). The meaning of the expression "place of jackals" (v 20) is not entirely certain, but the parallelism with "deathly darkness" suggests the devastation of defeat; the battlefield, where defeat was experienced, had become like the lonely palaces of postwar Babylon, inhabited only by the scavenging jackals and hyenas (cf. Isa 13:21–22). On "deathly darkness" (צלמות), see the *Comment* on Ps 23:4.

The concluding prayer (44:24–27). Neither the king nor the people have any solution to the perplexing questions raised in the lament; they can only conclude with a prayer that God not reject them *forever* (v 24). The language of the prayer evokes again the military context of the lament; on the expressions "wake up" and "arise," in a military context, see further Judg 5:12 and Num 10:35. The prayer is for divine aid in crisis (vv 24, 27), for though the battle had been lost, the war continued; but the prayer is uttered in the same perplexity as the lament, the two questions *"why?"* (vv 24, 25) separating the two explicit parts of the prayer. The final word of the psalm, "lovingkindness" (v 27), raises again the grounds of the plea. Though the covenant, in which the people had been faithful (v 18), had become a mystery, still it was only in the covenant lovingkindness of God that there remained any hope of redemption.

Explanation

In a sense, there is no simple explanation to the issues raised in Ps 44, any more than there is a simple explanation to the issues raised in the Book of Job. Indeed, from a certain perspective, Ps 44 may be perceived as a communal or national parallel to the more individual and international Book of Job. But whereas the Book of Job raises some of the fundamental perplexities of human existence for examination and reflection, Ps 44 raises them only in an agonizing *cri de couer* addressed to God. Job, before his crisis, had only "heard with his ears," but after the divine revelation, he could say: "now my eyes have seen you!" (Job 42:5). But the lamenters of Ps 44 could only say, "we have heard with our ears" (v 2); for them there was no vision of God, only a desperate prayer for help.

The problem in Ps 44 appears at first to be a problem of covenant theology. If king and people had been faithful to the covenant stipulations (vv 18–22), then why was God not faithful to his covenant commitment to provide

defense and deliverance? The root problem, in other words, is precisely the problem of the Book of Job, namely the problem of God. But while the psalmist neither elaborates on the problem nor points to a resolution in theology, he points nevertheless to a more existential resolution. It is to be found in the prayer with which the psalm concludes. At the rational level, it would seem rather futile to pray and to seek God's love, when the immediate experience suggested that God could not be relied on. Yet the prayer is rooted in a faith deeper than reason. The faith also went beyond theology, which implied that God's actions could always be anticipated, if not predicted, strictly in terms of the covenant theology; the faith recognized a mystery in God's ways, beyond both reason and theology, which made prayer worthwhile even in a time of crisis that was both military and theological in its proportions. And so ultimately, Ps 44 with its concluding prayer points in the same direction as the Book of Job, namely that there is an immense mystery in God and his ways, but one must continue to trust and to pray. The faith of the psalmist is not meek and acquiescent; his prayer follows a statement of downright insolence, in which he states that it was all God's fault that so many had been killed (v 23)! But the insolence is muted by the prayer; for if God would only arise, then the life of faith could return to some kind of fragile stability.

A Royal Wedding Song (45:1-18)

Bibliography

Couroyer, B. "Dieu ou roi? Le vocatif dans le Psaume XLV (vv 1–9)." *RB* 78 (1971) 233–41. **Emerton, J. A.** "The Syntactical Problem of Ps 45:7." *JSS* 13 (1968) 58–63. **Gaster, T. H.** "Psalm 45." *JBL* 74 (1955) 239–51. **Harman, A. M.** "The Syntax and Interpretation of Psalm 45:7." J. H. Skilton (ed.), *The Law and the Prophets. Old Testament Studies in Honor of Oswald T. Allis* (1974) 337–47. **Loretz, O.** "Psalmenstudien (II)." *UF* 5 (1973) 213–18. **Mulder, J.** *Studies on Psalm 45* (1972). **Porter, J. R.** "Psalm XLV.7." *JTS* 12 (1961) 51–53.

Translation

1   For the musical director. According to *Shoshannim*.ᵃ For the sons of Korah.ᵇ A *Maskil*.ᶜ
A love song.

2(1) *A noble theme moves my heart;*   (4+4+4)
I will recite my compositions concerning the king;
my tongue is the pen of a skillful scribe.

3(2) *You are the most beautiful* ᵃ *of human beings,*   (3+3+4?)
with your lips anointed with grace;
so God has blessed you forever.

4(3) *Gird your sword upon your thigh,*   (3+3)
your splendor and your majesty, O warrior! ᵃ

5(4) *Then dominate,*[a] *prosper, and ride out*   (3+4?)
      on behalf of truth, humility, and righteousness.
      Then may your right hand show you wondrous deeds,   (3+2)
6(5) *your arrows sharpened;*
      peoples shall fall beneath you,   (3+3)
      in the midst [a] *of the king's enemies.*

7(6) *The eternal and everlasting God has enthroned you;* [a]   (4+4)
      the scepter of your kingship is a scepter of uprightness.

8(7) *You have loved righteousness and hated wickedness;*   (4+4+3)
      therefore God, your God, has anointed you,
      rather than your companions, with the oil of exultation.

9(8) *All your robes are myrrh, aloes and cassia;*   (4+4)
      from ivory palaces, stringed instruments [a] *delight you.*

10(9) *A princess* [a] *is stationed among your noblest women,*   (4+4)
      the consort of your right hand, with gold of Ophir.

11(10) *Hear, O princess,*[a] *and look and listen;*   (4+4)
      and forget your people and your father's house.

12(11) *And the king longs for your beauty,*   (3+2+2)
      for he is your lord;
      so give him respect!

13(12) *Then a princess of Tyre will bring you a gift;*   (3+3?)
      the wealthiest [a] *people will court your favor.*

14(13) *A princess is all honor within;*   (3?+3)
      her garment is made from finely worked gold.

15(14) *In embroidered clothes, she is brought to the king;*   (3+3+2)
      the maidens, her companions, are behind her,
      being brought to her.[a]

16(15) *They are conducted with joy and gladness;*   (3+3)
      They enter the king's palace.

17(16) *Your sons shall replace your fathers;*   (4+4)
      you will make them princes over the whole land.

18(17) *I will make your name to be remembered through every generation;*   (4+4?)
      therefore, peoples will praise you for ever and ever.

Notes

1.a. Literally, "lilies" (rather than "roses," as in some old translations). The word refers to the tune, or musical setting, to which the psalm should be sung, and appears also in Pss 69, 80; see also Ps 60.

1.b. On the "sons of Korah," see THE COMPILATION OF THE PSALTER in the INTRODUCTION.

1.c. On *Maskil*, see note a on Ps 32:1.

3.a. There is no need to emend the text (as proposed in *BHS*); on the translation of יפיפית, "you are the most beautiful," parallel to Ugaritic *ttpp* ("she beautifies herself"), see J. C. de Moor, "Murices in Ugaritic Mythology," *Orientalia* 37 (1968) 124 (note).

4.a. For reasons of balance, גבור ("warrior") is taken with the second line of the verse, rather than the first line, as indicated in the punctuation of MT.

5.a. וֶהְדָרְךָ is pointed as a Hiph. imperative of the verb הדר, "to dominate, master." See also Dahood, *Psalms I*, 271, and on the Hebrew-Ugaritic root *drk*, Craigie, *ZAW* 90 (1978) 378.

6.a. Literally, "in the heart."

7.a. The translation of v 7a is that of Dahood, *Psalms I*, 273, vocalizing כסא as the Piel of a denominative verb, "enthrone." Though this rendition is not without difficulty, it appears to be the most appropriate to the sense and context of the passage, which is descriptive of the king. The following are alternative translations of the crux. (1) "Your throne, O God, is forever and ever," following the punctuation and obvious syntax of MT (viz. that אלהים is vocative); cf. *G*, Harman, art. cit., Porter, art. cit., and Couroyer, art. cit., the latter citing Egyptian analogies in support of the vocative. The problem of this rendition is the difficulty of the sense in context. (2) "Your throne is like God's throne, eternal," as proposed by NEB (cf. Emerton, art. cit.), but the syntactical argument in support of this rendition is not persuasive (see Harman, op. cit., 338–40). (3) "Your divine throne," as in RSV, but again the syntax raises problems (cf. GKC 128d). (4) "Your throne is God's for ever and ever," as proposed by Mulder, but the syntax does not clearly designate possession. While Dahood's translation suits the context best, (1) above is the most likely interpretation of the vocalization in MT.

9.a. מני is emended to מִנִּים, "stringed instruments" (cf. Ps 150:4); see Delitzsch, *Biblical Commentary on the Psalms*, II, 99–100.

10.a. Reading the singular (בת מלך); cf. *S*. The parallelism also implies the singular form.

11.a. Literally, "daughter"; the context (v 10) indicates "princess."

13.a. Dahood translates עשירי עם as "the guests," on the basis of Ugaritic *šr* (II), "to invite to a banquet" (see *Psalms I*, 275). The nuance "banquet" in the Ugaritic term is not certain; though many scholars have argued for it on the basis of the Ethiopic cognate *'ašur*, Ludolf has raised the question whether the Ethiopic term is not merely based on the hour ("tenth") at which a banquet was held (cited by Caquot, et. al., *Textes ougaritiques I*, 154). The regular parallelism of Ugaritic *šr* (II) with *šqy* indicates that the sense is "to serve with drink." The sense is strengthened by the apparent sense of the noun derived from *šr* (II), having the sense "victuallers"; see B. Cutler and J. McDonald, "The Unique Ugaritic Text *UT* 113 and the Question of Guilds," *UF* 9 (1977) 23–24. In summary the nuance of the Ugaritic term required by Dahood's argument is highly uncertain, and hence Ugaritic data should be omitted from the proposal.

15.a. Reading לה, with two Heb. mss, as implied by context.

Form/Structure/Setting

The initial problem in any examination of Ps 45 concerns the text and the related issue of the metrical analysis. The text is difficult to translate and interpret at many points, and the analysis of the poetic structure is equally uncertain. These problems, in turn, produce in clear form a problem of method inherent in all study of the Psalms; from one perspective, it would be ideal to establish the text and its meaning first (as attempted by Mulder, *Studies on Psalm 45*), before moving to the metrical analysis. On the other hand, as Loretz points out (*UF* 5 [1973] 216–17), a knowledge of the metrical (or stichometric) structure is of enormous assistance in determining the text. But the problem is essentially one of circularity from which there is no easy escape. Both the analysis of the psalm and its translation (above) are subject to some uncertainty, given the problems inherent in the text itself.

With respect to form, Ps 45 is basically a *royal psalm;* specifically, it is described in the title (v 1) as a *love song,* and the substance indicates that the love song should be interpreted as a *wedding song.* The content of the song focuses on the bride and groom, apparently in the context of the wedding ceremony as such. There are no precise parallels to this type of psalm elsewhere in the Psalter, so that little internal comparative evidence can be used in the interpretation of the psalm. The Song of Songs provides general parallels with respect to Hebrew love poetry, but little that is directly analogous to the psalm in form and setting; the closest parallel material is the "Song of Solomon's Procession" (Cant 3:6–11), though it is not a precise parallel.

For parallels from ancient Near Eastern literature, see Mulder, *Studies on Psalm 45.*

Gaster's view (art. cit.), that Ps 45 is a regular rather than a royal wedding song, is probably inappropriate with respect to the initial form and setting of the psalm. Indeed, it is possible that the tradition in later Judaism, whereby bride and groom were addressed as if royalty, is related to the later usage of texts such as Ps 45; with the passing of the monarchy from the history of Judaism, more royal texts were put to common usage, thus subtly shaping later tradition and custom.

The introduction of the song (v 2), in which the poet states his intentions and makes explicit reference to his "compositions," is reminiscent both of the earlier Near Eastern court poetry and also of the Arabic compositions of the bards of a later date, singing the praise of their patrons. The structure of the psalm can be set out as follows.

1. Title (v 1)
2. The poet's introduction (v 2)
3. In praise of the royal groom (vv 3–9)
4. In praise of the bride (vv 10–16)
5. Final words to the king (vv 17–18).

Thus, the psalm proper extends from v 3 to v 18, and the psalm is balanced by the *inclusio* device, signified by the use of the words עַל־כֵּן ("so, therefore") (vv 3, 18) and לְעוֹלָם ("forever") (vv 3, 18).

The setting should probably be found in some general wedding celebration, rather than in any specific temple or cultic context. This much may be implied by the poet's opening words (v 2), which are indicative of an artistic composition in celebration of the event, rather than a cultic or prophetic context. The possibility of a prophetic context is raised in vv 17–18, however, with respect to the identity of the word "I." If "I" has God as its antecedent, then the last two verses could be interpreted as a kind of prophetic declaration of God's blessing on the royal couple. But the context, together with the *inclusio* device linking v 18 to v 3, suggest that the "I" is none other than the poet of v 2, who has already referred to himself in the first person. Thus it is the poet, by means of his composition, who will cause the king's name "to be remembered through every generation" (v 18a).

There can be little doubt that this poetic composition originated in the wedding celebration for a particular king, composed for the occasion; subsequently, it would have been used frequently at royal weddings. But having affirmed in principle that the song, in its initial setting, should be related to a particular occasion, it should also be admitted that no firm decision can be made with respect to its historical origin. Thus, by way of example, the reference to the ivory palaces (v 9) and to the princes of Tyre (v 13) have been used to support an argument for setting the psalm originally in the context of the wedding of Ahab and Jezebel; but, as Kraus rightly points out, the evidence is thoroughly ambiguous and could refer to a variety of different occasions (*Psalmen 1–59,* 489). All that can be affirmed with reasonable certainty is that the psalm originated at some point in the history of the Hebrew monarchy.

Comment

The poet's introduction (45:2). The poet begins by declaring his intention to recite his composition on a "noble theme," namely the king's wedding. His "compositions" (literally, "works": מעשי), were no doubt oral, rather than written, compositions; that is to say, the creative process was an oral one, the product only later being recorded in writing (in contrast to the modern world, in which the composition of poetry is viewed primarily as a literary task). On oral composition (as distinct from transmission), see further Culley, *Oral Formulaic Language in the Biblical Psalms*, 5–9. Thus the poet is not a scribe; what the pen is to the scribe, the tongue is to the poet (v 2c). It is his tongue which articulates the words that will both praise and celebrate the participants in the wedding festivities.

In praise of the royal groom (45:3–9). The poet begins by declaring the king's beauty, but it is clear from the lines that follow that it is not primarily any physical kind of beauty with which he is concerned. It is the king's royal attributes and divinely approved functions which give rise to such celebration. Thus the first objects of beauty are the king's "lips," not because of their physical appearance, but because they are "anointed with grace" (v 3b). Thus anointed, they speak words of grace and kindness to the royal subjects, and the gracious speech in turn evokes the divine blessing of the king (v 3c). The royal attributes in vv 4–8 combine the military role and prowess of the king with the just causes for which he must fight. Thus, he has a warrior's sword, but its use (either literally or metaphorically) is such that he is accorded characteristics normally reserved for God, namely "splendor" and "majesty" (v 4; cf. Ps 96:6). His battles are on behalf of "truth, humility and righteousness" (v 5); his enemies, against whom he rides out in battle, are the enemies of the same virtues, and therefore must be conquered. The essence of the poet's praise of the king comes to a focus in v 7; the king's throne is the earthly counterpart to God's throne. And just as God's throne was assumed after the conquest of the evil forces of chaos (see further J. Gray, *The Legacy of Canaan* [2], 287), so too the king was enthroned by God as a consequence of his conquest of the enemies of righteousness (vv 6–7). Thus, "righteousness" and "wickedness" (v 8) correspond to order and chaos, and just as God's conquest of chaos established his orderly reign, so too the king's hatred of wickedness contributed to the righteous rule of order. The anointing with oil (v 8) refers poetically to the anointing of the king for his royal task, but the immediate point of reference is probably to be found in the activities of the wedding ceremony as such; the king would be anointed as a part of the preparation for the celebration itself (on Ugaritic parallels for such anointing, see A. Caquot et al., *Textes ougaritiques*, I, 161). After the anointing, the groom would be decked in royal robes, fragrant with precious perfumes (v 9a); in the background, the stringed instruments can already be heard striking up their music (v 9b). Thus the poet weaves the visual scene into his poetry, but though the words are evoked by the event, they point beyond to the deeper significance of the event. The "ivory palaces" are not buildings constructed from ivory, but furnished and decorated with precious ivory treasures.

In praise of the bride (45:10–16). The scene now shifts from the royal groom to the princess who is the bride, who is pictured as standing, perhaps in the palace, among the land's noblest women. The gold which adorns her (v 10b) is no doubt decorative, but again the poet has taken the visual element of gold and applied it, by implication, to the inner worth of the princess. The location of Ophir, which is mentioned frequently in the biblical text as the source of gold, is not known with certainty; recent discoveries in Saudi Arabia, however, have indicated that the remains of ancient gold mines at Mahdadh Dhahab (between Mecca and Medina) may perhaps have been the mines of ancient Ophir, the source of Israel's gold in Solomon's time (see further L. Berkowitz, "Has the U.S. Geological Survey found King Solomon's Gold Mines?," *BAR* 3/3 [1977] 1, 28–33).

The poet captures the sense of loneliness and homesickness in the princess, overwhelmed by the setting and the occasion, and urges her in his poetry not to lament the loss of her paternal home (v 11), but to look forward to the new love she will find in her groom, the king (v 12). She is not only to be married, but she is coming into a new position; no longer a daughter in her father's house, she will be a queen in her own house, whose favor is sought by men and women alike (v 13).

The poet returns again to the quality of the princess in vv 14–15. He has little to say about her physical beauty (in contrast to the Song of Songs), but indicates again how the extravagantly beautiful garments worn for the occasion symbolize the inner honor and integrity of her person (v 14a). The poet's words (in vv 15b–16) suggest a procession; perhaps the king, who is described first, is already in the palace, and the princess now comes in to him accompanied by her maidens. (A modern analogy would be the groom waiting in the church, and the bride and bridesmaids processing in to him there.)

Final words to the king (45:17–18). Though the words are ambiguous in English, the pointing of the Hebrew text (viz. the gender of the pronominal suffixes) makes it clear that the final verses are addressed again to the groom. The significance of "sons" (or children) is to be seen in the context of the continuity of the royal dynasty. The marriage was not only a covenant of love, but from the union would come the children upon whom would rest future responsibility for ruling in the kingdom. "I will make your name . . ." (v 18a): that is, the poet, through his composition, would prolong permanently the memory of the king in the land. Alternatively, if v 18 is interpreted as a prophetic declaration, then God is subject; God, through the children (v 17), would prolong the memory of the king (but see the comments in *Form/ Structure/Setting*, above).

Explanation

Psalm 45 is a superb example of what C. S. Lewis has called "second meanings in the Psalms" (*Reflections on the Psalms*, 101–15). The primary meaning of the psalm is clear; it is a wedding song, celebrating the marriage of a king to a princess. In its original sense and context, it is not in any sense a messianic psalm. And yet within the context of early Christianity (and in Judaism before that), it becomes a messianic psalm par excellence. The express evidence for the transition is to be found in Heb 1:8–9, where Ps 45:7–8 is quoted with explicit reference to Jesus Christ. But the "second meaning" extends to the whole psalm, not merely to the two verses quoted, and it develops further the way in which the OT's portrayal of human love and marriage may become the basis of an allegory of Christ and the Church, the Groom and the Bride. Thus Ps 45 supplements the positive allegory of the Song of Songs (in its "second meaning") and the negative allegory of Hosea 1–3; it is closer to the parable of Ezekiel 16, though it goes beyond that too. For Ps 45, in its second meaning, develops not only the allegory of love, but also that of royalty. Christ, the King, has been enthroned by God (v 7) and rules in righteousness. The Church, the Bride, is called upon to leave home and worship the King (v 12). But the ultimate blessing of the marriage is that of the children (v 17), the future generations through whom the kingdom would flourish.

A Psalm of Confidence   (46:1–12)

Bibliography

Eissfeldt, O. "Psalm 46." *Kleine Schriften,* IV, 8–11. **Kelly, S.** "Psalm 46: a Study in Imagery." *JBL* 89 (1970) 305–12. **Krinetzki, L.** "Jahwe ist uns Zuflucht und Wehr. Eine stilistisch-theologische Auslegung von Psalm 46 (45)." *BibLeb* 3 (1962) 26–42. **Neve, L.** "The Common Use of Tradition by Psalm 46 and Isaiah." *ExpTim* 86 (1974/ 75) 243–46. **Weiss, M.** "Wege der neuen Dichtungswissenschaft in ihrer Anwendung auf die Psalmenforschung." *Bib* 42 (1961) 255–302.

Translation

[1]	For the musical director. For the sons of Korah.[a] According to *'Alamoth.*[b] A song.	
2(1)	*God is our refuge and protection,*[a]	(4+4)
	a very present help in times of trouble.	
3(2)	*Therefore, we shall not fear when the earth quakes,*[a]	(4+4)
	or when the mountains slide into the midst of the seas.	
4(3)	*Its waters roar and foam;*	(3+3)
	the mountains shake at its swelling. SELAH.	
5(4)	*A river! Its streams cause rejoicing for the city of God,*	(4?+3)
	the holy dwelling place of the Most High.	
6(5)	*God is in its midst—it will not slip!*	(4+4)
	God will help it at the break of dawn.	
7(6)	*The nations roared!*	(2+2)
	The kingdoms slipped!	
	He gave forth his voice—	(2+2)
	the earth melts!	
8(7)	*The Lord of Hosts is with us;*	(3+3)
	the God of Jacob is our stronghold. SELAH.	

9(8) *Come, see the Lord's deeds,*   (4+4)
      the desolations he has done in the earth.
10(9) *He makes wars cease to the earth's ends;*   (4+4+3)
      he breaks the bow and shatters the spear,
      and burns war-wagons ª *in the fire.*
11(10) *"Relax, and know that I am God;*   (4+4)
      I will be exalted among the nations, exalted in the earth."
12(11) *The Lord of Hosts is with us;*   (3+3)
      the God of Jacob is our stronghold. SELAH

Notes

1.a. On *the sons of Korah* psalms, see THE COMPILATION OF THE PSALTER in the INTRODUCTION.
1.b. *'Alamoth* (lit. "maidens, young women") might be the name of the tune or musical setting
to which the psalm was sung. More probably, it may indicate a high musical setting, or being
sung by soprano voices; see Delitzsch, *Biblical Commentary on the Psalms*, II, 109.
2.a. Hebrew עז may mean "strength," or "refuge, protection"; the latter sense is implied
by the present context. On Hebrew-Ugaritic *'z,* "protection," see Craigie, *VT* 22 (1972)
145–46.
3.a. Dahood translates בהמיר by "jaws" (of the nether world), on the basis of Ugaritic *hmry*
(mhmrt); Psalms I, 278. But while the sense of the Ugaritic terminology is fairly well established
(the *mhmrt,* in *CTA* 5.i.17, are the "watery depths"), its association with the Hebrew term in
this context is not well established; see further Loretz, *Die Psalmen*, II, 445–51. The Hebrew is
interpreted as Hiph. (inf. constr.) of the root מור.
10.a. The sense "wagons, carts," for Heb. עגלות is somewhat uncertain. *G* has θυρεοὺς ("buckler, small shield"); on this translation, see further Dahood, *Psalms I*, 281, who cites 1 QM V1.15,
by way of analogy. But the common Hebrew usage of the noun עֲגָלָה is "cart"; it is only the
present context which raises doubt.

Form/Structure/Setting

Psalm 46 has the general character of a hymn, in which the refuge and
protection that God provides are the focal point of the praise; but it is probably
not a hymn in a more formal sense, lacking (as it does) an introductory
exhortation to praise and having a distinctive internal structure (below). Since
Gunkel's time, it has been recognized widely as a "song of Zion" (to which
Gunkel added the adjective *eschatological*), along with Pss 48, 76, 84, 87 and
122; see further Kraus, *Psalmen 1–59*, 496–99. But whereas there are clear
similarities between Ps 46 and the Songs of Zion, there are also grave problems
with such a classification of the form. The implied association with Zion is
to be found in v 5, with the reference to the "city of God" and the "holy
dwelling place"; nevertheless, the psalm differs from the clearly established
Songs of Zion in that it contains no explicit references to either Zion or
Jerusalem. Indeed, Weiss (art. cit.) has stressed the universal character of
the psalm, lacking reference to either Jerusalem or Israel; but against such
a stress, the terminology is distinctively Hebrew (e.g. v 7 "God of Jacob"),
although there are more universal elements as well (e.g. v 5: "Most High,"
or *Elyon*). Hence, after Krinetzki (art. cit.), it is best to classify the psalm as
a *psalm of confidence;* but though such a classification is appropriate in descriptive terms, it is insufficiently precise with respect to the particular peculiarities
of Ps 46 (see further below).

In terms of structure, the psalm falls into three units, each of approximately equivalent length, each separated by the word SELAH. (1) God's refuge in the context of natural phenomena (vv 2–4); (2) God's refuge in the context of the nations of the world (vv 5–8); (3) God's refuge in the context of both natural and national powers (vv 9–12). It is possible that the twice repeated refrain (vv 8, 12) originally occurred also after v 5 (cf. *BHS*, note). The three parts of this literary structure have been closely woven together by the particular usage of certain words. The key word in the whole psalm is *earth* (אֶרֶץ; cf. Kelly, art. cit.), appearing in all three sections (vv 3, 7, 9, 10, 11) and providing the overall unity of theme. The first two sections are closely related by the repeated use of the following terms: (a) עֵזֶר "help" (vv 2, 6); (b) מוֹט "slide, slip" (vv 3, 6, 7); (c) הָמָה "roar" (vv 4, 7). The second and third sections are linked through the repeated use of גּוֹיִם "nations" (vv 7, 11). The whole psalm is further rounded out in that the substance of the refrains (vv 8, 12) reflects the substance of the opening declaration (v 2). Thus the central theme of the psalm is *protection* (vv 2, 8, 12) in God's *earth* (vv 3, 7, 9, 10, 11).

The classification of the text as a psalm of confidence does not provide any sure guide as to its setting; a cultic setting may be supposed on the basis of v 5, though it is by no means certain. Again, the words of v 11, which have something of the character of a cultic or prophetic oracle, might be indicative of a setting; but, in view of the finely worked literary structure of the psalm as a whole, the divine words of v 11 might more appropriately be interpreted in literary terms. Verse 11 brings together the two subthemes of the early parts of the psalm (protection from nature and protection from nations); it is appropriate that the two sources of potential threat should be converted into praise by the divine declaration.

It is more likely that the particular and distinctive language and motifs of the psalm will provide a clue to its initial setting. There are elements of the chaos-motif, so familiar in Near Eastern mythology and, in adapted form, elsewhere in the psalms (e.g. Ps 29). But much more distinctive is the motif of the "river" (v 5), which is associated with the throne of El. Although both these themes were no doubt present in the ancient (pre-Hebrew) cult and mythology of Jerusalem, they are not distinctively "Jebusite" (contra Neve, art. cit.). El's throne, at the "head of two streams," is clearly illustrated in the Ugaritic texts (*CTA* 17.vi.47). Thus, following the suggestion of Eissfeldt (*Kleine Schriften*, IV, 10–11), it is probable that Ps 46 should be associated with the establishment of David's royal cult in Jerusalem. It brings together the ancient Hebrew traditions and blends them with the Jerusalem traditions. The Hebrew antecedent to the psalm is probably to be found in the Song of the Sea (Exod 15:1–18), for many of that song's themes are developed in the present psalm: (1) the Lord's strength and protection (Exod 15:2; Ps 46:2, 8, 12; cf. Craigie, *VT* 22 (1972) 145–46); (2) the Lord's subjugation of the chaotic waters (Exod 15:4–5, 8, 10; Ps 46:3–4; cf. Craigie, *TyndB* 22 [1971] 3–31); (3) the Lord's *dwelling*, secured by his victory (Exod 15:17; Ps 46:5). These ancient themes are worked into the language already known in Jerusalem, such as *Elyon* (v 5; see Gen 14:18–24), thereby establishing the Lord's rightful presence in the stronghold which was Jerusalem. The lack of specificity, in the absence of reference to Jerusalem or Zion in explicit terms, is no doubt to be explained by the original setting of Ps 46 in the very earliest period of the history of the Hebrew cult in Jerusalem. Thus Ps 46 appears to stand at a midway point between the very earliest of Hebrew traditions, represented by the Song of the Sea, and the later more classical representations of the tradition in the Songs of Zion.

Comment

God's protection in natural catastrophes (46:2–4). Verse 2 introduces the theme of the psalm as a whole, which reappears in the refrains (vv 8, 12) that give the psalm its total structure. The "times of trouble," in which God offers protection, are times when chaos attempts to reassert its primacy over order, both in the natural world and in the world of nations and human affairs. The affirmation of God's presence in a protective capacity is the basis for the confidence in the community's words: "we shall not fear . . ." (v 3).

In powerful poetry, the psalmist describes a fearful earthquake; mountains tumble into the sea, and the tumult and tidal waves of the ocean make the remaining mountains tremble again. Though the language is poetic and not strictly descriptive, it no doubt represents the experience of earthquakes, which were not unfamiliar to residents in the lands surrounding the great Rift Valley from the upper reaches of the Jordan to the Arabah in the south. The language is reminiscent of other contexts, in which the Hebrew poets employed language evocative of the shaking earth (Isa 24:19–20), the trembling mountains (Isa 54:10), and the disruption of land and sea alike (Hag 2:6). But at a deeper level, the poet is alluding to forces of chaos, never quite subdued and always threatening the order of creation; even in the face of chaotic powers, there would be no fear, for God had conquered chaos in creation. Thus the language of confidence here is rooted in creation, for God's order emerged from primeval chaos (Gen 1:1–2). But God's creation (Exod 15:17) of Israel had also been a consequence of his control of the chaotic waters, by which he conquered Pharaoh and redeemed his people (Exod 15:1–10); hence the psalmist now turns from confidence in the face of natural chaotic forces, to confidence in the face of national threats.

God's protection in national (or international) catastrophes (46:5–8). Whereas in v 2, it was God himself who was portrayed as the source of protection, now it is the city of God which is the immediate location of protection. And the city of God is safe because it is there, in his "holy dwelling place," that his presence might be experienced. The reference to the "river" and its "streams" describes the city in language reminiscent of Canaanite mythology. The throne of the high god El, at the head of two streams (*CTA* 17.vi.47), is localized in a particular place. But in the psalm, the ancient cult of El Elyon ("God Most High"), traditionally associated with King Melchizedek (Gen 14:18–19), is identified as the same true tradition as that associated with *Yahweh of Hosts*, the "God of Jacob" (v 8). Though the mountains, traditional symbols of stability, may "slide" (v 3, מוט) into the seas, God's city will not "slide" or "slip" (v 6, מוט), for God's presence there would give it stability even on the dawn of the day on which chaotic forces assert themselves (v 6).

The central section of this portion of the psalm is to be found in the reference to "nations" and "kingdoms" in v 7. It is these human powers which now threaten their chaotic might, but they "slip" (v 7: מוט) like the mountains before them, while the city of God does "not slip" (v 6). The divine protection is here depicted as true stability in a world where powerful foreign nations are fundamentally unstable. God speaks (v 7c; the allusion is to the *thunder* of God's voice, as in Ps 29 and the Ugaritic texts; see *CTA* 4.v. 70), and the very earth, which is the setting for the power of human states, "melts" beneath them (v 7d). In the refrain that concludes the section, the old titles or epithets for God, "Lord of Hosts" (or *Armies*) and "God of Jacob," refer back to Israel's ancient traditions. On the "Lord of Hosts," see further P. D. Miller, *The Divine Warrior in Early Israel* (HSM 5. Cambridge: Harvard University Press, 1973), 145–55; the title is particularly appropriate in this context, for it is the "Lord of Armies" who offers protection against the armies of foreign nations and kingdoms. The title "God of Jacob" evokes specifically the *protective* character of God; see further the *Comment* on Ps 20:1.

God's refuge in the context of both natural and national powers (46:9–12). The poetic invitation to *come* and *see* introduces the final section of the psalm, in which the two themes of the preceding sections are woven together in a passage forming a suitable climax. The worshipers can "see" what God has done in the earth (v 9), indicative of his control of the world of nature; and they can "see" what he has done to human powers, making peace and breaking the instruments of war (v 10), indicating thereby his control of the world of history. The divine words (v 11), which are probably not in the form of an oracle (see *Form/Structure/Setting*, above), indicate the transformation of all chaotic forces into instruments of divine praise. Both the "nations" and the "earth" (v 11), which earlier were depicted as posing a threat to orderly existence, are now harnessed in service to the exaltation of God. Hence the people may "relax" in appropriate confidence (v 11a); to know that God is God is to know his Lordship of nature and history, and therefore to be aware of his total capacity as Protector.

Explanation

Psalm 46 contains one of the clearest elaborations in the Bible of the theological implications of the faith in *creation*. The two versions of the fourth commandment provide the dimensions of Israel's creation faith. The primary faith in creation concerned God's creation of the world as such (Exod 20:11; cf. Gen 1); the secondary faith, given expression in the second form of the commandment, was rooted in God's redemption and creation of the nation Israel from Egyptian bondage (Deut 5:15; cf. Exod 15:1–18). In each case, creation represents the establishment of order where formerly there was chaos, either the chaotic primeval waters (Gen 1:1–2), or the bondage of Egypt which was crushed and ended by the waters of the Reed Sea. The first focus of creation faith established God's kingship and rule in the realm of nature; the second focus of creation faith established God's kingship in the realm of history (Exod 15:18).

In the psalm, the natural implication of this creation theology is drawn out and expressed in a statement of confidence. Because God controls both history and nature, the chaotic threat which both may offer to human existence may be faced fearlessly. The very worst manifestation of chaos is merely a threat, for the Creator has mastered chaos. And yet, as Gunkel rightly observed, there is an eschatological element in the psalm, though it is implicit rather than explicit. The order of creation has been established, and yet the reality of human existence is that there continue to be manifestations of chaos. Faith in God's protection, expressed so profoundly in this psalm, is both present and proleptic, reaching forward to the time of God's ultimate conquest of chaos and establishment of peace.

A Psalm of God's Kingship   (47:1–10)

Bibliography

Combs, A. E. *The Creation Motif in the "Enthronement Psalms."* Ann Arbor: University Microfilms, 1963. **Loretz, O.** "Psalmenstudien III." *UF* 6 (1974) 175–210. ———. "Psalmenstudien IV." *UF* 6 (1974) 211–14. **Muilenburg, J.** "Psalm 47." *JBL* 63 (1944) 235–56. **Roberts, J. J. M.** "The Religio-Political Setting of Psalm 47." *BASOR* 220 (1975) 129–32.

Translation

1   For the musical director. For the sons of Korah. A psalm.

2(1) *Applaud, all you peoples;* [a]   (4?+4)
       shout out to [b] *God with a cry of praise!*

3(2) *For the Lord Most High is to be feared,*   (4+4)
       a Great King over the whole earth.

4(3) *He subdues* [a] *peoples beneath us,*   (3+3)
       and warriors [b] *beneath our feet.*

5(4) *He chooses our* [a] *inheritance for us,*   (3+4?)
       the pride of Jacob, whom he loved. SELAH

6(5) *God has gone up with a great shout,*   (3+3)
       the Lord, with the sound of a trumpet.

7(6) *Sing praises to* [a] *God, sing praises!*   (3+3)
       Sing praises to our King, sing praises!

8(7) *For God is King of the whole earth;*   (4?+2)
       sing a maskil! [a]

9(8) *God has ruled over nations;*   (3+4)
       God has sat upon his holy throne!

10(9) *The princely ones of the peoples are assembled*   (3+3)
       with [a] *the people of Abraham's God;*
       for the earth's rulers [b] *belong to God,*   (3?+2)
       who has been greatly exalted!

Notes

2.a. Dahood (*Psalms I*, 283–84) translates העמים by "strong ones," but in context this is most unlikely, for עמים "peoples," is a theme running throughout the psalm (cf. vv 4, 10). See further note a at Ps 18:28 and Loretz, *UF* 6 (1974) 183–84.

2.b. Dahood translates "you gods," interpreting the ל as the vocative *lamedh;* *Psalms I*, 284. But in context, this interpretation is most unlikely; see Roberts, art. cit. 129 and P. D. Miller, "Vocative Lamed in the Psalter: a Reconsideration," *UF* 11 (1979) 632–33.

4.a. On the translation of the verb דבר, see note a on Ps 18:48.

4.b. On the translation of לאמים, see note b on Ps 2:1.

5.a. Alternatively, translate "*his* inheritance," with *G* and *S;* cf. Roberts, art. cit. 130.

7.a. Reading לאלהים, with several Heb. mss., and as is implied by the following line's parallelism.

8.a. On the meaning of the term *"maskil,"* see note a on Ps 32:1.

10.a. Reading עַם עָם, as implied by *G*, and assuming that MT represents a haplography.

10.b. For מגני "shields," סגני "rulers" is read with *BHS,* as implied by context.

Form/Structure/Setting

Psalm 47 is a *hymn;* the "peoples" (v 2), both Israel and foreign nations, are called upon to sing the praise of God's kingship. More precisely, Ps 47 is usually classified as an *enthronement psalm,* together with Pss 93, 96–99; various other psalms may also belong to this category (see further J. D. W. Watts, *TZ* 21 [1965] 341–48 and the section *Form/Structure/Setting* at Ps 29, above). While this subclassification is useful, the precise meaning of the word *enthronement,* and its implications with respect to setting, are open to debate (see below).

The psalm is a finely structured literary unit, and should probably be viewed as a hymn having two "verses," each verse repeating the call to praise.

I. 1. Call to praise (v 2)
   2. Praise of God's victories (vv 3–6)
II. 3. Call to praise (v 7)
   4. Praise of God's kingship (vv 8–10).

The literary structure is characterized by the following points. (1) The word כִּי ("for") systematically introduces the substance of praise (vv 3, 8) and a concluding declaration of praise (v 10c), providing a structure for the psalm as a whole. (2) The two verses introducing the sections of praise (vv 3, 8) are parallel in the use of מלך ("king") and כל־הארץ ("the whole earth") in both verses. (3) The first "verse" or strophe of the hymn is made complete and rounded by the device of *inclusio;* note the use of forms of רוע ("shout") and of בקול ("cry, sound") in vv 2 and 6. (4) The overall unity of theme in the psalm is provided by the repeated usage of the following words: עם ("people") vv 2, 4, 10; מלך ("king") vv 3, 7, 8, 9; and ארץ ("earth") vv 3, 8, 10.

The so-called *enthronement psalms* are joined by the common theme of the praise of the Lord's kingship. However, the setting in which the Lord's kingship was praised is far from clear and a variety of different hypotheses have been proposed. Thus Mowinckel interprets these psalms in the cultic context of his proposed New Year Festival in ancient Israel (*The Psalms in Israel's Worship*, I, 106–92), and Weiser interprets them in the context of a Covenant Festival (*The Psalms*, 27–62). But neither of these proposed cultic settings can be clearly established in the history of Hebrew worship, at least in terms of the reconstruction proposed by Mowinckel and Weiser (see INTRODUC- TION, THE PSALMS AND RECENT RESEARCH.), and both have been subjected to a thoroughgoing critique, which calls into question the viability of either a New Year Festival or a Covenant Festival as a setting for the so-called *enthronement psalms:* see Combs, *The Creation Motif in the "Enthronement Psalms,"* 238–85.

The *enthronement psalms* should probably be interpreted as the culmination of an ancient tradition, beginning with particular *victory hymns* (Exod 15:1– 18), developing into general victory hymns (Ps 29), and being represented eventually by the general praise of God's kingship (Pss 47, 93, 96–99); see further the commentary on Ps 29 and Craigie, *VT* 22 (1972) 143–51. Against this general background, the particular setting proposed by Roberts for Ps 47 (*BASOR* 221 [1975] 132) is very attractive. Roberts suggests that the setting for the psalm is to be found in the cultic celebration of the Lord's imperial accession, "based on the relatively recent victories of David's age, which raised Israel from provincial obscurity to an empire of the first rank"; see further the *Comment* (below). On this interpretation, the psalm should be interpreted relatively early during the period of the Hebrew monarchy.

At a later period in its history, Ps 47 was used in other settings. In the Jewish tradition, the reference to the trumpet blowing (v 6) was the basis for the utilization of the psalm in the synagogue on *Rosh ha-Shanah*, New Year's Day (the first day of Tishri). In early Christianity, the reference to God's ascension (v 6) was the basis for the use of Ps 47 as one of the proper psalms for Ascension Day.

Comment

Call to praise (47:2). While an invocation is the standard introduction to *hymns*, the call to praise in this psalm is distinctive in terms of the persons addressed. It is the *nations* or *peoples* who are to praise Israel's God, the same nations who have been defeated in war (v 4) and whose representatives and chiefs must be envisaged as being actually present in this celebration of God's kingship (v 10). The background is to be found in the covenant context of Israel's early military expansion and imperial power. Israel was bound in covenant to God, who was Israel's king. Any nation conquered by Israel, becoming Israel's vassal, automatically became concurrently a vassal of God. Thus, although the opening invitation could be viewed in a general and poetic sense, it is more likely that it should be interpreted literally. An act of worship is taking place in which both Israel and her subject peoples are to praise (and thereby acknowledge) the ultimate sovereignty and kingship of God.

The praise of God's victories (47:3–6). The terminology employed for God in these verses is instructive. He is addressed first as *Yahweh Elyon* ("Lord Most High"); *Yahweh* is the personal name of the deity and *Elyon* (a name utilized also in extrabiblical texts; see further the commentary on Ps 46:5) sets God in an international context. Indeed, the biblical uses of the term *Elyon* frequently are in a context where foreign peoples, in addition to the Hebrews, are present: see further Deut 32:8 and Craigie, *The Book of Deuteronomy*, 379. The poetic parallelism then sets the expression "Great King" in parallel with *Yahweh Elyon*. Although the title "Great King" is an appropriate general title for God, it evokes specifically the covenant-treaty context of Israel's faith. Just as a Hittite monarch was addressed as *great king* in the introductory sections of vassal treaties (e.g. *ANET*, 201–03), so too God is here the "Great King" in relation to all his vassals, both Israel and the "peoples" (v 2) who had become Israel's immediate vassals.

God's covenant-treaty character is further developed in v 4, which expresses the immediate ground of his kingship. The peoples, who had been called to praise (v 2), had been subjugated by God's military action; thus it is the victory of the Great King (v 4) which is the basis upon which all the peoples are invited to join in the praise of God (v 2). The parallelism "peoples" // "warriors" (v 4) emphasizes further the military context of the psalm and of the basis of God's kingship. The metaphor of subjugation, "beneath our feet," arose from the practice and artistic symbolism of victory, wherein a victor stood with his foot on the neck of the conquered foe; see Keel, *The Symbolism of the Biblical World*, 297.

The expressions "inheritance" and "pride of Jacob" (v 5) are poetically parallel, and refer not only to the Promised Land, but also to the surrounding lands of nations that were conquered during and after the reign of David; see further Deut 32:8, for similar terminology in the context of God as *Elyon*. In v 6, the poetic language probably refers to the triumphant procession of the ark following a military victory. "God has gone up . . ."; viz., God's ark, symbol of his presence in battle, has gone up (to Jerusalem?), accompanied by the shouting and trumpet blowing of the people who rejoiced in the divine victory.

Call to praise (47:7). The second "verse," or strophe, of the hymn begins again with a call to praise, though in this instance, the verse is not specific with respect to the persons addressed. Presumably they included both the "peoples" (v 2) and now also the Israelites (viz. "the people of Abraham's God," v 10); thus this second part of the psalm is broadened with respect to those who are invited to worship.

The praise of God's kingship (47:8–10). God's kingship over the *whole earth* repeats the introductory theme of the opening portion of praise (v 3). Though the meaning of *"maskil"* is not known with certainty (see Ps 32:1), it is clear that the term must be broad enough in meaning to incorporate a hymn of praise, as is implied in this context.

מלך אלהים (v 9); the appropriate translation of this clause has caused considerable debate. The translation above, "God has ruled" (or reigned), expresses what appears to be the most natural sense of the verb. Mowinckel translates "God has become King," interpreting the expression with respect to the actual moment of enthronement in the cultic ritual of the New Year celebration. But such a translation, despite Mowinckel's careful arguments (*The Psalms in Israel's Worship*, II, 222–24), has a number of grammatical and

syntactical problems; see particularly J. Ridderbos, "Jahwäh Mālak," *VT* 4
[1954] 87–93 and A. E. Combs, *The Creation Motif in the "Enthronement Psalms,"*
219–21. The sense of the expression is that God has ruled (and continues
to rule) over the earth's nations. The divine rule was not simply established
by virtue of the victory over foreign nations (v 4); rather, the victory had
been possible because of the ultimate sovereignty of God over peoples and
nations. The reference to God sitting upon his throne (v 9b) is in poetical
parallelism with God's reign (v 9a). The rulers of foreign nations, together
with Israel's representatives, are gathered to acknowledge God's sovereignty;
the actual occasion for the acknowledgment would have been some ceremony
in Jerusalem, where the allegiance of Israel and its vassals was pledged to
God, the Great King (see further *Form/Structure/Setting*). The fact that the
earth's rulers "belong to God" was an indication of their status as vassals.

Explanation

From the perspective of the NT, the psalms concerning the kingship of
God, and that of his earthly representative, the king, form the general background to the theme of the "Kingdom of God" in the teaching of Jesus.
For fuller details, see the *Explanation* at Ps 2. Psalm 47 contributes insight
into one dimension of this kingdom, from the NT perspective; although the
hymn was not eschatological in its initial setting, as Gunkel had proposed,
it assumes eschatological dimensions in its "re-reading." The psalm describes
a limited reality, which was present for only a short period in Israel's history,
namely the joining together in praise of Israel with other nations in the presence of God the King. In the preaching and salvific acts of Jesus, that ancient
but limited reality comes a step closer to fulfillment on a world-wide scale,
though it remains still within the area of eschatological hope. But the climax
of the ancient hymn (v 10) remains, to be someday a climax of a different
sort, when Israel and all the world's peoples recognize the God to whom
they belong.

A Hymn of Zion (48:1–15)

Bibliography

Clifford, R. J. *The Cosmic Mountain in Canaan and the Old Testament.* HSM 4. Cambridge:
Harvard University Press (1972) 142–44. Dahood, M. "The Language and Date of
Psalm 48 (47)." *CBQ* 16 (1954) 15–19. Gordon, C. H. "The Wine-dark Sea." *JNES*
37 (1978) 51–52. Palmer, M. "Cardinal Points in Psalm 48." *Bib* 46 (1965) 357–58.
Roberts, J. J. M. "The Davidic Origin of the Zion Tradition." *JBL* 92 (1973) 329–
44. Robinson, A. "Zion and SĀPHŌN in Psalm 48.3." *VT* 24 (1974) 118–23.

Translation

¹ A song. A psalm for the sons of Korah.
2(1) *The Lord is great*   (2+2)
    and most worthy of praise!

In the city of our God	(2+2)
is his holy mountain;	
3(2) its elevation is beautiful,	(2+2)
the exultation of the whole world!	
Mount Zion, the Heights of Zaphon,[a]	(3+3)
is the city of the Great King!	
4(3) God is in its citadels,	(2+2)
renowned as a stronghold.	
5(4) For lo, the kings have assembled;	(3+2)
they have crossed over together.	
6(5) They[a] saw—	(2+2+2)
they were totally dumbfounded!	
They were terrified, they hurried away!	
7(6) Trembling took hold of them,[a]	(2+2)
writhing like that of a woman in labor,	
8(7) like[a] the east wind that shatters	(3+2)
the ships of Tarshish.	
9(8) As we have heard,	(2+2)
so have we seen	
in the city of the Lord of Hosts,	(3+2+3)
in the city of our God,	
that God establishes it for ever! SELAH	
10(9) O God, we have reflected upon your lovingkindness	(3+2)
in the midst of your temple.	
11(10) As is your name, O God,	(2+2)
so is your praise!	
To[a] the ends of the earth,	(3?+3)
your right hand is full of righteousness.	
12(11) Mount Zion shall rejoice,	(3+3+3?)
the daughters of Judah shall be jubilant,	
because of your judgments, O Lord.[a]	
13(12) Walk around Zion, and go all the way round it;	(3+2)
count its towers.	
14(13) Consider its[a] fortress,	(3+2)
traverse its citadels,	
so that you may describe it	(2+2)
to the next generation.	
15(14) For this is God,	(3+3+3?)
our God, eternal and everlasting;	
he will guide us eternally.[a]	

Notes

3.a. Heb. צָפוֹן has the secondary sense "north," but its primary meaning is *Zaphon*, the sacred mountain. See further the *Comment.*

6.a. Dahood identifies הֵמָּה ("they") with Ugaritic *hm* ("lo, behold"), claiming the independent pronoun serves no useful purpose; *Psalms I*, 291 and *CBQ* 16 (1954) 15–19. But Ugaritic *hm* does not clearly have this sense; see the criticism of such a proposal in note a at Ps 9:8. In defense of the conventional translation (above), the pronoun הֵמָּה serves to produce metrical balance.

7.a. MT adds שָׁם, "there," but it is best omitted with S.

8.a. Reading כָּרוּח, as implied by the parallelism, with the support of a few Heb mss.

11.a Reading עַד "to," for MT's עַל ("upon"), with a few Heb mss and S.

12.a. יהוה, absent in MT, is added with the support of G and S.

14.a. Reading חֵיל ("fortress"), with the pronominal suffix הָ.

15.a. Reading עֹלָמוֹת, with Dahood (*Psalms I*, 293), after Krinetzki, *BZ* 4 (1960) 73, for MT's עַל־מוּת. Alternatively, עַל־מוּת may be retained, and may have been displaced from the title of Ps 49; on the meaning of the expression in psalm titles, see the *Notes* on Pss 9:1 and 46:1.

Form/Structure/Setting

Psalm 48 is a *hymn*, but more precisely it belongs to a subcategory of hymns, namely the *Songs of Zion;* see further Pss 76, 84, 87 and 122 (and the comments under *Form/Structure/Setting,* at Ps 46). Though the Songs of Zion do not normally have the customary introductory exhortation to praise, it is probable that v 2a-b should be interpreted in such a manner; see further the *Comment.* The substance of the Songs of Zion may appear superficially to be the praise of Mount Zion in the holy city; at a deeper level, it is the praise of God, whose presence and protection is symbolized by the holy mountain and its sanctuary.

The structure of the psalm is as follows. (1) There is a short hymnic introduction, expressing God's worthiness of praise (v 2a-b). (2) There follows the main section of the psalm, which is a celebration of the glories of Mount Zion (vv 2c-9). (3) The congregation then address their words directly to God (vv 10-12). (4) The psalm concludes with an invitation to the worshipers to circumambulate the mountain (vv 13-15).

The psalm must be interpreted in a cultic setting, and it is possible that it should be viewed as one part of a larger liturgy or ritual. The general setting is that of Mount Zion itself; the specific setting is that of an act of worship taking place in the temple (v 10). The invitation to "walk around Zion" (v 13) indicates that the act of worship represented by the psalm may have been only one part of a larger ritual, which was followed by a procession around the mountain-city. Presumably the entire ritual took place during one of the three annual pilgrim festivals, and though there can be no certainty, it is possible that the ritual implicit in this psalm was a part of the worship associated with the Feast of Tabernacles.

In the history of Christian worship, Ps 48 was employed as one of the proper psalms for Whitsunday (or Pentecost); the psalm is appropriate for this usage, in that Jerusalem (Zion) was the location of the "birthday" of the Christian Church.

Comment

Hymnic introduction (48:2a-b). Many translations link the first two lines of v 2 with the last two "The Lord is great and most worthy of praise in the city of our God . . ." (cf. the punctuation in RSV, NIV, et al.). But the separation of the first two lines as a distinct invocation is more appropriate to the sense and structure of the psalm as a whole; see further Dahood, *Psalms I,* 289. The invocation indicates that the central theme of the psalm is the praise of God's greatness; the particular expression which the praise takes is that of God's greatness as reflected in the symbolism of Mount Zion.

The glories of Mount Zion (48:2c–9). The "city of our God" is Jerusalem, and the "holy mountain" is Mount Zion, whose height (though not distinctive in the literal and physical terms of altitude) is "beautiful." The beauty of the mountain, and its source of human exultation (v 3b), is associated primarily with its religious significance as the place where God may be known and experienced in a particular and direct fashion.

Mount Zion is equated directly with the ancient (mythological) Mount Zaphon; see further Roberts, *JBL* 92 (1973) 334 and Clifford, *The Cosmic Mountain in Canaan and the Old Testament*, 142–44. In the Ugaritic texts, the word *Zaphon* (*ṣpn*) is used of the mythological mountain dwelling of the god Baal, but it was also localized in particular geographical locations. Thus, Jebel al-Aqraʿ, the mountain some thirty miles north of Ras Shamra (ancient Ugarit), was identified as Mount Zaphon. And in one text, it is possible that the "hill" of Ugarit itself is called Zaphon (*UT* 107; see Robinson, art. cit., 118–23). But the mountain north of Ugarit was probably not the "original" Mount Zaphon. The original was a mythological reality, and among different peoples, at different times and places, it was given an earthly location in a particular geographical point. Thus the place name *Baal-Zaphon* (Exod 14:2) probably indicates the site of a Baal temple in Egypt, constructed by a Canaanite community resident there (cf. J. Gray, "Canaanite Mythology and Hebrew Tradition," *Transactions of the Glasgow University Oriental Society* 14 [1953] 47–57). And there is evidence of the localization of the Zaphon tradition at other places in the Near East; see further F. E. Eakin, *The Religion and Culture of Israel* (Boston: Allyn and Bacon, 1971), 65–66. The significance of the psalmist's statement (v 3) is to be found in the linking of this ancient mythological tradition with Mount Zion in Jerusalem and God's temple there. The psalmist affirms, in effect, that the aspirations of all peoples for a place on earth where God's presence could be experienced were fulfilled in Mount Zion, the true Zaphon.

The view of Palmer (*Bib* 46 [1965] 357–58), that Ps 48 has four strophes, each concerned with the "theological geography" of Jerusalem, is to be rejected. He sees a reference to *north* in v 3, *east* in v 8, *south* in v 11, and *west* in v 14. The evidence for *south* and *west* (in vv 11 and 14) is extremely tenuous. The evidence for *north* depends upon the translation of *Zaphon* (צפון) by "north" (e.g., AV). But while Heb. צפון does have the sense *north* in other contexts, it does not carry that sense here, as clearly indicated by the context (cf. Kraus, *Psalmen 1–59*, 510). In Ugaritic, the word never means "north," but always *Zaphon* (cf. Gibson, *CML* ², 8), indicating the secondary derivation of the sense "north" in Hebrew. Hence, the "geographical theory" of Ps 48 is left only with the unambiguous "east" (v 8), which is clearly descriptive of a type of wind (see below).

Verses 5–9 must be taken together and interpreted as a striking contrast of two types of vision. The world's "kings" (v 5) came to Jerusalem and "saw" one thing (v 6); the pilgrim worshipers came to Jerusalem and saw (v 9) another thing, though in a literal sense it was the same sight that met their eyes. The focal point of the contrast is thus introduced in v 4: Mount Zion was a "stronghold" by virtue of God's presence there. When kings of

approaching armies saw that stronghold, they were horrified by its impregna-
bility (v 6); in poetic language, it is not merely the genuine military strength
of the stronghold that is stressed, but the awareness on the part of the kings
of the protective presence of God in that stronghold. The fear which affected
the kings is described in two similes. First, they writhe like a "woman in
labor" (v 7b); for other uses of this simile of fear, see Isa 13:8 and 21:3.
The second simile is that of a storm, whipped up by the powerful east wind.
(It was probably an easterly wind that caused the shipwreck in which Paul
was involved; see Acts 27:14.) The meaning of "Tarshish" is much debated;
it may refer to the Phoenician colony of Tartessus in Spain. On this and
other geographical possibilities, see Anderson, *Psalms I*, 370. But it is more
likely that the term "Tarshish" refers primarily to the "open-sea," from which
was derived the secondary sense of "far-off lands reached by ocean-going
ships"; see Gordon, *JNES* 37 (1978) 51–52. If this sense is correct, then
the meaning of the simile is that even as the powerful east wind shattered
the ocean-going ships, so too would the sight of Zion terrorize the world's
powerful kings.

But the sight the horrified kings saw was the same sight that thrilled the
eyes of pilgrims as they approached the city of Jerusalem (v 9). What they
perceived was not an impregnable fortress keeping them out, but a city permanently established by God, offering them joy and protection. Thus the contrast
of vv 5–9 presents poetically two different groups approaching Mount Zion:
the kings with their great armies who look and are horrified, and the pilgrims
who look and rejoice.

The words of the worshipers (48:10–12). The assembled worshipers now address God directly; whereas in the early portion of the psalm God was described in the third person, he is now addressed in the second person. If it
is correct that Ps 48 is one part of a larger ritual, which begins in the temple
and moves to the circumambulation of the city, it is possible that these verses
form a particular point in the proceedings. The invocation (v 2a–b) may
have been spoken by the leader of the worship; then the whole group joined
in declaring the glories of Zion, in language evocative of their recent pilgrim
arrival in the city of God (vv 2c–9). Now, in a moment of particular solemnity,
the focus of the ritual shifts from the holy place to the holy presence in
that place: God is addressed.

The substance of the address is a form of praise, in which the focus is
on the covenant characteristics of God: "lovingkindness" (v 10), "righteousness" (or perhaps "victory," v 11), and "judgments" (v 12). The words are
descriptive of the ritual proceedings: in the midst of the celebration, the
people pause to remember the meaning of it all, which is rooted ultimately
in God's lovingkindness.

The idiomatic expression of v 11 ("as is your name . . . so is your praise";
cf. v 9) is an indication of God's total reliability and hence worthiness of
praise. God's name was his honor; the idiom is similar to the English idiom
of being "as good as one's word." It emphasizes God's covenant faithfulness,
already introduced by the word "lovingkindness" (v 10: חסד).

Mount Zion, which was formerly the object of exultation (v 3), now becomes
the subject and rejoices (v 12) in God's "judgments." The "daughters of

Judah" is an idiomatic expression indicating the villages or towns of Judah.

The invitation to process around Mount Zion (Ps 48:13–15). The psalm ends with an invitation to the worshipers, delivered perhaps by the officiating priest; but though the psalm ends with these verses, the ritual presumably continues as the pilgrims rise and leave the temple in response to the invitation. Mount Zion, both city and temple, which had been the focus of words in the earlier part of the worship, was now to become the focus of sensory experience. As the worshipers processed around the mountain, seeing its "towers," "fortress," and "citadel," they would gain a profound impression of the reality of Zion which they could take home with them and share with their children (viz. the "next generation," v 14), who were as yet too young to participate in the pilgrimage. But the procession was designed to imprint upon the mind and heart of the worshipers a more profound reality, that of the Living God. "This is God": that is to say, this mountain is in a sense God. The mountain as such was not, of course, deity; the point of the words was to press home the symbolism of what was seen, so that it might be converted into a sense of reality. God's presence and protection were as eternal and real as the rocks and structures of Mount Zion and its city. The symbolic procession was a means by which the sensory perceptions could feed and strengthen faith in that greater, but intangible, reality, namely God.

Explanation

In much of Western Christendom, and especially in the Protestant tradition, worship has largely been reduced to words and thoughts, with only the added dimension of music. Psalm 48, and many like it, functions as a reminder of the added dimension which ritual, symbol and activity may contribute to the act of worship.

The psalm contains words, though the title makes clear that there was added to them the dimension of music and song. The object of praise was the Lord, yet the avenue through which the praise was channeled was the powerful symbol of a mountain, on which there were a temple and a stronghold. And the people not only addressed God in words, but also engaged in action, walking around that real, but symbolic, mountain and thus somehow making more immediate their awareness of the reality of a God who is ultimately beyond the grasp of the human senses. And all this was done in the midst of a great crowd of pilgrims, creating a knowledge in each one of the larger community of God's people to which they belonged. Just as the essence of such worship reaches beyond the capacity of human speech, so too is language ineffective in describing its power and influence on the worshipers. They gave of their praise to God in that act of worship, but received much more in return; the sights and sounds, the smell and touch, the pilgrim bustle and songs of praise, all contributed to a growth in faith which they would take with them from Jerusalem back to the distant communities and workaday world from which they had come. When one penetrates beyond the words of this ancient psalm to the larger experience of which it was a part, one begins to perceive something of the strength and greatness of worship in ancient Israel.

A Wisdom Psalm on Life and Death
(49:1–21)

Bibliography

Perdue, L. G. "The Riddles of Psalm 49." *JBL* 93 (1974) 533–42. **Slotki, J. J.** "Psalm 49:13, 21 (*AV* 12, 20)." *VT* 28 (1978) 361–62. **Tromp, N.** "Psalm 49: Armoede en rijkdom, leven en dood." *Ons geestelijk leven* 45 (1968/69) 239–51.

Translation

1   For the musical director. For the sons of Korah.[a] A psalm.

2(1) *Hear this, all you peoples;* (3+3)
       listen, all you inhabitants of the world,

3(2) *both humble and mighty,* (4?+3)
       rich and poor alike.

4(3) *My mouth shall speak wisdom,* (3+3)
       and the meditation of my heart concerns understanding.

5(4) *I will turn my ear to a proverb;* (3+3)
       with a lyre, I will expose my enigma.

6(5) *Why should I be afraid in evil days,* (3+3)
       when the iniquity of my treacherous foes [a] *surrounds me,*

7(6) *they who trust in their wealth* (3?+2)
       and boast of the magnitude of their riches?

8(7) *Surely* [a] *a man cannot redeem himself* [b] (4+3)
       and [c] *pay to God his ransom?*

9(8) *(For the redemption of his* [a] *life is costly;* (3+2)
       he should leave it alone forever. [b]*)*

10(9) *For then he should continue* [a] *to live forever* (3+3)
       and [b] *would not see the pit!*

11(10) *Surely he can see that wise men die,* (4+4)
       that fool and brute perish together. [a]

12(11) *Graves* [a] *are their homes forever,* (3+3)
       their dwelling places from generation to generation;
       they named lands with their own names, (3+3)
       but left their wealth for others. [b]

13(12) *But man, in his worthiness, does not survive;* [a] (3+3)
       he is like the beasts that are cut off.

14(13) *This is their way, their folly,* (4?+3)
       and that of those after them who approve their words. SELAH

15(14) *Like sheep shipped* [a] *to Sheol,* [b] (3+2)
       Death shall graze on them.
       The upright shall rule them at dawn, (4+4)
       their forms for Sheol's consumption, [c] *rather than their lofty abodes.*

16(15) *"Surely God will redeem me,*   (3+3)
      even from Sheol's grasp, for he will take hold of me!" SELAH

17(16) *Do not fear when a man becomes rich,*   (3+3)
      when the honor of his household increases,

18(17) *for in his death he cannot take it all along,*   (4+3)
      his honor cannot go down there after him.

19(18) *For he was blessed in his lifetime—*   (3+3)
      people praise you when things go well for you!—

20(19) *yet he* a *enters his ancestor's generation,*   (3+3)
      who will never again see the light!

21(20) *Man, in his worthiness, does not* a *understand;*   (3+3)
      he is like the beasts that are cut off.

Notes

1.a. On the Korahite psalms, see THE COMPILATION OF THE PSALTER in the INTRODUCTION. It is possible that עַל־מוּת ("on death") should be added to the title from Ps 48:15 (see the note on that verse); if inserted after מִזְמוֹר "psalm," it could be translated: "a psalm concerning death," which would be appropriate to the subject matter.

6.a. The translation is based on the pointing עֲקֵבַי; see Brockington, *The Hebrew Text of the Old Testament*, 131 and NEB. G renders "the iniquity of my heel," as from Heb עָקֵב "heel." On Dahood's translation *slanderers* (*Psalms I*, 296), based on the same pointing as adopted here, see note c on Ps 41:10 with respect to the Ugaritic evidence employed.

8.a. Reading אַךְ ("surely") for אָח ("brother"), with the support of a few Heb mss; while it would be possible to translate: "a brother cannot redeem a man," the normal idiom would require אָח followed by אָח, or אִישׁ ("man") followed by אִישׁ (see Briggs, *The Book of Psalms*, I, 413).

8.b. The verb is pointed as a Niph., with reflexive sense, as required by the change in note a (above): יִפָּדֶה ("redeem himself").

8.c. A conjunction is added (וְלֹא), with the support of many Heb mss.

9.a. Reading נַפְשׁוֹ (with G).

9.b. On the syntax of vv 8–10, which requires v 9 to be interpreted as a parenthetic insertion, see Delitzsch, *Biblical Commentary on the Psalms*, II, 130–31.

10.a. On Dahood's translation of עוֹד by "jubilant" (*Psalms I*, 298), see the critical observations in note b at Ps 39:2.

10.b. The conjunction is read with the support of many Heb mss.

11.a. Dahood interprets יחד as a verbal form (cf. (יֶחְדֶּה): "he gazes" (*Psalms I*, 298), but this is highly unlikely in terms of context; see O. Loretz, *Die Psalmen*, II, 500.

12.a. For MT's קִרְבָּם ("their insides"), it is preferable to read קִבְרָם (G, S, TC) or קְבָרִים as here; cf. NEB.

12.b. This line has been transposed, being the third line of v 11 in MT; see Brockington, *The Hebrew Text of the Old Testament*, 131.

13.a. There are a number of problems in this line. Slotki (art. cit.) and others propose the emendation בָּקָר "cattle," and translate: "man is as cattle. . . . ." This is a possible emendation, but the overall sense of the psalm dictates against it. The translation of יָלִין ("survive") is in effect a paraphrase; the precise sense is "to lodge," but context indicates one who "will not lodge" in this world any longer. Hence the emendation to יָבִין "understand," suggested both by v 21 and by G and S at this verse, is unnecessary.

15.a. שַׁתּוּ (from שׁתת) is similar in meaning to Ugaritic *št/yšt*: "to drag, haul" (cf. Caquot, et. al., *Textes ougaritiques*, I, 138).

15.b. The alliteration in the translation is an attempt to catch the flavor of the Hebrew, with the sequence ṣ, š, and š.

15.c. On the sense "consume" for the verb בלה, similar to Ugaritic, see Dahood, *Psalms I*, 301 and Gibson, *CML* 2, 68, 143.

20.a. Reading יָבוֹא (with G).

21.a. The conjunction in וְלֹא is omitted with the support of some Heb. mss and G.

Form/Structure/Setting

The psalm belongs to the general category of the *wisdom psalms*. It differs, however, from some other types of wisdom psalm, in which are developed the general themes of morality so basic to the wisdom tradition (e.g. Ps 1). Ps 49 is concerned with a single issue (a "proverb" or "enigma," v 5); the issue is death, but specifically death in the context of human wealth and power.

The wisdom literature as a whole falls into two general categories. There is first a basic category, in which the moral essence of the wisdom tradition is expressed in a didactic form; the Book of Proverbs is an example of this type. The second category contains works of a more theoretical nature, exploring the difficult intellectual and theological issues raised in moral wisdom (e.g. The Books of Job and Qoheleth); see further Craigie, *Crux* 15 (1979) 7–9 and 16 (1980) 7–10. Psalm 49 falls into the second category and has some similarity to the themes of the Book of Job, particularly that portion of the book in which Job raises the empirical problem of the apparent success and prosperity of the wicked and rich (Job 21:7–15). The psalm differs from Job in form and function; whereas the latter deals with the issues in a context that is primarily literary and theological, the psalm may have a more didactic function. Yet it is not didactic literature in the conventional sense, and hence an educational setting as such need not be supposed. It is possible that the psalm should be set in a context that would nowadays be called a "counseling situation." The person with the moral and intellectual dilemma approached a representative of the wisdom tradition (a *wise man*, in effect a counselor) and sought a solution. The psalm (recited or sung, v 5) was the response, but it contained no easy answers; it merely set the appropriate horizons within which the dilemma must be accepted and carried.

The psalm begins with an introduction (vv 2–5), addressed to all, though the specific addressees would have been the persons seeking counsel. Two main sections of the psalm follow, (a) vv 6–13 and (b) vv 14–21, each of which concludes with a similar, but not identical, refrain (vv 13, 21), expressing the essence of wisdom on the problem at hand.

Comment

The wisdom teacher's introduction (49:2–5). The introductory address has a remarkably international character, as befits the wisdom tradition which was in itself broad and international in substance and scope. The persons to whom the words are addressed are "all you peoples" and all the world's "inhabitants" (v 2); they are not literally addressed, of course, but the force of the words is to indicate that the wisdom about to be declared applies to all mankind, regardless of race and nation. Equally, the wisdom applies to all, regardless of their position in life, their wealth or poverty (v 3), but here the address in the introduction is critical, for often it seems that the issue at hand afflicts primarily those who are poor and of low estate. Indeed, it is probable that the persons who are directly addressed by the wisdom teacher are the poor and afflicted, but by addressing them in the broad terms of vv 2–3, their problem is set immediately in its wider context.

The words that the wisdom teacher will speak are called "wisdom" and "understanding" (v 4); they relate in turn to a "proverb" or "enigma" (v 5). The "enigma" (or "riddle") is not necessarily a riddle of the Samsonian variety (Judg 14:14-20), as implied by the study of Perdue (*JBL* 93 [1974] 533–42); it is something larger than that. G. K. Chesterton is reported to have said that "the Book of Job is great because all life is a riddle," and like Job, the wisdom of Ps 49 is addressed to one of the greatest riddles of life, the relationship of life to death. For such riddles, there may be no easy answer, but there is a framework of wisdom within which to accept and live with the riddle; it is this that the wisdom teacher will "expose" or explain (v 5b).

Wisdom concerning fearing the wealthy (49:6-13). The teacher's introductory question (vv 6-7) no doubt puts into words precisely the fear of those who had come for his counsel. In bad times, threatened by death, it was hard not to be afraid of powerful enemies, whose wealth and position seemed to make them so invulnerable to similar threats. But why should one be afraid of them, the teacher asks; what really is their situation? Their own estimation of their strength was clear: they "trust" in wealth and "boast" of riches (v 7), clearly thinking of themselves as freed from the fears that obsessed weaker persons. But were they really free and invulnerable? It is at this point that the wisdom teacher provides the perspective denied to the sufferer, for standing at a distance from the event, he can perceive more clearly the situation of all human beings.

For all a person's wealth, he cannot redeem himself; the world's richest person could not afford his own ransom (v 8). The context indicates clearly that it is *death* which is the background to these words. When facing death, the ultimate leveller of all human beings, wealth would finally be useless. (The parenthetic statement of v 9, perhaps a later editorial edition, indicates that further exploration of the matter should be "left alone"; redemption can't be bought.) If money were the criterion of death, then the rich would have everlasting life and never see "the pit" (v 10), or the grave; though the possibility of buying eternal life (or immortality) was patently absurd, it certainly did not seem absurd to the poor and afflicted inquirer. Threatened with death and vulnerable in his poverty, it seemed to the psalmist that the wealthy had everything going for them; it is that false vision of the wealthy which the teacher destroys.

In death, at least, all human beings are equal; that equality is expressed in the words of vv 11-12. The words carry particular force, for the wisdom teacher includes himself, by implication, in the description of those who must die: "wise men," "fool" and "brute." Yet there is a certain irony in the words, for though in a technical sense, the wise men were the wisdom teachers of ancient Israel, in a general sense, it was the wealthy and powerful who thought of themselves as wise people. But all are included in the end by death, regardless of whether one has perceived correctly or incorrectly one's position in life. For all, the "grave" is a perpetual home; the earthly homes the rich had possessed, named after themselves in the vain hope of a kind of perpetuity, would pass into the hands of others (v 12).

It is against this background that the first refrain is stated: "man" (or "mankind": אָדָם) "does not survive" (v 13). The word "survive" is more precisely "lodge overnight" and is probably used in irony: the wealthy persons of this world devoted much of life to constructing for themselves a solid lodging place in this world, but the reality of death was that the grave (v 12) would be their only permanent lodging place. Human beings and beasts were alike in this, that death cut them off from the continuity of life. In this first expression of the teacher's thoughts, there is not much that is positive by way of counsel, but an important delusion has been shattered, the delusion that the rich and powerful are somehow at an advantage when facing death. They are not; at death everyone is equal.

The folly of confidence in wealth (49:14–21). The teacher, who first addressed the fear of wealthy persons and their apparent advantage in the face of death, now turns his attention to the folly of their way of life as such; in exposing its folly, he attempts to remove the temptation to seek wealth merely as a safeguard against death.

The "folly" of the powerful and rich lies partly in their failure to understand the wisdom of v 13, but it is given most powerful expression in their words, quoted in v 16. But first they are depicted in the powerful poetry of v 15: they are "like sheep shipped to Sheol." On the meaning of "Sheol," see the *Comment* on Ps 6:6. Like dumb sheep, on their way to slaughter (see Ps 44:12), they don't know where they are going; but while they are "grazing" in the pleasant pastures of their life, thinking all is well with them, "death" is already "grazing" on them (v 15b)! Their destiny is not the "lofty abodes" on which the entire focus of their living has been directed, but their bodies ("forms," v 15d) are destined for consumption in Sheol.

Against this bleak picture of the destiny of the wealthy, the poet quotes their (imaginary) words of self-confidence: "Surely God will redeem me . . . ." (v 16). They think their position of privilege in this life will give them also a position of privilege when it comes to death. And their words, which if taken out of context could express an honest hope, have within them the haunting echoes of v 8, that a wealthy person could somehow buy his own redemption. But such is not the case, for death ends life, and honor and wealth cannot be taken along on the final journey (v 18). So again, the teacher urges his subjects not to be afraid of having no wealth when others become wealthy (v 17; see also v 6). There may well be grounds for fearing death, but wealth and position in society are irrelevant considerations when it comes to dying. It is the deceptive confidence about death which life's prosperity may create that the teacher wishes to destroy. A person "blessed in his lifetime" (v 19a) may easily become falsely confident about death, for human praise in times of prosperity feeds such confidence (v 19b); yet the basic reality, to which the teacher returns, is that life ends in the netherworld of the ancestors, where there is no light (v 20). So again the refrain is expressed, but this time with a slight variation (v 21). The real folly of the wealthy and powerful is their failure to "understand"; in failing to understand fully the dimensions of death, it is inevitable that they also fail to understand fully the dimensions of life. Nevertheless, the purpose of the teacher is positive. It is not only the wealthy and powerful who may fail to understand; the teacher's audience have also not understood. If they do understand, they will not make the mistake of succumbing to the temptation to seek a solution to death in wealth or position; they will recognize the wisdom of seeking fulness of life in the present moment in the experience of God's presence.

Explanation

Taken by itself, the content of Ps 49 may seem to be less than entirely positive and constructive: it contains some practical advice and destroys some dangerous delusions, but it does not seem to offer much more with respect to the issues involved. And yet it is important to read all the wisdom literature in the context of its most fundamental principle, which is that "the fear of the Lord is the beginning of wisdom" (Prov 1:7). The wisdom teacher in Ps 49 eliminates two possible kinds of human fear: the fear of foes in times of trial (v 6) and the fear that the wealthy have some kind of advantage in the face of death (v 17). The teacher eliminates those fears, without explicitly stating a more positive message; yet the positive message is clear in the whole tradition to which he belongs, that wisdom may be found in the fear, or reverence, of the Lord. That wisdom provides the meaning and purpose of living; that wisdom provides also acceptance and calm in the face of dying. And though the psalm, in keeping with the Psalter as a whole, has no explicit theology and hope of life after death, there is nevertheless a confidence in his instruction. For it is important that death be faced without delusions, without the false confidence that may arise from a life judged to be successful by human standards. If one perceives death correctly, from the perspective of wisdom, one may live life correctly, in the fear of the Lord. And conversely, a life properly lived will provide a more appropriate and clear-sighted confidence with respect to death.

Hence the wisdom of the teacher, though devoid of an explicit eschatology, is not without hope. But from the perspective of the NT, one of the possible avenues of hope, which the teacher negated, is opened up. Can a man buy his own redemption (v 8)? No, the psalmist strongly implies. Nevertheless, it is the essence of the doctrine of incarnation that the redemption of mankind can be secured and has been secured in the redemptive death of Jesus Christ. And it is the resurrection that followed that death, in turn, which adds the dimension of eschatology and life beyond the grave to the wisdom of the psalm. Yet, for all the added dimensions which the NT gives to Ps 49, the ancient wisdom of the psalm remains essentially the same: in the matter of death, a person's wealth and position in this world provide no guarantees or escape.

A Prophetic Covenant Liturgy (50:1–23)

Bibliography

Buss, M. J. "The Psalms of Asaph and Korah." *JBL* 82 (1963) 382–92. **Illman, K.-J.** *Thema und Tradition in den Asaf-Psalmen.* (Åbo, 1976). **Johnson, A. R.** *The Cultic*

Prophet and Israel's Psalmody. Cardiff: University of Wales Press, 1979. **Mannati, M.** "Les accusations du Psaume 50:18–20." *VT* 25 (1975) 659–69. ———. "Le Psaume 50 est-il un *rîb?.*" *Sem* 23 (1973) 27–50. **Ridderbos, N. H.** "Die Theophanie in Ps. 50:1–6." *OTS* 15 (1969) 213–16.

Translation

1 A psalm of Asaph.[a]
  El, God,[b] the Lord,   (3+3+3)
    has spoken and summoned the world
    from the rising of the sun to its setting.
2 From Zion, the perfection of beauty, God has shone forth;   (4+4)
3   our God comes and will not be silent!
  A devouring fire is before him,   (3+3)
    and a tempest rages around him.
4 He summons the heavens above   (3+3)
    and the earth to judge his people.
5 "Gather my devotees [a] to me,   (3?+3)
    those about to make a covenant with me by sacrifice."
6 Then the heavens proclaimed his righteousness,   (3+3)
    for God himself is judge. SELAH
7 "Hear, my people, and let me speak,   (3+3+3)
    and let me give testimony about you, O Israel.
    I am God, your God.
8 I will not reprove you because of your sacrifices   (3+3)
    or your burnt offerings that are constantly before me.
9 I will not take a steer from your household   (3+2)
    or billy-goats from your pens,
10 for every creature of the forest is mine,   (3+3)
    and the beasts of a thousand hills.[a]
11 I know every bird of the mountains   (3+3)
    and the domestic beasts are mine.
12 If I were hungry, I would not speak to you,   (3+3)
    for the world and its fulness is mine.
13 Do I eat the flesh of bulls   (3+3)
    or drink billy-goats' blood?
14 Sacrifice to God thanksgiving   (3+3)
    and fulfil your vows to the Most High.
15 And summon me on the day of distress;   (3+2)
    I will deliver you, and you will honor me."
16 But God said to the wicked:
  "What right have you to recite my statutes   (3+3)
    and to take my covenant upon your lips?
17 For you have hated instruction   (3+3)
    and have cast my words behind you.
18 When you saw a thief, you were delighted [a] with him,   (4+3)
    and your lot was with the adulterers.
19 You have surrendered [a] your mouth to evil,   (3+3)
    and your tongue designed deceitfulness.

²⁰ *You continue* ᵃ *to speak against your brother;*   (3+3?)
    you slander ᵇ *your own mother's son.*

²¹ *You have done these things, but I kept silent;*   (3+3+3)
    you thought that I was surely ᵃ *like you!*
    I will reprove you and accuse you to your face.

²² *Now understand this, you who forget God,*   (4+3)
    lest I tear you apart, and you have no deliverer.

²³ *The one whose sacrifice is thanksgiving honors me,*   (3+2+3)
    and to the one who makes fixed ᵃ *his path,*
    I will reveal to him the salvation of God."

Notes

1.a. On the "psalm of Asaph," see further the INTRODUCTION. The collection of Asaph psalms embraces a variety of different forms and literary types. In spite of attempts to find continuity and conformity within these psalms (e.g. Buss, *JBL* 83 [1963] 382–92), there is no formal conformity or distinctive commonality of theme that would make it possible to link them in some meaningful way with the Asaphite temple-singers (cf. Illman, *Thema und Tradition in den Asaf-Psalmen*).

1.b. It is possible that אל אלהים should be interpreted as a superlative; see Dahood, *Psalms I*, 306; against such an interpretation, see Kraus, *Psalmen 1–59*, 526 and Delitzsch, *Biblical Commentary on the Psalms*, II, 144.

5.a. Or "pious ones": חסידי (viz. those that know and exercise the quality of lovingkindness).

10.a. The expression is rather curious, and it might be preferable to read הררי־אל, translating "marvelous mountains (or *hills*)"; see note a at Ps 36:7.

18.a. Alternatively, the verb could be pointed וַתָּרָץ (cf. *G*), and translated: "you ran along with him."

19.a. On Dahood's proposal that שלח be translated "forge" (*Psalms I*, 309), see note a at Ps 18:15.

20.a. Alternatively, the phrase could be interpreted as hendiadys and translated, with Dahood: "you sit speaking . . ." (*Psalms I*, 309).

20.b. Literally, "you give fault."

21.a. For MT's היות (inf. constr.), היו is read (inf. absol.). On the syntax of the clause, see GKC § 157a.

23.a. The sense is "one who is absolutely determined." שם is interpreted as a Qal active participle of שום (not a passive participle, as proposed by Dahood, *Psalms I*, 310).

Form/Structure/Setting

Ps 50 is a liturgy, or a part of a liturgy, to be associated with the ceremony of the renewal of the covenant in ancient Israel. Its prophetic character is distinguished by the fact that major portions of the psalm are identified as the divine words (vv 5, 7–15, 16b–23), which were presumably uttered in oracular fashion by the cultic prophets conducting the worship (see particularly Johnson, *The Cultic Prophet and Israel's Psalmody*, 22–30). For other prophetic liturgies, see Pss 81 and 95.

The psalm has an introductory passage, followed by two principal sections. (1) God summons the covenant people to his presence (vv 1–6); the descriptive language is that of a theophany. (2) God states the true meaning of sacrifice (vv 7–15). (3) A warning is issued to those whose lives are not in accordance with the covenant stipulations (vv 16–23).

The psalm's cultic setting is difficult to determine with precision. The explicit reference to *Zion* (v 2) indicates a setting in the Jerusalem temple, and it may be that the names used of God are indicative of the fact that the psalm was employed in worship at a fairly early period in the history of the monarchy; this may be indicated by the use of both "El" (v 1) and *Elyon* ("Most High," v 14). See further the *Comment* on Ps 47:3 and Johnson, op. cit., 22–23. It is also possible that the liturgy took place at dawn. The reference to the "rising of the sun," though ambiguous (see further the *Comment* on v 1), followed immediately by a reference to God having "shone forth" in theophany, may be instructive. The language of theophany is entirely appropriate to any covenant ritual, being reminiscent of the Sinai theophany (see further Ridderbos, *OTS* 15 [1969] 213–16), but it may be that the "effect" of theophany in this liturgy was obtained by holding the service at dawn. The first dazzling rays of sunrise on the eastern horizon signalled the advent of God.

The first six verses form a summons to worship and were no doubt spoken by one of the persons officiating; but v 5 could have been uttered by a cult prophet, given the oracular form of the words. The two main sections of the liturgy (vv 7–15 and 16–23) would have been declared by a prophet; v 16a may be a liturgical rubric of some kind, indicating that a different group of persons was to be addressed.

One may presume that this prophetic liturgy was one part of a larger ritual, or that it introduced a series of events. If the translation of the summons is correct (v 5: see *Comment*), the people addressed were about to engage in the more formal act of making and renewing the Covenant. The actual sacrifices and fulfilment of vows still lay before them (v 14), as did the formal recitation covenant statutes (v 16). In this sense, the prophetic ritual formed a kind of solemn preparation for the more formal act of a covenant renewal ceremony; held at dawn, it preceded the principal act of worship which would extend throughout the day until sunset (v 1). It is probable that the entire proceedings were undertaken as an occasional part of the celebration of the Feast of Tabernacles (see Deut 31:10–11 and Craigie, *The Book of Deuteronomy*, 370–71).

Comment

The summons to worship (50:1–6). The psalm begins powerfully with a piling up of divine names. The poetic form is such that it may be too artificial to make fine distinctions between the names; nevertheless, the middle term ("God," אלהים) is the most general, flanked by "El" (אל "God"), which in conjunction with "Most High" (v 14) may be indicative of the ancient God of Jerusalem, who is also the "Lord" *(Yahweh)*, God of the Exodus and Sinai.

There follows a triple summons: (1) the "world" as a whole (v 1) is summoned to observe what is about to happen; (2) "heavens" and "earth" are summoned, as witnesses of the covenant event (v 4), and finally (3) the people themselves are summoned to gather in the divine presence (v 5).

The expression "from the rising of the sun to its setting" is slightly ambiguous. If the point of reference is the "world," the expression may mean from *east* to *west;* viz. the entire world. But it is more likely that the expression designates the passage of time; for a whole day, from sunrise to sunset, the world is summoned as an observer of the events about to take place. The summons must have been issued at (or just before) sunrise.

The language of theophany (vv 2–3) is reminiscent of the original Sinai theophany, when the covenant law was first given to Israel (Exod 19:16–19). But in this context, the theophanic language is also related intimately to the sunrise. At the moment the sun rose in the east (v 1), God "shone forth" from Zion; thus the liturgy was timed to coincide with a natural event, which symbolized dramatically the theophany of the law-giving God of Sinai. At the heart of the experience of theophany was the divine speech; God, who had remained silent long enough (cf. v 21), was now about to speak (v 3a). But first the "heavens" and the "earth" were summoned to "judge the people" (v 4); the role of heaven and earth in this context is clarified by Deut 32:1, the introduction to Moses' "Song of the Covenant." In the original making and renewing of the covenant, the people themselves had summoned heaven and earth to be the silent witnesses to their enactment of a covenant relationship with God; see further Craigie, *The Book of Deuteronomy*, 376. Now, the same silent witnesses are summoned, this time by God; though God was the "judge" in a formal sense (v 6), heaven and earth participated (symbolically) in that judgment as observers of all the actions of the covenant people.

Finally, the people themselves were summoned to gather together in God's presence, in the words of an oracular pronouncement (v 5). The word "devotee" (חסיד) designates specifically those who were committed to God in the relationship of covenant. The words "those about to make a covenant with me" (כרתי בריתי) are critical to the understanding of the text as a whole. RSV translates: "who made a covenant with me. . . ." (cf. NIV, NEB, et al.), but these translations fail to recognize the force of the participle כרתי. In this context, the participle functions as the "participle of the immediate future," as is commonly the case in covenant contexts; see further, P. Joüon, *Grammaire de l'Hébreu Biblique* (1947), 339, and W. F. Stinespring, "The Participle of the Immediate Future and Other Matters pertaining to Correct Translation in the OT," in H. T. Frank and W. L. Reed (eds.), *Translating and Understanding the Old Testament* (1970), 64–70. Thus the covenant members are summoned by God; later in the day, they will be making, or renewing, the covenant, but first they must go through the searching preparatory ritual of divine scrutiny, to ensure that they are ready for the ceremony itself, in which the covenant "sacrifice" (v 5b) would be offered.

The true meaning of sacrifice (50:7–15). The divine speech begins with a summons to "hear" (implying also "obey"), in a fashion reminiscent of an earlier covenant renewal occasion (Deut 5:1; 6:4). And God's words are also reminiscent of the preface to the Decalogue (Exod 20:2 and Deut 5:6); "I am God, your God" (v 7c) is the equivalent, in the Elohistic Psalter, to the more familiar "I am the Lord (Yahweh), your God."

The essence of the divine speech concerns the meaning and purpose of sacrifices, and it was vital that the people have the meaning clear in their minds before the actual sacrifices were offered later in the day. God did not need sacrifices; the people did need them. God possessed already all the animals of the world, birds and beasts, domestic and wild (vv 10–11).

He had no pressing need for an extra steer or a couple of billy goats, as if he were running short of provisions (v 13)! From one perspective, the language is comical, for it presupposes a rather weak and hungry God, waiting desperately for the next sacrifice to fill his belly, but the power of the language comes from its nature as caricature. To think of sacrifices as something that God literally required was precisely to reduce God to this absurdly hungry deity; yet a superficial and formal offering of sacrifices, based on obedience to stipulations and nothing else, was tantamount to such a view of God. The essence of the whole sacrificial system was to be found in "thanksgiving" and the fulfillment of "vows" (v 14); for at root, the covenant community did not exist for the temple, but the temple and its cult existed only as an avenue through which the worship and thanksgiving of the covenant people could be directed to God. Covenant was a relationship with God; thanksgiving to God could be expressed through the sacrificial cult, thereby enriching the relationship. And when the relationship with God was healthy, then the people in turn could confidently call upon God in times of distress and experience his deliverance and salvation (v 15).

The true meaning of the law (50:16–23). The words that follow are addressed to the wicked, those who knew the law but did not keep it. It is possible that in the liturgy, a group of people were set on one side to symbolize the wicked and that these words, still in the form of a divine oracle, were addressed to them. Such a procedure would be analogous to that of the division of the people into two (symbolic) groups, representing the blessing and the cursing respectively, at the covenant renewal ceremony at Shechem (Deut 27:11–13).

The second divine oracle contains a severe warning of the danger of hypocrisy among the members of the covenant community. In the actual ceremony later in the day, they would "recite the statutes" and formally declare their commitment to "covenant" (v 16); in so doing, it was vital that there be no hypocrisy, that speech and life coincided as one. Verses 17–20, in the form of a divine judgment, are proclaimed to all, but no doubt found a lodging place in the hearts and minds of the guilty. But for all present, they required an act of self-examination, prior to the covenant ceremony as such.

The substance of the divine judgment develops the seventh, eighth and ninth commandments of the Decalogue (Exod 20:14–16 and Deut 5:18–20; see further Mannati, *VT* 25 [1975] 659–69). Later in the day, the covenant members would take the words of those commandments on their lips; it was essential that they not be guilty of the crimes specified, taking pleasure in the company and activities of thieves and adulterers (v 18) and engaging in evil speech, even against a blood-brother (vv 19–20). The divine silence with respect to such evil living could give the wicked persons a false sense of confidence, as though God was somehow like them and didn't worry too much about such evil acts (v 21a-b). But the divine silence with respect to evil was always only a temporary phenomenon. Now, in the divine words of the prophetic oracle, the silence was broken; God declares that he will "reprove" and "accuse" (v 21c), indicating that the evil must be dealt with before the covenant renewal ceremony as such begins. To mouth the words of the law, but not to be obedient to them, was tantamount to forgetting God (v

22), and that was a dangerous path to take. Hence the words of v 22 must be understood both as a warning and as a directive to repentance on the part of those who are guilty in terms of the divine oracle of judgment. Not to repent would lead to the risk of being "torn apart" (v 22b); the metaphorical language is that of God as the fierce lion who would tear apart evildoers (cf. Hos 5:14).

The concluding verse (v 23) re-emphasizes the point of v 14; the true meaning of the sacrifice and recitation of the law in the covenant renewal ceremony was to be found in "thanksgiving," and in actually walking with determination in that divinely ordained path in which the salvation of God would be revealed.

Explanation

Just as the covenant was the very heart of the religion of Israel, so too Ps 50 lies at the heart of the meaning of the covenant. From the perspective of religion, the covenant was a relationship between God and Israel; the relationship extended from the community as a whole to each individual member of that community in particular. And while the covenant relationship covered every facet and every moment of human existence, there were particular times set aside in the life of the community when the covenant should be renewed. For some, the covenant renewal ceremony was a time of recommitment and of renewing an old allegiance; for others, the new generation, they were in effect forming the covenant with God for the first time, though its history extended back to generations in the distant past. The renewal ceremony involved specific ritual proceedings, the offering of sacrifice and the recitation of the words of the covenant stipulations. But the ritual was for the sake of the people, rather than God. While God was the ever faithful covenant partner, it was in the nature of human beings to forget that the fundamental meaning of their individual lives and national existence was rooted in the relationship with God. The great renewal ceremony brought back these primary realities of living into the forefronts of the minds of the covenant members.

But what, in reality, was the essence of the covenant life? It was a relationship with God, certainly, but the essence of that relationship did not lie in ceremonies as such. The ceremonies signalled the deeper reality of life, that above all God required "thanksgiving" (vv 14, 23). God did not need thanksgiving to bolster his own self-esteem, as if (in the words of C. S. Lewis) he were "like a vain woman wanting compliments, or a vain author presenting his new books to people who had never met or heard of him" (*Reflections on the Psalms*, 79). God wanted thanksgiving, for that in turn emerged from human lives full of joy; it was the joyful lives of the covenant members, expressed so vividly in the sacrifices and words of the ceremony, which fulfilled in God the richness of relationship which he had given to his people.

Index of Authors Cited

Index of Principal Subjects

Index of Biblical Texts
Old Testament

Old Testament Apocrypha and Pseudepigrapha

Index of Ugaritic Texts

Index of Key Hebrew Words

Index of Ugaritic Words

'abd	296	ṭb	78	ʿdb	123
'aylt	324			ʿẓ	243, 342
'alt	122			ʿẓm	122
'aṯr	319	ybm	140	ql	313
'iršt	189	yd	122, 223	qly	99
'ul	197	ydd	324	ʿpʿpm	132
		ymm	140	ʿqb	319
		ymn	223	ʿšr	337
bl'	160	yn	155		
bly	160	ypḥ	230		
bn 'ilm	242, 246	yṣ'a	258	ǵdd	123, 307
bnt	84			ǵzr	284
bqr	230			ǵyr	115
brt	210	knd	270	ǵr	115
		ks'u	122		
gʿr	170			pḫd	145
		l (preposition)	33ff	pʿl	258
dwd	324	l'imm	98		
dmm	78	lb	210	ṣḫrrt	301
drk	336	lḥm	144f	ṣpn	91, 353
drkt	58			ṣrrt	90f
		mdb	248		
hgg	84	mdbr qdš	248	ql	247
hgh	84	mhmrt	342		
hdrt	242	mmh	136	šdm	136
hll	84	mr'	179	šd 'ubdy	296
hm	115, 204, 229, 351	mšr	236	škllt	285
hmry	342			šlḥ	169
hrr	155	nbl'at	160	šm'al	223
		ndd	324	šʿtqt	285
ḥdy	79	ndy	290	šqy	337
ḥsp	243	nhr	210	št	357
ḥrr	155	nǵṣ	140		
		nǵr	115	tǵr	115
ḫlq	85, 136, 155, 284	npš	97f	ttpp	336
ḫmt	179				
ḫnn	284				
ḫnp	285	smkt	136	ṯny	105